SOCIAL PSYCHOLOGY:
PEOPLE IN GROUPS

SOCIAL
PSYCHOLOGY:
PEOPLE IN
GROUPS

BERTRAM H. RAVEN
University of California
Los Angeles

JEFFREY Z. RUBIN
Tufts University

JOHN WILEY & SONS, INC.
NEW YORK
LONDON
SYDNEY
TORONTO

This book was set in Caledonia by Vail-Ballou. It was
printed and bound by Vail-Ballou. The designer was
Jerry Wilke. The drawings were designed and executed
by John Balbalis with the assistance of the Wiley
Illustration Department. Picture research was done by
Marge Graham. Cathy Pace supervised production.
Chapter opening photo design by Jerry Wilke; photographer: Dan Lenore. Cover design: Jerry Wilke;
photographer: Dan Lenore.

Library of Congress Cataloging in Publication Data:

Raven, Bertram Herbert, 1926–
    Social Psychology.

    Bibliography: p. 521
    Includes indexes.
    1. Interpersonal relations.   2. Social inter-
action.   3. Social groups.   4. Small groups.
I. Rubin, Jeffrey Z., joint author.   II. Title.

[DNLM: 1. Psychology, Social. HM251 R253p]
HM132.R28   301.11   75-32693
ISBN 0-471-70970-0

Printed in the United States of America

10 9 8 7

Lovingly
dedicated
to
Celia,
Michelle,
and
Jon Raven
and to
Carol
and
David Rubin

PREFACE

Bert Raven Footprints in the snow. This was my earliest conscious association with the intricacies of social interaction. As a young child in the Midwest, I recall going out early on a wintry day and seeing the footprints of those who had gone out earlier. I found myself wondering about the unseen figures who had left their marks so vividly before me. How much could I tell about them? Some prints were large, both in sole and heel, and deep—a workman going off to catch the early bus to the local steel mill? Some were a bit smaller, lighter, and narrower—obviously those of a woman. And there were children's footprints, some walking, some running, sometimes suggesting a chase—a playful snowball fight? Dog prints had their unique paths—telephone pole to tree to fire hydrant. A lone child's path would often follow a meandering course, indicating that the child's attention was attracted first by one object and then another. A lone adult's path would generally be straight and direct, swerving only in response to another person or group coming from the opposite direction. But what puzzled me most was my observation of the paths of two persons walking together. Their paths, instead of following two straight parallel lines, formed a connected series of mirror-image arcs as the two paths converged and diverged in a regular pattern. At first, I thought this was some sort of unusual occurrence, or even a playful game, so I watched carefully on another morning and found similar patterns in the footprints of other pairs. Why? I rejected a few possible explanations—the repeated pattern did not seem like a playful game or dance, nor could it be two convivial drinking buddies, for the pattern was too regular. It occurred to me that I was seeing a pattern of mutual adjustment—the two persons were attempting to maintain a mutually acceptable distance between them. As they walked side by side their paths would gradually bring them closer together, closer than they perhaps felt to be appropriate or comfortable; they would then over-adjust by moving farther apart, beyond the appropriate distance, and then closer together again. I had formed a very simple hypothesis and could not wait to test it through actual observation. When I saw a pair walking together later one day, their behavior seemed consistent with my hypothesis, and I experienced that wonderful feeling of exhilaration that comes with having one's hypothesis supported by data. I also learned something else from the simple exercise—that one could sometimes learn more about how people behave by observing a trace or fragment of their behavior than by observing their total behavior.

Later, when I was taking courses in psychology and social psychology, I became more aware of the problems and pitfalls in informal observation, and of the ways in which one's hypotheses can bias one's observation. Did the pattern of adjustment in the pair really occur, or did my expectations lead me to see such patterns when they didn't actually exist? For a time, healthy skepticism led me to distrust any casual observational data. Nothing was a fact unless it was supported by careful experimental control, precise and reliable measurement, and statistical significance. All too often social science education serves to put blinders on our students, restricting their observations and speculation to the point that their interest in human behavior becomes restricted and sterile. Even more often, a social psychology course or text will be overly defensive, limiting its discussion to a series of controlled and contrived experiments on molecular details of social interaction, each supported by pages of statistical tables. In this way, a creative student may be lost to the field forever. The rich observations of social behavior in biographies, novels, and drama are rejected as entertaining but of no social scientific value. A student is encouraged to disregard the evidence of his or her day-to-day experience for the same reason.

Jeff Rubin | Our primary objective in writing this book has been to achieve a balanced presentation of social psychology. On the one hand, we are convinced that social scientists need no longer be defensive. Social psychology has established itself as a substantial and important area, and its students no longer have to prove themselves or the merit of their discipline. Social psychology, however, is more than a systematic statement of the social scientific method. We therefore encourage you, the reader, to continually relate the material presented in these pages to problems and issues in your everyday lives; to works in literature, drama, and the arts that you find stimulating; to current social problems in our nation and elsewhere. We hope to provide some tools that will help you understand these problems and issues better, some theories, some hypotheses, and some carefully developed research evidence. While we believe that you will appreciate the ingenuity of social psychologists in developing the research studies described in this book, please never lose sight of the direct social and personal implications of their findings. To illustrate the relevance of basic social psychological concepts, we will draw on our own experiences—observations made while traveling with a circus will illustrate certain principles of group structure, an introspective account of a first parachute jump will illustrate affiliation in the face of threat, and patterns of interaction in our own families will illustrate similar patterns that can be found elsewhere. We urge you, the reader, to follow our lead and look for the personal relevance of the theories we discuss.

Bert Raven | While we are thinking about applications of social psychological concepts, what about two people writing a book? Shouldn't we be able to see many of the principles of social interaction operating here? I started to write another book a number of years ago, and after many sporadic attempts managed to complete six chapters, which have been sitting in a file drawer ever since. Although I was clearly interested in the subject matter, the problem was that there always seemed to be other things that had to be done, obligations toward others that seemed to be more pressing. I still felt that I had something to say in a text such as this one, but to make sure that it would be completed I needed to work with someone else. The field is broad and diverse, of course, and it is useful to have another person's perspective—someone with whom I could check my ideas from time to time. But even more critical for me are the interdependence pressures that result from working with a collaborator. By having someone to whom I was obligated and who was obligated to me in turn, someone with whom I could work toward a mutually desirable goal, I could put off some of the immediate conflicting pressures to do other things. However, the collaborator could not be just anyone. It had to be someone for whom I would have personal as well as professional admiration. It would have to be someone whose perspective was not entirely consistent with mine, so that we could mutually supplement and occasionally challenge one another, but not so different in outlook that we would feel no affiliation and no sense of common purpose.

Of course, similar considerations entered my mind as we explored the possibilities of working together on this book. Indeed, it was our basic similarity in outlook and approach to teaching and research that originally drew us together—I had been using Sartre's play *No Exit* to illustrate group structure in my lectures, and I was amazed and delighted to hear of a social psychologist out on the West Coast who was doing the same thing. I had been carrying out research on bargaining behavior and conflict and was delighted to find that many of the concepts of social power, as presented by my future collaborator, meshed with and further clarified my own research. Thus, both similarity and complementarity of interests and views helped bring us together.

Jeff Rubin

The process by which we worked together can also be seen in relation to the stages of group problem-solving described by Robert Freed Bales and Fred Strodtbeck. Our first meetings were devoted largely to solving problems of orientation and communication, agreeing to a common language (though we were both social psychologists, it is interesting how frequently we used our terms somewhat differently); and problems of evaluation and common goals—deciding exactly what our final product should be like, how broad a field of social psychology should be covered, and what audience we should write for. There were problems of control—decisions about how the task should be divided and coordinated. We had our occasional disagreements as well, to be sure, and our tensions, but fortunately we were able to resolve these effectively. The point, again, is that the two of us were working as a group and following most of the principles discussed in this book.

Jeff Rubin and Bert Raven

How, though, do two separate individuals combine in working toward a joint product or goal? How do their individual characters merge into one in the process of communication? Most books are written in the third person or in the passive voice. But we wished to write a more personal book, and so we have often written in the first person. Where we present a common viewpoint we have used the first person plural, as in this sentence. Sometimes, however, we have described an experience or observation that occurred to only one of us. Our reviewers were sometimes taken aback when the text suddenly shifted to the first person singular ("A number of years ago when I decided that it might be fun to live dangerously, I enrolled in a skydiving school . . ."). "I thought this book was written by *two* people," one reviewer said. But only one of us enrolled in the skydiving school. "Well, which one of you, then?" Does it make any difference? This book was written by both of us, so we won't label our individual experiences; the illustration is important, not the identity of the actor. Of course, we don't really want to be secretive. If you are curious as to who did the skydiving, who sought solitude in the woods, who traveled with the circus, and so forth, please write to us and we will be happy to tell you. Or perhaps you would like to guess first and see if you can reconstruct our individual identities from our combined group product.

Our early decision to focus on interpersonal behavior and interaction in the small group was a very important one. We had decided that we wanted a text that would provide an introduction to social psychology but would not be encyclopedic or overly long. We could have attempted to cover the entire field within these pages, but in doing so we would not have done justice to any of it. It was our belief that an analysis of interaction between persons and the behavior of groups would present the reader with a good basic introduction to the field. These basic concepts can then be applied to an understanding of larger groups, social organizations, and indeed relations between nations. We hope that you, the reader, having read this book, will be stimulated to study such related topics as attitude formation and change, behavior in social organizations, cultural factors in group behavior, the process of language and communication, social psychology and legal affairs, and international behavior.

The Raven-Rubin dyad, as is customary, takes full responsibility for this volume and any errors that it may contain. However, we are both deeply grateful to a number of others who have assisted us in various ways. First of all, the interdependence pressures that led us to devote long hours to this venture meant that we had less time to spend with others toward whom we have deep feelings of love and obligation. We are grateful to Carol and David Rubin, and to Celia, Michelle, and Jon Raven for their sympathy, support, and understanding.

Even before this project was well under way, we discussed our book and its prospectus with a number of our friends, colleagues, and others conversant with the field. We cannot begin to remember and list all of those who offered us suggestions and comments on our prospectus. The final manuscript was read and evaluated by the following, all of whom offered valuable suggestions for revisions and improvements: Daniel Katz, Robert Zajonc, Bruce Biddle, Ruth Cline, Gregory Donnenworth, George Levinger, Zella Luria, Neil Malamuth, Michael Pallak, David Redfearn, Carol Milligan Rubin, Stephen Schiavo, Walter Swap, and Daniel Williams. To assist us in evaluating our text from a student perspective, we are indebted to a number of students at Tufts and UCLA. In particular, Joel Brockner, Audrey Frank, and Greg Denton read the entire manuscript and offered a number of suggestions for its improvement. Dr. Zoltan Rubin reviewed aspects of the book from the perspective of a nonpsychologist, physician, and father of one of the authors. His newspaper clipping collection provided a number of the relevant examples that are sprinkled throughout the text. Marianne Senko, Marian Perry, and Eileen Howard provided invaluable assistance in typing the manuscript in its original draft.

Finally, we owe our thanks to the production and editorial staff of John Wiley: To Jack Burton, who as psychology editor helped us through the early stages and provided us with reviewers for our manuscript; to Marge Graham, for help in selecting photographs; to Jerry Wilke for assistance in design and layout; to Jerry McCarthy for the artwork; and to Cathy Pace for assistance in production.

CONTENTS

PREFACE   vii

1

EVERYONE A SOCIAL PSYCHOLOGIST   2
SOCIAL PSYCHOLOGISTS: TWO PROMINENT
   EXAMPLES   2
      MOHANDAS K. GANDHI AND THE SALT MARCH   2
      COPING WITH DRUG ADDICTION   6
WHO IS NOT A SOCIAL PSYCHOLOGIST?   9
WHY STUDY SOCIAL PSYCHOLOGY?   13
SOCIAL PSYCHOLOGY: EVERYDAY AND SCIENTIFIC   16
      THREE SOCIAL PSYCHOLOGISTS BET THAT THE
         WORLD WILL NOT END   16
      A FURTHER TEST IN THE SOCIAL
         PSYCHOLOGISTS' LABORATORY   23
THE DISTINCTIONS BETWEEN EVERYDAY AND
   SCIENTIFIC SOCIAL PSYCHOLOGY   25
      THEORY CONSTRUCTION AND DEVELOPMENT   25
      FORMAL METHODS FOR TESTING THEORY   26
PEOPLE IN GROUPS AS A FOCUS   27
SUMMARY   29

2

THE PERSON ALONE   34
ALONE IN ISOLATION   34
      THE EXPERIENCE OF BEING ALONE   34
      EXPERIMENTAL STUDIES OF ISOLATION   37
ALONE IN THE PRESENCE OF OTHERS   38
WHY WE NEED PEOPLE   41
OTHERS HELP US TO ATTAIN REWARDS   41
      SATISFACTION OF PHYSICAL NEEDS   41

xiii

SATISFACTION OF THE NEED FOR LOVE AND
APPROVAL   42
AFFILIATION AND FEAR-REDUCTION   43
OTHERS PROVIDE US WITH INFORMATION ABOUT
OUR WORLD AND OURSELVES   45
SOCIAL COMPARISON THEORY   46
SOCIAL COMPARISON AND ABILITIES   47
SOCIAL COMPARISON AND OPINIONS   49
SOCIAL COMPARISON AND FEELINGS   51
SUMMARY   54

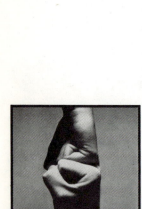

3
BECOMING AWARE OF OTHERS AND OURSELVES

58

BECOMING AWARE OF OTHERS   59
DEVELOPING IMPRESSIONS OF OTHERS   61
SIMPLIFYING OUR IMPRESSIONS OF OTHERS   68
ATTRIBUTING MOTIVES AND TRAITS TO OTHERS   73
THE ATTRIBUTION OF CAUSALITY   73
THE ELEMENTS OF ATTRIBUTION THEORY   75
PRESENTING OURSELVES TO OTHERS   89
THE DEGREE AND FORM OF SELF-DISCLOSURE   89
THE ART OF IMPRESSION MANAGEMENT   91
FINDING OUT ABOUT OURSELVES   93
ATTRIBUTION THEORY AND SELF-PERCEPTION   94
CONSIDERING HOW OTHERS EVALUATE US   96
SUMMARY   98

4
LIKING AND DISLIKING, FRIENDSHIP AND AGGRESSION

102

GETTING TO LIKE AND DISLIKE OTHERS   103
THE ELEMENTS OF BALANCE THEORY   103
BALANCE AND ATTITUDES   110

WHAT DETERMINES WHETHER WE LIKE OR DISLIKE
    ANOTHER PERSON?   111
    PERSONAL CHARACTERISTICS AND TRAITS   111
    A SENSE OF UNITY OR IDENTIFICATION   115
    LIKING THOSE WHO LIKE US   125
    LIKING THOSE WHO MATERIALLY BENEFIT US   129
    LIKING THOSE WHO ARE FAMILIAR   129
    LIKING OTHERS IN ORDER TO JUSTIFY OUR
        EFFORTS   132
    LIKING OTHERS WHO HELP US TO EVALUATE
        OURSELVES   133
HOSTILITY AND AGGRESSION   133
    THE FRUSTRATION-AGGRESSION HYPOTHESIS   134
    WHEN IS FRUSTRATION ESPECIALLY LIKELY TO
        LEAD TO AGGRESSION?   136
    WHEN DO WE AGRESS WHEN NOT
        FRUSTRATED?   141
    VIOLENCE, AGGRESSION, AND THE MASS
        MEDIA   144
    WHEN DOES FRUSTRATION NOT LEAD TO
        AGGRESSION?   147
    WHAT ARE THE CONSEQUENCES OF TRYING TO
        REDUCE TENSION THROUGH AGGRESSION?   148
SUMMARY   150

5
THE INTERDEPENDENCE OF PERSONS   154

THE PROBLEM OF COORDINATION   156
    CONVERGENT INTEREST COORDINATION   157
    DIVERGENT INTEREST COORDINATION   160
    MIXED-MOTIVE RELATIONSHIPS:
        COORDINATION CONVERGENT AND
        DIVERGENT INTERESTS   163
    SOCIAL EXCHANGE THEORY   164
    THE PRISONER'S DILEMMA GAME: A PARADIGM
        FOR MIXED-MOTIVE PROBLEM-SOLVING   166
    FACTORS THAT AFFECT COOPERATION AND
        COMPETITION IN THE PRISONER'S
        DILEMMA   169

COOPERATION AND COMPETITION AMONG KIBBUTZNIKS 173
COMPETITION AS A BY-PRODUCT OF URBANIZATION 177
INTERDEPENDENCE OF GOALS AND MEANS 178
COOPERATION AND COMPETITION REVISITED 181
INTERDEPENDENCE IN ESCAPE 187
CONFLICT AND BARGAINING 189
WHEN DOES BARGAINING OCCUR? 191
SUCCESSFUL BARGAINING 193
SUMMARY 194

6

INTERPERSONAL INFLUENCE AND SOCIAL POWER 200

POWER, INFLUENCE, AND CHANGE 201
SOCIAL DEPENDENCE AND SOCIAL INFLUENCE 202
THE IMPORTANCE OF SURVEILLANCE 202
POSITIVE AND NEGATIVE INFLUENCE 204
THE BASES OF SOCIAL POWER 206
INFORMATIONAL POWER—SOCIALLY INDEPENDENT INFLUENCE 206
REWARD AND COERCIVE POWER—SOCIALLY DEPENDENT INFLUENCE, SURVEILLANCE IMPORTANT 208
EXPERT, REFERENT, AND LEGITIMATE POWER—SOCIALLY DEPENDENT INFLUENCE, SURVEILLANCE UNIMPORTANT 212
COMPARING BASES OF POWER 222
COERCION-REWARD, EXPERT, AND REFERENT POWER 223
LEGITIMATE AND COERCIVE POWER 224
EXPERT AND REFERENT POWER 225
INFORMATIONAL AND EXPERT POWER 227
SECONDARY EFFECTS OF SOCIAL INFLUENCE 228
NEW PERCEPTIONS FOLLOWING SOCIAL INFLUENCE 228
ONE POWER BASE AFFECTS ANOTHER 230
DISSONANCE REDUCTION AND ATTRIBUTIONS FOLLOWING SOCIAL INFLUENCE 231

ENHANCING SOCIAL INFLUENCE 238
   ECOLOGICAL MANIPULATION 239
   GUILT-AROUSAL, OBLIGATION, AND INFLUENCE 239
   INFLUENCE BY GRADATIONS: THE FOOT-IN-
     THE-DOOR TECHNIQUE 241
SUMMARY 242

7
THE STRUCTURE
OF GROUPS 246

DIMENSIONS OF GROUP STRUCTURE 250
EVALUATION STRUCTURE 252
   SATISFACTION AND MORALE 254
INTERDEPENDENCE STRUCTURE 257
   THE STRUCTURE OF GOALS
     INTERDEPENDENCE 258
   THE STRUCTURE OF MEANS
     INTERDEPENDENCE 259
   INTERDEPENDENCE AMONG SUBUNITS:
     COALITIONS 260
COMMUNICATION STRUCTURE 267
   INTERACTION PROCESS ANALYSIS 267
   COMMUNICATION NETWORKS 270
ROLE STRUCTURE 274
   DEVELOPMENT OF ROLES IN INTERACTION 274
   CULTURE, TRADITION, AND ROLE DEFINITION 275
   ROLES AND COMMUNICATION NETWORKS 276
INFLUENCE AND POWER STRUCTURE 277
   COMMUNICATION AND INFLUENCE IN
     SOCIAL HIERARCHIES 281
   POWER AND ROLE STRUCTURE IN THE
     FAMILY 283
SUMMARY 285

8
GROUP INFLUENCES ON INDIVIDUAL BEHAVIOR 290

GROUP EFFECTS ON THE PERFORMANCE OF HUMANS
  AND OTHER ANIMALS 290
    SOCIAL FACILITATION 291
    SOCIAL INHIBITION 292
    OTHER GROUP EFFECTS THAT CONTRIBUTE TO
    INCREASED AND DECREASED PERFORMANCE 293
CONTAGION AND THE SPREAD OF GROUP EFFECTS 299
DEINDIVIDUATION AND GROUP EFFECTS ON
  BEHAVIOR 301
    LABORATORY STUDIES OF DEINDIVIDUATION 303
GROUP JUDGMENTS AND GROUP NORMS 310
    GROUP NORMS AND THE AUTOKINETIC
    EFFECT 310
    THE POWER OF A STUBBORN MINORITY 313
THE UNANIMOUS MAJORITY AND THE LONE
  DEVIANT 315
    MAJORITY INFLUENCES ON JUDGMENT 315
    PRESSURES TOWARD UNIFORMITY OF OPINION
    AND SOCIAL COMPARISON 319
    RESPONSES OF THE MAJORITY TO THE
    DEVIANT 322
    THE BEHAVIOR OF THE DEVIANT 326
THE STRANGE MYSTERY OF THE RISKY SHIFT AND
  THE RUNAWAY NORM 332
    CHOICE DILEMMAS AND RISKY SHIFTS 333
    WHY A RISKY SHIFT? 334
    RUNAWAY NORMS: THE NORMATIVE VALUE OF
    EXCEEDING THE AVERAGE 337
BYSTANDER INTERVENTION AND HELPING
  BEHAVIOR 339
    FACTORS THAT INFLUENCE HELPING
    BEHAVIOR 341
SUMMARY 350

9
GROUP PERFORMANCE, GROUP EFFECTIVENESS, AND LEADERSHIP 354

GROUP DECISION AND GROUP PERFORMANCE 355
  GROUP NORM AS A FIELD OF FORCES 355
THE QUALITY OF GROUP DECISIONS AND GROUP
  SOLUTIONS 360
  FACTORS THAT AFFECT THE QUALITY OF
    GROUP DECISIONS 363
LEADERSHIP 368
  WHAT IS A LEADER? 370
  WHAT FACTORS PRODUCE A LEADER? 371
  THE MANY FUNCTIONS OF LEADERSHIP 380
  THE DEVELOPMENT AND MAINTENANCE OF
    LEADERSHIP 381
  LEADERSHIP STYLE: THE BEHAVIOR OF
    LEADERS 387
  LEADERSHIP AND GROUP PERFORMANCE 393
SUMMARY 403

10
CONFLICT, HARMONY, AND TENSION BETWEEN GROUPS 408

SMALL-GROUP RESEARCH AND ITS RELEVANCE FOR
  INTERNATIONAL TENSIONS 410
  GENERALIZING FROM INTERPERSONAL TO
    INTERNATIONAL CONFLICT 410
  SMALL-GROUP DECISIONS AFFECT
    INTERNATIONAL AFFAIRS 412
HOW GROUPS IN CONFLICT MAKE DECISIONS 413
  GROUPTHINK 415
  THE NIXON GROUP AND THE WATERGATE
    AFFAIR 423

THE DEVELOPMENT OF INTERGROUP CONFLICT   433

    STUDYING INTERGROUP CONFLICT—SOME
      PERTINENT QUESTIONS   435

    FIELD EXPERIMENTAL STUDIES OF
      INTERGROUP CONFLICT   436

    DEVELOPMENT AND ESCALATION OF
      CONFLICT   442

    COMPETITIVE AND HOSTILE CONFLICT:
      ESCALATION OF CONFLICT BETWEEN
      NATIONS   448

REDUCING INTERGROUP CONFLICT   453

    REDUCING TENSION AND HOSTILITY IN THE
      SHERIF FIELD EXPERIMENTS   454

    REDUCING CONFLICT BETWEEN GROUPS,
      ORGANIZATIONS, AND NATIONS   456

    THE GRIT PROPOSAL FOR DE-ESCALATING
      INTERNATIONAL CONFLICT   465

SUMMARY   473

APPENDIX   475

GLOSSARY   496

REFERENCES   521

ILLUSTRATION CREDITS   563

AUTHOR INDEX   565

SUBJECT INDEX   574

SOCIAL PSYCHOLOGY:
PEOPLE IN GROUPS

ONE EVERYONE A SOCIAL PSYCHOLOGIST

Social Psychologists: Two Prominent Examples
Mohandas K. Gandhi and the Salt March
Coping with Drug Addiction

Who Is Not a Social Psychologist?

Why Study Social Psychology?

Social Psychology: Everyday and Scientific
Three Social Psychologists Bet That the World
    Will Not End
A Further Test in the Social Psychologists' Laboratory

**The Distinctions between Everyday and Scientific
    Social Psychology**
Theory Construction and Development
Formal Methods for Testing Theory

People in Groups as a Focus

1

SOCIAL PSYCHOLOGISTS: TWO PROMINENT EXAMPLES

Mohandas K. Gandhi and the Salt March

If one were to search for a social psychologist whose use of social psychological principles had affected the lives of millions, he would be hard-pressed to find a better example than Mohandas K. Gandhi and his role in the Salt March of 1930.

India was seething with labor and nationalist unrest after more than 200 years of British domination. The cry of "Freedom!" was heard throughout the land, and a number of Indian militants were screaming for extreme measures. In the province of Bengal, Subhas Chandra Bose had recruited a sizable following under his banner cry, "Give me blood and I promise you freedom!" But when Gandhi was asked about his role in the expected war of independence, he replied simply, "I would decline to take part in it." For, from his observations of group behavior and social interaction dating back to his experience in South Africa some 30 years earlier, he had developed what he considered a more appropriate means to attain the same end. The basic social psychological principles he had followed in South Africa were presented in his autobiography, *The Story of My Experiments with Truth,* written in 1925 (Gandhi, 1949).

In 1930 Gandhi hoped to influence a number of people and events. His ultimate aim was to get the British to grant some form of independence to India. Yet he wanted to avoid a bloody war of independence for both moral and pragmatic reasons—he was certain that in a shooting war with Britain, India would lose. Thus, he had to convince the militant young Indian revolutionaries of the correctness of his nonviolent principles. He also wanted to persuade many Indian functionaries who were cooperating with the British that the time had come to resist injustice and assert independence. Meanwhile, he had to convince the masses in India that British authority could and should be resisted. In the long run, Gandhi had faith in the world's conscience and in that of the British people, who seemed to live according to the principles of freedom, justice, and democracy at home, which contrasted sharply with the behavior of their administrators and military officers in the colonies. As a beginning, therefore, Gandhi tried to get the military and colonial administrators to relax a number of harsh laws and measures that had been foisted on the Indians.

At the outset he needed a specific target of protest—something equivalent to the tax on tea in Colonial America. It had to be something that would appear dramatically unjust and ridiculous. Gandhi chose the salt tax. This tax, which was imposed on the purchase and use of all salt, amounted to three days' income per year for the peasant. Besides the fact that his income was lower, the peasant used more salt than the well-to-do because of his heavy outdoor work which entailed greater perspiration.

After protesting the injustice of this tax, Gandhi believed in giving his adversary an opportunity to reconsider and negotiate before he took more drastic action. He tried to appeal to the British administrators' basic morality and ideals of justice, but it is clear that Gandhi was really not too hopeful. Thus, he wrote the following letter to Lord Irwin (later Lord Halifax), Viceroy of India:

Dear Friend,

Before embarking on Civil Disobedience and taking the risk I have dreaded to take all these years, I would fain approach you and find a way out. . . . Whilst, therefore, I hold the British rule to be a curse, I do not intend harm to a single Englishman or to any legitimate interest he may have in India. . . . And why do I regard the British rule as a curse? It has impoverished the dumb millions by a system of progressive exploitation and by a ruinous expensive military and civil administration which the country can never afford. It has reduced us politically to serfdom. It has sapped the foundations of our culture. . . . I fear . . . there has never been any intention of granting . . . Dominion status to India in the immediate future. . . . The British system seems to be designed to crush the very life out of [the peasant]. Even the salt he must use to live is taxed so as to make the burden fall heaviest on him. The tax shows itself more burdensome on the poor man when it is remembered that salt is the one thing he must eat more than the rich man. . . . Nothing but organized nonviolence can check the organized violence of the British government. . . . My ambition is no less than to convert the British people through nonviolence and thus make them see the wrong they have done to India. . . . I respectfully invite you to pave the way for immediate removal of these evils, and thus open a way for a real conference between equals. But if you cannot see your way to deal with these evils and if my letter makes no appeal to your heart, on the eleventh day of this month I shall proceed with such co-workers of the Ashram as I can take, to disregard the provisions of the Salt Laws. . . . It is, I know, open to you to frustrate my design by arresting me. I hope that there will be tens of thousands ready, in a disciplined manner, to take up the work after me [quoted in Fischer, 1954, p. 96].

Gandhi was not too surprised when he received an acknowledgment from Lord Irwin's secretary, but heard nothing from the viceroy himself. The letter was widely publicized, however, and on March 11, thousands of Gandhi's followers and onlookers gathered at his ashram (retreat) 241 miles inland from the Gulf of Cambay. That evening Gandhi held his last prayer meeting, followed by an exhortation to the Indian masses to begin civil disobedience against the Salt Act; according to British colonial authorities, unless the designated salt taxes were paid, it was unlawful to manufacture, possess, sell, or purchase salt, or even to carry away the natural deposits of sea salt.

On the morning of March 12, Gandhi and 78 men and women began their march from the gates of the ashram to the small coastal town of Dandi. For 24 days they walked through village after village. Peasants wet down the roads ahead of them and sprinkled the pilgrims with leaves. Two or three times a day, the ashramites stopped for prayer meetings, at which time the local villagers were exhorted to live pure lives and support the cause. The Indian village administrators, who had been cooperating with the British, now had some difficult choices to make about their own loyalty. Three hundred village headmen gave up their government jobs to support the cause. The residents of most villages would accompany the marchers on to the next village, and some would continue even beyond. From all over India sympathizers joined the ashramites so that when Gandhi reached Dandi, on the Bay of Cambay, on April 5, his original group of 78 had grown to thousands.

On the morning of April 6, the Mahatma led his followers to the seashore, where he picked up a handful of salt left by the waves. With this simple act, he defied the mighty forces of the British Empire. The dramatic effects were not lost on the populace. Subhas Chandra Bose, who had previously advocated more violent measures, now compared the Salt March to "Napoleon's march to Paris and his return from Elba." All along India's coast, peasants waded into the sea with pans and illegally took seawater, from which to extract salt. The authorities could no longer ignore what was happening, and they arrested hundreds of persons. At the Congress Party headquarters in Bombay, salt was produced by evaporating seawater in pans on the roof, which brought about a police raid. A crowd of 60,000 assembled to protest, and hundreds of these were arrested, as were prominent Indian leaders throughout the land.

Gandhi himself was not taken into custody until he announced that he would lead his followers in a raid on the Dharsana Salt Works. Despite his arrest, 2500 persons assembled to carry out that act. As the protesters advanced toward the great salt pans, 25 at a time, they were clubbed by hundreds of police. Each column of this ragged army waited its turn, groaning in sympathy at the sickening

Figure 1.1
(Top) Gandhi's fol-
lowers prepare to pro-
test the salt tax imposed
by the British through-
out India. (Bottom) As
Gandhi's followers are
about to raid a govern-
ment salt deposit, they
are clubbed down by a
mounted policeman.

sight and sound of the clubs crashing against the unprotected skulls
of those ahead of them, and then advanced without breaking rank.
This episode was repeated over and over for days, with lines of
stretchers carrying away bleeding protesters.

Although the Indian people had suffered before, never had it
been such a clear case of *choice* and protest. Commitment to the
cause was assured. Britain, and by extension the rest of Europe, had
suffered a blow to its prestige in Asia from which it would never

fully recover. Asia, though weak physically, could still fight back. For British subjects, the injustice and decadence of colonial rule was dramatically demonstrated. Lord Irwin and his administration were sorely wounded by the civil disobedience and loss of revenue. The next time Gandhi requested an interview, Irwin graciously obliged. One can picture the scene as the uniformed viceroy sipped tea with the "half-naked fakir," as Winston Churchill described him. Many meetings later a treaty was signed; it called for an end to civil disobedience and the release of prisoners. Salt manufacturing was again permitted on the seacoast, and delegates of the Indian Congress Party attended a Round Table Conference in London to discuss India's independence.

India, of course, did not achieve independence until after World War II, but from that first significant episode, India's course was set. Furthermore, Gandhi's nonviolent approach was adopted elsewhere as a model for social protest and social change, for example, by Martin Luther King, Jr., and the American civil rights movement, and by Danilo Dolci, who organized unemployed Sicilians to work illegally on improving public roads ("strikes in reverse"), thereby pressuring the authorities to develop an employment program (Dolci, 1959).

Clearly, then, if we were to search for someone who had effectively applied basic social psychological principles to implement social change, it would be difficult to find anyone who could equal Mohandas K. Gandhi.

Coping with Drug Addiction

Few social problems have received more attention in the 1950s and 1960s than drug addiction. After World War II the rate of addiction seemed to be increasing dramatically, and many people believed that narcotics addicts were hooked for life. Statistics seemed to support this pessimistic outlook. The United States Public Health Service Hospital in Lexington, Kentucky, which specializes in drug addiction, reported that 95 percent of the addicts whom they had "cured" returned as addicts later on. Most addicts who voluntarily went to Lexington did not really expect to be cured, but merely hoped to gain some control over their habit when the cost of a "fix" became too expensive; however, most of these people became addicted again after their release. Many health professionals were skeptical, therefore, when Charles E. Dederich said that he had made a significant step toward solving the problem through a program called Synanon (established in 1958).

Synanon utilizes certain social psychological principles, particularly those relating to the effects of the group on the individual, as well as certain assumptions about the character and personality of the drug addict. These are best described by Dederich, himself, in the following portions of a "manifesto" that he presented in a speech to Southern California parole officers:

The synanon can be defined broadly as a kind of group psycho- therapy. Synanon, which is a coined word, is used to describe a more or less informal meeting, which ideally consists of three male patients and three female patients plus one Synanist who is himself an addictive personality, but who has managed to arrest the symp- toms of his addiction for some considerable length of time, or seems to be progressing at a rate somewhat faster than his colleagues in the meeting. The Synanist acts as a moderator and by virtue of an empathy which seems to exist between addictive personalities, is able to detect the patient's conscious or unconscious attempts to evade the truth about himself. . . . The Synanist leans heavily on his own insight into his own problems of personality in trying to help the patients to find themselves and will use the weapons of rid- icule, cross-examination, or hostile attack, as it becomes necessary. These synanon sessions seem to provide an emotional catharsis and seem to trigger an atmosphere of truth-seeking which is reflected in the social life of the family structure. The Synanist does not try to convey to the patient that he himself is a stable personality. In fact it may very well be the destructive drives of the recovered or reco- vering addictive personality embodied in a Synanist which makes him a good therapeutic tool—fighting fire with fire.

Another device which in the opinion of the foundation has been successful, and which is paradoxical in the extreme is the "haircut." The "haircut" is a session which is attended by relatively few pa- tients and four or five of the significant figures of the family struc- ture, during which the patient is . . . "taken apart" and his perfor- mance to date, both constructive and destructive, is pointed out to him, together with suggestions for his future behavior. These ses- sions may even contain tones of the "third degree" and may become quite brutal, on a verbal level, of course. Surprisingly, the patient's reaction has been almost 100 percent favorable. As one of our members put it, "When the word gets around that haircuts are being given, people seem to get in line."

It might be that this device awakens in the subconscious of the patient a realization that someone cares about him. It may satisfy a desire to be the center of attention. It may help to make him realize that a loving father must also be a firm father. Many of the people who have experienced these "haircuts" reported a change in atti- tude or a shift in direction almost immediately. [Since this state- ment, it has become customary for the figurative haircut to be fol- lowed by a literal haircut.] [Quoted in Yablonsky, 1967, pp. 56–59.]

Synanon
3♂ + 3♀ patients +
a Synanist — moderator
(addictive personality)

uses personal insight

"haircut":
patient taken apart
by significant family
figures

Figure 1.2
(Top) Charles Dederich, founder of Synanon (in armchair at extreme right), responds characteristically to speaker in Synanon discussion group.
(Bottom) This drug addict has had his head shaved as a disciplinary measure for leaving a rehabilitation program. Following a verbal "haircutting" session, he was accepted back into the program and remained there.

The synanon (now called the synanon game) and the haircut session are two components of a drug addiction program that is actually far more complex. Participants in the Synanon program live and work together under the same roof as members of an extended family. They engage in a wide variety of activities, including housecleaning and cooking. Underlying all aspects of life in the Synanon family is Dederich's assumption that "a more or less autocratic family structure appears to be necessary as a pre-conditioning environment to buy some time for the recovering addict."

Has the Synanon model been effective? Apparently it has. At least it has kept hundreds of addicts off drugs for years—long enough in many cases so that the "cure" appears to be permanent. The Synanon Foundation has grown from a small group of addicts to a large corporation; the original unit in Santa Monica has been joined by separate establishments in San Francisco; San Deigo; Westport, Connecticut; Reno, Nevada; Detroit; and New York. It has become a successful multimillion-dollar business enterprise, consisting of automobile service stations, retail outlets, a ranch, and a computer center. These successful enterprises have provided the necessary funds to maintain the Synanon community. They have also offered meaningful employment and security for former addicts. Since the late 1960s, Synanon has also attracted a number of nonaddicts who have chosen to live or participate in the program because they found its life style satisfying.

Charles E. Dederich ended his academic studies in the middle of his sophomore year, when he quit Notre Dame. Thus, like Mohandas K. Gandhi, he took no formal university course in social psychology. Yet the principles and techniques he has espoused are quite consistent with a number of social psychological theories and findings. Dederich learned a great deal about group behavior through his long association with Alcoholics Anonymous. Indeed, he had been an alcoholic for more than 20 years. In 1958, while supporting himself on unemployment benefits in Ocean Park (near Los Angeles) and coping with his affinity for alcohol, he organized a weekly free-association group with some AA friends. This discussion group was joined by some drug addicts; the meeting each week was led by a rotating moderator. However, Dederich's superior analytic ability soon won him the role of permanent leader. As such, he attacked the deficiencies of the members and saw many positive changes take place in the group; his methods led to the later haircut sessions. When more addicts joined, the alcoholics quit, leaving the ex-alcoholic Dederich in charge of a group struggling against addiction. Gradually, the principles described above were developed, and Synanon was born (Yablonsky, 1967).

WHO IS NOT
A SOCIAL
PSYCHOLOGIST?

What is a social psychologist? We might be tempted to choose as our examples the hundreds of social scientists who have had formal training in a field called social psychology; who have received advanced degrees in psychology or sociology with a major in social psychology; who have carried out extensive research and either published books entitled "social psychology" or contributed articles to major journals such as the *Journal of Personality and Social Psychology, Journal of Experimental Social Psychology,* or the *European Journal of Social Psychology;* who belong to social psychological organizations such as the Society of Experimental Social Psychologists, the Division of Personality and Social Psychology of the American Psychological Association, the Society for the Psychological Study of Social Issues, or the social psychological section of the American Sociological Association. Yet, as our first two examples of social psychologists, we chose two very unusual and highly influential men, very different from one another, neither of whom would satisfy any of the criteria listed above. Both of these men would fit the following definition of a *social psychologist* given by Gordon Allport (1968) and accepted by many others: *someone who attempts to understand, explain, and predict how the thoughts, feelings, and actions of individuals are influenced by the perceived, imagined, or implied thoughts, feelings, and actions of others.* Obviously, this definition applies to the two men whom we have described above. They certainly did attempt to understand, explain, and predict the effects of certain individuals upon others, and they were quite successful.

There are numerous other social psychologists we could have discussed. Grigori Efimovich Rasputin, for example, evidently had a remarkable ability to understand, explain, and predict the behavior of the prerevolutionary Russian nobility. He very quickly sized up the potential power of Czarina Alexandra to influence Czar Nicholas

Social Psychologist:

Figure 1.3
Grigori Rasputin, seated with a group of admiring women, developed immense power over the Czar, Czarina, and all of prerevolutionary Russia.

who, because of his position, had almost absolute power in Russia. How, then, could he influence the Czarina? He decided upon her only son and heir, Czarevich Alexis. By means still not generally known, Rasputin was able to convince the Czarina that the pain and danger of her son's hemophilia would subside only if he, Rasputin, were present. Soon Rasputin was able to make his presence and approval indispensable to the royal household. By understanding, explaining, and predicting, Rasputin was able to control the behavior of others and to create for himself a position of real power (Fülöp-Miller, 1928).

In a later chapter, we will show how President John F. Kennedy developed keen insight into the basic principles of group behavior, which stood him in good stead when he was obliged to cope with the Cuban missile crisis. Florence Nightingale, without an astute awareness of the structure of the British military forces and their relationship to the home office, could never have brought about the changes that she achieved in military hospitals during the Crimean War. Mighty Cyrus, King of Persia, could have taken his cues from this book's chapter on influence, as he worked to achieve and maintain the loyalty of his men. Xenophon (trans. Warner, 1969) said of Cyrus:

Often, when he had had a particularly good wine, he used to send jars half full of it to his friends, with the message: "Cyrus has not for a long time come across a better wine than this; so he has sent some to you and wants you to finish it up today with those whom you love best." Often too he used to send helpings of goose and halves of loaves and such things, telling bearers to say when they presented these: "Cyrus enjoyed this; so he wants you to taste it too" [p. 52].

But does a social psychologist have to be famous or influential? Certainly not! Indeed, who is *not* a social psychologist? As Fritz Heider (1958) has written:

In everyday life we [all] form ideas about other people and about social situations. We interpret other people's actions and we predict what they will do under certain circumstances. Though these ideas are usually not well formulated, they often function adequately. They achieve in some measure what a science is supposed to achieve: an adequate description of the subject matter which makes prediction possible [p. 5].

The answer is clear. By our definition, everyone is a social psychologist. Without some ability to understand and predict the behavior of others, none of us would be able to function effectively in our social world. Too often it is our *errors* in understanding that are emphasized; the rather amazing accuracy of our predictions is so commonplace that it is frequently overlooked or taken for granted. We all know about the obvious errors in social coordination that lead to tragic collisions on our highways and freeways, but have you ever thought about the fantastic accuracy that is much more typical—as drivers speeding along at 70 miles an hour anticipate lane changes by other drivers and adjust accordingly?

To get some sense of *your own* rather remarkable ability as a social psychologist, try to solve the following hypothetical problem: You and a companion have unexpectedly had to parachute into an area with which neither of you is familiar; however, each of you has a map of the area (Figure 1.4). After landing, you look at the sur-

Figure 1.4
Understanding and predicting the behavior of others. *You and a companion have parachuted into unfamiliar territory. Each of you has a copy of this map. You estimate that you have landed approximately at point y. Although you do not know where your companion has landed, you must meet him as quickly as possible if you are to be rescued. Where should you go?* *(After Schelling, 1960.)*

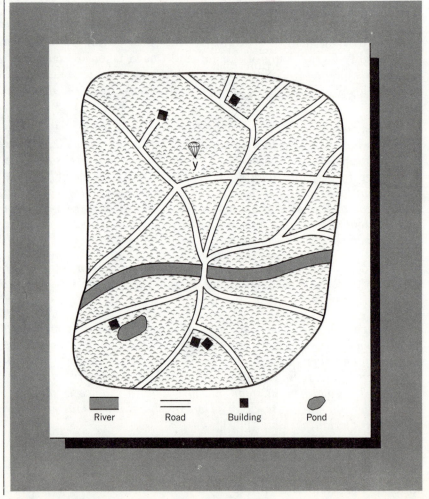

rounding territory carefully and study the map; you conclude that you are probably at point y. You have no idea where your companion has landed, and you have no way of communicating with him. Yet the two of you must get together quickly if you hope to be rescued. Think about this and look at the map very carefully. Where would you go to meet him? Write down your answer on a sheet of paper before reading further.

When the game strategist Thomas C. Schelling (1960) gave this problem to Yale University students, half of them were told (as you were) that they had landed at point y. The paired partners were told that they had landed at point x (at the lower right-hand corner of the map). Eighty-eight percent of the pairs succeeded in getting together by indicating a common meeting place. These successful "parachutists" understood their partners and the way in which they perceived the situation and the terrain; they were able to predict successfully what their partners' behavior would be, even in this highly ambiguous situation; thus, they were able to coordinate their behavior to match that of their partners. Would you have been successful? As social psychologists, we think that you probably would have been— that you would have immediately set out for the bridge where, according to Schelling, you would meet your partner.

WHY STUDY
SOCIAL
PSYCHOLOGY?

If everyone is already a social psychologist, why should anyone wish to study social psychology? If we already have an understanding, if we are able to predict successfully the behavior of others, if we can therefore coordinate our own behavior with theirs, then it might appear that we could spend our time more fruitfully doing other things rather than studying social psychology formally, that is, taking a course or reading a book in that field. There are, however, several good reasons why it seems useful to study social psychology:

1. Although we are all social psychologists, we are *imperfect* social psychologists. We can be surprisingly accurate in understanding and predicting the behavior of others, but there are obviously many instances when we are inaccurate. Have you ever brought together two mutual friends who have common interests and similar personalities, predicting that they would really "hit it off," only to discover later that neither one could tolerate the other? Our divorce courts are packed with couples whose problems can often be traced to a gross failure in their ability to predict and understand their behavior and interaction. Many social programs whose aim is to

relieve poverty, reduce prejudice and crime, and develop harmony among people, have been catastrophic failures because their originators had a woefully inadequate understanding of the basic principles of social interaction.

It is true that, even without a formal study of social psychology, some individuals are more effective social psychologists than others. The examples that we have presented—Gandhi, Dederich, Kennedy, Rasputin, Cyrus, Nightingale—together with many others embody extremely well the application of social psychological principles. However, these models and their behavior will be more meaningful if we can formally abstract the social psychological principles and relate them to a formal body of theory and research. Indeed, even the most skillful, practicing social psychologist must admit to gross errors and an inability to deal with many critical social events. Gandhi accurately understood and predicted the effects of the Salt March on the British and the Indians, but he was far less effective in understanding the intense feelings of animosity between the Hindus and Moslems. He was unable to bring his social psychological skills to bear on the problem of avoiding the bloody internal strife that accompanied independence and of maintaining a united India after independence. Dederich, while apparently successful in the development of Synanon and in the possible cure of many "incurable" addicts, still admitted that he had failed with a number of them. Furthermore, there is evidence that many of the "cures" depend upon continuing group support and participation in the Synanon community. Kennedy, although he was lauded for his skills in applying social psychological principles to the Cuban missile crisis, admitted to gross errors in predicting and understanding human behavior in the abortive invasion of Cuba at the Bay of Pigs (Janis, 1972).

Could these major figures have been even more effective if they had been knowledgeable about formal social psychological theory and research? We would like to think so. In any event, we can all gain greater insight into both the successes and the failures of these people by applying to them some of the concepts of the discipline of social psychology.

2. Even if one could be accurate in understanding and predicting the behavior of a given individual, understanding social behavior is much more difficult due to the problem of interaction. Interaction cannot be understood through knowledge of separate individuals. When two persons come together, their separate knowledge and skills may be used to try to outsmart one another, or their mutual concern for the other's welfare may lead to a less perfect outcome for both (as illustrated in O. Henry's *Gift of the Magi*). When three persons interact with one another, prediction and understanding are even more difficult, for two persons can form a coalition against the

third, or one person can play the other two off against each other, or
the three can unite or compete in any of various combinations. How
many times have small retail stores failed because each owner tried
to maximize his own profits by lowering his prices, thereby beginning an accelerating pattern of mutual loss? Or how often has it happened that the first lifeboat that was lowered from a sinking ship has
capsized because too many passengers—each focusing only on his
own desperate situation—all tried to climb on board? Many committees made up of relatively mediocre persons have jointly produced a
superior product, while other committees made up of outstanding
persons have collectively produced disasters. To understand these
successes and failures, it is helpful to utilize some of the tools provided by social psychological theory and research.

3. The fact that some people are more effective than others in
understanding and predicting social behavior is a matter of considerable political and social importance. There is always the danger that
those who acquire greater social psychological skills will utilize
them for self-seeking purposes or for ends that will be detrimental to
others. At times such misuse of social psychological skills will be
carried out in what the manipulator mistakenly believes are the best
interests of everyone. Machiavelli, either to gain personal favor or
because of what he believed were the best interests of the greatest
number, offered his remarkable social insights to his beloved
prince—who, in turn, utilized this knowledge to strengthen his own
power at the expense of many others. It often happens that social
psychological knowledge is most readily available to those with the
greatest resources because they can offer the most for it. It has been
demonstrated that, with proper financing and effective use of social
psychological principles, a lackluster political candidate can be
"packaged" and "sold" to the electorate and a jury can be persuaded
to acquit a defendant who would otherwise probably have been
judged guilty. Saul Alinski (1971) has offered his own insights into
the ways in which those with less power can better counter the
exploitative devices of those with more power. Another reason for
studying social psychology is thus to acquire a better understanding
of the methods used by more powerful or knowledgeable individuals
and groups to influence others. By developing a systematic statement
of our social psychological knowledge—utilizing scientific data—we
can encourage the widespread sharing of social skills for the benefit
of all.

4. Finally, a great deal of satisfaction can be gained by developing a clear statement of how people affect one another—giving structure and substance to our understanding of one another. We hope
that a careful presentation of social psychological theory and research can offer some of the same satisfaction that comes from read-

ing an exciting novel that provides new insights into life; from look-ing at a well-executed painting that provides new perceptions of the world around us; from listening to a carefully constructed musical composition that provides beauty and pleasure.

SOCIAL PSYCHOLOGY: EVERYDAY AND SCIENTIFIC

Although everyone is a social psychologist, there is also a discipline called social psychology, whose students are formally and exclu-sively concerned with understanding, explaining, and predicting so-cial behavior; for them, understanding is a significant goal in its own right and not just a means to achieve better relationships with others. In the following pages, we will point out several examples of how formally trained social psychologists differ from others in their analy-sis of social behavior. Despite our earlier assertion that *everyone* is a social psychologist, we will now use that term in its professional sense.

Three Social Psychologists Bet That the World Will Not End
In late 1955, three social psychologists—Leon Festinger, Henry W. Riecken, and Stanley Schachter—were intrigued by an interesting news item that appeared in the newspaper of a city on one of the Great Lakes: "PROPHECY FROM PLANET. CLARION CALL TO CITY: FLEE THAT FLOOD. IT'LL SWAMP US ON DEC. 21, OUTER SPACE TELLS SUBURBANITE." The article went on to describe the visions that were reported by a suburban housewife, Mrs. Marian Keech;[1] the visions were supported by many messages in automatic writing that would have cataclysmic or sublime implica-tions for those who accepted them as true. The city was to be de-stroyed by a huge flood from the Great Lakes, a flood that would create a huge inland sea ranging from the Arctic Circle to the Gulf of Mexico. A gigantic earthquake would submerge the Pacific Coast from Seattle to Chile.

Mrs. Keech had already told a number of her friends who lived in "Lake City" about her visions. She also aroused the interest of a cosmic exploration group headed by a Dr. Thomas Armstrong in "Collegeville," some distance away. Dr. Armstrong, a physician and research professor at a university in Collegeville, informed a number of his students who were interested in cosmology and the occult about them. Impressed by Mrs. Keech's visions, Dr. Armstrong and

[1] The names of most places and persons described here (other than Festinger, Riecken, and Schachter) are fictitious.

his student group traveled to meetings in Lake City. At these meetings, the "Seekers" exchanged their own ideas and thoughts about the impending catastrophe. If the world were coming to an end, they felt that they might as well prepare for it. Why should they continue to work if their future were to be so limited? A number of the Seekers gave up their jobs. They also canceled their debts and gave away their possessions. They stated their convictions publicly. Indeed, Dr. Armstrong lost his position when the administration at his university became embarrassed by his stated beliefs.

The Seekers' Commitment. It was the Seekers' deep commitment to their belief, and the resulting actions and implications for the members, that led Festinger, Riecken, and Schachter to infiltrate the group in the hope of studying it. For some time they had been interested in derivations of the theory of cognitive dissonance (Festinger, 1957), which postulated some rather definite things about what would happen when a person committed himself strongly, through words and actions, to a belief that would later be disconfirmed. The theory, developed from observations and some social psychological studies in the laboratory and in the field, has also helped to explain a number of historical events. Why, for example, did Jewish followers of the seventeenth-century false messiah, Shabbetai Z'vi, continue to believe that he was still their messiah, even after he had acceded to the Turkish sultan's request and converted to Islam? Why did other messianic groups, such as the Millerites and the Anabaptists, continue to believe in the doctrines of their prophets even after these doctrines had been renounced? When events prove us wrong, one might expect that we would quietly reject the discredited beliefs; yet here were instances in which the disconfirmed beliefs were held even more strongly than before, and in which the followers organized to proselyte and convince others that they were right.

Testing Dissonance Theory in a Natural Experiment. Essentially, Festinger, Riecken, and Schachter postulated that people have a strong need for consistency (consonance) among their beliefs and actions. (Would anyone disagree that such a need exists?) If a belief turns out to be false, however, one of the ways in which consistency can be satisfied is by changing the belief—as so often happens. But let us examine this idea more carefully: If you cancel your debts, give up your job, prepare for the millennium, and endure the ridicule and sarcasm of erstwhile friends and neighbors, are you going to admit to yourself that your underlying belief was false? No, for the psychological costs are usually too great. However, if you have some group support, you can reduce your state of inconsistency (dissonance) by reinterpreting your initial belief without actually destroying it. You can add further support for your own belief by seeking out

Cognitive
Dissonance

others in your group with a similar need to buttress the same belief, so that you can mutually support one another. Then your group can organize to win new converts to the belief. All of these things might make your original belief seem more reasonable. From an initial common-sense assumption about consistency, Festinger, Riecken, and Schachter thus logically arrived at a conclusion that would otherwise have seemed farfetched—even bizarre.

How excited our social psychologists must have been at the prospect of having the opportunity to test this theory by predicting what would happen to the Seekers who were at the beginning stages of the belief disconfirmation process, for Festinger and his colleagues believed quite firmly that the beliefs would be disconfirmed—that the world would *not* come to an end—and that they, the social psychologists, would live to write up the results of this study. It is one thing to reinterpret past history in terms of your theory, but how much more satisfying it is to be able to predict from your theory something that has not yet occurred and then see your prediction substantiated.

In order to test their theory, Festinger and his colleagues needed a situation in which a belief would lead to very specific predictions which, in turn, would be clearly and dramatically disconfirmed. In this case, Mrs. Keech had predicted that prior to the destruction of the world on December 21, the faithful Seekers would receive midnight visitors, members of a cosmic group called the Guardians. A Guardian would escort the Seekers to a flying saucer, and then they would whir off into outer space seven hours before the cataclysm.

To recapitulate, both the Seekers and the social psychologists had made specific predictions about what would happen on and after December 21, 1955. The Seekers based their predictions on the following: their collective knowledge of the cosmos; their particular understanding of people and of their relationship with the universe; the visions and dreams of one of their members—Mrs. Keech; conversations with the Creator by another member, Bertha Blatsky; extensive study of the sacred writings of Hinduism, the Apocrypha, *Oahspe*, theosophy, Rosicrucianism, and George Adamski's writings about his travels in a flying saucer, *The Flying Saucers Have Landed*. The social psychologists' main prediction was that the Seekers' predictions, and thus their beliefs, would be dramatically disconfirmed. They were so convinced that the world would *not* come to an end and that the space visitors would not arrive that they took it as an unstated assumption. Their other predictions were based upon their own particular knowledge of the nature of people and of their relationship with the universe; the theory of cognitive dissonance as presented by Leon Festinger; an extensive study of history; and the writings of Kurt Lewin, Fritz Heider, Hadley Cantril, Max Werthei-mer, Wolfgang Köhler, Kurt Koffka, and others.

The social psychologists predicted that so long as the Seekers were confident of their own beliefs, they would look within their own group for support and reject the inconsistent beliefs of outside groups. This did, in fact, happen, for after the appearance of the initial newspaper article, the Seekers refused to meet and discuss their plans and beliefs with reporters and others from outside. Indeed, Festinger and his colleagues felt that they would only be accepted as group members if they professed to be Seekers themselves; and so it was only after the Seekers had expressed considerable hestitation and reluctance that the social psychologists were finally accepted. The social psychologists also predicted that there would be a dramatic change once the Seekers' predictions had been disconformed. At that point, the Seekers would look for outside support for their beliefs; they would invite in the news media, reinterpret their beliefs for the benefit of the outside world, and strengthen their organization in an attempt to win new adherents. Thus, they could hope to gain additional support for their shaken beliefs.

A Night of Apprehension for the Social Psychologists and Seekers. Imagine the tension that gripped the small group of Seekers as they began to congregate on December 17 to prepare for the Day of Reckoning. Sixteen Seekers, including five infiltrators (the three social psychologists and two observers who were working with them), waited at Mrs. Keech's home. Eleven members of Dr. Armstrong's Collegeville contingent could not get to Lake City, and so Dr. Armstrong had instructed them to go about their affairs and to have faith that the Guardians would arrange to pick them up wherever they might be. Most of these student Seekers went home to spend their last Christmas holiday with their doubting families.

The Seekers had clearly invested a great deal of themselves in their beliefs and in their predictions of salvation and calamity. How important it was for them to have their predictions confirmed! But what about the social psychologists? Hadn't they spent many, many hours developing their theory, infiltrating the Seekers (which caused some feelings of guilt about this illicit venture), attending numerous meetings which required them to travel from Minneapolis to suburban Lake City (often on very short notice), and recording their observations on 65 hours of tape. Further, just as the Seekers had adopted beliefs that were contrary to those of their friends, relatives, and colleagues, the same was almost the case with the social psychologists. Festinger, Riecken, and Schachter were experimental social psychologists; they had established their reputations by means of careful laboratory studies of individual and group behavior. Now they were engaged in a field study that was obviously not well controlled, and in which there were enormous measurement problems. It was a study more in the tradition of anthropology than of social psychology and quite unorthodox anthropology at that. Although they tried to conduct their investigation in relative secrecy, they could not help communicating something of it to other social psychologists, who probably greeted their plans with raised eyebrows or worse. What consequences would Festinger and his colleagues have to face if their predictions about the Seekers' behavior were disconfirmed? Thus, every member of this small group must have awaited the confirmation or disconfirmation of his or her beliefs with some apprehension.

One might speculate that the Seekers were less apprehensive than the social psychologists, since they had developed a well-organized system of beliefs and enjoyed mutual group support (which included the distinguished physician and his wife from Collegeville and an intelligent group of "converts" from Minneapolis). It fit the initial predictions of the social psychologists that, at this stage at least, the Seekers did not need converts. Therefore, several persons who expressed an interest in joining at this time were discouraged. Recall that the social psychologists had been accepted only with reluctance. Many reporters and feature writers who requested interviews and who could have broadcast the Seekers' message to an audience of millions were summarily excluded.

During the final days, the group made increasingly frenetic preparations. Among other things, they searched their clothing for bits of metal that might be affected by the wave of radioactivity they believed would accompany the moments of salvation and destruction. One of the women observers had the heels of her shoes ripped off by a Seeker because the heels had nails in them; the metal buttons were also ripped from her coat. When it was pointed out that her brassiere probably had metal fastenings, she removed it. She had to be careful when she spoke for fear that the metal fillings in her teeth might show.

The Tribulations of Dr. Armstrong. The last word received by the Seekers was that the Guardian and his flying saucer would arrive at midnight, December 20. The Seekers assembled at the home of Mrs. Keech and waited anxiously as the seconds and minutes ticked away. At 11:35 P.M. Leon Festinger nearly caused a panic when he suddenly discovered that he had not removed the metal zipper from his trousers. Dr. Armstrong rushed him into the bedroom where he performed emergency surgery with a razor blade. Hands trembling in a manner uncharacteristic of a physician and glancing at the clock every few seconds, he cut out the zipper and wrenched out the metal

Figure 1.5
The group of Seekers (as well as Riecken, Schachter, and Festinger) anxiously await the appointed hour.

clasps with wire cutters. It took until 11:50 to sew up the trousers with a few rough, unsurgical stitches, leaving Dr. Festinger somewhat less mobile for the critical observations he hoped to make. Such are the costs of social psychological research.

Two clocks in the living room ticked loudly; one was 10 minutes faster than the other. As the faster clock reached 12:00, the tension increased. When nothing happened, the group simply acknowledged that the slower clock was more accurate. When the slower clock read 11:59, Mrs. Keech, her voice strained and high pitched, exclaimed, "And not a plan has gone astray!" Finally, the Seekers heard the slow painful chimes as the slower clock struck 12. There was silence, apprehension, no overt sign of tension (although Dr. Armstrong and Bertha Blatsky later admitted that the shock was overwhelming). At 12:05, the Creator spoke slowly and haltingly through Bertha Blatsky's voice: "There will be a slight delay, just a slight delay." Minutes dragged into hours. At 4:00 A.M., one of the social psychologists stepped out the front door to get some fresh air. It looked as if he might be abandoning the group, and the thought of losing a member at this time—when group support was so desperately needed—was intolerable to the Seekers. Dr. Armstrong was particu-

larly distressed and so he dashed out the door to reinspire the de-
parting comrade. His words reflected his own dissonance clearly:

*I've had to go a long way. I've given up just about everything.
I've cut every tie. I've burned every bridge. I've turned my back on
the world. I can't afford to doubt. I have to believe. And there isn't
any other truth. . . . I've taken an awful beating in the last few
months, just an awful beating. But I do know who I am and I know
what I've got to do. I know I've got to teach just as Jesus knew, and
I don't care what happens tonight. I can't afford to doubt. I won't
doubt even if we have to make an announcement to the press tomorrow and admit we were wrong. You're having your period of doubt
now, but hang on, boy, hang on [Festinger, Riecken, and Schachter,
1956, p. 168].*

Fortunately for them, the Seekers were spared the problem of
having to admit that they were wrong. At 4:45 A.M., Marian Keech
announced that she had received a message, which she read aloud:

*And mighty is the word of God—and by his word have ye been
saved—for from the mouth of death have ye been delivered . . .
[because] not since the beginning of time upon this Earth has there
been such a force of Good and light as now floods this room [Fest-
inger, Riecken, and Schachter, 1956, p. 169].*

The power of goodness had spared the group and the world. The
message was greeted with jubilation and rejoicing. A few days later,
the Seekers gathered in front of the Keech residence to sing
Christmas carols to some 200 curious onlookers. With what fervor they
must have sung "O come all ye faithful, joyful and triumphant!"—a
carol that must have held a special meaning for the Seekers, not fully
understood by others. Meantime, special press releases were prepared and newsmen were invited in, whereas only a few days before,
reporters and potential members had been discouraged.

Although the group of Seekers in suburban Lake City rejoiced
together, the dispersed members from Collegeville simply disbanded and suffered the intense pain that accompanied the disconfirmation of their beliefs.

In reading the account by Festinger, Riecken, and Schachter
(1956), it seemed to us that the Seekers' beliefs were clearly and
dramatically disconfirmed. It should be pointed out, however, that
the Seekers who remained faithful to the end did not perceive their
beliefs as disavowed, nor their predictions as unsupported. Instead,
it appeared to them that new elements had entered the picture. Who
would have expected the Creator, seeing all of the goodness and

light in the Keech living room, to call off the cataclysm?

For the Social Psychologists: Beliefs Confirmed. And what about the social psychologists? It appears that their predictions were confirmed. Didn't the Seekers, who had avoided publicity and new adherents before the fateful night, now search out the news media and attempt to proselyte? And what about those Seekers who did not wait with the group in suburban Lake City and gave up their beliefs? The social psychologists had said that their predictions would hold true for groups that had some group support. The Collegeville Seekers who had gone to their respective homes for the Christmas holiday not only lacked group support, but were actively encouraged and pressured by their families to give up their beliefs. These predictions were also supported.

What would have happened if the social psychologists' predictions had been disconfirmed? Tongue-in-cheek, Robert W. White (1958) suggested that, according to their own theory, Festinger and his colleagues would have had to find some explanation for their failure (perhaps a new factor had entered the situation, or the Seekers had manifested some personality or social class peculiarity that produced an opposite effect than the one predicted). Faced with dissonance themselves, the social psychologists would then have had to organize and proselyte for new adherents to dissonance theory, possibly by establishing a new journal and a professional organization. In this way, they would be able to assure themselves that their efforts had not been in vain.

White's comment, although meant as a satirical criticism of dissonance theory, need not be read that way. He could have been saying that, to the extent that social psychological theory is correct, it should be generally applicable—even to social psychologists themselves.

A Further Test in the Social Psychologists' Laboratory

As mentioned earlier, the punishment suffered by Gandhi's followers at the Dharsana Salt Works served to consolidate their support for the Indian independence movement. Similarly, Dr. Armstrong's endurance of the many unhappy consequences of his beliefs seems to have made these beliefs all the more important to him ("I've taken an awful beating. . . . I can't afford to doubt"). His "awful beating" was due not only to his beliefs but to his association with the Seekers.

The Festinger, Riecken, and Schachter study, Festinger's book *Theory of Cognitive Dissonance* (1957), and other cognitive dissonance studies were enough to win over two formidable converts to dissonance theory: Elliot Aronson and Judson Mills. (Note that we didn't say that disconfirmation was the *only* way to win converts.) These two social psychologists set out to examine systematically the effects of taking a beating on the consolidation of a belief system.

Members of fraternal and sororal organizations have long believed that the allegiance of a new member would be more secure if his indoctrination included some sort of painful (or at least uncomfortable) initiation—wearing silly clothes, scrubbing the floor of the fraternity house with a toothbrush, paying a large initiation fee, undergoing painful paddling, and so forth. In a similar vein, psychiatrists have also contended that their high fees serve, in part, to make the therapeutic relationship more important to the patient. On the other hand, one could argue that the negative association of a painful initiation might carry over to the organization itself and cause the initiate to lose interest. These alternative predictions could be tested, of course, by comparing organizations—those with and those without uncomfortable initiations—and observing which members liked their organization more. This test poses a problem, however. If it is known beforehand that a certain club has a rigorous initiation, only those who want to join it very badly will allow themselves to go through such an ordeal—and if the members show that they like their club very much, this could be due to self-selection rather than to the rigor of the initiation. Aronson and Mills, therefore, decided to carry out an experimental test of these two predictions under more controlled laboratory conditions.

Their subjects were 63 college women who had individually volunteered to join a group (made up of college women) that was to discuss the psychology of sex in a series of meetings. After volunteering, each woman was randomly assigned to one of three experimental conditions: Severe Initiation, Mild Initiation, or No Initiation. Preliminary measures indicated no differences among these three groups of subjects with respect to their initial evaluations of their prospective groups. Those assigned to the Severe Initiation condition were told that they would first have to take an "embarrassment test" (presumably designed to screen out those who become extremely embarrassed in sex discussions) before they could join the group. In this so-called embarrassment test, each subject had to read 12 obscene words written on 3x5 cards and then two passages taken from recent novels giving elaborate and vivid descriptions of sexual activities. The subjects assigned to the Mild Initiation condition were given the same explanation and then were instructed to read five words that were sex related but not obscene. All of the subjects in both these conditions were told that they had passed the screening test and could thus join the group. The subjects in the control group (No Initiation) were given no tests.

Before the women were introduced to the other group members, who had already begun to meet, the "new members" were asked to listen to a tape recording of the group (and the *same* recording was played for all subjects). It was a discussion about a book the group had read—*Sexual Behavior in Animals*. Hesitantly and in halting fashion, the group members discussed the secondary sex characteristics of lower animals. Their comments were full of inconsistencies and *non sequiturs*, lots of hemming and hawing, and there was no clear, logical flow of ideas. The discussion was obviously boring.

Having heard the expected group in action, each of the subjects was asked to rate the group and its discussion on a series of scales, indicating their own personal interest and enjoyment. After this, the experiment ended, and the actual purpose of the study was carefully explained to the subjects.

The results of this experiment clearly supported dissonance theory prediction: Those subjects who had undergone a Severe Initiation tended to rate their group and its discussion as interesting and enjoyable. By contrast, the subjects in the Mild Initiation or No Initiation condition tended to rate the group and its discussion as extremely boring (Aronson and Mills, 1959).

THE DISTINCTIONS BETWEEN EVERYDAY AND SCIENTIFIC SOCIAL PSYCHOLOGY

Earlier we suggested that professional social psychologists differ from others in their basic goals. Although everyone must be a social psychologist in order to navigate his way through life toward his own objectives, the professional social psychologist wants to explain social behavior as a goal in and of itself. In order to do this, he must be able to understand the meaning not only of his own private social experiences, but of those of other people in a variety of situations. In order to develop some insight into social behavior, the social psychologist must cast a wide net on experience and, in so doing, attempt to explain and integrate diverse, often contradictory, observations as parsimoniously as possible. This net, as well as the conceptual lens through which it is viewed and interpreted, constitutes the social psychologist's *theory* of social behavior.

Theory Construction and Development

Earlier we discussed the fact that one's commitment to and affiliation with a group are determined in part by the extent to which he has ex-

erted effort, suffered pain, or otherwise given up something in order
to be a member of that group. Gandhi and Dederich may have had
some earlier experiences in life that led them to accept this principle. However, Festinger, Riecken, and Schachter (as well as Aronson
and Mills) were acting, as social psychologists, according to a previously conceived and developed theory—namely, Festinger's
theory of cognitive dissonance. This theory posits a tendency toward
consistency—the individual will experience pressures to make his attitudes and behavior consistent (or consonant) with one another. An
individual's knowledge that he has exerted considerable effort to join
a group, that he has experienced hardship in order to belong to that
group, that he has given something up as a result of group membership, and that he has done all of this voluntarily is dissonant with
his having a weak affiliation with that group. One way in which he
can reduce such dissonance is by increasing his positive evaluation
of the group so that his previous efforts and punishments seem
worthwhile. Festinger developed this theory by observing his own
experiences and those of others and then integrating these observations with the findings of earlier research. Dissonance theory has
deep roots in the Gestalt theory of perception in psychology (for example, Köhler, 1929; Koffka, 1935; Wertheimer, 1923), the field
theory of Kurt Lewin (1951), the concepts of balance and consistency
of Fritz Heider (1958), and elsewhere.

Formal Methods for Testing Theory

In order to test the adequacy of a theory, a social psychologist must
utilize a body of existing evidence—data that he obtains from his
own experiences and evidence that he finds in social psychological
research. Does the theory fit the data? If not, how could the theory
be reformulated? Of course, in any assessment of theory against existing evidence, the social psychologist must be aware of his own
limitations; he must understand that his own personal investment in
a theory may cause him to look at the data selectively. In examining
the writings of various social psychologists, Berkowitz (1971) has
pointed out that there is a tendency to report experimental data
rather selectively and in such a way that the experiment fits the
theory more clearly than the data justify. Berkowitz is not suggesting
any conscious attempt by social psychologists to distort their data; he
is simply saying that social psychologists are subject to the same
forces that affect the behavior of the people whom they study. Scientific social psychologists try to be aware of their fallibility and guard
against its effects upon their own behavior as scientists.

Prediction is a major test of understanding. Therefore, after the
social psychologist has stated his theory carefully, defined its con-

cepts precisely, and established postulates and derivations, he may then frame some hypotheses and attempt to test them. Over the years, social psychologists have developed a variety of rather intriguing methods to test predictions, each of which has its own advantages and limitations. These methods include: *review of relevant historical documents,* such as biographies, archives, public records, or newspaper accounts; the *field survey,* a technique that utilizes a large field staff of trained interviewers who obtain evidence by questioning a representative sample of a preselected population; the *field study,* a method that requires close, careful examination of a single social unit, such as a community, club, or work group; the *natural experiment,* a technique in which the investigator observes behavior before, during, and after some naturally occurring event (such as an earthquake, a strike, or an election); the *field experiment,* in which the researcher observes natural behavior, but attempts to obtain greater control over that behavior, its causes, and consequences by systematically manipulating certain (independent) variables and examining their effects on various (dependent) measures; and the *laboratory experiment* (perhaps the most important, and certainly the most widely used, technique available to social psychologists), in which the researcher systematically introduces independent variables and dependent measures in an artificial environment (the laboratory) which gives him maximum control over the social situation being studied. Each of these research techniques is described and illustrated in greater detail in the Appendix.

PEOPLE IN GROUPS
AS A FOCUS

The discipline of social psychology has much in common with both sociology and psychology. Psychology is generally concerned with the ways in which an individual is affected by the environment, while *social* psychology focuses on the ways in which an individual is affected by his *social* environment—namely other people. In that sense, social psychology is often considered a subdiscipline of psychology.

Sociology, on the other hand, is the study of social aggregates and groups, their internal forms and organization, and the factors that encourage their stability or produce change. The sociologist is particularly interested in social structure and the relationship among units in a social system. In analyzing social structure, he often focuses on the individual in the social system. Accordingly, social psychology is often considered an important subdiscipline of sociology.

At various times, therefore, social psychology has been claimed by university departments of sociology and psychology. However, knowledge does not come in neat packages, nor does it easily fit into academic pigeonholes. Social psychology as a discipline has drawn heavily from both sociology and psychology, as well as from political science, economics, and anthropology; it has much to offer these areas in return.

Since World War II, the boundaries of social psychology have expanded to an unprecedented extent. In the area of psychology, social psychological research has been conducted in social learning, personality development, psycholinguistics, language development, and psychological adjustment and maladjustment. In the area of sociology, social psychological research has encompassed communication and mass media, political behavior, international relations, culture and national character, economics, and industrial organization.

We have decided to limit the scope of this book to an analysis of interaction in small groups. It is our belief that most, if not all, of the basic concepts in social psychology can be examined through such an analysis, but we will apply our concepts more generally from time to time. Among the questions to be covered are the following:

People Alone and Together. What is it like to be alone? Is a person ever *really* alone? Can one be alone even when there are others present? What effect does isolation have on people? Why are social contacts so important? When do social contacts become oppressive?

Becoming Aware of Others and Ourselves. How do we get to know others? How is new information about another person integrated into the information that we already have? How do our prior conceptions and prejudices affect our learning about others? How do we select and control the information that others receive about us? How do we evaluate ourselves in relation to others?

Liking and Disliking, Friendship and Aggression. What determines the way in which we evaluate another person? Why do we seek out some people and avoid others? Do opposites attract? Do "birds of a feather flock together"? How do we go about trying to get others to like us?

The Interdependence of Persons. What determines whether we cooperate or compete with other persons? What are the effects of cooperation and competition upon our relationships with other persons? Are we always aware of the extent to which cooperation and/or competition take place? How can we understand cooperation, competition, and bargaining in everyday life?

Interpersonal Influence and Social Power. By what means do we attempt to get other people to do as we wish? What are the effects of different methods of influence—promise of reward, threat of punishment, expertise, legitimacy, mutual identification, and information? Who is responsible for the change that occurs—the person who attempted to influence another or the person who decided to accept it?

The Structure of Groups. How can we study communication, attraction, role assignment, interdependence, and prestige as structural dimensions? More generally, how can we examine the structural patterning of groups, and how are these dimensions of structure interrelated?

Group Effects and Individual Behavior. Under what conditions will people in groups engage in activities that they would object to as individuals? Why do groups often choose riskier courses of action than do individuals? Under what conditions does an individual's identity become lost in a group, and what are the effects of such deindividuation? Under what conditions do people help one another or refuse to help?

Group Performance, Group Effectiveness, and Leadership. What are some of the factors that influence the performance and effectiveness of small groups? In particular, how is group performance affected by the quality of its leadership? What are the determinants of good or bad leadership? How does the style of leadership affect the members of a group? What are the determinants of leadership style?

Conflict, Harmony, and Tension between Groups. To what extent can we apply our theories about the interrelationships of individuals to an analysis of the interrelationships of groups? What factors affect conflict or cooperation between groups? What effects do the relationships between groups have upon the individuals in these groups? How can we study group conflict and international tensions in the field and in the laboratory? What clues from social psychological research will help us to live together more harmoniously?

Summary

There is nothing magical about a social psychologist—in fact, in a sense every person is one, even though he may not think of himself as such. The distinguished psychologist, Gordon Allport, has defined a social psychologist as someone who attempts to understand, explain, and predict how the thoughts, feelings, and actions of individuals are influenced by the perceived, imagined, or implied thoughts, feelings, and actions of others. Obviously this definition applies to many of the world's great leaders such as Mohandas K. Gandhi, who used basic social psychological principles so effectively to implement social change in India; it also applies to Charles E. Dederich, whose understanding of the group and its effects on the individual enabled him to found Synanon and make it into an effective drug-addiction program. This definition likewise applies to each of us. Without some ability to understand and predict the behavior of others, none of us would be able to function very effectively in our social world. We understand other people's goals and perceptions, and we coordinate our behavior with theirs in a variety of simple and complex ways, drawing on skills of which we may not be aware. Furthermore, we use our knowledge to influence others—and we each have our own ideas about how to do that. Everyone, in short, is a social psychologist.

If everyone is a social psychologist, why should anyone wish to study social psychology? One reason is that, although we are often accurate in understanding and predicting the behavior of others, we are sometimes mistaken. On occasion our ability to adapt to different social situations is impaired, particularly when we are under stress. Second, although we may be accurate in our predictions of individual behavior (someone else's or our own), our understanding of social behavior is greatly complicated by the problem of interaction. People constantly do things to and with one another, and their interaction cannot be fully understood even though we may know the separate individuals. Interaction is more than the sum of the actions of the participants. Third, since some people seem to be more skilled at understanding, predicting—and manipulating—social behavior than others, it behooves us all to familiarize ourselves with their techniques. By developing a systematic understanding of scientific social psychology, we can encourage the widespread sharing of social skills for the benefit of all. Finally, the preparation of a clear, systematic statement of how people affect each other may give one a certain degree of aesthetic pleasure and intrinsic satisfaction.

Although everyone is a social psychologist, there is also a professional discipline called social psychology, whose students wish to understand, predict, and explain social behavior as a goal in and of itself. In order to accomplish this, the professional social psychologist attempts to develop a theory of social behavior. A theory, however, cannot suddenly emerge full grown, like Athena from the head of Zeus. Rather, it must emerge from a body of existing evidence (data), and it must be tested and revised frequently in relation to this evidence.

The discipline of social psychology has much in common with both sociology and psychology and draws heavily from both of these academic fields, as well as from political science, economics, and anthropology. There are numerous areas that are relevant to and encompassed by social psychology. Rather than attempt to cover all of them in this book, we have chosen to present an analysis of what we consider to be the most central, basic concept in social psychology: the interaction of people in groups.

THE PERSON ALONE

TWO

Alone in Isolation
The Experience of Being Alone
Experimental Studies of Isolation

Alone in the Presence of Others

Why We Need People

Others Help Us to Attain Rewards
Satisfaction of Physical Needs
Satisfaction of the Need for Love and Approval
Affiliation and Fear-reduction

**Others Provide Us with Information about Our
        World and Ourselves**
Social Comparison Theory
Social Comparison and Abilities
Social Comparison and Opinions
Social Comparison and Feelings

33

For those who spend much of their lives in crowded, noisy, bustling cities, the thought of being alone, completely alone, might seem quite appealing. In the daily struggle to cope with the teeming world of people who inundate, and even threaten to overload, our senses, we often seek privacy behind a variety of simple dividing barriers: doors that can be opened or closed; windows through which we hope to see, but not be seen by, the world; and receptacles such as drawers and safes, in which we can secrete our most valuable personal possessions. Given this need and the substantial effort to obtain privacy, how wonderful is the thought of being adrift in solitude, "far from the maddening crowd."

ALONE IN ISOLATION

But have you ever been really alone, not merely by yourself—but alone? I remember a time several years ago when, filled to the gills with teeming humanity, I set out to create for myself an experience of existential solitude. I went off to an isolated cabin, equipped with neither telephone nor mailbox—I was all alone in a beautiful spot in the north woods. For the first few days I was deliriously happy. I hiked through the surrounding forest, exploring my new environment as Thoreau had done at Walden Pond. I floated for hours in the waters of a nearby lake. My mind was alive and resonant with peaceful thoughts and feelings. At night, the stillness enveloped me in a wonderfully soft cocoon. After about a week, however, things began to change. Instead of comforting me, the stillness of the night began to feel oppressive. Orderly, peaceful thoughts became a torrent of frightened questions: What if something happens to me? Who will know? Who can hear me scream? Or laugh? And what is there to laugh about anyway? Soon I began to look for reminders of my social world. First, I made nocturnal visits to the nearest town to glimpse houses, shop windows, and factories; then came day trips to the town and some quiet mingling among its unfamiliar inhabitants; later I brought a radio back to the cabin, then a TV set (Johnny Carson had become an old and faithful friend); and finally, I implored my friends to come up and visit me for a while!

The Experience of Being Alone

To fully appreciate the importance of other people and the groups in which they are arranged, let us think about what life would be like without them. In the late 1700s, Alexander Selkirk was cast away on a deserted island on which he remained totally alone for more than

Figure 2.1
Admiral Richard E.
Byrd prepares a meal in
the hut beneath the Ant-
arctic snow where he
lived for six months.

four years. Survival on the island was not a problem; however, his desire for human contact at times became unendurable. As a substitute for human companionship, he took in several animals as pets and would talk to them at length. But, without the stimulation of human company, he would sometimes sink into a trancelike state. After his rescue Selkirk found that he was unable to interact effectively with others; in fact, he was never the same again after this period of isolation.

In his book *Alone* (1938), Admiral Richard E. Byrd related his experience of being buried in a small hut under the Antarctic snow for six months. He undertook his confinement voluntarily "to taste peace and quiet and solitude long enough to find out how good they really are" (p. 4). However, his dream of serenity soon turned to unbearable torment. He became severely depressed after only three months.

Another voluntary isolate was Dr. Alain Bombard (1953), who set out to cross the Atlantic in a small life raft, completely alone, in an attempt to test how open-sea accident victims and other castaways might be able to survive until they reached land or were rescued. He believed that sustenance, including liquids, could be taken from the sea with the most primitive equipment, provided that one had enough confidence in his ability to survive. A quote from Bombard's

trance-like state

✓ *poor interaction*

depression

log seems to be typical of the experiences recorded by many who
have experienced this intense sort of solitude:

> *I had begun to understand the difference between solitude and
> isolation. Moments of isolation in ordinary life can soon be ended; it
> is just a question of going out of the door into the street or dialing a
> number on the phone to hear the voice of a friend. Isolation is
> merely a matter of isolating oneself, but total solitude is an oppres-
> sive thing and slowly wears down its lonely victim. It seemed some-
> times as if the immense and absolute solitude of the ocean's expanse
> was concentrated right on top of me, as if my beating heart was the
> center of gravity of a mass which was at the same time nothingness.
> . . . It was a vast presence which engulfed me. Its spell could not be
> broken, any more than the horizon could be brought nearer. And if
> from time to time I talked aloud in order to hear my own voice, I
> only felt more alone, a hostage to silence [Bombard (trans. Connell
> 1953), p. 144].*

Fortunately for Bombard, the activities he had to perform in order to
survive kept him busy and prevented him from slipping into apathy.
Also, a school of dolphins became his daytime associates, providing a
form of companionship. When human beings are not available, it
would appear that some people accept animal companionship as a
substitute; indeed, in such cases, there is often a tendency to attribute human characteristics to the animals.

Visions and Hallucinations. Among Laplanders and others who live
in the Far North, isolation is a frequent occurrence. Hallucinations
are accepted as more or less normal among those who are isolated,
and social groups in the Far North have developed modes of dealing
with hallucinating individuals. In order to prevent hallucinations
and probable drowning, the Eskimos always go out fishing in their
kayaks in groups, never alone.

The quest for visions was important in the lives of the American
Plains Indians. To experience these visions, a young man would
isolate himself in a lonely place for several days and await a visita-
tion from benevolent spirits. These visions (or hallucinations) were
sought during crises and as part of the rite of passage to adulthood.
In addition, various religious sects, especially those in the Orient,
practice solitude and meditation in an attempt to reach a certain state
of stillness in which there is disengagement from the external world.
For these groups the effects of isolation—such as hallucinations and
lassitude—are a prerequisite for important religious experiences.

Isolation and Psychopathology. Solitary confinement in prison is another instance of extreme isolation. Christopher Burney (1952) re-

lated his experiences of spending 18 months in solitary confinement during World War II in a German prisoner-of-war camp. When he was returned to the company of other prisoners, he was afraid to speak to anyone for fear that others might consider him insane. For Burney, as well as for the American servicemen who were captured during the Korean War and subjected to brainwashing, there was a breakdown of the normal sources of consensual validation of one's own value standards and behavior.

In reviewing the autobiographies of people who had endured extreme isolation, the psychiatrist J. C. Lilly (1956) concluded that, in spite of the self-censorship imposed on these autobiographies, "persons in isolation experience many, if not all, of the symptoms of the mentally ill" (p. 4). It is certainly evident that isolation is an unusually stressful experience and, according to Lilly, one from which an individual is not always able to recover fully.

In addition to the accounts of isolated prisoners, sailors and airmen lost at sea, hermits, and others, much has been learned from scientific research on isolation. Many personality theorists stress the importance of adequate early mothering for the proper emotional development of the child. Nowhere has this need been so clearly demonstrated as in the work of René Spitz (1945). Spitz used the term "hospitalism" for the syndrome he had observed among infants in orphanages. Although these infants received adequate food and enjoyed a clean and healthful environment, their mortality rate was nearly 100 percent. Spitz concluded that the isolation experienced by these infants and the lack of mothering, that is, cuddling and other kinds of physical and emotional contact with an adult, led to the death of most of the children and to permanent emotional and intellectual damage to the few who survived.

Experimental Studies of Isolation

In a rather simple but dramatic experiment, Bexton, Heron, and Scott (1954) paid subjects to do nothing for as long as possible. Each subject would be brought into the laboratory, asked to lie on a comfortable bed in a small cubicle, fed, and taken to the toilet on request; otherwise, he would do nothing. A set of frosted glass goggles was placed over the subject's eyes, a sponge rubber pillow over his ears, and heavy gloves with cardboard cuffs over his hands. It was observed that, during their stay in the cubicle, all of the subjects experienced a sharp decline in their ability to concentrate, an increase in anxiety, and other behavior changes—including some rather complex and bizarre hallucinations.

Since Bexton, Heron, and Scott's study, the topic of sensory deprivation has been of considerable interest to psychologists. Of course, the subjects being studied were isolated not only from other human beings but from all external stimuli—through the use of certain apparatus and restraining devices. We cannot, therefore, include these data in a discussion of isolation without making it clear that the deprivation of all external stimuli, by itself, greatly affects behavior.

A study conducted by Schachter (1959) focused on just the social isolation. His subjects were removed from other people but were *not* deprived of all external sensory stimulation. Students were paid $10 a day for volunteering to remain alone in a locked, windowless room for periods ranging from two to eight days. Of five subjects, one broke down after two hours, banging on the door to get out, and one of the three who remained a total of two days was unwilling to repeat the experience. Obviously people respond differently to isolation. Two subjects did not seem to be terribly upset by two days of isolation, but the one who was isolated for eight days admitted that he had grown uneasy and nervous and was, therefore, delighted to see people again; otherwise, he was not significantly affected by the experience. Perhaps because the students knew that they could terminate their isolation at will and that it was only for a short time anyway, the effects were not too serious (as in some of the anecdotal accounts).

It has been found that isolation not only increases anxiety, decreases the ability to concentrate, and produces bizarre hallucinations, but also increases suggestibility. For example, the phenomenon of brainwashing in the Chinese prisoner-of-war camps during the Korean War took place even when the prisoners were not physically isolated but were merely forbidden to speak under pain of punishment (Schein, 1961). The heightened suggestibility required for brainwashing is probably created by the prisoners' intense need for social approval following prolonged isolation. Susceptibility to the influence of others, it would seem, is greater after social deprivation—a fact that has been borne out by research with both children and adults. In a study of children (Gewirtz and Baer, 1958) who had been isolated for 20 minutes, it was found that they became more responsive to verbal approval. In another experiment (Scott, Bexton, Heron, and Doane, 1959), male college students were isolated for several days and then subjected to recorded propaganda. These students showed not only a greater change in attitudes than a control group, but also an inability to concentrate and impaired judgment.

↑ suggestibility

ALONE IN THE PRESENCE OF OTHERS

One can, of course, experience the acute pain of isolation while being with others. I well remember a visit to my uncle Alex, an invalid who lived with his wife and son in a crowded section of Brooklyn, New York. Down in the street below their tenement apartment, children yelled and screamed while playing stickball, punchball, hide-and-seek—all the games of city streets; radios and TV's were blaring away through the open windows of adjacent apartments. Yet there Alex sat at the kitchen table, eating a bowl of cereal, a worn and dying spectre of a man—engulfed in a sea of other people, yet bitterly and utterly alone. I remember him sitting at that table, pleased to see me and yet suspicious as well. The ravages of cancer were visible in his face, the skin drawn taut in folds of pain. Feeling awkward and uncomfortable, and not knowing what to do or say, I offered to give him a haircut (which, because of his illness, he could not have at a barber shop). Alex seemed pleased with the idea, so I proceeded to snip off the hair that had grown out over his ears and neck. When I had finished, he studied my work in the mirror and thanked me for a job well done. Then a gleam of pride and pleasure played over his angry, ravaged face. He was a man, and although we both knew that he would never again put on his favorite suit and tie and walk out into the streets of the city, this simple act had restored some of the pride and self-respect he felt as a man.

And how many others are there, young and old, sick and well, dwelling in the country and in our crowded urban centers who, surrounded by others, nevertheless feel uprooted and alone? Perhaps it is these very feelings of alienation that have helped to bring about such programs as group psychotherapy, T-groups, encounter groups, sensitivity groups, and even communes. People, it is clear, need others. And perhaps, hoping to overcome in part the feelings of isolation in a crowded society, they have formed groups in which feelings and experiences can be compared and presumably better understood. These groups tender not only the promise of greater relatedness with others but often the seductive lure of "instant change" as well. If only we would scream loudly and sincerely enough (as in primal scream therapy), or if only we could learn to give and be receptive enough to feedback (as the leaders of T-groups would have us do), perhaps a persistently ineffective life style could be suddenly altered and a confusing, distant world better understood. At a time when human beings feel increasingly remote from and impatient with world events, it is tempting (although not necessarily effective) to seek instant redress of grievances by participating in groups such as these.

But now, let us look more closely at the feelings and experiences of isolation and alienation. Are people ever *really* alone? Can we ever truly escape the social world in which we have been born and raised? Don't we all, even in our most private moments, remain aware of other people? Of course, there are times when we may want

*Figure 2.2
How often do people
feel alone, even when
they are surrounded by
others?*

to isolate ourselves for brief periods, as when we have suffered a painful social encounter, or when we must meet a work deadline but have been continually interrupted. We may look for a room or a quiet place where no one can find us, but, in that very act, we are thinking of others because we are anticipating their possible behavior and moving toward those places where we think they will not go. When we get there, we may think about the expectations of others and our obligations to them, even though they are not physically present. In fact, even in the privacy of our own room, with the door closed and the shades drawn, we may feel and act as if we were on a stage of sorts, being closely and critically scrutinized by an audience made up of those who comprise the world of our past and present. And doesn't this awareness of others continually shape our behavior?

Think of Robinson Crusoe, for example, or the boys in Golding's book *Lord of the Flies*. Abandoned on a deserted island, far away from civilization, they constructed for themselves not a strange and unfamiliar world, but a replica of the society they once knew. For Robinson Crusoe, it was a world replete with timepieces, a shelter, and a type of moat to protect himself against the "hostiles." For the boys in Golding's book, the replica included such things as special uniforms, a division of labor (hunters and fire builders), a list of rules, and eventually systematic violence, death, and destruction—all imported, so Golding would have us believe, from jolly old civilized England.

And what about Uncle Alex? Is he really alone? Is not his alienation due in part to the anger he directs at those whom he feels have abandoned him? Even in the midst of his suffering and impending death, he still wants to be seen and thought of as a man.

WHY WE NEED PEOPLE

It may be, as the sociologist Emile Durkheim suggested, that the individual is little more than an abstraction. It is difficult to imagine a person for whom others are not present, either physically or psychologically. There are times when we all want to be alone, yet often when people are not readily available, we seek them out. My experience in the isolated cabin reflects a common conflict, one with which the child must deal at the very earliest stages of his development. Everyone wishes to become independent, to be able to stand on his own two feet, to be free from the interference of others and from obligations to them. On the other hand, everyone needs other people; it seems that very few people can really get along well without others for any length of time. This conflict has been thoroughly discussed by Erich Fromm (1941).

Why do we need others? Essentially, we need them for the rewards they can offer us and the costs they can help us avoid; we also need others for the information they can provide about our world and about ourselves.

OTHERS HELP US TO ATTAIN REWARDS

Satisfaction of Physical Needs

The infant, at birth, is in many ways an asocial creature—almost totally dependent upon others, yet unable to interact with them effectively. He cannot readily differentiate among people nor can he communicate very well with them. Yet, the infant cries when he is cold, and someone comes to provide warmth; he cries when he is hungry, and someone comes with food; he gets tangled up in his covers, and someone comes to help. Even though the infant does not know how to manipulate his environment, he is able to utter sounds and behave in ways that lead to the satisfaction of his needs.

Satisfaction of the Need for Love and Approval

It does not take very long for the baby to associate the signals he emits with the actions of others—actions that permit him to obtain rewards and avoid costs. By the time the child is a year old, he has become a full-fledged member of the human race. H. R. Schaffer (1971) describes this transformation as follows:

> *He has learned to distinguish familiar people from strangers, he has developed a repertoire of signalling abilities which he can use discriminatively in relation to particular situations and individuals, and he is about to acquire such social skills as language and imitation. Above all, he has formed his first love relationship: a relationship which many believe to be the prototype of all subsequent ones, providing him with that basic security which is an essential ingredient of personality development [p. 13].*

Physical rewards—food, drink, warmth, dryness—soon become generalized to social rewards—approval, companionship, and love. Spitz's (1945) studies of hospitalism indicate that the comforting love relationship between adult and child is just as important as the satisfaction of physical needs, for without love and approval the child will withdraw from interaction, will deteriorate physically, and may even die.

We all want and need to be liked; we want and need approval, support, companionship, and prestige; we want and need to avoid appearing foolish in the eyes of others. It is somehow ironic that the satisfaction of these very needs—of such central importance in our lives—can *only* be obtained from others. No matter how hard we try, we cannot compel others to like or approve of us; they must choose to do that of their own accord. We can smile at them, say that we like them, offer them various rewards, and perhaps even threaten them, but they alone must decide how they feel about us.

The fact that people need so desperately to be liked and therefore seek out the socially rewarding companionship and support of others is illustrated in the following anecdote: I was driving across the United States several years ago and stopped to pick up a lone hitchhiker along the way. He was a young man, a worker in an automobile factory in Detroit who, having been laid off from his job, decided to leave his wife and family for a while, take his few belongings and a little money, and go to Los Angeles in search of a new job and a better life—the American Dream. Since I happened to be going to Los Angeles, I offered to give him a lift the whole way, and the two of us set out together on a trip that lasted several days. We chatted along the way about nothing in particular, gradually developing a friendly, although by no means close or significant, relationship with each other. Upon arriving in Los Angeles, I gave the young man my phone number and dropped him off in the center of the city, as he had requested. The following afternoon, to my surprise, he phoned. "Do you need money?" I asked. "No," he said. He had enough to live on for a while. "Do you need a place to stay?" I inquired. "No." He had found himself a room. The reason he had called, he said, was because he simply wanted to *talk* for a while. He didn't know a soul in Los Angeles and, although the people he had met were friendly enough, they were all strangers and he wanted to hear the sound of a familiar voice. So we chatted together for a while. During the next few months I heard from him occasionally. He got a job, his wife and family came out to Los Angeles to live, they made new friends, and eventually we lost contact.

As can be seen, this young man did not simply need to talk—millions of people in Los Angeles could have served that purpose. Rather, he needed to make contact with someone he knew and liked—someone who might care whether he was well or ill, alive or dead; someone who might acknowledge his special, distinct individuality. I did not completely fulfill that need, since our relationship had been so brief and casual, but for his purpose I was the best person available. He felt isolated and alone, which undoubtedly filled him with anxiety (as had been true for me in the north woods), and thus he needed to seek me out.

Affiliation and Fear-reduction

As Berscheid and Walster (1969) point out, when people feel anxious, afraid, lonely, or unsure of themselves, they will probably find that just the mere presence of others is rewarding. They suggest the following simple experiment:

Come to class a few minutes early on a regular school day. You will probably find that few of your classmates approach you. Then, sometime when an exam is scheduled in one of your classes, arrive a few minutes early. You may be surprised to see the number of classmates who approach you with friendly remarks or joking com-

*ments. . . . Students seem friendlier on days when an exam is
scheduled than on days when one is not [p. 32].*

The fact that anxiety increases one's tendency to affiliate has
been demonstrated in a clever experiment by Stanley Schachter
(1959). Individual women undergraduate students were ushered one
at a time into a laboratory at the University of Minnesota, where each
was met by the experimenter—a rather formidable-looking man who
wore a white doctor's coat, carried a stethoscope, and introduced
himself as Dr. Gregor Zilstein of the Medical School's Department of
Neurology and Psychiatry. The experimenter told each young
woman that she would be taking part in a study to determine the effects of electrical shocks. Each subject was then placed in one of two
experimental conditions—High Fear or Low Fear. Those in the High
Fear Condition were told:

*What we will ask each of you to do is very simple. We would like
to give each of you a series of electrical shocks. Now, I feel I must be
completely honest with you and tell you exactly what you are in for.
These shocks will hurt; they will be painful. . . . What we will do is
put an electrode on your hand, hook you into apparatus such as this
[pointing to the equipment behind him], give you a series of electrical shocks, and take various measures such as your pulse rate,
blood pressure, and so on. Again, I do want to be honest with you
and tell you that these shocks will be quite painful but, of course,
they will do no permanent damage [p. 13].*

The subjects in the Low Fear Condition were given the following instructions:

*I have asked you all to come today in order to serve as subjects
in an experiment concerned with the effects of electrical shock. I
hasten to add, do not let the word "shock" trouble you; I am sure
that you will enjoy the experiment. What we will ask each one of
you to do is very simple. We would like to give each of you a series
of very mild electrical shocks. I assure you that what you will feel
will not in any way be painful. It will resemble more a tickle or a
tingle than anything unpleasant. We will put an electrode on your
hand, give you a series of very mild shocks, and measure such things
as your pulse rate, blood pressure, measures with which I am sure
you are all familiar from your visits to your family doctor
[pp. 13–14].*

The students in each of these two experimental conditions were
then told that before the study began, there would be a delay of

about ten minutes while the experimenter finished setting up the apparatus. During this time they could either wait alone in a private room (which was described as comfortable and spacious, with armchairs and plenty of books and magazines) or wait in a room together with some of the other women. They were asked to specify on a questionnaire whether they preferred to wait alone, together, or had no preference. This was the end of the experiment; no shocks were actually given.

Schachter had predicted that those who were anxious would be especially likely to prefer the company of others. The results clearly supported this hypothesis, for 63 percent of the subjects in the High Fear Condition said that they wanted to wait with others, while only 33 percent of those in Low Fear chose this alternative. In general, then, when people are lonely, fearful, anxious, or under stress, they are especially apt to seek out the companionship of others, and the mere presence of others in these situations is likely to be rewarding in and of itself.

Figure 2.3
When people feel anxious, afraid, and under stress, they are often comforted by being with others. These Cambodians who fled from the advancing Khmer Rouge insurgents in 1974 face an uncertain future.

OTHERS PROVIDE US WITH INFORMATION ABOUT OUR WORLD AND OURSELVES

Just as the young child is dependent upon others for the satisfaction of his physical needs, he is dependent upon them for information about his world. If he is ever going to be able to satisfy his own needs, he must know what his world is like and how to deal with it. Thus, the young child observes his parents carefully, watching how they pick up food with a spoon and trying to imitate their behavior; watching how they open a door; watching how they turn the light off and on; observing how they fasten and unfasten the pin on his diaper. This information supplements his own exploratory trial-and-error learning. As soon as he is able to speak, he will bombard them with a myriad of questions about the world.

As we grow older, we continue to depend upon others for information about our world, but we become more discriminating in choosing our experts—selecting the weatherman for information on the day's weather forecast, the doctor for information about curing a backache, and the next-door neighbor for information about whether the mail has arrived.

Social Comparison Theory

In our transactions with the world, we need to evaluate ourselves. We want to know whether our opinions, judgments, beliefs, and attitudes are correct—is democracy good and fascism bad? We want to know whether our emotions are warranted by a given event—should we be frightened by a certain noise we just heard? should we be apprehensive about a visit to the dentist? And we also want to be able to evaluate our abilities—to know just how well we are doing and whether we are performing as well as we might. Our need to evaluate ourselves and the world varies from time to time according to what we expect to face in the near future (a student's evaluation of his abilities in mathematics is especially important before a critical examination), according to whether our previous evaluations have been threatened (our disbelief in flying saucers may be shaken by seeing an eerie object in the sky on a moonlit night), or according to whether we confront dangerous or frightening situations (we are awaiting surgery and wonder if it will be painful). Whenever possible, of course, we turn to physical evidence to obtain clear-cut evaluations; for example, using field glasses to observe an object in the sky or getting an objective measure of our abilities. When these physical means for evaluation are not possible or adequate, we often turn to other people.

A number of years ago, the social psychologist Leon Festinger (1954) proposed a rather simple but elegant theory to account for people's need to use others as a source of information about physical and social reality. Festinger's formulation, which is called *social comparison theory*, begins by postulating that people need to hold (what they consider to be) correct opinions about the world and have an accurate concept of their own abilities. One of his co-workers, Stanley Schachter, later extended social comparison theory to feelings and emotions as well. To the extent that objective, nonsocial means of appraisal are available and acceptable, Festinger said, these will be sought out in preference to other people; but if they are not available, one will tend to evaluate his own abilities, opinions, and feelings by comparing them with those of others. The nonsocial means of appraisal, of course, must be not only available but adequate or *acceptable.* For example, a man could try to determine his physical capacity by simply seeing how many 100-pound sacks of stones he could lift to a specified height within a given period of time, or he could try to determine his intelligence by seeing how high he could score on an IQ test. But how acceptable are these measures? The man probably wants to know not only how strong or smart he is, but how he stands in relation to his friends and associates; therefore, he must rely on social comparison.

Given a wide range of people with whom comparisons could be made, Festinger said that a person will ordinarily choose someone who is seen as similar in abilities, opinions, or feelings. Notice that the theory says that we will seek out not simply the company of other people but the company of rather *special* people—those whom we perceive as comparable to ourselves. Finally, Festinger suggested that there is a "unidirectional drive upward" in the case of abilities but not in the area of opinions or feelings. In other words, we place a positive value on strength and intelligence—the more capable you are, the better. To evaluate our abilities, then, we look toward others who are somewhat better than we are—but not *too* much so. By contrast, we do not necessarily believe that it is good to hold opinions that are more extreme than those of others or to feel something more intensely than they do.

This, in a nutshell, is the essence of social comparison theory, although it is actually somewhat more complex than we have suggested here. The theory has given rise to some interesting and extensive social psychological research. We will examine abilities, opinions, and feelings in turn, together with some of the research in these areas, to see how each is affected by the process of social comparison.

Social Comparison and Abilities

Imagine that you are a devoted, but rather mediocre, chess player. You love the game and want to play it as well as you can, but you are not one of the stars at your local chess club. On your birthday, you receive a book by an outstanding chess master that presents an apparently ingenious approach to the game and includes a number of chess exercises that you can do to improve your skills. For months you stay away from your chess club, pleading other commitments, while you quietly and diligently practice these exercises. Now you are ready for your first game, one that will test whether all of your efforts have been worthwhile. Your major concern is to learn just how good you are now, a most important matter since the autumn chess tourney is approaching and you must have some objective assessment of your abilities before you sign up. You have four friends you can call upon (none of whom happen to be members of your chess club), and each would be willing to play with you. Tom is a relative beginner whom you could undoubtedly defeat with ease; Dick and Harry have both played at about your level—Dick has been somewhat less skilled than you, while Harry has been somewhat more skilled; Charlie is a real pro, a champion who has won a number of exhibitions and knows chess backward and forward. Which one would you call? Before answering this question, let us look at a relevant experimental study.

In an experiment conducted by Ladd Wheeler and his colleagues (1969), groups of nine subjects were each assigned an identification letter and given the same written test. The experimenters told some groups that the test measured a "desirable" trait—intellectual flexibility—while others were told that it measured a rather "undesirable" trait—intellectual rigidity. After the subjects had completed the test, they were given false information about their performance. Each subject received his own score on the test, plus a rank ordering of all the members of his group (without scores). The rank ordering indicated to each subject that he had placed fifth, the middle rank in the group of nine. (For experimental purposes each subject was given the identical ranking and score.) The experimenter then offered the subjects an opportunity to obtain more information:

I would like to give you some information about the scores of the other members in the group. For reasons that I can't go into right now but will later, I can't show you everybody's score, but I would like to give you the score of one other person in the group. This will give you some relevant information. So, on the card in front of you, please write the identification letter of the person whose score you would most like to see [p. 223].

Social comparison theory would predict that each subject would want to see the score of the person who had performed just slightly better than he had—a group member who was either slightly more intellectually flexible or slightly less intellectually rigid. This is precisely what Wheeler found. First, the tendency to look toward someone who performed better was clearly indicated—in nearly every

case, the subject chose to see the score of someone who had performed better (rather than worse) than he. Furthermore, most subjects chose a person whose score was close rather than distant.
Among those who thought that the test was measuring intellectual
flexibility, most of the subjects asked to see the score of the person
who ranked just above them; for those who believed that the test was
measuring intellectual rigidity, most of the subjects asked to see the
score of the person who was ranked as just slightly less rigid.

Going back to the chess example then, the answer becomes
more clear. If you really want to evaluate your chess skills, you
would probably choose Harry, the player who had been slightly better than you. Although you could beat Tom easily, a game with him
would teach you very little about your own skills. Similarly, Charlie
could beat you hands down: you might learn some new plays, but
you wouldn't be able to assess your abilities by playing with him.
Dick and Harry would both offer you some means for comparison,
but since it has been empirically demonstrated that people tend to
look upward in order to evaluate themselves, the choice would be
Harry, the somewhat better player.

These predictions are based on the assumption that you sincerely want to evaluate your skills. If your real motive, however, is to
show off your abilities, you might prefer Tom since you could beat
him by a wide margin; or if you really want to learn a few additional
pointers about technique, you might select Charlie.

Social Comparison and Opinions

We also tend to look toward others in an attempt to evaluate our
beliefs and opinions. When something threatens our beliefs or opinions, we are especially anxious to have them confirmed by others.
For example, during the 1971 Los Angeles earthquake, many people
telephoned or went in person to see if their impressions about the
earthquake and its dangers were correct. During election campaigns,
many people join political organizations to work with others who
share their view that a certain candidate should be elected. They
may also join in order to obtain support for and evaluate the correctness of their opinions at a time when these opinions may be
threatened by charges and accusations made by the opposing side.
Part of the motivation of the Seekers (as described in Chapter 1) was
precisely this: the Seekers found that their opinions about the
cosmos were being threatened by others, and so they joined together
for mutual protection and support.

The tendency to affiliate with others when one's own opinions
must be evaluated has been demonstrated in an experiment by Roland Radloff (1961). He asked groups of college students in an intro-

*Figure 2.4
Advertisements often
capitalize on our desire
to be like others.*

In Philadelphia nearly everybody reads THE BULLETIN

ductory psychology course to answer an opinion survey on how a
college education should be financed. Specifically, they were asked
to state what percentage of the cost they believed should be met by
students and their families and what percentage by the government.
The importance of the issue was emphasized by pointing out that
college costs would rise markedly in the years to come and that they,
the subjects, would be the parents and taxpayers of the future. After
completing their answers, the subjects were placed in one of four experimental conditions. Some were shown a summary of the opinions
on this issue given by a group of high school sophomores (inferior information); others were shown an opinion summary of sophomores at
their own university (peer information); still others were shown a
distribution purportedly summarizing the opinions of leading econo-
mists, university presidents, and state legislators (expert information); and the rest were given no information about the views of

others (no information). The subjects were then told that groups made up of college students (like themselves) were being organized to discuss the problem of financing college education, and they were asked to indicate the extent to which they would be interested in joining one of these groups.

The significant thing to remember here is that the students were asked to express opinions about an important topic and then were given some information that would allow them to evaluate their opinions. The more expert the opinion the students were exposed to, Radloff hypothesized, the less they should have wanted to affiliate with others in order to assess their individual opinions. The results clearly supported this interpretation. Of those who saw the opinions of the experts, only 14 percent expressed an interest in joining a discussion group; of those who saw the opinions of other college students, 19 percent said that they wanted to join a group; of those who saw the views of high school sophomores, 30 percent wanted to join a group; and of those who were given no information, 40 percent indicated a desire to affiliate. Further support for this hypothesis came from the students' own statements about why they wanted to join a discussion group—the most frequent reason given was the desire to evaluate their own opinions.

Thus, at a time when people are uncertain about their opinions, views, or tastes, they are especially inclined to engage in a process of social comparison by seeking out the company of relevant others.

Social Comparison and Feelings

A number of years ago when I decided that it might be fun to live dangerously, I enrolled in a skydiving school and learned how to use a parachute. After a few hours of instruction, which consisted mainly of falling out of trees into stacks of hay and learning how to roll forward, backward, and to either side, I was ready for my first jump. Parachute on my back, excitement and adventure in my adolescent heart, I boarded a small plane (a Cessna 500) with a group of other skydivers and off we went. As the plane gained altitude and the countryside began to fall away below, the time for my jump drew near and I began to feel increasingly anxious. Why had I committed myself to such a madcap adventure? I wondered to myself. Could I manage to get out of it somehow? (Not without looking like a sissy and a fool, I thought.) And what was I feeling, exactly? Excitement? Fear? A sense of adventure? I looked around the cabin at my fellow lemmings. Some of them were obviously far more experienced at skydiving than I. They had their own equipment—colored helmets with their names blazoned on the vizor, and timers and altimeters strapped around their waist to track their descent. These experienced skydivers seemed to be having a helluva good time. They were laughing and joking with the pilot and with each other, guzzling beer, and assuring me that everything was going to be okay. I found their assurances mildly comforting (after all, they had survived, so why shouldn't I?), but while they were providing me with useful information about how I *ought* to feel, they couldn't help me understand my inner turbulence. So I did some more looking around. Seated near the front of the plane, just behind the pilot, I spotted two men. Both were wearing rented equipment like my own; neither seemed to have any fancy, personalized gear; and both seemed to be acutely agitated! Their knees were knocking together and their eyes had a wild, staring look about them—just like my own. As I studied their demeanor, I began to understand what I was feeling: neither excitement nor an existential spirit of adventure, but fear. I wanted to go over and sit next to them. But before I fully realized what was happening, I was "out on the strut," one foot dangling in the air, and was given the command to jump. I did jump, like an automaton following orders, had a wonderful trip down (it seemed to last forever), and lived to tell this tale.

Studies of Fear and Anxiety. Led by Schachter, his colleagues, and students, many social psychologists have investigated the ways in which people use others to evaluate their own feelings. As we saw in the Gregor Zilstein experiment (see page 44), misery loves company. When an individual feels anxious or afraid, the mere presence of others is likely to be rewarding. But why, exactly? Is it because other people provide a distraction, thereby enabling him to reduce his anxiety? Or is it because the individual is uncertain about his feelings and therefore seeks out others in the same plight in order to better evaluate them?

To decide between these two alternatives, Schachter conducted a second experiment that was similar to the Gregor Zilstein one. In this case, *all* of the subjects were told that they would receive painful electric shocks—that is, all were placed in a High Fear Condition. Again, they were given a choice between waiting alone or with a group, but the characteristics of the group were systematically varied. Some of the subjects were told that the group consisted of students sitting down the hall, waiting to see their faculty advisers (Different State Condition); others were told that the group consisted of subjects (like themselves) waiting to take part in the same shock experiment (Same State).

If an anxious person affiliates in order to find distraction, he might prefer to wait with others who do not have the same problem (Schachter's Different State Condition). If, on the other hand, as social comparison theory predicts, the anxious individual affiliates in order to better assess his own feelings, he would probably prefer to wait with others who are sharing the same experience (Same State). The latter prediction received unequivocal support. Of ten subjects in the Same State Condition, six chose to wait in a group and four chose to wait alone. All ten subjects in the Different State Condition, however, chose to wait alone. Thus, it appears that anxious people affiliate primarily to evaluate their own feelings.

Schachter's findings have been further substantiated by John Darley and Elliot Aronson (1966) in a subsequent experiment. Using Schachter's fear of shock paradigm, each of 78 women subjects was assigned to two female experimental confederates. After the shock procedure was described in gory detail to each group of three, the subject was asked to give her reactions by specifying how painful she thought the shocks would be and how nervous or anxious she felt about being shocked. The experimenter then asked the subject to read her nervousness rating aloud, and the two confederates did likewise. One confederate indicated that she was one point more nervous than the subject, while the other stated that she was two points less nervous than the subject. At this time, the subject was given the choice of waiting with one of the two confederates or of waiting alone. This ended the experiment.

If the subjects wanted to reduce their anxiety, they probably would have chosen to wait with the calmer (but more dissimilar) other; if, however, they wanted to evaluate their own feelings (as social comparison theory predicted), they probably would have chosen the more similar (but also more nervous) confederate. The social comparison prediction was clearly supported: most of the subjects preferred to wait with the more nervous but *more similar* other.

Affiliation thus appears to provide the anxious person with information. But what kind of information, exactly? Does it pertain to the experience he is about to undergo? If so, what better source than others who have already been through it all (like the experienced skydivers)? Or does it pertain to the kind of feelings that are appropriate? In this latter case, those who are in the same psychological state (novice skydivers) would be more suitable.

To decide between these two possibilities, Zimbardo and Formica (1963) conducted another experiment using Schachter's shock paradigm. The subjects were all told that they would receive painful shocks, and they were given the choice of waiting alone or with a group. As in Schachter's experiment, the characteristics of the group varied: One group was composed of subjects who had not yet participated in the experiment, while the other consisted of those who had already completed it. Zimbardo and Formica found that, given the choice of waiting alone or with others in the same state as themselves, most subjects chose the latter. By contrast, those subjects who were given the choice of waiting alone or with others who had already completed the experiment (people who could have provided the subjects with information about what the experience would be like) tended to choose the former as often as the latter. Thus, it seems that misery does not love company as such but, as Schachter put it, "misery loves miserable company."

Summary

To fully appreciate the importance of groups, it is well to think about what life would be like without other people. Case studies of hermits, castaways, prisoners in solitary confinement, and others indicate that isolation is an unusually stressful experience—one from which an individual may not always be able to recover fully. Social psychologists have found that isolation increases anxiety, decreases one's ability to concentrate, and sometimes produces bizarre hallucinations; it also increases enormously one's need for social approval and hence susceptibility to influence by others.

Of course, people may experience the acute pain of isolation even when they are surrounded by others. The sick and elderly who live in small rooms or apartments and sit all day watching television; the residents of our crowded, impersonal big cities; and countless others of all ages who are struggling to overcome their feelings of separation from others. Perhaps it is these feelings of alienation that have helped to popularize such programs as group psychotherapy, encounter groups, sensitivity groups, and communes.

People, it is clear, need others. But for what purposes? First, other people help us to attain the rewards that we need and seek. People are uniquely qualified to meet the physical needs of others (for example, a mother provides her infant with the rewards of food, warmth, and stimulation). People, moreover, need love and approval—rewards that can generally only be secured from others. Finally, when people feel anxious, afraid, lonely, or unsure of themselves, they often find that the mere presence of others is rewarding in and of itself.

People need others in a second major way. Other people provide us with information about our world and ourselves—information that can help us resolve the complexity and ambiguity of our experience. In our transactions with the world, we are continually evaluating ourselves in order to know whether our opinions, judgments, beliefs, and attitudes are correct; whether our feelings are appropriate in a particular situation; and whether we are performing as well as we might. Other people are uniquely able to provide us with such information.

Leon Festinger's social comparison theory attempts to account for people's need to use others as a source of information about physical and social reality. This theory is based on the assumption that people try to appraise their abilities, opinions, and feelings by seeking out others who are somewhat similar in these areas. Someone whose abilities, opinions, or feelings are comparable to your own is probably able to provide you with far more useful information, and therefore will probably be far more influential, than someone who is totally different.

Because of the fact that we need others for direct satisfaction of our needs and for information about our environment and its meaning, we are uniquely vulnerable. It is precisely because we are dependent on others that they can significantly influence our behavior. How this influence is exerted, generally and within the context of a group, will be discussed in later chapters. For now, though, let us look more closely at the processes by which we learn to become aware of other people, and the consequences this awareness has for our behavior. How do we form first impressions of others? How do we attempt to discover what other people are really like? How do we present ourselves to others? And in so doing, how do we learn about ourselves? These issues will be discussed in Chapter 3.

BECOMING AWARE OF
OTHERS AND OURSELVES

THREE

Becoming Aware of Others
Developing Impressions of Others
Simplifying Our Impressions of Others

Attributing Motives and Traits to Others
The Attribution of Causality
The Elements of Attribution Theory

Presenting Ourselves to Others
The Degree and Form of Self-disclosure
The Art of Impression Management

Finding Out about Ourselves
Attribution Theory and Self-perception
Considering How Others Evaluate Us

Strangers on a Train. Imagine that you are a college student on your summer vacation, about to take a train trip across the country by yourself. You purchase a round-trip ticket to Los Angeles, California, board a train at Pennsylvania Station in New York City, and set out on your adventure. For the first day or so, you keep busy exploring your new physical environment—studying maps and timetables, looking out of the window at the passing countryside, wandering through the train, and so forth. In addition, you begin to explore your social environment—trying to make some sense of the sea of unfamiliar faces around you. Some of these faces seem to stand out (the attractive young man or woman at the other end of the car, the conductor, the mother with her bawling infant, the old man in the rumpled suit), and gradually you begin to wonder about them. Who are they? Where are they going? What are they like? Without speaking to any of them and relying entirely on your impressions of their appearance and manner, you begin to spin fantasies about each of them and their lives—and, of course, you realize that they may be doing exactly the same thing about you.

As the train slowly makes its way into the vast Midwest, many of the original passengers depart, new ones board to take their place, and the daydreaming process of imagined acquaintance with your fellow passengers continues. Eventually, a miniature social world begins to develop. Certain faces seem to appear with regularity, while others disappear and are never seen again. The gentleman across the aisle, whom you barely noticed when the train left New York, is still there, sitting in the same seat, leaving for the dining car at regular (and by now predictable) intervals. The conductor and the waiter, whose manner you found harsh and brusque in New York, are still with you and have, by virtue of their mere presence and the regularity of their behavior, become "friends" with whom you exchange smiles of recognition. These smiles eventually lead to conversation, and soon you find yourself getting to know the other people on the train, just as they are getting to know you.

You exchange information about who you are, where you are from, where you are going, and so forth, and gradually you begin to develop some hypotheses about what the others are like—based on both the manner in which they present themselves to you (the impression they seem to want to make) and your own private guess about what they are *really* like. They, of course, are in the process of developing hypotheses about you as well—something you are probably acutely aware of. The topic of conversation, you notice, seems to vary from person to person. You discuss working conditions, trains, and timetables with the conductor; food with the waiter; living conditions in New York City with the young lady in the seat in front of you; and college life with the student at the end of the car. In some of these conversations, you may find yourself trying to impress the other person in a particular way, while in other conversations you may feel freer to reveal yourself as you really are. Through this repeated process of information disclosure and exchange, you begin to discover what the other person is like, and he does the same with you. By the time the train arrives in Los Angeles, the chances are that you will have made several new friends (perhaps an enemy or two as well), and in the process possibly discovered a bit more about what you, yourself, are like.

As we have seen in Chapter 2, people need one another for a variety of reasons: to acquire information about reality, to obtain social rewards and avoid costs, and so forth. Because of these needs, people are motivated to want to know what others are like and how others perceive them. Beginning with our first (often fleeting) impressions of others and our subsequent interaction with them, we attempt to discover why they behave as they do. In the process of acquiring information about them, we inevitably disclose things about ourselves as well. Through this process of self-disclosure, and the subsequent responses and reactions of others, we learn what we, ourselves, are like—why *we* behave as we do. The processes of acquiring information both about others and ourselves are thus intertwined in close, often complex, fashion. Let us begin, therefore, with an examination of how we become aware of others and then later discuss the implications of this for self-perception.

BECOMING AWARE OF OTHERS

An Infant's First Impressions. The infant is not born knowing people. Indeed, it cannot even distinguish the inanimate features of its environment from other human beings. It smiles at dots on a piece of paper as readily as at its mother's face. However, by the time it is about 1 week old, it has come to prefer social to nonsocial stimuli. The reason for this preference is not entirely clear, but it may be due to the fact that the infant seeks out a variety of perceptual encounters with its environment and finds some stimuli more distinctive or interesting than others (Schaffer, 1971). R. L. Fantz (1963), for example, has demonstrated that, beginning at about 1 week of age, infants prefer stimuli that are visually complex. In a rather simple, but elegant, experiment, Fantz placed infants inside a stimulus chamber, exposed them to pairs of visual stimuli, and then measured the amount of time they spent looking at (visually fixating) each. He found that these infants seemed to prefer stimuli that were striped,

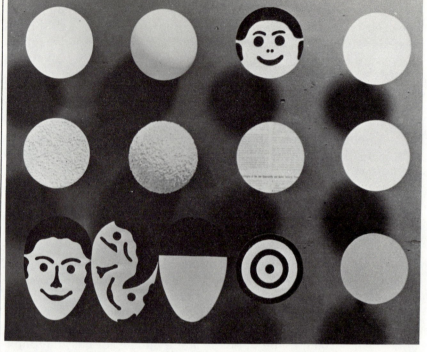

Figure 3.1
R. F. Fantz used these objects in an experiment to determine the visual preferences of infants. He found that, even at 1 week of age, babies prefer objects that are visually more complex. Of the items pictured here, the infants focused most of their attention on the one in the lower left-hand corner—which has most of the features of a human face.

face-like, or composed of concentric circles, to those that were plain or undifferentiated. When presented with pairs of face-shaped stimuli, infants spent more time looking at the face that had a larger number of features (see Figure 3.1).

Finally, Fantz found that young infants preferred stimuli that were bright, moving, and solid—characteristics, of course, represented in the visual pattern known as the human face. The eyes, in particular, appear to be distinctive for the infant: they are bright, complex, solid, full of information, and can move independently of the face. Thus, the infant may show a preference for people (especially faces) over inanimate objects not because they are people as such, but because they possess features that are inherently interesting.

By the time the infant is 3 or 4 months old, he can distinguish not only social from nonsocial stimuli, but familiar social stimuli (his mother and/or father) from those that are unfamiliar (strangers). The ability to make these distinctions is by no means trivial for such a young, primitive creature. For, to differentiate between familiar and unfamiliar social objects, the infant must be able to compare his present with his past sensory experiences—he must be able to remember. Thus, according to Schaffer (1971), the 3- or 4-month-old infant "does not merely ask of the stimulus 'Is it interesting?' but also

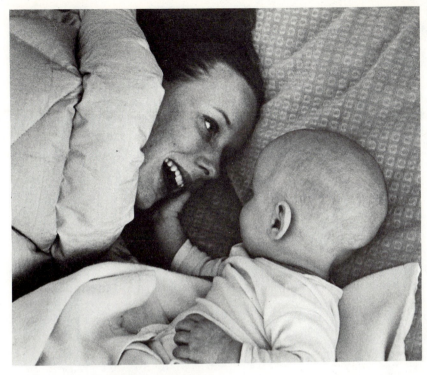

Figure 3.2
Infants prefer familiar
social objects.

'Have I seen it before?' " (p. 32).

Once the infant has acquired what Schaffer (1971) describes as the " 'aha' reaction . . . that is responsible for the young infant's pleasure in catching sight of his mother's face" (p. 105), he is ready to take the next step in his socialization: formation of a powerful emotional bond of attachment—his first love relationship. By the time the infant is 9 months old, social objects are no longer interchangeable. The mother and/or father (the primary caretakers) have become the objects of attraction; the infant seeks them out and stays close to them; strangers, conversely, have become the objects of fear and avoidance. Thus, in less than a year, the infant has learned to distinguish between people and objects, parents and strangers; attachments have developed; and the infant has begun to be truly aware of others.

Developing Impressions of Others
The infant soon becomes a child, then an adolescent, and finally an adult who is surrounded by an often bewildering world of social objects. It is a world peopled by a few close friends and loved ones, numerous acquaintances, and millions of strangers. To survive and function effectively amid these strangers, we need to form impres-

sions of them. These impressions will enable us to develop a picture of what other people are like, how we feel about them, and how we should interact with them—if at all.

Forming an Impression as an Integrated Whole. Years ago, Solomon Asch (1946) pointed out that in forming impressions of others, we tend to develop a gestalt (the German word for "shape" or "form"). This gestalt is a global, integrated picture of what another person is like; it permits us to organize our perceptions of others—including the discrepant, contradictory aspects of their behavior and manner— into a unified whole. Based on only a few superficial glimpses of some of the other passengers on the train to Los Angeles, we may develop elaborate fantasies and hypotheses about all aspects of these people's lives.

The Impact of a Single Attribute. The most trivial aspects of another person's appearance or manner may be enough for us to develop a gestalt about who he is and what he is like. For example, a prop as trivial as a pair of eyeglasses may, depending upon the type, allow us to classify the wearer as an intellectual, a businessman, a hippie, or a Hell's Angel. According to *Esquire* magazine (September, 1972):

Glasses are the new way to proclaim identity, a kind of disguise. They are used to project a persona which, for some reason, the wearer thinks desirable. There are frames and tints for people who want to glower, who want to look tough, who just want a little privacy, who want to say: "I hate Martha Mitchell," who want to say: "I am Martha Mitchell." Seeing is the smaller part of believing [p. 125].

The impact of status and prestige. A single attribute of another person may lead us to make inferences about additional, often unrelated, characteristics. In an experiment conducted by Paul R. Wilson (1968), a single confederate (a "guest lecturer") was introduced to five groups of Australian college students. Each group was told that he had a different academic status. In one group, he was introduced as a professor of psychology at Cambridge University, in the second group as a senior lecturer (a position of lower status), then a lecturer, a demonstrator, and finally a student. After the introduction, the students in each group were asked to estimate simply the height of the guest lecturer, as well as the height of the regular class instructor (a person who had the same status in each of the five groups). Wilson found that the greater the ascribed status of the confederate, the taller he was judged to be—in fact, the "full professor" was rated as a full 2½ inches taller than the "student." In contrast, estimates of the regular class instructor's height varied by no more than ¾ inch

Figure 3.3
For that serious or chic
look, select your eye-
glasses accordingly!

among the five groups. Thus, importance along a psychological dimension (status) tended to be generalized to importance along a physical dimension (height). Of course, the reverse may be true as well. Big or tall people (at least in Western nations) may be perceived as more important than their smaller, shorter colleagues.

The fact that people often develop a general, integrated impression of others based on minimal information can be seen in some of the early pioneering research in this area. Back in 1936, Irving Lorge asked a number of subjects to read the following passage: "I hold it that a little rebellion, now and then, is a good thing, and as necessary in the political world as storms are in the physical." Lorge found that when the statement was attributed to Thomas Jefferson, most of his subjects (who were Americans) agreed with it, but when it was attributed to Lenin, they tended to disagree. He concluded from this study that people are more likely to concur with the views of someone they consider to be a prestigious figure (Jefferson) than with the views of someone they perceive as less prestigious (Lenin).

Solomon Asch was not satisfied with this explanation, however. He believed that the subjects in Lorge's experiment had not simply agreed or disagreed with the passage in an automatic, blindly conforming fashion. Rather, he felt that the attribution of authorship to Jefferson or Lenin had led the subjects to define the *meaning* of the passage in two completely different but integrated ways. In order to test his hypothesis, Asch (1946) repeated Lorge's experiment and then asked the subjects to write a short essay describing the meaning of the statement. Those who thought the quotation was from Jefferson perceived the word "rebellion" as denoting a peaceful shift in political power and emphasized the word "little." Those who thought the statement had been made by Lenin, however, perceived "rebellion" as meaning revolution and tended to overlook the word "little."

"Warm" and "cold" as central traits. It could be argued that Asch found these sharp differences in meaning only because the two "authors" (Jefferson and Lenin) represented such prominent, polar opposites in the minds of his subjects. However, these clear-cut differences in perceived meaning emerged even when far more subtle cues were used. Asch (1946) presented each of two groups of subjects with a list of character traits describing a single hypothetical individual, and he asked the subjects to write a brief sketch giving their impressions of this person and rating their impressions on a series of adjective scales. For one group, the list of traits was as follows: intelligent-skillful-industrious-warm-determined-practical-cautious. For the other group, the traits were: intelligent-skillful-industrious-cold-determined-practical-cautious. Notice that the two lists are identical, except for the words "warm" and "cold." Asch found that the subjects were able to take this simple list of discrete traits and form an integrated impression of the hypothetical individual. Moreover, the impressions formed by the two groups turned out to be dramatically different. Those subjects who had received the "warm" list tended to rate the individual as generous, happy, good-natured, humorous, and humane; those who had received the "cold" list rated him as ungenerous, unhappy, unstable, humorless, and ruthless. Thus, a subtle difference in stimulus traits produced two very different, but coherent, impressions of the hypothetical individual.

One of the criticisms of Asch's warm-cold study concerns its artificiality—the subjects' judgments were not based on exposure to a real person. Harold H. Kelley (1950) answered this criticism with a study of the warm-cold variable as it operates in the classroom. Kelley told the students in a psychology course at M.I.T. that a guest lecturer would lead the class discussion for the day. Before the "lecturer" (a confederate of the experimenter) arrived, the students were given a short, written biographical sketch of him. Half of the students received the following sketch:

Mr. _____ is a graduate student in the Department of Economics and Social Science here at M.I.T. He has had three semesters of teaching experience in psychology at another college. This is his first semester teaching Economics 70. He is 26 years old, a veteran and married. People who know him consider him to be a rather cold person, industrious, critical, practical and determined [p. 433].

The other students received the identical sketch, except that the word "warm" was substituted for "cold." The "guest lecturer" then appeared and conducted a 20-minute discussion, during which the experimenter kept track of the number of times the students asked questions or made comments. After the "lecturer" had left, the students were asked to give their candid impressions of him on a series of adjective scales and in a short, written descriptive statement.

Kelley found that the "warm" instructor was liked far more than the "cold" one. Even though the subjects were judging identical behavior, those given the "warm" sketch rated the instructor as more considerate, informal, sociable, popular, good-natured, humorous, and humane than those who had been told he was "cold." Interestingly, the warm-cold variable affected not only the students' impressions but also their behavior: 56 percent of the students who had received the "warm" sketch participated in the class discussion, while only 32 percent of those who had received the "cold" sketch did so.

Kelley's experiment is important for two reasons: first, it corroborates the findings of Asch's earlier, less realistic study, thereby lending greater support to the importance of subtle cues in the development of an integrated impression; second, because it was found that students were more apt to interact with an instructor who impressed them favorably than with one who did not, the experiment shows that people's impressions have behavioral consequences that may be important.

What's in a name? Consider one of the most basic attributes of an individual—his or her name. Do you generally have the same initial reaction to a man named John or Joe as you do to one named Oscar or Julius? Is your impression of a woman named Betty or Sue different from one named Hortense or Janellen? And don't these first impressions sometimes color your behavior? Perhaps you view Oscar as stuffy, Joe as casual, Betty as pretty, Hortense as ugly—and act toward them accordingly. Herbert Harari and John McDavid (1973) have demonstrated that what's in a name has important (and sometimes unfortunate) consequences for the way teachers treat pupils. Harari and McDavid asked a number of elementary-school teachers to grade several different compositions written by fourth- and fifth-graders whose essays were identified by a signed first name only. Some of the papers were supposedly written by students named Michael and David (nice regular names), while others were attributed to Elmer and Hubert (unpopular names). Harari and McDavid found that Elmer and Hubert tended to receive letter grades that were nearly one whole letter lower than Michael and David—regardless of which papers carried their names.

The Importance of First Impressions. Just as the teachers in Harari and McDavid's experiment appear to have formed a global, sometimes unfavorable, impression of these pupils merely on the basis of their first names, we do similar things ourselves. Like the student on the train to Los Angeles, we are always forming first impressions of other people and using these impressions to develop a gestalt.

Solomon Asch (1946) conducted one of the earliest experiments on the importance of first impressions. He presented one group of subjects with a list of traits describing a hypothetical person: intelligent-industrious-impulsive-critical-stubborn-envious. A second group was given an identical list, but the order of the adjectives was now reversed: envious-stubborn-critical-impulsive-industrious-intelligent. Asch found that those who received the list presenting a "good–bad" order of traits (intelligent . . . envious) were far more likely to develop a positive impression of the hypothetical person than those given a "bad–good" order (envious . . . intelligent). From this he concluded that the *first* traits listed in a series will determine the manner in which subsequent traits will be interpreted.

Consider the thought processes that an individual might go through in forming an impression of someone with the following order of traits: intelligent ("He must be a pretty bright fellow"); industrious ("Great! He knows how to work hard and put his clever ideas to good use"); impulsive ("He doesn't waste any time—a fellow who is intelligent and industrious can't wait to do things with his abilities"); critical ("That doesn't mean he will accept just anything—he has high standards and expects others to live up to them as well"); stubborn ("He sticks to his guns—he is not going to let people push him into doing or accepting sloppy work"); envious ("He really feels badly when somebody is doing something better than he does—he is always working hard but is still uneasy when somebody else is doing better—what a fellow!"). Now look at the reasoning that might be used for the reverse order of traits: envious ("That means jealous—if there is anything I can't stand, it is a jealous person"); stubborn ("Yes, it figures, a fellow who is jealous of you won't listen to what you say—he just won't give an inch"); critical ("We should expect this, too—always finding fault with others—after all, he can't do much good himself"); impulsive ("He is awfully hard to get along with—flies off the handle at the slightest provocation"); industrious ("He'll work hard at it, trying to beat you out—but where does it get him?"); intelligent ("He sure is a crafty one. Would you buy a used car from someone like him?").

Primacy and recency effects. Our first impressions of others, then, may be of great importance. They provide us with a framework within which we can and do interpret or ignore subsequent cues. Social psychologists refer to this simple principle of person perception—in which information presented first is more influential in shaping a final impression—as a *primacy effect*. The reverse pattern, in which the information presented last is more important, is referred to as a *recency effect*.

Asch, of course, had observed a primacy effect in his "good–bad" versus "bad–good" trait experiment. In order to verify this finding, Abraham Luchins (1957) constructed two paragraphs about a boy named Jim and then asked a group of subjects to write their impressions of him. Jim was described as either friendly, outgoing, and extroverted (paragraph E), or as shy, seclusive, and introverted (I). Some of the subjects were given only *one* of the two paragraphs; of these, the subjects who received the description of Jim-E alone saw him as friendlier than those who received Jim-I alone. The other subjects were asked to read *both* paragraphs before describing their impressions of Jim; half of these subjects read the paragraphs in an I–E order, while the others read them in an E–I sequence. Like Asch, Luchins found that the subjects who read the E–I order rated Jim more favorably (as friendlier, more outgoing, and extroverted) than those who read the I–E order.

In order to study the conditions under which a primacy effect breaks down, Luchins (1957) ran a follow-up study in which another group of subjects was presented with the two Jim paragraphs in an E–I or I–E sequence. Some of the subjects were simply given one of the two orders, as before. Others, however, in addition to being given one of the two orders, were admonished not to make a hasty decision:

I want each of you to try to suspend judgment of the individual about whom you are to read until you have completely finished reading all that is written about him. Don't make any snap judgments. Take into account all that you read [p. 66].

Still another group was asked to solve several simple arithmetic problems (such as addition and subtraction) after reading the first paragraph but before reading the second.

Luchins found the usual primacy effect among the subjects who had simply been given the two paragraphs to read. However, it was not found among those who had been admonished not to make snap judgments or who had been given arithmetic problems. Among these two groups, the subjects who received the E–I order did not tend to rate Jim as friendlier than those who received the reverse sequence. In fact, a number of subjects who were asked to solve arithmetic problems displayed a recency effect: they rated Jim as friendlier in the I–E than in the E–I order.

Despite Luchins's findings, it is generally the first, rather than the last, impressions that are the most important—they are the ones that will probably shape the individual's gestalt. In the general area of attitudes and the conditions under which they may change, however, it is not so clear whether a primacy or a recency effect is likely to prevail. If I want to change your attitude on a certain issue, and want to present preliminary arguments both in favor of and against my position, it would help me to know whether you would be more inclined to change your view according to my wishes if I presented my arguments in a pro–anti or anti–pro order. Although an enormous amount of research has been done on this issue, the answer is not entirely clear. In general, however, it seems that you would be more inclined to change your view if: (1) I presented the pro argument first, followed immediately by the anti position, and then waited several days or weeks before asking you your opinion (a primacy effect); or (2) I presented the anti argument first, waited quite a while before telling you the pro position, and then immediately asked your opinion (a recency effect).

Simplifying Our Impressions of Others

Underlying the process of impression formation is a remarkably simple but important assumption: People need to simplify their social world. We need to transform the often bewildering array of impressions we receive from others into a simple, coherent explanation of their behavior. The gestalt we develop, in other words, reflects an overwhelming, and occasionally treacherous, need to reduce the complexity of our social environment.

Implicit Personality Theories and Stereotyping. Because of our need to understand other people's behavior, we tend to construct what social psychologists have described as *implicit theories of personality*. We entertain private hypotheses about the ways in which other people's traits and attributes are organized. Perhaps we view fat people as placid and jolly; those who are muscle-bound as outgoing and domineering; or people who are skinny as ascetic and withdrawn. In the course of our lifetime, we encounter thousands or perhaps millions of people. Often we must react to these people quickly and with as much accuracy as possible. Thus, our ability to characterize them on the basis of a few simple cues may be not only a matter of convenience, but an important determinant of effectiveness and the appropriateness of behavior. If we meet a person in foreign dress in the United States, we may assume certain things about him, for example, that he is not fluent in English; therefore, we may begin to speak to him in a slow and distinct fashion. (Occasionally, we may be quite surprised to discover that his command of English is even better than our own.) If we see a person with dark glasses and a cane, we may help him as he gropes for the curb. If we see an automobile driver with glassy eyes making uncertain movements, we may conclude that he is drunk and react accordingly. Regardless of the particulars of our hypotheses, we tend to categorize others in terms of a few, basic traits that we believe somehow go together.

Sex stereotyping. This tendency to develop a unified picture has been demonstrated rather cleverly in a paper by Seymour Rosenberg and Russell Jones (1972). These men wanted to develop a methodological tool that could be used to represent an individual's implicit personality theory. Instead of choosing a laboratory experimental setting, however, they decided to see how implicit personality theory was expressed in Theodore Dreiser's book *A Gallery of Women* (1929), a collection of short stories about 15 different women. Each story presents a self-contained, detailed description of a number of men and women; using short stories, it was not necessary to comb through an entire novel to discover Dreiser's characterization of a particular person.

Rosenberg and Jones began their analysis by recording *every* physical or psychological trait mentioned by Dreiser about each character. The researchers wanted to determine whether there was anything systematic in Dreiser's descriptions of people—were there certain traits that seemed to cluster together? They found that Dreiser did have a system—certain characters tended to be described as attractive, graceful, sensual, defiant, understanding, cold, and clever. Others tended to be great, poetic, sincere, careful, and intellectual. Can you guess what else distinguished the characters with the first set of traits? They were all women, while those with the second set of traits were men. Thus, if you knew a character's sex, you could predict with considerable accuracy what traits that character would have. From this, we can get some idea about Dreiser's implicit (if somewhat sexist) theory of personality.

Ethnic stereotyping. Implicit personality theory is really the same thing as stereotyping. The beliefs that Jews are secretive and clannish, that blacks are lazy and musical, that professors are absent-minded, and that bearded students are radicals represent implicit theories of personality that allow us to ascribe a set of characteristics to a group of people. This pigeonholing process is obviously functional, since it enables us to reduce the complexity of our social environment and summarize our impressions of others with a few simple adjectives or epithets. It is also a treacherous process because it labels others in ways that deprive them of their uniqueness. Moreover, stereotypes are typically formed at an early age and, once implanted (like most first impressions), are extremely difficult to change.

A Scottish psychiatrist, Morris Fraser, has studied the development of bigotry in Northern Ireland. As reported in the *New York Post* (October 4, 1972), he found that by the time a child has entered elementary school, his stereotyped views of others are firmly entrenched. Protestants (all Protestants) are seen by Catholic children as members of a "master race" that is attempting to suppress the "inferior" Irish; the British army is an armed aggressor similar to the forces of Nazi Germany. Catholics, in turn, are viewed by Protestant childen as reckless, lazy, dirty, and oversexed—traits not unlike those sometimes attributed to blacks in our own country. In fact, Protestant children sometimes refer to the Catholics as "niggers," and they even have a song that begins, "I'd rather be a nigger than a Taig [a Catholic]." According to Fraser, this frightening process of indoctrination begins at home, is strengthened in the rigidly segregated schools where there is almost no contact between Catholics and Protestants, and is encouraged by the presence of overt hostility and fear.

Effects of being labeled "schizophrenic." Of course, we don't have to go to Northern Ireland to discover the sometimes tragic effects of labeling others. David L. Rosenhan (1973) investigated the diagnostic procedures used in admitting patients to mental institutions. Giving fictitious names and occupations, Rosenhan and seven of his colleagues went to 12 American mental hospitals on the East and West coasts, feigned symptoms of mental instability, and asked to be admitted. They all told exactly the same story, complaining that they had been hearing voices that said "empty," "hollow," and "thud." Otherwise they told the truth in discussing their joys, satisfactions, frustrations, and upsets, as well as their relationships with their family and friends. Upon admission to the psychiatric ward, the pseudopatients stopped simulating *any* symptoms of instability. They spoke to the patients and staff members as they would normally speak to anyone; when asked by the staff how they were feeling, they said that they were fine and were no longer experiencing any abnormal symptoms; they accepted medication—but flushed it down the toilet, as the other patients did from time to time.

With lots of time on their hands, the pseudopatients took copious notes of what was happening around them. Initially they did their note-taking in secret, but when they found that no one cared, they did it openly. Although no one on the hospital staff ever questioned the note-taking, one nurse apparently saw it as a symptom of a crazy compulsion. "Patient engages in writing behavior," she wrote on his medical chart. Some of the patients were more suspicious, voicing such views as: "You're not crazy." "You're a journalist or a professor." "You're checking up on the hospital."

All except one of the pseudopatients was admitted with a diagnosis of schizophrenia and, despite their public display of sanity throughout their stay, *all* were discharged with a diagnosis of "schizophrenia in remission." The tragedy of this diagnosis is that labels tend to persist. "A diagnosis of cancer that has been found to be in error," said Rosenhan, "is a cause of celebration. But psychiatric diagnoses are rarely found to be in error. The label sticks, a mark of inadequacy forever" (p. 257).

To see if the tendency to diagnose the sane as insane could be reversed, Rosenhan conducted a second experiment in which the staff of a mental hospital was told that sometime within the following three months one or more pseudopatients would seek admission to their hospital. Of 193 patients admitted during this period, 41 were thought to be pseudopatients by at least one member of the staff. However, it turned out that Rosenhan had sent *no* pseudopatients to the hospital at all.

Rosenhan's study is important both because it points to gross errors in diagnosing mental illness and because it documents the possibly tragic consequences of stereotyping. Labeling pseudopatients as "schizophrenic" because of one symptom (hearing voices) led to their being categorized and treated as abnormal; labeling also creates a stigma that real patients may have to live with for a number of years. Each new observation of the pseudopatients tended to be interpreted in terms of the stereotype (recall the Asch study of the order of traits)—taking notes was seen as compulsive behavior, joyous laughter was euphoria, and serious thought was depression.

Labeling newborn infants. Let us look at one final example of the stereotyping process—the labeling by parents of their newborn infants. The infant at birth is a largely undifferentiated creature. It appears to be little more than a tiny ball of hair, fingers, toes, cries, gasps, and gurgles; superficially, at least, it often seems that "if you've seen one, you've seen them all." But babies are not all alike, especially to their parents. Since parents want and need to view their newborn child as a special creature, much of their early contact with the infant may focus on a search for distinctive features. Once the parents have established that the baby is healthy, other questions arise such as: "Who does the baby look like?" "How much does it weigh?" or "How long is it?"

Of all the concerns that parents have about their newborn infant, one seems to be particularly prominent and important—namely, the infant's gender. The gestalt of boy or girl may lead the parents to organize their perception of the infant with respect to a wide variety of attributes—ranging from its height and weight to its activity, attractiveness, or intelligence.

In order to study the sex-typing process at the outset, Jeffrey Z. Rubin, Frank J. Provenzano, and Zella Luria (1974) interviewed the parents of 15 sons and 15 daughters within the first 24 hours after delivery. Besides asking the parents several questions about the baby's resemblance to someone in their family and their preference for a boy or a girl, the parents were independently asked to rate their baby on a series of adjective scales.

The results of this simple study are striking. The parents saw their sons as resembling the father and their daughters as resembling the mother; they said they preferred a boy if theirs was a boy and a girl if theirs was a girl. Of even greater interest were the parents' responses to the adjective scales. Even though the male and female infants did *not* differ in over-all birth length, weight, or Apgar score (a measure of normal physical activity and functioning), the parents described the baby girls as being softer, smaller, finer-featured, and even less attentive than the baby boys. Moreover, it was primarily the fathers who were responsible for this differential labeling of male and female infants. The fathers thus appear to be the major sex-typers.

The central implication of these findings is that sex-role development appears to begin its course at the time of the infant's birth. The labels that parents ascribe to their newborn infants may well affect the parents' subsequent expectations about both their infant's behavior and their own behavior. Michael Lewis (1972) has pointed out that girl babies are looked at and talked to far more than boys (perhaps because the girls are perceived as softer and smaller). By the time they are a year old, girls are encouraged and permitted to spend more time touching and hovering near their mothers than are boys. Thus, the chance characteristic of an infant's sex leads to labeling and differential behavior by its parents, and eventually to the child's own perception of what it means to be a boy or a girl—a perception that the child, when it grows up, will probably transmit to its own offspring.

ATTRIBUTING MOTIVES AND TRAITS TO OTHERS

Obviously it is important for us to find out what others are like. This information can enable us to learn what to expect of others and their behavior so that we can judge what kind of relationship (if any) we want to have with them. We sometimes jump to conclusions about others on the basis of very minimal, superficial cues—height, sex, race, age, dress, type of eyeglasses, and so forth. Sometimes we can observe another person's behavior—the way he interacts with other people and objects in his environment—and conjecture about the consequences of this behavior for himself and others. We observe the behavior carefully, look at the context in which it has occurred, and then, taking into account any other information we may have about the person, attribute certain qualities or characteristics to him. We have a strong tendency to draw conclusions about motivations and personality characteristics, and we often do so after observing persons or objects for only a minimum time; on occasion we even attribute human qualities to objects.

The Attribution of Causality

In an early study of the manner in which people attribute human motivations and causality to inanimate objects, the Belgian psychologist Albert Michotte (1946) projected onto a screen two rectangles that were either moving toward or away from each other at various speeds and that were tangent to each other ("in contact") for varying lengths of time. A group of subjects was shown one rectangle (A) moving toward the other (B) until contact was made—and then B moving off in the opposite direction. Michotte found that the subjects' explanations of what they had seen depended upon both the speed with which A and B moved and the amount of time that they were in contact. When A approached faster than B moved away, the subjects thought that B's movement was caused (or launched) by A; B was a pawn in the hands of A. On the other hand, when A approached more slowly than B moved away, the subjects thought that B's movement was autonomous; B moved not because it had to, but because it wanted to. The greater the amount of time A and B spent in contact, the more likely the subjects were to view them as two "friends" getting together or as "accomplices" planning some devilish act. The subjects often used the language of human emotions: "A joins B; then they fall out, have a quarrel, and B goes off by himself"; "It is as though B was afraid when A approached, and ran off."

If human motivation can be attributed to two simple objects moving only toward or away from each other in a straight line, what about three objects involved in a more complex relationship? Fritz Heider and Marianne Simmel (1944) asked a group of subjects to view a short film (an animated cartoon), in which three solid shapes—a large triangle (T), a small triangle (t), and a small circle (c)—moved in, out, and around a large hollow rectangle (see Figure 3.4). The three shapes moved close to one another, became attached or enclosed within the rectangle, and then moved apart. At the end of the film, all of the shapes disintegrated, and the subjects were asked to report what they had seen. Two major findings emerged: First, the subjects tended to attribute human characteristics to these inanimate shapes. The large triangle (T) was seen as aggressive and bullying, t as heroic and defiant, and c as timid and fearful (and, we might add, female). Second, the movements of the inanimate shapes were interpreted in causal fashion. They were seen as chasing, leading, fighting, fleeing, and so forth. In fact, the subjects even made up scenarios to explain the movements they observed; for example, a

Figure 3.4
A test of the perception of causality. *Each of the three shapes used in Heider and Simmel's (1944) animated cartoon—a large triangle, a small triangle, and a circle—moves in, out, and around the large hollow rectangle.*

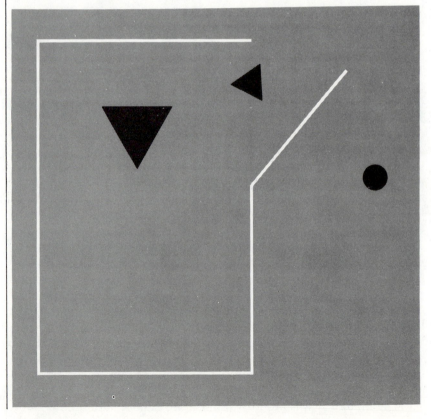

mother (*t*) and a father (*T*) were seen as fighting with their child (*c*); two men (*T* and *t*) were thought to be vying for the same woman (*c*); *t* was perceived as protecting *c* against the threatening advance of *T*. Thus, even though the subjects had been presented with nothing more than simple geometric forms moving around in a two-dimensional space, they tended to explain these movements in terms of a social, behavioral, cause-and-effect system.

Since the three shapes in Heider and Simmel's study were seen as causally related, Ronald E. Shor (1957) decided to assign two sets of attributes to one of the "characters" and observe how the subjects perceived the other two. Before being shown the Heider and Simmel film, one group of subjects was told that *T* was an aggressive person, disliked by most people; another group was told that *T* was a fair-minded person who was generally liked. Shor found that the subjects' impressions of *t* and *c* depended upon their concept of *T*. Those who saw *T* as likable were unfavorably impressed with *t* and *c,* and those who thought *T* was aggressive tended to see *t* as brave and *c* as defenseless. It is almost as if the presence of a "good guy" in the subjects' minds required the development of oppositional "bad guys"—a social world of good and evil.

As Krech, Crutchfield, and Ballachey (1962) pointed out, the research findings of Heider, Simmel, Shor, Michotte, and others are tremendously important:

> *The tendency to perceive cause and effect is basic to man's cognitive processes. If this is true of the perception of moving rectangles, how much truer it must be of the perception of social events which involve the actions of human beings. To ask people to refrain from assigning blame, responsibility, or credit for events until "all the facts are in" is to ask them to do a very difficult thing. Our cognitive organizing processes force us to jump to conclusions about causes. No matter how cogently the logician may argue against the concept of cause, our perception will pay him no heed [p. 30].*

The Elements of Attribution Theory

Let us now return to the world of human beings, and see how we attempt to explain the reasons for other people's behavior. Harold H. Kelley (1967) and Edward E. Jones and Keith E. Davis (1965), as well as Fritz Heider (1958) before them, have proposed an explanation known as *attribution theory.* It assumes that we have an implicit theory of human behavior. Look at Figure 3.5, which has been adapted from an article by Jones and Davis (1965). In observing another person, we assume that he has certain traits or dispositions—that he is kind or cruel, generous or tightfisted, friendly or hostile,

INFERRED　　　　　　　　　　　　　　　　　　　　　　　　**OBSERVED**

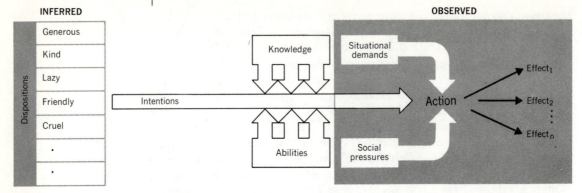

Figure 3.5
Attribution of disposi-tions from observed ac-tions. We assume that the sequence of behav-ior moves from left to right: Personal disposi-tions produce inten-tions; these, modified by one's knowledge and abilities, as well as situ-ational demands and so-cial pressures, lead to a specific action which, in turn, produces effects. However, we observe only the right side of the diagram. From that in-formation, we reason backward and make inferences—first about knowledge and abilities, then intentions, and finally dispositions (after Jones and Davis, 1965).

and so forth. His traits or dispositions lead him to want to do specific things, and he attempts those things that are within his range of knowledge or ability. He thus acts in a given way, depending upon the situation in which he finds himself, and these actions have cer-tain effects that may be good or bad for us. A kind, generous person wants to help others; and if he has the knowledge or ability and if the circumstances permit, he will help an unfortunate motorist in distress—which pleases us, especially if we are that motorist. Al-though we assume that all behavior occurs in this fashion, we can only observe another person behave in certain ways under given cir-cumstances; we must then either infer or learn more about his knowledge or ability, intentions, and dispositions. We thus work backward—from observations to inferences, from acts to dispositions.

Suppose that we are motorists, sitting in a car that has engine trouble on a deserted road. Suppose that we are obliged to spend the night there in the pouring rain and that we are cold and hungry. Sud-denly we see a man driving by in a tow truck and speeding up as he passes us—even though our car's emergency lights are flashing and we have tied a white cloth to the car's antenna. From the fact that he is driving a tow truck, we assume that the man has both the knowl-edge and the ability to help us, but that he does not want to do so. We therefore jump to the conclusion that he is cruel, inconsiderate, and untrustworthy. Later, we may learn certain facts about the man that change our initial impression, for example, that it was not his own tow truck (he had borrowed it); or that he was not a garage man and knew nothing about repairing cars; or that he was afraid to stop for fear of being robbed or mugged; or that he had really wanted to stop and help us, but was rushing to the hospital where he had just learned that his wife was undergoing emergency surgery. We thus formed our impression of this man without possessing sufficient in-formation—but we did not hesitate to do this any more than the sub-jects participating in the Michotte or Heider and Simmel studies hesitated to attribute human qualities to various inanimate objects.

In this example, it is important to note the relationship between the effects of the driver's actions and his intent. Did he *want* to cause the effect (leaving us without assistance all night in a broken-down car), or was the effect caused by circumstances beyond his control? (Note that there is a resemblance to the analysis of causation in Michotte's study of the movement of the two rectangles. Was the movement of the second rectangle caused by the first, or was the movement totally independent?) This question of internal versus external locus of control (elsewhere referred to as the "origin-pawn question" [deCharms, 1968]) is especially important in legal matters. Often a jury or judge must decide whether an individual is responsible for a crime. When a motorist injures someone, did he do it intentionally, or were the circumstances such that he could not avoid doing so? And what about the man who kills someone in a barroom brawl—to what extent was he responsible for his act? Legal experts would customarily assign three levels of intentionality with respect to the death in the barroom: (1) intentional—the man really wanted to kill the victim; (2) incidental—he killed the victim unintentionally while engaged in another crime (for example, attempted robbery); (3) accidental—the two men were simply testing their strength in a wrestling match, and the one happened to hit his head on the corner of a table. Of course, the greater the intention to kill, the greater the penalty—and, by implication, the more negative the dispositions and character traits of the guilty party.

Considering the Effects of the Act. Suppose a child knocked over and broke a cup from his mother's favorite set of china. Is he fully responsible for this act? Well, we might want some additional information before reaching a conclusion. Would it help if we knew that he had knocked down a total of 15 cups? Logically it shouldn't. If he broke one cup, he did it—whether it was alone or among a group of 15. Yet, in fact, we tend to determine causality in part by the consequences of acts. After studying the attribution of causality and intention in children, the Swiss psychologist Jean Piaget (1948) concluded that young children seem to disregard extenuating circumstances and assign blame solely on the effects of an act. Piaget told his subjects two stories and asked them to judge which protagonist should be punished more severely for his offense. In one story, a boy named John was called to the dinner table. He came immediately, but as he entered the dining room, he knocked over a tea cart that, unknown to him, had been placed directly behind the door. Fifteen cups were broken as a result of the collision. The boy in the other story, Henry, had been forbidden to take any jam. When his mother left the room, however, Henry climbed up to the cupboard where the jam had been

Figure 3.6
Who should receive the
greater punishment—
John, who accidentally
broke 15 cups, or Henry,
who knocked down 1
cup while disobeying
his mother?

placed and, in his attempt to get the jam, knocked a cup down to the floor and broke it.

Young children (under 7 years of age), Piaget found, tend to focus on the objective aspects of a situation, that is, on the *number* of broken cups. Since John broke 15 while Henry broke only one, they felt that John should be punished more severely. Older children (9 years of age and over), however, are more concerned about subjective responsibility, that is, with a person's reasons for acting as he does. In Piaget's study the older children felt that Henry should receive the greater punishment because his offense was committed while he was in the act of disobeying an order, whereas John's offense was purely accidental. Henry was therefore a "nastier" boy than John.

In a related experiment, Elaine Walster (1966) asked undergraduates to listen to one of several taped versions of a story and to ascribe blame on the basis of the facts provided. The story dealt with a car that had been parked on a hill and had accidentally rolled down. In one version, the car struck a tree, incurring little damage. In another, the car missed the tree and struck another vehicle, damaging its bumper. In a third version, the car rolled down the hill and into a shop, seriously injuring a small child and the shopkeeper. Walster found that greater blame was assigned according to the seriousness of the accidents. When the damage was minimal, the subjects did not feel that the car's owner was particularly blameworthy—accidents do happen, after all. However, when people were injured by the runaway car, the subjects felt that the owner should be punished for not having had his brakes checked recently. Thus, it appears that adult respondents also judge guilt, at least in part, on the basis of the effects of acts.

Of course, this is especially apt to happen when the act has negative effects for a specific person. The wife of the man killed in the bar incident will undoubtedly perceive the other man in the brawl as responsible; she will probably disregard any evidence that both men were drunk, or that they had been engaged in a friendly wrestling match at the time of the accident.

Attribution of causality for the My Lai massacre. In 1970 the American public—as well as the world—was shocked at reports of the massacre of an entire village of unarmed Vietnamese civilians by U.S. armed forces personnel. Eventually, a minor officer in charge, Lt. William Calley, was convicted for his actions in the My Lai massacre. Despite the gravity of Calley's act, there was considerable disagreement as to the justice of his conviction and sentencing. And this disagreement was not especially related to people's views of the war itself. It turned out that a major factor in the approval or disapproval of the court's action pertained to the attributions of causality and the intentionality of the act. Herbert C. Kelman and Lee H. Lawrence (1972) conducted an extensive post hoc analysis of people's views about Calley and the court decision. A total of 989 subjects, representing a cross section of all Americans 18 years of age or older, were interviewed by the Roper organization (a public opinion survey group) under Kelman and Lawrence's supervision. The respondents were first asked: "Do you approve or disapprove of Lieutenant Calley having been brought to trial?" They gave the following replies: 34 percent approved, 58 percent disapproved, and 8 percent didn't know. Then each of the respondents was given a list of five reasons for approving or disapproving of the trial and was asked to select the one that was most important to him or her. Among those respondents who *approved* of the trial, two reasons accounted for 45 percent of their choices:

1. *Even a soldier in a combat situation has no right to kill defenseless civilians, and anyone who violates this rule must be brought to trial.*
2. *The trial helps to put across the important idea that every man must bear responsibility for his own actions* [p. 184].

Among those who *disapproved* of the trial, two reasons accounted for 90 percent of their choices:

1. *It is unfair to send a man to fight in Vietnam and then put him on trial for doing his duty.*
2. *The trial used Lt. Calley as a scapegoat: one young lieutenant shouldn't be blamed for the failures of his superiors* [p. 184].

Interestingly, these four reasons turned out to be more influential in shaping the respondents' views about Calley's trial than their attitudes toward the Vietnam War. Study the four reasons for a moment and see how they fit together.

Notice that the respondents who approved of Calley's trial saw him as morally responsible for his action and therefore blameworthy. Beginning with the effects of his actions, they inferred that he had both the knowledge and the ability to behave in a variety of ways. He acted as he did because he wanted to, not because he had to. He did not simply perform the duties (role) of a soldier. Rather, he deliberately and intentionally violated the moral code against killing defenseless civilians. He willingly chose to commit a crime and was a reprehensible human being; therefore, he certainly deserved to be brought to trial.

On the other hand, those who disapproved of Calley's trial perceived him as the victim of environmental and circumstantial contingencies beyond his control. He was a pawn in a great war machine—a soldier merely doing his duty. He acted as he did not because he wanted to, but because he had to. He could not know what was in the minds of his superiors, nor could he—as a soldier—defy their orders. Given his role as a soldier, he behaved appropriately. Thus, looking at the identical action, the disapprovers inferred that Calley had neither the knowledge nor the ability to act otherwise, did not intentionally kill innocent women and children, was not a heinous individual, and therefore should not be held responsible for his actions.

Observing front stage and backstage behavior. The problem of figuring out what an individual is *really* like is presented in a clever analogy by Erving Goffman, a sociologist who has offered many insightful analyses of social behavior through his careful and keen observations of everyday events. In his lively book *The Presentation of Self in Everyday Life* (1959), Goffman likens behavior in social situations to a theatrical performance. In the course of our daily encounters with others, he says, we each attempt to present ourselves in ways designed to create a given impression; we also tend to assume that others are doing the same thing. Like the passengers on the train, we are each *actors* in some sense, playing out our parts before the *audience* of other people whom we hope to impress in particular ways. If an individual is a good actor, if he stages a good *performance* (that is, puts up a good front), if the setting and lighting are appropriate, and if he works effectively with the other members of the cast (his team), the performance will probably be convincing and successful. We will explore Goffman's analysis of what is required for a good performance later on. For now, though, let us see how this dramaturgical metaphor permits us to better understand what others are really like—as we, the audience, witness the actor's performance.

The "expressiveness of the individual (and therefore his capacity to give impressions)," Goffman writes, "appears to involve two radically different kinds of sign activity: the expression that he *gives*, and the expression that he *gives off*" (p. 2). The expression the actor *gives* is the information about himself (the impression) he deliberately conveys; it consists of those aspects of his performance that he wishes us, his audience, to see. The expression he *gives off*, on the other hand, is the information that the actor unwittingly discloses about himself; it can inform us about what he is really like.

Our observations of actors, then, based solely on the information that is available to us on the right-hand side of Figure 3.5, provide us with a very limited amount of information. It is somewhat like being in a theater where we see the performer front stage, behaving according to his role, trying to convince us of the genuineness of his behavior. How much can we learn from this performance about what the actor is like backstage, where he is reasonably confident that no one from the audience can intrude? Goffman illustrates the stage-to-life analogy with a quotation from George Orwell's book *Down and Out in Paris and London* (1951), which describes the remarkable transformation of a Paris waiter as he moves from front stage to backstage:

It is an instructive sight to see a waiter going into a hotel dining-room. As he passes the door a sudden change comes over him. The set of his shoulders alters; all the dirt and hurry and irritation have dropped off in an instant. He glides over the carpet, with a solemn priest-like air. I remember our assistant maître d'hôtel, *a fiery Italian, pausing at the dining room door to address his apprentice who had broken a bottle of wine. Shaking his fist above his head he yelled (luckily the door was more or less soundproof):*

"Tu me fais—Do you call yourself a waiter, you young bastard! You a waiter! You're not fit to scrub floors in the brothel your mother came from. Maquereau!"

Words failing him, he turned to the door; and as he opened it he delivered a final insult in the same manner as Squire Western in Tom Jones.

Then he entered the dining-room and sailed across it dish in hand, graceful as a swan. Ten seconds later he was bowing reverently to a customer. And you could not help thinking, as you saw him bow and smile, with that benign smile of the trained waiter, that the customer was put to shame by having such an aristocrat to serve him [pp. 68–69].

Suppose we were to ask an attractive, young woman diner what the waiter was like. Her response might be based on the waiter's front stage behavior—she might say that he was friendly, helpful, courteous, dignified, and charming. Suppose, however, that she really needed to know what he was like because he had asked her for a date. The young woman must now decide whether the observed behavior in the restaurant or the manner in which he asked her for a date best typifies what he is really like. In trying to learn more about him, she might well discount some of his observed actions as she tries to make inferences about his disposition and character traits by analyzing his behavior.

Considering the Role and Situational Demands. Obviously, when he was working and when he was asking the young woman for a date, the waiter was behaving according to the demands of the situation. But the young lady would probably like to have the opportunity to

Figure 3.7
Backstage and front
stage performance by
the assistant maître
d'hôtel.

observe the waiter's behavior in situations where he would display his true self. We are always engaged in the performance of one or another role, such as student, employee, man, woman, teacher, colleague, friend, or parent. In order to find out what another person is really like, we try to observe the various roles he portrays, study his performance carefully, and attempt to find instances in which his behavior is inconsistent with his role. The information an actor provides when he is playing a role is not too useful for anyone who wants to learn about him. But when he acts out of role—that is, when he does things that we might not typically expect of him—his behavior is far more revealing.

For example, we can learn far more about what a waiter is really like if we see him fighting in the kitchen (presumably out of role) than we can while he is gliding over the dining-room floor (in role). We can possibly understand more about what a little boy is like when we see him playing with dolls than with toy trucks or fire engines. After all, trucks and fire engines are considered boys' toys—they are consonant with society's stereotype of the male role. A boy playing with dolls, however, is considered to be a sissy—he is behaving in a sex-role-discrepant way. Similarly, a Jew who takes an anti-Israeli position (or an Arab who takes a pro-Israeli position) may be seen as revealing more of his true feeling than one who takes a pro-Israeli (or pro-Arab) position. This is precisely what Stuart Katz and Eugene Burnstein found.

Undergraduates at the University of Michigan were asked to listen to a taped job interview between an "applicant" and the "headmaster" of a school where the applicant wished to teach. In one experimental condition, the applicant (a confederate of the experimenter) was named "Cohen" and was reported to be active in the Hillel organization and other Jewish groups on campus. In the other condition, the same applicant was presented to the subjects as "an Arab who was born and raised in the Near East and sent to the U.S. for his university training." The subjects then listened to one of two versions of the taped interview in which they heard the applicant make a series of either strongly positive or strongly negative statements about Israeli policies. At the conclusion of the tape, the subjects were asked to evaluate the candidate's statements on a series of adjective scales. Katz and Burnstein found that when the Jewish applicant made anti-Israeli statements he was seen as more independent, disloyal, and open about his true beliefs than when he took a pro-Israeli position. When the Arab applicant took an anti-Israeli stand, on the other hand, he was seen as more conforming, loyal, and secretive about his true beliefs than when he made pro-Israeli statements (Katz and Burnstein, 1973).

Social psychologists have devoted considerable research to the consequences of behaving in role-consonant or role-discrepant ways. In one study, Edward E. Jones, Keith E. Davis, and Kenneth J. Gergen (1961) asked a group of subjects to listen to one of four taped interviews between a psychologist and a student applying for a job as either an astronaut or a submariner. Those subjects who listened to the interview for the astronaut job heard the interviewer describe the ideal astronaut as an *inner-directed*, self-sufficient person. Those who heard the submariner interview heard the ideal submariner described as gregarious, friendly, and *other-directed*. The student interviewee (in reality, a confederate of the experimenter) followed a prepared script. In one of the astronaut interviews he described himself as inner-directed (consonant with the role of astronaut); in the other he described himself as other-directed (role discrepant). In one of the submariner interviews the interviewee described himself as other-directed (role consonant), and in the other as inner-directed (role discrepant). After listening to one of these four tapes, the subjects were asked for their opinion on what the interviewee was really like as a person as well as their own confidence in this opinion.

After listening to the two in-role tapes, the subjects rated the interviewee as moderately gregarious and moderately self-sufficient, but they showed little confidence in their rating. In other words, hearing a person behave in a role-consonant fashion did not provide much information about his true nature. The out-of-role interviewees, on the other hand, were rated in a more extreme fashion and with greater confidence by the subjects: the inner-directed, role-discrepant submariner was seen as being truly inner-directed (extremely self-sufficient); while the other-directed, role-discrepant astronaut was perceived as actually other-directed (extremely gregarious). Thus, the subjects believed that the behavior of a person in a role-discrepant situation provided valuable information about his true nature.

Considering the Demands and Pressures from Others. While riding in a train or a bus, you may see a small boy sitting very quietly, behaving correctly and courteously. Initially, you might conclude, "What a quiet, well-behaved, restrained child!" But then you may notice the stern, harsh look on his father's face, obviously conveying the message: "Behave yourself on this trip, or else!" Now what do you really know about the child's disposition? Not too much. The boy's behavior is obviously restrained because of his father's presence; otherwise, he might possibly be quite active. When we see a less powerful person respond to a request made by a more powerful one, we know little about the characteristics of the former. We would know much more if it were the *more* powerful person who was responding to a request made by a less powerful person. This is the essence of a study conducted by John W. Thibaut and Henry W. Riecken (1955).

Twenty male college freshmen were individually escorted to a room, where the experimenter introduced them to two confederates who had been instructed to behave like naïve subjects. One of the confederates (High Status) was introduced as a member of the faculty and a recent Ph.D.; he was neatly dressed in a suit and tie. The other confederate (Low Status) was introduced as an army veteran who had just finished his freshman year in college; he was casually dressed in shirtsleeves and without a tie. The confederates alternated playing these roles from subject to subject.

After the introductions, the experimenter seated the three men in separate rooms and informed them that one would be randomly selected as a communicator. This person would have the task of attempting to persuade the other two (the audience) to donate blood for a Red Cross drive. Although lots were drawn, the subject was always assigned to be the communicator, and he was asked to prepare a single persuasive written message that would be sent to both of the others. Before sending his persuasive message, the subject was asked to rate his initial liking for each of the two other men on an "acceptance" scale. This same scale was completed once again at the end of the experiment.

After receiving the message, both confederates said that they had been persuaded and that they would donate blood. The subjects (all of whom had been successful persuaders) were then interviewed by the experimenter, who asked the following question: "Suppose you had to decide that one of the members of the audience said 'yes' (that is, complied) because you forced him to (that is, put pressure on him) and the other said 'yes' because he just naturally wanted to anyway. Which one would you say you forced and which one just wanted to anyway?"

Thibaut and Riecken found that of the 19 (out of 20) subjects who were able to decide on an answer, 18 reported that the High Status confederate was the one who "just wanted to anyway," while the Low Status confederate had been "forced." In response to the question pertaining to their "acceptability," the High Status confederate was initially seen as more acceptable (likable) than the Low Status one. Moreover, this discrepancy in liking—favoring the High Status confederate—increased further in the final ratings. Thus, despite the fact that the two confederates had responded in exactly the same way to the identical persuasive argument, the subjects attributed different motives to the two confederates and indicated a greater liking (and an increase in liking) for one rather than the other. What might be a possible reason for this? Perhaps the subjects perceived the Low Status confederate as behaving in a role-consonant fashion; he complied because he felt obliged to, and there is nothing particularly likable about a person who blindly acquiesces. And perhaps they saw the High Status confederate as behaving in a role-discrepant fashion; surely he didn't *have* to comply, since in an academic community an individual with a Ph.D. has status. So he must have complied simply because he wanted to. Although Thibaut and Riecken did not ask their subjects to specify which of the two confederates they felt they knew more about, it is entirely possible that they would have chosen the High Status one.

Learning from those who can get "backstage." If we cannot get backstage personally to learn about somebody, we can sometimes learn about him from others. The young lady who would like to know more about the waiter before agreeing to a date would be lucky if she knew someone else who worked in the kitchen and could observe the waiter backstage.

Goffman (1959) has listed several types of people who may have access to backstage information about an actor: (1) An *informer*— someone who has access to backstage, is trusted by the performers, and then discloses their secrets to the audience. (2) A *shill*—someone who pretends to be a member of the audience (such as a claque or professional applauder), but is actually in league with the performers. Goffman provides an example:

> At informal conversational gatherings, it is common for a wife to look interested when her husband tells an anecdote and to feed him appropriate leads and cues, although in fact she has heard the anecdote many times and knows that the show her husband is making of telling something for the first time is only a show [p. 147].

If we could only persuade the wife to tell us what she knows, how much we could discover about her husband! (3) A *go-between*— someone who is trusted by both the audience and the performers, and who leads each group to believe he will guard its secrets and be more loyal to it than to the other. Mediators and marriage brokers often perform the function of a go-between. (4) A *non-person*— someone who witnesses the interaction between performers and audience, going backstage at will, but occupying neither role. A servant, says Goffman, is a classic example of a non-person: "He is defined by both performers and audience as someone who isn't there" (p. 151). Mrs. Trollope, in her book *Domestic Manners of the Americans* (1832), provides a good example of a non-person in the following passage (cited by Goffman):

> I had, indeed, frequent opportunities of observing this habitual indifference to the presence of their slaves. They talk of them, of their condition, of their faculties, of their conduct, exactly as if they were incapable of hearing. I once saw a young lady, who, when seated at table between a male and a female, was induced by her modesty to intrude on the chair of her female neighbor to avoid the indelicacy of touching the elbow of a man. I once saw this very young lady lacing her stays with the most perfect composure before a Negro footman [pp. 56–57].

Thus, assuming that we cannot go backstage ourselves, we could still hope to learn about life behind the curtain through the services of an informer, a shill, a go-between, or a non-person.

In many laboratory experiments, the experimenter may also serve as an informer by telling the subject certain things about another person that the other person himself may not know—or would, at least, be reluctant to disclose. In a number of studies of interpersonal attraction, the experimenter provides a subject with information about another person that the experimenter has obtained from attitude or personality measures. In this case, the experimenter acts like Goffman's go-between.

Sometimes we can learn certain things about an individual simply by observing how others act in the same situation; if we see a number of people acting in a different fashion than the individual in question, we would be inclined to attribute his behavior to himself alone. In the evaluation of Lt. William Calley (Kelman and Lawrence, 1972), this was undoubtedly one reason why he was held responsible for his crimes. Those who blamed him were probably aware of the fact that many men, in similar wartime circumstances, did *not* wantonly kill innocent civilians. Those who believed he was not at fault were probably inclined to think of others in comparable circumstances who *had* committed similar acts. They reasoned that if others had also done the same thing, it must be the circumstances that should be held accountable for the acts and not the individuals themselves.

To recapitulate, we are each continually forming impressions of those around us; these impressions lead us to develop a gestalt—a way of viewing others in elementary, parsimonious terms. However, since we know that these impressions are often simplistic, we try to discover what others are *really* like. We can try to explore directly the backstage areas of their behavior to see what they are like when their masks are removed; or we can try to enlist the help of third parties who have access to these areas; or we can look for behavior that is role discrepant, hoping for a clue about these people's true nature. In searching for the underlying causes of other people's behavior, we typically begin with an analysis of their actions and the resulting effects, and then draw inferences about their intentions. From our inferences about their intentions, and the extent to which their behavior is either internally or externally determined, we attempt to reach conclusions, whenever possible, about what other people are really like.

Thus, as we sit on the train to Los Angeles and observe the man across the aisle raising an eyebrow, jiggling a jowl, or letting his teeth glitter in a little grin, we want to know whether he is an actor—choosing to give a certain impression—or a real person. We observe his behavior in a variety of situations—interacting with other people and talking about many different topics—and try to decide if he is playing a role. If we believe he is, we will probably conclude that his behavior does not reveal very much about his true nature or motives. On the other hand, if we decide that he is behaving in a free manner, we may conclude that we really know something about his true self.

PRESENTING
OURSELVES
TO OTHERS

Thus far, we have focused on the way we, as members of an audience, perceive another person, his behavior, his surroundings, and his contextual situation, and then try to draw conclusions about what that person is really like. Let us now take the perspective of the actor who is being observed by others and who is sensitive to the ways in which others perceive him. We have already alluded to the actor's perspective, for it is impossible to divorce completely the actions of the actor from those of the observer. As we indicated in the example of the strangers on the train, we often think a great deal about the impressions we are probably making and would like to make on other people; and in interpreting the behavior of others, we generally take into account the fact that they are also trying to make certain impressions on us.

The Degree and Form of Self-disclosure

The Threatening Nature of Self-disclosure. Sidney M. Jourard (1964) and others have pointed out that we often think about how much we reveal ourselves to others. We often fear if we reveal too much, others will be able to exert control over us; or perhaps we fear that they will think less well of us if they really know us. This fear of self-disclosure, as well as the fear of knowing another too intimately, are illustrated most dramatically by Eldridge Cleaver, the black political activist and author, in a letter to his attorney (a woman), with whom he had become quite intimate:

The reason two people are reluctant to really strip themselves naked in front of each other is because, in doing so, they make themselves vulnerable and give enormous power over themselves to the other. How awful, how deadly, how catastrophically they can hurt each other, wreck and ruin each other forever! How often, indeed, they end by inflicting pain and torment upon each other. Better to maintain shallow, superficial affairs; that way the scars are not too deep, no blood is hacked from the soul. You beautifully–oh, how beautifully!! spoke in your letter of "what an awful thing it is to feel oneself on the verge of the possibility of really knowing another person . . ." and "I feel as though I am on the edge of a new world." Getting to know someone, entering the new world, is an ultimate, irretrievable leap into the unknown. The prospect is terrifying. The stakes are high. The emotions are overwhelming [Cleaver, 1968, p. 139; as quoted in Altman and Taylor, 1973, p. 41].

As we trust others, we disclose more. As we get to know one another, we tend to reveal more about ourselves (Jourard, 1964) and, in the process (perhaps contrary to our initial expectations), we tend to feel more secure. Such is the pattern you might follow as you continued your train trip from New York to Los Angeles. Indeed, you would probably begin to talk more and more with one person, perhaps the young lady sitting in the seat in front of you. As you talked more and became better acquainted, she might begin to reveal more of herself to you. What you would disclose to her, in turn, would not be an unsystematic assortment of scattered facts. Rather, we might expect a series of successive revelations, beginning with the superficial layers and then moving toward more private areas. At first, you might restrict your conversation to such things as your personal history, your occupation, where you live, and what you have studied. Next, you might reveal some of your less emotional attitudes and beliefs, such as whether you like the train, the fact that the Midwest landscape is a bit boring, and so forth. Then, as you become more mutually trusting, you might disclose some of your views about politics and perhaps religion. Eventually, you might reveal something about your family and your very close friends, and perhaps even discuss your difficulties in relating to other people; your more intimate feelings about sex, love, and marriage; your thoughts about the nature of life and death; and then your secret hopes, fears, and psychological hangups. Perhaps before you reached a very intimate level, you might feel threatened and call off your relationship. If you continued, however, you might begin to sense a very deep feeling of relief and even affection for the person who has listened to you and who has probably revealed something of herself in the process.

Reciprocating Self-disclosure by Others. That we do, indeed, reveal more of ourselves to others roughly in accordance with how much they reveal to us has been demonstrated in a clever field experiment, conducted by Zick Rubin (1975) in the departure lounge of Boston's Logan Airport. In this study a student experimenter would approach a lone passenger waiting in the lounge and ask him (or her) for assistance in a study of handwriting. If the passenger agreed, the student would write a few sentences, telling the passenger about himself (the student); the passenger would then be asked to write a few sentences about himself (or herself). In some cases the student wrote a sentence of very low intimacy ("I'm in the process of collecting handwriting samples. . . . I will stay here a while longer, and then call it a day"). In a High-Intimacy Condition, the student wrote a more revealing statement ("I think that I'm pretty well adjusted, but I occasionally have some questions about my sexual adequacy"). The passengers generally tended to reciprocate: If the student experimenter wrote an intimate statement, the passenger's statement would also be longer and more intimate (for example, "I've just been attending . . . my 40th [college] reunion. I still feel sexually adequate—never felt otherwise"). This tendency to reciprocate, however, took place only when the student experimenters appeared to be composing the sentence extemporaneously and thus seemed to be revealing their true selves. There was no such reciprocation if the experimenter merely appeared to be copying sentences that had been written by someone else.

Personality and Cultural Differences in Self-disclosure. There are vast individual, and often cultural, differences in the tendency to reveal things about oneself. Kurt Lewin (1936, 1948), for example, made some interesting informal observations of differences between Germans and Americans. He suggested that Americans *appear* to be more open and self-revealing than Germans, but that this openness extends only to the peripheral layers. He observed that Americans are more apt to reveal superficial things about themselves, but then you encounter a stone wall; Americans are extremely reluctant to share their innermost secrets. Germans, on the other hand, are somewhat more difficult to get to know casually; they are reluctant to reveal some of their superficial attitudes and values. However, once one has managed to gain the Germans' confidence, they are much more open about their inner secrets. Lewin's observation is an intriguing one, but there is not yet much systematic research on this topic.

Jourard (1964) believes that self-disclosure is especially difficult for men in our society. Traditionally men have been expected to be unemotional, strong, stoic, self-composed. Therefore, it has been considered unmanly to reveal too much—one must present a strong masculine image to others. In his letter, Cleaver seems to exemplify this male reticence. Jourard believes that because men restrict their feelings, they pay a heavy price in terms of poor personal adjustment and self-confidence.

The Art of Impression Management
Not only are we often concerned about how much we reveal to others, but we are concerned about the manner in which this revelation occurs. What we reveal and how, will vary according to the company and situation in which we find ourselves. On the train, clearly, we will reveal differing social selves as we discuss one topic with the waiter, another with the conductor, another with the young lady in front of us, and still another with the distinguished looking gentleman across the aisle. Furthermore, back in our home community we present still other social selves—at work, at school, and with our fam-

ilies. Goffman (1959) assumes that in our social encounters we try to give a variety of impressions and, like actors on the stage, attempt to present the best and most appropriate performance in each encounter. Let us look, for example, at a physician who is seeing a succession of patients in his office during the course of a day. What impression does he want to create in their eyes? Perhaps he wants to look as if he is a master of his art, knowledgeable in medicine, efficient, friendly, dependable, and self-confident. How can he go about trying to create this impression?

1. *A proper front.* Just as the actor needs a proper stage and proper scenery, so does the physician. Front, as defined by Goffman is "that part of the individual's performance which regularly functions in a general or fixed fashion to define the situation for those who observe the performance" (p. 22); it has three components: setting (such as furniture, decor, and diplomas on the wall), personal setting (such as clothing and insignia), and appearance and manner. Think of a typical visit to your family doctor. You enter the waiting room, sit down on one of the comfortable chairs or sofas, and perhaps leaf through a copy of *National Geographic, Reader's Digest,* or *Better Homes and Gardens* that is lying on the table. Then the smiling doctor appears, wearing a white coat and conservative tie; he may have a stethoscope draped around his neck. His appearance and manner suggest that he is a professional who is very much in control of the situation. Taken together, these aspects of the doctor's front produce an effective performance—they tend to inspire your confidence in the doctor and his ability. By contrast, how would you feel if your doctor's waiting room were lined with folding chairs and the reading material consisted of *Screw* and *Playgirl* magazines; and suppose your doctor came out wearing faded and torn dungarees with shoulder-length hair; and suppose his manner were rather unfriendly and abrupt?

2. *Involvement in one's role.* It is absolutely essential that the actor be fully involved in his role. Undoubtedly it would be helpful if he actually believed in the role, that is, felt himself totally a doctor. In any event, a good actor, either in the theater or on the stage of everyday life, can perform well only if he is personally involved enough to be able to present the role convincingly.

3. *Dramatic realization and idealization.* The doctor must know what type of role the audience *expects* and take this into account in his performance. Sometimes he must do things that are not actually necessary for the performance of his function but that are expected of him. The physician may be sufficiently experienced and insightful that he can diagnose a patient's problem by merely glancing at the color of his skin or the dilation of his pupils. If that were all he did, however, before prescribing an appropriate medicine, the patient

might feel cheated and probably a bit suspicious: What kind of doctor is this anyhow? What am I paying him for? To avoid such problems, the doctor may go through an entire routine—stethoscope,
thermometer, pulse check, tongue depressor—even though it is really not necessary for the diagnosis.

4. *Mystification.* Finally, Goffman writes, for many roles a good
performance requires the maintenance of a certain social distance
between actor and audience. The physician must maintain an appropriate distance with his patients—he cannot become too familiar or
friendly, lest the mystery and awe of his role be lost in the process.
Many of us want to think of the President (despite, or perhaps because of, the Watergate scandals) as a person who is endowed with
special virtues and talents that mysteriously set him apart and above
the rest of us. Sitting in the Oval Office behind his large desk, surrounded on either side by the American flag and the bald eagle, he is
a person we want to respect and admire—and not just another man in
the street.

These, then, are the characteristics of a good performance, according to Goffman—characteristics that enable us both to make the
impression we wish and to learn something about our own effectiveness.

FINDING OUT
ABOUT OURSELVES

In the very act of trying to create a particular impression, we inevitably reveal clues about our real selves that other people pick up, interpret, and use in responding to our behavior. Their view of us, and
thus our view of ourselves through them, enable us to develop a concept of self—to discover what we are really like.

The "I," the "Me," and the "Looking Glass Self." As a matter of fact,
the sociologists Charles Horton Cooley (1902) and George Herbert
Mead (1934) have argued that it is *only* through others that we can
acquire an awareness of ourselves. Cooley, for example, likens our
concept of self to a "looking glass," a social mirror in which we learn
to view ourselves from the perspective of significant others. Like the
three characters in Sartre's play, *No Exit*, we see ourselves only
through the eyes of other people. Cooley writes:

*As we see our face, figure, and dress in the glass, and are inter-
ested in them because they are ours, and pleased or otherwise with
them according as they do or do not answer to what we should like
them to be; so in imagination we perceive in another's mind some*

*thought of our appearance, manners, aims, deeds, character, friends,
and so on, and are variously affected by it [p. 152].*

In a similar fashion, Mead suggests that the child learns to distinguish between himself as the perceiver of the world around him (the
"I") and himself as the object of his own perception (the "me"). It is
only when the child has acquired the concept of "me"—when he has
learned to see himself through the eyes of others—that he has truly
developed a sense of self.

The important implication of Cooley's and Mead's analysis is
that we need other people in order to discover what we, ourselves,
are like. Through them we learn to view ourselves from a more realistic, social perspective, to see ourselves as object rather than subject. And, as Jourard (1964) has pointed out, one of the things we
gain by exposing ourselves to others is a greater knowledge of ourselves:

*No man can come to know himself except as an outcome of
disclosing himself to another person. . . . When a person has been
able to disclose himself utterly to another person, he learns how to
increase his contact with his real self, and he may then be better
able to direct his destiny on the basis of knowledge of his real self
[p. 5].*

Attribution Theory and Self-perception

Daryl J. Bem (1967) and Harold H. Kelley (1967) have suggested that
the process of arriving at inferences about oneself is basically identical to that of making inferences about others. Just as we observe the
effects of another person's actions and use these to draw inferences
about his intentions and dispositions, we may observe our own actions (kicking a door, for example) and then make attributions about
our own underlying state ("I must be feeling angry"). Often, of
course, we have a particular feeling or attitude first and then trans-
late it into action ("I agree with the views of candidate X; therefore, I
will vote for him"). There are other situations, however (especially
those that are ambiguous), in which we begin an analysis of our behavior by initiating some action, and then interpret this action in
light of how we think we were feeling at the time ("I voted for candidate X; therefore, I must agree with his views").

Think about the following example, suggested by Kelley's (1967)
analysis of attributions to oneself. You go with a group of friends to
the movies one night and see a double feature: the Marx brothers in
Horse Feathers and Charlie Chaplin in *The Great Dictator*. Later in
the evening, back in your room, you relax and think about the films

you have seen. *Horse Feathers*, you decide, was enormously funny—it was a truly great film. But, wait a minute, you think to yourself. Was *Horse Feathers* really funny, or were you perhaps in a mood to enjoy anything that evening, no matter how trite—or are you generally a person with a good sense of humor who enjoys most comedies? How might you go about answering these questions?

There are four criteria, according to Kelley, that should be considered: (1) *entity*—was it *Horse Feathers* alone that you found enjoyable, or did you find *The Great Dictator* funny also? Do you find other comedy films funny? (2) *persons*—did you alone enjoy *Horse Feathers*, or did your friends find it funny as well? (3) *time*—if you were to see *Horse Feathers* a second time, would you still find it funny? (4) *modality*—would you have enjoyed *Horse Feathers* if you had seen it at the grubby $.50 student theater rather than at the $3.00 Roxie? Would you enjoy it at a drive-in or on television? Each of these criteria (or questions), Kelley has argued, needs to be kept in mind as you attempt to decide whether it was the movie or your mood that was responsible for your enjoyment. If, for example, you concluded that you liked *Horse Feathers* but not *The Great Dictator*, that your friends liked *Horse Feathers* also, and that you enjoyed it when you saw it again and in a different setting, you would probably be justified in concluding that your enjoyment was due to the film. If, on the other hand, you liked both movies, your friends did not like either one, and you enjoyed *Horse Feathers* only on that one occasion in that particular movie house, you would probably decide that your enjoyment was due to the particular mood you were in that evening.

As mentioned earlier, we typically analyze the causes of other people's behavior by observing the effects first and then making attributions about dispositions; through this process we try to decide whether the behavior is externally or internally caused. Similarly, in analyzing the causes of our *own* behavior, we often begin with an effect (laughter during a movie we enjoy) and then try to decide what our underlying attitude was. Was our enjoyment externally or internally determined? Was it due to the movie (external) or the mood we were in (internal)?

Although Figure 3.5 (the Jones and Davis paradigm) depicts the attribution of dispositions and traits to others on the basis of their observed behavior, it also applies to attributions to oneself. One important difference, of course, is that we *think* we already know quite a bit about ourselves, have less need to make inferences, and therefore are more resistant to changing our self-perception as a result of observing our actions. But there are still many situations in which we try to make our self-perception more accurate, especially when our self-concept is threatened—by new and unfamiliar situations and behaviors, by disparate information about ourselves conveyed by others, and by challenges that require us to be certain of our own image.

We follow the same pattern as the one we use in evaluating others: (1) *Effects*—when we have done something that has produced unusually good or bad effects, we reevaluate ourselves accordingly. One would hope that those who participated in the My Lai massacre felt that they had to reconcile the deaths they caused with their self-perception. As a professor, I like to think of myself as someone who is careful in his evaluations, but when a student comes to my office and tells me that as a result of my reasonable grade he has flunked out of college and his career plans have been ruined, I must admit that I usually feel compelled to reexamine my actions and motives. (Often, of course, the student's technique is to suggest that I *alone* am responsible for his misfortune; I can sometimes assuage my guilt by realizing that the grades of other professors have also been responsible. In this way, I can reinterpret the effect as due to an attribute of the student rather than myself.) (2) *Considering role, situational, and social demands*—in analyzing your reactions to *Horse Feathers,* we wanted to find out whether it was the film or the locale that affected your enjoyment. A policeman, while writing a traffic ticket for an elderly driver, may sometimes think (and perhaps also say), "I hate to do this, but it is my job [that is, I am not a heartless person]." Similarly, the defense usually given by soldiers who have been accused of war atrocities is: "I did what I was ordered to do; I am *not* a bloodthirsty, cruel person when I am only doing my duty and carrying out orders." (3) *Considering the opinions and behaviors of others*—when we are uncertain of ourselves, we are especially inclined to look to others for an evaluation of ourselves. This tendency was noted in Schachter's study (1959) of affiliation under threat (see page 44). Let us now look at several additional studies conducted by Kenneth J. Gergen and his colleagues.

Considering How Others Evaluate Us

In one experiment (Gergen, 1965), the subjects were asked a number of questions about how they viewed themselves. In one condition, the interviewer (a confederate of the experimenter) positively reinforced the subjects' positive self-evaluations (by smiling, nodding her head, and stating her agreement), and she negatively reinforced their self-critical evaluations (by shaking her head, frowning, looking puzzled, and stating her disagreement). In the other condition, the interviewer did not respond in any way to the subjects' answers. Gergen found that those subjects who were given verbal and nonverbal support by the interviewer became increasingly positive in their self-evaluation; in the presence of someone who seemed to like them, they came to like themselves more and to increase their self-esteem—at least temporarily. However, in the other group (where the subjects received no response from the interviewer), the subjects showed no change in their self-evaluation.

Gergen and Barbara Wishnov (1965) subsequently demonstrated that an individual's self-concept can be temporarily changed by even more subtle cues than the nods or frowns of another person. Pairs of college women were brought into the laboratory and were asked to write descriptions of themselves which, they were told, would be exchanged. Instead of exchanging the descriptions, however, the experimenter handed each subject an evaluation that had been prepared in advance. One group of subjects was led to believe that the other member of the pair was extremely self-centered and egotistical, while the second group was led to believe that the other member of the pair was self-effacing and humble. The experimenter then asked the subjects to describe themselves once again in response to what they had learned about their partner.

Gergen and Wishnov found that those subjects who were presented with a self-centered partner became increasingly positive in their own evaluation of themselves. As Gergen (1972) pointed out, they seemed to be saying, "You think you're so great; well, I'm pretty terrific too" (p. 34). Those presented with a self-effacing partner, however, became increasingly negative in their self-evaluations. They acknowledged that they had a number of shortcomings, which they had not admitted before. They seemed to be saying, "I know what you mean; I've got problems too" (p. 34). When Gergen and Wishnov asked the subjects if their self-evaluations were completely accurate and if they had been influenced by what their partner had said about herself, 60 percent responded that their self-evaluations were completely honest and accurate and had *not* been influenced by their partner in any way. Thus, these subjects' views of themselves appear to have been altered with little conscious awareness of the process.

In yet another study of an individual's self-concept, Stanley J. Morse and Kenneth J. Gergen (1970) recruited a number of male undergraduates who wanted to apply for a lucrative "summer job." Upon their arrival at the laboratory, each subject was seated alone in a room and was given a variety of tests, including a self-evaluation questionnaire. While the applicant was busy with these tests, another applicant entered the room (actually a confederate of the experimenter). In one condition, the second "applicant" (Mr. Clean) was neatly dressed in a dark suit and appeared well groomed and self-confident; from his attaché case he took a number of neatly sharpened pencils, a statistics book, a slide rule, and a copy of Plato. In a second experimental condition, the confederate (Mr. Dirty) wore an old, smelly sweatshirt, torn pants, and no socks; appeared dazed and confused; and had a battered copy of *The Carpetbaggers* and no pencils. In neither condition did the confederate speak with the subject at any time.

Morse and Gergen compared the subjects' self-evaluations both before and after the appearance of Mr. Clean or Mr. Dirty. They found that the self-evaluations became increasingly positive after exposure to Mr. Dirty and increasingly negative after exposure to Mr. Clean. In other words, Mr. Dirty helped to raise the subjects' self-esteem—he made them feel more confident, optimistic, and even more handsome. Mr. Clean, however, produced a lowered self-esteem, perhaps because he made the subjects feel ignorant, sloppy, and inferior by comparison. The implication of Morse and Gergen's research is that we discover, at least in part, what we are like by comparing ourselves with others—significant others especially, but strangers as well. We evaluate our own abilities, opinions, judgments, and feelings through the process of social comparison. And the clues we obtain from other people—such as their approval of us, their manner, and their appearance—shape our views of ourselves.

Summary

In order to function effectively in our complex social world, we need to understand what other people are like. We tend to simplify our social world by assembling the array of impressions we receive from others into a coherent explanation of their behavior. One way in which we do this is by relying on our first impressions. Categorizing others as sane or insane, nice or nasty, stereotypically male or female early in our relationship allows us to organize and explain their subsequent behavior with considerable ease. Unfortunately, the picture we develop of others from first impressions is usually oversimplified or distorted; since it fails to tell us what others are really like, we may be inclined to act toward them in stereotypic, prejudicial ways.

There are at least four interrelated ways in which one can try to learn what another person is really like. First—and most important—we can observe his behavior, assess the consequences of this behavior for himself and others (taking into account the particular context in which it took place), and then attribute certain personal qualities to that person. Because we typically assume that people behave as they do because of their particular character traits, we work backward in trying to learn what another person is like—we go from observations to inferences, and from acts to dispositions. Second, we can observe whether there is some congruence between the information a person deliberately conveys about himself and what he discloses unwittingly. Thus, following Erving Goffman's sociological analysis, to understand what an actor is really like we must observe not only his "front stage" behavior (when he is wearing a costume and makeup, and enacting a role) but also his "backstage" behavior (when he is no longer wearing his costume and makeup or acting a role). The information an actor provides about himself in a given role is not particularly useful, but when he acts out of role—when he does things that we probably would not expect of him—his behavior is far more revealing. Third (and this is closely related to the second point), we can note the demands and pressures on an individual by others and try to distinguish those situations in which he behaves as he does because he has to from those in which he behaves as he does by choice (obviously acts of free choice reveal more about the given individual). Finally, even if we cannot get backstage ourselves, we can sometimes learn about a person through third parties who have access to him.

As we attempt to discover what another person is like by interacting with him, we ask certain questions and respond in special ways that probably disclose various things about ourselves: interaction, after all, is a two-way process. People are typically concerned about what and how they reveal themselves, and there are vast individual and cultural differences in this area. As a result, people often try to control the impression they make on others; like actors on a stage, they attempt to give their best and most appropriate performance at each encounter.

The process of drawing inferences about oneself is basically the same as drawing inferences about others. Just as we observe the effects of another person's actions and then make assumptions about his intentions and dispositions, we sometimes observe our own actions and then make attributions about ourselves. We may take into account the various role, situational, and social demands we face (did we behave, believe, or feel as we did because of necessity or because of free choice?). We may also consider the opinions and behavior of others, especially in situations that are not clear, for the purpose of evaluating ourselves.

Our emerging awareness of others and ourselves has a number of important consequences: it affects the kinds of interdependent relationships we enter or that trap us; it affects our susceptibility to particular forms of influence, whether exercised by individuals or groups; and it very much determines whether we will like or dislike certain others. Chapter 4 will address itself to this last important consequence of interpersonal perception and awareness—the development of liking and affection or disliking and hostility in a relationship.

Getting to Like and Dislike Others
The Elements of Balance Theory
Balance and Attitudes

**What Determines Whether We Like or Dislike
  Another Person?**
Personal Characteristics and Traits
A Sense of Unity or Identification
Liking Those Who Like Us
Liking Those Who Materially Benefit Us
Liking Those Who Are Familiar
Liking Others in Order to Justify Our Efforts
Liking Others Who Help Us to Evaluate Ourselves

Hostility and Aggression
The Frustration-Aggression Hypothesis
When Is Frustration Especially Likely to Lead to
    Aggression?
When Do We Aggress When Not Frustrated?
Violence, Aggression, and the Mass Media
When Does Frustration Not Lead to Aggression?
What Are the Consequences of Trying to Reduce
    Tension through Aggression?

LIKING AND DISLIKING, FRIENDSHIP AND AGGRESSION

FOUR

101

Omens of Love in Folklore. "He loves me . . . he loves me not . . . he loves me. . . ." How many young men and women have turned to the daisy for answers to this most important question? For some, the ritual is carried out half-jokingly; for others, it is a very serious matter. Hundreds of other methods have also been devised to discern who one's lover might be: Sleep with a piece of wedding cake under your pillow and you will dream of your future spouse. Or, if no wedding cake is available, you can wink three times at the brightest visible star before going to bed. Or you can learn the initial of your lover's name by observing the shape of an apple peel thrown over your left shoulder, or in the trail left by a snail that you have caught on Halloween.

For those who would prefer to take a more active role, there are other techniques. To attract lovers, Ozark girls have carried around the beard of a wild turkey; Texas girls have hidden horned toads on their persons; Balkan girls have quietly selected a piece of earth on which their favorite man has stepped and planted a marigold there—as the flower blooms, presumably so does her man's love. Men have also utilized all types of love potions, incantations, talismans, and other rituals—some amusing, some bizarre (Hill, 1968).

Look through any popular magazine, watch television, or read billboard signs and you will learn even more about the many available methods to make yourself more attractive to others—beauty aids, perfumes, deodorants, clothing, and fancy automobiles. Then, of course, there are numerous articles and books, such as Dale Carnegie's *How to Win Friends and Influence People* (1936).

From these examples we can see that being liked or loved, disliked or hated, is one of our major concerns in interacting with other people; we want to know if others like or dislike us, and we want to be able to make ourselves more attractive to others. The benevolent ruler wants the loyalty and devotion of his subjects, and the subject wants the good favor of the ruler; the young man wants the love of his lady fair, and the young lady wants the love of her favorite man. On the negative side, witches and sorcerers stand ready to provide information about one's enemies and to supply voodoo dolls and pins for doing them in. It is virtually impossible to fathom the tremendous expenditure of time, resources, and intellectual energy that mankind has spent in developing armaments to fight his enemies.

Long before social psychologists began to formulate principles of interpersonal attraction, there were a number of popular "theories," although they were often inconsistent with one another:

"Birds of a feather flock   "Opposites attract"
together"

"Familiarity breeds
   contempt"

"Blood is thicker than water"

"Absence makes the heart
   grow fonder"

"Old friends (like old shoes) are
   best"
"To know him is to love him"

"You choose your friends; fate
   chooses your relations"

"Out of sight, out of mind"

The fact that folk sayings often contradict one another has been used to discount their validity altogether. However, social psychological research on interpersonal attraction often indicates that two opposing folk sayings may be correct, depending upon the circumstances. We will examine some of the evidence for this here.

GETTING TO LIKE AND DISLIKE OTHERS

Much of the research on interpersonal attraction and hostility can be fruitfully examined within a framework developed by Fritz Heider (1946, 1958) and elaborated and modified by others (for example, Newcomb, 1953, 1961, 1963; Cartwright and Harary, 1956; Osgood and Tannenbaum, 1955; Backman and Secord, 1959). Fritz Heider was the one who argued that scientific social psychology can progress by first understanding and then systematizing common sense. And this is the procedure that Heider seems to follow in *balance theory*. For his analysis he borrows some simple ideas from formal logic, from the algebra of sets and relations, and from graph theory (a branch of topology).

The Elements of Balance Theory

The person on whom we are focusing is designated with the letter p, and other people with the lower-case letters o, q, r, s, and t. The letters x, y, and z are usually reserved for objects. These persons and objects may have a variety of relationships with one another. In balance theory, Heider uses two different kinds of relations—L for a liking relationship, and U for a unit-forming relationship. Both L and U can be represented in positive or negative forms. Thus, a typical statement in Heider's algebra of social relations would be $p +Lo$, which means "the person p likes the other person o. The symbol $+L$ can designate a number of positive feelings between persons and objects—"likes," "approves," "agrees with," "views favorably," "loves," and so forth. The negative form, $-L$, designates "dislikes," "disapproves," "disagrees with," "views unfavorably," "hates," and so forth. Often the plus sign is omitted in the statement so that pLx means that p likes x; the minus sign is reserved for dislikes. Heider borrows the concept of the unit-forming relationship (U) from the classical Gestalt theory of perception. Because certain objects and people seem to go together quite naturally, they form a unit. Members of the same family or people who are closely associated with one another are often seen as a unit. Sometimes the unit relationship is accentuated by the surroundings. Two Brooklynites waiting for the same subway together with hundreds of other Brooklynites may not think of themselves as forming a unit. However, if they happen to run into each other in Los Angeles, they suddenly become two Brooklynites in the midst of hundreds of Angelenos, and thus they may feel very much like a unit. Heider illustrates the effects of background on unit formation in the following example:

A Kansan boasts about the Empire State Building. Where is this most likely to happen, in Topeka (Kansas), New York, Paris, or Chicago? The obvious answer is Paris. Boasting implies that the person who does the boasting and the object about which he boasts form a unit. This is equally true of being proud or ashamed or something. For the Kansan this unity with the Empire State Building would exist only outside of the United States, or at least it is much more likely to occur there [Heider, 1958, p. 180].

Thus, U in the statement pUx can mean "is part of," "owns," "identifies with," "is associated with," "belongs," "created," "is a member of," and so forth. Similarly, $-U$ indicates "is distinct from," "disowns," "does not identify with," "destroys," and so forth.

Some Examples of Balanced and Imbalanced Relationships. One of Heider's major contributions is the concept of *balance*, applied when there are two or more relationships—a "harmonious state in which the entities comprising the situation and the feelings about them fit together without stress." Here are some examples of two entities in balance or imbalance:

1. $pUx, p-Lx$ Bill wrote a book with which he is dissatisfied. Mary is a member of a club that she finds distasteful.

2. pUo, pLo Bill and Mary are husband and wife, and Bill loves Mary.

3. pLo, oLp Bill likes Charlie, and Charlie likes Bill.

4. $pLs, s-Lp$ Mary likes Sarah, but Sarah dislikes Mary.

5. $p -Lo, o -Lp$ Bill and Stanley dislike each other.

If you were asked to indicate which of the above relationships seemed balanced or imbalanced, would you have any difficulty?
Now let us look at a few relationships among three entities:

6. pUx, pLo, oLx Bill wrote a book; his friend Charlie likes that book.

7. $pLo, oLx, p -Lx$ Bill likes Charlie; Charlie likes Los Angeles; Bill dislikes Los Angeles.

8. $p -Lo, o -Lx, pLx$ Bill dislikes Sarah; Sarah dislikes the Democratic Party; Bill likes the Democratic Party.

9. $pLo, p -Lq, qUo$ Bill likes Mary but does not like Sarah; Sarah and Mary are sisters.

Judging balance here may be a little more difficult, but you have probably been able to pick out the imbalanced relationships: 1, 4, 7, and 9. How did you do it? It seems reasonable that there would be some imbalance if a person were dissatisfied with something he had made, or if he loved Los Angeles while his best friend disliked it. Is there a rule that applies? Balance theorists suggest that the answer is clearer if the same relationships are presented graphically. In Figure 4.1, we can see the representation of one person p, another person, o, and an object, x, when p either likes or dislikes o, o either likes or dislikes x, and p either likes or dislikes x. Heider (1958) and Cartwright and Harary (1956) have pointed out that you can determine balance by multiplying algebraically around the triangle as follows: p to o to x and back to p again. (In this operation, the direction of the arrows should be ignored.) Thus, in Figure 4.1(a), *plus* times *plus* times *plus* gives you the product *plus*, a balanced relationship. In Figure 4.1(b), *plus* times *minus* times *minus* equals *plus*, also balanced. But in Figure 4.1(e), *minus* times *plus* times *plus* equals *minus*, and so the relationship is imbalanced. Therefore, if you have a relationship with either no minuses or an even number of minuses, the cycle will be balanced. Furthermore, in his initial statement of balance theory, Heider said that the balance or imbalance will occur regardless of whether the relationships are U-relationships or L-relationships.

You may notice that our examples 6, 7, 8, and 9 are represented by Figures 4.1(a), (g), (d), and (g), respectively. (The basic form of the relationship is the same for both examples 7 and 9, even though the letter-labeling differs.)

Achieving or Restoring Balance. Heider predicted that imbalanced relationships would tend to create stress and discomfort, and thus

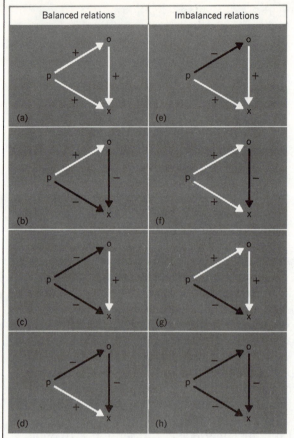

Figure 4.1
Balance and imbalance in the relationships between two persons and an object. *The two persons are represented by the letters* p *and* o, *and the object by* x. *The plus arrows indicate either liking or unity; the minus arrows indicate either disliking or nonunity. According to balance theory, imbalanced relationships are stressful and thus there is a tendency to change the values of the relationships from imbalance to balance (after Heider, 1958).*

there would be an impetus toward achieving balance. As an illustration, let us look at Figure 4.1(f), which might represent the following situation: John (*p*) likes Bill (*o*); Bill says that jogging (*x*) is a lot of nonsense, but John believes it is one of the most beneficial exercises. John experiences stress at the imbalance. What might happen?

1. **Change in evaluation of object.** *John might reconsider and decide that jogging was not so beneficial after all. By changing pLx to p−Lx, balance has been restored.*
2. **Rejection of other.** *John might reject Bill—anybody who can't appreciate jogging cannot be a worthwhile friend.*
3. **Persuasion.** *John might try to convince Bill that jogging is really an excellent activity; if o−Lx can be changed to oLx, then balance can be restored.*
4. **Misperception of other.** *John might misperceive Bill's evaluation—"He really approves of jogging; I don't believe he meant what he said about it being a lot of nonsense."*
5. **Minimizing relevance or importance.** *John might minimize the*

importance or the relevance of the issue—"We may disagree about jogging, but it is not an extremely important issue in our relationship."

6. ***Dividing the other.*** *Another method is to separate Bill into two parts, o_1 and o_2: "Bill is really a wonderful fellow, except that he has a quirk about exercise, probably going back to the time when he became overexhausted as a child. One part of him (o_1) abhors exercise (such as jogging), but this is not an essential part of him. I am willing to overlook that one part since Bill (o_2) is basically a very nice fellow, and I do like him very much."*

Do people actually reduce imbalance in these ways? It appears that they do, at least within certain limitations that we will spell out later. Ivan Steiner and Stanley C. Peters (1958), for example, designed a study in which the subject found himself in disagreement with another subject (actually an accomplice) in evaluating a sketch. They had been asked to judge whether a given sketch adequately resembled a specific object (such as the Empire State Building). Following the disagreement, Steiner and Peters offered the subject four possible means for reducing the imbalance: (1) *changing* his own

MANNY WAS MY BEST FRIEND BUT MILLIE SAYS HE'S INFANTILE. / SCRATCH MANNY.

MICKEY WAS MY CHILDHOOD FRIEND BUT MILLIE SAYS HE'S ENVIOUS. / SCRATCH MICKEY.

MILTY WAS A CLOSE FRIEND BUT MILLIE SAYS HE'S WEAK. / SCRATCH MILTY.

MURRAY WAS AN OLD FRIEND BUT MILLIE SAYS HE HAS HOMOSEXUAL LEANINGS TOWARDS ME. / SCRATCH MURRAY.

NOW I DON'T HAVE A FRIEND LEFT WHO I KNEW BEFORE I MARRIED MILLIE.

MILLIE SAYS NOT TO WORRY. / SHE'S MY FRIEND.

COPYRIGHT © 1973 JULES FEIFFER.

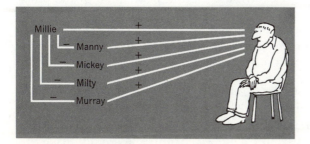

Figure 4.2
A balance analysis of a man, his wife Millie, and his old friends, as presented by Jules Feiffer. Here is one way in which a person's friendship patterns might change after marriage. Note that this man's bond with Millie was the major source of imbalance. Why wasn't Millie "scratched"? Although some men might have rejected her, apparently this man had a stronger relationship with her than with any of the others. After each decision to remain with Millie and reject a friend, he may have experienced post-decisional dissonance, which could have led him to be even more attracted to Millie.

evaluation of the sketch, (2) *misperception*—minimizing the amount of disagreement, (3) *minimizing the importance*—saying that the task was not really too important, and (4) *rejection* of the accomplice as not being qualified or competent to make such an evaluation. All four of these means were, in fact, selected to reduce imbalance. The subjects differed markedly in their tendency to use one means rather than another. However, once one method had been selected, the subject seemed to use it consistently, disregarding all of the others. For example, a subject who tended to change his own evaluation in order to achieve balance seldom rejected the accomplice, or minimized the discrepancy, or minimized the importance of the task.

The theory of balance, as applied to interpersonal attraction, is quite intriguing in its simplicity. Have you ever found that your best friend disagreed with you on an important political issue? Did you try to convince him to change, change your own opinion (sometimes after he had tried to reduce *his* imbalance by persuading *you* to change), reject him, minimize the issue, misperceive his position, or separate the political issue (as some sort of eccentricity) from your esteem for him as a person? If so, why did you choose one particular means? Here we must acknowledge certain limitations in the theory of balance. For one thing, our evaluation of other people and objects is not simply all good or all bad; we like or dislike them in varying degrees. You may feel very strongly about the issue of whether the United States should engage in a particular conflict in the Middle East. In this case you would probably not change your opinion, but you might try to convince your friend to change his or, if this were impossible, you might reject him. Your evaluation of your friend may also vary in its intensity—if you liked him a great deal, you would be less inclined to reject him and more inclined to try to convince him. The intensity of feeling between two people in a relationship is not shown in Heider's simple pluses and minuses. However, there is no reason why finer gradations of plus or minus could not be used as well.

Furthermore, your relationship with a given person and object is not limited to the simple triad—you, the other person, and the object. Many other relationships contribute to your evaluation of the other person: other objects that you may evaluate similarly or differently, other unit-forming relationships, and other persons who like or dislike you and the other person. Your evaluation of the other person and object is thus a function of all these relationships.

Brutus and Caesar—A Balance Analysis. How would a balance theorist analyze the change in Brutus, who loved Caesar but then helped to destroy him (according to Shakespeare)? Let us look at the extended balance analysis in Figure 4.3. Brutus's love for Caesar was

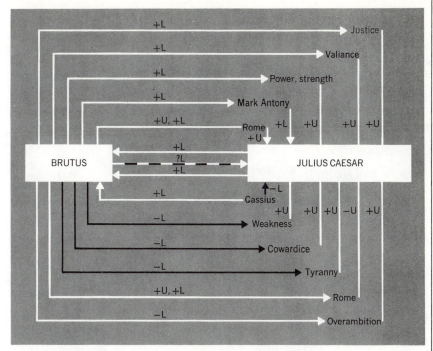

Figure 4.3
**Brutus's changing atti-
tudes toward Caesar.**
*Brutus's initial love for
Caesar is represented
by the balanced cycles
at the top of the
figure—Brutus loved
Rome and felt that Cae-
sar also loved Rome;
Brutus admired Mark
Antony, who loved Cae-
sar; and so forth. The
cycles below indicate
imbalance with a love
for Caesar—Brutus dis-
liked cowardice, and he
learned that Caesar was
sometimes cowardly;
Cassius admired Bru-
tus, but disliked Caesar;
and so forth. When the
number of imbalanced
cycles exceeded the
number of balanced cy-
cles, Brutus's love for
Caesar changed in
order to restore bal-
ance.*

strengthened by a number of factors: (1) Caesar's deep love for Brutus, (2) Caesar's love for Rome (which Brutus also loved), (3) Caesar's
close identification with Rome (with which Brutus was also identified), (4) Mark Antony loved Caesar, and Brutus admired Antony,
and (5) Caesar's exercise of strength, power, justice, and wisdom—
traits that Brutus admired. Of course, there were other relationships
that involved Caesar and Brutus, and they were all balanced with
Brutus's love for Caesar.

Enter Cassius; he and his co-conspirators were determined to
destroy Caesar. Cassius desperately wanted Brutus to join the con-
spiracy. His strategy included a careful evaluation of Brutus: What
things did Brutus like? Which people did he love and hate? Why did
he love Caesar? Then Cassius proceeded systematically to introduce
imbalance into Brutus's evaluation of Caesar: (1) Cassius expressed
admiration for Brutus and disdain for Caesar; (2) He claimed that
Caesar was not strong; Caesar had been weakened by epilepsy and
might have drowned in the Tiber, except that Cassius saved him;
(3) Cassius alluded to Caesar's cowardice in the Spanish campaign to
counter Brutus's view of him as a valiant warrior; (4) Cassius pointed
out that Caesar had become associated with injustice and tyranny; (5)
Cassius argued that Caesar could not love Rome because he was destroying it. The force of Cassius's arguments was not lost on Brutus
nor was the opposition to Caesar by others whom Brutus respected.

Undoubtedly there were other personal reasons that led Brutus to find these arguments against Caesar especially compelling. In any event, in terms of the theory of balance, the number of balanced cycles favoring Brutus's love for Caesar were soon far outweighed by the cycles that could be balanced only by Brutus's dislike for Caesar. Although the weightings of the cycles differed, the most powerful (according to Brutus) was his perception that Caesar was dangerous to Rome, which Brutus loved above all else.

Balance and Attitudes

The basic principles of balance apply to any analysis of attitudes. *Attitude* refers to the positive or negative evaluation of an object. Much of the research on the nature and change of attitudes in social psychological literature pertains to persons as well as objects. The extension of balance theory to attitudes has been quite useful. In Figure 4.3 one could replace the person Caesar with other persons (such as Jews or blacks) or impersonal objects (such as school desegregation, the use of evidence obtained by wiretap, what constitutes pornography, automobile seat belts, or fluoridation of water supplies). These could be related to evaluation by respected public officials, confirmation or denial of important values (such as freedom, equality, wisdom), and positive or negative evaluation by one's friends.

In one of the earliest applications of balance theory to attitudes, Milton Rosenberg (1956) found that he could predict students' attitudes on the issue of allowing members of the Communist Party to address the public by knowing: (1) the individual respondent's positive or negative evaluation of values such as "being respected by others," "being well educated," and "letting people make their own decisions," and (2) the extent to which the Communist speakers either supported ($+U$) or negated ($-U$) each of these values. Fishbein (1963) later conducted a similar study on attitudes toward blacks, but he went beyond values to such characteristics as having a dark skin; being religious, athletic, ambitious, tall; and so forth. Again, the respondents' views about blacks could be predicted from the combination of U- and L-relationships. With such a model, it should also be possible to change people's attitudes. Earl Carlson (1956) found that he could alter students' feelings about blacks who move into white neighborhoods by having them write essays stating that integrated neighborhoods could contribute (U) to: greater American prestige abroad, increased property values, equal opportunity, and broadmindedness. Rosenberg (1960) was able to bring about the same change in views by means of hypnosis. However, one drawback to the use of this method was that when the hypnotic suggestion wore off, there was a tendency for people to revert to their earlier views.

WHAT DETERMINES WHETHER WE LIKE OR DISLIKE ANOTHER PERSON?

It appears that balance theory can provide a means for organizing a substantial amount of what we know about how people come to like or dislike one another. We will now apply balance analysis specifically to some of the existing research on interpersonal attraction, as we discuss certain factors that affect your liking or disliking of another person. We will discuss seven reasons for liking others: their personal characteristics or traits, a feeling of unity or identification with them, their liking for us, the fact that they offer us some material benefits, the fact that we feel comfortable with them, justification of our efforts on their behalf (reduction of dissonance), and the fact that they offer us a means of evaluating ourselves.

Personal Characteristics and Traits

Obviously, we like people who have traits that appeal to us. An extensive literature in social psychology has attempted to delimit exactly what those traits are. Some studies show that people generally like those who are intelligent and competent (particularly if that competence and intelligence benefits the one who is doing the liking), and those who are honest, understanding, and sincere; they tend to dislike those who are deceitful, malicious, dishonest, and lazy. One social psychologist went so far as to develop a catalog of 555 traits, classified according to positive or negative evaluation in varying degrees (Anderson, 1968). Despite a general tendency to evaluate a given trait positively or negatively, there are obviously individual differences in judging personal traits. Although intelligence is generally valued, undoubtedly some people feel threatened by a person with higher intelligence and therefore would prefer to avoid contact with him. Assessing traits may also be affected by circumstances—an honest person who tells everything will not be sought out by a gang of thieves. Further, there are great variations in the extent to which traits determine evaluation. As we pointed out in Chapter 3, certain central traits, such as warmth or coldness, may have far-reaching effects, influencing the evaluation of other traits attributed to the person. Let us examine the surprising effects of one important personal trait—physical appearance.

Physical Appearance and Attraction. How important is a pleasing physical appearance in getting a job, in getting a loan at a bank, in getting a good grade in a course, in receiving favorable consideration during a trial, in being promoted at work, or in developing a friendship? Although most people might agree that a physically attractive person does have certain advantages, few would admit that their own evaluations of others would be affected to any great extent by such considerations. Certainly, other factors should be much more important—competence, honesty, knowledge, skills, temperament, kindness, experience, reliability. Giving someone a job, a promotion, or a good grade on the basis of his or her appearance, we should admit, is a form of bias—to be abhorred or even punished. Even if we know that others have such a bias, we generally do not like to acknowledge it in ourselves. Yet, it has been shown that physical appearance extensively affects our evaluations of others, suggesting that beauty may be a much more significant trait than warmth or coldness. As is well known, consumers spend huge amounts of money, time, and energy on cosmetics, clothes, and other aspects of personal grooming—pointing to the importance of physical appearance in our society. Many appearance-based stereotypes can be found in our works of art, novels, drama, and poetry. Schiller (1882) expressed it most succinctly: "Physical beauty is the sign of an interior beauty, a spiritual and moral beauty. . . ." The pervasiveness of the stereotype can be seen in the once widely accepted theories of the nineteenth-century Italian criminologist, Cesare Lombroso (Lombroso-Ferrero, 1911). Lombroso felt that he could identify criminal types by their physical appearance; his typology made certain assumptions (now largely discredited) about evolution, heredity, and the relationship between appearance and brain physiology. Yet, it is also true that the criminal characteristics that he emphasized—such as facial asymmetry, narrow forehead, and receding chin—are still considered aesthetically displeasing, at least in Western culture.

Although Lombroso's formal theories have not been supported, apparently people still think that common criminals have an abnormal appearance—a prejudice that can be regularly seen in crime dramas on television and in films. Even social workers, who are trained to be aware of their biases, find it hard to believe that a pretty girl could be guilty of committing a crime like shoplifting (Monahan, 1941).

The prevalence of the "what is beautiful is good" bias (presented in just those words by the Greek poet Sappho) has been demonstrated by Karen Dion, Ellen Berscheid, and Elaine Walster (1972) in a study of judgments made by college students. The researchers had previously requested other college students to rate the physical attractiveness of a large number of photos of college-age men and women. Each subject in the experiment was then given three photos: one that had been judged very attractive, one average, and one unattractive. The respondents consistently rated the unattractive person as being less socially desirable, of lower occupational status, less competent in marriage, less marriageable, and less happy socially and professionally. The attractive person received the highest rating on all of these characteristics, though the difference between the attractive and average person was not as great as that between average and unattractive. Moreover, the attractive person was consistently favored whether the rater was a male or female and whether the photo was a male or female.

In dating, physical attractiveness plays an especially important role. Elaine Walster and her colleagues (1966) studied dating preferences by means of a computer dance. Students took a battery of tests, such as the Minnesota Multiphasic Inventory, the Berger Scale of Self-Acceptance, and scholastic aptitude measures. Dates were then randomly assigned for the dance (except that no man was matched with a woman who was taller than himself). As the students entered the large armory where the dance was being held, each was rated for physical attractiveness by four independent judges (the rating was done without the knowledge of the participants). After 2½ hours, the men and women were given questionnaires, asking them to evaluate their partners. Four to six months later, the students were contacted again to learn if they had attempted to arrange further dates with their partners.

What characteristic was most prominent among the partners who liked each other and wanted to continue the relationship? It was not dominance or submission, masculinity or femininity, introversion or extroversion, maturity, courtesy, sexual attitudes, intelligence, or academic competence. The overriding trait was physical attractiveness. A point of further interest here is that the ratings of physical attractiveness were made by the *judges*. Although we might generally assume that judging physical attractiveness is a highly subjective matter, in this case it was the *judges'* ratings of physical attractiveness that correlated most highly with the students' liking for one another and their subsequent attempts at dating. The extent to which physical attractiveness overshadowed all of the other variables was quite striking.

Now these data must be treated with some caution. Perhaps 2½ hours was not enough time for other factors to manifest themselves significantly; they might have become more prominent if the couples had continued to meet over an extended period of time. It may also be true that the traits that are important in selecting a partner for a short-term dating relationship are not the same as those that would be important for a marital relationship. A study of 300 Canadian students showed that on the issue of traits that one desired in a marriage partner, males ranked "attractive, good-looking" as twelfth out of a total of 32 traits listed; females ranked attractiveness as twenty-second. A higher ranking was given to such traits as "dependable, honest"; "faithful, loyal in marriage"; "considerate, under-standing"; and "good sense of humor" (Wakil, 1973). Although these questionnaire data suggest that physical appearance is not so important in choosing a marriage partner, the results are not conclusive. We cannot be certain that the students' responses on the questionnaire will bear any relationship to the traits that would actually be found in their eventual spouses.

In another study of attractiveness, Karen Dion (1972) dealt with children's perceptions of transgressions. A group of elementary-school girls was given a description of a serious (but fictitious) incident in which a second-grade child threw some sharp rocks and injured a sleeping dog in the school playground. Accompanying the description was a picture of the child who had, presumably, committed the act. If the child in the picture looked attractive, Dion found, the respondents tended to minimize the incident, saying that the child had just had a bad day and that the rock-throwing was not at all typical of the child. If the child was unattractive, however, the event was perceived as more serious; the child was seen as having a chronic behavior problem that would continue to give his teachers trouble. Furthermore, the unattractive child was believed to be less honest. This response implies that if any unattractive child denied that he had committed a wrongdoing or tried to explain it as due to other circumstances, he would probably not be believed. It is not unreasonable to expect that teachers will behave toward unattractive children just as the respondents did—with prejudice. (In Chapter 3 we discussed a study in which children with less common names received lower grades on their compositions.) If this is generally true, it could be expected that children would respond accordingly, being molded according to the expectations and treatment of their teachers.

Even more serious are the implications of an observational study of cases brought into the emergency ward of a county hospital (Sudnow, 1967). The most common death in the emergency ward is DOA (dead on arrival). Yet the pronouncement of DOA requires a judgment first by the ambulance driver and then by a physician. Sudnow observed that one patient "was brought into the emergency room with no registering heartbeat, respiration, or pulse—the standard signs of death"—but a large team of doctors and nurses, applying heart stimulation and resuscitation, managed to revive an apparent corpse. Yet another patient with the same physical signs and no discernible difference in skin color or warmth was pronounced DOA and sent off to the county morgue. What was the difference? Sudnow observed that doctors were less inclined to make a DOA pronouncement if the patient was younger, well-to-do, nicely dressed, clean, and without the smell of alcohol—generally of pleasing appearance!

A Sense of Unity or Identification

From the theory of balance, it can be surmised that we should like people with whom we feel some identification and mutuality (pUx and oUx induces pLo). Such identification can develop for a variety of reasons: (1) membership in the same social unit—same race, same sex, same social organization, or same religion; (2) possession of similar characteristics, beliefs, or attitudes; (3) the existence of common goals and/or mutual threats.

Mutual Identification and Group Membership. The United States has often been characterized as a melting pot, in which differences among groups are minimized so that race, class, and ethnic origin eventually become insignificant. If this characterization is a fact, the melting is a very slow process. There have been numerous indications that ethnic, racial, socioeconomic, and religious similarities and differences have played a major role in the development of friendships and out-group prejudices. The tendency for marriage partners to be members of the same group has been clearly documented (Schiller, 1932; Blood and Wolfe, 1960); but today there is a growing number of out-marriages, which tend to be viewed with alarm by close adherents to those groups.

In an ambitious study of friendship choices by Edward O. Laumann (1969), 1013 white males in the greater Detroit area were interviewed by a University of Michigan research team; the men were asked to name their three best friends and to describe them. There was a marked tendency for men to choose those who were similar in group identification—Jews chose Jews, Catholics chose Catholics, whites chose whites, Republicans chose Republicans, and working-class people chose working-class people. Friends also tended to be highly similar in education, socioeconomic level, and age. The similarity was especially great when viewed in terms of the respondent's misperception of his friends (sometimes a respondent would identify his friend as a Democrat, when in fact he was a Republican). These errors typically attributed one's own group membership to the friend.

The quest for association with similar others is obvious in many studies. For example, Theodore M. Newcomb (1961) reported that college students who lived in the same dormitory were more apt to form friendships with others who were majoring in similar subjects—the liberal arts and engineering majors tended to form separate cliques. A study of the relationships among psychiatrists, clinical psychologists, and psychiatric social workers (Zander, Cohen, and Stotland, 1957), showed that in their leisure time, members of each occupational group preferred the company of others in their own group, despite the frequency with which they all worked together in

Figure 4.4
A feeling of unity pre-
vailed among these
hard hats as they
paraded in support of
U.S. policies in South-
east Asia in 1970. Their
unity may have been
due to similar social
characteristics (race,
sex, work group, social
class), similar beliefs
and attitudes, and a mu-
tual sense of threat
(from the antiwar ac-
tivists).

hospitals and clinics. Those who emigrated to the new state of Israel
from the Soviet Union have asked to be housed near other Soviet immigrants; in some cases, the demands are quite specific—Georgians
have asked to be near other Georgians. Certainly, the great resistance by American whites, and since the 1960s by many blacks as
well, to integration in housing and schooling can be viewed in terms

of a desire to associate with similar others. The impetus to integrate has, of course, come about because of evidence that limited association perpetuates the disadvantages of the minority groups.

Similarities in Beliefs, Attitudes, Values, and Other Characteristics. People tend to like others who agree with them. Probably few other findings in social psychology have been confirmed with such regularity and consistency. In an early study of student attitudes at Bennington College, Theodore Newcomb (1943) found that the women who adopted the prevailing political and social attitudes of the college community were the most popular; those with differing views tended to associate with those who shared their views. Newcomb was able to demonstrate the same phenomenon in a more careful fashion later on at the University of Michigan (Newcomb, 1961). In that study, he offered male students entering the university free board and room in return for filling out a series of questionnaires periodically. Thus, he was able to measure their attitudes toward politics, school, baseball, chess, interracial marriage, and so forth. Newcomb found that, as they lived together, these students tended to form friendships with those who had similar attitudes on various issues, while they rejected those whose views were different. As time passed, however, the differences in attitude among members in a given subgroup (or clique) seemed to diminish and a consensus was developed. Thus, the attitudes within a given clique became more homogeneous, while those between cliques became more disparate (Newcomb, 1963, 1965).

Figure 4.5

A group member whose opinions and attitudes conform to the norms of the group will be liked much better by his fellow group members, and will also tend to be selected for more favorable treatment; by contrast, a deviant group member is apt to be punished. Stanley Schachter (1951) established a number of student clubs at M.I.T. At the first meeting of each club, he asked the members to indicate their attitudes toward, and recommendation for treatment of a juvenile delinquent. Most members of each club were sympathetic toward the delinquent and recommended that he be treated with kindness and understanding. Schachter arranged for one member of each group (a confederate) to state a position that was in keeping with that group norm; another confederate, by prearrangement, held the delinquent fully responsible for his actions and recommended firm punishment. The club members clearly preferred the confederate who agreed with them, and they tended to assign that member to prestigious positions in the group (such as the executive committee); the deviant member was not liked and was assigned to the tedious and undesirable correspondence committee. (This study is described in greater detail on pages 322–324.)

Even more drastic were the choices offered in a later experiment conducted by Jonathan Freedman and Anthony Doob (1968): A group was asked to assign its members to either of two jobs; one job allowed the jobholder to earn some extra money, while the other job required him to receive painful electric shocks. In this study, the group voted to assign the money-making job to members whose personalities appeared to be similar to the majority, while those whose personalities appeared to be different were assigned to the job that required receiving electric shocks.

Donn Byrne (1971) and his associates have perfected an unusually good device for studying the effects on similarity and difference on attraction. At a preliminary session, the respondents are given an "interpersonal judgment scale" on which they indicate their opinions, attitudes, and beliefs about a number of social and political issues. At a later session, the subject is given the same scale on which the responses of another person are recorded. Actually, the experimenters have prepared the responses: In some cases the responses are almost identical with those of the subjects; in others they are almost completely different; in still others there is 33 percent agreement, 50 percent agreement, and 66 percent agreement. The subjects are asked to look at the responses of the fictitious other person and then indicate on a series of scales how much they like that person. The results are surprisingly predictable—the greater the similarity, the greater the liking (Byrne and Nelson, 1964; Byrne, Nelson, and Reeves, 1966).

Lest this simple paper-and-pencil test appear too artificial, a follow-up study by Byrne, Ervin, and Lamberth (1970) matched 44 male-female pairs for a Coke date. The greater the similarity in attitude and the greater the physical attractiveness (as rated by the experimenter), the more the students (1) said that they liked their partner, (2) sat close to their partner during their date, (3) wished to have future dates with their partner, (4) remembered their partner's name accurately some time later, and (5) actually contacted their partner at a later time. Essentially the same result has been replicated in a number of laboratory experiments in which a subject's opinion or attitude is solicited, he is given information about another's attitudes, and then he has an opportunity to respond to the other in some way. As in the Byrne studies, the subject tends to like

the person who agrees with him and to dislike the one who disagrees. The dislike may be shown by indicating rejection on a questionnaire, voting to exclude the person from the group, or assigning
him tasks or roles that are unpleasant or carry little prestige. As we
mentioned earlier, the subjects may distort the amount or importance
of the disagreement, or they may attempt to convince the other person to change his views in order to increase agreement (for example,
Emerson, 1954; Schachter, 1951; Smith, 1957; Stein, 1966; Steiner
and Peters, 1958; Triandis, 1960; Triandis and Fishbein, 1963; Worchel and Schuster, 1966). These processes also take place between
marriage partners (Levinger and Breedlove, 1966).

Similarity and competence. Although it was mentioned earlier
that competent people tend to be liked (especially by those who
benefit from their competence), most people also have feelings of
ambivalence toward competent others—even though they may benefit from them.

When I visited Israel shortly after it achieved independence, I
was particularly struck by the attitudes expressed toward the
German-Jewish immigrants who had arrived there in the late 1930s
and thereafter. The earlier Jewish settlers, mainly of Eastern European origin, had a favorable image of these *yekkes* (*yekke* [from the
German *Jacke*] was the word for the distinctive short jackets worn by
the German immigrants and later applied to the Germans themselves). These German immigrants were a highly educated group,
and they brought valuable skills to a developing nation. The earlier
settlers admired the *yekkes* for their well-kept homes, their gardens,
and neatly trimmed lawns and trees; and for their diligent work and
their dedication. However, I heard several of these same Israelis
say: "It is good to have a *yekke* in the office. They see to it that you
do your work properly; they see that you don't waste too much
paper, that you don't spend too much time at your tea break, that you
don't leave too early, that your work is carefully done, neat, and
clean. Yes, it is good to have a *yekke* in the office. Every office
should have one." The implication was "Please, no more than one!"
Thus, we often have mixed feelings about those who are more competent. We are pleased to have a capable person help us, yet the very
fact that he is more capable—by definition—makes him different.
Dissimilarity again may lead to some rejection, accompanied perhaps
by feelings of personal threat and discomfort. In addition to being
different, the superior person may also be a threat to one's self-esteem, suggesting that one is inferior (Morse and Gergen, 1970).

The value of a pratfall. Occasionally, an extremely competent
person may inadvertently increase his attractiveness by making a
mistake, thus proving that, despite his supposed superiority, he is essentially no different from anyone else. Elliot Aronson, Ben Willer-

man, and Joanne Floyd (1966) demonstrated this point in a laboratory experiment. Their subjects listened to tape recordings of a young man who was a candidate for a "College Quiz Bowl." The candidate was sometimes presented as a "nearly perfect" person, who answered 92 percent of the questions correctly and identified himself as an honor student, editor of the yearbook, and member of the track team. In other cases, the candidate was presented as a mediocre individual who had average grades in school, worked as a proofreader on the college yearbook, and had not made the track team; he answered only 30 percent of the questions correctly. When the subjects were asked to evaluate how much they liked the candidate, they rated the "nearly perfect" one much more favorably. Half of the subjects then listened to the "nearly perfect" candidate commit a clumsy blunder. They heard a lot of commotion, scraping of chairs, and rustling of papers; then he said, "Oh my goodness, I've spilled coffee all over my new suit." This mishap endeared him to the subjects more than ever; however, when the mediocre candidate spilled coffee, he was liked even less. Somehow, then, a blunder seems to make a paragon seem more human and thus more likable. This pratfall experiment was replicated in a later study, which also found that an average performer will reject another average person who has such an accident, but that he will increase his liking for a superior person. It was further determined that superiority by itself was not the crucial factor, but rather relative superiority—if the observer himself was superior, he tended to be especially harsh in judging another outstanding performer who committed an awkward blunder (Mettee and Wilkins, 1972).

Aronson (1972) suggests that people's tendency to like a superior person who makes a mistake might help to explain why President John F. Kennedy reached new heights of popularity after the abortive Bay of Pigs invasion of Cuba; if he had been less admired, such a fiasco would have led to greater rejection. By contrast, recall that President Nixon's popularity dropped dramatically after many of the facts about the Watergate affair became known. It is tenuous to make an analogy between a coffee-spilling mishap and the Bay of Pigs invasion, for obviously there might be another explanation for Kennedy's increased support (such as the nation rallying behind the flag during a time of international censure). Yet Aronson's suggestion is certainly an intriguing one.

Do opposites attract? In the face of many studies supporting the idea that "birds of a feather flock together," a few have tried to show the opposite. Robert Winch (1955) has become the primary exponent of a theory of complementary needs in mate selection. He argues quite convincingly that a dominant person, for example, would not choose another dominant person for a mate, for how could a marriage endure in which each spouse attempted to dominate the other? A more submissive spouse would be much more satisfactory. Similarly, a sadistic person would probably prefer a masochistic mate, and vice versa; a motherly woman would probably select a man who needed to be mothered. Winch and his colleagues provided some initial evidence that appeared to support the complementarity hypothesis. (Winch, Ktsanes, and Ktsanes, 1954).

Alan Kerckhoff and Keith Davis (1962) have developed the hypothesis further in a long-term study of college couples who were considering marriage. Periodically they questioned the couples about their progress toward either a permanent union or a dissolution of their relationship. The researchers also measured the degree of the couple's similarity on the most important values in marriage (having happy and healthy children, companionship, economic security, and so forth) and their complementarity of needs (do those who have a need to control others tend to pair off with those who would like to be controlled? do those who have a strong need for affection tend to be matched with those who have a need to express affection?). And the researchers included data about such factors as the subjects' socioeconomic class, religion, and ethnic background. Kerckhoff and Davis found that the subjects went through an initial "filtering process" very early in their relationship, pairing off according to similarity in socioeconomic class, religion, and ethnic background. During the first 18 months, similarity in marital values played an especially important role in the development of the relationship. Thereafter, complementary needs became the most important factor in the couple's progress toward marriage. The implication, therefore, is that similarity in status and values is necessary in order for the partners to become attracted to one another and begin a relationship. However, unless complementary needs emerge at a later time, the relationship will end.

Another study (Levinger, Senn, and Jorgensen, 1970) also found that couples will be initially attracted to one another because of similar characteristics and attitudes. As the relationship continues, however, they found that there will be an active development of complementarity—a meshing of needs—with each partner gradually adjusting to the other. One may become more of a talker, the other more of a listener; one may become more dominant and the other more submissive; thus, complementary needs and behaviors become more prominent in their relationship.

In social psychology, those who uphold the view that similarity is most important in a relationship often take issue with those who feel that complementarity is most significant. But why must complementary needs necessarily be dissimilar? As George Levinger (1964) has pointed out, similar needs are sometimes complementary:

Two persons who each have a high need to affiliate may become friends and interact intensively, thus complementing one another's needs. Other needs that are non-complementary could eventually lead to the termination of a relationship; for example, if both members of a couple have a low need for achievement, they may not perform the work that is necessary to sustain the relationship. In some cases similar needs are antagonistic: If each member of a pair has a high need for dominance, an attempt by one to satisfy his own need will prevent the other from satisfying his.

Whether similarity or complementarity factors increase a person's attractiveness will also be affected by a given situation, social norms, and role relationships. Both Levinger and Roland Tharp (1963, 1964) have pointed out that similar needs will be significant under certain conditions (a man and his drinking buddy may have similar needs for affiliation), while complementary needs will predominate elsewhere (a nurturant-dependent relationship in the family or a dominant-submissive relationship at work). In many cases, socially-determined roles may define what characteristics are combined in a given social relationship. In the *traditional* Western family, the typical male role calls for such characteristics as dominance, aggressiveness, and ambition, while the typical female role calls for such traits as submissiveness, gentleness, affection, and understanding. For heterosexual couples to accept the traditional role relationships, they must behave and expect their partners to behave according to the society's expectations. A traditional female would probably be unhappy with a husband who was extremely gentle; the traditional male would probably be unhappy with a wife who was rather aggressive. On a questionnaire, such as the one that was used by Winch, these discrepancies in needs and expectations lend support to the complementarity analysis of interpersonal attraction.

An ideal androgynous society? The fact that these different roles and expectations are largely determined by the culture was demonstrated many years ago by the anthropologist Margaret Mead in her extensive studies of sex roles in New Guinea. Among the peaceful Mountain Arapesh, she found that both men and women displayed the gentle, maternal, responsive qualities that are usually associated with women in the Western world. These people were not unhappy that both sexes shared similar needs and behaviors; the same was true for the warlike Mundugumor, whose men and women both showed the aggressive characteristics that we usually expect of men. In yet another society, the Tchambuli, there was an accommodation with complementary and clearly different roles and expectations for men and women, but here the sex roles were the opposite of ours: among these people the men were typically more gentle, responsive, dependent, and maternal, whereas the women tended to be more aggressive, dominant, and independent (Mead, 1935).

More recently, the social psychologists Sandra and Daryl Bem, together with other persons who are associated with the women's liberation movement, have advocated an "androgynous" society that would blur the differences in roles and expectations for men and women; both would be freer to follow their natural inclinations rather than have male and female roles forced upon them. The Bems glowingly describe their own happy marriage, in which they both do certain things that are associated with the traditional male role and other things that are associated with the traditional female role; some of their activities reverse the usual role expectations (Bem and Bem, 1970). They point out approvingly that the trend in our society is toward greater freedom in self-fulfillment and self-expression, which means less differentiation in the role requirements for men and women. Testing her newly developed androgyny scale (Bem, 1974) on others, Sandra Bem (1975) found that "androgynous" subjects were more flexible and responsive to given situations and less affected by role demands. Both androgynous men and women showed more "masculine" independence when they were under pressure to conform and greater "feminine" playfulness when given an opportunity to interact with a small kitten. She also pointed out that the nonandrogynous subjects ("masculine" men and "feminine" women) showed signs of having greater problems adjusting to various stresses in life, especially the "feminine" women.

Whether our society could ever reach the androgynous ideal presented by the Bems, and whether androgyny could provide the greatest opportunity for an optimal relationship between men and women (whether in marriage or out) will doubtless be debated for some time.

Similarity and insecurity. We necessarily miss out on certain things if we confine our relationships to those who are similar to ourselves. We do not hear divergent opinions and views; we do not have our own beliefs challenged; we do not have many opportunities to gain new insights; we lack the stimulation of new and different experiences. Why, then, do we isolate ourselves in this way? Probably it is because we feel more comfortable with similar others: With them, we don't have to think too much about what we say and we don't have to worry about being misunderstood. Perhaps we have some built-in fear of unknown things and people; consequently, our lives are narrower, as are those of others whom we don't allow to have contact with us. Maslow (1970) said that being willing to expose oneself to different attitudes, beliefs, accents, clothing, and customs may be a sign of self-actualization and personal growth.

New immigrants and disadvantaged minorities will often seek one another out in an attempt to find security in what may seem like a hostile environment. In some cases, however, where a minority group member has gained a measure of acceptance from the majority and wants to identify with the majority and accept its advantages (to assimilate), he will also accept its prejudices. The individual who has been somewhat successful in "passing" into the majority culture may appear to be even more hostile toward his former minority group than the majority group is. Lewin (1935, 1941) has discussed at length the pathetic problems of such marginal men, who may develop hateful attitudes toward their former group and ultimately toward themselves.

Common Threats and Goals. Just after World War II in Europe, some American visitors were shocked to hear Europeans say, in moments of intimacy, that they missed the war. This admission was usually followed by a guilty qualification, "Well, I don't really miss it. It was a horrible time. Fear, danger, death, hunger. . . . But there was something there that we have not had since—a warm feeling for one another. We talked to each other during and after the raids. We helped one another. We cared for one another. This is something that I miss more than I can say." The intense positive, personal feeling that arises from a common threat cannot be imagined by those who have not experienced it. I have heard similar admissions from Japanese-Americans who miss the sense of unity they experienced in the relocation centers where they were unjustly imprisoned during World War II. In fact, the disaster researchers E. L. Quarantelli and Russell Dynes report that people who are victims of serious disasters—such as floods, hurricanes, tornadoes, and earthquakes—tend to develop such a strong in-group feeling that they sometimes resent the appearance of outside agencies such as the Red Cross or government rescue teams. They seem to feel that it is *their* disaster, and they don't want impersonal outsiders who haven't experienced their tragedy butting in (Quarantelli and Dynes, 1970). The tendency to affiliate when threatened has also been documented in accounts of what happened in New York City during the Northeast power failure of 1965 (Zucker, Manosevitz, and Lanyon, 1968) and in Los Angeles during the earthquake of 1971 (Hoyt and Raven, 1973), as well as in controlled laboratory experiments (Lanzetta, 1955).

The impact of a common threat can be so powerful that it overrides strong negative personal feelings and prejudices. In the Netherlands, for example, there is a strong individualistic, anti-cooperative tradition among the small shopkeepers—the butchers, greengrocers, bakers, dairy shopkeepers, and grocers. Yet, two social psychologists, Mauk Mulder and Ad Stemerding (1963), were able to arouse a high degree of cohesiveness and mutual attraction among these retailers by posing the threat that a supermarket chain would establish itself in their communities. The individualism of the shop-keepers was so great that it was very difficult even to persuade them to attend an initial meeting. Mulder and Stemerding were able to do so only after talking with them at length, obtaining support from the shopkeepers' organization executives, and placing notices in trade journals. The meetings were arranged by a fictitious "Scientific Agency for Middle-class Shopkeepers." At the first meeting, the credentials of the agency were presented to the shopkeepers who attended, followed by an agency report. The report said that there was a possibility that a major supermarket chain would enter their towns and compete with them. The likelihood of this event and the agency's estimate of the potential drop in sales were systematically varied among the shopkeepers from different towns. The experimenter said that the agency was not planning to arrange any further meetings, but that some of the groups had expressed a desire to meet more frequently and become more permanent. Then he asked them how they felt about this. If the threat was slight (10 percent chance that a chain would open, causing a 6 percent drop in sales), then the mutual attraction of the shopkeepers was relatively low; if the threat was great (80 percent probability, with a potential drop in sales of 30 percent), then their desire to affiliate and meet together was much greater. The common threat produced feelings of unity and mutual attraction.

Similarly, Samuel Stouffer and his colleagues (1949), observed that prejudice against blacks was less among white men who had been in combat with blacks during World War II. Laboratory experiments have yielded parallel results (Burnstein and McRae, 1962; Feshbach and Singer, 1957). In his study of affiliation, Stanley Schachter (1959) found that there was a strong desire to affiliate only with those who faced a similar threat (see page 44). The results, which were presented in terms of social comparison theory, are nonetheless consistent with the Heider balance analysis—a mutual threat leads to a feeling of unity and consequently to mutual attraction and liking. The same feelings of unity and attraction can also be produced when people are working toward a common goal (Raven and Eachus, 1963). By the same token, people tend to dislike those with whom they are competing (Deutsch and Krauss, 1962).

Liking Those Who Like Us

The Gain-Loss Hypothesis. The simplest formulation of balance theory suggests that we tend to like those who like us and dislike those who dislike us (see, for example, Backman and Secord, 1959; Tagiuri, Bruner, and Blake, 1958; Newcomb, 1963; Festinger,

Schachter, and Back, 1950; Dickoff, 1961). More interesting and somewhat less obvious is the question of the gain or loss of affection. One might imagine that the greater the expression of affection for us on the part of another person, the more we might like that person. Although there is a measure of truth to this statement, Elliot Aronson and Darwyn Linder (1965) carried out an interesting experiment showing that the *gain* or *loss* of affection is more critical. They arranged for a female subject to overhear someone (actually a confederate) talking about her. Over the course of several sessions, the subject heard one of four different patterns of remarks: (1) In one pattern, the confederate said very nice things about the subject throughout all of the sessions. (2) In the second pattern, the initial comments were very favorable, but then they became increasingly unfavorable in later sessions. (3) In the third pattern, the initial comments were negative, but then became more positive as the sessions progressed. (4) In the fourth pattern, the confederate made unflattering remarks about the subject from beginning to end.

Now a simple reinforcement hypothesis would predict that we would like best those who said the most positive things about us and that we would like least those who said the most negative things; therefore, the subject should like the confederate in the first condition best and the confederate in the fourth condition (all negative comments) least. Aronson and Linder found, however, that the best-liked confederate was the one who started by saying negative things about the subject and then became increasingly positive; the least-liked confederate was the one whose initial remarks were positive and then became increasingly negative. In a parallel study, the subjects observed a videotaped interaction between a woman (actually an actress who was following a prescribed role) and a man. In this case, the woman communicated by means of non-verbal cues (or "body language"). Previously, it had been determined that the woman could communicate warmth and positive feelings by such actions as sitting and facing the man directly, smiling, and nodding her head affirmatively; she could convey coldness and negative feelings by looking around the room, frowning, and playing with the ends of her hair. As in the Aronson and Linder study, the order of communication was varied: warm–warm, cold–cold, warm–cold, cold–warm. The subjects were asked to rate the extent to which the man would probably like the woman under these four conditions. The results also paralleled those of Aronson and Linder: the subjects decided that there was greatest attraction in the cold–warm sequence and least attraction in the warm–cold sequence (Clore, Wiggins, and Itkin, 1975). The increasing affection in the cold–warm sequence has also been found in a number of other studies, but the loss effect in the warm–cold sequence has not been found too often. It is interesting that in both the Aronson and Linder and the Clore, Wiggins, and Itkin studies—where both effects were clearly demonstrated—the communication of positive and negative feelings was subtle and indirect (these studies used overheard statements and body gestures, rather than direct speech). One possible explanation is that words expressing warmth are sometimes perceived as attempts at flattery or ingratiation, especially if they are expressed after only a brief period of interaction, and so they tend to be discounted. In any case, it appears that we are often more impressed by the gain or loss of affection shown toward us by others than by the total number of nice things they say about us.

Elsewhere, Aronson (1972) draws some interesting implications from this research for husbands and wives. It is ordinarily the case, he says, that the most positive things a husband and wife say about each other are expressed during courtship or soon after the wedding. It is also likely that such positive expressions diminish afterward, with fewer positive and more negative things being said. From the Aronson and Linder experiment, one would expect that, on this basis alone, love in marriage would diminish over time. However, the trend is often accelerated as each partner becomes more aware of and comments on the other's limitations, thus approximating even more the warm–cold sequence. Small wonder, then, that love wanes rapidly and marriages end in divorce. Even if the lovey-dovey relationship of the courtship and honeymoon were to continue, its effects on mutual love would be less than optimal, since expressions of affection should *increase* in order for love to maintain itself. Perhaps, then, marriages that begin with restrained expressions of affection and continue with increasing expressions of love over time stand the best chance of success. The husband or wife who complains, "I feel that I am being taken too much for granted," is probably expressing concern that his/her partner's expressions of affection have followed the warm–cold sequence.

Self-esteem and Being Liked. Although we tend to like people who think highly of us, what about the person who has a low opinion of himself? In that case, anyone who likes him is thereby disagreeing with him. Balance theory can view the person as an object of evaluation to himself (p_i); thus, the relationship $p -Lp_i$ is possible. One might conclude from balance theory, then, that if we dislike ourselves ($p -Lp_i$) we would dislike the person who likes us (oLp_i). Actually, a number of clinically oriented psychologists have concluded that unless we love ourselves, we cannot be loved by others or love them in return (for example, Rogers, 1951; Fromm, 1939; Maslow,

1942; Stock, 1949). However, the opposite conclusion can also be drawn. According to balance theory, it is clear that the person is part of himself (pUp_i). Thus, disliking oneself (pUp_i and $p -Lp_i$) is inherently an imbalanced relationship. One who has a low opinion of himself should, therefore, welcome the opinion of someone who says something positive about him and like that person.

Elaine Walster (1965) devised a clever experiment to test these two interpretations of balance theory. While a female subject was waiting to participate in two experiments, a male student (actually a confederate) arrived. Presumably he, too, was waiting to participate in an experiment. He struck up a conversation with the subject, told her about himself, and eventually asked her for a date. (It may be of interest to note that in practically every case, he was successful.) At this point the female subject was called in for the first of two experiments. She was given a word-association personality test and the Rorschach Inkblot Test. The results of the tests were quickly analyzed, presumably by a professional clinical psychologist, and then conveyed to her. Half of the subjects received a very positive evaluation ("one of the most favorable personalities analyzed by the staff . . . [shows] sensitivity to peers, personal integrity, and originality and freedom of outlook"); the other half received a negative evaluation ("weak personality, antisocial motives, lack of originality and flexibility, and lack of capacity for successful leadership"). These "test results" had the expected effect—the subjects were either elated at their own positive self-image or dejectd at the negative evaluation.

For the second experiment, the subject was asked to rate anonymously her liking for five people, one of whom was the confederate who had asked her for a date. The results showed that the subject liked the confederate much more if her self-esteem was low. Being asked for a date by a nice young man was just what she needed to bolster her sagging ego. By contrast, the girls who had received a positive evaluation did not need his support, and thus did not like him as well.

A case can be made, however, for the clinical view of self-esteem and affection. If a person has a low opinion of himself, he is somewhat less likely to recognize affectionate overtures when they are made (he may overlook them or interpret them as attempts at ingratiation). Once he recognizes affection for what it is, however, he will grasp it eagerly (Jacobs, Berscheid, and Walster, 1971). Certainly a person's desire for bolstering has limits—if he performs extremely poorly on a task, he will not rush to embrace someone who tells him that he did extremely well. Undoubtedly he will prefer a frank and honest evaluation (Deutsch and Solomon, 1959). *Obvious* attempts at ingratiation do not lead to affection (Jones, 1964).

Liking Those Who Materially Benefit Us

A game of tennis or chess, a bicycle ride with others, our wish to raise a family, our desire to compare notes before taking an exam—all of these require that we somehow get together with someone else. In doing so, we undoubtedly have to give up something in return. Thus, most social relationships can be viewed as a *social exchange*—we give up something in order to get something. Earlier, when we pointed out that common goals or threats may bring people together, we were discussing the perception of unity in terms of balance theory. Obviously, we get together with others because we need them in order to attain certain ends.

John W. Thibaut and Harold H. Kelley (1959), as well as others who are called "exchange theorists," view people as continually going through some sort of accounting process. In order to maintain a given relationship, we carefully evaluate the *costs* and the *benefits*—the things we must do for the other person and the satisfactions that we receive. We weigh these costs and benefits against a subjective picture of what a satisfactory relationship is like. Our concept is developed according to our past experiences with others and our knowledge of what other relationships are like. After weighing the costs and benefits of a given relationship, we can decide whether we are satisfied with it.

A cost-benefit analysis seems rather cold and calculating. Yet, there is evidence that many relationships between people such as working relationships, bargaining relationships, and marriage relationships can be fruitfully analyzed in this fashion.

Liking Those Who Are Familiar

In 1972, Picoaza, Ecuador, a coastal town with a population of 4000 was faced with the question of how to deal with their new mayor, Pulvapies. Pulvapies was constitutionally elected, beating his nearest opponent by a comfortable margin. There was one problem, however—Pulvapies was a foot deodorant. During the municipal election, the manufacturer thought that it would be clever to plaster the billboards and distribute leaflets saying, "FOR MAYOR: HONORABLE PULVAPIES." Little did the manufacturer dream that his honorable foot deodorant would be elected (Reuters, July 17, 1972).

In an American election, a candidate was elected to political office as the result of a saturation advertising campaign to familarize the public with this nearly unknown aspirant. On billboards, in newspaper ads, and in facsimile telegrams, during a four-month period, the same simple message was communicated: "THREE CHEERS FOR PAT MILLIGAN." Milligan was elected overwhelmingly. Robert Zajonc (1970), who called this phenomenon to our at-

*Figure 4.6
Following frequent exposure of the populace to signs such as these, a foot powder was elected mayor of Picoaza, Ecuador.*

tention, has a ready explanation for the tremendous success of this election campaign. "What else but the effects of mere exposure?" We feel that we would need to have somewhat more information before coming to this conclusion about the election of Pat Milligan, or about the similar but more startling election of Pulvapies. At least, we ought to know something about the opposing candidates. Nonetheless, these two examples, as well as a growing body of research, suggest that mere exposure to objects seems to make them much more attractive to us. Advertisers have assumed this to be the case for many years.

Zajonc has collected an impressive array of evidence to support this concept. Words used over many centuries have gradually taken on more favorable meanings. The word "nice" originally meant "ignorant," later "foolish," and then "finicky"; now it has a favorable connotation. "Pretty" once meant "sly" or "deceitful." Zajonc has found that he can take an unfamiliar Turkish word like *dilikli*, ask an American subject if the word means something good or bad, and the subject will usually say that it means something unfavorable. However, the more the word is presented to the subject, the more he will be inclined to attribute a favorable meaning to it.

Another experiment demonstrates that familiarity through exposure may also increase the attractiveness of people. Susan Saegert, Walter Swap, and Robert Zajonc (1973) arranged for female subjects to go into a number of booths, ostensibly to participate in a study of taste preferences. Each booth had a different solution in it, and the subjects went from booth to booth in a prearranged order. The scheduling called for two subjects to be in a booth, tasting the same solution at a given time, but the number of times that each woman was in a booth with a specific other woman varied—once, twice, five times, ten times, or not at all. Later each subject was asked to fill out a long questionnaire, which included a question about how much she liked each of the other women who were participating in the experiment with her. The results were quite clear: the greater the exposure, the greater the liking. Could it be that the easy, pleasant experience of tasting various solutions would carry over to the evaluation of the group members? The experimenters dealt with this possibility by varying the types of solutions tasted; in some cases, the subjects were paired with others while tasting pleasingly sweet substances (three flavors of Kool-Aid); in others they tasted unpleasant, tart substances (vinegar, quinine, and citric acid). The results showed that it made no difference whether the solution tasted pleasant or unpleasant: The greater the frequency of exposure, the more the liking. Could it be that this was an example where common fate was important—that the women felt closer to someone who was enjoying and working toward a pleasant goal or to someone who was also enduring an unpleasant experience? A second part of the experiment controlled for this: It was arranged that in each pairing in a booth, one subject would taste while the other observed. Again, this factor seemed to make no difference; it was the amount of exposure that the women had to each other that was crucial in determining their liking.

The exposure effect seems to be especially likely to occur when a person is exposed to *novel* stimuli—whether these stimuli are unfamiliar Turkish words, strangers, or Chinese characters (Zajonc, 1968). However, when people are asked to look at little known but familiar objects (for example, the names of such U.S. Presidents as Zachary Taylor, James Buchanan, or William Henry Harrison), the typical exposure effect is not found (Swap, 1973). There thus appear to be some limitations to the simple exposure and liking hypothesis. In a recent exposure experiment, patterned after the Saegert, Swap, and Zajonc (1973) Kool-Aid study, Swap had pairs of subjects play a game in which they were either rewarded or punished, and in which the responsibility for these outcomes was attributable either to the experimenter or their partner. When the experimenter was seen as responsible, the usual exposure effect was found—in both the Reward and the Punishment Conditions. When the partner was seen as responsible, however, a rather different pattern emerged: in the Reward Condition there was an enhancement of the usual "exposure leads to liking" effect, while in the Punishment Condition it was found that the greater the frequency of exposure, the greater the *dislike* for the partner. Thus, the more we are exposed to a person who is responsible for our own unfavorable situation, the more negative our evaluation of this person tends to be (Swap, 1975).

Within a residential community, it has been demonstrated that people tend to like those with whom they have most contact. Contact is frequently dependent upon geographical location. In a small apartment house the person whose apartment happens to be near the main stairway and entrance may have many friends in the building, while the person who has a separate entrance to the street may have fewer friends there (Festinger, Schachter, and Back, 1950). Moreover, an early study of desegregation in housing (Deutsch and Collins, 1951) indicated that racial prejudice may be reduced through this kind of contact between whites and blacks.

Liking Others in Order to Justify Our Efforts

In Chapter 1, we presented several studies showing that the greater the hardship experienced by someone in joining or maintaining membership in a group, the greater would be his attraction toward that group—as he tried to reduce his dissonance. Recall the beatings suffered by the Indian marchers at the Dharsana Salt Works, the ridicule and suffering endured by Dr. Armstrong because of his affiliation with the Seekers, and the effects of haircutting sessions on Synanon members; in each case the individual's identification with and attraction toward his group were strengthened. The same effect was demonstrated experimentally in the laboratory "initiation experiments" by Aronson and Mills (1959) and Gerard and Mathewson (1966). We have all known of instances in which parents have disapproved of their son's or daughter's choice of a spouse. This disapproval can be very punishing in its own right, but it is often accompanied by threats and sanctions; often the combined effects are enough to impel the son or daughter to end the relationship with his (her) intended. However, if the young person decides to go through with his (her) plans, dissonance theory would predict that his (her) attraction toward the new spouse would be all the greater—he (she) would have to justify the punishment he (she) had chosen to receive from the parents.

Just as the recollection of past efforts often leads to increased attraction, so does future anticipation. If you know that you will be working with someone for a considerable time, that fact, by itself, will tend to make the other person more attractive. This prediction follows from both dissonance theory and balance theory (pUo induces $p+Lo$), and a number of studies have provided evidence. In one, conducted by John Darley and Ellen Berscheid (1967), women subjects were scheduled to meet in pairs to discuss acceptable dating behavior. Each woman received folders containing personality descriptions of two other women and was told which one of these had been randomly selected to be her partner. Then she was asked to indicate how much she thought she would like each of the women. The prospective partner was always rated more positively. In a later study, the subjects were again given two folders, one describing a woman with positive traits and the other describing a woman with negative traits; the subjects were told that they would be paired with one of these two. Of particular interest are the responses of the subjects who were told that they would be paired with a negative partner. These subjects showed a clear tendency to distort the information they had received and to view their prospective partner as quite attractive. In fact, when it was later announced that they could actually choose their own partners, many of the subjects chose the more negative one. Undoubtedly, there are limitations to how much our evaluation of others can be affected by knowledge of future interaction. Nevertheless, it is good that we can perceive as attractive those people with whom we must live, work, and play.

Liking Others Who Help Us to Evaluate Ourselves

As mentioned earlier (page 44), Schachter's (1959) studies of threat and affiliation showed that subjects who were going to experience a severe shock wanted very much to be with others who were in a similar predicament. Schachter believed that a major factor in this desire for affiliation was the person's wish to learn if he was responding appropriately.

HOSTILITY AND AGGRESSION

Having discussed several reasons why we like or dislike others, let us now consider precisely when we are apt to behave hostilely or aggressively toward others. As we shall see, liking and hostility are intertwined in complex, non-obvious fashion. Just because you do not like someone does not mean that you feel hostile; and an understanding of liking does not necessarily imply an understanding of why hostility and/or aggression may arise.

During the evening hours and Saturday mornings of just two weeks in 1967 and 1968, nearly 800 persons were left dead or injured on the television screens of the three major networks. These programs had been monitored by investigators working under the direction of the National Commission on the Causes and Prevention of Violence (Baker and Baker, 1969). Eight out of every ten programs included some form of violence or aggression, averaging about five violent episodes per program. The National Commission was established as the result of a growing conviction that, because our nation seems to be becoming increasingly violent and aggressive, something should be done to learn more about the causes of this aggression and ways in which it could possibly be reduced. Not to minimize the present aggressiveness in America, it is not entirely clear that our country is more aggressive now than others are or have been. A quick perusal of the Bible, or Xenophon's account of Cyrus and the Persian expedition (1969), or Caesar's Gallic Wars will reveal a catalog of horrors that man has wrought against his fellow man. Newspaper accounts from Northern Ireland, Biafra, and the Middle East attest to the fact that the United States does not have a monopoly on violence and aggression in the late 1960s and the 1970s. One is sometimes tempted to agree with pessimistic social philosophers such as Thomas Hobbes (1904), who saw mankind as inherently in a state of "war of all against all." Sigmund Freud, who became disillusioned following the bloodbath of World War I and even more by the holocaust of the Nazi era, advanced the notion of *thanatos*—a death instinct leading to a desire for destruction. Turned inward, it leads to suicide; turned outward, it takes the form of hostility, aggression, and war.

The Frustration-Aggression Hypothesis

A somewhat less pessimistic analysis of the origins of human aggression was presented by a team of eminent Yale psychologists—John Dollard, Neal Miller, Leonard Doob, O. H. Mowrer, and Robert Sears (1939). They minced no words in postulating that "aggression is always a consequence of frustration," and that "whenever frustration occurs, aggression of some kind and in some degree will inevitably result" (Dollard et al., 1939, p. 1). They defined *frustration* as interference with the attainment of some goal (later, they also included receiving punishment or insult from another person). *Aggression* was simply defined as behavior by one person that injures another in some way.

Later psychologists have emphasized that aggression involves the *intentional* injury of another. A related distinction is made between *hostile* aggression, the primary purpose of which is to harm someone, and *instrumental* aggression, or hurting someone as a by-product of trying to attain some goal or defend oneself against a negative consequence (Sears, Maccoby, and Levin, 1957). The steam-boiler frustration-aggression analysis refers to hostile aggression—pent-up hostility that is released against someone. However, instrumental aggression is carried out with a specific (but not necessarily hostile) goal in mind: a purse-snatcher will knock down an elderly woman because he wants her money; the woman in turn will try to scare off the robber by sticking him with her hat pin; the tough kid will punch the smaller child in the nose so that he can take his new toy; and the husky football lineman will hurl his bulky body against the player with the ball so that he can recover a fumble. To be sure, a case can always be made for frustration preceding even goal-oriented aggression. Yet, we must recognize that the purpose of such aggression is clearly different, as are its implications. Instrumental aggression can sometimes be avoided by the potential victim by merely surrendering to the aggressor; in the case of hostile aggression, however, surrender would presumably encourage the aggressor.

It is clear, of course, that a person who is frustrated cannot always act out his aggression immediately—a motorist rushing to get home may be stopped (frustrated) by a traffic policeman, or a child may be frustrated by a teacher who insists that he stay after school. In both cases, there are many forces restraining the person from acting out his aggression. The motives for aggression may build up in a manner analogous to steam in a stopped-up hot water heater—eventually they must burst forth. When they do, it may not be against the source of the frustration, because of severe restraints against such behavior. Thus, the person will select someone else—a scapegoat—who is both similar *and* available. (This is called *displacement* of aggression.) The child, frustrated by the teacher, cannot strike back at her. Where then? At his father? Not unless his home is unusually permissive. At his mother? Probably not. His older brother? No, he wouldn't get away with that. His younger sister? Perhaps, if no one is watching. As a last resort, there is always the dog.

Typical of some of the evidence presented by the Yale group was their analysis of lynching and the cotton crop. They suggested that the white Southern cotton farmers were frustrated when the price of cotton was low at a time when the South was faced with economic depression. Toward whom could they aggress? The weather? The federal government in Washington? The easiest target was their black neighbors. In fact, between 1882 and 1930, there was a correlation between the increased number of lynchings of blacks in the South and the decline in the price of cotton (Hovland and Sears, 1940; Mintz, 1946). Unfortunately, this study suffers from many of the problems described in the Appendix—attempting to draw conclusions about causality from correlations.

In a more precise field experiment, 31 young men in a work camp were frustrated by being restricted to camp on a night when they normally attended the local theater (and therefore missed a chance to win money at the weekly theater raffle). The attitudes of the men toward Japanese and Mexicans were measured before and after the frustration. Consistent with the frustration-aggression hypothesis, the men expressed more hostile attitudes toward those two minority groups after the frustration (Miller and Bugelski, 1948). In selecting a target for aggression, these two studies point out the importance of such factors as one's initial negative feelings toward the target.

The work of Dollard, Miller, Doob, Mowrer, and Sears has stimulated a tremendous amount of research in the years since their book *Frustration and Aggression* (1939) was first published. As the dust has settled, the proud and bold Yale banner still flies, though somewhat tattered; like most bold hypotheses, it has had to be qualified. Yes, frustration does tend to lead to aggression, but not always—it sometimes leads to other things. And yes, aggression is caused by frustration, but not always—aggression is sometimes due to other factors. We will pose a series of questions that have been suggested by the initial frustration-aggression formulation and then discuss some of the subsequent research.

When Is Frustration Especially Likely to Lead to Aggression?

The tendency to aggress when frustrated is quite strong. However, it seems that certain conditions lead to greater aggression, while others suppress aggression altogether.

Attributing Responsiblity for the Frustration. We are more likely to aggress against someone who appears to be responsible for our frustration than against someone who does not. Obviously we will be more angry if someone hits our car as he tries to beat us to a parking place than if the car is damaged accidentally. Although we will probably be quite angry at someone who coldly and deliberately grinds his heel into our toe, we will probably not be too angry at someone who inadvertently steps on our toe in a crowded subway—even if the pain seems greater. As discussed in Chapter 3, we go through a process of attributing intentions and dispositions in analyzing acts that hurt us. It was pointed out that very young children are more inclined to attribute blame according to the outcome of an act and less inclined to consider the intentions and extenuating circumstances.

A related study (Rule and Percival, 1971) was done on aggression against subjects who performed poorly on a learning task. One subject (actually a confederate) attempted to learn a series of syllables, while the actual subject presented the syllables. The task was explained as a joint endeavor—the subject was to be evaluated according to the confederate's performance. The confederate, however, performed quite poorly. Frustrated, the subject was given the opportunity to shock the confederate (presumably to improve his learning, but actually to allow for an expression of aggression). The results clearly indicated that the greater the frustration experienced by the subjects, the greater their aggression. This was especially true if the syllables were easy—then blame for frustration was attributed to the confederate. The subjects' aggression was manifested by giving longer and more intense shocks and by verbal expressions of hostility toward the confederate.

Characteristics of the Situation. Leonard Berkowitz and Anthony Le Page (1967) have demonstrated that objects visible to a frustrated person may suggest and thus encourage aggressive behavior. In their study, 100 male university students received either one or seven shocks, administered presumably by another student as part of a learning task. The second part of the experiment allowed each subject to administer shocks in return. As the subjects sat down at the table where they were to give the shocks, they saw various objects lying near the shock key—some saw a .38 revolver and a shotgun: others saw two badminton rackets and shuttlecocks. Given the opportunity to retaliate, those subjects who had received the greatest number of shocks (seven) and who saw the two guns lying near the shock key delivered the most shocks. The effect was even greater if the subject believed that the guns belonged to the confederate.

Since the assassination of President Kennedy, there has been a growing interest in federal legislation to control the sale and possession of firearms. Those who advocate such legislation point to the very high homicide rate in the United States as compared with countries where guns are not so readily available. In Tokyo, for example, where few people can legally possess weapons (other than the police and the military), there were 213 homicides in 1970 for a population of more than 11 million; in New York City during that same year, there were 1117 murders for a population of less than 8 million (Halloran, 1971).

It has been pointed out that the state of Texas, which has virtually no restriction on the possession of firearms and where many people have guns and other weapons, also has a much higher homicide rate than other states where guns are not so available. The following are possible explanations for this phenomenon: The large number of homicides might lead people to want guns for self-protection. The "frontier tradition" might contribute to one's desire for a gun. The availability of guns may make homicide easier (though the rate is also high for murder with other weapons). To these possibilities, let us add another, suggested by the Berkowitz and LePage (1967) study. Suppose an individual has a serious argument with his wife, his boss, or his girl friend's lover and then happens to look into the drawer of his night table and sees the revolver he had put there as protection against burglars? Or suppose a spurned wife happens to see the pistol that belongs to her unfaithful husband? The point is that, aside from the fact that the presence of the gun makes homicide easier, the mere sight of it, following frustration and instigation, may encourage any type of violence.

Characteristics of the Frustrator. It is understandable, of course, that aggression is more likely against a frustrator if we don't like him to begin with. In displacing our aggression, we will be more inclined to select a target whom we also dislike, and to punish him according to the degree of our dislike. Leonard Berkowitz and James Green (1962) demonstrated that when an experimenter frustrated a subject, and the subject was then offered two other people against whom he could displace his aggression, he was more inclined to aggress against the person he did not like. (On page 118 we discussed the experiment in which group members who had a different personality [and were, therefore, strange] were selected for jobs in which they would receive electric shocks rather than have the chance to earn money [Freedman and Doob, 1968].)

Berkowitz and his co-workers planned a series of interesting studies in which they first frustrated a subject and then determined what factors led to greater or lesser aggression when he was given an opportunity to shock another person. First, they found that the student subject delivered more shocks when the other person was identified as a boxer rather than a speech major (the student subjects were majoring in fields other than physical education—none were boxers); this tendency was heightened when the subject was shown a film about boxing (Berkowitz, 1965). In another study (Berkowitz and Geen, 1966; Geen and Berkowitz, 1966), a number of subjects were shown a particularly bloody seven-minute scene from the film *Champion,* in which a boxer, played by the actor Kirk Douglas, was beaten to a pulp. Some subjects were then introduced to a confederate named "Kirk"; other subjects were introduced to the same confederate, but in their case he was called "Bob." When named "Kirk," the confederate was much more apt to be given severe shocks by the subjects. Note that in the film, Kirk Douglas played the role of the *victim,* not the aggressor. The aggressor in the film was named "Kelly," but that name did not arouse as much aggression as did "Kirk." The subjects apparently identified the aggressive boxer with the name of the actor, and not with the name in the story. Identifying Kirk as the aggressor continued, even though parts of the film were rerun showing that he was the victim of unjustified aggression (Berkowitz and Geen, 1966). Apparently, the mere association of Kirk's name with aggression was sufficient to increase the aggression of the subjects toward the confederate using that name.

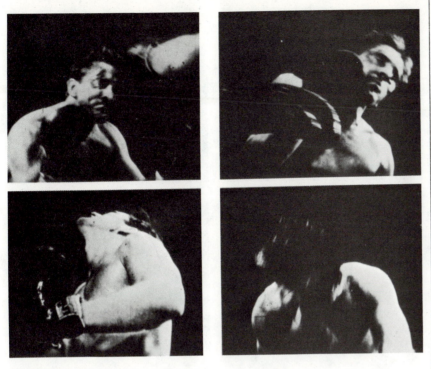

*Figure 4.7
After seeing the actor
Kirk Douglas beaten up
in this boxing sequence
from the film* Cham-
pion, *a group of sub-
jects tended to act ag-
gressively toward a
confederate named
"Kirk" (Berkowitz and
Geen, 1966).*

Social Facilitation, Imitation, and Aggression. When the frustrated
white Southern sharecropper takes out his aggression against blacks,
his choice of a target is to some degree facilitated by the attitudes
and behavior of other Southern whites. There is evidence that when
we are frustrated, we select our target and form of aggression by observing the norms of our own social group. Albert Bandura and his
colleagues have demonstrated imitation and aggression in an impressive series of experiments. Their subjects were preschool children
who were frustrated in a simple task. After the frustration, the children saw an adult approach a large plastic Bobo doll (a clown doll
that bounces up when you knock it down) and push it down, hit it
with a mallet, throw it into the air, sock it, and sit on it. As he did
these things, the adult shouted such aggressive things as, "Sock him
in the nose . . . hit him down . . . throw him in the air . . . kick him
. . . POW. . . ." The adult then left the room.

The children, given the freedom of the room, tended to copy the
adult; some of them added a few innovations of their own, such as
taking a toy gun and shooting at Bobo. In a control condition, in
which the adult model played with tinker toys instead of hitting the
Bobo doll, there was very little evidence of aggressive behavior in
the children. It was found that imitation was greater for a like-sex
model—boys showed more aggression than girls after being exposed

LIKING AND DISLIKING,
FRIENDSHIP AND
AGGRESSION

140

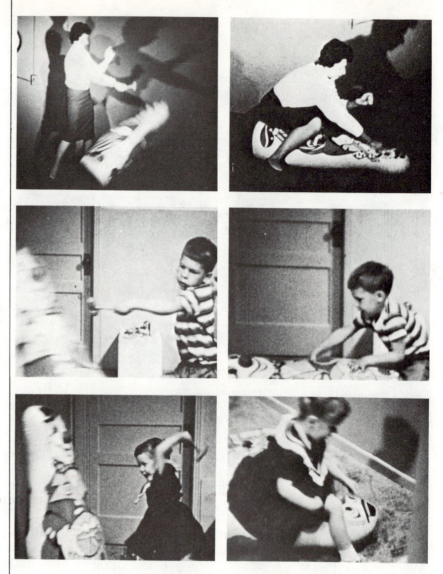

Figure 4.8
Children can learn how
to behave aggressively
by copying an adult
model (Bandura, Ross,
and Ross, 1961).

to an aggressive male model; girls showed more aggression than
boys after being exposed to an aggressive female model. However,
the increased level of aggression took different forms: the boys
tended to display more physical aggression and gun play, whereas
the girls were more inclined to engage in verbal aggression (Bandura, Ross, and Ross, 1961).

General Emotional Arousal. The first boxing film study (Berkowitz,
1965) suggests that greater aggression is likely to occur when hostile
emotions have been aroused. However, Dolf Zillman (1971) found

that aggression will take place even when other emotions have been aroused. He showed one group of subjects a travel film, another group a boxing film, and a third group a highly erotic sex film. Later, when angered by a confederate, the subjects aggressed more if they had seen the boxing or sex film than if they had seen the travel film; in fact, the greatest aggression was committed by those who had seen the sex film.

The effects of general emotional arousal on the expression of anger were demonstrated by Stanley Schachter and Jerome Singer (1962). In their experiment, they injected subjects with epinephrine, a drug that produces physiological responses similar to those experienced in certain emotional states (flushing of the face, tremors, increased heartbeat, and increased perspiration). In some cases, the subjects were informed that the injection had each of these effects; in other cases they were not told. Later, they were given questionnaires to answer. A confederate, who was also filling out a questionnaire, suddenly burst into anger at the experimenter and the situation. If the subject had been informed of the effect of the drug, he did *not* follow the confederate's example. However, if he had not been informed, he also acted in an angry and aggressive manner. It is as if the subject in the latter situation were saying to himself, "Why am I feeling this way—hot, perspiring, on edge? Of course! It is because I am angry." In a parallel version of this experiment, the confederate behaved in a euphoric fashion, and the subject who did not know about the effects of the drug also behaved likewise. Many of us have had moments when we were on edge or uneasy and didn't know precisely why. It could have been due to a new medication we had taken or something we had eaten or drunk. Women often experience emotional changes during certain stages of the menstrual cycle. If we can't account for our feeling, we are especially likely to grasp for a convenient explanation. We may seize upon a minor, untoward remark made by someone that would provoke only slight annoyance under ordinary circumstances. "*That* is why I feel this way. After being insulted like this, what can you expect!" We may then proceed to express our anger and hostility in retaliation, which may sometimes lead to a real insult, which will then provide us with even more justification for our psychophysiological state.

When Do We Aggress When Not Frustrated?
A major limitation of the frustration-aggression hypothesis is the clear finding that aggression occurs even when there is no obvious frustration. We will examine five such instances: (1) instrumental aggression, (2) imitative aggression, (3) aggression on command, (4) aggression as a social role, and (5) aggression and group effects.

Instrumental Aggression. We mentioned earlier that aggression has an instrumental value in some instances, allowing us to attain certain goals or avoid certain punishments. Arnold Buss (1966) has illustrated this point in a study in which students were told that they were to help someone learn to distinguish light patterns. The learning was to take place by means of the student giving shocks to the other person for his incorrect responses. When the student was told that learning would be facilitated by high shock levels, he shocked the learner more. In this case, it was the instrumental factor that led to increased shocking, rather than the satisfaction of hurting the other person; for whenever the learner informed the subject that the shocks were painful, he reduced the level of the shocks. If the subject had been motivated by hostile aggression, however, this feedback would have led him to increase the shocks.

Imitative Aggression. It was pointed out earlier that after being frustrated, people tend to increase their aggression and to select their targets according to the prevailing social norms. Aggression also seems to take place by imitation, without any obvious frustration. Police have long observed that similar violent acts often take place in close succession. They assume that newspaper reports of a kidnapping encourage others to commit the same crime, and the wave of airplane hijackings has been likened to the spread of a disease. From time to time, a particularly dramatic television program depicting violence will be followed by similar acts committed by the viewers. A simple experiment by Ladd Wheeler and Anthony Caggiula (1966) illustrates this point quite clearly. The subjects were navy enlisted men who worked in groups of three and communicated with one another by telephone. To maintain experimental control, the voices of two of the men were tape recordings. One of the voices expressed a number of unconventional opinions: "All religions [other than my own] should be illegal," "Most people one meets are probably bastards," "Liquor should be banned," "Wives should be allowed to play around with other guys." In some conditions, the subject heard the second navy man reprimand the first one by calling him such names as "bastard," "ass," "creep." Hearing the navy man use verbal aggression against the deviant encouraged the subject to behave in the same way. This occurred even when the navy man with the unconventional views retracted his statements and, in effect, apologized. When no verbal aggression was expressed by the second man, little aggression was expressed by the subject.

Aggression on Command. In a rather disturbing experiment, Stanley Milgram (1963) demonstrated that an individual will deliver shocks to another person, even at a level he believes is harmful, simply on command. The study was presented as a "learning experiment," and

Milgram - shocks

the experimenter ordered the subject to play the role of "teacher"
and to shock a second subject each time he made a mistake—increasing the shock level after each succeeding mistake. The second subject (who had expressed fear that the shocks might be dangerous to
his heart condition) was, of course, a confederate; he did not actually
receive electric shocks, but the "teacher" clearly thought he did. All
too often, Milgram found, the subjects were willing to obey the commands of the experimenter—delivering severe, apparently dangerous, shocks to the victim. (We will discuss this important study in
greater detail in Chapter 6.)

Martin Orne and Frederick Evans (1965) present an equally disconcerting illustration of aggression on command. They had been
conducting research on hypnosis and wanted to determine the extent
to which subjects could be induced to do things under hypnosis that
they would not do otherwise. Six subjects were hypnotized; another
six were told to pretend that they had been hypnotized and to act accordingly; and another six were told that they were controls for a
hypnosis experiment. Each subject met individually with the experimenter and was instructed to perform the same series of acts. The
first requests were straightforward and innocuous: pick up a coin,
pick up and identify a piece of chalk, pick up a harmless lizard. Then
the subject was asked to pick up a venomous snake (a plate of glass
stopped the subject's hand before it reached the snake). Next, the experimenter put a glass beaker in front of the subject, and he poured
concentrated nitric acid into it. Then he dropped a penny into the
liquid and it began to dissolve. The experimenter instructed the subject to remove the dissolving coin as quickly as possible with his
bare hand and then plunge his hand and the coin into a nearby basin
of soapy water. While the subject was busy washing his hands
(which were not harmed), the experimenter replaced the acid with
an identical-looking, harmless liquid. At this point the experimenter's assistant, who had been responsible for recruiting the subject for the experiment, arrived. The experimenter suggested that the
subject was very angry at the assistant and would have an irresistible
urge to throw the acid into his face; authoritatively he ordered the
subject to do so. It was found that the subjects complied almost completely with the instructions of the experimenter. Of the six hypnotized subjects, five obeyed all commands (one subject had become
hysterical at the sight of the harmless lizard, and so she was removed
from the experiment). All six subjects who were pretending to be
hypnotized complied with every request. Of the six controls, three
refused to touch the poisonous snake, but five of the six obeyed the
other commands, including throwing the acid into the face of the assistant.

The extent to which people are willing to commit aggression on command appears to be virtually unlimited, as can be seen from the actions of American soldiers who massacred innocent civilians at My Lai, in South Vietnam, in 1968, and from the behavior of German civilians who commanded Nazi concentration camps during World War II.

Aggression as a Social Role. Aggression can be committed simply by assuming the role of someone whom we believe is aggressive. Philip Zimbardo (1972) simulated a prison on the campus of Stanford University. Students were randomly assigned roles as either prisoners or guards. Zimbardo found that the "guards" did not have to be ordered to act aggressively toward the "prisoners." Their behavior was sometimes brutal—even sadistic—and the student "guards" shuddered at the thought of it when they were asked to discuss their behavior after the study had been completed. We all know that prison guards aggress against prisoners. Thus, when the students were placed in such a role, they tended to behave in a similar fashion. (This study will be discussed in greater detail in Chapter 8.)

Aggression and Group Effects. It has been pointed out that aggression is generally inhibited by social norms, suggesting that aggression is an unacceptable form of behavior. When we see others acting aggressively (as in the imitation study cited above), or when we are part of a group where our identity is disguised (as in the case of the Ku Klux Klan), we feel less inhibited and thus freer to aggress against others. This loss of individuality—deindividuation—often allows an individual to aggress with impunity; this accounts for acts committed in group demonstrations, riots, and mass lynchings. (We will discuss these situations in greater detail in Chapter 8.)

Violence, Aggression, and the Mass Media

We began this section on "Hostility and Aggression" by mentioning the violence committed regularly on our television screens. We could also have pointed to the violence that is presented to us in the movies, newspapers, magazines, books, and other mass media. The critical question is: Does this constant diet of overt aggression lead to greater violence among those who consume it so avidly? Several studies cited earlier give us reason to expect that it would. The experiments by Bandura and his colleagues provide several illustrations of what happens to those who view aggressive acts committed by others; since children will often imitate an adult who acts in a hostile manner, isn't it possible that they would also imitate a violent adult whom they see on the television screen? Similarly, might we not expect certain adults to imitate other adults? Actually articles do appear in the newspapers from time to time about bank robberies, plane hijackings, and even murders, where the criminal reports that he got his idea from watching a television program or a movie. Studies have been made of emotional arousal (such as those carried out by Berkowitz and his co-workers) indicating that the mere sight of a violent act in a movie (*The Champion*) may lead an observer to act more violently toward an innocent subject later on.

Other experimental studies and surveys also suggest that seeing violence in the media may increase one's own aggressiveness. In one study, 7-year-old children listened to radio serials about taxi drivers. For some children, the serials presented the taxi drivers as quite violent and aggressive, while other children heard serials in which the taxi drivers were more friendly and nonviolent. Later, the children from both groups were given a newspaper story to read that described the activities of a real-life taxi driver. The effects of the radio serials were quite clear: those who heard the violent serials tended to interpret the real-life taxi driver's behavior as violent and aggressive, whereas those who heard the nonviolent serials tended to see the real-life taxi driver as less violent (Siegel, 1958). One might reasonably conclude that children form their concepts of the world in part from what they hear over the radio and see on television. The next logical step would be to assume that if children are exposed to people who are violent and aggressive, they may behave in a similar fashion themselves.

That logical step may be supported by a subsequent finding: children who reported that they viewed many violent programs on television tended to be seen as more violent and aggressive by their peers (Eron, 1963). This evidence should be interpreted cautiously, however, since children who would like to appear tough may report that they like violent programs.

In order to get some hard facts on the causes of violence, the United States federal government established the National Commission on the Causes and Prevention of Violence, under the direction of Milton Eisenhower (Eisenhower et al., 1969). After gathering a large amount of data and interviewing many outstanding authorities who had been doing research on violence, the commission reported: "It is reasonable to conclude that a constant diet of violent behavior on television has an adverse effect on human character and attitudes. Violence on television encourages violent forms of behavior, and fosters moral and social values about violence in daily life which are unacceptable in a civilized society" (Eisenhower et al., 1969, p. 202). The report also stated that "The preponderance of the available evidence strongly suggests, however, that violence in television programs can and does have adverse effects upon audiences—particularly child audiences" (p. 5).

With such statements from a national commission that had carefully studied the problem, together with the studies and experiments that we mentioned earlier, as well as what many of us intuitively believe to be the case, the issue would seem to be closed. However, the national commission also noted that the results of a number of studies were not wholly consistent or conclusive.

The national commission's report was criticized for relying too much on indirect evidence and on contrived laboratory studies, rather than on field studies or studies in natural settings. Since then, one major field experiment has been conducted on the subject of television viewing by Seymour Feshbach and Robert Singer. They used 625 boys, aged 10–17, who were attending three private boarding schools and four state residential schools. The boys were randomly assigned to watch six weeks of either "aggressive" or "nonaggressive" television programs. The aggressive programs (such as "I Spy," "FBI," "Combat," and "The Untouchables") depicted killing, beating, fighting, and other forms of violent behavior. The nonaggressive programs included such shows as "Gilligan's Island," "Ed Sullivan," "the Lucy Show," and "Yogi Bear." All of the boys in the study were required to watch at least six hours of television a day, and the programs had to be chosen from a designated list.

Contrary to earlier findings and expectations, watching violent programs for six weeks significantly reduced the boys' aggressiveness, as shown on tests of aggressive tendencies, peer ratings, and supervisor ratings. The boys who viewed the aggressive programs engaged in only half as many fights as did those who watched the nonaggressive programs. The major differences were apparent among the boys in the public institutions; there was little difference among the boys in the private schools.

The Feshbach and Singer study suggests that viewing violence may have a cathartic effect—the boys who watched the violent programs could let out their aggressive and hostile tendencies there rather than on the playground (Feshbach and Singer, 1970). Of course, it is also possible that the boys were influenced by the general results of the violence that they saw on television—of seeing the criminal eventually punished and brought to justice. If so, this would support Bandura's (1965) finding on the effects of seeing aggression punished (described on page 147).

Obviously there are cases in which violence in the mass media induces violence in those who are exposed to it, yet there are also cases in which viewing such violence may reduce one's own hostile tendencies. And, of course, there are people for whom viewing violence makes little difference one way or the other. One's propensity to commit acts of hostility is also affected by many other variables. The general social climate in which the individual lives may be significant. For example, in families where parents discourage children from being aggressive or hostile, the correlation between viewing violent TV programs and aggressive behavior is virtually zero; however, if the parents place little stress on nonaggression or perhaps encourage their children to fight back, there is a decided association between viewing numerous violent TV programs and more aggressive behavior (Chaffee and McLeod, 1971).

When Does Frustration Not Lead to Aggression?

As we have noted, aggression sometimes takes place without frustration. It is also clear that frustration does not always lead to aggression.

Other Responses to Frustration. Frustration may lead to increased striving toward a goal. It has been found, for example, that children who were frustrated in a task (placing marbles in holes in a board) often intensified their efforts, particularly if they were about to reach the goal, and sometimes they released their frustration in another way—such as by pressing down very firmly on a plunger (this move signaled the end of a trial, but a light touch would have accomplished the same purpose) (Haner and Brown, 1955). Demosthenes responded to the frustration of his speech defect not by committing aggression, but by increasing his efforts and becoming a great orator. Franklin Roosevelt responded to the frustration of his partial paralysis from polio by developing his political talents. Leonard Berkowitz (1960) presents other evidence, indicating that extreme frustration may simply lead to a reduction of striving toward one goal and a seeking out of other goals, with no evident signs of aggression. Gandhi advocated a nonviolent response to frustration, hoping that the aggressive colonialists might be induced to feel sympathy (or guilt) and thereby reduce their aggression. Such a response to aggression, of course, requires great self-discipline; one may also ask whether this response is actually a form of nonviolent aggression (Pelton, 1974).

Inhibition of Aggression. It has been demonstrated that aggression may be inhibited under certain circumstances, either by observing the behavior of a model or by observing the consequences of aggression. Following up on their study of aggression against the Bobo doll, Bandura and his associates varied the rewards or punishments that the model received—if the aggressive adult model was rewarded after attacking the doll, the children were much more likely to aggress when given the chance; if, however, the model was punished, then the children were less apt to commit aggression (Bandura, 1965; Bandura, Ross, and Ross, 1963). Rewards for aggression or nonaggression can, of course, be administered more directly. In a study of 7- to 9-year-old children, Joel Davitz (1952) began with a training session in which he lavishly praised some children for cooperative, task-oriented activity, while praising others for aggressive, hostile activity. Then he frustrated them by interrupting a movie that they were watching. When they were allowed to play freely, the children who had been praised for aggression acted even more aggressively, while those who had been praised for cooperative, constructive activity behaved even more constructively.

The evidence is clear that in some families where aggression at home is punished severely, children do show less aggression—at home. Unfortunately, there is also evidence that these same children sometimes express quite a bit of aggression outside the home (Sears, Whiting, Nowlis, and Sears, 1953).

Reducing Aggression by Changing Attributions. As pointed out earlier, we feel less hostile toward someone who injures us, and are less likely to blame him, if we do not hold him responsible for his actions. Accordingly, any communication that might lead us to attribute responsibility for an aggressive act to a third person should reduce our hostility toward the one who committed the act. Shahbaz Mallick and Boyd McCandless (1966) conducted an experiment with third-grade children who were paid to construct a block tower. When they had finished, a sixth-grade confederate appeared and proceeded clumsily to knock down the construction, making sarcastic remarks as he did so. Mallick and McCandless found that the children developed hostile and aggressive feelings toward the sixth-grader. Among the various techniques the experimenters used to try to reduce this hostility, the most effective proved to be an explanation of the sixth-grader's behavior; specifically, they pointed out that he was sleepy and upset at the time he knocked down the blocks, so that he really wasn't responsible for his act.

What Are the Consequences of Trying to Reduce Tension through Aggression?

Both the adherents of the frustration-aggression hypothesis and others (including the followers of Freud) argue that it is beneficial—even necessary—to ventilate the tensions that build up as a result of frustration. We are all frustrated in some way, they suggest, and we need to let off steam through aggression or catharsis—a direct or indirect expression of hostility through actions, words, or fantasy. It has been contended that violence on television, in films, and in pulp magazines helps to reduce tension (Feshbach and Singer, 1970). The clinical psychologists George R. Bach and Peter Wyden, in their book *The Intimate Enemy: How to Fight Fair in Love and Marriage*

*Figure 4.9
George R. Bach demon-
strates to a wife how to
use a bataca club to
express hostility (in a
non-hurtful way) to-
ward her husband.*

(1968), urge couples to vent their hostilities on one another, but to do so in a way that will permit catharsis without permanent injury.

Some contemporary therapy groups encourage the free expression of verbal hostility and the release of pent-up emotions (for example, Perls, 1969; Janov, 1970; Bach and Wyden, 1968). The assumption is that many people's problems today stem from an overemphasis on intellectual approaches to life—at the expense of the free and direct expression of emotion. By encouraging patients to express verbal hostility and harmless aggression, therefore, it is believed that their underlying tensions will be alleviated.

But aggression apparently does *not necessarily* reduce the tensions of frustration. In a short, pointed statement, Leonard Berkowitz (1973) observed that although there are data showing that aggression committed after frustration may sometimes reduce one's feelings of hostility toward the frustrator (Hokanson, 1961; Feshbach, 1955), there is also evidence to the contrary—that aggression (both actual and fantasy) committed after frustration may *increase* one's feelings of hostility. Feshbach (1956) has found that boys who initially showed little aggression or hostility demonstrated a substantial increase after playing with guns and other war-like toys. The Mallick and McCandless study (which reported that children reduced their hostility toward a frustrator after the reason for his actions was explained to them) also found that when the children were given some means for letting out their aggression—by playing with guns and shooting at a target that resembled the frustrator—their hostility toward the frustrator increased. Although some studies have found that our hostility toward a given person will be reduced if we see or hear him suffer (Bramel et al., 1968), other studies have demonstrated the exact opposite—that if we see someone who has harmed us suffer, we will feel even more strongly that he is guilty and deserves to suffer and thus will behave all the more aggressively toward him in the future (Patterson, Littman, and Bricker, 1967). Also, as one might expect, giving praise for aggression after frustration leads to still greater aggression (Walters and Brown, 1963).

In short, it is not at all clear that aggression serves to reduce frustration. It would be desirable if individuals and nations could search for ways to reduce their frustration by means other than aggression.

Summary

The mass media, advertisements, folk sayings, and everyday experience all attest to the fact that people share an ongoing desire to be liked or loved by others, as well as a desire to avoid being disliked or hated. Equally apparent is the fact that social relationships vary in the extent to which they are characterized by liking, friendship, or love on the one hand, and disliking, hostility, or aggression on the other. Underlying interpersonal attraction is an important assumption—that of cognitive consistency or balance. Fritz Heider and others have suggested that people need to maintain consistency in their attitudes and beliefs, and that they will experience discomfort or tension if these are inconsistent. In the language of interpersonal attraction, there appears to be a tendency to view our friend's friend as our friend, our friend's enemy as our enemy, our enemy's friend as our enemy, and our enemy's enemy as our friend.

Social psychological research has found that people tend to like or dislike others for at least seven related reasons. First of all, we like those who have personal characteristics or traits that appeal to us; those who appear to be physically attractive, intelligent, competent, honest, understanding, and sincere are generally liked more than their opposites. Second, we tend to like those with whom we feel some sense of unity or identification—members of the same race, sex, religion, or group; those who have similar beliefs, attitudes, values, or abilities; and those with whom we share common goals or common threats. Third, we tend to like those who like us and to dislike those who dislike us—especially when their attitudes crystallize and become more obvious over time. Fourth, we like those who can or do materially benefit us. Fifth, we like those with whom we are familiar or whom we see on a regular basis. Sixth, we tend to like certain persons simply to justify our efforts; the very fact that we have worked with someone in the past, or will do so in the future, is enough to make that person seem more attractive. Finally, we like those who help us to evaluate ourselves—especially when those evaluations are favorable.

An understanding of why people like or dislike others does not necessarily explain why people display social aggression. One particularly influential and important explanation of aggression—the frustration-aggression hypothesis—holds that aggression is invariably a consequence of frustration, and that frustration always leads to aggression. There is increasing evidence, however, that the frustration-aggression hypothesis, at least as initially stated, is an overly narrow and often inaccurate formulation.

There are obviously cases in which frustration is likely to lead to aggression: for example, when a given person is specifically responsible for our frustration, when instruments of aggression are readily available, when the frustrator is someone we dislike anyway, when group norms sanction aggression as an appropriate response to frustration, and when our hostile emotions have been aroused. However, aggression often occurs without any frustration: aggression can be instrumental in attaining a particular goal; it can result from imitating an aggressive "model"; it can occur by obeying the commands of someone in authority; it can be produced by assuming the role of someone believed to be aggressive; and it can result when an individual's inhibitions are reduced because of his group membership. Finally, there are important cases in which frustration does not lead to aggression; for example, frustration may motivate a person to strive harder toward some coveted goal; or it may lead him to change his assignment of blame from one person to another.

Underlying the issue of liking or disliking other people is a simple but important assumption: we come to like or dislike others because we are interdependent with them; we need them and they need us, and as a consequence other people are the focus of our strongest positive and negative feelings. Chapter 5 will examine the many forms of interdependence, as well as its effects on the kinds of relationships that evolve.

THE INTERDEPENDENCE OF PERSONS

FIVE

The Problem of Coordination
Convergent Interest Coordination
Divergent Interest Coordination
Mixed-Motive Relationships: Coordinating Convergent
  and Divergent Interests
Social Exchange Theory
The Prisoner's Dilemma Game: A Paradigm for Mixed-
  Motive Problem-solving
Factors That Affect Cooperation and Competition in
  the Prisoner's Dilemma
Cooperation and Competition among Kibbutzniks
Competition as a By-product of Urbanization

Interdependence of Goals and Means
Cooperation and Competition Revisited

Interdependence in Escape

Conflict and Bargaining
When Does Bargaining Occur?
Successful Bargaining

153

Interdependence during an Uneventful Day. In the course of a single, not especially eventful day in the lives of most of us, we are expected and required to make an extraordinary number of judgments that pertain to the complex ways in which we are interdependent with others. Here, for example, is a sequence of events that happened one day in the life of a professor of social psychology.

Beginning in the late morning, at the conclusion of my weekly graduate seminar in social psychology, the students and I are discussing plans for our next meeting. We agree to spend our next session critiquing a body of social psychological research and decide that, in order to have a really fruitful discussion, each person will read the same set of experimental papers. I have most of the articles the students are to read, but many of them are too long to duplicate. As a consequence, the students must decide on some sharing arrangement. Phone numbers are exchanged, and an elaborate plan is established for coordinating the reading. Since there are five students in the seminar and five articles to be reviewed, each student will read a different article on the first day and then, round-robin fashion, pass the article along to someone else. In this way, each student will be able to study each of the papers by the following meeting.

After the seminar, I join several other faculty members and students for lunch at a local restaurant. Midway through our meal, we overhear four businessmen at the next table each insisting that today *he* must pay the check. Soon, however, it becomes clear that none of them *really* wants to pick up the tab; the bill is lying in the middle of the table, and any one of them could easily pick it up if he really wanted to. Why, then, this elaborate ritual? And what strategy is each using to make his offer seem honest—while not getting stuck with the bill?

Later in the day I have a brief meeting with the department chairman. After our other business has been completed, I decide to broach the subject of my salary for next year. With as much delicacy as I can muster, I inquire about the possibility of a raise. His response is surprisingly disarming. He points out, first of all, that he considers me worthy of a raise, and that he will do his very best to help me. But, he cautions, I must remember that his hands are tied. The university administration has allotted him only a fixed amount of money for departmental salaries, which he must distribute as he sees fit. Thus, if I get the raise that I deserve, someone else will not. I experience pangs of guilt at the thought that one or more of my equally competent and deserving colleagues may suffer because of my avarice. After a moment or two, I suggest that we solve the problem by encouraging the administration to allocate a larger sum of money to our department, thereby allowing all who deserve raises to receive them. The chairman assures me that he will try his hardest.

154

That evening, my wife and I set about the task of preparing dinner. Following our usual division of labor, I fix the salad while she prepares the meat and salad dressing. After dinner, I wash the dishes and empty the garbage, while she waters the plants. Since it is Friday, and thus the end of a work week, we decide to go out for the evening. But where? During the course of our conversation, the following dialogue takes place:

Me: Why don't we go to a movie?

My wife: That's fine with me. Or we could go to a play.

Me: It sounds like you'd rather see a play.

My wife: That would be nice—but a movie is fine also. I'm easy.

Me: Me too.

(Silence)

Me: So how are we going to decide?

My wife: What movie did you want to see?

Me: *Cries and Whispers.*

My wife: It may be difficult to get seats.

Me: That's true. What play did you want to see?

My wife: *Don Juan in Hell.*

Me: It'll probably be just as difficult to get seats for that as for the movie.

(Silence)

Me: So how are we going to decide?

My wife: What would you like to do?

Me: I'd like to go to a movie—but only if you'd like to also.

My wife: *Cries and Whispers* is fine.

Me: Okay. But do you *really* want to go—or are you just saying that because you know I want to go and are being nice?

My wife: *Cries and Whispers* is fine. (Pause) Look, why don't you stop fooling around and decide. I made the decision last time.

Me (thinking to myself): She says she's willing to go to the movie, but I suspect she really wants to see the play. She's saying the movie is okay because she knows my preference and wants to please me. But her impatience with my ambivalence suggests that she isn't as "easy" about what we're going to do as she's letting on. I think I'll give her a pleasant surprise.

Me: Okay. Let's go to the play. We'll see the movie another time.

And so it goes—one example of interdependence following another. But now, let us examine this scenario of events, the details of which vary from person to person, and from day to day. In what ways are the events recounted here similar? In what ways do they differ? And, most important, what are the consequences of these similarities and differences for the ways in which people behave with one another?

THE PROBLEM OF COORDINATION

The individual actors in our drama of an uneventful day were busily, and characteristically, engaged in a process that we shall call *coordination:* they were each trying to phase their preferences, intentions, and/or expectations with those of others. It is by means of coordination that people transform their interdependent relationships into behavioral reality. Coordination, in other words, is interdependence made visible.

People are often fully aware of the coordination process in which they engage. For example, I knew perfectly well that my wife preferred a play to a movie and plant-watering to dishwashing. At other times, however, people are only dimly aware of their interdependence or have no awareness at all. Thus, while speaking to another person, we may adjust the tone of our voice and our articulation so that we will be understood by, but not annoy, him. If he is socially sensitive, he will adjust his own speech in turn. And all this may take place without either person being consciously aware of it.

In order to study the coordination process that emerges when neither person is aware of his interdependence with another, three psychologists conducted a rather interesting experimental study of a "minimal social situation" (Sidowski, Wyckoff, and Tabory, 1956). Two subjects were placed in separate rooms, but neither was told of the other's existence. Each subject was presented with two buttons; although he was not informed of the purpose of the buttons, he was told that he could press them in any manner or order that he wanted. He was further informed that he would receive points on a counter in front of him, but that he might also receive a shock through an electrode that was attached to him. He was instructed to try to get as many points as possible and to avoid shocks. Unknown to the subjects, one of Subject A's buttons was wired to give a point to Subject B and the other was wired to shock Subject B. B's buttons were similarly wired to Subject A. Note that neither subject could reward or shock himself, but only the other.

You might think that in a situation such as this, complete and utter chaos would result. To the contrary, the experimenters found that the number of shocks received by both subjects steadily decreased, while the number of points obtained increased. Thus, despite the subjects' ignorance of their interdependent relationship (not to mention their ignorance of one another's existence), they still learned to help, rather than hurt, each other. But how could this happen? It appears that, over time, each subject learns to adopt the identical, simple strategic rule—"win-stay, lose-change." That is, each person tends to repeat (stay with) his last response after receiving a positive outcome (a point), but he tends to change it after getting a negative one (a shock). For example, if Subject A receives a point and B receives a shock, then we might expect A (who "won") to repeat his last response and B (who "lost") to change. Now both A and B would get a shock. If they both changed their response, then they would both get points. And, since they have both "won" now, both might be expected to repeat their last response—and continue to win.

In many relationships people are unaware of their interdependence. The central implication of the "minimal social situation" research is that in any relationship where people are uncertain about which of several courses of action to pursue, they may adopt the strategic "win-stay, lose-change" rule. But note the inherent conservatism of this rule: If things are going well, it says, continue doing whatever you have been doing ("you must be doing something right"), but if things are not going well, change ("you have little to lose—and possibly much to gain"). By adhering to this rule, we learn to persist in behavior for which we are rewarded (by ourselves, but even more so by others) and to change behavior for which we are punished (or at least not rewarded).

Now that we have seen how coordination may occur even when people are ignorant of one another's existence, let us look at the more frequent case in which people do know about their interdependence. In analyzing this situation and the various strategies that result, it may be useful to distinguish among three types of coordination problems: those in which people's interests are either *convergent* (common), *divergent* (different), or both *convergent and divergent*.

Convergent Interest Coordination

Try to solve the following problem (taken from Schelling, 1960): You and a total stranger, whom you have never met and with whom you cannot communicate, are seated in separate rooms. On a table in front of each of you is a pencil and a piece of paper. Your task is to write down a sum of money. If you and the stranger both name the same amount, you can each have as much as you have named. But, if you and the other person write down a different amount, neither of you will win anything.

Guessing what the other person will do. Okay; what amount did you indicate? $1.00? $5.00? $1 million? Next, ask yourself how you went about trying to solve this problem. Perhaps you said something like this to yourself: "Since I know nothing at all about this other person, why not assume that he is just like me? I will figure out the amount of money *I* want to write down, and then assume that he will do exactly the same thing." Or perhaps you reasoned as follows: "I cannot really assume that the other person is just like me [I'm probably a bit smarter], but I'll try to guess what he [an average person] might put down and then give the same answer myself." Or perhaps, if you were especially clever, you thought to yourself: "In order to decide what amount to put down, I will first have to figure out how much the other person thinks *I'm* going to write down—which will be the amount *he* will then specify to match my choice—which will be the amount *I* will put down to match his guess about my choice." And so on, perhaps endlessly, this cycle of interpersonal perspectives might continue, each person making his choice dependent upon his guess about the other's guess about his guess about the other's guess . . .

Picking a prominent solution. Obviously, in attempting to solve a problem like this, each person must try his best to coordinate his preferences, intentions, and expectations with those of the other. In this particular problem, each person knows only that the other person is in exactly the same interdependent relationship as he—and that the other is aware that he knows this. Given this limited information about one another, perhaps the wisest course for each to take would be to seek out a "solution" that is somehow prominent (what Schelling, 1960, has called the "focal point"). Thus, $1.00 is a more prominent solution than $0.73. Heads is more prominent than tails in the flip of a coin, and so forth. Of course, if you knew anything at all about the other person, this would greatly increase your chances of finding a prominent solution. If, for example, you thought he was a student, you might guess that he would write down a relatively small amount of money—$1.00, $10.00, or $100.00 perhaps, but certainly not $1000.00. On the other hand, if you were a millionaire playing with Howard Hughes in a game conducted by Aristotle Onassis, $1000 or even $1 million might emerge as a more prominent solution.

Using additional information about the other person. What we have done so far is to take the "minimal social situation" and modify it by letting each of our two people know that there is another with whom he is interdependent in a particular kind of way. Let us now further enrich and complicate this situation by systematically introducing new information about the other person. The following example is based upon a study conducted by Arlene F. Frank and

Jeffrey Z. Rubin (1975). Suppose that you and the stranger are once again seated in separate rooms without any means of communication. On the table in front of each of you is a pencil and a piece of paper, on which six circles have been drawn in a horizontal row. The circles are of equal size and are spaced evenly apart. Your task is to put a check mark in *one* of the six circles. If both of you check the same circle, you will each win some identical (but hypothetical) sum of money. But if you and the other person check different circles, neither of you will win anything. Let us suppose that you are a native-born American who reads from left to right; therefore (other things being equal), you have a natural preference for the extreme left circle.

If I were to tell you that the stranger was also an American, you might readily assume that he had the same left preference and thus check off the extreme left circle. But suppose I informed you that the stranger came from a Middle Eastern country (where words are written from right to left). Then you could assume that he would have a preference for the extreme right circle and simply pick that one. Fine! But wait a minute. Does *he* know that *you* are an American? If so, he might expect you to choose *left,* and so he would do likewise—despite his own inclinations—in order to coordinate with you. Then you would both lose, although each had been trying to accede to the other's inclinations.

To go one step further, suppose that before making your choice, I told you your partner's preference and told him yours (and informed you of this). Now your partner knows that you prefer the extreme left circle, but he does *not* know that you are aware of his preference for the extreme right. What would you do? Probably you would stick with your initial preference. After all, if he knows your preference (and you are aware of this), but he does not know that you are aware of his preference, it will probably be incumbent upon *him* to change his preference to match yours. However, if each of you knows not only the other's preference, but also that the other person is aware that you know, you would both be in a quandary again about what to choose.

Knowing the other too well may hinder coordination. In sum, perfect knowledge about the other (and his knowledge about you) may not facilitate a coordinated solution; to the contrary, it may hinder progress. Recall the example of my wife and I trying to decide how to spend Friday evening. She wanted to see a play, while I wanted to see a movie, and we were each aware of the other's preference. Given this state of knowledge, as well as our shared desire to spend the evening together, it was difficult to make a decision. If only my wife had not known that I wanted to see a movie, yet had known that I was aware of her desire to see a play (or vice versa), we might have easily settled on a course of action and been relatively satisfied. The one who was ignorant of the other's choice would "stay," while the one who knew would "change." However, we each knew the other's choice and were aware that we both wanted to do whatever the other preferred. It was extremely important for us to please each other. Therefore, how could I know that when my wife said that seeing a movie was fine with her, she really meant it? Perhaps she only said it in order to please me. If only I had been ignorant of her desire to please me, I could have accepted her offer to go to the movie at face value and been pleased with our solution. And if only I had not been so intent on trying to please her, I might not have invested so much energy in trying to determine what she "really" wanted to do. But such is life!

People are forever trying to "get inside one another's heads"—to take the other person's perspective in order to coordinate behavior. A humorous aspect of such role-taking is presented in the Jewish folklore of Eastern Europe as, for example, in the tragicomic stories of the ghetto community of Chelm. One of the "wise men of Chelm," while visiting the big city, wrote home to his wife:

Please send me your slippers. I say send me your slippers because I really want my slippers. But if I had written "Please send me my slippers" then you would have read "my slippers" and you would have sent me your slippers. But I do not want your slippers, I want my slippers. And that is why I write and ask you to please send me your slippers.

Divergent Interest Coordination

The Aalsmeer Flower Auction. For a study of coordination of divergent interests in a natural setting, one would be hard-pressed to find a more colorful example than a Dutch flower auction. In the small town of Aalsmeer, the preparation begins at night, as barges arrayed with the most amazing concentration of color and fragrance float down the canals into the village. Early the next morning, the buyers assemble in a large sales room, each with an assigned and numbered seat that is equipped with a signal button. The flowers are wheeled in before the buyers in huge lots. As each lot number and a description of the flowers is announced, the auctioneer sets in motion a large clock-like meter, which starts ticking down the price of the flowers: "100 guilders, 95, 90, 85." Suddenly the meter stops, and the result flashes on a board: Buyer number 16 has pressed his button to stop the clock at 85 guilders, and so the lot is now his. The next lot is then brought forth, and the auction continues. The whole proceeding takes place rather quickly so that a large number of flowers can be shipped off early in the morning for sale to the public.

Imagine that you are a merchant bidding for flowers at the Aalsmeer auction. A cart full of especially attractive flowers has just been
wheeled in. You would like to buy this lot, since you know that the
sale of these flowers will bring you a handsome profit, and you suspect that the other bidders feel very much as you do. The meter
begins ticking down the price of the flowers. How long should you
wait before stopping the clock? The longer you wait, while the meter
lowers the purchase price of the lot, the greater will be your potential profit when the flowers are sold at retail later in the day. However, the longer you wait, the greater will be the chance that another
bidder will stop the meter and buy the flowers instead. What you
need to do, therefore, is to try to stop the meter just a few guilders
ahead of anyone else. However, other buyers may be watching you,
trying to figure out when you will make your bid, so that they can bid
just a moment earlier. You may decide to stage something of an act—
pretending to have no real interest in a given lot of flowers—until
you are ready to make your move. But perhaps other buyers seem
disinterested also—and perhaps they are also play-acting for your
benefit.

Of course, the buyers at the Aalsmeer flower auction may not
always engage in this sort of strategic reasoning and behavior. They
probably meet each other on a daily or weekly basis, know each
other quite well, and know what each is likely to bid; therefore, they
may not try to disguise their intentions by bluffing. Moreover, since
the buyers are aware that many lots of flowers are to be auctioned off,
they may believe that even if they don't get a particularly desirable
lot, they can probably get another one that is almost as good at a
reasonably good price; therefore, they may not bother to try to figure
out what the other buyers are going to bid. Trying to outfox others at
an auction may be more likely to occur when the bidders know little
or nothing about one another and when they are vying for a single,
highly coveted item such as a rare stamp, an unusual antique, or any
unique acquisition (Roby and Rubin, 1973; Rubin, Greller, and
Roby, 1974).

Comparing Convergent and Divergent Interest Coordination. Let us
now examine some of the points of similarity and difference between
problems of convergent and divergent interest coordination. Both
require the use of complex chains of interpersonal reasoning that are
fundamentally alike. In trying to decide how to act, one must first try
to take into account the other's expected behavior, his expectations
of your behavior, and so forth. Then each must correctly coordinate
his own behavior with his guess about the other's. Convergent and
divergent problems differ, however, in the purposes for which these

guesses are made. In the former, interpersonal information is used in order to reach a solution that is mutually beneficial; if you make a mistake, *everybody* loses. In the latter, information is used for the purpose of obtaining a competitive advantage; if you make a mistake, *you* lose!

To successfully outwit the other bidders at an auction, one must first figure out what the highest other bid is likely to be and then bid just more than that oneself. If your judgment is incorrect, you stand to lose in one of two ways: either you fail to get the object you seek (if you bid too little) or you end up paying more for it than you really had to (if you bid too much).

As the Democratic primaries were drawing to a close in the late spring of 1972, four Democratic senators—McGovern, Muskie, Humphrey, and Jackson—were still in contention. Senator McGovern was building up a commanding lead, and it appeared increasingly probable that he would have the support of a majority of the delegates by convention time. Among his rivals, there appear to have been two prominent goals: to win the nomination or, failing that, to obtain a position of prestige and influence within the party. Think about the dilemma facing Senator Muskie during the late California primary: At what strategic point should he concede and throw his support to McGovern? To do so too early would mean giving up any chance of winning the nomination as well as any possible bargaining power with McGovern. To do so too late would mean that all or most of the other candidates would have already done so; McGovern's candidacy would be assured and Muskie's endorsement would have little value and gain him little bargaining power.

Finally, recall the example of the four businessmen "fighting" over the luncheon check. In trying to decide how many times to offer to pick up the tab, so that he does it one time less than the next guy, each man must first make a shrewd guess about the probable behavior of the other three. Up to this point, it can be seen that the problem is somewhat similar to that which confronts the participants in a convergent coordination task: each wants to have an accurate understanding of the other. However, each person's guess about the other's probable behavior is then used not for mutual, but for individual, advantage. Each businessman, in effect, said to himself: "In order to solve this problem, I must estimate how many times each of my colleagues (none of whom really wants to pay the bill) will offer to pay. Then I will try to coordinate my actions with theirs so that I avoid two possible mistakes: the Scylla of offering to pick up the tab *too often,* in which case I'll get stuck, and the Charybdis of *not offering often enough*—in which case I may be seen as cheap by the others. So I should offer to pay exactly one time less than the man whom I believe will make the greatest number of offers."

In some instances it is neither knowledge alone nor ignorance alone, but the coupling of one person's knowledge with the
other person's ignorance that makes convergent interest coordination
problems relatively easy to solve. My ignorance of your preference,
coupled with your knowledge of my preference (and your awareness
of my ignorance) can result in a mutually beneficial, coordinated
solution: I stick with my preference, while you change your choice
accordingly. He who is ignorant "stays," while he who knows
"changes." Does this "ignorance-stay, knowledge-change" rule
apply to divergent coordination? The answer is no, for the following
reason: If our interests are divergent, and I am ignorant of your preference while you know mine, you would surely win and I would
surely lose. You would be able to exploit your knowledge and my ignorance to your competitive advantage. Similarly, in order to be able
to outwit you, I would have to begin with some knowledge (or at
least a good guess) about your preference.

Of course, one person could *pretend* to be ignorant of the other's
preference, in order to gain a strategic advantage in the relationship.
Suppose you and another driver are approaching an unmarked intersection at right angles, each apparently wanting to cross first. How
might you manage to prevail in this conflict of interest? One possibility would be for you to adopt a strategy of staring straight ahead into
space, thereby communicating your total unawareness of his desire
to cross the intersection first—and even your ignorance of his very
existence. Assuming that he has good eyesight and can see that you
"don't see him" (which is untrue, of course, but hopefully he doesn't
know that), your "unawareness," coupled with his knowledge of this,
compels him to cede the right of way. What you have done, in
Thomas Schelling's (1960) language, has been to "bind" (irrevocably
commit) yourself to a course of action, thereby shifting the locus of
control over a possible collision from your shoulders to his. Note,
however, that if the other driver even suspects that you are only pretending, he is far less likely to yield (Rubin, Steinberg, and Gerrein,
1974).

Mixed-Motive Relationships:
Coordinating Convergent and Divergent Interests
Although many relationships exist in which the parties' interests are
either purely convergent or divergent, the most common interdependent situations are those that contain both convergent and divergent
interests. These situations are called "mixed-motive" since the parties are motivated both to cooperate and to compete.

Many relationships that appear, at first glance, to be examples of
pure divergent interests are, in fact, mixed-motive relationships—

they contain convergent interests as well. The two drivers racing to be the first to cross the intersection appear to be in a purely competitive relationship. Yet, although they want to beat each other, they also share a common interest in getting across the intersection safely and thus avoiding a collision. Similarly, in the event described earlier, my colleagues and I appeared to have purely divergent interests with respect to our salaries (the larger my raise, the smaller theirs would be, the chairman argued). Our interests would also be convergent to the extent that we might collectively urge the administration to increase the departmental budget, or to the extent that we might use one professor's raise to try to extract raises for the others.

Minimizing Divergence through Redefinition. Under some circumstances, a relationship that is characterized by divergent interests can be redefined as a convergent one. Consider the behavior of two boys in a badminton game, as observed so sensitively by the psychologist, Max Wertheimer. The 12-year-old boy (we'll call him Johnny) was obviously much more skilled than the 10-year-old (Billy), and was defeating him in game after game. Billy finally threw down his racket and said that he would not play anymore. Johnny was puzzled and a bit angry. He had enjoyed the game and especially the winning. Billy had enjoyed playing at first, but he did not like being beaten over and over again. Johnny tried to persuade Billy to continue the game, for without Billy he could not play and, thus, could not win. Suddenly he thought of a solution: "I have an idea—let us now play this way: Let's see how long we can keep the bird going between us, and count how many times it goes back and forth without falling. What score could we make? Do you think we could make it ten or twenty?" Billy agreed readily, and so they played the game that way. Billy enjoyed it more, of course, and so did Johnny—for apparently he realized that beating the younger boy at a game at which Billy was unskilled was not really such a rewarding experience. In fact, what had happened was that both boys had redefined a divergent interest situation as a convergent one (Wertheimer, 1945).

In many respects our interaction with others day in and day out can be viewed as a game in which we have both convergent and divergent interests. In Chapter 4 we briefly discussed social exchange theory as a way of analyzing interpersonal attraction and rejection. Let us see how this theory applies to mixed-motive relationships.

Social Exchange Theory

The social exchange approach in social psychology originated in economic analysis and game theory (von Neumann and Morgenstern,

1944). Although it has been presented in various forms (for example, Blau, 1964; Homans, 1961; Schelling, 1960), our approach is the one proposed by John Thibaut and Harold Kelley (1959). Thibaut and Kelley began by examining the limited social interaction of two people and later extended their analysis to more complex interaction in larger groups. The social exchange relationship is often represented in matrix form, as in Figure 5.1, which depicts the exchange relationship between a husband and a wife on a Sunday afternoon. Each has five possible activities in which he or she may engage. Clearly, they have both divergent and convergent interests. The satisfaction or dissatisfaction that each receives is a function of the combination of what they both do. (The wife's costs and rewards are above the diagonals, and the husband's are below.) Note that the wife would most enjoy going with her husband to the museum (+10). The husband would not like to go to the museum at all (−5), but, if he does go, he would rather go with his wife than alone (the other cells in that row show −8). What does the husband want to do? He really

	Wife's Possible Activities				
Husband's Possible Activities	Go to museum	Read Sunday newspaper	Go bicycling	Visit Aunt Suzie	Write article
Go to museum	+10 / −5	−2 / −8	+4 / −8	+4 / −8	+5 / −8
Read Sunday newspaper	−5 / +4	+6 / +3	−3 / +4	+4 / +4	+7 / +4
Go bicycling	−5 / +7	−5 / +7	+8 / +5	+4 / +3	+5 / +7
Visit Aunt Suzie	−5 / −5	−5 / −5	−5 / −5	+9 / −2	+5 / −5
Play squash	−5 / +10	+1 / +10	−5 / +10	+4 / +10	+5 / +10

Figure 5.1
A social exchange analysis of a husband's and wife's activities on a Sunday afternoon. In each box, the value above the diagonal represents the wife's costs or rewards, and the value below the diagonal represents the husband's. The wife prefers most of all to go to the museum with her husband, while he prefers most of all to play squash—regardless of what she does.

wants to play squash (+10); furthermore, he wants to play no matter what his wife does (the other cells in that row also show +10). Although the wife's first choice is to go to the museum with her husband, she would rather do anything with him than by herself. But playing squash is not available as an alternative to her (since she doesn't even belong to the squash club), so, in all likelihood, the husband will spend the afternoon playing squash and the wife will do some more work on an article she is writing—the most attractive activity in that row (+5).

Social exchange theory provides a useful conceptual scheme for analyzing a variety of social interaction phenomena. A matrix analysis is, of course, not without its limitations. For example, it is often difficult to determine the values that should be assigned to the cells; moreover, only a few activities can be included in a simple matrix. Obviously, we did not deal with the possibility of the husband nagging his wife or of being inconsiderate to her at a later time if she refuses to let him play squash. Nevertheless, analyzing social interaction in terms of mutual rewards and costs has proved to be very useful. In fact, many of the convergent and divergent relationships we have discussed could be examined in the matrix analysis of social exchange theory. In Chapter 4 we pointed out that the maintenance of a social relationship depends upon how an individual evaluates its potential outcomes, costs and rewards, and the probability of attaining these in view of the other person's costs and rewards. We can now see that in the badminton game, Billy had examined his potential gains and losses and decided to break off the relationship, until Johnny cleverly redefined the values in their matrix.

The Prisoner's Dilemma Game:
A Paradigm for Mixed-Motive Problem-solving
Let us now apply the exchange analysis of costs and rewards to a research problem that has captured the imagination of large numbers of social psychologists—the Prisoner's Dilemma. Imagine that you and an incommunicado stranger are seated in separate rooms. In front of each of you are two buttons, one black and the other red. Your task is simply to push *one* of these buttons. Depending upon the choices made by both you and the other person, you will each win or lose an amount of money, as follows: If you both push black, you will each win $1.00; if you both push red, you will each lose $1.00; and if one pushes red while the other pushes black, the one who pressed the red button will win $2.00 while the one who pressed the black button will lose $2.00. The amounts of money you and the other person can win or lose, depending upon your combined choices, are summarized in Figure 5.2.

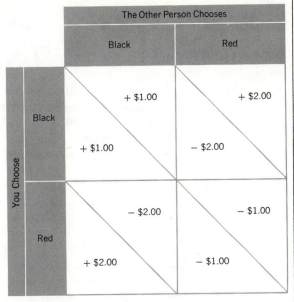

Figure 5.2
Black-red problem. *The
number in the lower
left-hand corner of each
box is the amount of
money you can win or
lose by choosing black
or red. The number in
the upper right-hand
corner of each box is the
amount of money your
partner can win or lose
by choosing black or
red.*

When confronted with this problem, many people are inclined to
choose red, perhaps reasoning as follows: "Since I don't know anything about the other person, I don't know whether he would be
more likely to choose red or black. What I should do, therefore, is to
figure out what choice to make if he pushes black and what to do if
he chooses red. Let's see. If he pushes his black button, I can make
more by choosing red ($2.00) than by choosing black (only $1.00);
therefore, I should push my red button. If, on the other hand, he
pushes his red button, I'm going to lose regardless of what I
choose—but I will lose less by choosing red (−$1.00) than by choos-
ing black (−$2.00); therefore, I should push my red button in this
case as well. In other words, regardless of what the other person
does, I should choose red because I stand both to make the most (if
he presses black) and lose the least (if he presses red)."

Sound logic, indeed! The only problem is that the other person
may have reasoned in exactly the same way—in which case, you will
each choose red and lose $1.00, whereas you could have each chosen
black and won $1.00!

This particular situation is called the "Prisoner's Dilemma"
game, because of the example originally used by R. Duncan Luce
and Howard Raiffa (1957) to illustrate this type of coordination problem. In their example, which is not too far afield from some real-life
situations, two burglary suspects are apprehended together by the
police. Since the evidence is not sufficient to convict either one, the
police interrogators devise a clever stratagem. One of the suspects is
isolated in a room and told: "Look. We know we don't have the evi-

dence to convict you, but we are questioning your partner. We will make it worth his while to squeal on you, and we believe he will. If so, you will get four years for burglary and he'll get off scot-free. But you can make it a bit easier on yourself by telling on your partner; you will then get a reduced sentence for turning state's evidence—only eighteen months. If your partner doesn't tell on you, we will still get you on a vagrancy charge, which will keep you in jail for six months. And even then, it would be worth your while to squeal on him, for then we would let you free." The prisoner correctly guesses that his partner has been told the same thing. The payoff matrix is presented in Figure 5.3.

Assuming that the prisoners cannot communicate with each other, and that neither one would do anything to the other in retaliation afterward, what would you do in this situation? Try this problem out with a friend and see how he or she would choose. As in the black-red problem, you will find that if you and your friend are only interested in saving your own skin and in getting the best possible deal for yourself, you will probably both choose to squeal and thus end up with 18 months in jail, whereas you could have gotten off with six.

Of course, the possibility that you both end up in the reduced sentence cell of the matrix in the Prisoner's Dilemma, as well as in the −$1.00 cell of the black-red game, is due in part to your inability to communicate and work out a convergent arrangement. Communication is obviously important. (In the badminton game, if Billy and Johnny had become so angry that they could not speak to one another, Johnny could never have conveyed his plan for a convergent relationship.) It should be stressed, though, that communication is meaningless without mutual trust. If the two prisoners had met and were suspicious of each other, then a mutual agreement to remain silent still might not be honored when they were separated again. Each might suspect that the other was using him to get off free. When there is communication without trust, we try all sorts of stratagems to mislead the other person.

Consider, for example, the old parable about the two competing merchants (call them A and B) who meet at the train station one day. A turns to B and inquires where he is going, to which B replies "To Minsk." After some thought, A retorts: "You say you are going to Minsk in order to make me think that you are going to Pinsk, but I know you are *really* going to Minsk. Do you think you can fool me?" Notice that A has a choice in this situation. He has the option of trusting B and simply accepting his reply ("to Minsk") at face value. But, instead of this, he appears to proceed from the assumption that B is untrustworthy and out to fool him. Paradoxically, through this double-think process, A ends up by accepting B's statement as fact

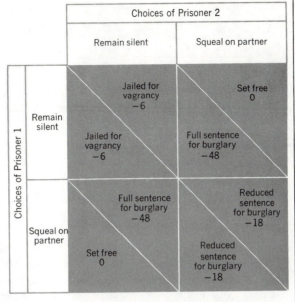

Figure 5.3
Prisoner's Dilemma.
Here are the jail sentences for each of two burglars, depending upon whether each remains silent or testifies against his partner.

after all. Question: By what path of reasoning could B best outwit A?

A participant in a mixed-motive relationship has a choice not unlike that confronting A. He can view the relationship as one of convergent interests, in which case he should behave cooperatively (while expecting the other person to do the same). Or he can view the relationship as one of divergent interests, in which case he should attempt to outwit and exploit the other person. Whether he decides to view the relationship as one of convergence or divergence depends upon both how much he *trusts* the other person to behave cooperatively and how much he *can be trusted* to behave cooperatively himself. Two hostile nations that can decide either to limit their arms production to an agreed upon level or to compete with each other for military superiority are in very much this sort of situation.

Factors That Affect Cooperation and Competition in the Prisoner's Dilemma

Mixed-motive games, particularly the Prisoner's Dilemma, have given rise to hundreds of experiments in the past decade—largely, we suspect, because of the intrinsic interest, importance, and prevalence of relationships that contain a mixture of cooperative and competitive motives. This extensive research literature has been reviewed in Rubin and Brown (1975). Let us now look at a few of the factors that affect the degree of cooperation.

1. *Number of interactions.* As you might expect, when pairs of

Turn	Person A		Person B	
	Choice	Outcome	Choice	Outcome
1	Black	+1	Black	+1
2	Black	+1	Black	+1
3	Black	+1	Black	+1
4	Red	+2	Black	−2
5	Red	−1	Red	−1
6	Red	−1	Red	−1
7	Red	−1	Red	−1
8	Black	−2	Red	+2
9	Red	+2	Black	−2
10	Red	−1	Red	−1

Figure 5.4
Hypothetical choices in the Prisoner's Dilemma game (black-red version). *The two players typically begin the game cooperatively (black-black). Eventually one person (A) defects, and then both compete and miscoordinate to their mutual disadvantage.*

strangers are asked to play the black-red version of the Prisoner's Dilemma game just once, they tend to act less cooperatively than when they play the game repeatedly. Why? Because when playing just once, each person knows that he cannot be held accountable for his future behavior and is therefore more willing to attempt to exploit the other (by choosing red). Both players thus tend to choose red, and both lose.

When the Prisoner's Dilemma game is played over a series of turns, and both players are told the other's choice at the end of each turn, there is more likely to be cooperation, although it may eventually deteriorate. In general, social psychologists have observed a pattern of choice behavior in games with multiple turns like the hypothetical one depicted in Figure 5.4.

Assuming that neither Person A nor Person B begins with prior information about the other or how to act toward him, our two players might start by choosing black on their first turn. In this way, each shows that he is willing to trust the other and to be trustworthy himself; the result is a set of outcomes (+1, +1) that is mutually and equally beneficial. Once A and B have established this kind of cooperative relationship, they typically maintain it for quite some time. After a while, however, one person, A (turn 4 in our diagram), may decide to defect. The reasons for this defection are not completely clear. Perhaps A decided that B was an "idiot" who could be exploited readily and indefinitely; perhaps A simply became more greedy, rivalrous, or even just plain bored with so much cooperation. In any event, he defects, while poor B (totally unaware of A's decision) once again gives a trusting and cooperative response. As a result, A succeeds in exploiting B. On the following turn (5), things typically deteriorate further. A, in effect, says to himself: "It worked once. Why shouldn't it work again? And anyway, if B gets angry, he will surely choose red to protect himself. So I should choose red in either case." B, on the other hand, probably thinks: "That dirty, rotten S.O.B.! I can't afford to trust him anymore. I've got to choose red to protect myself against further exploitation." So both choose red, and both lose. For the next several turns, this mutually competitive pattern will probably continue, A hoping that B will slip back into a trusting black choice, and B remaining totally committed to defending himself against A's aggression. After a while, however, as the pair continues this costly, destructive course, losing money on every turn, one person (typically the one who defected in the first place) tries to return the relationship to its earlier, more prosperous state. Perhaps A thinks to himself: "Wow, did I make a mess of things! If it weren't for me and my errant ways, we'd still be riding the high road to mutual fortune. I've got to show B that I want to change. I will choose black." B, however, knows nothing of A's plan to reform, and so he continues to choose what he feels he must in order to protect himself—namely, red. The result (turn 8) is that A loses, while B inadvertently exploits A and wins. Now A may say to himself: "Things are hopeless. It's just not going to work. I've made an irreconcilable enemy of B. He's going to continue to defend himself. Therefore, I've got to defend myself as well. I'll choose red." B, meanwhile, is thinking: "Wow! A has finally seen the light. I'll choose black and everything will be okay again." So A chooses red, while B chooses black (turn 9), and the pair miscoordinates once again. And so, in this Kafkaesque way, A and B may continue—one person making a cooperative overture while the other behaves competitively (or defensively). Eventually what often happens is that the pair slips back into a pattern of mutually competitive, costly behavior (turn 10), locks into this pattern, and remains there.

Gloomy? Indeed it is! However, some pairs eventually manage to find a way out of this impasse. This happens when one person chooses black not once but at least *twice consecutively*, thereby indicating his willingness to trust the other and conveying his conviction that cooperation represents the only reasonable course of action. Such persistent attempts at cooperation by one person, especially after the pair has pursued a mutually destructive course of action, typically enable the pair to restore a cooperative relationship. And once restored, cooperation tends to continue.

2. *Initial orientation to the situation.* By varying the introduction to the Prisoner's Dilemma game, experimenters have elicited vastly different behaviors on the part of the two participants. When the players are told that they are in a competitive game and that their goal is to try to get a higher score than their partner (and that he will be doing the same thing), the participants almost invariably end up in the red-red square. However, when the situation is presented as a

cooperative game, in which each player is supposed to try to help the other beat the bank and to get the banker to pay out as much as possible, the players generally finish in the black-black square. And finally, when the game is presented as an individualistic endeavor, in which each player is supposed to try to get the highest score for himself (without regard for the other's winnings or losses), there is greater variability in behavior. However, the players typically end up in the red-red cell (with both of them losing) more often than in the black-black cell (Deutsch, 1958; Scodel et al., 1959).

3. *Personality predispositions.* Individual differences in personality are especially inclined to affect behavior in the Prisoner's Dilemma game when the players begin with an individualistic orientation. A person who is inherently suspicious of others, distrusting, or malicious is especially apt to make a red response. He expects his partner to be untrustworthy, and so he chooses competitively, causing his partner to do likewise; therefore, his own expectations are confirmed as a self-fulfilling prophecy. If both partners are open and trusting, however, a black-black response is much more probable (Deutsch, 1960; Loomis, 1959).

4. *Communication.* As we have mentioned, communication may help to reduce competition, so that the players can redefine the situation as a cooperative one. An explicit cooperative communication (for example, "I would like you to choose black. I intend to choose black. But if you continue to choose red, then I shall choose red also") will probably elicit a cooperative response (Deutsch, 1960; Loomis, 1959). But once distrust and hostility have been initiated, they are extremely difficult to change (Deutsch and Krauss, 1960; Scodel et al., 1959).

5. *Partner's strategy.* When the Prisoner's Dilemma game is played for a series of turns (as depicted in Figure 5.4), each choice becomes a form of communication. A black response is perceived as an intention to be cooperative; a red response is viewed as an intention to be competitive. A series of black responses may elicit cooperative responses in return, so that the more favorable black-black cell pattern is established. However, there is one danger. Sometimes a succession of cooperative responses is perceived as a sign of ignorance or naïveté, and so it invites exploitation. There is evidence that a more realistic strategy for eliciting cooperation from one's partner requires some form of matching—after one's partner chooses black once or twice, one should begin to reciprocate by choosing the same color as he did on the preceding turn. If your partner chooses red, retaliate with red on the next trial to show that you mean business. Turning the other cheek is often not the best strategy (Solomon, 1960; Meeker and Shure, 1969).

6. *Cultural factors and cooperation.* Cultural norms can influ-

COURTESY WILLIAM STEIG
FROM *THE LONELY ONES.*

IF YOU ARE GOOD-NATURED,
PEOPLE STEP ALL OVER YOU

*Figure 5.5
An unconditionally co-
operative strategy may
not lead to cooperation
from others.*

ence a person's cooperative or competitive orientation in a manner
that is very similar to one's personality predisposition. As the cultural anthropologist Margaret Mead demonstrated many years ago
(1937), some cultures encourage a cooperative, trusting orientation
toward people, while others foster competition, distrust, and hostility. We will illustrate the effects of culture in two settings—an Israeli
kibbutz and a Mexican community—using two different mixed-
motive games.

Cooperation and Competition among Kibbutzniks
The collective agricultural community in Israel (kibbutz) is one in
which a communal, cooperative orientation is explicitly emphasized.
Private property is minimal; by mutual agreement, property that has
been produced and is used by the community rightfully belongs to
the entire community. Competitiveness is considered antithetical to
a full and happy life. Children of the kibbutz are perceived as a valuable asset of the entire community; they are typically brought up in a
common children's section, and they sleep apart from their parents.
Private gifts of any real value that are received by individual kibbutzniks are supposed to be shared by the total kibbutz. This orientation, explicitly stated by leaders of the community, by teachers in
the kibbutz schools, and in the literature studied by kibbutzniks,

Figure 5.6
In an Israeli kibbutz, a cooperative ideology quite clearly governs everyday working relationships, but it may not carry over to their chess tournaments.

probably ought to foster a cooperative spirit in interpersonal relations (Weingarten, 1959).

The Prisoner's Dilemma in the Kibbutz. It might be expected, then, that the kibbutz youth, presented with a Prisoner's Dilemma game, would tend to end up in the black-black square almost immediately. Raven and Leff (1965) attempted to test this prediction with a group of young kibbutz residents who had just completed their last year of secondary school and were at a special retreat, receiving some additional orientation toward kibbutz life before beginning their military service. The entire setting probably ought to have encouraged cooperation.

The Prisoner's Dilemma game was played for points (which could later be exchanged for books) and with an individualistic orientation (each player was to try to get as many points for himself as possible). Further, each player was separated from his partner and did not even know who he was, so that privacy was assured. To the researchers' surprise, the kibbutzniks played a highly competitive game; overwhelmingly they chose the square that would give them maximal benefit at the expense of their partner. Furthermore, when one partner was "programmed" to behave in a consistently cooperative way, the paired kibbutznik responded by making competitive (exploitative) choices. So strong was the competitive orientation of the kibbutzniks that plans were abandoned for a comparative study of Israeli urban youth. (Interestingly, far more evidence of cooperation was found among American youths who were planning to spend several months in a kibbutz.)

It was difficult to understand why there would be such competitive behavior in a community that was ostensibly so cooperative. The researchers finally decided that the kibbutz youth had interpreted the Prisoner's Dilemma as a competitive game, such as chess, which is very popular in the kibbutz. There is no evidence that the cooperative spirit of life in the kibbutz carries over to a game of chess; indeed, it is entirely possible that there is even greater ritualized competition in certain well-defined activities in societies where everyday competition has been restricted. The researchers were somewhat reassured at a later time, after the purpose of the research had been explained to the young people. Unanimously, the youths decided that the money that had been earmarked to purchase the book prizes should be contributed to a fund for a farewell party—to be enjoyed by everyone.

The Madsen Cooperation Board. In a study comparing kibbutz and non-kibbutz children, conducted by Ariella Shapira and Millard Madsen (1969), rather different results were obtained using the Madsen Cooperation Board (pictured in Figure 5.7). The board is 18 inches square with an eyelet at each of the four corners. There is a metal cylinder in the center of the board with four strings attached to it, and each string goes through an eyelet. Four subjects, each seated at a corner, hold a string with which they can move the metal cylinder. A ball-point pen in the center of the cylinder records the movements of the cylinder on a piece of paper that covers the board.

The first stage of the study (trials 1–3) dealt with convergent goals. The four circles on the board, one between every two subjects, were numbered 1, 2, 3, and 4. The subjects, Israeli urban and kibbutz children, were told:

> *The aim of the game is for you to draw a line over the four circles within one minute. If you succeed in doing this, each one of you will get a prize. If you cover the four circles twice, everyone will get two prizes, and so on. But if you cover less than four circles no one will get a prize* [pp. 612–613].

Both the urban and kibbutz children succeeded in drawing smooth

Figure 5.7
Madsen Cooperation Board. *This is a device for studying cooperation and competition under conditions of convergent and convergent-divergent interests. In the Convergent Interests Condition, the four subjects were told that if they pulled the metal cylinder so that all four numbers were crossed, they would receive a prize. In the Convergent-Divergent Interests Condition, each subject was asked to write his name in a circle in front of him and was told that he would receive a prize each time the cylinder crossed his own circle (after Madsen, 1967).*

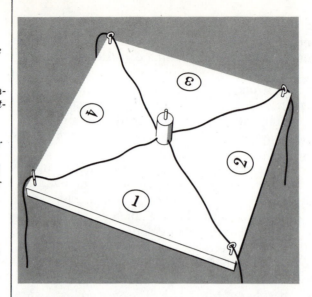

sets of lines going through the four circles with few wasted motions.

The second stage of the study (trials 4–6) dealt with a mixture of convergent and divergent interests. Each child wrote his name in a circle directly in front of him. The subjects were then told:

Now, when the pen draws a line across one of the circles, the child whose name is in the circle gets a prize. When it crosses David's circle, David gets a prize; when it crosses Ron's circle, Ron gets a prize, and so on. You will have one minute to play before I stop you [p. 613].

The kibbutz children performed this task as easily as they had the convergent one; in fact, they seem to have structured the task as a purely cooperative one, even though there was a possibility of competition. They said such things to one another as: "Okay, gang, let's go in turns" or "Let's help each other." They had decided on the order of turns before they even began the game. In contrast, the urban children behaved quite differently; they seemed to structure the task in terms of divergent interests—a four-way tug of war. Even though the prizes were of little value (candy, gum, small plastic charms), the urban children seemed to want to win them individually, at the expense of the others. As a result, they won very little. This occurred even though the urban children were aware of the bind in which they had been placed. They obviously did not enjoy the competition. Yet, once the task had been structured in this way, divergent interests seemed to prevail. Sometimes one child would suggest taking turns, but he was always refused by the others. If one child began to cooperate with a second, the other two would pull harder and return the game to competition.

These results seem to contradict the findings of the kibbutz Prisoner's Dilemma game. As mentioned earlier, one reason may be that the kibbutzniks viewed the Prisoner's Dilemma as a game in which the norms of cooperation did not apply. Also, in the Raven and Leff study, the subjects were allowed to make their choices in private, whereas in the Shapira and Madsen study, the subjects were face to face. Perhaps the kibbutz norms for cooperation are weaker in private, for, once the subjects came face to face, they decided that the prize money would be shared. Although the Prisoner's Dilemma subjects were older, there is evidence that cooperation among kibbutz children in the Madsen Board problem increases with age (Shapira, 1970).

Competition as a By-product of Urbanization
Among the kibbutz children, the norms for cooperation seem strong enough to structure a convergent-divergent task into a purely convergent one (as happened in the case of the young badminton players). There is also evidence, however, that a society's technological development (causing it to change from a relatively simple rural culture to a more complex urban society) tends to increase an individual's competitive orientation.

*Figure 5.8
In a rural area near
Lancaster, Pennsylvania, a group of Amish
people are cooperatively raising a barn.*

The anthropologist Oscar Lewis (1961) has observed such changes in Mexico. As the village of Tepoztlan was transformed from a quiet farm town into a busy international tourist center between 1943 and 1956, there were many other developments as well, including a marked change in child-rearing practices. In 1943 children were trained to be passive and submissive, but by 1956 they were not punished as much, and there was greater emphasis on achievement and individualism. Madsen (1967) found experimental support for Lewis's observation in his original study with the Madsen Cooperation Board. He compared rural poor and urban middle-class Mexican children. The rural Mexican children, like the kibbutz children, worked with the board cooperatively, graciously offering the first prize to the winner with *para tu* (for you). By contrast, the urban middle-class children tended to pull hard, emphasizing their competitiveness with *para mi* (for me). One urban child even pulled so hard that he cut his hand on the cord. The middle-class teacher, standing in the background, murmured approvingly, "This is the new Mexico."

INTERDEPENDENCE OF GOALS AND MEANS

One way in which an interdependent relationship can be analyzed, as we have pointed out, is in terms of the underlying coordination process. When two or more people engage in convergent interest coordination, their relationship may be described as one of *positive* interdependence. On the other hand, when the coordination process stems from divergent interests, the relationship is one of *negative* interdependence. And, as we have attempted to demonstrate, the nature of people's interdependence has important consequences for the strategic interaction that ensues.

In order to understand more fully the similarities and differences in our illustrations of interdependence, a second major distinction must be made—between interdependence with respect to *means* and interdependence with respect to *goals*. In other words, besides knowing whether people are positively or negatively interdependent, one needs to know whether it is with respect to means or goals.

Consider the following illustration of interdependence provided by Robert Woodworth (1925):

Two boys, between them, lift and carry a log which neither could move alone. You cannot speak of either boy as carrying half

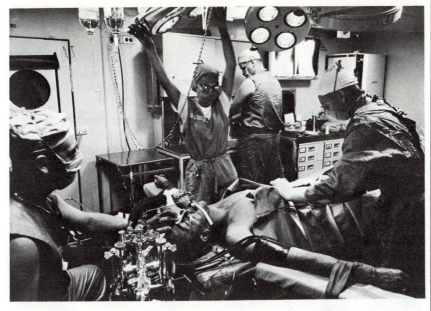

*Figure 5.9
The surgeon, anesthe-
tist, and surgical nurse
are interdependent with
respect to both means
and goals.*

*the log, in any concrete sense, for the log is not in halves. Nor can
you speak of either boy as half carrying the log, for there is no such
concrete fact as half-carrying the log. The two boys, coordinating
their efforts upon the log, perform a joint action and achieve a
result which is not divisible between the component members of
their elementary group. To insist that the pair of boys consists simply of two individuals is to commit an abstraction. It leaves out the
log. By acting together upon the same object, the individuals composing the group coordinate their behavior, and the total behavior
consequently possesses a unity analogous to that of a group of mus-
cles in a coordinated movement [p. 105].*

Presumably the two companions are moving toward some shared
goal—the log might provide fuel for a fire by which both could warm
themselves, or it might be used to build a cabin that both could
enjoy. There is thus *interdependence with respect to goals*—
achievement of the goal by one boy affects the satisfaction of the
other. There is also *interdependence with respect to means*—each
boy depends upon the other to help him achieve his goal. The interdependence in each case is positive (the boys' interests are convergent), since a gain for one is also a gain for the other.

Various Patterns of Interdependence of Means and Goals. Obviously, many group relationships are characterized not by positive,
but rather by negative interdependence (divergent interests) with respect to either goals, means, or both. And in other relationships there

		Goals		
		Positive interdependence	Independence	Negative interdependence
Means	Positive interdependence	Subgroup division of labor; joint discussion at next meeting. (A)	Subgroup division of labor; non-curved exam at next meeting. (D)	Subgroup division of labor; curved exam at next meeting. (G)
	Independence	Everyone does own reading (multiple copies); joint discussion at next meeting. (B)	Everyone does own reading (multiple copies); non-curved exam at next meeting. (E)	Everyone does own reading (multiple copies); curved exam at next meeting. (H)
	Negative interdependence	Everyone does own reading (limited copies); joint discussion at next meeting. (C)	Everyone does own reading (limited copies); non-curved exam at next meeting. (F)	Everyone does own reading (limited copies); curved exam at next meeting. (I)

Figure 5.10
Means-goals inter-dependence. Here are several options by which a graduate seminar in social psychology may prepare for its next meeting.

is positive or negative interdependence with respect to goals and *independence* (non-interdependence) with respect to means, or vice versa.

In order to better understand the variety of forms that interdependent relationships may assume, as well as their consequences (in terms of people's feelings and actions toward one another), it may be useful to examine the above distinctions in the context of a single example. Recall the illustration in which my students and I were discussing plans for the next meeting of our graduate seminar in social psychology. We agreed that each student would read five articles and that we would simply discuss them at the next meeting. To the extent that the class shared my desire for a fruitful discussion, they (we) were positively interdependent with respect to goals. However, if I had instructed them to prepare for an examination based on their reading, which would be graded on a "curve" (a relative basis), the students would have been negatively interdependent with respect to goals. Finally, if I had said that I would grade them on an absolute (rather than a relative) basis, then the students' goals would have been independent: one student's good grade would not affect another's chances of getting a good grade as well.

Continuing with the example of the graduate seminar, let's look at the issue of means interdependence. Although I had most of the articles the students were to read for the next class, many of them were too long to duplicate, and so some type of sharing arrangement was necessary. The students were, therefore, negatively interdependent with respect to means. If multiple copies had been available so that each student could have a complete set of all of the articles, the students would have been independent with respect to means. And finally, if a subgroup of the class had decided to prepare for the following class session by adopting a division of labor (in which, for example, one student would read articles 1 and 2, a second would read 3 and 4, and so forth, and each would make copies of their critiques for the others to study), this subgroup would have been positively interdependent with respect to means.

Cooperation and Competition Revisited

Each of the ways in which people are interdependent with respect to means, goals, or both has important consequences for the kind of relationship that emerges. Let us, therefore, address ourselves to two related questions: Under what circumstances will a *cooperative* relationship between people probably develop? And under what circumstances a *competitive* relationship? Although we have already discussed these questions in relation to mixed-motive coordination problems (such as the Prisoner's Dilemma game), let us now examine the terms "cooperation" and "competition" to see what they mean with respect to a more general analysis of means-goals interdependence.

Cooperation, Competition, and Goals Interdependence. Morton Deutsch (1949a, 1973) defines a purely cooperative situation as one in which "the goals of the participants are so linked that any participant can attain his goal if, and only if, the others with whom he is linked can attain their goals" (1973, p. 20). In a purely competitive situation, on the other hand, the goals are linked in such a way that one person can reach his goal only if the others do not. According to Deutsch (1973), "In a cooperative situation . . . everybody 'sinks or swims' together, while in the competitive situation if one swims, the other must sink" (p. 20). Notice that Deutsch defines cooperation and competition in terms of positive or negative *goal* interdependence. Although goal interdependence is obviously of primary importance in determining the cooperative or competitive nature of a relationship, we shall see that means interdependence is also important.

Cooperation and competition, writes Deutsch (1973), can be characterized according to several underlying, theoretical features: (1) In a cooperative relationship, Person A's movement toward his goal facilitates Person B's movement toward his goal; thus, there is little need for the two persons to duplicate each other's activities. My wife prepares the meat while I fix the salad, and both of us end up enjoying the meal. In a competitive relationship, on the other hand, A's successful actions reduce B's chances for success; therefore, each tries to cover the same ground as the other by imitating or outdoing him, and a division of labor is impossible. (2) In a cooperative relationship, A's movement toward his goal as a consequence of B's actions increases A's liking for B—a situation that is apt to lead to mutual trust, open communication, and a tendency for A to be receptive to B's attempts to engage him in activity that benefits B. In a competitive relationship, however, B's actions tend to retard A's progress toward his goal, and so A is apt to come to dislike and distrust B, and to resist any attempt on the part of B to induce him to do something that would benefit B.

From Deutsch's theoretical analysis, it can be seen that cooperation would be most likely to develop in a relationship where *both* goals and means are positively interdependent (Box A in Figure 5.10). In this situation, people are best able and most highly motivated to facilitate one another's progress. The two boys carrying a log toward a common goal exemplifies this type of relationship.

On Means Interdependence. Social psychologists have conducted a number of experiments that document the cooperative consequences of positive interdependence of goals and means. In one study (Thomas, 1957), groups of women employees of a large private utility company were given the task of constructing cardboard houses. To construct a house, five steps were necessary: tracing the pattern, cutting out the pattern, scoring the folding points with a knife, gluing the pieces together, and painting the house. In a condition of independence with respect to means, each subject performed all five operations herself; in a condition of high positive interdependence with respect to means, each subject performed two of the steps in a double assembly line. All of the subjects were told that they would be graded on a scale of "general work intelligence" according to their participation. Some, however, were told that they would receive an individual score based only on their own performance (they were thus independent with respect to goals), while others were told that the whole group would get the same score (they were thus positively interdependent with respect to goals). These two variations of goal-interdependence were each conducted under two conditions of means-interdependence, yielding four experimental conditions (which correspond to Boxes A, B, D, and E in Figure 5.10). As predicted by the experimenter, the more positive the interdependence with respect to either means or goals, the greater the concern shown by the women for the effects of their actions on others, and the higher their rate of production.

When Does Competition Increase Productivity? In another experiment (Deutsch, 1949b), the students in an introductory psychology course at a large university were divided into ten groups of five students each. These groups were first rated on their ability to solve a complex human relations problem, and from these ratings pairs of groups were matched according to the productivity of their discussion. By a random procedure, each of the two comparable groups in a pair was assigned to either of two experimental conditions—Cooperative or Competitive. During the class meetings, the groups were given puzzle problems ("tests of your ability to do clear, logical thinking") and human relations problems to solve. Each group in the Cooperative Condition was told that it would be rated as a group (by comparing it with other similar groups) according to the members' performance on these problems; grades for the psychology course would be awarded accordingly—each member of the group receiving the identical grade. The group members were thus positively interdependent with respect to the goal of getting a good grade, but negatively interdependent with respect to the other groups in the Cooperative Condition. By contrast, the groups in the Competitive Condition were told that their grades would be decided on an individual basis according to the contribution of each member. Each member of the group would be ranked with respect to the other members, so that only one person in the group could receive a top grade. As measured by ratings and questionnaires, members of those groups with a Cooperative orientation (as compared with those that were negatively interdependent with respect to goals) showed a greater awareness of their mutual interdependence and a greater coordination of effort. They also had greater motivation and seemed to enjoy their work more; they surpassed the Competitive groups in both the quality and quantity of work produced. They tended to pay closer attention to and to help one another, as well as to evaluate each other more positively.

At first glance, Deutsch's (1949b) findings appear to contradict the results of other studies showing that people are more highly motivated and productive in competitive (rather than cooperative) situations. One of the more interesting of these studies was conducted way back in 1898 by Norman Triplett (who is reputed to have been the *first* experimental social psychologist). Triplett observed that bicycle racers often achieved much faster times when they raced against others in direct competition rather than against the clock. Bringing this problem into the laboratory, he studied pairs of children, each of whom was asked to wind a fishing reel, which in turn pulled a flag. In one condition, the subjects were instructed to try to move their flag to an end point more rapidly than their opponent; in another condition, the subjects worked alone and were told to wind their fishing reel as quickly as they could. Triplett found that most of the children worked faster when competing with others than when alone.

Competition and means interdependence. One important difference between Deutsch's (1949b) study and Triplett's (1898) experiment is that in the latter case, the subjects were asked to work on a parallel task; although the competitive subjects were negatively interdependent with respect to goals, they were *independent* with respect to means (Box H in Figure 5.10). In Deutsch's experiment, the subjects were *positively interdependent* with respect to means, even when they were negatively interdependent with respect to goals; therefore, they could have benefited by sharing information and dividing their labor (Box G). Thus, the subjects' failure to cooperate in the Competitive Condition led to a failure in mutual assistance; because of their high interdependence in means, their failure to share information and work assumed greater importance in the lowering of their efficiency and morale.

The likelihood that people will develop a cooperative relationship depends upon the nature of their goals interdependence as well as their means interdependence. This point is illustrated dramatically in a study conducted by Raven and Eachus (1963). In this experiment, each member of a three-man group (a triad) was seated at one corner of a triangular board, as shown in Figure 5.11. Each subject had a set screw that he could turn to raise or lower his corner of the board. He also had in front of him a carpenter's spirit level that was perpendicular to his line of sight and parallel to the side opposite him. Readers familiar with carpentry will know that the carpenter's level consists of a glass tube filled with alcohol (spirits) and having an air bubble. The air bubble will rise toward whichever end of the tube is higher and will be centered only if the tube is exactly horizontal. A careful examination of the triangular board, as illustrated in Figure 5.11, will reveal why this apparatus is particularly useful in studying the issue of interdependence: none of the three subjects can do anything that will directly affect the centering of his own spirit level. If the right side of one person's level is higher than the left, it will remain that way, no matter how much he raises or lowers his corner of the board. However, the slightest turn of one set screw would affect the plane of the levels at the other two corners.

The subjects were thus positively interdependent with respect to means.

At the beginning of each of the four times (trials) that the game was played, the board was set with one side raised 1 inch, the second side 2 inches, and the third side 3 inches, so that none of the bubbles was centered. Twenty of the 40 experimental triads were told that their objective was to "see how fast the three of you can level the board." The subjects in this condition were told that if their group performed well in comparison with other similar groups—in terms of the total time required to make the board horizontal over all four trials—each member of their group would get a paperback book as a prize. These subjects were thus positively interdependent with respect to both means and goals (Box A in Figure 5.10). The other 20 triads were told that their objective was to "see which one of you can level his corner first." Only the fastest person in the group—in terms of total time taken on the four trials—would receive the prize. These subjects were thus positively interdependent with respect to means but negatively interdependent with respect to goals (Box G).

Figure 5.11
Raven and Eachus board problem. *A triangular board with set screws at the corners was used to study the effects of interdependence of means and goals. The subjects were instructed to center the bubbles in their spirit levels by raising or lowering their respective corners. In the arrangement depicted here, no subject can directly control the bubble in his own spirit level (after Raven and Eachus, 1963).*

As in the case of Deutsch's classroom study, the subjects in the Cooperative Condition of the Raven and Eachus experiment were more efficient in getting the board horizontal, showed more interest in their task, evaluated their team members more favorably, and demonstrated less hostility. Interestingly, the experimenters observed that the difference between the Cooperative and Competitive groups was greatest during the first of the four trials. By the fourth trial, the Competitive groups showed greater improvement than the Cooperative groups (in terms of the time required), though they were still less efficient. Interviews with the subjects afterward indicated that, as the experiment progressed, some members of the Competitive groups began to care less about winning individually and to care more about the group finishing the task quickly. Thus, it appears that a high degree of positive interdependence in means coupled with negative interdependence in goals can lead to a restructuring of the latter and ultimately to cooperative behavior; it is uncomfortable, after all, to compete with someone whose help you need in reaching your goal.

To summarize, cooperation is most apt to emerge when people are positively interdependent with respect to both means and goals. Such was the case in our example of the subgroup of graduate students who were working together to prepare for a joint discussion at the following class meeting (Box A in Figure 5.10). Assuming that goals interdependence is more important than means interdependence, cooperation is probably next most apt to occur when positive goals interdependence is coupled with independence of means. Accordingly, there would be less cooperation among the graduate students when each had all of the necessary reading materials, and therefore did not need one another's assistance, but who still shared the goal of having a fruitful class discussion (Box B). Similarly, so long as the students remained positively interdependent with respect to goals, they would probably resolve their negative means interdependence (limited copies of the articles) through some sharing arrangement and act cooperatively (Box C). This was also the case in the example of my wife and I trying to decide where to spend the evening. Even though we were negatively means interdependent (she preferred to see a play, while I wanted to see a movie), so long as we shared a common goal (spending the evening together) we were likely to work out a satisfactory solution.

Even when there is no longer any positive goals interdependence, cooperation will probably continue if people remain positively interdependent with respect to means. The subgroup of students preparing for class through a division of labor would probably develop a cooperative relationship even though they were studying for a non-curved examination (Box D). Indeed, as the research by

Raven and Eachus (1963) suggests, even if this examination were a competitive one (curved), cooperation might still occur since the subgroup's division of labor would help each student progress toward his goal, and it would be uncomfortable to compete against those whom you need (Box G).

If a cooperative relationship is most likely to come about in situations where people are positively interdependent with respect to goals and means, it stands to reason that *competition* is most probable in situations where there is negative interdependence with respect to both goals and means. Such was the case in the example of the graduate students who had only a limited number of copies of the articles, yet each had to read all of them in order to prepare for the competitive examination (Box I). Instead of working out some kind of sharing arrangement, as they would probably do if they were positively interdependent with respect to goals (Box C), the students would probably "hoard" their resources greedily—as each attempted to prevent the others from obtaining the information necessary to perform well on the exam. Thus, instead of trying to facilitate each other's progress, the students would probably go out of their way to hinder it, and the result could be mutual dislike, distrust, and even overt hostility.

Competition is also apt to develop in a relationship in which people are negatively interdependent with respect to goals, but independent with respect to means. Even when each graduate student had all of the necessary reading materials to prepare for the examination, the competitive nature of the exam might color their attitudes toward each other (Box H). They would probably be angry and mistrustful (although less overtly so than if they were negatively means interdependent), and therefore tend to act competitively.

INTERDEPENDENCE IN ESCAPE

Still another relationship in which competition is likely to emerge is one in which people are independent with respect to goals, but negatively interdependent with respect to means (Box F in Figure 5.10). This relationship is especially interesting because it reflects the many unfortunate, but real, situations in which people exhibit panic behavior. The infamous Cocoanut Grove fire (in which so many people helplessly died because they were jammed up against a door that opened in) and the Titanic disaster (in which an incredible number of passengers drowned because too many of them desperately wanted to get into the first available lifeboat) can be analyzed as relationships in which people were negatively interdependent with respect to means and independent with respect to goals.

In order to study the circumstances in which panic arises, a social psychologist (Mintz, 1951) conducted the following intriguing experiment. Groups of 15 to 21 subjects were given the task of pulling wooden cones out of a large bottle. Each subject was given a piece of string that was attached to a cone in the bottle; the neck of the bottle was large enough so that only one cone at a time could pass through. However, the simultaneous pulling of several strings resulted in traffic jams at the neck of the bottle; consequently, no cones could be pulled out. Mintz found that there were more traffic jams when high individual motivation was introduced—in the form of rewards for getting the cone out quickly and fines for not getting it out. Although the subjects were not instructed to compete, the high negative interdependence with respect to means led them to do so. The traffic jams became even worse when the experimenter increased the subjects' stress by having water flow into the bottom of the bottle and imposing additional fines on those subjects whose cones became wet. By contrast, when the experiment was conducted at a leisurely pace, and the subjects were allowed to discuss the situation among themselves, Mintz found that there were fewer traffic jams. Sufficient time and discussion permitted the subjects to coordinate their effort and thus reduce their negative means interdependence. The jamming was reduced even further when the situation was turned into a cooperative one by telling the subjects that their score as a group would be compared with that of other groups (Box C in Figure 5.10).

Thibaut and Kelley (1959), as well as Roger Brown (1965), have pointed out that panic situations contain many of the ingredients of a mixed-motive coordination game (like the Prisoner's Dilemma), in which the participants' interests are both convergent and divergent. Assuming that the individual wishes to escape as rapidly as possible (from the proverbial crowded theater in which someone has yelled "fire!"), it makes sense for him to rush the exit—but only if he expects everyone to take turns. However, if everybody rushes the exit, everybody loses, except perhaps for the very first few who beat the crowd. Thus, it makes more sense for the individual to wait his turn—but only if he expects everyone else to do the same. If he is mistaken in judging the behavior of the others—if they rush the exit while he patiently awaits his turn—he will end up being a nice guy, but also a fool, for everyone knows that nice guys finish last! The problem is that in matters of life or death nobody wants to risk finishing last, and, under stress, no one can be certain that a proper queuing arrangement will develop so that the last person may escape. Fire and ship drills may help to give that assurance. A culturally or formally defined ordering system is also helpful in this regard. The

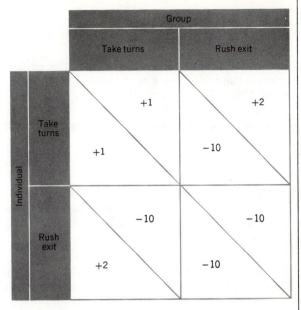

Figure 5.12
Matrix representation of a panic situation. *If both the individual and the group rush the exit, everybody loses. If one rushes the exit while the other waits, the latter is the big loser. However, when both the individual and the group take turns, everybody can win.*

slogan "women and children first" may be more than mere gallantry; it may be an assurance of survival for the greatest number.

CONFLICT
AND BARGAINING

Of the various examples of interdependence presented at the beginning of this chapter, several appear to be relationships in which *conflict* exists. By conflict, we mean any situation in which people are *negatively interdependent*—with respect to goals, means, or both. Thus, the relationships represented in Boxes C, F, G, H, and I in Figure 5.10 are all examples of conflict.

One of the curious and important characteristics of many conflicts is that the ease with which they are resolved is often a question of how they are viewed by their participants. Conflicts of means, as you might expect from our discussion of cooperation and competition, are generally easier to resolve than conflicts of goals. For example, a group of teachers who all want to raise the reading level of elementary-school children, but disagree about how to accomplish this, is far more likely to resolve its differences than another group that disagrees about the general objectives of an educational system. But even the latter group, to the extent that it can redefine the situation as one of means conflict with common goals ("C'mon, we all believe in the fundamental importance of imparting the skills of reading, writing, and arithmetic, or we wouldn't be teaching"), should be able to reduce its goals conflict and resolve its differences of opinion.

Earlier we mentioned the example of two drivers approaching an unmarked intersection. Although they clearly have a conflict of interest, this conflict can be defined as one either of goals or means. To the extent that they each want to cross the intersection before the other, their goals are negatively interdependent, and they may be inclined to act in a somewhat belligerent and infantile fashion—quite possibly at their own mutual expense. But, to the extent that they choose instead to view their goals as independent (crossing the intersection as quickly as possible) and to define the conflict as one of means (only one of them can cross the intersection first), they are far more likely to resolve the conflict amicably.

Obviously, conflicts can be resolved in a variety of ways. One person can simply attempt to overpower or eliminate his opponent; one person can flee the scene, thereby withdrawing completely from the conflict; or the two antagonists can try to settle their conflict by verbally making offers and counteroffers (bargaining) until they reach a mutually acceptable settlement. Of these possibilities, bargaining is perhaps the only one that represents a true resolution of conflict.

People bargain with one another all the time, and not just in smoke-filled conference rooms, used-car lots, or around the Paris peace table. Some everyday examples include: a husband and wife trying to decide where to spend their evening together; a family discussing plans for its summer vacation and convening a "family council" in order to resolve differences of opinion; a teacher and a student exchanging ideas about a grade; and of course the controversial procedure known as "plea bargaining" by which, in return for a guilty plea, a prosecuting attorney agrees to recommend a lenient sentence to the judge (thereby saving the state the time and expense of a trial, and assuring the defendant of a lesser sentence than he would probably get if he were tried and convicted).

The Characteristics of Bargaining. Because bargaining is such a pervasive phenomenon in our society, and because it flows so directly from an analysis of interdependence, it may be useful to analyze some of the characteristics of this process. The term "bargaining" typically refers to the process whereby parties attempt to settle what each shall give and take, or perform and receive, in some transaction between them. Such a definition, possibly because it is a definition, is much too general to be very useful. In their book on the social psychology of bargaining and negotiation, Rubin and Brown (1975) state that bargaining can occur if and only if a relationship has the following characteristics: (1) there are two or more parties, (2) they have a conflict of interest, (3) their relationship is a voluntary one, (4) the focus of activity is the resolution of one or more tangible or intangible issues, and (5) the parties interact through a series of offers and counteroffers.

When Does Bargaining Occur?

Let us now examine each of these characteristics as it relates to an understanding of interdependence. The requirement of at least two parties is obvious, for bargaining is a *relational* concept. It can take place not only between individuals, but between groups or nations as well. And, as we shall see, adding more parties to a bargaining relationship increases enormously the complexity of the process.

To say that bargainers have a conflict of interest simply means that bargaining is a *mixed-motive* relationship, not unlike the Prisoner's Dilemma game. The parties must be sufficiently competitive that bargaining is necessary and also sufficiently cooperative that bargaining is possible. Bargaining thus takes place within a range where interests are both positively and negatively interdependent. Because of the mixed-motive nature of the relationship, each party must attempt to chart a course between two kinds of risk: by being too competitive (that is, by driving too hard for an advantageous agreement), one party may drive the other from the relationship; but by being too cooperative (that is, by not driving hard enough), one party may provide the other with too favorable an outcome, thereby settling for less than was necessary. Harold Kelley (1966) has called this bargaining dilemma the "dilemma of goals."

For bargaining to occur, the relationship must be voluntary in *two* respects: each party must feel free to choose whether to enter into, and remain in, interaction with the other, and each must feel free to choose which of several possible demands to make and which, if any, to accept ultimately. Both kinds of choices must be available because they (and the fact that both parties are aware of their existence) enable each party to exert leverage in their relationship. Consider the example of a young man entering a used-car lot, hoping to sell his old car. One way in which he can attempt to pressure the used-car salesman into a favorable settlement is by systematically varying the size of his opening and subsequent offers. He might, for example, begin with a very high opening demand and then, after listening to the salesman make a series of counteroffers and concessions, make some concessions himself until an agreement is reached. However, if the salesman promptly pulls a "blue book" out of his vest pocket (before the young man has said anything) and announces the current market value of the car (the exact amount he is willing to pay), the young man's offers no longer have any meaning and thus there is no possibility of bargaining. The young man might also try to obtain a favorable agreement by threatening to leave the relationship (and perhaps go elsewhere) unless the salesman makes a more generous offer. Note, however, that for this strategy to be effective, there must be at least one meaningful alternative for the young man to choose or threaten to choose. If this is the *only* used-car lot within a 500-mile radius (and both parties know this), the young man is trapped in his relationship with the salesman, and there cannot be any real bargaining.

Most bargaining relationships focus on at least one tangible issue, such as the selling price of an old car, where a family will spend its vacation, the shape of the Paris peace table, or who should be nominated as vice-president at a major political party convention. At least as important as the tangible issues, however, are the less tangible ones that so often arise in the course of bargaining. People seem to have a general need to look good in the eyes of others: They want to be liked, respected, and admired, and they certainly do not want to appear foolish. The need to look good probably arises in all interdependent relationships, especially in relationships of conflict. For example, the young man who is trying to sell his old car is probably concerned not only with the amount of money he will receive, but also with his appearance in the eyes of significant others, such as the salesman and his own friends. Because he does not want to be viewed as "a sucker," the young man will probably act accordingly. Similarly, when two drivers "bargain" over who will go through an intersection first (the tangible issue), they are probably also thinking about an intangible issue (whoever goes second "eats crow," and therefore looks weak and foolish). To the extent that they define their conflict as one of negative interdependence of goals (rather than means), this intangible issue is apt to be of paramount importance.

The fact that bargaining takes place by means of a series of offers and counteroffers seems obvious, yet it is important. By making offers, each party tries to acquire information about the other's true preferences and intentions, while disclosing only selective information about his own. One party may try to provide the other with (possibly misleading) information about his own preferences while trying to use this offer to extract accurate information about the other's.

Notice the extreme complexity of the process of exchanging offers and counteroffers. In the coordination problems we discussed, the interpersonal reasoning process was difficult enough when two people were placed in separate rooms and were simply asked to make a simultaneous choice. Introduce these two people into a bargaining setting, where choices (or offers) are made not simultaneously but sequentially, and the exchange of information becomes far more complex. Suppose, for example, that I made you an initial offer, and you responded with a counteroffer; then I made a second offer. In order for you to figure out the true meaning of my second offer, you would have to be able to determine to what extent it was an accurate reflection of my true preferences and intentions (and not merely a response to my own first offer and/or to your response). Obviously, as the number of offers and counteroffers increases, the task of working through a complicated chain of reasoning becomes much more difficult. And if more than two people are participating in the bargaining process (as was the case at the four-party Paris peace talks to end the war in Vietnam), the problem of deciphering each party's true intentions becomes exceedingly complex, if not impossible.

Successful Bargaining

To recapitulate, bargaining is one of the ways in which people can resolve conflicts. In order for it to succeed (that is, for each party to feel he has achieved an agreement that is at least minimally satisfactory), the bargainers must be able to cope successfully with three central issues: first, they must be able to find out as much as possible about the other's true preferences, intentions, and expectations, while revealing only limited information about their own. Through this complex process of information exchange, the bargainers learn to coordinate their respective actions. Secondly, they must be able to recognize and deal with both the tangible and intangible issues. To the extent that a conflict of goals can be satisfactorily redefined as a conflict of means, it is possible that such intangible issues as the "loss of face" will fall away and that a settlement can be reached. Finally, the bargainers must learn to deal with the mixed-motive nature of their relationship; since they are both negatively and positively interdependent, they must compete *and* cooperate with each other in order to reach a mutually satisfactory agreement.

Taking the Role of the Other Can Be Nonproductive. Rubin and Brown (1975) estimate that social psychologists have conducted more than 1000 experiments in the field of bargaining during the decade beginning in the early 1960s. By way of concluding our discussion of bargaining, let us look at the findings of one important study carried out by Schenitzki (1962) and addressed to the possible pathology of a cooperative bargaining relationship. Schenitzki asked pairs of bargainers to take part in a bargaining game, in which the subjects were given information about their own range of profits (that is, what they would gain by reaching a particular agreement), but were told nothing about the other's. They could communicate with each other only by making written offers and counteroffers. Half of the experimental pairs were explicitly instructed to make every attempt to maximize their *joint* profits (Cooperative induction); the others were simply told to try to maximize their *own* profits (Individualistic induction). From our earlier discussion of interdependence, one might imagine that the Cooperative pairs (those who were positively interdependent with respect to goals) would reach a more mutually advantageous settlement than those who were Individualistic (independent with respect to goals). Instead, Schenitzki found exactly the opposite: Those with the Individualistic induction obtained a high joint profit more often than those with the Cooperative induction. In explanation, Kelley and Schenitzki (1972) pointed out that the cooperators may have been too busy trying to "get inside the head" of the other. Instead of beginning their bargaining session by making extreme initial offers (thereby communicating accurate information about the outcomes they most preferred), the bargainers with the Cooperative induction tried to be nice guys. They began by demanding less than the maximum share of the profits, thereby providing the other with misleading information about their own real preferences. In the absence of information about the other person's true needs and preferences, bargainers are most apt to reach an optimal agreement if they both focus on a clear and honest presentation of their own. For example, a bargainer who sets his opening offer below that which he really wants (perhaps because he likes the other, or because he doesn't want to appear greedy) often ends up with a less satisfactory agreement than he might otherwise have obtained by being more "selfish"; and if both bargainers act in this fashion, they are both likely to obtain less than a maximal division of resources. Thus, one of the potential pathologies of an otherwise beneficial, mutually cooperative relationship is the possibility that the cooperators, in their desire to "take the role of the other," may come to the wrong conclusion and therefore act upon incorrect expectations about the other's preferences and intentions, and the result may be mutually detrimental miscoordination.

Summary

By virtue of the fact that people are continuously engaged in social encounters, they are interdependent with others in a variety of complex and interesting ways. At the most fundamental level, interdependence requires the parties to a relationship to attempt to coordinate (accurately phase) their preferences, intentions, and expectations with those of others. Sometimes coordination occurs implicitly, as when two persons who are speaking to each other adjust their tone of voice, articulation, and interpersonal distance without being aware of doing so. At least as often, however, coordination emerges from people's explicit awareness of their interdependence and their deliberate attempts to get "inside the head" of one another.

Three fundamentally different types of coordination may be distinguished, depending upon whether convergent (common) interests, divergent (antagonistic) interests, or a mixture of both are at issue. The most prevalent (and perhaps the most interesting) interdependent situations are those that contain both convergent and divergent interests; these situations are called "mixed-motive" since the parties are motivated both to cooperate and compete. A particularly useful and influential tool to study mixed-motive relationships is the Prisoner's Dilemma game, a paradigm in which each of two persons must choose whether to trust the other and whether to be trustworthy himself. Each person can view the relationship (and the problem of coordination) as one of convergent interests, in which case he will probably behave cooperatively while expecting the other person to do the same. Or he can view the relationship as one of divergent interests, in which case he will probably try to outwit and exploit the other person.

In addition to knowing whether a relationship is one of convergent or divergent interests, it is necessary to understand the extent to which the participants are interdependent with respect to means, goals, or both. Goals interdependence exists when two or more persons have a relationship in which one person's attainment of his goal affects the other's chances of reaching his goal. Similarly, means interdependence exists when the means that one person needs in order to reach his goal affect the means available to the other. Relationships may thus be characterized according to the participants' interdependence with respect to means and/or goals, and the extent to which this interdependence is positive (based on convergent interests) or negative (based on divergent interests).

Social psychological research has found that a cooperative relationship is most likely to develop between two people when they are positively interdependent with respect to *both* goals and means. Cooperation may also emerge when positive goals interdependence is coupled with independence, or even negative interdependence, of means. Indeed, even when there is no longer any positive goals interdependence, cooperation will probably still continue if people remain positively interdependent with respect to means. Conversely, a competitive relationship is most likely to develop between two people who are negatively interdependent with respect to both goals and means and, to a lesser extent, between people who are either negatively goals interdependent but independent with respect to means, or negatively means interdependent but independent with respect to goals.

Whenever a relationship is characterized by negative interdependence of goals, means, or both, a state of conflict exists. Conflicts may be resolved in a variety of ways, including: redefining the conflict by the participants, attempting to overpower or eliminate one's opponent, fleeing the scene, or bargaining. The last technique, bargaining, represents perhaps the only true resolution of conflict; it has five defining characteristics: First, there must be at least two parties. Second, each party has both convergent and divergent interests with respect to one or more different issues. Third, the relationship is a voluntary one, in that each party can choose which of several possible demands to make, which (if any) to accept, and how long to remain in interaction with the other. Fourth, bargaining consists of resolving one or more tangible or intangible issues among the parties or their representatives. Finally, bargaining typically includes the presentation of demands or proposals by one party, evaluation of these by the other, followed by concessions and counterproposals.

Now that we have examined the various ways in which people are interdependent, as well as some of the consequences of interdependence for the kinds of relationships that emerge, several questions arise: What are the implications of interdependence for behavior? Granted that there is an interdependent relationship, how do people go about doing things to and with one another, that is, how is *influence* exerted? What influence techniques do people typically employ in different situations? How do these techniques compare with one another, and what are their immediate and secondary consequences? How can the effectiveness of social influence be enhanced? Chapter 6 will address itself to these issues.

SIX INTERPERSONAL INFLUENCE AND SOCIAL POWER

Power, Influence, and Change
Social Dependence and Social Influence
The Importance of Surveillance
Positive and Negative Influence

The Bases of Social Power
Informational Power—Socially Independent Influence
Reward and Coercive Power—Socially Dependent
    Influence, Surveillance Important
Expert, Referent, and Legitimate Power—Socially
    Dependent Influence, Surveillance Unimportant

Comparing Bases of Power
Coercion-Reward, Expert, and Referent Power
Legitimate and Coercive Power
Expert and Referent Power
Informational and Expert Power

Secondary Effects of Social Influence
New Perceptions following Social Influence
One Power Base Affects Another
Dissonance Reduction and Attributions following
    Social Influence

Enhancing Social Influence
Ecological Manipulation
Guilt-Arousal, Obligation, and Influence
Influence by Gradations: The Foot-in-the-Door
    Technique

199

¹ The *lira* (plural *lirot*) is the basic unit of Israeli currency.

Dear Mr. Customs Officer:

1. *I can well understand your reasoning in assessing 42 lirot* [1] *for the 14 ladies' slips I ordered from abroad. Obviously you must have thought that I planned to sell these for profit. How could you have known that I have three marriageable daughters? Please consider the situation of my daughters so that I can marry them off as befits them. The hope of three girls lies in Haifa port. . . . Ask your wife how many slips she has in her wardrobe. . . . Are 14 slips so many for three who are about to be married?*

2. *Your decision to charge duty on my imported Volvo transmission undoubtedly was based on your best judgment. However, I beg to inform you that I have studied customs law intensively at the University of Leipzig and more recently at Tel Aviv University. You can take it on good authority that your charges were totally inappropriate.*

3. *I am writing you as one Jew to another. Surely we should have understanding for one another after all we have been through together. . . .*

4. *Surely you are aware of the fact that in emigrating from Chicago to live in the harsh climate of Dimona, I have given up a great deal. As a new immigrant dedicated to my new homeland, I am only demanding my just rights. Please send me my shipment immediately!*

5. *When we fled from Cairo to Cyprus, we lost all of our possessions. My husband did not survive, and the few things I was able to gather together in Cyprus I had to sell in order to support myself and my four young children. Now you are holding my small bundle. . . . Have you no heart, sir?*

6. *You do not know me, but I have heard about you from my cousin, S—— M——, in your central office. He tells me that you are a very effective customs officer and that it is likely you will be considered for a promotion shortly. I am particularly pleased to know that my problem is in such good hands. . . . Now, what I wanted to ask you is this. . . .*

7. *I know that mine is not the only complaint you have received. Among my immediate friends alone there are at least six who have been very angry at the abrupt treatment they received from your office. We will not stand for this much longer. There are ways in which a citizen can make his concerns known to higher authorities. I hope, however, that such action will not be necessary.*

Although the above letters are fictitious, each is based upon *real* requests made by Israelis of their customs officers (as suggested by Katz, Gurevitch, Danet, and Peled, 1969). Suppose that you were the customs officer who had received these letters. Which of these appeals do you find most persuasive? Which one might make you feel most kindly toward the writer? Which one might anger you? Can you see the vast differences in the manner in which a person might phrase essentially the same request? What does the form of these appeals tell you about the people who make them? And what type of person would or would not be influenced by each?

This kind of analysis might be applied to many other situations in which one person is trying to influence another. If a parent is alarmed at the large amount of time his child spends watching television, how should he try to change the situation? Should he try to convince the child that television will stunt his intellectual growth? Should he emphasize that he, an experienced adult and parent, knows best? Should he point out that he, the parent, does not watch television very often, and so the child should do likewise? Should he stress that parents have the right to determine their children's activities and thus that the child should do as he is asked? Should he offer a reward (such as a higher allowance) if the child watches television less? Should he threaten punishment if the child does not comply?

If you will compare the parent's options with the Israeli letters, you will see a close resemblance. (The letters written by the immigrant to Dimona [letter 4] and the widow from Cairo [letter 5] are merely different forms of a very similar appeal.) Indeed, parallel forms of influence can be seen in countless everyday situations—a policeman urging a motorist to watch his speed on the highway, a teacher trying to persuade a student to learn a new method for solving algebra problems, a doctor trying to get his patient to give up smoking, a door-to-door salesman attempting to convince a housewife that she needs a new vacuum cleaner, Gandhi trying to persuade the British to abolish the salt tax, or Charles Dederich working to induce drug addicts to break their habit.

POWER,
INFLUENCE,
AND CHANGE

Notice that in each of the above examples, any change taking place in one person's behavior has its origin in another person or group. This, then, is what we generally mean by *social influence*. An individual's *power*, that is, his ability to shape another's behavior, may be defined as *potential influence* (French and Raven, 1959).

Social influence is often so continuous and pervasive that we are not generally aware of the extent to which it operates in our daily lives. Yet, as the examples suggest, influence is exercised in *six* fundamentally different ways: information, reward, coercion, expertise, reference and identification, and legitimacy (French and Raven, 1959; Raven, 1965). Before discussing these six types of social influence (bases of social power) in greater detail, let us first consider three further concepts: *social dependence, surveillance,* and *positive* and *negative influence.*

Social Dependence and Social Influence

The relationship between the one who does the influencing and the one who is influenced is illustrated quite vividly in Fritz Heider's description of the two ways in which a hand may affect the movement of a ball:

> *In one case, a ball is pushed so that it rolls across a plane. In another case, the ball is guided by a hand and its movements are dependent at each moment on the movement of the hand. . . . In the first case, an influence from the outside is active once . . . in the other case, when the ball is guided during the whole movement, the course of events is continuously influenced from the outside* [Heider, 1959, pp. 4–5].

All influence, of course, begins with an influencing agent. Most influencing agents wonder about how much they must *continue* to exert influence in order for change to be maintained. The parent who tries to persuade a son to reduce his television viewing obviously wants to change the child's behavior, but the father or mother generally wants more than just that. The parent would like him to change his television viewing habits because the son, himself, *wants* to. As in the case of the first ball, the parent would like to take the first step and then have the child be *socially independent* of him. If, however, the child continued to relate his changed behavior to the parent ("I watch television less only because you ask me to"), as in the case of the ball being continuously guided, then the change would be *socially dependent.* In our analysis of the bases of social power, we will examine the factors that lead to either socially dependent or socially independent influence.

The Importance of Surveillance

A number of years ago, Richard L. Schanck (1932) carried out an intensive field study of "Elm Hollow," a small rural community. He found that its residents were nearly unanimous in stating their opposition to card playing, drinking alcoholic beverages, and smoking. Yet, Schanck reported, he himself had played cards, drunk hard cider, and smoked with many community residents—but always behind closed doors and drawn blinds. The small community church and several older residents seemed to be very influential in shaping the stated attitudes of the community. There was thus a clear, near-unanimous, *publicly stated* norm about many behaviors, and the *stated* attitudes of individual community members seemed to be grouped at one end of the opinion scale. But people's *private* attitudes and behavior differed substantially. Some strongly favored drinking, some were vehemently opposed, and the rest were distributed somewhere in between. When Schanck asked the residents how *other* people in the community felt about these issues, their responses closely paralleled the publicly stated, rather than the private, attitudes. This phenomenon, which Schanck called "pluralistic ignorance," is readily understood if you think about the secrecy with which "deviant" attitudes were held—the villagers, after all, could not possibly find out how their neighbors *really* felt if these neighbors could only permit themselves to express what would be considered "acceptable" dogma.

It turned out that the major proponents of the public attitudes were the young minister of the church and, even more so, the dowager widow of the previous minister—an ardent and outspoken fundamentalist. Shortly after she died, it became apparent that even the young minister's personal views were not as extreme as those that he had expressed from the pulpit; he managed to bend his behavior, even to the point of playing cards within sight of some of the town's more vocal residents. Had his actions deviated as much from the community's *private* attitudes as they did from its *public* attitudes, he might have been chased out of town. But, instead of that, Schanck reports that there was a very rapid change in the community's publicly stated attitudes, which brought them into much closer line with its private ones. As a consequence, therefore, pluralistic ignorance was eliminated.

Schanck's study preceded many other field and laboratory investigations of the discrepancy between private beliefs and public actions. As pointed out in Chapter 1, when our public actions do not correspond with our private beliefs, we ordinarily experience some tension or dissonance—together with a desire to reduce this discrepancy. Nevertheless, we often do things in which we do not believe. This occurs most frequently when we wish to do something for which we will be rewarded, or when we must do something in order to avoid severe punishment. In those cases, surveillance by the influencing agent is of critical importance.

Positive and Negative Influence

I recall observing a woman who had brought her young son to our psychological clinic. They sat together for a while in the waiting room, and then the woman left to go to the rest room. Before leaving her son, she said, "Now I will be back in just a minute, and you will have to wait out here. But while I am in there, please do *not* touch that fire extinguisher—you must *not* touch it." I saw the boy staring with interest at the bright red fire extinguisher fastened to the wall beside him. As Carl Sandburg once observed: "Why is it that Johnny always wants to stick beans up his nose when the very thing I ask him not to do is to stick beans up his nose." How like my own children, who seem to be exceptionally eager to watch television just when their mother has told them not to.

The Boomerang Effect. Most social influence studies have examined only *positive* influence, where the person changes in the direction of greater similarity to the influencing agent or in the direction desired or requested by him. However, as the above examples indicate, influence can also be *negative*. During World War II, a group of social psychologists was asked to assess the effects of a film series (*Why We Fight*), which was shown to U.S. armed forces personnel. One of the films (the *Battle of Britain*) had been designed to encourage more favorable attitudes toward Great Britain. It showed the valor and sacrifice of the British people as they fought alone against the overwhelming forces of Nazi Germany. The social psychologists, however, found that those who had seen the film came away with much more *negative* attitudes toward Britain than they had had before (Hovland, Lumsdaine, and Sheffield, 1949). This "boomerang effect" was later investigated in a series of laboratory experiments (Kelman and Hovland, 1953; Hovland and Weiss, 1952). These studies showed that when a communicator is disliked or distrusted, there is a tendency to adopt an opinion that is exactly the *opposite* of the one advocated.

Since I was one of the soldiers who saw the *Battle of Britain* film, the discovery of the "boomerang effect" did not surprise me in the least. The senior officers at our training center were apparently unimpressed by the need to show soldiers *Why We Fight*. They probably felt that we fight because we are ordered to fight, and the job of the training center is to teach new soldiers *how* to fight. The officers resented the film series's intrusion into the tight training schedule, and so they decided that we would be roused one hour earlier than usual (at 5:00 A.M. instead of 6:00 A.M.) so that we could see the *Battle of Britain* before breakfast. I can well recall our hostility, directed at both our officers and the film-makers who had deprived us of an hour of precious sleep during our exhausting basic training. Had my attitudes been tested, I am quite certain I would have shown a "boomerang effect." Even among the soldiers who were not awakened at 5:00 A.M. to see the *Battle of Britain*, many were negatively disposed toward those who were responsible for showing them the film (and may have been suspicious of their motives and the circumstances under which it was shown). In any event, they tended to change their opinions in the opposite direction of the one intended.

Robert Abelson and James Miller (1967) conducted an interesting field study of negative influence, using as their subjects 80 persons of various ages and backgrounds who happened to be sitting on park benches in New York City's Washington Square Park. After the interviewer had asked a subject privately about his views on discrimination in employment, he asked the respondent to state his opinions aloud for those around him to hear. A nearby park-bench dweller (a confederate, of course) listened to the opinion and then proceeded to insult him: "That's ridiculous . . . just the sort of thing you'd expect to hear in this park . . . obviously wrong . . . terribly confused . . . no one really believes that." Somewhat later the respondent was asked to state his opinions again—this time privately. The results indicated *negative* influence, a "boomerang effect"—the positions of the respondents were even further removed from those presumably held by the confederate. There is a resemblance here between the subjects' behavior and that of voters who discover (or suspect) that a certain candidate is up to some "dirty trick"; the result is negative influence in the form of a vote for his opponent. There was no negative influence when Abelson and Miller ran a control condition in which the confederate did not insult the respondent.

There are undoubtedly many factors that contribute to negative influence, as suggested by the balance theory analysis presented in Chapter 4. (As you may recall, p-Lo and oLx may lead to p-Lx, since pLx would be imbalanced.) It is imbalanced, inconsistent, and disturbing to like someone whom our enemy likes. Can you imagine the strain that Northern liberals must have felt in the summer of 1973 when their archenemy, Governor George Wallace of Alabama, appeared to support their favorite, Senator Edward Kennedy of Massachusetts? This tension was probably equaled by the Southern conservative enemies of Kennedy who thought that he was supporting their friend, George Wallace. No doubt many people on both sides changed their views about their idol as a result of this negative influence.

Reactance—A Response to a Threat to Independence. It also appears that, apart from disliking the influencing agent, negative influence may arise from a need for independence. Jack Brehm (1966) has reported a number of studies in which an individual displays what he calls "reactance," a form of negative influence that comes about when that person feels that his freedom (his status as a free agent) has been threatened. The adolescent boy whose parents tell him not to date may be exceptionally eager to do so on the sly; he may even react against his parents by doing more dating than he would have done otherwise. Similarly, the apparent negative influence upon the young boy who disobeys his parent's strictures against watching too much television, or playing with the fire extinguisher, may actually be due to his need to demonstrate personal freedom. However, playing with the fire extinguisher could also be a by-product of the influence attempt itself; possibly the boy would never have thought of doing such a thing otherwise. He may have heard only the informational aspect of the parent's command and not the stricture.

An English school once tried to reduce sexual promiscuity by conducting a sex education campaign. A schoolboy described most dramatically its apparent ineffectiveness: "The parson came to school and told us not to do it, the doctor came to school and told us how not to do it, and then the headmaster came and told us where not to do it." In attempts to exercise influence, the agent all too often inadvertently communicates information suggesting behavior that is precisely the opposite of what he desires.

THE BASES
OF SOCIAL POWER

Informational Power—Socially Independent Influence
Suppose that a Mr. X asked you to solve this problem: "A number of ducks swim downstream in formation. Two are in front, two in the middle, and two bring up the rear. What is the smallest number of ducks that could pass by in such a formation?" Your answer would probably be six, since everyone knows that three times two equals six. Then suppose that Mr. X told you that the correct answer was four, and he showed you a picture of the ducks swimming in single file—the first and second in front, the second and third in the middle, the third and fourth bringing up the rear. Suddenly you see it, and it becomes crystal clear. If Mr. X or anyone else were to present you with this problem in the future, it is unlikely that you would ever give a different answer.

This is an example of pure informational influence, for the *content* of the communication is the critical factor. As a result, you experience a dramatic cognitive change—you see the problem in a totally different light. Cognitive change, then, is the principal characteristic of informational influence. And once this change has taken place, it is completely independent of the influencing agent. Would you change your mind about the answer to this problem if Mr. X left the room and was never seen again? Would you return to your initial answer if your friend told you that Mr. X was not an expert in mathematics or the movement of ducks, or even if you learned the following week that he was mentally incompetent? Would it make any difference if you suddenly took a dislike to Mr. X, or if another friend pointed out that he really had no right to be giving you answers or directions? It is not likely, since in this example it is the information itself (and not the influencing agent) that is significant.

Informational influence is characterized by its dependence on the informational content of the communication, though elements of other bases of power may also be present to a lesser extent. Look at letter 1 to the Israeli customs officer. This correspondent, who is trying to convince the officer that the 14 ladies' slips were imported for personal use, implies that his three daughters need the new slips in order to be able to marry well. While the letter also seems to be an appeal for altruism and sympathy, its major basis of power is information. By conveying the plight of his three unmarried daughters, the writer attempts to convince the customs agent that the slips are for personal use and not for sale. The parent who tries to convince his child that television will stunt his intellectual growth is also relying on informational influence. Other examples would be: the vacuum cleaner salesman trying to convince the homemaker of his product's value; the teacher attempting to explain why a different method of solving mathematical equations is superior to the one the student had been using; or the traffic policeman trying to convince the motorist of the likelihood of a serious accident if he continues to make right turns from the center lane.

Social psychologists have done extensive research on the conditions under which different forms of communication are apt to change people's attitudes and opinions. In Chapter 4 we pointed out one example of this: by presenting someone with convincing arguments that the desegregation of housing will support important values (greater American prestige abroad, higher property values, equality of opportunity, open-mindedness), it is possible to change his views about desegregation (Carlson, 1956).

Using Information to Highlight Inconsistency. In a similar vein, Milton Rokeach (1971) demonstrated rather dramatically that the attitudes and behavior of people can be changed by making them aware of the inconsistency between their attitudes and values. He asked a group of students to rank 18 basic values according to their importance. The two that were of special interest in this study were "free-

". . . in assessing 42 lirot for the 14 ladies' slips I ordered from abroad. Obviously you must have thought that I planned to sell these for profit. How could you have known that I have three marriageable daughters? . . ."

dom" and "equality." The students tended to rank "freedom" quite high and "equality" rather low. Rokeach then informed them of their inconsistency, making such statements as: "Hmm. I see that you think your own freedom is pretty important. You must think that your own freedom is much more important than the freedom of others, since you rank 'equality' as much lower." Many of the respondents were deeply impressed with their inconsistency. In later measures, they tended to rate "equality" much higher; also, their attitudes and behaviors became more consistent with their changed value. For example, these students became more favorably disposed toward civil rights and were more inclined to respond to appeals for financial support from the National Association for the Advancement of Colored People. They were also more likely (than a control group) to enroll in an ethnic studies course. Although one could speculate that these changed attitudes and behaviors were merely attempts on the part of the students to give the experimenter what he wanted, the appeals from the NAACP came by mail, and the students had no reason to believe that the experimenter had anything to do with the NAACP or the ethnic studies course. Even 17 months after their inconsistency had been pointed out to them, the students still showed evidence of their new attitudes and behaviors. Clearly, Rokeach was utilizing one type of informational influence, not unlike the pure example we presented in the duck problem. The students' changed behavior seemed to be totally independent of the influencing agent, and there was no indication that surveillance had played a significant role. Rokeach's studies have now been replicated by several other investigators in different research settings. More recently, Rokeach has demonstrated how long-term value change can be accomplished even more efficiently through computerized feedback (Rokeach, 1975).

". . . my cousin . . . tells me . . . that it is likely that you will be considered for a promotion shortly. . . . Now, what I wanted to ask you is this. . . ."

". . . There are ways in which a citizen can make his concerns known to higher authorities. I hope, however, that such action will not be necessary."

Reward and Coercive Power—
Socially Dependent Influence, Surveillance Important

Whereas informational influence is independent of the influencing agent, reward and coercion typify the exact opposite, that is, social dependence. Compare letter 1 to the customs official with letter 6 (suggesting that if the writer gets favorable treatment, his cousin might be able to do something nice for the official) and letter 7 (threatening to bring pressure from a higher authority on the customs official if he does not accede to the request).

Other examples of reward include: a parent offering his child a higher allowance if he curtails his television viewing; a supervisor offering higher pay for increased productivity; and a teacher promising a student an *A* if he completes his assignment in a prescribed manner. Examples of coercion include: a parent threatening to spank his child if he does not reduce his television viewing; a supervisor threatening to fire a worker who does not increase his productivity; and a teacher threatening to give a student an F unless he completes his assignment in a prescribed manner. Other forms of reward and punishment are more personal: approval, love, acceptance, liking, and agreement can be viewed as personal commodities to be offered or withheld on the basis of compliance or noncompliance. Disapproval, dislike, hatred, rejection, and disagreement can be either implicit or explicit threats for noncompliance. The potency of such personal rewards and punishments can be as great, if not greater, than the impersonal forms. How often do we hear or read about a youth who has committed a petty crime (or even murder) because he wanted the approval of the members of his gang? How often do parents use threats of disapproval in order to make a child conform to their requests?

Promise of reward and threat of punishment have often been thought to be almost synonymous with power (as that term is commonly used) and thus highly effective techniques of influence. Yet, in fact, both coercion and reward are more fragile than informational power because they are both highly dependent upon the influencing agent and require the agent to be aware of whether the person has complied or not. Surveillance is thus important. Sometimes, of course, surveillance can be maintained easily. The letter-writers will be able to determine quite readily whether the customs official has acceded to their requests. After threatening the child with loss of his allowance or promising him an increase if he cuts down on his television viewing, the parent would have only a little more difficulty than the letter-writers in maintaining surveillance to see if the child has complied. (Of course, the child could watch TV at his friend's house, or while his parent is away from home.) Generally, though, surveillance is quite difficult—if not impossible—to maintain when coercion and reward are used.

Differentiating Reward and Coercion. At this point, it may be asked: "Why should we consider reward and coercion as two *different* bases of power? Isn't the absence of reward punishing, and isn't the failure to receive an expected punishment rewarding?" If your supervisor says, "Your promotion depends upon whether or not you increase your productivity," is this a threat of punishment or a promise of reward? This is an important point in the analysis of reward and punishment. Certainly the supervisor's statement will be interpreted by some as "reward power" and by others as "coercive power." A request that is phrased ambiguously will bring forth both different interpretations and different responses, depending upon whether the request is viewed as reward or coercion. Furthermore, the resources of the influencing agent (to recommend for or against promotion) enable him to phrase his request in such a way that he can emphasize one base of power or the other. Several empirical studies suggest that it would be preferable for the supervisor to use reward ("I am ready to recommend you for that promotion if you can increase your productivity") rather than coercion ("Unless you raise your productivity, I am not going to recommend you for that promotion"). There are several reasons for this:

1. When coercive power is used, the person tends to dislike the influencing agent and to feel negatively about the situation; by contrast, there is a greater probability that he will like the influencing agent who uses reward (Rubin and Lewicki, 1973; Rubin, Lewicki, and Dunn, 1973; Horai et al., 1970). As we shall see, when the influencing agent is disliked, his ability to use other bases of power effectively (such as referent power) is greatly diminished. Thus, the agent can probably continue his influence with reward power, but not with coercive power (Kipnis, 1958).

2. By the same token, coercion may impel the person to try to leave the situation entirely, whereas reward may encourage him to continue his relationship with the influencing agent in order to receive the reward. This is precisely what happened several years ago in a voluntary Upward Bound program, where the students came for tutoring on Saturday mornings. When they were offered a small monetary reward for doing their assignments during the week, they were more apt to show up with their assignments completed. However, when they were given a lump sum for attending, and then told that they would be fined for not doing their assignments, they simply tended to stay away.

3. Although surveillance is necessary for both reward and coercion, it appears that surveillance is easier to maintain for reward. In order to obtain his reward, the person will find it advantageous to make the agent aware of his compliance. When coercion is used, however, the person will try to conceal his noncompliance in order to avoid punishment (Thibaut and Kelley, 1959). Kenneth Ring and Harold Kelley (1963) demonstrated this point in a study in which students were asked their opinions about mental illness. According to a prearranged plan, the experimenter disagreed with certain opinions and agreed with others. For some subjects (Reward Condition), the experimenter simply expressed disagreement with some of their opinions, while lavishly praising them for others ("That certainly shows that you have a lot of insight, Mr. _____; most persons don't get that one"). For other subjects (Coercive Condition), the experimenter merely agreed with their "correct" opinions, while pointedly criticizing the others ("Well, I'm sure that you must have a reason for

Figure 6.1
Coercive power
requires surveillance.
Variants of this coercive sign appear frequently in Great Britain. Other bases of power are also found in signs.

A PERSON IN
CHARGE OF A
DOG WHICH FOULS
A FOOTWAY
IS LIABLE TO
A FINE OF £20

that choice, Mr. _____, but I'm darned if I can see what it could possibly be"). Since no reasons were given for the experimenter's judgment, coercive and reward power seemed to be operating so that the results were pretty much as predicted. The subjects in the Coercive Condition were much more inclined to try to conceal their opinions than those in the Reward Condition, and they were far less likely to accept the opinions of the experimenter. In real life, then, a supervisor who uses threats of punishment will probably find that his workers dislike him, refuse to accept his suggestions as valid, conform only so long as surveillance is possible, and try to conceal their work from him. Therefore, he will have to use threats not only to try to obtain compliance with his requests, but also to prevent any concealment of work.

4. Surveillance, which seems to be required especially under coercive conditions, seems to make the influencing agent somewhat suspicious of the person he is observing. Lloyd Strickland (1958) illustrated this point neatly in a study in which a supervisor was assigned to direct two workers—both of whom could be punished for not following his requests. At the end of the first work session, the supervisor examined the goods produced by the two workers, and he found that both had performed in pretty much the same fashion. However, the experimenter had arranged (by making it appear to happen by chance) that the supervisor would carefully observe the performance of worker A but not observe worker B at all during that work session. At the beginning of the second work session, the supervisor had a real choice: he could watch either worker A or worker B. He chose to watch A, probably because of his distrust of A ("Since B worked well without my watching him, he must be doing so because he *wants* to. On the other hand, A, whom I have been observing, might well be conforming just because I have been watching him"). This is an example of attribution theory—A was perceived as conforming because of external circumstances, whereas B was seen as internally motivated. Thus, distrust occurred when the workers had been threatened with punishment. In a later, follow-up study, it was found that there was no special distrust of the observed worker when a reward was offered for conformity (Kruglanski, 1970).

Expert, Referent, and Legitimate Power—
Socially Dependent Influence, Surveillance Unimportant

Three bases of power lead to influence which, while still dependent on the influencing agent, does not rely on surveillance for its effectiveness. In each case, the person continues to relate his changed pattern of behavior to the influencing agent ("I did it because he asked me to do it [or because he was doing it]"). However, fear of punishment or hope of reward from the other may not be critical, and surveillance by the other may not be important.

Expert Power. Look at letter 2 to the Israeli customs official. The writer is attempting to persuade the official that he, the writer, is

". . . I have studied customs law intensively at the University of Leipzig and more recently at Tel Aviv University. You can take it on good authority that your charges were totally inappropriate."

COURTESY WILLIAM STEIG
FROM *THE LONELY ONES*.

**WHOEVER WANTS THE
ANSWER MUST COME TO ME**

*Figure 6.2
In order to command respect as an expert, it is often important to present an impressive front; to maintain it, one must carefully withhold information and keep the basis of one's knowledge a mystery.*

knowledgeable about customs law and that the official should take him at his word. Our guess is that this letter would not be effective since the customs agent probably will not concede that the writer has superior knowledge. Examples of how we *are* affected because we attribute superior knowledge to an influencing agent include: (1) acceptance of the doctor's word regarding the nature of our illness and the medicine we should take; after all, he has studied medicine and has had a lot of experience with medical problems such as ours. Also (as pointed out in Chapter 3), the doctor has gone to great lengths to set the stage so that he will appear as an expert, with diplomas, (dusty) medical books on the shelves, and a lot of impressive, complicated equipment in his office; (2) acceptance of much of a teacher's expertise ("Use this formula, and take my word for it—it is correct. Later, perhaps, you will understand why"); (3) acceptance of a paint salesman's recommendation for a particular brand of paint that he has successfully used himself for painting a damp bathroom, which is precisely your purpose (Brock, 1965); and (4) acceptance of the word of a little boy you encounter in a small rural town about how to get to the town hall. In this example the boy has expert power even though he is not an "expert" in any formal sense; nonetheless, we assume that he has superior knowledge about this particular town.

Negative expert influence. Whenever we suspect that a person is using his allegedly superior knowledge to influence us in a way that will benefit him rather than us, we are inclined to do the opposite; this is known as *negative* expertise. If we suspect that the paint salesman wants to sell us a particular brand simply because he will get a larger commission or because that brand requires several coats (so that we will have to buy more), we will probably refuse to buy it. In one of their experiments on the "boomerang effect," Hovland and Weiss (1952) presented a group of subjects with an article arguing that a steel shortage, which was plaguing the country at that time, was due to labor union demands, rather than to the steel industry. When the article was attributed to a prominent newspaper columnist who was known for his pro-steel industry and anti-labor position, the subjects rated the communication as unfair and changed their opinion so that it was precisely the opposite of the one advocated. When the same article was attributed to the "Bulletin of National Resources Planning," the subjects felt that the communication was generally "justified by the facts" and changed their views accordingly.

"I am writing to you as one Jew to another. Surely we should have understanding for one another after all we have been through together. . . ."

Referent Power. Letter 3 to the customs official appeals to the similarity between the official and the writer. If two people have had the same experiences or if they are members of the same group, it is more likely that they will look at things in a similar way. Referent influence, then, depends upon a person's identification with the influencing agent, or at least his desire for such identification. We have discussed referent power indirectly with respect to social comparison processes and the ways in which people use others as a basis for evaluating themselves (page 46), and with respect to cognitive balance and Cassius's attempts to convince Brutus that they should think alike since they were both Romans and very similar (page 108). The term "referent" comes from studies of reference groups (Hyman, 1942; Merton and Rossi, 1957), which show how people refer to others in order to evaluate their own opinions, beliefs, behavior, and even emotions. Even without the direct threat of punishment for being different, one often derives personal satisfaction from being similar to others, particularly those whom one likes or admires. Referent power can be exercised by people with whom one has no formal affiliation or common membership, for example, the girl who effects the speech mannerisms of her favorite movie actress, or the boy who eats the same breakfast cereal that his much-admired baseball hero ate so heartily in the television commercial.

The referent power of groups or individuals varies in saliency at different times, depending upon whom we happen to be identifying with at a given moment. Thus, an American in Paris will probably be more conscious of his identification as an American than when he is at home. As a result, when he is in Paris his expressed opinions may more nearly reflect what he thinks American opinions are or ought to be. When Catholic students are asked for their *own* opinions on a questionnaire, they are more likely to give typical Catholic opinions if their group membership is salient at that time (Charters and Newcomb, 1952).

Negative referent influence. Referent influence also has its negative forms. There are times when we deliberately dissociate ourselves from others, when we adopt a different opinion or attitude merely because someone we dislike holds that opinion. Parents sometimes try to make a negative referent salient by such remarks as: "Cut your hair. Do you want to look like that awful Hubert Smith? None of us can stand him." Such an attempt may backfire, of course—especially with adolescents, whose positive reference group usually consists of other adolescents.

The use of negative referent power in election campaigns has a long tradition. Evidently, the ancient city of Pompeii was in the midst of an election campaign when it was destroyed by the eruption of Mt. Vesuvius. When modern-day excavators and archeologists scraped the ashes from its walls, they found such slogans as: "VOTE FOR VATIUS, ALL THE WHOREMASTERS VOTE FOR HIM." "VOTE FOR VATIUS, ALL THE DRUNKS AND SLUG-A-BEDS VOTE FOR HIM." "VOTE FOR VATIUS, ALL THE WIFE-BEATERS VOTE FOR HIM." Did this use of negative referent power help Vatius's opponent to defeat him? We will never know, since lava from the volcano destroyed the city and all of its written records. (White, 1973, p. 369)

The effects of the salience of positive and negative reference groups on opinions was illustrated in a study we conducted at the time of the 1960 presidential election (Raven and Gallo, 1965). We expected that the political parties would serve as positive and negative reference groups during the months preceding the nominating conventions. To check this out, we asked a group of students to evaluate a number of potential candidates both before and after the Republican and Democratic party conventions. The day after the Democratic convention ended, its nominee, John F. Kennedy, was evaluated much more favorably (than before the convention) by those who identified themselves as Democrats; he was evaluated more negatively at that time by those who identified themselves as Republicans. A similar effect occurred after the Republican conven-

Figure 6.3
The use of negative referent power in a political campaign. *This election shenanigan was uncovered on a wall in ancient Pompeii.*

tion—Richard Nixon became more attractive for Republicans and less attractive for Democrats. Apparently the electioneering hoopla during the following months served to increase party identification further—an evaluation of the two candidates a few days before the election showed a very high degree of party polarization. But what was the effect of the election itself? The day after Election Day, questionnaires were distributed to the students again. At this time, the political parties had less referent power, and national identification was more important. The new president-elect, Kennedy, was clearly liked more by Republicans right after the election. To a lesser extent, the negative referent power of the Republican party was diminished for Democrats as well—they didn't find Nixon quite so distasteful the day after his defeat.

Legitimate Power. The basic statement of conformity to legitimate power may be phrased as follows: "I do as he says because he has a right to ask me to do this, and I am therefore obliged to comply." *Should, ought, oblige,* and similar words signal a legitimate power relationship. Legitimate power is evident in formal social organizations—military units, industrial organizations, governmental agencies—where each person has a specific place on the organization chart, and it is clear who has power over whom (see Chapter 7). What else is implied in Tennyson's phrase, "Theirs is not to reason why/ Theirs but to do and die," but the military dictum that the line soldier is subject to legitimate power and should neither expect nor demand information?

Even in less formally organized social units where roles are prescribed for group members, legitimate power is also exercised. In the traditional family, the father often assumes legitimate power to determine where the family will live; the mother may have legitimate power to decide how the house will be decorated or what the family will eat for dinner; the children have less legitimate power, although perhaps they may be given the right to decide where the family will go for a Sunday outing. To be sure, the role relationships in a modern family, as well as the designations of legitimacy, are not what they used to be 50 or more years ago.

Legitimate power of the powerless. It seems almost paradoxical that powerlessness can become a basis of legitimate power. This is especially the case in societies whose social norms emphasize the obligation of those with means to help the less fortunate (Berkowitz and Daniels, 1963; Goranson and Berkowitz, 1966). A blind person may legitimately request a sighted person to assist him in crossing the street. A helpless-looking young motorist, with a disabled automobile, may legitimately request a capable-looking older motorist for assistance. A child, who has little formal legitimate power in the family, can legitimately request his parent for help in tying his shoe. The powerless often assert their power by emphasizing their helplessness. For example, the Jewish beggar in the *shtetl* (a small ghetto community of Eastern Europe) would knock at the door boldly and then present himself—erect, domineering, almost imperious—demanding his rights as a beggar (Zborowski and Herzog, 1952). The legitimate power of the powerless is evident even at the international level. When Britain and Iceland were at the height of a dis-

Figure 6.4
Power strategy. *If an appeal based on power-lessness doesn't work, one can try coercion.*

"When we fled from Cairo to Cyprus, we lost all of our posses-sions. . . . Now you are holding my small bundle. . . . Have you no heart, sir?"

". . . As a new im-migrant dedicated to my new homeland, I am only demanding my just rights. Please send me my shipment imme-diately!"

pute over fishing rights, the London *Daily Mirror* complained: "Ice-land must stop exploiting the fact that she is a small and weak country up against a large and powerful one."

Look at the two remaining letters to the Israeli customs official (letters 4 and 5). Both are examples of the attempted use of legiti-mate power. The first is somewhat stronger—the writer feels that a new immigrant has the right to make certain demands—even excep-tions—to the usual customs law, and the letter is stated quite firmly. In the second, the writer is relying on the "power of the powerless" in its purer form. She has lost nearly everything; she is helpless to do anything about it; and the customs official is in a position to do some-thing for her—surely he will take pity on her situation and help.

Elihu Katz and Brenda Danet (1966) wanted to find out what a group of Israeli army recruits would do in certain hypothetical situa-tions where they (as clients) sought services from a bureaucrat and were refused. They presented the following problem to each subject: "You go to the bank to request a loan. The manager . . . refuses to grant the loan." Or, "You are sick and request emergency medical treatment at the Sick Fund Clinic, but you have forgotten to pay your monthly dues. The clerk refuses to let you see the doctor." The ex-perimenters found that the two most common responses represented different forms of legitimate power. One stressed formal role rela-tionships and obligations ("Giving loans is one of the services a bank is supposed to provide. As a client of this bank, I have the right to demand such service"); the other stressed powerlessness ("I'm sick and this is an emergency. You cannot turn away a sick, helpless person, regardless of the rules"). Katz and Danet also found that Israelis with a "more modern background" (those who had been there a long time, were of Western origin, had at least some high-school education, and had a higher-status occupation) were much more inclined to emphasize formal role relationships and obligations. The "more traditional" Israelis (those who were newcomers from the Middle East and North Africa, had only an elementary-school education, and had a lower-status occupation) were much more likely to emphasize powerlessness. It also appeared that the longer the "Oriental" Israeli had lived there and the greater his contact with the bureaucracy, the more he was inclined to adopt the formal approach to legitimate power. Of course, it sometimes happens that after a number of ineffective attempts to use the power of the powerless, the frustrated party may adopt an extreme form of coercion, as did the North African immigrant to Israel who finally exploded: "If I don't get what I've asked, I'll blow up the office!" (Katz et al., 1969, p. 447).

Legitimate power of the experimenter. In most reports of psychological experiments, the experimenter is presented as someone outside of the situation; although he sets up the experiment, reads the instructions, and passes out the questionnaires, his role and his personal relationship with the subject appear to be irrelevant to the experiment. Since the early 1960s, there has been a growing awareness that the experimenter apparently plays a much more active role than many social scientists ever realized before (Rosenthal, 1966). As part of a psychological study of satiation, Jerome Frank (1944) asked student subjects to eat dry soda crackers in order for him to observe the conditions under which they would eat more or less. The original project was abandoned when Frank discovered that the subjects were eating huge quantities of these crackers simply because he, the experimenter, asked them to; they continued to eat the crackers until he told them that the experiment did not require them to glut themselves. How far, then, will subjects go in accepting the legitimate power of an experimenter?

Stanley Milgram (1963, 1965) attempted to test the limits of subject obedience in a series of experiments. Imagine that you are a resident of New Haven, Connecticut. You decide to answer a classified advertisement in the newspaper that offers the sum of $4.50 for your participation in an experiment. When you arrive at the designated place, you are greeted by a man in a lab coat. Another person—a mild-mannered, 47-year-old accountant—has also answered the ad. One of you is to be a teacher, the other a learner. You draw slips and find out that you are to be the teacher. The man in the lab coat then explains that the purpose of the study is to determine exactly what effect punishment has on learning. Punishment will be in the form of

*Figure 6.5
(Upper left) This is the shock generator used in Stanley Milgram's experiments. (Upper right) The learner is strapped into his chair and electrodes are attached to his wrist. He gives his answers by pressing switches that are connected to an answer box. (Lower left) The teacher (subject) receives a sample shock from the generator (the experimenter is in the background). (Lower right) Unlike most other subjects, this "teacher" refuses to continue the experiment.*

an electric shock delivered by the teacher to the learner each time he responds incorrectly. The learner is placed in an adjacent room and you watch him being strapped into a chair. At about this time, he indicates that he has had some heart trouble and wonders if the shock may be dangerous. The experimenter tells him that the shock may be painful, but that it will not result in permanent injury. You receive a sample shock yourself and find that it really is quite painful. Now you read a series of words to the learner. On many trials, he answers incorrectly. In accordance with the experimenter's instructions, you shock the learner after each error, beginning at 15 volts. Then you throw a toggle switch over to the next higher voltage on the Shock Generator. As instructed, you increase the voltage after each error: 15 . . . , 30 . . . , 45 . . . , 60 . . . At 75 volts the learner begins to grunt and moan. At 150 volts he demands to be let out of the experiment. At 180 volts he cries out that he can no longer stand the pain. At 300 volts he refuses to respond with any more answers to the memory test, insisting that he is no longer a participant in the experiment and must be freed. Coping with this last tactic, the experimenter instructs you to treat the learner's refusal to answer as equivalent to a wrong answer, and to "follow the usual shock procedure." If you hesitate at all, the experimenter insists that you must continue and that the experiment cannot be stopped until it has been completed. At what voltage level would you decide to stop and absolutely refuse to participate any more in this experiment? Think seriously about this question for a few moments before you continue reading.

If you are like most people who have been asked about this verbally, you will probably insist that you would not give very many shocks before quitting. On the other hand, if you are like most subjects who actually participated in this experiment, you will probably continue on—past the learner's moans at 75 volts, past his demands to be let out at 150 volts, past his pleas that he cannot stand the pain at 180 volts, past the 300-volt point when he refused to continue and insisted upon being freed, and all the way past 390 (DANGER: Severe shock) to 450 (XXXX).

It is extremely interesting that people tend to underestimate the extent to which others will comply with demands made by a legitimate power in situations such as this. When Yale undergraduates were asked to predict the amount of obedience that could be expected in this experiment using 100 hypothetical subjects ("Americans of diverse occupations, and ranging in age from 20 to 50 years"), they estimated that an average of 1.2 percent would go all the way to 450 volts, and no student predicted that more than 3 percent would go that far (Milgram, 1963). When a number of psychiatrists were asked for their predictions, they also expected very little compliance. Milgram's initial study was done with 40 adult males from the New Haven area, including skilled and unskilled workers, businessmen, white collar workers, and professionals. Of these, a total of 26 (or 65 percent) went all the way to the most extreme shock level, and not one stopped before the 300 (Intense Shock) level.

Of course, the "learner" with the heart condition was an accomplice of the experimenter. His voice was recorded so that each "teacher" heard exactly the same set of responses. It has been suggested that the "teachers" did not really believe that the "learner" was receiving the shocks. However, anyone who has seen Milgram's excellent film of this experiment would probably not accept this explanation, for the accomplice was an excellent actor, and the pained, conflicted, tortured behavior of the "teachers" clearly indicated that they felt the experimental situation was authentic. (Questions have been raised about the propriety of placing human subjects in this type of painful predicament. Such questions are discussed in detail in the Appendix.)

Why, then, did they follow the experimenter's instructions and inflict what they obviously felt was severe pain (and perhaps worse) on an innocent human being who had never harmed them? It appears that legitimate power can be extremely compelling, and evidently the subjects in these experiments were ready to grant almost limitless legitimate power to the experimenter.

Milgram's first experiment was followed by a series of others to determine what factors might increase or decrease the legitimate power of the experimenter. (1) *Closeness of the victim.* If the teacher was placed in a room that was situated some distance away so that he could not even hear the subject, then the shocking became particularly intense. The tendency to obey the experimenter and shock the victim was reduced when: the victim's voice was heard, the victim sat next to the teacher so that he could be seen and heard, and the teacher had to touch the victim and press his hand against the shock electrode (this caused the greatest reduction in the amount of shocking). (2) *Closeness of the experimenter.* If the experimenter transmitted his instructions by telephone from the next room, there was less obedience to his authority. If the experimenter was in a separate room and communicated only by means of a tape-recorded message, there was even less obedience. (3) *The scene.* As pointed out on page 92, a doctor can increase his legitimate power by means of the setting of his office. Similarly, Milgram found that when the experimenter was not wearing his white lab coat—when the experiment was conducted in a dingy, unprofessional looking laboratory—there was less conformity. But, even then, 48 percent of the subjects went to the limit in shocking their victim. (4) *Group pressure.* When two other "teachers" (confederates) were present and encouraged shocking, it increased; when they refused to shock their own "learners," the subject tended to refuse also. (This could be viewed as the referent or expert power of the others, which helped to either increase or decrease the legitimate power of the experimenter.) (Milgram, 1974.)

Stanley Milgram apparently decided to undertake this study of obedience because of a deep concern about atrocities committed under orders in wartime. He began shortly after the trial of Adolf Eichmann, the former Nazi agent who was held responsible for the murder of millions of people in wartime concentration camps. Eichmann pleaded that he was not guilty because he had only been following orders. Milgram's studies anticipated the trial of Lieutenant William Calley, who used a similar defense for his participation in the massacre of innocent civilians at My Lai during the Vietnam War.

COMPARING BASES OF POWER

So far, we have described six bases of social power and pointed out differences in their operation. We emphasized that reward and coercion depend upon surveillance in order to be effective (though it appears that surveillance is easier to maintain with reward power than with coercion). Expert, referent, and legitimate power do not require surveillance, but do entail a continued, dependent relationship with the influencing agent. Informational power is almost immediately independent of the agent; it is based upon the content of the communication itself and the cognitive change produced. We have also suggested that the person's evaluation of the influencing agent will probably be determined according to the base of social power that is utilized.

Research on the bases of social power is complicated by the fact that several bases may be operating at the same time. It sometimes happens that the same attempt to influence may increase the operation of one power base but decrease or even negate another. For example, the use of coercion may lead to public compliance, but cause the agent to be so disliked that there is private noncompliance. A parent may threaten his child with severe punishment if he uses "improper" language. As a result, the child may comply so long as the parent is within hearing distance (coercive influence), but he may privately resent the parent and want more than ever to use the forbidden words (negative referent); he will, of course, do so at the first opportunity.

Let us now compare the differing bases of power and examine the ways in which they may interact with one another.

Coercion-Reward, Expert, and Referent Power

Working with somewhat different definitions of power bases, Herbert Kelman (1958) carried out an interesting comparison of three power combinations. His study was conducted at an all-black college in the early 1950s—a time when most black students felt that total integration of schools and colleges was a desirable goal. A preliminary questionnaire indicated that this was indeed the overwhelming view of the students at that college. Kelman played them a tape-recorded communication which argued that in the interests of preserving Negro culture, all-black universities should be maintained as such, even if other universities were integrated. This same message was played to different groups of students, but attributed in each case to a different communicator. In a condition that combined reward and coercive power, the communicator was identified as a very powerful president of a foundation for Negro colleges; he promised to support the college and the students who agreed with him, and punish (by withholding financial support and blackballing) all those who disagreed. The students who heard the message under these conditions changed their views on the position advocated, but only if their names were written on the forms (they were not about to take a chance on being punished by the vindictive communicator). If they felt that they would not be personally identified, the respondents did not change their views significantly in the direction advocated.

Another group that heard the message was told that it came from the very popular president of the student council at a leading all-black university—in short, a source of referent power. Those who heard this communication changed their views on this issue in the direction advocated, both on the confidential and the identifiable questionnaires. The change did not last, however; when the questionnaire was administered again several weeks later, the students had reverted to their earlier positions. A third group of students heard from an "expert" source—a professor of history with considerable knowledge about minority groups, including the Negro community. This communicator proved to be the most effective—the students changed their opinions and maintained this change when they were given the same questionnaire again several weeks later; surveillance was irrelevant to these students. One might wonder why the change would continue longer for an expert source of power than for a referent one, since both are socially dependent forms of influence. We suspect that the students may have listened more carefully to the expert power source, so that the informational influence was thereby increased.

Legitimate and Coercive Power

The advantages of legitimate power over coercion were demonstrated in a study (Raven and French, 1958), in which groups of women university students were given the job of cutting patterns out of cardboard. In describing the task to each group, the experimenter pointed out that an effective group must have a supervisor, and so it was decided that a supervisor would be elected. Each group included two confederates—Ellie and Barbara. One of these two was always "elected" supervisor (since the experimenter counted the ballots). Sometimes the experimenter announced that Ellie had been elected, in which case she continued as legitimate supervisor throughout the session. In other groups, where Barbara was elected, she would serve as supervisor briefly, but then Ellie would ask if they could exchange jobs (hinting that her hand hurt so that she could not use the scissors). Thus, in every group, Ellie served as supervisor, but sometimes with legitimate power and sometimes as a usurper. In either case, Ellie would tell each woman in the group that she was working too fast and carelessly; she would then ask her to cut more slowly and accurately. The women resisted this order somewhat, since they were being paid for each piece cut. For half the groups, Ellie was permitted to fine the workers for non-compliance (coercive power), while in other groups she was not. Thus, there were four experimental conditions: legitimate coercive, non-legitimate coercive, legitimate non-coercive, and non-legitimate non-coercive. There were measures of compliance under surveillance (the extent to which the subjects actually slowed down in response to orders) and private acceptance (the extent to which the subjects confided to the experimenter that they should have been cutting more slowly).

As predicted, using surveillance, Ellie was equally effective in gaining compliance whether her power was based on legitimacy or coercion or both. Privately, however, the workers accepted the propriety of Ellie's request when her power was legitimate, but rejected it when her power was coercive. When Ellie's position was legitimate, she was also better liked and her supervisory ability was more highly rated than when her power came from coercion.

An interesting side issue arose when non-legitimate coercive power was coupled with close surveillance. Although we had expected compliance, some had complied in the extreme—they cut only one piece in a four-minute period when it was typical to cut ten. This high level of conformity under coercion puzzled us initially, particularly since it was often coupled with the greatest dislike for the supervisor. After discussing the matter with individual workers, the explanation became clear. In the coercive power situation, *over-conformity* was a means of indicating disagreement and hostility. It was as if the workers were saying, "You want me to go *still* slower. Okay, let me show you how ridiculous your command is!" Similar techniques were used in the early part of this century by the colorful "wobblies" (Industrial Workers of the World), a workers' movement that is known today by many people largely through their hero, Joe Hill, and the song that he inspired. The IWW used overconformity as a device for dealing with their bosses, whom they felt were illegitimate and coercive. If the "wobblies" were asked to slow down, they slowed down to a near stop. If they were asked to work more quickly, they worked so quickly that most of the work was ruined. Then, when admonished, they could truthfully answer that they had only done what they had been asked to do (Brissenden, 1957).

Expert and Referent Power
One of the problems frequently encountered by those in positions of authority is the conflict between referent power (which stems from identification and similarity) and other bases of power, such as legitimacy and expertise (which depend upon dissimilarity). The army officer often wonders "how close" he should allow himself to be with his subordinates. On the one hand, he thinks that his soldiers will follow his commands more readily if they have a sense of camaraderie with him. On the other hand, he fears that if he becomes too familiar, they will fail to recognize his superiority and his legitimate power. Thus, the same factors that increase the effectiveness of ref-

erent influence may simultaneously reduce the effectiveness of expertise. Our daughter's piano teacher once told us how much she liked our daughter. "I would really like to be Michelle's friend," she said, "but I am afraid that our friendship would make it more difficult for me to be her teacher." These feelings are undoubtedly experienced by many teachers who would like to have closer relationships with their students.

The interaction between expert and referent power is illustrated in the following experiment (Raven, Mansson, and Anthony, 1962): Groups consisting of four women subjects were each asked to try to receive ESP (extrasensory perception) images, which a "sender" in another room was presumably transmitting to them. Each subject could indicate if she had received the image by pressing either of two buttons in front of her labeled "receive" or "not receive." There was, in fact, no "sender." Even so, we found that if we gave a subject false information, indicating that the other three had received an image, she was more likely to report receiving an image and also to have a more positive belief in ESP. In those cases where the subject said that she had received an image, she could provide us with a vivid description of it.

We then varied the perceptual ability attributed to the other three. Some subjects were told that their co-participants had been tested in the "Perceptual Training Laboratory" and were found to have very keen and reliable perceptual ability. Other subjects were told that the test showed that their three co-participants were only slightly above average, and therefore presumably quite similar to themselves. The "superior" partners were thus high in expert but low in referent power; the "average" partners were high in referent but low in expert power. Which, then, would be more influential?

We predicted, and indeed found, that both expert and referent power prevailed, but in different ways. When the "average" perceivers reported that they had received ESP images, the subjects also reported receiving them. Even though a subject's responses would not be seen or identified by her co-participants, she seemed to enjoy doing as the others had done. However, her belief in ESP was not noticeably affected. When the "superior" perceivers reported that they had received ESP images, the subject was much more inclined to believe in the existence of ESP, but not to report receiving the images. Were such subjects bothered by this discrepancy? Apparently not, since they had a ready rationale: "If the superior perceivers are able to receive an image, there must be something to ESP; but, since I am just an average perceiver, it is not surprising that I do not receive the image myself."

The differential effects of expert and referent influence on behavior and beliefs raise some important questions. Suppose a clergyman denounced racial prejudice from his pulpit. Would this reduce racial prejudice among his parishioners? We might expect that it would, in the sense that the parishioners probably tend to respect his opinion; if he says that racial prejudice is wrong, immoral, and inhuman, they may well believe that he is right. Yet, where any view really counts—in one's everyday actions—his sermon may have no effect whatsoever. The parishioners may feel that he is different from them—morally superior—and therefore believe that they should be excused if their behavior does not measure up to his standards. Perhaps someone whom they admire but who is more nearly similar—a best friend or companion—would have a greater impact on their behavior. Similarly, it is not likely that the model behavior of physicians, scientists, and other experts could be too effective in convincing dope addicts, habitual smokers, alcoholics, and overweight people to change their habits. However, the referent power of one's peers, who have given up their injurious habits, may account for the effectiveness of such programs as Synanon, anti-smoking group discussions (Janis and Hoffman, 1971), Alcoholics Anonymous, and Weight Watchers.

Informational and Expert Power
In discussing the social power of those who purportedly favored the maintenance of all-black universities (Kelman, 1958), we mentioned that people seem to pay closer attention to a message from an expert; therefore, the information he conveys will be more persuasive and have more long-lasting effects. Often, then, expert and informational power go hand in hand. Occasionally, however, the effects of information are negated by a negative expert (one whom we distrust) or by a negative referent (one whom we dislike). The "boomerang effect," mentioned earlier, represents such an instance. The informational power of the film *Battle of Britain* was negated because of the soldiers' overwhelming negative attitudes toward the authorities who presented it (Hovland, Lumsdaine, and Sheffield, 1949). When a lecture was given on the value of antihistamines as a cold remedy and it contained some persuasive information, it was influential when it was presented by a "trustworthy" source (a professor of biology and medicine). However, when it was given by an "untrustworthy" source (a drug manufacturer with a vested interest), there was greater negative expert influence than there was positive informational influence (Hovland and Weiss, 1952). It seems that informational influence (which is less dependent upon the source) has a more permanent effect, but that any negative expert power is gradually dissipated. Therefore, if attitudes are measured several weeks later, the respondents tend to show what has been called a "sleeper

effect," that is, a change toward acceptance of the views presented by the negative expert or negative referent. The investigators were surprised that the subjects did show a more favorable attitude toward Great Britain and toward antihistamines later on, although this result seems consistent with the concept of the relative permanence of informational and expert influence. Subsequent research showed that if the subjects were again reminded of the nature of the communicator, they tended to revert to their earlier opinions (Kelman and Hovland, 1953).

SECONDARY EFFECTS OF SOCIAL INFLUENCE

Our emphasis thus far has been on the primary effects of social power—immediate changes produced in someone by an influencing agent. We have suggested that coercive and reward power require surveillance in order to be effective, and that only informational power leads to internalized change. However, in many cases people eventually accept and come to believe in certain changes that had initially been forced upon them. Secondarily, coercion and reward may lead to private dependent, or even independent, change. Eventually, legitimacy, expertise, and reference may also result in socially independent change. The ways in which a person's attitudes and opinions change following a forced compliance in his behavior have been of particular interest to social psychologists. Three such secondary changes will be considered here: (1) new perceptions following after social influence on behavior; (2) new perceptions of the influencing agent due to his use of power; and (3) attempts by the influenced party to reduce any inconsistency between his behavior and his belief or attitude, or between his own inconsistent perceptions about himself.

New Perceptions following Social Influence

"Johnny, taste your porridge."
"I don't like it."
"Johnny, I said taste your porridge."
"I don't like it."
(Sternly) "Johnny! Taste . . . your . . . porridge!"
(Tastes) "Hmmm. I like it."
This not-too-uncommon incident exemplifies private acceptance

of a change in behavior (socially independent change) after coercion. We assume that there was a threat of punishment in the parent's voice. We also assume that Johnny (who really seemed to like the porridge after tasting it) will continue to eat it even after his parent is out of sight—indeed, even after he has forgotten that he was *ordered* to change his behavior in the first place. Social psychologists have been particularly curious about why people change their behavior in this way. The simplest explanation seems to be that Johnny changed his perception of the porridge after being influenced by his parent. Why didn't he want to eat it in the first place? Probably because its appearance did not appeal to him—perhaps he thought it resembled something else that he knew was distasteful. If so, then he probably never would have tasted it if he had had a choice; and so long as he did not taste it, he would have continued to assume that it was distasteful. Why does he like it now? Probably because he finds that it does not taste the way he had imagined it would. Sometimes psychologists overlook the simple explanation in favor of the more complex one. Yet it seems to us that many of the findings of private attitude change following "forced compliance" can be explained in this fashion.

A Tale about a Short Hoe. Since the turn of the century, California truck farmers have insisted that their predominantly Mexican American farm laborers use a short (12-inch) hoe to thin the crops and chop the weeds in their fields. They believed that the short hoe, requiring the laborer to stoop down and remain close to the ground, produced better results since he could see the weeds better and be closer to his work. They believed that changing to a longer hoe would increase their costs by reducing the laborers' efficiency 25–50 percent. Even though medical authorities testified that the short hoe leads to back problems and greater fatigue, thus reducing productivity, this expert opinion was rejected. The workers' representatives, attempting to use their legitimate power of the powerless, pleaded with the growers to think about the physical damage caused by the short hoe and the effect that this would have on the poor worker and his family. The United Farm Workers' president, Cesar Chavez, also argued with logic that the long-range effects of the short hoe would inevitably be detrimental to all concerned, pointing to his own back injuries sustained when he was a young field hand. None of these bases of social power was able to change the minds of the truck farmers. Finally, in 1975, the California State Division of Industrial Safety, utilizing a ruling made by the Orange County Superior Court, forbade any further use of the short hoe. This combination of the legitimate power of established government and the coercive power of threatened fines led the growers to comply, but only after considerable resistance and complaint. However, after the longer hoe had been in use for a while, a major lettuce producer announced that production had increased by 10 percent, adding, "We fought this thing and worried over it and now it turns out not to be a problem. Frankly, I feel like a goddamn jackass." The longer hoe is here to stay; what had initially been a socially dependent change, produced by the combination of legitimate and coercive power, eventually led to private acceptance (Jones, 1975).

The Acceptance of Forced Desegregation. When the Supreme Court decided in 1954 that *de jure* school segregation was illegal (*Brown* v. *Board of Education*), many people were up in arms. Some agreed that racial prejudice was bad, but they said, "You can't legislate morality." Yet, as a result of subsequent decisions and the threat of fines and imprisonment, schools were desegregated throughout much of the South. People's attitudes seem to have changed reluctantly in accordance with their behavior. It has been found that white parents who had been obliged to send their children to desegregated schools later adopted a more favorable view of integration as compared with those in areas where desegregation had been forestalled (Brigham and Weissbach, 1972). Now, with the schools in the North engulfed in controversy over court-ordered busing of school children, it remains to be seen whether a similar change in behavior and attitudes will occur.

One Power Base Affects Another

As pointed out earlier, the use of coercion—the threat or actual use of punishment by an influencing agent—will cause him to be disliked by the person affected. That person, then, associates the effects with the agent. The illegitimate use of power will also lead to personal rejection. The teacher who punishes a student—by corporal means, verbal reproof, or unmerited poor grades—will generally be disliked by the student. Since dislike may lead to negative referent power, the result may resemble the "boomerang effect"—a negative change in private attitude (Raven and French, 1958). There may also be a negative "halo effect"—the influencing agent will be seen as less expert and less legitimate, and thus any information he presents will be less persuasive. On the other hand, when reward power is used, the result may be a positive attitude change. When students are well rewarded for advocating in a debate the merits of a position that is exactly the opposite of their own, they will tend to adopt the position they have advocated. There is a general tendency to associate a reward received with the person who has been attempting influence and with the position that has been advocated (Elms and Janis, 1965).

Dissonance Reduction and Attributions following Social Influence
It may seem obvious that if a person has been generously rewarded
for doing something, he may begin to enjoy that activity; the greater
the reward, the more he will like the act. Now consider a rather
different and opposing position—that a person may enjoy doing
something even more if he is rewarded only *moderately*, just
enough to persuade him to do it. This was the conclusion reached by
Leon Festinger in his theory of cognitive dissonance (1957). The
results of his first study, which tended to support this view (Festinger and Carlsmith, 1959), seemed to be so counter-intuitive that
they caused a raging controversy among social psychologists—one
that has not yet been fully resolved. Let us first review the theory
of cognitive dissonance.

The Theory of Cognitive Dissonance. Festinger views an individual's
world as composed of a large number of cognitive elements, that is,
things of which we are aware—"knowledges," if we may use the
plural of that word. We are aware of our behavior: that we are smoking, that we are wearing a woolen suit, that we have just purchased a
new Volkswagen, and so forth. We are also aware of certain facts and
our own beliefs and attitudes: that we like smoking, that smoking
may lead to lung cancer, that the Volkswagen has a good resale
value, that citrus fruits are raised in Florida and California, that the
highest mountain in North America is Mt. McKinley. Most of these
cognitive elements are not related to each other—my knowledge that
I am smoking is not related to my knowledge that citrus fruits are
grown in Florida and California; the fact that Mt. McKinley is the
highest mountain in North America is not related to the fact that VWs
have a good resale value. On the other hand, other pairs of elements
are related to each other. If the implications of one piece of knowledge are opposed to another, the two elements are dissonant. The
knowledge that smoking may lead to lung cancer implies that we
should not be smoking. Thus, the knowledge that we *are* smoking is
dissonant with the knowledge that smoking is harmful. On the other
hand, the knowledge that smoking is enjoyable suggests that we
should be smoking; therefore, these two elements are consonant.
The same is true for the knowledge that we have just purchased a
VW and VWs have a good resale value.
  Festinger goes on to state that dissonance is uncomfortable and
produces tension, and that when we become aware of cognitive dissonance we tend to make a cognitive or behavioral change in order to
reduce that dissonance and restore consonance. If we are smoking
and know that smoking may lead to lung cancer, we may do one of
the following: give up smoking, reject the information that smoking
leads to lung cancer, try to obtain information on the positive values

of smoking, contribute money toward the development of a noncarcinogenic cigarette, and so forth.

As an example in decision-making, imagine that we wish to purchase a car but do not know whether to get a Ford or a VW. It is difficult to decide between them since the Ford has many positive features (it is roomy, aesthetically pleasing, quieter in operation, and easier to have repaired) as does the VW (it is less expensive, it has a good resale value, and it has lower repair costs). The Ford also has many negative features (it has high repair costs, it has a low resale value, and it is difficult to park) as does the VW (it makes one feel cramped inside, it is rather ugly, and it has unpleasant wartime associations). All of these cognitive elements make the decision difficult, but decide we must. Afterward (let us say we bought the VW) our dissonance is increased. Why? Because all of the negative factors of our choice are still cognitively present (the VW is still small, ugly, and unpleasant) as are all of the positive factors of the rejected alternative (the Ford is still roomier, prettier, and quieter). Festinger says that after making a decision, the individual has a special need to reduce his dissonance—by finding out additional factors that make his choice seem a good one, by trying to convince friends to make the same decision, by reading articles or pamphlets showing that the rejected alternative is a poor product, and so forth. The greater the conflict was before the decision, the greater the dissonance will be afterward. Have you ever seen someone who has just given up smoking trying with great vigor to get his friends to stop? Possibly he is extremely pleased with his own decision and wants to share its benefits with those whom he loves. But all too often, the vehemence of his behavior suggests that he is also trying to satisfy himself that, despite all of the pleasures he is forgoing, his decision was a good one; effectively convincing others will also help him to convince himself. (See the discussion about the proselyting behavior of the Seekers on page 16.)

Dissonance and Forced Compliance. Festinger's theory of cognitive dissonance after making a decision can readily be applied to our analysis of social power. A person who is asked to do something that he really does not want to do is, almost by definition, undergoing conflict: should he comply or not? If he decides to comply, he must again resolve his dissonance; the greater the conflict he experienced before the decision, the greater will be his dissonance afterward. This concept is illustrated in Figure 6.6.

It is reasonable to assume that there are very few acts that most people would *not* commit if the power exerted on them were great enough (say, the threat of death). But, to take a less extreme example, think about the issue of cheating on an examination. We hope that

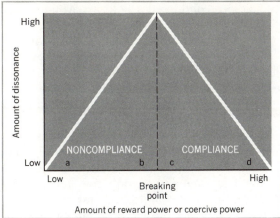

Figure 6.6
"Forced compliance":
Dissonance as a func-
tion of the magnitude of
reward or coercive
power. Before an indi-
vidual decides to
comply with an un-
desirable request, his
inner conflict is highest
around the "breaking
point," the point above
which he complies and
below which he does
not. When the reward or
punishment offered is
very high or very low,
the individual experi-
ences no conflict before
making a decision and
no dissonance after-
ward. Both his disso-
nance and his conflict
are greatest around the
breaking point (after
Festinger, 1957).

most students would never contemplate such a thing. But at some price, for example $1000, some students probably would. Suppose that only $1.00 were offered for a student to take an exam for a classmate. Most students would probably reject this offer without hesitation. But what if the offer were $10,000? Undoubtedly some students would consent to cheat with very little hesitation. In rejecting the $1.00 offer or accepting the $10,000 offer, there would be no conflict before making the decision. The rejected offer would require no explanation, for the reward is so small. The accepted offer would also carry its own justification—cheating may be bad, but for $10,000! Suppose that $1000 is the breaking point, the point at which the offer is just large enough to balance all of the arguments against cheating. At this point, conceivably, nothing would happen, and the student would just fluctuate back and forth. Let us make it $1001. There may be a lot of hesitation and soul-searching, but finally it is accepted. If the amount is $999—not quite enough—there may also be a lot of hesitation and conflict, but finally the offer is turned down. In both cases, the student must resolve his post-decisional dissonance. *Compliance:* "Why did I compromise my morals by agreeing to cheat? Did I do it for only $1001? No. (Possible dissonance reduction:) I guess that cheating is not all *that* bad. Most people have done it at one time or another. Besides, that exam is stupid." *Noncompliance:* "Why did I reject $999—money that I could have used so nicely to do so many things I would like to do? Obviously because cheating is a terrible thing—now that I think about it, worse than I had ever imagined. Anyone caught cheating should be strung up from the nearest lamp post."

This tendency for an individual to change his views to make them consistent with his behavior has led to much research in social psychology on the issue of forced compliance. When Judson

Mills (1958) conducted a field experiment with sixth-grade children, he found that those who cheated for high rewards, or did *not* cheat for *low* rewards, did not change their views about cheating. However, those who cheated for relatively low rewards became more lenient in their views about cheating. And those who did not cheat, despite attractive inducements, became very harsh and critical in their attitudes toward anyone who would even consider it.

Cognitive change for one dollar? The first major test of the dissonance and forced compliance hypothesis was carried out by Leon Festinger and J. Merrill Carlsmith (1959). The subject was asked to participate in a "measure of performance." Imagine yourself filling a tray with 12 spools using only one hand, then emptying the tray and refilling it again, over and over, for half an hour. You would probably be relieved when the experimenter tells you that this test is over. But then he gives you a board with 48 square pegs and instructs you to turn each of these one quarter turn, again with only one hand. When you have finished this, you must start again and turn each one another quarter turn for an additional half hour. And that is the experiment—performing unusually monotonous tasks for an hour. When it is over, you prepare to leave. But wait. The experimenter tells you of a problem and asks your help:

> *There are actually two groups in this experiment. In one, the group you were in, we bring the subject in and give him essentially no introduction to the experiment. . . . In the other group, we have a student that we've hired that works for us regularly . . . and I introduce him [to the subject]. . . . I say: This is so-and-so, who's just finished the experiment, and I've asked him to tell you a little of what it's about before you start. The fellow who works for us then, in conversation with the next subject, makes these points [about the experiment]: "It was enjoyable, I had a lot of fun, I enjoyed myself, it was very interesting, it was intriguing, it was exciting. . . ." Now the fellow who normally does this couldn't make it today . . . so we've been looking for someone that we could hire to do it for us. You see, we've got another subject waiting [Festinger and Carlsmith, 1959, p. 204].*

At this point the experimenter offers you either $20.00 or $1.00 (depending upon the experimental condition) to tell another subject that the task was enjoyable, intriguing, and so forth. Practically all of the subjects (like you, perhaps) agree to cooperate and then proceed to tell an innocent-looking young woman (who is an accomplice) a convincing story about how enjoyable the task has been. Now (following her instructions), the accomplice says, "But my roommate took part in this experiment and said that it was really very dull and

boring." "Oh, no," you respond (if you are like the typical subject).
"She must have been in another experiment. This one is really very
interesting and enjoyable." The experimenter then thanks you for
helping him out in the emergency, pays you the $20.00 or $1.00, and
you leave.

An hour or so later, you are interviewed by a departmental investigator elsewhere on the campus (presumably he has no relationship
with the experimenter). The investigator is trying to find out what is
happening in various psychological experiments that are being conducted on campus and specifically asks you about the experiment in
which you participated. Did you find the task you were given (spool-
packing and peg-turning) enjoyable?

You have cooperated in an extremely dull experiment, have
been inveigled into telling another innocent "subject" that it was interesting and enjoyable (for $20.00 or $1.00), and are now asked how
interesting and enjoyable you really thought it was. Under which
condition ($20.00 or $1.00) would you say that it was truly enjoyable?
What prediction would you have made if this situation had been described to you before you became familiar with dissonance theory?
What prediction would you make now?

From dissonance theory, you can see that the $1.00 subjects
would be at about point c in Figure 6.6; the $20.00 subjects would be
at about point d. Each subject may ask himself: "Why in the world
did I tell that poor, innocent girl that turning those pegs and packing
those spools was such an interesting and enjoyable experience?"
The $20.00 subjects can respond to this question rather easily: "For
$20.00, that's why. The task was boring, but for $20.00 I can compromise somewhat on my usual penchant for telling the truth." The
$1.00 subjects would have more difficulty. They might say, "Well it
wasn't for $1.00—that is not enough to get me to do much of any-
thing. I guess the reason I said the task was enjoyable and interesting is because there were certain things about it that *were* enjoyable
and interesting. While turning the square pegs, I could pretend that I
was operating a complicated switchboard in a space station. And I
saw the spool-packing as something of a challenge—a chance to test
my own manual dexterity." In any event, although Festinger and
Carlsmith did not discover the exact reasons that the subjects gave
for their compliance, they did find dramatic evidence that those who
received only $1.00 were much more inclined to consider the task
pleasurable.

The findings of this study—that the *more* you pay someone to do
something he really doesn't want to do, the *less* you will affect his
opinion—certainly seem to run counter to our intuitive beliefs. It
flies in the face of much of the traditional work done in psychology,
which holds that the larger the reward, the greater the effect. Yet, the

Figure 6.7
Attitude change following behavior change. *Cognitive dissonance theorists would say that Linus was simply reducing dissonance. Self-perception theorists would examine the change in his self-attributions. However, we cannot rule out the possibility that after viewing the program Linus saw features in it that were unexpectedly pleasing.*

Festinger and Carlsmith study was followed by many others that seemed to support the same conclusion. Furthermore, it appears that other bases of power may operate similarly, particularly the socially dependent ones; could it be, for example, that complying with an authority because of his high legitimate power might lead to *less* private acceptance (since the legitimacy justifies the compliance)?

How to get people to eat grasshoppers—and like them. One of the more intriguing studies of referent power and forced compliance was conducted by Ewart Smith (1961) and developed further by Philip Zimbardo and his associates (Zimbardo et al., 1965). It consisted of trying to persuade army reservists and college students to eat fried grasshoppers. One communicator was very friendly, relaxed, casual, and generally likable; another was cool, stiff, forbidding, and unlikable. Those who ate the grasshoppers at the request of the unlikable communicator were much more inclined to say later on that they found them tasty; why else would they eat them? Those who complied with the request of the "nice guy" had a built-in explanation for their behavior—they did it for that fellow because he was so nice; they did not need to reduce their dissonance by *liking* the grasshoppers.

Self-attributions following Forced Compliance. From our discussion of dissonance reduction following forced compliance, it appears that the individual goes through a process of self-attribution, very similar to that which we discussed on page 94. This analysis is somewhat different from the strict dissonance theory position of Festinger, which postulated a simple move toward consonance. The self-attribution (or self-perception) analysis of forced compliance was first presented by Daryl Bem (1967, 1972). He postulated that the individual tends to reconsider his past behavior (like the televised instant replay), trying to understand why he did certain things. He might analyze his own behavior just as he analyzes the behavior of others, reasoning backward—as Jones and Davis (1965) suggested—from the effects, to the behavior, to the extenuating circumstances, and then back to his own beliefs, attitudes, predispositions, and so forth.

Believing one's false confessions. In a particularly interesting study, Bem had a group of subjects rate a series of cartoons on a "very funny–very unfunny" scale. Then he "conditioned" the subjects, through a large number of trials, to lie whenever an amber light lit the room and to tell the truth whenever a green light appeared. (He, of course, varied the lights so that for some subjects green was associated with lying and amber with truth-telling.) Then he requested the subjects to say that some cartoons were funny and that others were not funny; sometimes they were answering truthfully and sometimes untruthfully. At the same time, the room was bathed in either the "lie light" or the "truth light." He found that when the subjects lied while the "truth light" was shining, they began to believe their own lie—that is, if they originally believed that the cartoon was "unfunny" and yet they said that it was "funny" while the "truth light" was shining, then they would begin to believe that the cartoon was truly funny. They did not change their beliefs, however, when they lied at the same time that the "lie light" was shining. The signal for "lie," as in our attribution discussion, provided the extenuating circumstances that the subject needed: "Of course I said it was funny. The light called for that." Bem suggested that the $20.00 payment in the Festinger and Carlsmith experiment functioned as a "lie light" and the $1.00 as a "truth light." This explanation is very appealing. Although it is sometimes cited as a criticism of dissonance theory, we do not believe this to be the case; rather, we believe that this analysis enhances a dissonance position. In any event, what this study demonstrates is that if we can be subtly persuaded to do something that runs counter to our beliefs or attitudes, we will tend to restore consistency by changing our beliefs or attitudes (Bem, 1965).

Philip Zimbardo (1970) compared these forced compliance, self-attribution studies to police interrogations and confessions. The police rely heavily on confessions to solve crimes, since many would not otherwise be solved, and the police and the courts can save a lot of time and effort if the suspect confesses. At times, the police have been known to use extreme measures—the "third degree," threats of harsh punishment, and other forms of coercion—in order to obtain confessions. However, a number of major Supreme Court and lower court decisions in the 1950s forbade many of these harsh measures. Use of the rubber hose and other forms of physical punishment have virtually been eliminated now. In their place, the police use more subtle means to induce confessions. Manuals on criminal interrogation (for example, Inbau and Reid, 1962) suggest that the suspect should be interrogated in an unfamiliar room that has few pictures or decorations. The suspect should be required to sit in a straight-backed, armless chair so that he may tire more quickly. The interrogator should be firm, but not overwhelming; in a friendly manner, he should ask his questions carefully, repeating and rephrasing them from time to time. He should indicate that he understands why one might be tempted to commit a crime such as the one the suspect is accused of, permitting the suspect to save face by confessing.

This subtle approach to interrogation would seem to be more favorable to the suspect. Yet, Zimbardo argues, some suspects may be harmed even more as a result. Occasionally a suspect falsely confesses to a crime that, as later demonstrated, he could not possibly have committed. If harsh measures have been used to extract a false confession, the suspect can later attribute his confession to that punishment. But if a false confession is extracted through subtle means, the suspect has more difficulty explaining his confession to himself; in fact, he may become confused about what he actually did. In one particularly dramatic case, a man confessed to the rape and murder of two young women, and he was convicted for this capital crime. Although he did not repudiate his confession, he might have been executed, except for the fact that a second man was apprehended for another crime, was identified, and later confessed to this rape and murder; the evidence was unquestionable that the second man was the real criminal. To provide the greatest protection against such unrepudiated false confessions, Zimbardo urges that careful records be maintained of all police interrogations, with every possible precaution taken to forestall subtly induced, as well as coercive, false confessions.

ENHANCING SOCIAL INFLUENCE

This chapter has examined the six bases of social influence, individually, in combination, and in relation to the complex secondary effects that may emerge. There is, of course, no guarantee that a person in a position of power can effect a particular change, despite the means that he has available. However, a clever influencing agent may be able to enhance his social power by carefully preparing the scene and by developing strategies to make full use of that power. If he has expert power, he may augment it by setting the proper scene (see our discussion of the doctor's office on page 92). Or the agent can attempt to strengthen his power base by changing the perception of power itself: for example, a lord may usurp the power of a legitimate king by force and then prepare a genealogical chart to convince his subjects that he should indeed be their legitimate king. A twentieth-century dictator who assumes power by force may similarly try to rig an election in order to establish his legitimacy. Strategies to enhance social influence thus have both political and conceptual importance. Let us, therefore, analyze several of these techniques.

Ecological Manipulation

Imagine that you are having a party at your home. The guests arrive and seem very cold and stiff. In order to make them feel more relaxed and receptive, you may serve alcoholic beverages. Alcohol tends to reduce inhibitions and facilitate social interaction. You may also note that all of the men are wearing their jackets. You think that they would relax somewhat more if they took them off, but you suspect that they might resent your suggestion. So, when nobody is looking, you turn up the thermostat. Soon the house is sweltering. Now you can turn to the men and say, "It's awfully warm in here. Wouldn't you be more comfortable with your jackets off?"

This device has been called "ecological manipulation" (Cartwright, 1965). By changing the environment, you set the stage for social influence. City planners sometimes seem to use this strategy in planning the expansion of cities. If the goal is to have a city composed of small community clusters, rather than a sprawl of continuous housing, one could try to persuade people to move to certain areas. But such an effort would not be as effective as planning the number and location of freeway exits or train stops.

A similar technique was used by Lewin (1943, 1952) during World War II to try to change people's meat-eating habits. His task was to try to persuade Americans to ease the meat shortage by switching to nutritious but less popular cuts of meat (for example, sweetbreads, lungs, and hearts). He assumed that if those cuts could be put on the family's table, people would eat them and eventually like them. Thus, he developed means for influencing those who decide what goes on the table—namely, homemakers. Through the homemaker, he knew he could reach others. The U. S. government funded this research, which proved to be effective among the groups of homemakers in the few communities that were studied. (The methods that he used to influence the homemakers are described in Chapter 8.) Unfortunately, the government did not support the implementation of Lewin's techniques on a nationwide basis; even though meat was rationed, most Americans continued with their same preferences.

Guilt-Arousal, Obligation, and Influence

Mother (on telephone to son): "Hello, Sam? I just wanted to tell you that that coat you left here had three buttons missing. Yes, I have sewed them all on now, ironed it, and took out the shine. It's as good as new. You can pick it up when you come for dinner tonight. What? You may have work to do? Oh well, don't worry if you can't make it. Even if I made a big dinner, what does it matter? I didn't have any-*

Figure 6.8

Momma   By Mell Lazarus

COURTESY OF MELL LAZARUS AND FIELD NEWSPAPER
SYNDICATE © 1974 FIELD NEWSPAPER SYNDICATE.

*thing else to do anyway. And most of it won't get wasted. It will
keep. I can have it for lunch tomorrow, and dinner, and maybe I can
give some away to the neighbors. . . . No; it doesn't matter at all;
don't you worry about that one bit. You must have other things to
think about—it will all work out—like last week, right? . . . So do
go ahead and enjoy yourself. Better it should happen to me and not
to you. . . . But, of course, if you really think that you would like to
come, and it isn't too much trouble. . . ."*

Perhaps you have recognized elements from Dan Greenburg's
whimsical *How to Be a Jewish Mother* (1964). These influence techniques are not unique to Jewish mothers, or even to mothers in general, but they can be extremely effective. Their relationship to the
bases of social power is not entirely obvious. There are elements of
the legitimate power of the powerless, especially an appeal to the legitimate obligations of a son to his mother. However, these techniques emphasize a *preparation* for influence, a setting of the stage.
You invoke obligations on the part of another person by first helping
him or doing him a good turn. You induce guilt feelings, making the
person less able to resist the influence attempt that follows. (We
would particularly encourage you to read that portion of Greenburg's
book in which he shows how you can offer a person an ash tray with
your right hand and then sweep it away just in time—so that you
catch the flicked ashes in your left hand! "Don't worry about it," you
say, and, with guilt assured, you are ready to make your request.)

The effectiveness of guilt arousal in setting the stage for influence has been demonstrated in several experimental studies (Carlsmith and Gross, 1969; Freedman, Wallington, and Bless, 1967). The
experimenter typically tricks the subject into committing some sort
of transgression—for example, he has a confederate tell the subject
about the experiment and then gets the subject to lie and deny that
he knows anything about it; he has the subject believe he has broken
an expensive piece of equipment; or he leaves notes around the lab-

oratory that the subject happens to notice, and then remarks that it is good that he has not seen those notes since that would ruin the experiment. Regardless of the type of transgression, it appears that the guilt experienced by the subject is such that he is quite ready to comply with any request (for example, making a telephone call to help save the California redwoods, or volunteering for extra experimental hours); those who are not made to feel guilty comply far less frequently.

Influence by Gradations: The Foot-in-the-Door Technique
When Jerome Frank's subjects had reached the point where they would not eat another soda cracker, Frank found that he could persuade them to change their minds by using the gradation technique. "Would you at least pick up a cracker? Now smell it. Now touch it to your lips. Taste it. Now would you eat it?" (Frank, 1944). This approach has long been used by salesmen, military conquerors, seducers, and others. Jonathan Freedman and Scott Fraser (1966), who called it the "foot-in-the-door" technique, demonstrated that if you can get someone to comply with a small request (signing a petition to encourage safe driving), he will more readily comply with a larger request (agreeing to allow a large, ugly sign—"DRIVE CARE-FULLY"—to be posted on his front lawn). The technique can be seen as an aspect of Festinger's cognitive dissonance paradigm (Fig. 6.6): if you apply just enough pressure to induce someone to comply with a request, then he will reduce his cognitive dissonance by agreeing with the behavior (yes, since I have done this, then safe driving must be important); and since his attitude has changed, he will be prepared to engage in even more extreme behavior. It is also possible that the influencing agent, by successfully persuading the individual to comply with a small request, has helped to establish his power position for future use.

People in the Netherlands have told me that during World War II the Nazis would have encountered stiff resistance from the Dutch people if they had immediately started arresting Dutch Jews and deporting them to concentration camps and gas chambers in Germany. However, their technique was far subtler. First of all, they required the Jews to wear yellow stars of David (a bit silly, but nothing to get upset about); then the Jews were forbidden to use public parks; then they were restricted in their employment; then they were forbidden to live in certain areas; then they were forced to move into a restricted ghetto area; then that area was sealed off with barbed wire and gun emplacements. After waiting an appropriate length of time, the Nazis spirited the first Dutch Jews to "work camps" in Germany. Each step seemed less severe, once there had been compliance with the previous step.

Summary

Social influence, defined as a change in one person's behavior that is attributable to another person or group, is a ubiquitous phenomenon. Indeed, it is so much a part of social interaction that we are seldom aware of it in our daily lives. Although social influence has a number of complex and interesting forms, John R. P. French, Jr. and Bertram H. Raven have singled out six that are quite common: information, reward, coercion, expertise, reference, and legitimacy.

Informational influence (or power) stems from the persuasive content of an influence communication per se, rather than the attributes of the influence agent himself or the relationship between him and the person he is trying to influence; a math teacher who explains to a student the logic behind solving an equation in a particular manner thus exercises informational power. Reward power arises from the influence agent's ability to mediate rewards or benefits for the one who is being influenced, where it is clear that the agent will reward him only if he complies with the agent's request. Similarly, coercive power derives from the ability to mediate punishments, where punishment is exercised only if the person being influenced does not follow the agent's instructions; a teacher who promises a student an A if he completes his assignment in a prescribed manner, or who threatens to keep the student after school if he fails to do so, is exercising reward and coercive power, respectively. Expert power emerges from the fact that the one being influenced attributes superior knowledge or ability to the influence agent; a teacher who asks a student to accept and use a particular formula because the teacher is an expert ("take my word for it, the formula is correct—perhaps later you will understand why") exercises expert power. Referent power comes about because the one being influenced identifies with the influence agent, perceives some commonality with him, or wishes to form a unit with him; for example, a teacher would exercise referent power if he asked a student to adopt a particular position on a certain issue because both teacher and student shared certain underlying values, group affiliations, and so forth. Finally, legitimate power arises when the one being influenced accepts the agent's right to influence him, thereby feeling an obligation to comply; a teacher who asks a student to carry out a certain request because it is a rule, and an experimenter who asks a subject to behave in a specific way because it is "part of the experiment" are each exercising legitimate power.

The six bases of social influence differ from one another in several important ways. Informational power is socially independent since, if effective, the one being influenced does not continue to relate his changed behavior, belief, or attitude to the influence agent. In contrast, the other five bases of power require the person to relate his changed behavior, belief, or attitude to the influence agent, and are therefore socially dependent. Among the five socially dependent forms of influence, reward and coercive power differ from expert, referent, and legitimate in that, to be effective, the former require the influence agent to maintain surveillance (he must check to see whether the person complies), while the latter do not. Finally, depending upon the particular situation in which they are employed, all six bases of power may result in varying degrees of positive influence (influence in the direction desired by the influence agent) or negative influence (in a different direction than desired).

In addition to producing the immediate changes desired by the influence agent (the primary effect), social influence may produce a number of complex secondary effects, leading to the eventual acceptance of and belief in changes that were initially forced upon the one being influenced. These secondary effects include the acquisition of new perceptions following social influence, a generalized effect of one power base upon others, and a tendency to experience and reduce cognitive dissonance. There is no guarantee, of course, that a person exercising power can produce a particular primary or secondary effect, despite the means that he has available. However, a clever influence agent may be able to enhance his social power using such techniques as "ecological manipulation" (altering some aspect of the other person's environment), arousing feelings of guilt and obligation in the other person, and the "foot-in-the-door" technique (influence by gradations).

In this chapter we have discussed the influence process primarily as it occurs at an interpersonal level, typically with only two persons—the target person and the influencing agent. Influence, however, is exerted not only between individuals, but between and within groups. The remaining chapters of this book will explore the role of influence and other processes in increasingly complex social settings. Chapter 7 will introduce this analysis by examining the structure of groups; Chapter 8 will explore the ways in which groups affect the behavior and feelings of their members; Chapter 9 will deal with the problems of group performance, group effectiveness, and leadership—how an individual characteristically exercises influence in his group; and Chapter 10 will discuss influence and conflict as these occur among and between groups.

Dimensions of Group Structure

Evaluation Structure
Satisfaction and Morale

Interdependence Structure
The Structure of Goals Interdependence
The Structure of Means Interdependence
Interdependence among Subunits: Coalitions

Communication Structure
Interaction Process Analysis
Communication Networks

Role Structure
Development of Roles in Interaction
Culture, Tradition, and Role Definition
Roles and Communication Networks

Influence and Power Structure
Communication and Influence in Social Hierarchies
Power and Role Structure in the Family

THE STRUCTURE OF
GROUPS

SEVEN

245

Caste and Status in a Circus Community. In our daily lives, our relationships with friends and acquaintances tend to become so much a part of us, so accepted as facts of life, that we seldom question them. But when we suddenly find ourselves immersed in a new and different life style (for example, participating in a group that has markedly different relationships), we have the opportunity to become truly sensitive to what our various relationships, new as well as old, may mean for us. I had an experience very much like this one summer when I had the job of clarinetist in a circus band.

The circus I joined the summer before finishing high school was one of the last remaining traveling tent circuses. We slept in bunks on a large circus train, awoke early in the morning in a strange town, and walked to the circus grounds. Breakfast was served in the large "cooktent"—one of the first tents to be set up—before dawn. Then we had several hours to relax, practice, and socialize before lunch and the matinee show. Afterward we had a few additional hours before dinner in the cooktent and then the evening show. We finished by midnight and then returned to the train, which was being loaded up for our night trip. The next morning found us in yet another town, prepared to start the day all over again.

The circus with its itinerant life tended to perpetuate itself as a separate little community; socially and psychologically the circus community maintained its own life style and developed its own norms, values, and social structure. At the time I thought of myself as a musician, and so I felt a strong kinship with and interest in other musicians. One morning, shortly after I had joined the circus, I was walking from the train with my friends and fellow bandsmen, Jack and Barry. We spotted two other musicians walking toward the circus grounds, and I suggested that we go over and introduce ourselves. Barry, who had been with the circus for some time, rejected this suggestion immediately: "They're no good. Don't mess around with them." I didn't understand. I said that I had heard them play in front of the Side Show tent, and thought they played terrific Dixieland. "Exactly," Barry added. "They're Side Show. They don't play good and they're no damn good. And you should steer clear of them, if you know what's good for you." Later, this admonition was driven home even more clearly. The Big Top band, of which I was a member, felt that it was time for a cost of living raise, and so a representative of the American Federation of Musicians came to serve as our negotiating agent with the management. It would have made sense for us to maintain a united front with the musicians in the Side Show band, who were also members of the AFM and poorly paid. Yet the senior spokesman for the Big Top band would have no part of this; indeed, he repeatedly emphasized to the AFM negotiator that only the Big Top and not the Side Show band was bringing these grievances.

Shortly thereafter, we were having lunch in the cooktent during a very busy hour, and a waiter seated two Side Show people at our table. My fellow bandsmen were furious—what sort of ignorant waiter was this, seating Side Show people at the Big Top table! The Big Top bandsmen became loud and abusive and were almost on the verge of a fight when the Side Showmen scowled and moved away to a Side Show table. My friend said that he would report this incident to the cooktent manager and make certain that the facts of life were explained to the waiter.

I had never lived before in a society that maintained such a clear caste system. There was the Big Top and its personnel, and then there was the Side Show and its personnel. The major performances took place in the Big Top. That is where the stars were—the trapeze artists, animal trainers, tumblers, and high-wire walkers—and I was proud to be identified as part of the Big Top. The Side Show had its freaks, its magicians, the tattooed lady, the sword swallower, the half-woman-half-alligator, the hula dancers, and the traveling shell games complete with shills. These were hardly the people one would want to associate with. There was, to be sure, a status hierarchy within both the Big Top and the Side Show—usually associated with the importance of the person and his act, as well as the level of his salary. Some people received more admiration and respect than others. Yet, to a Big Topper, even the highest paid Side Show person was not as worthy of respect as the lowliest Big Topper—even though his salary might be several times larger. Interestingly, the Big Top-Side Show caste division in the circus was even stronger than the black-white caste division of the larger society (during the 1940s), even in this community where many of the personnel came from the Deep South where antiblack prejudice was particularly intense at that time.

The otherwise rigid and impermeable caste system of the circus was breached at only one visible point. Several of the performers in both the Side Show and the Big Top were male homosexuals. Quite a few of the clowns in the Big Top were homosexuals, while a number of the Side Show dancers were male homosexuals and transvestites. Indeed, the most popular hula dancer (who was so attractive and such a good dancer that "she" often performed outside the tent to help lure male customers) was a transvestite. ("She" was accepted as a female among the circus people and was referred to with a feminine pronoun.) I was told that having a male transvestite dancer was a traditional part of many traveling circuses and carnivals and that this tradition dated back to former local blue laws that restricted the display of the female (but not the male) body in public. In any event, homosexuality was generally accepted in the circus community. Furthermore, association among homosexuals was even permitted across caste lines; the circus people just looked the other way when the homosexual Big Toppers got together with the homosexual Side Showmen. After the matinee and before dinner, the Big Top clowns often had refreshments with the Side Show dancers, including the popular hula dancer who was now dressed modestly in a skirt and blouse. Occasionally this breach of the caste system fulfilled a definite community function—the homosexuals could sometimes mediate or settle disputes between the Big Top and the Side Show.

In addition to the caste system, the circus had its share of association groups—friendships that had formed along occupational lines. Although the Big Top bandsmen might have an occasional conversation with a juggler or horseback rider, this was very rare. The only real contact the band had with anyone else was with the "Colonel," the Big Top's master of ceremonies. The seating arrangements in the cooktent tended to follow occupational as well as caste lines. There were, of course, quite a few sexual pairings, couples who stayed together in hotels when the circus remained in one town for several days. But even these couples tended to be of equivalent status—a cowboy might pair off with a dancer ("ballet broad"), the trampoline star with the lady who rode the waltzing horse, a roustabout with a kitchen helper, and so forth.

As in most social organizations, those of higher rank had certain status symbols and privileges. Some of the obvious symbols were one's salary, a dressing room on the circus grounds rather than in a tent, the size and location of one's tent, the quality of the tablecloth on one's table in the cooktent (red and white checked cloth or clean white linen), and so forth. The most obvious indication of rank, however, was one's sleeping accommodations on the circus train. These accommodations differed substantially: The owner, who traveled with his family on the train, had one whole luxurious car for his personal use. The top headliners and their families had ample compartments, each comprising one-fourth of a car. Lesser headliners had smaller compartments. The Big Top bandsmen, clowns, and cowboys had separate bunks, arranged in upper and lower tiers on both sides of a car. And the lesser personnel (work crews and roustabouts, for example) had shabby three-tier bunks, and usually two people were assigned to a bunk.

One's location on the train was also significant. The preferred place was toward the rear, since there was less engine noise, less smoke and soot, and less jerking of the train (the forward cars cushioned the later ones from sudden changes in speed). Look at Figure 7.1; as you can see, the circus people were arranged on the train according to their status and caste, with occasional exceptions. The one major exception was due to general social norms and state laws requiring separate sleeping accommodations for men and

Figure 7.1
(Opposite page)
The caste and status systems aboard a circus train. *In general, the closer one is situated toward the front of the train, the lower is his position in the status hierarchy.*

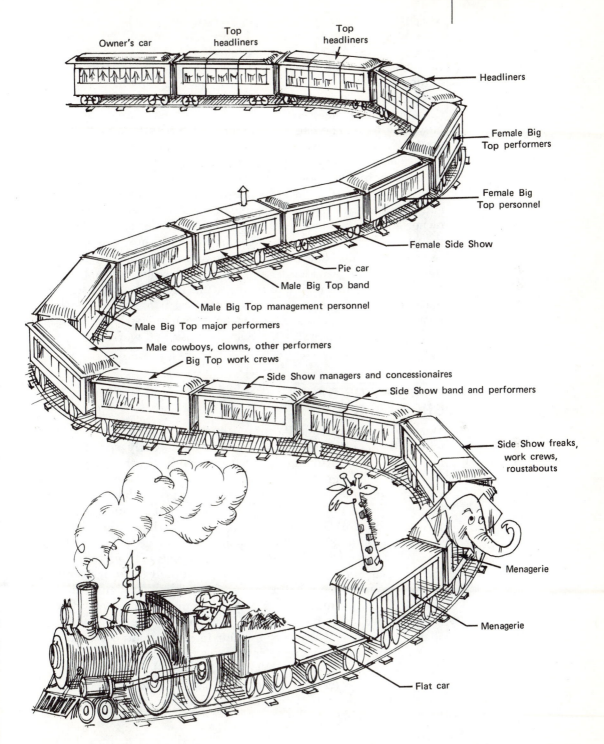

Owner's car

Top headliners

Top headliners

Headliners

Female Big Top performers

Female Big Top personnel

Female Side Show

Pie car

Male Big Top band

Male Big Top management personnel

Male Big Top major performers

Male cowboys, clowns, other performers

Big Top work crews

Side Show managers and concessionaires

Side Show band and performers

Side Show freaks, work crews, roustabouts

Menagerie

Menagerie

Flat car

women. With a note of chivalry, perhaps, the women were generally situated toward the rear of the train. Thus, some of the lower-caste women (the Side Show) had better locations than some of the higher-caste men (Big-Top major performers). The male and female halves of the train were connected by a "pie car," actually half of a car that was made into something like a club car, where alcoholic beverages (if permitted by state law) and sandwiches were served on particularly long trips. The car also had a card table and a long row of slot machines. Men and women could socialize in the pie car while traveling. The owner of the circus and his family had the best car and the most desirable location. The compartments of the top headliners were also situated toward the rear of the train. (The top headliners and headliners, of course, included both men and women. The owner and the two groups of headliners would have to walk through the women's cars in order to reach the pie car.) Thus, with occasional exceptions, as noted, among both men and women, one's location on the circus train provided a rather clear indication of his status and caste. Among both men and women, the Big Top caste had preference over the Side Show caste. Within each of these groups, the headliners and stars had better locations than the performers, and the managers were better situated than the unskilled workers.

DIMENSIONS OF GROUP STRUCTURE

Many of our most significant encounters with others take place within the context of a particular, rather orderly social arrangement—the *group*. Although you have probably never been a clarinetist in a traveling circus, think about the enormous variety of groups you have undoubtedly been a member of during your life. To mention a few possibilities, there is your family, your kindergarten class, your Brownie or Cub Scout troop, your religious education class, your cabin at summer camp, your high school debate or basketball team, and your college dormitory or frat house. And think of the many social roles you have probably occupied (or will occupy) in various groups: infant, child, adolescent, sibling, student, colleague, teacher, friend, parent, and so forth. The range and number of groups to which we each belong is truly immense! Groups come in all shapes and sizes. They vary in their formality, purposes, and composition; indeed, they are as variable as their members. Yet, despite the differences, *all* groups, like the individual members who give them life, *share* certain important characteristics that enable the trained observer to understand their particular nature and the way they tend to function.

Physical scientists have advanced the hypothesis that all substances consist of small particles of matter (atoms), and that there are
several different kinds, corresponding to the various elements. This
hypothesis provides a plausible explanation for the previously observed but unexplained chemical reactions among substances. Its
central implication is that any kind of matter, such as a molecule of
water, can be understood most parsimoniously in terms of its *structural* composition—atoms of oxygen and hydrogen bound together in
a precise way.

Analogously, a group may be thought of as a social molecule
whose atoms consist of *individuals* (Jane, Dick, John) or of positions for which individuals have not yet been designated (such as
foreman, laborer, or secretary within an organization). These atoms
are systematically bound together through the set of *relationships*
that the individuals maintain with one another. Thus, if we use a
lower-case letter to denote an individual, and a capital letter to sym-
bolize a relationship, *aRb* means that person *a* exists in some relationship *R* with person *b*. It is this set of all possible relationships, *R*,
that defines the *social structure* of a group.

Although there are many and varied relationships among group
members, five appear to be of particular importance. As we pointed
out in Chapters 3 and 4, people are continuously engaged in the process of *evaluating* one another. As part of our ongoing interest in
how we appear to others, we form relationships that range from the
height of romantic love to the depth of intense hatred. We have also
emphasized in Chapter 5 that people are *interdependent* with respect to one another in a variety of ways, each of which helps to determine the kind of relationship that will emerge. And we have discussed (Chapter 6) the complex and interesting ways in which
interdependence is transformed into behavioral reality through the
language of power and *influence*. A fourth process, which crosscuts
the other three and therefore requires separate consideration, is
communication—who can and does talk with whom. Fifth, groups
also tend to be structured according to *roles* and positions. Formally
or informally the group will be differentiated into a number of positions (for example, leader, follower; father, mother, child; teacher,
student). Each position carries with it a certain pattern of behavior
(or role) that is expected of the person who occupies that position.
Taken together, these five dimensions of social structure—evaluation, interdependence, influence, communication, and roles—enable
us to analyze the organization and function of almost any group: a
circus, a classroom, a Boy Scout troop, or an industrial work group.
Although our discussion will focus on these five, several other dimensions of social structure have also been discussed in the literature, including status (or prestige) structure and locomotion structure

(in formal organizations especially, movement in the group is restricted to certain paths—in the army, for example, a private must become a corporal before he can become a sergeant).

Of course these five processes are not independent of one another. Rather, as so often happens in social psychology, they are linked together in a complex, multidirectional chain of causality. Thus, it seems reasonable to assume that evaluation (positive or negative) and feelings of interdependence (positive or negative) will affect one's inclination to communicate and to both exert and be receptive to influence. We know, for example, that people tend to behave in a friendly, accommodating fashion toward others whom they need and like. It is also reasonable to assume that feelings of positive or negative interdependence, and the ability to exert influence, will affect communication and evaluation. For example, people tend to dislike and to avoid speaking to those with whom they must compete and who resist attempts at persuasion. And, of course, a person's positive or negative evaluation, coupled with his ability to exert influence, may well affect his perception of interdependence and his inclination to communicate. People, for example, speak to and feel cooperatively disposed toward those whom they both like and are able to influence. A person's role may also include expectations regarding whom he may communicate with, whom he can influence, or who can influence him. Role will determine and be affected by the patterns of interdependence.

Evaluation, interdependence, communication, roles, and influence are thus distinct and yet intrinsically related—a fact that should be kept in mind as we explore the nature and functioning of groups. These structural dimensions both affect *and* are affected by variations in one another.

EVALUATION STRUCTURE

Suppose that each student in a class were asked to write down the names of those classmates, beside whom he would most like to sit. By studying the responses, we would probably be able to obtain a fairly accurate picture of the attraction (or, as it is also called, sociometric) structure of the class and how the class is likely to function. If we found that sociometric choices tended to be mutual (for example, John indicates that he would most like to sit next to Jack, and Jack says the same about John), we would probably conclude that the class consisted largely of pairs of friends who share positive feelings about each other. Or, if we found that one particular person was

Pairs of friends	Centralized evaluative structure	Imbalanced group

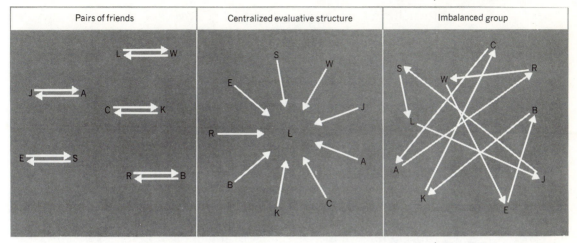

Figure 7.2
Three sociometric patterns.

chosen by virtually everyone in the class, we would conclude that this group had a rather centralized evaluative structure, in which one student was the focus of the group's affective attention. If we found that the choices were almost never reciprocated (that is, John puts down Jack's name, Jack puts down Joe's, Joe puts down Jim's, and so forth), we might infer that the group's affective structure was relatively unstable, and we might predict that the group's functioning would be marred by a large amount of interpersonal tension and discord. According to Heider's formulation (see page 103), the group would probably be in a state of "imbalance."

An individual may find other members of his group personally attractive for a variety of reasons. Perhaps a freshman gets some pleasure from associating with the football lettermen in his fraternity. Perhaps he wants to join the Sociology Club in order to meet some of the attractive girls there. Perhaps he wants to live in a certain dormitory in order to be close to his long-time friend. Regardless of the reasons, when the members of a group evaluate one another either positively or negatively, they tend to affect their own as well as the group's behavior in a number of ways.

Social psychologists have examined two aspects of evaluative relations and group functioning: the role of the affective ties among *particular* group members (their interpersonal attraction) and the *over-all* pattern of evaluative relations in a group (the group's "cohesiveness," defined as the sum of the positive forces acting on all the members of a group to remain in, rather than leave, that group). Remembering that interpersonal attraction may be both a cause *and* an effect of group cohesiveness (we feel attached to groups whose members we like, and we tend to like the individual members of groups to which we are attached), let us look at several major research findings on the effects of positive and negative evaluative relationships in groups.

Satisfaction and Morale

Working with the supervisors and foremen of work groups and a representative of top management, R. H. Van Zelst (1952) studied the effects of two types of work groups composed of carpenters and bricklayers who were constructing houses. Some groups were made up of workmen who had indicated a mutual liking for one another on a questionnaire, while others were composed of fewer individuals who liked one another. The highly cohesive groups demonstrated significantly less absenteeism, had a lower turnover rate, had lower labor costs, and voiced greater job satisfaction. Van Zelst introduced controls to remove the possibility of any initial differences in individual abilities among those in the two types of groups; thus, the effects he observed could clearly be attributed to differences in cohesiveness.

Patterson and Willett (1951) attempted to study the effects of group cohesiveness in a British coal mine. Instead of studying changes in personal attractiveness through sociometric assignment, they introduced a number of group activities, such as concerts, trips to football games, and informal parties. They also made the workers aware of their positive interdependence with respect to goals. As a result, they were able to report a 54 percent reduction in accidents.

Perhaps one reason for the greater attractiveness of cohesive groups (like the Big Top band)—for their small turnover, for their lower absentee rate, and for their lower accident rate—is the increased security they offer. Individuals who evaluate one another and their work situation positively do not need to be too concerned about their interpersonal relationships and so they can concentrate on their work instead. The group can provide support for the individual in his encounters with an anxiety-producing world. Analyzing work groups comprising a total of 5871 workers in a manufacturing company, Seashore (1954) found that the greater a group's cohesiveness, the less likely its members were to feel "jumpy or nervous" or "under pressure to achieve higher productivity."

Task Performance and Morale. As one might expect, a number of social psychologists have found that work groups composed of friends tend to be more productive in accomplishing some task than groups not composed of friends (Bjerstedt, 1961; Husband, 1940; Van Zelst, 1952). Other studies, however, have failed to demonstrate a relationship between evaluative relations and productivity (Horsfall and Arensberg, 1949; Marquis, Guetzkow, and Heyns, 1951; Philp, 1940). Although it appears that negative evaluative relations within a group inhibit group performance, the opposite is not necessarily true, that is, positive evaluative relations do not inevitably facilitate group performance. As McGrath (1964) has pointed out, "Too much friendship within a work group can result in the group's spending most of its time on social activities rather than on the task" (p. 85). If, for example, an individual belongs to a group primarily because he wants to be with his friends, the rewarding consequences of high group productivity are not likely to have much effect on his behavior. Schachter and his colleagues (1951), as well as Berkowitz (1954), have found that high-cohesive groups tend to be more responsive to group norms, so that when the norm calls for low productivity, these groups tend to decrease their productivity to a greater extent than low-cohesive groups with the same norm.

Interpersonal Influence. As Collins and Raven (1969) have pointed out, one of the most thoroughly documented consequences of high group cohesiveness is the fact that individual group members tend to both exert and be susceptible to influence. For example, Back (1951) demonstrated that the members of two-person groups who like one another make more attempts at mutual influence and are more successful in these attempts than members of groups who do not like each other. In general, it appears that increased cohesiveness results in greater pressure toward uniformity in the group. Individual members are more inclined to use other members of the group in order to evaluate their own behavior, beliefs, or attitudes. This may result in persuasive communication directed at deviant members; in a change in one's own behavior, beliefs, or attitudes to bring them in line with those of the group; or in the rejection of deviant members.

Evaluative Relations in No Exit: *An Aside.* Considerable social psychological research has focused on the behavior of groups that are task- or work-oriented. But obviously not all groups can be characterized as such. A family, for example, certainly constitutes a group, yet it is not really work- or task-oriented—and to treat it as such would probably limit our understanding of its most important functions. Therefore, let us consider briefly the processes of attraction and cohesiveness in a group that is decidedly *not* task-oriented. Our example is taken from Jean-Paul Sartre's magnificent play *No Exit* (1955). This play is a caricature rather than an accurate representation of reality and, like most good caricatures, it provides some insight into the real world from which it is drawn.

There are three characters in *No Exit*, each of whom has been condemned to eternity in Hell, but for different reasons. The first, Garcin, is a pacifist journalist from Brazil who mistreated his wife, was a coward during wartime, and was condemned to Hell for his betrayal of his comrades. Garcin, in short, is *cowardly*. The second character, Inez, is a French lesbian condemned to Hell because of her responsibility for the suicides of three people (including her female lover and herself). Inez, in Sartre's words, is a "devourer of souls . . . a live coal in others' hearts" who continually seeks to force her mate to see the world as she sees it. We may characterize Inez as *overbearing*. The third character is Estelle, a French woman condemned to Hell for the murder of her child and the deception of her husband. Estelle is tantalized by her own physical presence and is hopelessly in need of male attention; she will do anything, even lie, to get this attention. Estelle, in short, is *vain*. Put these three people in a Holiday Inn-type of motel room, as Sartre does, from which there is no escape ("no exit")—not by sleep, the blinking of an eyelid, tears, looking out of the window (there are no windows), awareness of the passage of time, or even minimal control over the environment (the objects in the room are too heavy to lift, and a service bell sometimes works and sometimes does not)—and there is Hell.

Each member of this tortured group needs something that can be provided by only one of the others. Estelle craves Garcin's male body and attention; Garcin, in turn, craves Inez's respect ("only Inez can love a coward"); and Inez craves Estelle's female soul. Each is thus attracted to one of the other two. This bizarre pattern of interpersonal attraction is heightened by the fact that each member of the group receives attention *not* from the one whose attention he desires and needs, but from the other. Garcin seeks attention from Inez, but gets it from Estelle; Inez wants Estelle's attention but receives it from Garcin; and Estelle craves Garcin's attention but gets it from Inez. The one who can provide the needed attention becomes the object of attraction, while the one who proffers unwanted attention becomes the object of repulsion. The result is a state of tantalizing conflict from which none of the three characters can extricate himself.

Lest you think that such a pattern of evaluative relationships can occur only in fiction, consider the possibility of a classroom in which the students' sociometric choices go unreciprocated. Or consider the (perhaps) pathological possibility of a family of three (mother, father, son), in which the father seeks the attention of the mother, the mother prefers the company of her son, and the son craves the companionship of his father—each for his or her own reasons—and where the need for attention is not reciprocated. Perhaps the mother views the father as "brutish," the son views his mother as "suffocating," and the father views his son as a "rival." An unholy trio, indeed!

Do the three characters in *No Exit* constitute a cohesive group? Apparently they do, for when the door of the room finally opens (for a brief moment toward the end of the play), *no one* chooses to leave. Apparently the forces of attraction are greater than those of repul-

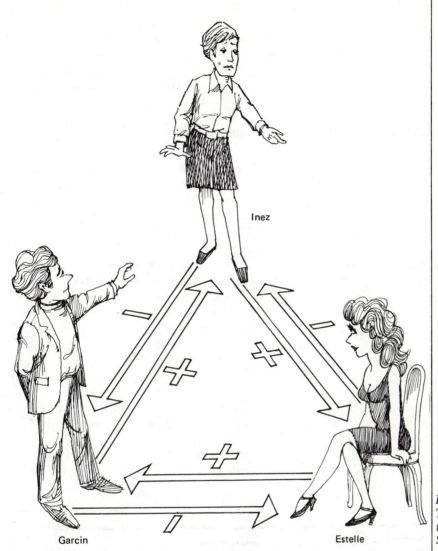

Inez

Garcin

Estelle

Figure 7.3
The sociometric rela-
tionships in Jean-Paul
Sartre's play No Exit.

sion, and yet each character is continually being tortured by the attentions of the one whom he does not like and by the rejection of the one to whom he is attracted. No wonder that Garcin finally exclaims: "There's no need for red-hot pokers. Hell is—other people!" Indeed it is, in such an eternally imbalanced social situation.

INTERDEPENDENCE
STRUCTURE

As pointed out in Chapter 5, every day we must function in a variety of interdependent relationships with other people. Some of these relationships, such as those among members of an athletic team, are based upon convergent interests (trying to win games) and therefore are of positive interdependence. Other relationships, like that between two drivers who would each like to cross an intersection first, are based upon divergent interests and thus are of negative interdependence. In still other relationships, such as the example of the two boys who together lift and carry a log that neither could move alone, people may be positively or negatively interdependent with respect to means (carrying a log), goals (using the log to build a fire), or both means and goals. Keeping these distinctions in mind, let us now look at some of the consequences of the structural dimension of interdependence for the nature and functioning of groups.

The Structure of Goals Interdependence

Imagine that you are an industrial psychologist, hired by the management of a large company to offer advice about structuring the company's incentive system to increase worker productivity. Three possibilities occur to you: recommending that the workers' pay be based solely on their individual productivity (goals independence); recommending that incentives be structured in such a way that there would be competition among the workers—for example, by establishing a system in which the worker who was most productive would receive a bonus in pay (negative interdependence with respect to goals); or recommending that the workers' pay be based on their joint, collective output (positive goals interdependence). What recommendation would you make?

In general, it appears that a group is likely to function most effectively when its members are positively interdependent with respect to goals. In a classic study of cooperation and competition in groups (see page 183), Deutsch (1949b) found that positive goals interdependence results in a higher quality and greater quantity of work than negative goals interdependence. Similar findings have also been reported by Raven and Eachus (1963), Smith, Madden, and Sobel (1957), Thomas (1957), and Zander and Wolfe (1964).

Positive goals interdependence leads not only to improved productivity, but to an increased willingness to help (and accept influence from) the other members of one's group. Deutsch (1949b) found that members of cooperative (as compared with competitive) groups are more inclined to be aware of their mutual interdependence, to coordinate their efforts, and to be attentive to one another. Similar results have emerged in experiments by Thomas (1957); and by Zander and Wolfe (1964), who reported that members of cooperative groups are also more likely to trust one another. Finally, as might be expected, Deutsch (1949b) and others have found that group members who are positively interdependent with respect to goals tend to like one another more and to display greater work satisfaction and morale than do members of competitive groups.

What incentive system would you suggest to the company's management for increasing productivity? Based on the above research, you should probably recommend a system in which the workers are paid according to their joint, collective output. Of course, management might object to such a proposal (possibly believing that it represented "creeping socialism") as might the workers (their pay would be limited by the productivity of the slowest worker). But you could point out to both groups the demonstrable benefits of positive goals interdependence. Thus, you could tell management that productivity, job satisfaction, and morale would probably all rise. And you could point out to the workers that their own sense of solidarity would probably improve under a system in which they worked with, rather than against, one another, and that the resulting probable rise in their productivity would surely benefit them as well as their bosses.

The Structure of Means Interdependence

Suppose that the management of our hypothetical company also asked your advice about one of three alternative arrangements designed to increase worker productivity. One arrangement (means independence) would have the workers perform a parallel (identical) task—constructing hi-fi cabinets, for example—and give each worker all of the necessary tools for its completion (a Phillips head screwdriver); the second arrangement (negative means interdependence) would be like the first, except that there would be fewer screwdrivers than workers; the third arrangement would have the workers perform complementary tasks (some would wire radio chassis, while others would construct cabinets), requiring a division of labor (positive interdependence with respect to means). Which of the three would you recommend?

While less research has been undertaken to determine the consequences for group functioning of means (rather than goals) interdependence, it has been found that groups are generally more effective when their members are *positively* interdependent with respect to means. Raven and Eachus (1963), for example, discovered that groups whose members are positively means interdependent (even when they are negatively interdependent with respect to goals) tend to restructure their goals and to function with increasing efficiency. It is uncomfortable to compete with those whom you need in order to reach your goal. Conversely, it has been demonstrated in a number of studies of panic behavior (see, for example, Mintz's experiment, page 188) that groups tend to function least effectively when their members are negatively interdependent with respect to means.

Returning to the advice you might give, you should probably recommend an arrangement in which the workers perform complementary tasks, requiring a division of labor (so that there would be positive interdependence with respect to means). This arrangement, however, has certain disadvantages. Although a division of labor increases the efficiency with which tasks can be performed and enhances a group member's view of himself as an expert, workers also want to have the feeling of accomplishment that comes from seeing a task through from beginning to end; no one wants to be just a cog in a large, impersonal machine. A second disadvantage of task specialization stems from the fact that it is, in Ivan Steiner's (1972) words, a "conjunctive" arrangement. A conjunctive task is one in which success is defined in terms of the *least* effective member (for example, a team of mountain climbers can move only as fast as the slowest member). According to Steiner: "Nobody can succeed unless everyone succeeds, so any incompetent or recalcitrant person can substantially impair everyone else's prospects of goal achievement" (p. 148). Whenever a group's progress is limited by the productivity of its slowest, least competent members, these "slow" members may become the object of considerable group pressure—what has been called a process of "push and pull." The slow worker on an assembly line is "pushed" along by the person who precedes him in line (the one who drops ever increasing piles of work onto the slow worker's table), while being "pulled" by the worker who is next (the one who stands around twiddling his thumbs). Thus, although a division of labor will probably achieve greater output, it may also result in lower morale and an increased vulnerability of the group and its slowest members.

Interdependence among Subunits: Coalitions

So far we have focused on goals-means interdependence in the group as a whole. In addition, however, there are numerous occasions in which patterns of interdependence emerge among individual members, resulting in the formation of subgroups.

Look at Figure 7.4, which is based on the Raven and Eachus (1963) triangular board study. In our earlier discussion of this experiment (see page 184), each subject was seated at a different corner of a triangular board and had a set screw that he could turn to raise or lower his corner. Each person also had in front of him a carpenter's spirit level that was perpendicular to his line of sight and parallel to the side opposite him. This arrangement produced high positive means interdependence among the three members of the group (a, b,

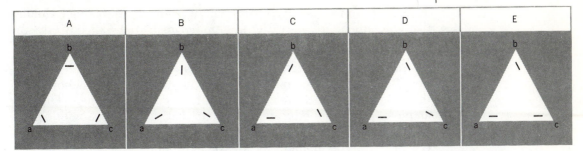

and c), since the levels were situated in such a way that each subject had no control over the bubble in his own level, but was totally (and equally) dependent upon the other two (Figure 7.4, Pattern A). Obviously, by changing the arrangement of the three spirit levels, other patterns of interdependence can be created.

Pattern B illustrates a situation in which there is minimal interdependence with respect to means, since each person has substantial control over the positioning of the bubble in his own level. Pattern C shows an asymmetrical relationship in which each person is dependent upon someone who is not dependent upon him (a depends on c, c on b, and b on a). Notice the strong resemblance of this pattern to the relationships in *No Exit*. Pattern D, also asymmetrical, depicts an arrangement in which a and b are both more dependent upon c than c is on either of them. (Could one perhaps predict, from this structure, that c would become the "leader" of this group?) Finally, if we turned c's level in Pattern D so that it pointed toward a, then a and c would be highly dependent upon each other and largely independent of b—even though b would still be dependent upon c. This particular pattern (Pattern E) is important for our discussion of subgroup formation, for it is here that we might expect to find two members of the group (a and c) forming a mutually cooperative relationship (a coalition) at the expense of the third (b).

Although coalitions can and do form because of means interdependence (as we predict would occur in Pattern E), they are more likely to form when subunits of a group are positively goals interdependent with respect to one another and negatively goals interdependent with respect to other subunits. In other words, coalitions emerge when members of a subgroup decide that they share certain goals that differ from the goals of the others. When Churchill, questioned about a possible alliance between Britain and the U.S.S.R. uttered those now-famous words, "To beat the Nazis I would form an alliance with the devil himself," he was saying, in effect, that Great Britain and the Soviet Union shared a common goal and faced a common threat that far exceeded any possible differences between them. Among the nations of the world (the group), Britain (a subunit) was

Figure 7.4
Possible patterns of interdependence in the triangle board problem (Raven and Eachus, 1963). *The letters* a, b, *and* c *denote players, each of whom is seated at a corner of a triangular board (see Figure 5.11). The positions of the players' spirit levels are indicated by the small lines near each letter.*

desirous to form a coalition with another subunit (the Soviet Union) that was sufficiently powerful to help her resist the Axis powers.

Interdependence Structure in Soviet Boarding Schools. The formation of subgroups has important consequences for the functioning of the subgroups themselves as well as of the group as a whole. One example of this is the educational system that prevails in Soviet boarding schools, as described in some detail by Urie Bronfenbrenner (1962). From the moment the Russian child enters school in the first grade, he is socialized to view himself not as an individual but as a member of a widening series of subgroups.

Like most classrooms the world over, the Soviet classroom has rows of seats. The basic subgroup to which the Russian pupil belongs, and to which he is held accountable, is the *row*. From his first day of school, he learns to develop a relationship of positive interdependence (cooperation) with the other members of his row, and one of competition with the members of all other rows. Thus, Bronfenbrenner describes an educational manual in which the teacher is advised that the first thing she should say upon entering her newly assembled class is: "Let's see which row can sit the straightest." Records are kept for each row on a daily basis. Charts are posted in the classroom showing the performance of each row in a variety of activities, as well as its over-all standing. Occasionally the members of the winning row are photographed together.

Much, but not all, of the cooperation and competition in Soviet boarding schools occurs within and between rows. The children who

*Figure 7.5
An elementary-school classroom in the Soviet Union. Each row is placed in competition with every other. If Vanko slouches, he will disgrace his entire row—and will have to explain himself to its members.*

are exceptionally responsible or able are designated as monitors in each row for each activity, and the others are invited to compete with the monitors in order to "beat them at their own game." Competition is also encouraged between classrooms. The winning classroom and the winning row within the class are sometimes visited by children from other classrooms so that they can learn how to reach the same level of excellence.

It seems clear that the administrators of Soviet boarding schools assume that children can best be motivated to learn and achieve by encouraging positive interdependence within groups and subgroups but negative interdependence between them. Like the dialectical Soviet ideology itself, the educational system assumes that from thesis and antithesis will emerge a synthesis. The purpose of promoting conflict between rows, the Russians believe, is to achieve not only row excellence, but also class and school excellence. And, lest you imagine that such a system is alien to American society, think of the troops of Boy Scouts and armies of men whose activities in groups, subgroups, and sub- subgroups are organized along similar lines and seem to flow from similar implicit assumptions.

A Jigsaw-Puzzle Method for Reducing Interracial Tensions. An interesting American variant of the Soviet row system has recently been proposed by Elliot Aronson. Aronson's deep concern about continuing racial tensions in the nation's schools led him to examine the possible contributing role of the elementary-school classroom. In a typical classroom, he suggested, pupils compete with one another for the respect and approval of the teacher, rather than learning to like, understand, and use one another as resources. The result of this competition is often the exacerbation of racial conflict: "When one adds racial tensions to a pot that already is brewing one-upmanship, envy, and suspicion, it is little wonder that violence often seasons the stew" (Aronson et al., 1975, p. 47).

Aronson proposed 'an alternative to the traditional educational system, which he dubbed the "jigsaw-puzzle" method. It does not require changing the curriculum itself, but simply the method of teaching. Suppose, for example, that the children were expected to learn about the life of Thomas Edison. Traditionally, the children might be required to read the identical material and then come to class prepared to compete for the teacher's attention and approval. With the jigsaw-puzzle method, however, the pupils would work together in cooperative subgroups, which would each be made up of about six children. Each child in the group would be given a paragraph describing a different aspect of Edison's life (his early childhood, his education, his years as an apprentice, his most important inventions, and so forth), asked to teach the group the content of this paragraph, and informed that the group would be tested on its knowledge of Edison's life later on. Thus, just as a jigsaw puzzle consists of many pieces that must all be fitted together before the puzzle is complete, Aronson's method gives the group members different pieces of information that must be pieced together in order to master the material. Every group member, regardless of his race, holds a piece of the puzzle and is therefore a valuable and necessary resource.

The jigsaw-puzzle method is characterized by positive interdependence within subgroups, and independence between them (rather than negative interdependence, as is the case in the Soviet row system). Aronson's preliminary tests of this new method have yielded promising results: Fifth- and sixth-graders in Austin, Texas, who were taught by this method showed more positive attitudes toward school, a greater liking for their peers, and higher self-esteem than did children who were taught in the traditional manner. Furthermore, these benefits were not achieved at the expense of learning: When the children were tested on the material they had studied, there were no significant differences between the traditional and experimental groups (Aronson et al., 1975).

Coalitions and Group Size. While groups can be, and are, divided into interdependent subunits (as in the Soviet boarding schools), there are also several structural properties of groups that affect the likelihood of subgroup formation. Perhaps the most important of these properties is a group's size.

A dyadic group is elegant in its simplicity: there is but a single relationship, that between its two members. But now consider the rapidity with which the number of relationships multiply as we increase the size of a group. A three-person group (triad) consisting of members A, B, and C, for example, has built into it the possibility of not one but *four* relationships: AB, AC, BC, and ABC. A group of four (A, B, C, D) contains not four but *eleven* interdependent relationships: six dyads, four triads, and of course the total group (ABCD). And this is without even taking into account each of the possible coalitions that could be formed! The point we wish to stress is simply that as the size of a group grows, the number of possible interdependent relationships among its member multiplies, as does the problem of interpreting the group's behavior in clear and systematic fashion. And it is perhaps because of this very fact that social psychologists have devoted so much of their attention to trying to understand the simple, elegant little dyad.

Early in this century, the sociologist Georg Simmel (1902) observed that a triad is inherently unstable, often resolving itself into a coalition of two persons and exclusion of the third. More recently,

Theodore Mills (1953) has coded the interaction in discussion sessions among 48 triads and has found that, over time, two of the members generally begin to communicate with each other, leaving out the third. Experimental evidence is consistent with the common belief that triads are somehow unstable. The old saying, "Two is company, three is a crowd," is readily documented by our own everyday experience. A lover's triangle is usually an extremely uncomfortable relationship for at least one of the participants, and it usually ends with an alliance of two and exclusion of the third. If we can believe Freud's psychoanalytic theory of human behavior, a family of three (mother, father, son, for example) is likewise an unstable social structure. The son forms an Oedipal attachment to his mother, the queen, and hopes to wrest her away from the king, only to find that his mother and father are bonded together in an intimate relationship from which he is excluded. And we can even observe a stable instability in the relationships among the United States, the Soviet Union, and the People's Republic of China. Each hopes to form an alliance with a second nation at the expense of the third; and each nation, aware of the dangers of a coalition between the other two, goes out of its way to prevent such an alliance from forming. The United States, for example, either wittingly or unwittingly, tries to promote conflict between the Soviet Union and China by playing off one against the other and by making seductively friendly overtures to each.

The unstable triad—a familiar theme in literature. One can also turn to the world of literature and find abundant examples of unstable triads. In Tennessee Williams's play, *A Streetcar Named Desire*, Blanche DuBois forms an unholy threesome with her sister Stella and Stella's husband Stanley. Blanche (or perhaps it's Tennessee himself) appears to be a pretty fair social psychologist. She understands the inherent instability of a triad and attempts to take advantage of it. As Blanche enters the Kowalskis' home, she finds Stella and Stanley very much in love—in a coalition, if you will, from which Blanche is excluded. Desperately, she tries to break into this dyad, first trying to unite Stella and herself against Stanley, and then trying to join forces with Stanley at the expense of Stella. Her attempts, of course, are in vain. Blanche slips off into oblivion, as Stella and Stanley give birth to a child, forming their own cozy (or will it be cozy?) threesome.

Consider the inherent instability of the *No Exit* triad. Each person would like to form a coalition with one of the other two (the person each needs) and to exclude the third: Garcin with Inez, Inez with Estelle, and Estelle with Garcin. And, as Sartre informs us, each of these coalitions is possible—at least in theory. Garcin and Inez alone could sit forever in silence, but the presence of the talkative Estelle prevents this; Inez and Estelle alone could both pay atten-

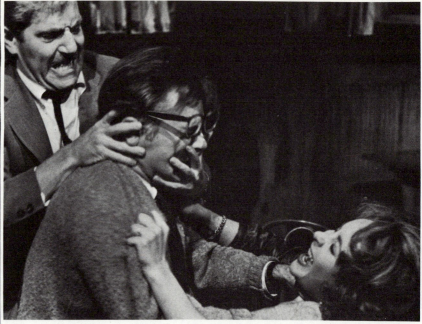

Figure 7.6
An unstable triad in Edward Albee's play Who's Afraid of Virginia Woolf? *When George (Richard Burton) attacks his wife Martha (Elizabeth Taylor), Nick (George Segal) comes to her assistance.*

tion to Estelle (since Estelle craves the attention of others, and Inez is only too willing to comply), but the presence of the male Garcin prevents this; and Estelle and Garcin alone could, according to Sartre, "throw dust in each other's eyes," but Inez, whose respect Garcin craves, prevents this from happening. Thus, no lasting coalitions are really possible in *No Exit.* Each person acts as "torturer" of one of the other two and therefore, indirectly, of both.

In contrast with the triad, whose inherent instability has been amply illustrated, it appears that larger groups are less inclined to form subunits that exclude a single member. A family of four (mother, father, son, daughter), for example, seems to be structurally more stable than a family of three. To the extent that coalitions form, they are not likely to consist of three people at the expense of the fourth, but of two and two. The son and daughter, for example, may view themselves as partners in opposition to the alliance of their parents. The mother and daughter may act as if they were allied against the father and son. And finally, in keeping with the psychoanalytic assumption of cross-sex identification, the son may feel that he and his mother are united together against the father and daughter.

A similar patterning of coalitions, two against two, occurs elsewhere as well. In Arthur Miller's play *Death of a Salesman,* one can observe the shifting formation of alliances among the four characters—Willy, Linda, Happy, and Biff—as each tries to or succeeds in uniting himself with one of the others against the remaining two.

The ongoing crisis in the Middle East can be thought of as involving four major participants: the United States, the Soviet Union, Israel, and the Arab states. Any number of coalitions are theoretically possible in this system, yet only one pattern has emerged: the United States and Israel have been partners in an alliance against the Soviet Union and the Arab states. Note the symmetry of this arrangement: each coalition includes a "big guy" and a "little guy," a superpower and a relatively small nation (or nations). To some, it might seem that the two superpowers had decided that a direct confrontation with the other would be too costly and so, as a consequence, they chose to wage their conflict indirectly—through less powerful allies whose victory they hope to assure.

COMMUNICATION STRUCTURE

Take a group of complete strangers, assemble them together in a room, and, unless instructed otherwise, they are apt to begin speaking with each other before very long. If the group has been brought together to undertake some task (for example, a jury that has been instructed to reach a verdict), its members will probably get right down to the business of talking "shop." If the group's purposes are less clear-cut (as in the case of a T-group), its members may begin by introducing themselves or trying to find out why they are there. In any case, communication is likely to begin right away and to continue throughout the life of the group. As the members speak with each other, several things will often happen: people begin to disclose information about themselves—what they themselves are really like and what they would like others to think of them; they begin to form attachments, liking some, disliking others, and remaining indifferent toward the rest; they begin to sound themselves and others out; they try to get a better sense of their own identity in the group—whether they are viewed as powerful, competent, friendly, likable, secretive, and so forth; some of the members, perhaps because they are dissatisfied, may eventually withdraw from active participation in the group, while others may begin to take a more active role, emerging as leaders. In any event, during the course of speaking with one another, certain patterns begin to develop that appear to be similar in a wide variety of groups.

Interaction Process Analysis

Social psychologists have long been interested in charting the course and consequences of communication in groups. One man in particular, R. Freed Bales (1950), has developed an impressive coding system called "interaction process analysis" that can be used to observe and classify the interaction in any group, regardless of its history, function, or composition.

Bales has conducted his research over a number of years and in a variety of ways, but a rather typical procedure is the following: Between three and six strangers (often college students) are brought to the laboratory and are asked to meet together as a group for four weekly sessions. Each group is instructed to think of itself as the administrative staff of a central authority, and each week it is given a detailed summary of an administrative personnel problem to review. The members are requested to review the facts in each case history and to return a report with their recommendation for a course of action. Each group has 40 minutes in which to reach a decision. After giving these instructions and waiting for the case histories to be read, the experimenter leaves and steps into an adjacent room from which he can observe the group. The experimenter arbitrarily assigns numbers to the participants so that he can write down who speaks to whom. For example, the notation "1–5" means that member "1" has spoken to member "5." He then proceeds to code their communications according to the category system depicted in Figure 7.7.

Bales's analysis of many groups shows that there is a highly consistent pattern of interaction. Groups that are problem-oriented, such as those in the study described above, typically begin by trying to deal with the task itself—by orienting themselves to the problem (categories 6 and 7). Then there are problems of evaluation —deciding what the group's goals are (categories 5 and 8). Next, there is the problem of how to reach the goals. Questions of procedure are raised and answered (categories 4 and 9). In the process of working on the task, differentiation of roles usually develops, accompanied by a division of labor. A prestige and power hierarchy may emerge, with some persons giving more suggestions (category 4) and others following. With the development of a power and prestige structure, and with the onset of fatigue from working on the task, tensions and hostility may arise. Sometimes disagreements and antagonism become so intense that the group can no longer continue with its job. (The responses then begin to center on categories 10, 11, and 12). Prolonged interaction in categories 10, 11, and 12 will eventually threaten the group's existence. Consequently, one or more group members will typically respond with reconciliatory comments (categories 1, 2, and 3). Disagreements are thus resolved, tensions released, and group solidarity restored. The group can then continue its work until further tensions arise. The procedure is not always as clear-cut as this, and some investigators have questioned the generality of Bales's results. However, there is no doubt that Bales's tech-

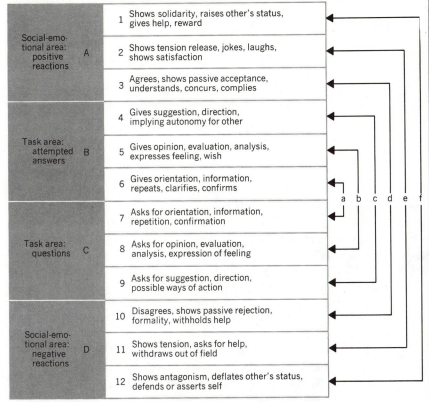

Key: a: problems of orientation, b: problems of evaluation, c: problems of control, d: problems of decision, e: problems of tension-management, and f: problems of integration.

Figure 7.7
Bales's interaction process categories (Bales, 1950). *Using this category system, one can systematically record the pattern and content of communication in groups.*

nique provides a useful tool for analyzing communication in groups and describing a group's structure and functioning.

Interaction process analysis in Albee's play. You may find it useful to test the validity of Bales's system for yourself by applying interaction process analysis to some group that you know: either one that you belong to (such as your family, your fraternity, or your sorority) or one that is fictitious. Edward Albee's play, *Who's Afraid of Virginia Woolf?,* for example, can be analyzed rather neatly in this fashion. As the play progresses, we find that of Albee's four characters (George and Martha, Nick and Honey), George and Martha are doing almost all of the speaking (communicating may not be the best word to describe this process!). George and Martha speak to each other, to Nick, and occasionally to Honey; Nick speaks to George and to his wife Honey; and Honey speaks only to Nick. If we were to code their communication using Bales's system, we would probably find that George and Martha score very high in the areas of Negative

Reactions and Attempted Answers; Nick (being an ingratiating Young Turk) scores high in Positive Reactions and Questions; and Honey scores high in Questions and Negative Reactions. Try analyzing Albee's play yourself.

Communication Networks

In order to exercise tighter control over the process of communication in groups than is possible with an observational technique such as the one developed by Bales, social psychologists have devised a rather ingenious method of studying the effects of communication structure in groups. As initially described by Bavelas (1950) and Leavitt (1951), five subjects were brought into the laboratory and were seated in individual booths, separated by partitions that contained slots. Each of the five members of the group was given a card that had five symbols written on it (for example, #, $, %, ¢, &), but only *one* symbol was the same on all of the cards (for example, #). The subjects' task was to discover the common symbol as quickly and accurately as possible by passing notes through their slots. The subjects could not communicate with one another except by means of these notes, but they could write anything they wished in the notes.

The slots connecting the subjects' individual booths were either open or closed, creating the four predetermined communication networks shown in Figure 7.8. A line between any two elements (*a, b, c, d, e*) denotes the possibility of two-way communication; conversely, no communication is possible between elements not connected by a line.

By following a procedure similar to the one described above, social psychologists have been able to answer a number of important questions, such as those posed by Bavelas (1950):

> *Do certain patterns have structural properties which may limit the group performance? May it be that among several communication patterns—all logically adequate for the successful completion of a specified task—one will result in significantly better performance than another? What effects might pattern, as such, have upon the emergence of leadership, the disruption of organization, and the degree of resistance to group disruption* [p. 725]?

Centrality in Communications. Bavelas (1950), Leavitt (1951), and others have suggested that the answer to each of these questions will be determined primarily by a single attribute of the group's communication structure—its *centrality*. Centrality is defined according to the number of communication linkages from a given position (ele-

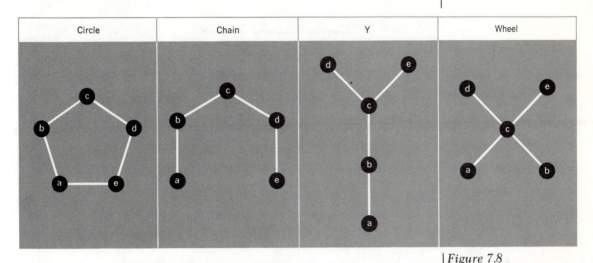

Circle	Chain	Y	Wheel

Figure 7.8
Four communication networks. The letters denote people, who can communicate with one another only along the pathways indicated by the lines.

ment) to each of the other positions. Thus, of the four networks in Figure 7.8, the wheel is the most centralized (one person, *c,* can communicate with all four others); next comes the Y (in which *c* can communicate with three others); then the chain; and finally the circle. Expressed another way, in the wheel, *c* occupies the most central position; in the Y, *c* is more central than *b* who, in turn, is more central than, *a, d,* or *e;* in the chain, *b, c,* and *d* are equally central and more central than *a* and *e;* and in the circle, everyone is equally central (or equally peripheral, if you will).

What social psychologists have typically found, using a simple problem, is that the more centralized nets solve problems faster and with greater accuracy than the less centralized ones (in descending order: the wheel, Y, chain, circle). As it turns out, however, the greater efficiency of the most centralized pattern of communication (the wheel) is related to the nature of the problem. Finding a missing symbol is a relatively simple task, which is solved most efficiently when all of the information is channeled to one person who collates it, finds the answer, and then relays it to the others. However, in the case of a more complex problem, such as deciding what is the most efficient way to move the furniture of a large company with a limited number of trucks, the circle is the most efficient (Shaw, 1954). Errors are more common with the wheel network because an incorrect approach by the central person cannot be checked by the others. Also, if the central person is given a complex task, he may have more decisions to make than he can handle; therefore, a peripheral person with less information at his disposal may be obliged to make the key decision.

Social psychologists have also consistently found that the person who occupies the most central position in a group communication network is quite often viewed as its leader. For example, of the 25 subjects placed in each of the four networks in Leavitt's (1951) study, 23 members of the wheel agreed that c was the leader, 17 members of the Y designated c, 12 in the chain, and there was no clear agreement on this issue in the circle.

A highly centralized group network (such as the wheel) is, in a way, more vulnerable than less centralized arrangements, and this greater vulnerability is closely related to the emergence of a single individual as the leader. The wheel depends for its effectiveness on the competence of one person—the man in the middle. But if this person should prove to be incompetent, the performance of the centralized network may suffer. (We actually observed this happen one day in a social psychology class that was trying out a version of the network experiment. Given a simple problem to solve, the wheel actually took longer and made more errors than any of the other groups!) Conversely, a decentralized group, such as the circle, is apt to be much more stable; because each member is equally central and peripheral, he is equally responsible for the group's performance.

A particularly intriguing finding that has emerged from the research on communication networks is the fact that there is greater over-all group satisfaction when the network is *less* centralized (the decreasing order of satisfaction is: circle, chain, Y, wheel), although the individual satisfaction of the "leader" is usually higher in the more centralized networks. Perhaps the most central persons obtain greater satisfaction because they are continually receiving communications about the status of the problem. Everyone's attention is focused on them. They have the clearest idea of what is going on—of how the group is attempting to reach its goals. Perhaps they view themselves as more powerful, or less dependent, than the others. Whatever the explanation, it seems clear that peripherality in a communications network may produce considerable dissatisfaction.

If we examine the organization chart of a typical factory it will seem clear that the workers at the bottom of the chart are peripheral in the communications network, while the top-level management is central. Possibly the low morale that results from dependence upon those with whom one cannot communicate (as well as from unsatisfactory pay, poor working conditions, and the powerlessness of individual workers to bargain alone) led to the eventual development of unions—with union representatives functioning as communication links between the workers and top management. Today it is middle-level management that has become more peripheral. They complain that the decisions that affect them are being reached between top management and the workers, without consulting them (middle management) first.

Stage 1	Stage 2	Stage 3	Stage 4

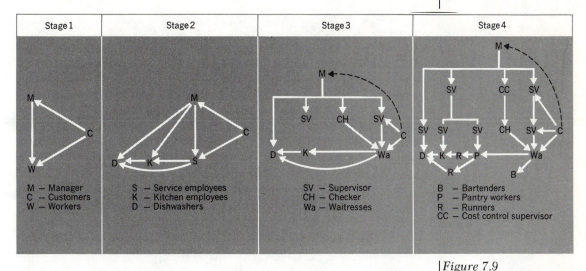

M — Manager
C — Customers
W — Workers

S — Service employees
K — Kitchen employees
D — Dishwashers

SV — Supervisor
CH — Checker
Wa — Waitresses

B — Bartenders
P — Pantry workers
R — Runners
CC — Cost control supervisor

Figure 7.9
The costs of success. The small, short-order lunch counter develops into a large, successful restaurant—but at what expense in structural complexity! Note the increasing strain on the waitresses who, although low in the status structure, become the center of a highly complex communication, influence, and interdependence network (after Whyte, 1961).

The Social Structure of a Restaurant: An Aside. The sociologist, William F. Whyte (1961), has provided an insightful analysis of the peripherality and tension that often accompany the growth of a group. Describing the expansion of a restaurant owned by a fictitious Tom Jones, he reported:

Jones begins with a small restaurant where he dispenses short orders over the counter (Stage 1). He has two employees working for him, but there is no division of labor and all three work together as cooks, countermen, and dishwashers. . . . The business expands and we see the beginning of a division of labor (Stage 2). . . . Now, if the organization is to function smoothly, the work of waitresses, cooks, and dishwashers must be coordinated [pp. 82–83].

In Stage 3, Jones is no longer able to supervise all the work.

He hires a service supervisor, a food-production supervisor, and places one of his employees in charge of the dishroom as a working supervisor. He also employs a checker to check on his waitresses. In Stage 4, he adds runners and pantry girls—one more group of workers to be supervised, so that new levels of supervisors must be added [p. 84].

As the business grows, Jones no longer has the close informal relationship with his employees that he once had. The communication network has become too complex and extensive. Now he also encounters the problem of friction between supervisors and employees. Those at the lowest level of the hierarchy feel that they are separated from the sources of control, which produces even more frustration and friction. Eventually, they will become unionized and this will mean new problems of communication.

The dilemma faced by the waitresses, as seen in Figure 7.9, is particularly acute, since they must serve as a relay for so much of the flow of power and communication. Furthermore, as waitresses they must "give orders" to the cook, either directly or through the counterman. The cook, who is often male and believes that he has high prestige, may reject what appears to be an inversion of the power structure, thereby aggravating the dilemma of the waitresses. This problem was solved by installing a high counter between the waitresses and counterman. Now the waitresses, who cannot be seen by the counterman, can place the written orders on a spindle above the counter. With this change, they appear to be delivering messages rather than giving orders, and the counterman and cooks can fill the orders as they see fit. Under this new system, the tension among the employees was substantially reduced.

ROLE
STRUCTURE

Development of Roles in Interaction

Considered together, the careful observational research of psychologists such as Bales and the experimental work of network theorists such as Bavelas, Leavitt, and Shaw provide a rather informative picture of the communication structure in groups. As the observers of group interaction have demonstrated, members vary in the quantity of their communication, as well as in the number of others with whom they communicate. And, as communications network research has shown, patterns of interaction have a number of important consequences for the way in which groups tend to function, including the over-all level of group productivity, the emergence of leadership, and member satisfaction and morale. In addition, one of the most important findings to emerge from both observational and communications network research pertains to the development of *roles*. A role consists of the set of behaviors that is required or expected of the person who occupies a certain position in a group (Biddle and Thomas, 1966).

Over time, Bales and other observers of group interaction have found, a group's functions tend to become differentiated into a series of often complementary roles. One person, for example, may eventually assume the role of "social smoother," attempting to settle arguments among members; others may become "clarifiers," explain-

Figure 7.10
Within the family, roles
often depend upon cul-
tural patterns. At a fam-
ily picnic the husband
will frequently do the
outdoor cooking, while
the wife will prepare
the other food, set the
table, and take care of
the children's needs.

ing new situations to the group, or "questioners," criticizing group decisions. Moreover, two rather distinct leadership roles often emerge, usually occupied by different members of the group: the "task" specialist, who is responsible for generating ideas that move the group toward the completion of its job, and the "socioemotional" specialist, who is responsible for maintaining harmony and good feelings within the group. Even though these roles are not formally designated, the group may expect certain members to assume them and may look to these members when the need arises.

Culture, Tradition, and Role Definition
Roles are often based on traditional or cultural patterns. Some behaviors are considered appropriate for or expected of women but not of men, and children are often expected to behave in a special way ("to be seen but not heard"); depending upon the cultural setting, blacks may be expected to behave differently from whites. In what many people believe is a liberal Northern university, it was found that black students normally tended to be less ascendant and more acquiescent than whites. The blacks seemed to accept this role, and the whites expected it of them. But after the blacks had been given assertiveness training and had been encouraged to participate more actively in group discussions, they tended to be rejected by the whites (Katz and Cohen, 1962). Women are also expected to be less domi-

nant and more acquiescent. Those who deviate are apt to be called "bitchy" or "castrating." The college woman who wants to achieve academic success and shows little interest in being cute or attractive may find that she is not popular among men or among women (Horner, 1972). Fortunately, these role expectations for blacks and women seem to be changing (Frieze et al., 1976).

Occasionally a person finds himself in a situation of role-conflict—where he simultaneously occupies two positions with differing and conflicting roles. What happens, for example, when a woman is appointed to an executive position in business? Her formal role requires her to be assertive and directive. Yet her role as a woman requires her to be essentially non-assertive. Role-conflict sometimes occurs in the family too, where a woman, as mother, is expected to assume the major responsibility for running the household and caring for the children—even though the traditional female role is to be somewhat submissive to the male. Although the strain can be quite intense, women faced with such role-conflicts often develop subtle means for exercising influence while not appearing to do so (Johnson, 1974; 1976). Rather than using commands ("Please do such-and-such immediately"), they are more likely to mask their attempts at influence ("Wouldn't it be a nice idea if we . . . ?").

Roles and Communication Networks

Roles emerge not only in task-oriented groups such as those observed by Bales, in groups governed by tradition or culture, in formal organizations, and in informal gatherings, but also in the various communication networks discussed earlier. Guetzkow (1960) placed a group of subjects in one of three five-man groups—a wheel, a circle, or an all-channel network (a circle in which each person could communicate directly with every other person). When the participants were allowed two minutes in which to organize, the circle tended to develop a three-level hierarchy: One person would become "key-man" (similar to the circus owner) who would collate the information, solve the problem, and send back the information; two men would serve as "relayers" (the Big Top and Side Show managers), communicating information from the remaining two to the "key-man" (in Figure 7.9, the person in position b of the Y is a good example of a "relayer"). The remaining two become "end-men" (similar to the circus work crews) who merely passed in their information to the "relayers" and then received the final solution. The members of the wheel soon discovered that only a two-level hierarchy was possible—one key-man and four end-men; there seemed to be no place for relayers. The members of the all-channel network had considerable difficulty organizing the roles in their group; they ultimately settled on either a two-level or a three-level hierarchy. The results generally showed that the wheel enjoyed the same advantage found in earlier studies: since their role structures had already been established for them by the communication network, they didn't have to waste time developing such an organization for themselves.

Guetzkow found that the organization of roles, once established, effectively dispensed with some of the communication links and consequently the end-men were peripheral. Consistent with earlier findings, the end-men were less satisfied with the solution that was worked out for the problem than were the key-men. Where the organization was allowed to develop freely and where the structure did not dictate the role, personality factors usually determined role assignment. Those subjects who were highly ascendant (as measured by the A-scale of the Guilford-Zimmerman test) were especially likely to become key-men, partly because of their inclination to nominate themselves. Personal ascendance proved to be more of a determinant of role than intellectual ability. However, in another experiment (Berkowitz, 1956) utilizing the four-person wheel, it was found that the communication structure itself could be even more significant than personality in the determination of role assignment. When a low-ascendant person was placed in the central position of the network, he would initially assume a very passive role, while the high-ascendant person in the peripheral position would take the real responsibility. Over time, however, centrality in the communication network proved to be significant, and the low-ascendant person in the c position became more prominent in achieving solutions for the group problems. It thus appears that one's position in the communication structure may alter his behavior, even as one's personality may determine what position he is assigned.

INFLUENCE AND
POWER
STRUCTURE

We come now to the last of the five structural dimensions that we believe are necessary for understanding the nature and functioning of groups. As pointed out in Chapter 6, interdependent relationships are transformed into behavioral reality through the process of *influence*. Even in the most elementary dyadic relationships—parent and child, teacher and student, policeman and citizen, foreman and worker, husband and wife, and so forth—influence is continually being exerted in a variety of complex and interesting ways, as each person attempts to alter the behavior of the other. And, of course, the process of influence also takes place in larger groups.

All groups—whether they are formed in order to undertake a particular task or not, whether they represent a formal assembly of their membership or only a casual congregation, whether they are composed of friends or strangers—depend upon the ongoing exchange of influence; through this process, the individual members change their ideas and attitudes toward themselves, one another, and the world at large. As will be discussed in later chapters, groups systematically affect their own members; individual members, in turn, deliberately attempt to shape the behavior of the group as a whole; and groups affect other groups.

As a group develops, its members engage in the ongoing process of "jockeying for position"—exercising one or more of the six bases of power discussed in Chapter 6: reward, coercion, expertise, legitimacy, reference, and information. Which of these bases of power is invoked depends upon the nature and structure of any given group. Among the members of a street gang or a group of young boys on a playground, influence may depend primarily upon physical prowess—one boy's ability to beat the others into submission (coercive power). On the other hand, in a Boy Scout troop, power may be related to the expertise or legitimacy that is presumed to accompany a particular rank (Tenderfoot vs. Eagle Scout). Similarly, among the members of a "think-tank" (a task-oriented group, such as those at the RAND Corporation, whose task is to generate as many high-quality ideas as possible), the greatest prestige may accrue to the person who seems to have the best ideas (informational power); among the members of a T-group, prestige may be associated with the person who appears to be most successful in embodying the values and feelings of the group (referent power); and among politicians, influence may depend upon one's ability to mete out favors of various kinds (reward power). Regardless of how the members of a group go about jockeying for position, the result is a general pattern of power relations, similar across a wide variety of groups, that has important consequences for the functioning of the group as a whole.

Biologists, ethologists, and other students of animal behavior have long known that groups of animals tend to establish certain patterns of social power that persist in one form or another throughout the life of the group. These patterns, known as "dominance hierarchies," lend a certain degree of stability to the group and help ensure its collective survival. As Washburn and DeVore (1961) have observed, a troop of baboons maintains a fixed, symmetrical configuration as it moves across open terrain (where it is most vulnerable to attack). Out in front (and also bringing up the rear) are the young, dominant males, who act as "scouts" for the troop and fend off possible attackers. Behind them, in turn, come the less dominant

males, the females, and the very young; in the center (the most protected part) of the advancing group, one finds the pregnant females,
the females with young, and (interestingly) the most dominant males
in the troop. Like generals in an advancing army, these male troop
leaders manage to sequester themselves in the safest, most congenial
place.

Pecking Orders among Chickens and Other Species. One of the most
interesting and important animal dominance hierarchies is the
"pecking order," first observed among chickens, although it also
occurs among other animals as well. The Norwegian ornithologist
Schjelderup-Ebbe (1938) noted that many species of birds tend to establish a set of power relations among themselves, characterized by
the use of coercive power in the form of pecking. Among a group of
three birds, for example A, B, C, it is not uncommon for A to peck
both B and C while being pecked by neither; for B to peck C only;
and for C to peck neither A nor B but to be pecked by both. The
power relations among the three are thus patterned in a clear hierarchy (a linear arrangement), with A at the top of the pecking order, B
in the middle, and C at the bottom.

This pecking order pattern of power relations is particularly important because it occurs with such regularity among people as well
as animals. Recall the status hierarchy on the circus train. Or think of
a Boy Scout troop. At the bottom of the pecking order is the Tenderfoot; above him, in turn, come the Second Class and First Class
scouts, then the Star, Life, and Eagle scouts. Each rank can peck
those beneath them in the hierarchy and can be pecked, in turn, by
those above. Consider any military, governmental, or industrial organization that has a direct chain of command. At the top of the power
structure is the general, president, or chairman; beneath him appear
the various subordinates that he controls; then come the lower-
echelon subordinates that they, in turn, control.

A pecking order can also be found in a less formally constituted
group, such as the dyad of George and Martha in Albee's *Who's*

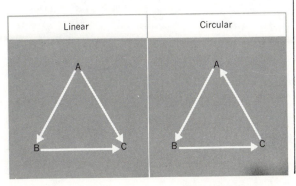

Figure 7.11
***Two pecking orders: lin-
ear and circular.*** *The
arrows indicate the di-
rection of pecking. In
the linear arrangement,
A pecks B and C, B
pecks C, and C pecks no
one. In the circular ar-
rangement, A pecks B, B
pecks C, and C pecks A.*

Afraid of Virginia Woolf? George and Martha are engaged in an ongoing struggle throughout the play to determine who is "top dog." In every way she can, Martha tries to convince George of his inadequacy. She tells him that he is ignorant ("Don't you know anything?"), effete ("You're going bald"), fat ("Paunchy over there isn't too happy when the conversation moves to muscle"), and a professional failure ("Georgie didn't have the stuff"). And George, in turn, tries to let Martha know how woefully inadequate she is. He tells her that she is vulgar ("Don't you touch me! You keep your paws clean for the undergraduates"), old ("You've taken a new tack, Martha, over the past couple of centuries"), loud ("We got lonely for the soft purr of your little voice"), and a drunk to boot ("My god, you can swill it down"). While Nick and Honey sit idly by, tongues lolling about in their mouths, George and Martha go at each other with scissors and tongs, each trying in any possible way to establish himself at the top of the conjugal heap.

Psychiatrists, psychologists, and psychiatric social workers. A less dramatic, but nonetheless interesting example of a "pecking order" sometimes emerges in the social structure of a mental health team, composed of a psychiatrist, a clinical psychologist, and a psychiatric social worker. Zander, Cohen, and Stotland (1957) conducted a series of comprehensive interviews with 156 psychiatrists, 165 psychologists, and 159 psychiatric social workers who were members of such teams in order to gain some insight into their power and role relations. In general, there appeared to be clear-cut agreement that the psychiatrists were at the top of the power hierarchy, followed by the clinical psychologists and then the psychiatric social workers. For example, with respect to the diagnosis, therapy, and assignment of mental patients, 51 percent of the psychologists reported that the psychiatrists possessed greater authority, while 85 percent of the psychiatrists also believed that they, themselves, had substantially more power.

All psychiatrists reported that, given another opportunity, they would again choose to be psychiatrists. However, 42 percent of the psychologists and 39 percent of the social workers said that they would rather be psychiatrists. As this finding might suggest, the psychologists and social workers displayed a strong tendency to communicate upward in the hierarchy—to the psychiatrists—and they limited themselves to comments that might obtain for them greater support and liking by the psychiatrists. Related to this finding is the fact (observed in a later study by Leff, Raven, and Gunn, 1964) that while psychologists are influenced equally in making their diagnoses by both psychiatrists and psychologists, psychiatrists tend to be more affected by the views of other psychiatrists than by those of psychologists.

Communication and Influence in Social Hierarchies

As this study shows, one of the important consequences of a pecking order appears to be a general tendency for those who are lower in the hierarchy to want to communicate with those who have more prestige and power, and for those at the top to prefer to communicate among themselves. This pattern has been confirmed in several laboratory studies. In one (Kelley, 1951), eight subjects at a time were brought to the laboratory and given the following general instructions before being divided into two subgroups of four:

The purpose of this experiment is to determine how well a group of people can perform a complicated task when the possibilities for communication among them are limited to written messages. Your group will be divided into equal-sized subgroups, working in separate rooms. The first of these subgroups will be given a specific pattern of rectangles. They will write messages to the second subgroup in the adjoining room, so as to enable the latter group to reproduce the pattern by placing the bricks in the proper position on the floor. All communications between and within the two subgroups will be restricted to written messages, each addressed to a single specific person. . . . You may write messages about anything you wish. Your task is simply to work together so as to reproduce quickly and accurately in one room the pattern given in the other room [p. 41].

Both subgroups of four were actually given the identical task of laying bricks. The experimenter served as messenger, and he collected for analysis all of the notes written by the subjects while delivering to them instead notes that had previously been prepared. Some subgroups were told that their own task—laying the bricks—was quite important and challenging, while the paired subgroup's task was relatively unimportant, menial, and did not require much intellectual ability. Other subgroups were told that their brick-laying job was relatively trivial, requiring only the carrying out of instructions, while the subgroup in the other room had the more challenging task. As predicted, those subjects who believed they had the more important job of the two subgroups were more likely to write messages to the other members of their own group, whereas the subjects who were told that their task carried less prestige tended to direct more of their communications to the "more prestigious" other subgroup. This tendency to communicate upward in the prestige hierarchy was especially great when each subgroup was told that it would continue to work on the same task throughout the experiment. When the subjects were told that they might be able to switch from the low-prestige task to the high-prestige one, upward communication was reduced. In explanation, Kelley suggested that communication may serve as a substitute for upward mobility, especially among low-status persons who have little possibility of being promoted to positions of higher prestige (such as the psychologists and social workers on the mental health teams).

The generality of these results was demonstrated by Hurwitz, Zander, and Hymovitch (1953) in a study of the residents of a midwestern community, all of whom were working on problems of mental health. As participants in a conference, these people were assigned to groups and given a problem to discuss. Before the meetings, the participants had been ranked according to prestige by two knowledgeable community residents using local standards. These two persons clearly agreed that some participants (such as directors of social agencies and psychiatrists) had high prestige and would probably be influential in making decisions at the conference; other participants (such as YMCA group workers or nurses) would have less prestige and power. With this ranking, the participants were assigned to discussion groups—two high-prestige and two low-prestige persons to each group. The prestige factor was emphasized in the participants' titles, which were carefully prepared and included after their names on the assignment sheet.

During the discussion, trained observers kept track of the number of remarks made by each group member, as well as the person to whom these remarks were directed. It was found that those of lower status spoke less often than those of higher status and that they tended to address their comments to the higher status persons. Those of higher status, on the other hand, were more inclined to speak to one another. Later on, when the participants were asked to rate the other members of their group on a scale of "liking," their preferences reflected the communication structure—both the higher and lower-status participants expressed a preference for the high-status members.

Similar results have been reported by Strodtbeck and his associates (1957) in a laboratory study of jury deliberations, in which it was found that men (rather than women) and people of higher socioeconomic status have more influence: they are chosen more often as foremen of juries, they speak more, and their recommendations are more likely to be heeded.

Taken together, these findings suggest that groups tend to establish dominance hierarchies, sometimes without regard to the competence of individual members, and that these hierarchies affect the flow of communication and the exercise of influence. However, although many groups form pecking orders, others do not—at least not in a simple, linear fashion. A family, for example, may be divided occupationally, with the husband taking responsibility for performing certain tasks and the wife taking responsibility for others.

Power and Role Structure in the Family

The pattern of power relationships in the family has been studied in a rather novel way by Herbst (1952); rather than asking a married couple to characterize their own relationship, he questioned their children, asking them such questions as: "Who sees to it that you get out of bed at the right time?" "Who decides when you have to get up?" and "How often do your parents disagree about what time you should get up?" The first question was intended to learn who performed the activity; the second, the person who made the decision about the activity; the third, the degree of tension or disagreement associated with that activity.

Family activities were then classified according to whether they were performed predominantly by the husband or by the wife. Six categories were established, as follows:
1. **Wife's household duties:** *for example, ironing.*
2. **Common household duties:** *for example, doing the dishes.*
3. **Child control and care:** *regulating the child's table manners.*
4. **Husband's household duties:** *mowing the lawn.*
5. **Social activities:** *inviting guests.*
6. **Economic activities:** *financing family vacations.*

If the husband performed any of the above duties, he would also perform all of those that followed it in the list. If he performed only three duties, these would almost certainly be numbers 4, 5, and 6. Of 74 husbands investigated, only 10 deviated in any way from the above pattern. Child control and care, an activity in the middle, was often handled by both parents, and it also led to the greatest amount of disagreement and tension in the family.

Family activities were also categorized in terms of who made the decisions about them. Some decisions were labeled "husband dominant" and some "wife dominant." If a decision was made jointly, it was called "syncratic." If the area of decision was divided by mutual consent, with the husband assuming responsibility for some decisions and the wife for others, but without consultation, the term "autonomic" was applied. It was found that most disagreements occurred over decisions that were either husband dominant or wife dominant.

Later studies by Wolfe (1959) and Blood and Wolfe (1960) attempted to learn why families followed one pattern of authority rather than another. They interviewed 731 wives in Detroit and generally found that: (1) Husband dominance was more likely to occur when the husband was occupationally successful and had a relatively

Figure 7.12
The power structure in the Raven household, as seen by Jon Raven at 7 years of age. *So who is really the boss? The relative size of the two power figures is grossly inaccurate, perhaps reflecting a tendency to see a more powerful figure as physically larger. However, when asked why his mother was drawn so large, the artist responded, "Because she is angry."*

My Mom pretends to beat up my Dad. My Mom screams at my Dad when he lets us stay up late. My Dad cheats by eating the wrong things. My Mom says that he is boss, but she seems to be the boss.

high income. (2) Wife dominance increased when the wife was employed. (3) The wife's power decreased the more she needed love and affection. (4) The wife's power increased with age. (5) Marital satisfaction was greatest in husband-dominant and syncratic families; it was least in wife-dominant families. Parallel findings were reported later in a similar study in Los Angeles in which both husbands and wives were interviewed (Centers, Raven, and Rodrigues, 1971).

Thus, although many groups structure their power relations in the form of a linear pecking order, the family generally shows greater variability in its power structure; dominance tends to vary according to the task to be performed, and it changes over time. Yet another pattern of power relations that occasionally emerges in groups is one in which each member has control over a different other person. Schjelderup-Ebbe (1938), who discovered this pattern among certain groups of birds, called it "circular pecking." This rather unusual pattern is illustrated in Figure 7.11.

Instead of A pecking B and C, B pecking C, and C pecking neither (the usual linear arrangement), A pecks B, B pecks C, and C pecks A. As you may recall from our discussion of *No Exit*, Sartre's three characters follow this power pattern exactly: Garcin needs Inez but controls Estelle; Inez needs Estelle but controls Garcin; and Estelle needs Garcin but controls Inez. The person each character needs is *not* the one he controls. As a consequence, each can attempt to satisfy his own needs only by exerting control over a second person who, in turn, controls the one whom he needs. At one point in the play Estelle turns to Inez and spits in her face, whereupon Inez immediately screams at Garcin: "You'll pay for this!" Inez can satisfy her need for Estelle only by attempting to exert control over Garcin who, in turn, controls Estelle.

This peculiar, intriguing pattern of power relations helps to explain why the conflict among the three characters in *No Exit* neither increases nor decreases, but remains hellishly the same (a "creeping pain that gnaws and fumbles and caresses one and never hurts quite enough"). The conflict cannot escalate because there is always the tantalizing possibility of a three-way "pat-on-the-back" relationship. If only the first person could satisfy the second, the second might do the same for the third who, in turn, could satisfy the first. But there is also a second cycle, running counter to the first, that prevents any amelioration of the conflict. Thus, there is always the infernal possibility of a three-way "stab-in-the-back" relationship: the first person tortures the second, the second the third, and the third the first.

The *No Exit* pattern of circular pecking is certainly not typical of most group relationships, although, as we have pointed out, some families are structured this way. The circular pecking pattern is just one of a wide variety of power structures within groups, each of which has important implications for the ability of the group's individual members to exert influence.

Summary

A group may be thought of as a social molecule whose structure is determined by the relationships among its members. Although these relationships are many and varied, five appear to be of particular importance; they correspond to the processes of evaluation, interdependence, communication, roles, and influence. It is important to bear in mind that these processes are not independent; they are linked together in such a way that they both affect and are affected by one another.

Social psychologists have examined evaluative relations in groups primarily with respect to group "cohesiveness," where cohesiveness is defined as the sum of the positive forces acting on the members of a group to remain in, rather than leave, that group. It has been found that high group cohesiveness provides greater satisfaction and morale among the group members, enables the members to both exert and be susceptible to influence, and yields greater productivity. Of course, since high cohesive groups also tend to be more responsive to group norms, when the norm calls for low productivity, these groups tend to decrease their output and may actually become less productive than low cohesive groups with the same norm.

The type of interdependence among group members also has important consequences for the functioning of a group. In general it appears that a group tends to function most effectively when its members are positively interdependent with respect to goals; the result is not only improved productivity, but an increased willingness to trust, like, and help the other members of the group. While less research has been done on the consequences for group functioning of interdependence with respect to means, it has been found that groups are generally more effective when their members are positively means interdependent. Finally, when two or more group members decide that they share certain goals that differ from those of the others, coalitions tend to form, and the result is often increased cooperation and liking within subgroups and increased competition and hostility between them.

The effects of communication in groups have typically been studied in two rather different ways: by careful observation of the interaction among the members who are brought together to discuss some problem, and by studying the consequences of experimentally imposing one of several communication patterns (networks) on a group. The observational study of communication in groups shows that, over time, members begin to vary in the quantity of their communication and in the number of others with whom they communicate. Groups also tend to become differentiated into a series of often complementary roles: one person may take the role of "social smoother" (attempting to settle arguments among members), another may become a "clarifier" or "questioner," and still others may assume one of two distinct leadership roles—the "task specialist" (responsible for generating ideas that help the group move toward its goals) and the "socioemotional specialist" (responsible for maintaining harmony and good feeling within the group). The experimental study of communication networks indicates that the more centralized the communication structure of a group (that is, the greater the extent to which one or a few members can receive messages from all or most of the others), the greater the group's speed and accuracy in solving simple problems, the lower the satisfaction and morale of most members, and the greater the members' tendency to view the most central members of the communication network as leaders.

While social roles typically develop during the process of communication, groups may also be differentiated into positions according to tradition and culture. Sometimes these positions are formally defined—doctor and patient; supervisor and subordinate; teacher and student; wife-mother, husband-father, and child. Each position carries with it a prescribed role, a pattern of behavior that is expected of the person occupying that position. Sometimes these roles may be in conflict—the traditional role assigned to women may conflict with the role requirement of a particular woman who is a major executive of a business organization.

In order to function, all groups depend upon the ongoing exchange of influence. As a group develops, its members tend to "jockey for position," which leads to a general pattern of power relations (a "dominance hierarchy"). Dominance hierarchies lend a certain degree of stability to a group and help ensure its collective survival. The most prevalent and important power structure is the pecking order, first observed among chickens and other animals: the most dominant group member, a, is able to peck each of the others (and not be pecked in return), b can peck all of the group members except a, c can peck all but a and b, and so forth. One important consequence of such a power arrangement is that those who are lower in the hierarchy generally want to communicate with those who have more prestige or power, and those at the top tend to prefer to communicate among themselves.

Now that we have looked at a number of the relationships that typically exist among the members of a group, let us examine the group from another vantage point and consider the many ways in which it influences its individual members. Does the mere presence of a group affect individual behavior? To what extent and in what way does a group motivate its members to modify their attitudes, feelings, and behavior with respect to their willingness to take risks and their desire to perform antisocial or prosocial acts? How do groups typically deal with deviant members? These questions will be addressed in Chapter 8.

Group Effects on the Performance of Humans and Other Animals
Social Facilitation
Social Inhibition
Other Group Effects That Contribute to Increased and Decreased Performance

Contagion and the Spread of Group Effects

Deindividuation and Group Effects on Behavior
Laboratory Studies of Deindividuation

Group Judgments and Group Norms
Group Norms and the Autokinetic Effect
The Power of a Stubborn Minority

The Unanimous Majority and the Lone Deviant
Majority Influences on Judgment
Pressures toward Uniformity of Opinion and Social Comparison
Responses of the Majority to the Deviant
The Behavior of the Deviant

The Strange Mystery of the Risky Shift and the Runaway Norm
Choice Dilemmas and Risky Shifts
Why a Risky Shift?
Runaway Norms: The Normative Value of Exceeding the Average

Bystander Intervention and Helping Behavior
Factors That Influence Helping Behavior

Social Facilitation and the **Camponotus** *Ant.* When one is considering who has the greatest reputation for industrious work, no living creature surpasses the lowly ant. The ant can and does carry objects many times its own weight, transporting these at amazing speed to its nest. Among ants the *Camponotus* is particularly energetic and worthy of study. Professor S. C. Chen (1937) of the National Tsing Hua University of Peiping was so intrigued with them that he decided to observe them with extreme care and detail. By collecting and counting the number of tiny pellets of earth kicked up by the worker ants as they dug their nests, he was able to keep a careful and precise record of their productivity, which could be plotted on a graph over time. To most of us, all ants may look alike—at least those of the same species. Professor Chen observed otherwise—some ants work more rapidly than others and appear to have a higher energy level. These hard-working ants seem to be genetically different. They are particularly susceptible to starvation and drying, and are especially sensitive to ether and chloroform. The number of pellets kicked up per minute is remarkably constant for a given ant under ordinary circumstances and even under unusual circumstances such as being placed alone in a milk bottle half filled with dry, sandy soil.

Chen carefully measured the isolated ant's rate of productivity and then noted what happened when one or two other ants were added to the milk bottle. As soon as a second ant was added, the first one began digging with noticeably less delay. If the two ants had originally worked at about the same rate, the arrival of the second ant led the first one to work more actively and with greater productivity. The speedup in digging, moreover, was greater for ants that usually worked more slowly. When two ants with different levels of activity were placed together, there was some convergence in their work rate—the slower ant increased its rate while the faster ant slowed down. The ant with an intermediate level of activity was especially susceptible to influence, increasing its work rate when paired with faster ants and decreasing it when paired with slower ants. These results are quite interesting if we realize that the normal rate of activity of the *Camponotus* ant seems to be physiologically determined and is probably innate. Yet that activity level can be significantly affected by the presence of a co-worker.

GROUP EFFECTS ON THE PERFORMANCE OF HUMANS AND OTHER ANIMALS

Similar group effects have been observed in the action of other animals. When other members of their own species are doing the same thing, chickens (Bayer, 1929), fish (Welty, 1934), and rats (Harlow, 1932) will eat more; cockroaches (Zajonc, 1968), horses (Triplett, 1897), and dogs (Vogel, Scott, and Marston, 1950) will run more quickly; pairs of rats will copulate more (the group effect is especially noticeable for senescent rats) (Larsson, 1956); little chicks will peck more rapidly (Tolman, 1964); and children and adults will laugh more heartily (Chapman, 1973; Wolosin, 1975). The pecking rate of chicks can be accelerated by rapid tapping sounds, such as those made by tapping a pencil on a table within the chick's hearing (Tolman, 1964). What, then, of other group effects on the performance of human beings?

During the Industrial Revolution in the late nineteenth century, there was considerable emphasis on productivity in industry; accordingly, factory managers wanted to know what factors would enable industrial employees to work more rapidly and efficiently. In the case of those who worked in a pre-mechanized shoe factory, it was observed that they seemed to tap nails into the leather more rapidly when other people were present than when they were alone (Moede, 1920). Could an analogy be drawn between the pecking behavior of the chicks and the tapping behavior of the shoe workers?

One of the first experimental social psychologists, Norman Triplett (1897) (whose work we discussed briefly in Chapter 5), arrived at the study of group effects through his interest in bicycle racing He carefully studied the record books of the League of American Wheelmen, and from his statistical analyses found that cyclists in training pedaled much faster when they were paced by another bicycle (often a tandem) that managed to keep just slightly ahead of them. In actual races where there was explicit competition, the cyclists were even faster, but it appears that competition was not required for group-induced acceleration. The slowest speeds were recorded when the cyclist was merely racing against the clock on his own. Later on, Floyd Allport (1924) examined the "group increment"—increased activity that is due to the presence of co-acting others. He suggested that two major factors might be responsible: "rivalry"—increased motivation due to competition; and "social facilitation"—increased activity due to the stimulation of merely seeing or hearing the parallel movements of another person.

Social Facilitation

The social facilitation analysis was later viewed from the perspective of stimulus-response theories. With respect to chicken pecking, each pecking movement produces a stimulus (a pecking sound that stimulates the ear of the chicken) as well as a visual cue. The lone chicken responds to that stimulus by pecking again, which provides yet an-

Figure 8.1
Social facilitation in horse racing. *Floyd Allport's analysis suggests that if horse no. 7 has been leading throughout most of the race, horse no. 2 will receive extra stimulation, pull ahead, and win.*

other stimulus, to which it responds, and so forth. When another chicken is pecking nearby, the sight and sound of that chicken provide an additional stimulus to which the first also responds. The second chicken also responds to its own stimulus and to that of the first chicken, so that the pecking rate for both increases. This analysis is consistent with the finding that one can increase the pecking rate of a chicken by tapping a pencil (Tolman, 1964). A shoemaker's tapping would have the same effect on a co-working shoemaker as the movements and sounds of one cyclist on an adjacent cyclist. Allport (1924) pointed out that there is a maxim among bicycle racers that if two racers have precisely the same capabilities, and if one happens to get a slightly faster start and to maintain his lead over the initial section of the course, he is bound to finish as the loser. Why? Because the cyclist in front provides a visual and auditory stimulus for the one behind him, but he does not have a similar stimulus to activate him. Thus, social facilitation would enable the second cyclist to pull ahead and eventually win.

Social Inhibition
The presence of others may sometimes have an inhibiting effect. Allport (1924) reported such social inhibition in a study that required a group of subjects to read and disprove philosophical passages. The quality of the counterarguments was evaluated independently, and it was found that three-fourths of the subjects had prepared better statements when they were alone than when they were in the presence of others. Social facilitation was evident in the quantity of the arguments produced, but not in the quality. The subjects reported

that they had been distracted while they were with others who were working on the same task. Thus, the stimuli from others that had produced an increased number of responses may also have reduced the subject's ability to evaluate his responses clearly. Since all of us have probably been distracted while working with others, and it seems like such a commonplace phenomenon, this may explain why it has not been the focus of much experimentation.

Other Group Effects That Contribute
to Increased and Decreased Performance

The analysis of social facilitation in terms of increased stimuli leading to increased responses is appealing in its simplicity. But obviously there are limitations to this analysis. First, there is evidence that people can increase their performance when others are present only as an audience. Second, there are some tasks, such as solving mathematical problems, learning finger mazes, and memorizing lists of nonsense syllables, where the presence of others appears to have a negative effect. Third, the presence of someone who is explicitly evaluating an actor can, under certain circumstances, motivate him to increase the level of his performance, while at other times lead him to decrease it.

Presence of Others as a Source of Arousal. Elaborating on the earlier formulations of Allport, Robert Zajonc (1965, 1968) suggested that the major factor in group effects is arousal. The other person or group, which is functioning as co-actor or observer, increases the actor's motivation to perform. Zajonc admits that the evidence for this view is indirect. Although he cites research on group effects indicating arousal in animals, there is more direct evidence. It has been demonstrated that when subjects are paired off with others while working on a parallel color-learning task, they show a higher level of galvanic skin response (a common physiological measure of emotional arousal) when compared with subjects who are working alone (Shapiro and Leiderman, 1964).

If it is true that the presence of others leads to increased emotional and motivational arousal, why does this sometimes lead to improved performance and sometimes to decreased performance? Zajonc suggests that arousal elicits the actor's dominant responses (those that he has best learned at some earlier time in his life). If he is working on a task that he has mastered, these dominant responses will be correct. But if the task is new, then the dominant responses, although learned under somewhat similar stimulus conditions, will often be incorrect. Under conditions of greater arousal, then, an increase in dominant responses will lead to poorer performance when the task is relatively new, but to better performance if the task has been well mastered. To illustrate this point, Zajonc cited an experiment by Pessin (1933):

Pessin gave his subjects three tasks: (1) a rotor-pursuit task (requiring the subject to keep a pointer in contact with an object that moves in a circular fashion on a turntable); (2) a maze-learning task; and (3) a nonsense-syllable-learning task. The subjects performed these activities both in front of an audience and alone. The rotor-pursuit task was learned and performed better in front of the audience rather than alone. Zajonc says that this would follow from the arousal theory, if we assume that the rotor-pursuit task is similar to many eye-hand coordination activities that we perform quite often and do quite well. The maze and nonsense-syllable tasks, however, differ more from our everyday activities, calling forth a number of previously learned responses that may not be correct. As an example, the subject may be presented with the nonsense syllable "WAK" and instructed to respond with "BOF." Since he has probably never had to make such an association before and since "WAK" looks like "WALK," the subject may have a strong inclination to respond with "RUN." Under conditions of high arousal, which are due to the presence of others, the subject will frequently respond with "RUN" and will have great difficulty saying "BOF."

The Pessin study provides additional support for the Zajonc interpretation. When the subjects were later asked to repeat the maze-learning task and the nonsense-syllable task—after they had finally mastered them—they performed *better* in front of a group than they had alone. Zajonc thus concludes that performing well-learned responses—doing things with which we are quite familiar—will be facilitated by the presence of another person or group, but learning new material and performing difficult tasks will be inhibited by the presence of others. Presumably, then, he would advise a student who was studying very difficult, new material for a test to do so in the privacy of his room (assuming, of course, that he doesn't need to consult anyone about the material). Once he has mastered the material, he might do well to review it with another student.

The observer effects will be heightened if the actor is explicitly told that he will be evaluated by an observer or an audience (Henchy and Glass, 1968). But evaluation need not be explicit: Even casual observation by a Lieutenant Colonel is sufficient to lead to more effective light-monitoring performance by groups of National Guardsmen (Bergum and Lehr, 1963).

The value of increased arousal—as provided by an audience—is generally recognized by accomplished musicians, dancers, and actors. Indeed, when a play is nearing the end of its run or whenever the audience is sparse, the actors may urge the theater management to "paper the house" (give out complimentary tickets) so that they will be able to perform in front of a full house. On the other hand, young music students who are performing at a recital planned for them by their teacher will typically not play as well in front of an audience.

Presence of Others as a Source of Anxiety. While Zajonc emphasizes the effects of others in arousing dominant responses, there is also reason to believe that "evaluation apprehension" (Rosenberg, 1956)—fear that the observer will devaluate the actor—may arouse anxiety and thus diminish his performance (Steiner, 1972). Such anxiety may occur, at least to some extent, whenever one performs in front of an observer, but the anxiety will probably be greater when the evaluation is explicit and when the performer truly fears failure. When an audience responds negatively, this can have a devastating effect upon the performers. This was clearly demonstrated in a study in which fraternity pledges were asked to perform before a group of active members, who then proceeded to razz them (Laird, 1923). When a young girl performs poorly at her first piano recital, this may merely reflect her heightened arousal which leads her to give incorrect dominant responses. But the child may actually be experiencing severe anxiety, which causes her to freeze and be unable to play at all. Aside from the question of one's mastery of a task, a person who undertakes an activity with anxiety and fear about a negative evaluation will perform less adequately (Aronfreed, 1964). Irwin Katz (1967) has applied this analysis to the test performance of lower-income black students. He postulated that due to frequent criticism of their academic performance by white teachers, black students might be unduly anxious about being evaluated by a white tester. On relatively simple tasks, black students performed better when the tester was white rather than black; conceivably, the black student, feeling confident about his performance, was motivated to show the white tester that he could do well. But on difficult tasks, anxiety about poor performance apparently caused the black student to perform less well for a white tester than for a black. This study was carried out in the 1960s; it would be interesting to see if changes in the schools and greater emphasis on self-confidence among minority groups would produce different results today.

Thus far, we have examined three factors that may increase the level of performance of a person who is in the presence of others: (1) increased stimulation from the sight and sound of others who are performing similar tasks; (2) increased motivational arousal from the presence of a co-actor or an observer, leading to a higher level of dominant responses (provided that the task has been mastered and that the dominant responses are correct); and (3) increased motivation due to competition with another person. Three factors that may decrease an individual's level of performance are: (1) responses from others that are distracting and thus make it more difficult for the person to evaluate his acts; (2) increased motivational arousal, where a task has not been mastered, leading to an increased number of incorrect responses; and (3) evaluation apprehension, which may increase anxiety and thus inhibit performance.

Two additional social factors may also contribute to either better or worse performance: *group norms* and *interdependence pressures*.

Group Norms. An individual will often determine the appropriate level of performance for himself by referring to a group with which he identifies and which he uses as a standard for self-evaluation. Thus, there is a tendency for those who belong to an industrial work group to have a similar performance rate. Various work groups that are performing essentially the same task will have different rates of productivity, but within a given work group the variation will be relatively small, especially when that group is cohesive (Seashore, 1954). The effects of the group norm will sometimes increase and sometimes decrease production; in either case, there will be greater uniformity.

The analysis of group norms helps to explain why there is prolonged reduction in productivity when a work group's usual procedures are changed. In a classic study of productivity in a pajama factory, it was observed that when there was a change in the procedure for packaging pajamas, a substantial decrease in productivity took place. This was, of course, to be expected. However, since industrial engineers had determined that the new method was not intrinsically more difficult than the old, management expected that the production rate would return to its former level once the new procedure had been learned. But this did not happen. Therefore, two industrial social psychologists, Lester Coch and John R. P. French, Jr., were asked to analyze the situation and suggest a solution (Coch and French, 1948). In accordance with the theory and research of Kurt Lewin and his co-workers (1947), it seemed that the work group had developed a norm of production that everyone tended to follow. Those who might have been inclined to produce at a lower level raised their production to that of the group as a whole. More frequently, though, those who performed at a higher level tended to lower it to that of the group norm.

Coch and French described the case of one new worker who joined a work group at the pajama factory, learned her job very quickly, and was soon producing well above the group norm. However, this did not last long; her productivity level soon fell. To test their ideas further, Coch and French removed the woman from her usual group and allowed her to work on her own. Her productivity level rose dramatically, but then, when she returned to her group, it fell again. Coch and French's suggestion for dealing with the problem of lowered productivity will be described in greater detail in Chapter 9.

It has been suggested that group norms may also operate in the case of academic performance (Backman and Secord, 1968). In most schools, children are grouped together according to age; they may also be grouped according to intellectual ability, and in neighborhood schools most children are of the same ethnic and socioeconomic background. Thus, the child, continuing in the same school with many of the same classmates, probably feels a degree of similarity and identity with the others. He may then use his classmates as a basis for evaluating himself to determine his level of performance. He receives many cues as to how the others are performing—by hearing classroom recitations and teachers' remarks, and by comparing papers turned in and grades received. A pupil who is assigned to a class where the general level of performance is higher than his own will be pressed to improve—by studying harder, doing more assignments, and so forth. Similarly, a pupil who is assigned to a class whose level of performance is lower may reduce his efforts. These pressures toward uniformity will oppose the tendency to compete (as described in Chapter 5), which is often fostered by the school. Indeed, the normative pressures may serve as a defense against the extreme pressures of competition. One study of medical students described how those enrolled in a certain course arrived at a norm for the number of medical summaries that would be handed in to the professor; any student who exceeded that number was rejected by his classmates (Hughes, Becker, and Geer, 1962).

The effects of group norms are limited, however: If the others in a group perform either too far above or too far below a given individual, he will reject that group as a standard for comparison and his performance will not be affected. Furthermore, Festinger (1957) has suggested that, with respect to performance, people tend to compare themselves with those whose level of performance is just slightly above their own.

Interdependence Pressures. As part of the Industrial Revolution, there was division of labor, which became the hallmark of the modern, efficient production system. Each worker became interdependent (rather than independent, as in the case of the pre-mechanized shoe factory mentioned earlier), working at one small part of the task in coordination with others. The modern assembly line, which Henry Ford perfected in the automobile industry, became the model for the modern industrial system. Its efficiency is due in part to the fact that the worker needs to learn only one simple task which he repeats over and over again. To some extent, the assembly line leads to greater productivity because of interdependence pressure. Each worker on the line is highly interdependent—with respect to means—with the person who precedes him and the person who follows him in the line. Industrial psychologists have called these joint pressures "push" and "pull": Each worker has to keep up with the one behind him who is piling up products that require his attention; he may also be pressured by the worker ahead of him who works so quickly that he keeps waiting for something to do. The moving belt of the assembly line may add to both of these pressures. Thus, the worker is compelled to work more quickly than he would normally.

In Chapters 5 and 7, we have discussed interdependence as a dimension of group structure and the ways in which it can lead to greater group identification. Here we are also examining the intense pressure that interdependence can place on the individual. On the assembly line even today, the pressures can become so great that a worker will collape. This pressure from means interdependence is illustrated quite dramatically in Charlie Chaplin's classic film *Modern Times*, in which Charlie plays the role of a worker who must tighten the bolts on an infinite number of nondescript objects that keep coming at him on the assembly line, and that must then be

Figure 8.2
Charlie Chaplin, in a scene from the 1936 film Modern Times, *goes to pieces under the extreme "push and pull" pressures of the assembly line. Though uproariously funny on the screen, this scene satirizes very real and serious problems that have confronted workers in the modern factory.*

passed on, bolts tightened, to the next man in line. Charlie works increasingly fast until he can no longer bear up under the strain. The scene is uproariously funny until one begins to realize that the depiction is a caricature of the pressures that have actually occurred in production lines. Small wonder that labor unions came into being to counter the incredible strains of the modern industrial system.

CONTAGION
AND THE SPREAD
OF GROUP EFFECTS

Groups are clearly able to facilitate or inhibit the performance of their individual members. In addition, groups can also affect the behavior and emotions of individuals through example, implicit suggestion, or contagion. Two examples will be presented here:

Fainting among British Schoolgirls. On an otherwise insignificant Thursday afternoon in October 1965, the Blackburn Medical Office of Health in Lancashire, England, received a distress call from the headmistress of a girls' secondary school. It seems that earlier that day several girls had complained of feeling dizzy and peculiar, and then they had fainted. Later on the "affection" assumed epidemic proportions and the girls were "going down like ninepins." The medical officer rushed to the school to examine the frightened and shocked girls. Eighty-five were taken away in ambulances, and the rest were dismissed for the weekend. There were no new cases over the weekend, but when school reopened on Monday the epidemic returned and 54 girls were hospitalized. There was another major outbreak the following Monday. During the entire course of the epidemic one-third of the 550 girls enrolled in the school were affected. The general symptoms included swooning, moaning, chattering of teeth, muscle spasms, and rapid and deep breathing. For those who were hospitalized, the symptoms continued for as much as four days, and then they often reappeared among the same girls during the next outbreak. Yet careful laboratory tests showed no signs of a virus, bacterial infection, or other organic disorder; the girls' temperatures were normal or a bit low and their blood count was normal. The investigators then looked at the problem from a social point of view; they administered questionnaires to the entire school. The following interesting findings were established:

(1) Several years earlier, there had been a polio epidemic in Blackburn (the town where the school was located), which had received widespread publicity (lorry drivers had refused to make deliveries to the "polio town"), and the girls had been quite frightened

and upset by this. (2) Just before the fainting epidemic, there had been a ceremony at the Anglican cathedral under Royal patronage. Due to the late arrival of the dignitaries, the girls had waited outside in the sun for three hours, and about 20 girls had fainted. (3) The epidemic, particularly in its early stages, was more apt to occur after an informal mingling among the students—as in the assembly hall or during class breaks; fainting was less common when the girls were in class and their attention was directed more to the teacher or their classwork than to other students. (4) The initial outbreaks were among the 14-year-olds (the middle age group), spreading first to other students in the same age group and then to the younger (rather than the older) students. (5) Students seemed to be paricularly susceptible to the fainting if they scored high in extroversion and hysteria on the Eysenck Personality Inventory (Eysenck, 1965). (6) It was found that the school was quite strict and that there was substantial pressure on the students to perform at a high level (Moss and McEvedy, 1966).

The June Bug Mystery. In the United States, a somewhat similar event occurred in a textile factory in a small Southern town. Sixty-two of the 200 women employees of the plant reported serious side effects from strange insect bites—severe nausea, nervousness, numbness, a rash breaking out over the whole body, and numbness. Some of the stricken women could actually point to what looked like gnat bites. The initial reports suggested that the strange bug had been imported in a shipment of cloth that had recently arrived from England! Could it be?

When local health officials, entomologists, professional exterminators, and experts from the U.S. Public Health Service's Communicable Disease Center carried out a careful search of the factory, they found only one black ant, a housefly, a couple of gnats, a small beetle, and one mite—none of which could have caused the severe reactions experienced by the women. Two Duke University social psychologists, Alan Kerckhoff and Kurt Back, then undertook a careful study to determine if this was another case of "hysterical contagion" (Kerckhoff and Back, 1968). A careful investigation, including observations and interviews with plant personnel soon indicated that this might indeed be the situation.

As in the case of the British school girls, the bug epidemic seemed to occur during a period of strain and tension—at the height of the production season when many of the workers were doing some unusually intensive overtime work. Kerckhoff and Back developed a four-point "strain" index based on reports from the workers; it included the amount of overtime worked, the extent to which a woman employee was providing more than half of her family's income, her unwillingness to reveal any tension or discuss complaints with her supervisor, and the extent to which she worked with others who had a very high work output. It turned out that those women who scored highest on the strain index were the most susceptible to the "bug bites."

The first women to suffer from the "bites" were the "social isolates." They had few friends, were not too popular, had little group support, and were less affected by the group norms (which might have precluded any signs of unusual behavior or symptoms). They were also unhappy with their work and had had previous fainting episodes. (These women might have also scored high on Eysenck's hysteria scale.) Yet, these women were less apt to malinger or feign illness to escape from work, which closed off one common means of avoiding strain and tension. As in the case of the Blackburn school, the epidemic first spread within one work group. Later, the "bites" seemed to spread according to a specific pattern—a given woman was more apt to be "bitten" if her friend had been "bitten." The symptoms seemed to follow a communication network, which approximately paralleled the sociometric network. As the epidemic reached its peak, however, friendship seemed to be less of a determinant; a general group norm seemed to prevail, and the symptoms appeared regardless of friendship.

It is intriguing and disconcerting to note that just as opinions, beliefs, and behaviors may spread through a group in systematic fashion, so may the hysterical symptoms of severe physical illness. A person evaluates his physical health in relation to the health of similar and desirable others in the same way that he evaluates his opinions.

DEINDIVIDUATION
AND GROUP EFFECTS
ON BEHAVIOR

Of Yoko Ono, Auto Vandals, Sharks, and Lynch Mobs. In the case of both the British school and the American textile factory, it has been postulated that succumbing to the group hysteria served some function for the affected individuals. At the school, it gave the students a "legitimate" means to escape from a highly pressured environment. There were many more outbreaks of fainting when the pressures were greatest. (The fainting spells generally subsided as the weekend approached and increased as the new week began.) At the factory, it gave the workers an opportunity to free themselves from the demands of work and family responsibilities. Although we do not believe that the process was generally a conscious one, it is entirely possible that group norms helped to facilitate the behavior toward which the individuals were inclined.

Let us examine the "audience-participation" act (the so-called Cut Piece) developed by Yoko Ono (the wife of the former Beatle John Lennon). Wearing a favorite dress, Yoko sits in front of her audience and offers any interested person a pair of scissors with which to cut off a piece of her dress. There is silence, uneasy laughter, tension, and uncertainty until finally someone comes up and cuts off a piece of the dress; then another person comes up, and then another. Soon the audience goes wild, scrambling for the scissors to cut the next piece, until the entertainer is left naked. Philip Zimbardo (1969), who discovered the Yoko Ono example in a 1969 issue of *Look* magazine, saw some obvious parallels with a study he had conducted with a colleague, Scott Fraser. They had purchased a 1959 Oldsmobile, removed its license plates, opened its hood slightly, and left it parked on a street just across from the Bronx campus of New York University. Within ten minutes, a man, a woman, and their 8-year-old son appeared, searched the car, and removed the battery and the radiator. They were followed by a steady parade of vandals who removed practically everything else—air cleaner, antenna, windshield wipers, chrome strips, hubcaps, gas cap, and the only usable tire—all within 26 hours. Then some adolescents smashed the headlights and windshield. In less than three days, the car was a complete wreck—an ugly trash can in which people threw their refuse.

This phenomenon is amazingly similar to the sharks' terrifying "dance of death" observed by the underseas explorer Jacques Cousteau. The sharks first circle a baby whale until the first shark takes a bite. Then the others join in a savage attack, soon reducing the whale to little more than a skeleton (Zimbardo, 1969). Although there is an apparent similarity between Yoko Ono's Cut Piece, the auto vandals, and the sharks' "dance of death," the underlying dynamics are probably quite different. Undoubtedly the impetus for the mass assault of the sharks is the sight, odor, and taste of the whale's blood. The human assault may be largely the result of overcoming social and moral restraints.

Before the turn of the century, the French sociologist Gustav LeBon offered an explanation for the unusual behavior of individuals in crowds and mobs. LeBon referred specifically to the behavior of revolutionary mobs bent on death and destruction, as in the French Revolution (LeBon, 1896). He suggested that in a crowd, the individual loses his sense of individual identity. He gains strength and support by merging with the larger social entity; losing his individuality frees him from the usual social restraints—a highly satisfying experience. Emotion (not intellect) rules, thus: "In a crowd men always tend to the same level, and on general questions, a vote recorded by forty academicians is no better than that of forty water-carriers" (LeBon, 1895).

The process of deindividuation, reduction of restraint, and satisfaction is dramatically illustrated in William V. Clark's classic story of *The Oxbow Incident* (1940). Even normally restrained, upstanding citizens—such as the respectable, mild-mannered general store merchant—in this Western town get caught up in the excitement of a posse hunt for the murderer of a popular neighbor. When three itinerant cowhands are discovered sleeping by their campfire, the posse becomes a bloodthirsty mob bent on lynching these men immediately, without a trial or hearing. After the lynching, it is learned that the men are innocent. Only when the mob has accomplished its purpose and disbanded, and each person again resumes his own identity, does he feel any shame or self-denigration for what he as an individual has done in killing three innocent men.

Laboratory Studies of Deindividuation

The deindividuation hypothesis was subjected to laboratory examination by three social psychologists, Leon Festinger, Albert Pepitone, and Theodore Newcomb (1952). Groups of four to seven students were first told of a fictitious study indicating that 87 percent of a large sample of students had a "strong, deep-seated hatred of one or both parents, ranging from generalized hostility to consistent fantasies of violence and murder." Furthermore, "of the 13 percent in whom no trace of hostility was found, the great majority thought they probably hated their parents and were willing to discuss every aspect of their feelings with the investigator." The students were then asked to discuss their personal feelings about their parents, and, as one might expect from the introduction they were given, most expressed considerable hostility toward their parents. During the discussion, an observer made a note of all of the hostile statements made and also who had made which statement. After the discussion, the recorded remarks were read to the group, together with some additional comments that had not been made at all. The subjects were asked to identify which remarks had been made in the group and by whom. Three variables were measured for the members of each group: (1) *hostility*—this was based on the number of hostile statements made by each individual and the group as a whole; (2) *cohesiveness*—this was based on a questionnaire asking each member how much he had enjoyed participating in the group; and (3) *deindividuation*—this was based on the number of errors each person made identifying who had said what (many identification errors would indicate that individual identities had been obscured, so that one could not be sure exactly who had said what). The experimenters had expected that when the group was deindividuated, with individual identities deemphasized, each member would feel less inhibited and thus would make more hostile remarks about his parents; the experimenters also expected that the loss of identity and inhibition would be pleasurable, so that deindividuation would help achieve greater group cohesiveness. Consistent with their hypotheses, the investigators found the three variables were highly interrelated (Festinger, Newcomb, and Pepitone, 1952). Unfortunately, in this study (as well as other correlational studies), one cannot be certain that the direction of causation was what the experimenters had predicted. Did freedom of expression lead to greater cohesiveness, or was it the reverse? Did deindividuation cause both disinhibition and cohesiveness, or did greater cohesiveness lead to a perception of similarity (and thus deindividuation) among members? Additional research was, therefore, necessary.

The deindividuation phenomenon has since been tested in other studies where individual identity was varied more systematically. Singer, Brush, and Lublin (1965) compared the behavior of groups of women who were asked to discuss pornographic literature. In one condition, each subject in the group was asked to wear her best clothes, wear a name tag, use her first name, and emphasize her individuality wherever possible. In a contrasting, deindividuated condition, the subjects wore baggy lab coats and their individual identity was not known to the others. Consistent with the experimenters' predictions, the subjects whose individuality was minimized were less restrained in their speech. They tended to use obscene words and to have livelier discussions.

In a later study by Zimbardo, women subjects were told that their "empathic ability" would be studied by the researcher as they (the women) shocked another woman "subject" and then rated her reactions. Each subject was led to believe that she would be doing the actual shocking. (Of course no shocks were actually administered, but the subjects could see a girl through a one-way mirror writhing, wincing, and grimacing in pain each time she supposedly received a shock.) When the subject who was to do the shocking was part of a "deindividuated group," where each member was dressed in a hood, was not identified by name, and was unknown to the others, she was more inclined to administer many shocks of high intensity and duration. By contrast, the identifiable subjects (who wore no hoods) were generally reluctant to deliver the shocks, and they showed greater pity for the unfortunate girl they believed was receiving the shocks (Zimbardo, 1969).

Additional Disturbing Examples. There is strong evidence that dein-

Figure 8.3
(Top) In Zimbardo's study, women subjects disguised with hoods (who were deindividuated) were more inclined to give high-intensity electric shocks to a woman student than were those without hoods (who were easily identifiable). (Bottom) Would deindividuation similarly affect the actions of these Georgia Ku Klux Klan women?

dividuation also functions outside the laboratory—in situations where there is real physical harm. A study was made of 27 different cultures, using data that had been collected by a number of anthropologists. There was a clear indication that when men go into battle with reduced personal identity (disguising themselves by means of body paint, haircuts, masks, special garments, and so forth), they are much more apt to act in an extremely violent manner against an enemy (torturing prisoners, killing all enemies on the spot, headhunting, or mutilating the enemy wherever possible). On the other hand, when the men's individuality is preserved in battle, such extreme treatment is far less likely (Watson, 1973).

The results of this study must be carefully assessed, however, since there may be other reasons for the findings; for example, in cultures in which individuals disguise themselves with battle ornamentation, there will also be greater emphasis on warfare and heroism (represented by the battle regalia); or perhaps aggression itself leads to a greater desire for deindividuation. Yet the implications are consistent with other observations. Members of the Ku Klux Klan certainly took care to disguise their identity in white sheets before going out to lynch blacks in the 1920s and 1930s. Before capital punishment was abolished in most states, penitentiaries often found it difficult to hire executioners. Then it was found that electrocutions could be performed with less personal anguish if there were three executioners, each of whom would press a button simultaneously; although only one button would complete the electrical circuit, none of the three would know whether his had been the fatal button. A similar method has been used by military firing squads, where some rifles have been loaded with blanks and others with real bullets. During a number of the violent student demonstrations in the 1960s, the police squads that were summoned took special care to mask their individual identities, even though they were already wearing uniforms, sunglasses, helmets with visors, and so forth. It was noted that just before a final charge, the police would often remove their badges and name plates. By doing this, the police presumably reduced the possibility that reprisals might be taken against them or their families. Yet it is also possible that this deindividuation permitted the squads to be that much more vicious.

A Simulated Prison. A particularly dramatic study of how groups can influence extreme behavior was conducted by Zimbardo and his co-workers at Stanford University (Zimbardo et al., 1973). Eighteen male students were selected from a group that had answered an advertisement offering $15.00 a day to participate in a two-week, live-in study of prison life. These 18 were chosen after it had been determined, by means of various tests and interviews, that they were normal, "average" college students, with no serious emotional problems. After being selected, each student was told that a coin would be flipped to determine whether he would be assigned as a "guard" or a "prisoner" in a simulated prison. When asked if they had a choice, every single student said that he would prefer to be a "prisoner." The assignment of nine of the students to be "prisoners" and nine to be "guards" was indeed totally random, and test results showed that there were no initial differences between these two groups.

The participants were not told that the Palo Alto police force was going to cooperate in helping to make the study realistic. Thus, the nine prisoners were not prepared for the way in which they learned of their assignment—they were "arrested" in their homes or on the streets, searched and handcuffed, and brought to the "Stanford County Jail" (a specially prepared section in the basement of the university's psychology building). The prisoners were fingerprinted, stripped naked, sprayed to remove lice, and forced to stand naked outside their "cells" during a long orientation in which they were informed about the prison rules. Then, clothed alike in white, shapeless smocks, their hair covered with stocking caps, they were herded by groups of three into three 6-by-9-foot cells. The other group of students was assigned to be "guards" in three 8-hour shifts. They were dressed alike in khaki trousers and open shirts. Their eyes were covered with large sunglasses, and each guard carried a club, a whistle, and cell keys. The guards had been told that they were to use no physical violence against the prisoners.

Although Zimbardo and his co-workers never claimed that what they had constructed was an exact duplicate of a prison, their simulation had many of the characteristics of real prisons. The guards were almost totally in control; they could require all sorts of unusual behavior from the prisoners at whim. The prisoners were largely dependent upon them for privileges and necessities. They had to ask the guards' permission to go to the toilet, and smoking was strictly limited. Outside visitors were forbidden, except for one visitors day.

Within a few days, both the guards and the prisoners seemed to have thoroughly adopted their respective roles. The guards often punished the prisoners rather cruelly: they called roll in the middle of the night to disrupt the prisoners' sleep, they denied them privileges (such as bathing) on whim, and they required them to do push-ups as punishment (with a guard sometimes putting his foot on a prisoner's back while he was doing the exercises). As time passed, the guards became increasingly brutal. It is entirely possible that the guards' loss of individuality contributed to this, as well as the fact that they had internalized their role so well. The "prisoners" also behaved as actual prisoners, calling each other and themselves only by their identification number. Demoralized, impassive, and smelly,

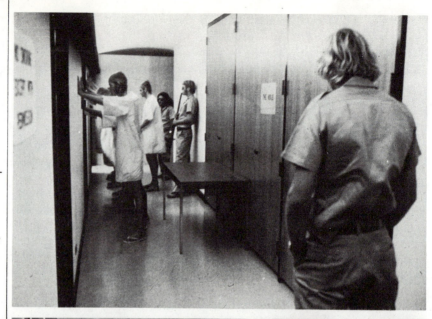

Figure 8.4
(Top) In Zimbardo's simulated prison experiment, the "guards" (in khaki uniforms) watch, as the "prisoners" (in white, shapeless smocks and stocking caps) line up against the wall. Deindividuation seemed to lead the guards to punish the prisoners more severely and the prisoners to accept this treatment more passively. (Bottom) Could the deindividuation of these troops have been partly responsible for the brutality of their attack on antiwar demonstrators outside the Pentagon in October 1967?

they hated their guards with a vengeance but, with the exception of one brief attempt at revolt, they complied with the guards' extreme demands.

After a few days of this existence, however, the prisoners began to show signs of psychosomatic disorders, severe emotional depression, outbreaks of rashes, crying fits, moroseness, and so forth. Although the experiment was scheduled to last for two weeks, it was called off after six days. Zimbardo said that by the sixth day it had passed beyond the point of being an experiment—it had, in fact, become a prison for all of the participants, even the experimenters.

Clearly, Zimbardo and his co-workers did not anticipate the extreme transformation in behavior and attitudes that took place among the guards, prisoners, and experimenters (serving as staff) in the simulated prison. They had expected group effects, but not the rapidity and intensity with which they developed; in this sense, there may be a parallel with the extreme compliance of the "teachers" who shocked the "learners" in the Milgram obedience experiments (see page 219). It has been argued that these behaviors could be explained simply in terms of compliance with role demands (Banuazizi and Movahedi, 1975). The students had agreed to participate in the experiment, were assigned roles as prisoners or guards, and then had simply acted according to their stereotyped views of how guards and prisoners typically behave. Although role demands may have had some initial impact, the nearly complete transformation of behavior seems to belie such a simple explanation. Zimbardo and his co-workers have reason to believe that deindividuation led to reduced restraints on the part of the guards, allowing them to engage in vicious behavior which they probably would not have done otherwise.

For the prisoners, deindividuation seems to have brought about a totally different effect—the loss of independence and a sense of powerlessness, which led to passive compliance. Furthermore, deindividuation served a special function for the prisoner, allowing him to lose his identity in front of the guards, thus reducing the possibility of his being singled out for special work assignments or punishment. The value of being a "faceless prisoner" lost in the crowd has been presented especially forcefully by Alexander Solzhenitsyn in his autobiographical novel about a prisoner in a Soviet labor camp (Solzhenitsyn, 1963; McDonough, 1975).

There is also some evidence that group norms affected behavior— the guards who were reluctant to act in an extreme fashion toward the prisoners were pressured to do so by their fellow guards, and the prisoners who were too independent were called "troublemakers" by their fellow prisoners. Since the prisoners and guards were completely separated from the reality of the outside world, Zimbardo and his co-workers argued that they had developed a new reality, that is, new perceptions and judgments as to what their isolated world was really like and what would constitute appropriate behavior. The group pressures and the entire social environment affected not only behaviors, but judgments and beliefs about reality as well. This analysis is consistent with descriptions of changes in perceived reality that took place in Nazi concentration camps (Bettelheim, 1943) and Siberian labor camps (Solzhenitsyn, 1963). Let us now turn to some laboratory studies that will help to pinpoint the effects of group pressures on belief and judgment.

GROUP JUDGMENTS AND GROUP NORMS

It should be noted that in our discussion of the effects of groups on individual performance, we have gradually moved away from a stimulus-response analysis, such as Allport's social facilitation theory. Allport essentially worked from the individual to the group—the responses of individual group members (hammering a nail into a shoe, tapping a pencil, or pedaling a bicycle) produce stimuli (sounds of tapping, images of moving cyclists), which cumulatively stimulate additional responses from the individual. Zajonc's later analyses move from the observing or co-acting individual to the actor, focusing on his arousal or increased motivation that is due to the presence of another person. Then we presented studies emphasizing the fact that collective group behavior serves as a norm or standard for expected modes of behavior. The individual who is aware of the collective behavior of his group forms a judgment about what is "correct" and evaluates his own behavior against that standard; as a consequence, he may alter his own level of activity upward or downward. In many cases, a person will improve his performance because of increased stimulation from others. This group norm analysis is cognitively oriented and has the virtue of being able to explain adjustments both upward and downward. It is also consistent with other studies of the effects of groups on individual judgment.

Group Norms and the Autokinetic Effect

Estimating the Movement of a Stationary Point. The norm analysis of the effects of groups on individual judgment was presented most effectively in a series of studies by Muzafer Sherif, who began his research in his native Turkey and then continued it in the United States. Sherif pointed out that psychophysical experiments had already clearly demonstrated what most of us know intuitively—that our judgments of objects or events are affected by the background against which they are judged. If we live in a warm climate where the daily temperature is around 80°F., we would be inclined to judge a 70°F. day as rather cool; on the other hand, a visiting Laplander who was accustomed to temperatures in the freezing range would probably think that 70°F. was quite warm. In an experiment in which the subjects were first given a series of weights ranging from 10 to 30 grams, they typically concluded that an 80-gram weight was quite heavy, whereas those who had initially been given weights in the 200- to 300-gram range concluded that the 80-gram weight was rather light.

Sherif studied the effects of group norms on the formation of judgments in an area where there would be only minimal effects from previous experience. It had been demonstrated that when a person is presented with a stationary pinpoint of light in an otherwise pitch-dark room, the light will appear to move. The perceived movement of any object is typically dependent upon its relation to other objects, but in a darkened room there are no background objects. When a subject in a darkened room is asked how much a pinpoint of light has moved, he will often give rather precise estimates: 5 inches, 17 inches, 3 inches. If he is asked to make a series of 100 judgments, there will be some variation at first, but then his judgments will generally stabilize within a given range. It appears that in the absence of other background stimuli against which he can form a judgment, the subject essentially creates his own background—his earlier estimates become the basis for his later estimates; of course, none of the estimates is correct, since the light has not moved at all. In addition, Sherif found that if he asked the subjects to come in on successive days for a total of three series of 100 judgments, each day's judgments would depend upon the preceding day's, with the range of judgments and mean remaining about the same, but with decreased variability each day. The mean judgments, of course, varied considerably from one person to another.

Next Sherif studied the influence of group norms on an individual's judgment by bringing together several persons and asking them to make their estimates in one another's presence. The means for one group of three subjects is presented in Figure 8.5. Notice that when these subjects had previously made their judgments alone, their means for 100 judgments varied considerably—approximately 1 inch, 2 inches, and 8 inches, respectively. When each of the three then made their judgments in front of the others, there was a drastic reduction in variation; the subject who had had a mean judgment of about 8 inches while alone reduced this to about 4 inches during the group's first session. By the third group session, the means of the three subjects converged toward a common point—approximately 2 inches. This new range of judgments, then, had become characteristic of this particular group.

By contrast, when other subjects who had never made any judgments before were brought together in groups of two or three, the convergence was very rapid; although there was substantial agreement during the first group session, there was an even greater con-

Figure 8.5
The funnel-shaped group effect on an individual's judgment of the movement of a point of light in an autokinetic experiment. *Three subjects judged the movement of a point of light (in inches) in a series of 100 individual judgments. Then they were brought together for three group sessions of 100 judgments each. This figure presents the mean judgments for one group of three subjects at each session.* (Sherif, 1935).

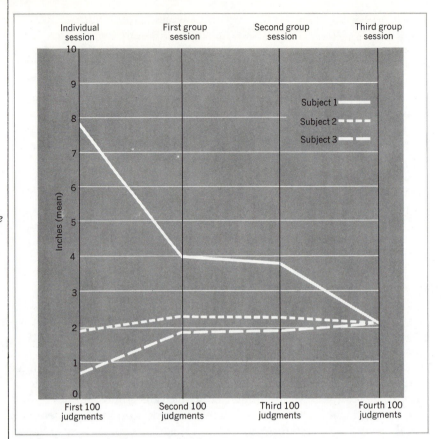

vergence during the next two sessions. Then these subjects were asked to make their judgments in individual sessions. Although the others were no longer present, the separated group members gave very similar responses. According to Sherif, when the subjects made their initial judgments alone, they developed their own frames of reference based upon their unique 100 judgments; these individual frames of reference then affected the subjects' later judgments and so they were less susceptible to the group effects. However, when the subjects made their initial judgments in a group, the series of group judgments provided the frame of reference so that later on, when they were alone, the subjects' individual judgments were decidedly influenced by the group.

In general, the development of a group normative judgment represents something of a compromise, with the individuals at both extremes changing more. However, as demonstrated in Figure 8.5, the final norm for three individuals is not the average of their separate mean judgments. One person will have a greater influence on the group than another, and one will be inclined to change his own judgments more quickly than another. An individual's personality characteristics, attributed expertise, personal attractiveness, degree of self-confidence, and previous group experiences will all affect his relative dominance or submissiveness in the creation of group norms. Sherif found that when one member took an extreme position and maintained it, the group norm tended to move toward that position. This may explain the relative dominance within a group of someone who has a large degree of self-confidence. A recent experiment indicates that a lone deviant can substantially enhance his ability to influence the opinions and judgments of a majority by occupying the chair at the head (rather than at the side) of a rectangular table around which the group is seated (Nemeth and Wachtler, 1974).

The Power of a Stubborn Minority

The influence on a group norm can be even greater when *two* persons in a group consistently report a deviant judgment. A team of French social psychologists (Faucheux and Moscovici, 1967; Moscovici, Lage, and Naffrechoux, 1969) demonstrated the effect of such a minority in a color-determination task. In a preliminary session, groups of six women subjects were tested on their ability to distinguish colors. After it had been clearly established that all of the women had normal color vision, they were shown a series of 36 color slides and asked to identify the colors out loud. The slides had been carefully pretested, and it had been verified that, under usual conditions, the slides were always seen as blue on the color spectrum. Two of the subjects in each experimental group were stooges; when presented with the slides, they consistently reported that they were green. Under this condition, 32 percent of all of the naïve subjects were led to report that four or more slides were green. The percentage varied from group to group; some groups were scarcely affected at all by the stooges, while others were influenced on more than half of their responses.

One assumption that could be made is that the "independent" groups thought for themselves and refused to be swayed by the stubbornly wrong minority. But a second part of the experiment casts doubt on this interpretation. After each group had finished identifying the color slides, a second experimenter came into the room, presumably to conduct an independent study on vision. He separated each of the six members in each group with cardboard screens and then showed each woman 16 disks in the blue-green end of the spectrum. The subjects were asked to rate these disks on a blue-green dimension, recording their individual responses on separate answer sheets. These private ratings indicated that the perceptual framework of the respondents had changed because of their exposure to the persistent stooges—there was a clear tendency for the subjects to judge the blue-green disks as greener as a result of their experience. What is even more interesting is the fact that the groups that had appeared not to be unduly influenced publicly by the stooges showed an even *greater* tendency to rate the disks as green *privately*. It is entirely possible that what appeared to be independence and certainty of judgment in the intimacy of face-to-face groups was actually a group effect in its own right—the tendency on the part of group members to want to identify publicly with the majority rather than with the minority. Privately, however, they tried to reconcile the discrepancy and took the stooges' judgments into account.

A Simulated Microculture. In some cases, a strong, persistent individual may affect the norms of a group over several generations, even after the original group members have been replaced several times. The maintenance of norms in a group "microculture" was illustrated in an experiment by Robert Jacobs and Donald T. Campbell (1961). They set up an autokinetic experiment similar to that of Sherif and found that groups of subjects tended to settle on a group norm of approximately 3.5 inches in their estimates of the movement of the light. After determining the norm, the experimenters assembled a special group of three subjects that included a confederate. During the first session of 30 judgments, the confederate maintained his judgment of 15 or 16 inches. During the second session the confederate was replaced by a naïve subject; during the third session one of the original naïve subjects was replaced; during the fourth session the remaining original subject was replaced; and then for each succeeding session, the longest term member of the group was replaced. It was found that the confederate had noticeably affected the norm of the group. Furthermore, the effects of his extreme judgment were still evident in the inflated group estimate five "generations" later. Finally, the effects of the strong, persistent confederate diminished and disappeared, but not until he and his original co-participants had been replaced six times over.

Sherif believes that his studies have significant implications, not only for the development of norms in small groups, but for large organizations, societies, and even whole cultural groups. As he pointed out, when a group of people is faced with a new, different, or unusual situation, the result is not chaos but a meaningful adaptation and common understanding among the members. The group norm helps to achieve orderliness and meaning in what might otherwise be seen as an ambiguous, uncertain, and perhaps threatening situation. Once established, a norm can become quite firm, even after those who originally established it have passed from the scene and been replaced by others. Conservatism in maintaining group norms, then, has important social psychological functions for those who inherit the norms. An outside observer can often spot customs, patterns of behavior, attitudes, or beliefs within a society that appear to be functionless—an unquestioned inheritance from a distant past. Western anthropologists can readily note such examples when they visit exotic cultures. An anthropologist from the Trobriand Islands would undoubtedly be fascinated by such items as the closed buttonhole in the lapels of our men's suits or the buttons on men's and women's coat sleeves; he might also wonder why we ask "How do you do?" when no answer is expected. A brand-new school teacher who is just beginning his career undoubtedly will ask all sorts of questions about why certain rules and customs are followed at his new school. The teachers who have been there several years will probably answer, "That is how we have always done things." In a school or elsewhere, someone typically initiates a habit or a custom; after many years have gone by, the fact that no one remembers who started the custom or why does not stop us from following it.

THE UNANIMOUS MAJORITY AND THE LONE DEVIANT

Majority Influences on Judgment

In one of his dramatic illustrations of social behavior, Allen Funt (in a "Candid Camera" television program) focused on conformity in a military situation. An officer (in fact, the television performer Garry Moore) is shown giving an orientation talk in his office to six young recruits, all of whom are beginning their basic training. Unknown to one recruit, the other five men have been instructed beforehand to follow a specified pattern of behavior. They take off their hats, and the unknowing recruit follows suit; they sit down on their haunches, and the young man looks around uneasily and then does likewise. He also follows them as they stand up again, put on their hats, turn their backs on the officer (who is still lecturing), and stare at a blank spot on the wall. Finally, the five recruits in turn walk up to the officer's desk, tear off a page from his desk calendar, salute smartly, and march out of his office. The sixth recruit, calendar page in hand, then marches out briskly behind them, apparently oblivious to the fading sound of the officer's voice.

Figure 8.6
Typical comparison lines used in Asch's study of group effects on judgments. *Here the standard line is 5 inches in length, while the comparison lines are 5 inches, 4 inches, and 6¼ inches, respectively. To study the group effects, Asch arranged for paid participants to answer in order, stating that line b or c was like the standard line; the experimenter then looked to see if the lone naïve subject (who responded next to last) would give a similar answer.*

Standard
line

a   b   c

Comparison lines

*Figure 8.7
In Asch's experiment,
seven students were
asked to judge which of
three lines was like the
standard line (see Fig-
ure 8.6). Subject no. 6
(from the left) has just
heard the preceding five
subjects (all of whom
are paid participants)
answer incorrectly.
Now it is his turn to an-
swer; note the look of
consternation and puz-
zlement on his face
(Asch, 1955).*

It is quite possible that this "Candid Camera" sequence was inspired by a classic experiment conducted by Solomon Asch (1956). He presented groups of subjects with a series of cards, each of which showed a standard line (s) together with three other lines (a, b, and c); the subjects were asked to estimate which of the three lines was closest in length to the standard line. (For example, a standard line of 5 inches in length was shown with lines that measured 4 inches, 5 inches, and 6¼ inches.) In each group there were from 2 to 19 subjects. All except one of the subjects in each group had been asked beforehand by the experimenter to give incorrect responses to a number of the cards. During the experiment the subjects answered out loud, one at a time, with the naïve subject answering next to last. (In the two-person groups, the naïve subject answered last.) When the other subjects in each group had responded incorrectly (saying, for example, that the 6¼-inch line was closest in length to the 5-inch standard line), the naïve subject could either answer correctly and deviate from the group or answer incorrectly and conform.

Surprisingly, about one-third of the naïve subjects conformed to the group norm. The amazing influence of the group was evident so long as there were at least three other subjects who responded identically. The subjects in the Asch experiment were college students, and some critics have pointed out that the experiment showed nothing more than that students were conformists (at least in the mid-1950s). However, a number of later experiments using other subjects—teachers, administrators, businessmen, participants in industrial leadership training programs, and telephone workers—have produced very similar results (for example, Deutsch and Gerard, 1955; Crutchfield, 1955).

Various Forms of Yielding. A careful reading of Asch's monograph shows that he was actually quite astonished at the degree of conformity to a patently false group norm. He even seemed rather disdainful toward the "yielders"—those who did not stand up for what they must have known was right—but he admired the "independents"—those who would not allow themselves to be swayed. Although earlier studies had demonstrated that groups can affect the judgments of individuals when the judgments required are rather ambiguous (such as estimating the movements of a pinpoint of light in a completely dark room [Sherif, 1935]), there was no ambiguity in Asch's study. In order to find out why the subjects answered as they did, Asch questioned them afterward. A few of the yielders insisted that their perception had been affected: By the time it was their turn to respond, they really "saw" the 6¼-inch line as closest in length to the 5-inch standard. It would appear that the group's influence on these subjects was *socially independent*; that is, their responses were stimulus-bound, dependent upon the length of the lines *as they perceived them.* The largest group of yielders showed distortion of judgment; even though they didn't see the 6¼-inch line as closest in length to the standard line, they believed that it probably was. Some suggested that there was an optical illusion involved, or that they were seeing the lines at a peculiar angle. The group's influence on these subjects was probably *socially dependent* since they continued to attribute their responses to the majority ("Perhaps the others were right"). The remaining yielders showed distortion of behavior. They knew that the 6¼-inch line was not closest to the standard line and they knew that the rest of the group was wrong, yet they went along with the group. These subjects either craved approval or feared disapproval. For them it was important that the others not *see* them responding differently. In that sense, then, the group's influence was dependent on surveillance. These subjects also gave interesting reasons for their answers; they indicated that they were responding according to the various bases of power (see Chapter 6).

A group can obviously utilize some of the same bases of power as an individual. In the Asch experiment some of the explanations given by the yielders for their conforming, but grossly incorrect, responses were: *informational*— "That is the way it looked to me"; *expert*—"I think a majority is usually right"; "There's a greater probability of eight being right [than one]"; *legitimacy*—"After all, the majority rules"; *referent*—"You always like to go along and be like everybody else"; "I felt the need to conform. . . . It was more pleasant to agree than to disagree." *Coercion* and *reward* were not spelled out as clearly in Asch's interviews, though further questioning might have shown that the subjects feared rejection by the others for nonconformity or felt that conformity would ensure acceptance.

Pressures toward Uniformity of Opinion and Social Comparison

In an important theoretical paper, Leon Festinger (1950) attempted to explain why there tends to be uniformity of opinion in groups. He postulated two factors: First, he said, there is the need for *group locomotion*. In order for any organization to move effectively toward its goals, there must be common agreement on certain basic principles as well as shared attitudes, values, and opinions. Second, the group serves as a means for establishing and maintaining *social reality*. Everyone needs to believe that his opinions, attitudes, and actions are correct and appropriate. If one belongs to a group that is valued and respected, but finds that the members of that group differ from him in their opinions, attitudes, or actions, this discrepancy is seen as a threat to his own conception of reality. This threat is, of course, particularly serious if one has no physical reality check.

Factors That Contribute to Pressures toward Uniformity. Some of the factors that have been found to contribute to greater uniformity of opinions in a group are the following: (1) *The amount of opinion discrepancy* in the group. There will be greater pressure toward uniformity if a group is unanimous except for one member. In his line-judgment experiment, Asch (1956) found that introducing one stooge into the group who gave the correct response (who deviated from the group norm) was sufficient to reduce dramatically the amount of conformity by the lone subject. Related to the amount of opinion discrepancy is the history of agreement in the group. A group that has had a tradition of agreement on many issues in the past will lean more toward uniformity than one that has typically disagreed. (Julian, Regula, and Hollander, 1968; Julian, Ryckman, and Hollander, 1969). (2) *Relevance of the opinion to the functioning of the group*. The more relevant the opinion, the greater the resulting pressure toward uniformity is likely to be. The residents of a housing project are apt to experience far more uniformity pressure over an issue such as the need for a tenants' organization than the advantages of a legalized state lottery. (3) *Group cohesiveness.* A group that has close, positive, interpersonal relations (common goals, personal friendships, group prestige, attractive group activities) will exert greater pressures toward uniformity than one with low cohesiveness (see pages 255 and 258). (4) *Personality characteristics of the members.* The following types of persons are especially apt to experience pressure toward uniformity: those who are authoritarian (rather than egalitarian), those who have low self-esteem, those who tend to be self-blaming, those who have a high need for affiliation, those who are less intelligent, those who are anxious, and those who have a low tolerance for ambiguity (Costanzo, 1970; Crutchfield, 1955; Hovland, Janis, and Kelley, 1953; Janis, 1955; Janis and Field, 1959; Janis and

Hovland, 1959). (5) *Cultural factors.* David Riesman (1950) has pointed out that cultures differ in the extent to which individuals use others to evaluate themselves. In those societies where the population is changing rapidly because of a high birth rate and a high death rate, an individual tends to rely upon tradition for guidance as to correct behavior. In societies that are undergoing rapid growth (a high birth rate, but a lower death rate), an individual tends to establish his own unique set of standards and values; he is "inner-directed." In stabilizing societies (a low birth rate and a low death rate), other people become important as a measure of what is correct, and the pressures toward uniformity are high. Riesman has characterized Americans as being "other-directed," citing the conforming, compliant behavior of college students of the 1950s as evidence. His case seemed quite convincing until the 1960s, when students, presumably members of the same society, became defiant, nonconforming, and rebellious. Perhaps these later students were no less other-directed, but simply shifted their orientation from those in authority to their peers.

One of the few experiments to determine how cultural factors affect pressures toward uniformity of opinion was conducted by Stanley Milgram (1961). Using Norwegian and French students, Milgram set up an experiment that paralleled Asch's: groups of six students were asked to judge the similarity in length (duration) of acoustic tones. Using these tones, he could simulate the Asch situation with better control; the five "confederates" were actually tape-recorded voices. His findings were quite similar to Asch's; there was a high degree of conformity among the naïve subjects to the false responses of the "majority." However, the Norwegians conformed substantially more (62 percent) than the French (50 percent). This difference was even greater when the tape-recorded "majority" members criticized the lone deviate for nonconformity ("Are you trying to show off?" "Do you want to look conspicuous?"). After that, the French students conformed on 59 percent of the judgments, whereas the Norwegians' conformity rose to 75 percent. Furthermore, the Norwegians tended to accept the criticism passively, while the French students tended to retaliate in kind and use abusive language.

Milgram suggested two possible factors that could account for these differences. First, the Norwegian people are generally more homogeneous in appearance, religion, and political opinions. Because of its relatively isolated geographical position, Norway has not been subjected to either the waves of invaders that France has experienced or as much contact with other nationals. Thus, at a societal level, Norway illustrates our first factor that contributes toward uniformity of opinion in groups—little history of discrepancy. France, by contrast, is more heterogeneous; thus, for the Frenchman, other

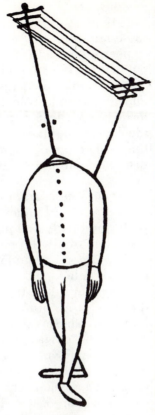

COURTESY WILLIAM STEIG
FROM *THE LONELY ONES*.

I DO WHAT IS
EXPECTED OF ME

*Figure 8.8
Other-directed people
appear to be going
around with their an-
tennae out—trying to
determine how others
think and act so that
they can do likewise.*

persons and groups provide a less stable basis for self-evaluation. Secondly, Milgram believes that the Norwegian people are more cohesive and have greater positive feelings of identification with the nation and with their fellow citizens (this is similar to our third factor above—group cohesiveness). Although these suggestions seem plausible, they should probably not be accepted without question. Milgram's sample was both extremely small and not particularly representative of the Norwegian and French people at large. Moreover, as our colleague Daniel Katz has pointed out, there is a strong cultural norm against exhibitionism in Norway, and this fear was specifically invoked among the Norwegians in the experiment. If a similarly strong cultural norm had been invoked among the French students— such as sneering at the language of the deviant—there might have been similar dramatic increases in conformity among them as well.

A more recent experimental study, with much larger samples,

demonstrated even more conclusively the effects of culture on conformity pressures: A comparison of 12-year-old children showed that those raised in the Soviet Union were much more likely to conform to peer pressure than were Israeli children. The investigators point out that in Israel "childhood is thought of as a time of mischief and adventure that prepares the young person for a (self-confident, independent) adult role," while in the U.S.S.R., "childhood is a time for learning the discipline and obedience required by Communist ideology." The study also found that children raised in collective settings, where group identity is stressed, tend to be more conforming than those raised in individual family settings (Shouval et al., 1975).

Uniformity as a State of Equilibrium. Festinger's analysis of the pressures toward uniformity is essentially an equilibrium model that posits uniformity as a preferred end state and then suggests that any disruption of it will produce activity and cognitive change that will, in turn, restore the uniformity. Thus, if there is sufficient similarity of opinion, belief, or behavior that a clear group norm is evident, then any member's deviation from that norm will lead to pressures in the direction of restoring uniformity. Festinger hypothesized that three basic mechanisms are utilized: (1) the group members try to influence the deviant to change his views; (2) the group members change their own views to bring them more in line with those of the deviant; (3) the boundaries of the group are redefined, thereby rejecting the deviant. The last mechanism will often result in the personal rejection of any deviant, as well as simple ejection from the group. On rare occasions, of course, members of the group will adopt the views of the deviant, especially when he remains as a member, is respected, and is deemed necessary to the group. The film *Twelve Angry Men* illustrates rather dramatically such a change toward the deviant. It depicts a murder trial in which initially the jury is split eleven to one in favor of a guilty verdict. The lone deviant continues to argue forcefully and effectively, despite personal vilification and rejection by the others. Eventually he succeeds in convincing the others to switch to a unanimous verdict of innocent. The lone deviant on the jury had a strong trump card, however, for the judge insisted on a unanimous verdict (a hung, indecisive jury would not be acceptable); unanimity was required for the jury to be released from its "imprisonment" in the jury chamber.

Responses of the Majority to the Deviant

One of the first significant tests of Festinger's theory was carried out by Stanley Schachter (1951). Schachter described four different types of ongoing clubs—case study, editorial, movie, and radio—to a group of college students who were then asked to indicate their degree of interest in joining each one. Two types of clubs (case study and movie) were composed of students who had made these clubs their first choice, while the other two (editorial and radio) were made up of students with little interest in such clubs. By varying the attractiveness of the club to its members, Schachter varied the clubs' cohesiveness, creating 16 high- and 16 low-cohesive groups.

Each club, composed of from eight to ten members, was asked to discuss the case history of a juvenile delinquent ("Johnny Rocco"), who was about to be sentenced for a minor crime, and recommend a course of action—either harsh or lenient. In some of the clubs, the discussion of this case was made relevant to the group's activity. (It was clearly relevant to the case study club, and the experimenter made it relevant to the editorial club by telling the members that they would use the case study in writing a feature article on juvenile delinquency.) The experimenter made the Johnny Rocco case irrelevant to the other clubs (movie and radio) by telling the members that he wanted them to help out—just this once—by giving their opinion on an issue in which someone else was interested. Thus, four experimental group conditions were created: High Cohesive-Relevant (case study), High Cohesive-Irrelevant (movie), Low Cohesive-Relevant (editorial), and Low Cohesive-Irrelevant (radio). There were eight clubs in each of these conditions.

The Johnny Rocco case was deliberately written in such a way that almost all of the club members recommended leniency. After the five to seven naïve members of each club had expressed their view of the case, the three remaining group members (who were actually carefully trained confederates of the experimenter) spoke up, taking the following roles: (1) a "deviate" favored harsh treatment for Johnny Rocco and maintained this position steadfastly; (2) a "mode" favored the popular lenient position and also maintained this view throughout; (3) a "slider" took the deviant (harsh) position initially, but then gradually shifted toward the lenient group norm. During the discussion of the case, observers kept track of who spoke to whom and for how long. Afterward, in order to measure the subjects' attitudes toward the three confederates, they were asked to recommend the names of fellow club members for several committee assignments. One of these, the "correspondence" committee, was made to seem extremely uninteresting and tedious, while the others (the "executive" committee and "steering" committee) appeared particularly attractive and important. In addition, the subjects were told that it might be necessary to reduce the size of the clubs, and so they were asked to indicate how much they would like to have each of their fellow members remain in the club.

As Schachter had predicted, the deviate was more apt to be rejected than either the mode or the slider. He was seen as a less desirable group member (as more expendable) and was often recommended for assignment to the correspondence committee. In contrast, the mode was frequently selected for the steering or executive committee assignments and was seen as a valued member of the group. In further support of Festinger's theory, it was found that the deviate was most clearly rejected in the High Cohesive-Relevant groups, since he was often rated as the least desirable group member. This finding was predicted because one would expect both high cohesiveness and relevance to increase the pressure toward unanimity and to lead to the rejection of a member who deviated markedly from the group norm. In the Low Cohesive-Irrelevant groups, there was *no* clear tendency to punish the deviate through unpopular committee assignments. If we don't particularly want to belong to a club, and a disagreement with one of the members is not relevant to the club anyway, why should we care if this person disagrees with the general opinions held by the other club members?

With respect to the amount of communication that was directed at each of the three confederates in each group, Schachter found that more persons spoke to the deviate (and for longer periods) than to either the mode or the slider—presumably in an attempt to persuade him to change his opinion. Similarly, more persons spoke to the slider than to the mode, particularly during the early part of the discussion—before the slider adopted the group norm.

One might expect high pressures toward uniformity to motivate group members to speak to the deviate more often in an attempt to persuade him to change his views. However, one might also expect the same uniformity pressures to lead the group to reject the deviate, at which point the members would stop speaking to him altogether. Actually both tendencies were observed in the groups with the greatest pressure toward uniformity—the High Cohesive-Relevant clubs. Initially, the number of times (and length of time) members spoke to the deviate in this condition increased rapidly, but then toward the end of the discussion there was a sharp dropoff. Indeed, the curtailment of speech was especially obvious in the case of those group members who rejected the deviate personally. (If we are in a group where having a uniform opinion is important, we may try very hard to persuade a deviate that he is wrong, but, failing that, we may write him off as a lost cause.)

The Tyranny of the Majority. Groups can sometimes be quite merciless in their treatment of a deviant member. British workers have been known to carry the "silent treatment" to an extreme, as in the case of a worker who is "sent to Coventry." In this form of ostracism, no one will speak to the deviant or his family unless it is absolutely

necessary. The effect can be devastating to the point of suicide. Industrial workers in the United States have been known to playfully,
yet painfully, "bing" a worker who exceeds the generally agreed
upon work norm—by snapping a bent index finger on his arm. A few
years ago, I learned of a young British boy who was visiting the
United States and was subjected to continuous taunting from his
American classmates. His parents consulted a clinical psychologist,
who finally figured out the reason why. The boy was considered to
be a deviant because of his British National Health Service eyeglasses with their large round lenses and wire rims. The parents
could not understand why anyone would tease their son for that, yet
once the glasses were exchanged for some less obvious American
ones, the taunting quickly faded.

Let us see how a deviant is typically treated in the Asch conformity situation. Although most of Asch's studies were conducted with
a group of paid participants and one naïve subject, he did undertake
one line judgment study in which there was a naïve majority of 16
and only one paid participant, seated seventh in line. The confederate followed exactly the same pattern of incorrect responses that had
been followed by the majority in the earlier study. Asch (1952) reported:

> At the outset they greeted the estimates of the dissenter with
> incredulity. On the later trials there were smiles and impromptu
> comments. As the experiment progressed, contagious, and in some
> instances uncontrolled, laughter swept the group. At one point, as
> the group reported their correct estimates, the sudden impact of the
> single wrong response appeared so droll that the experimenter, who
> had created the situation, was seized with an irrepressible tendency
> to join in the laughter [pp. 479–480].

Although the naïve majority had no doubts about the correctness
of their own judgments, they seemed to have little patience with the
strange deviate; two members reported later: "I felt a pitying contempt for a person who so misinterpreted directions as to be comparing the wrong lines," and "I felt annoyed at the constant disagreement with my judgment." The group also impugned the motives of
the minority member (Asch, 1952).

We have thus far examined three methods by which a group can
respond to a deviant member who threatens the group's uniformity:
attempting to change the deviant's views, changing the group's opinion in the direction of the deviant, and rejecting the deviant. There
are, of course, more subtle group responses that correspond to the
methods of reducing imbalance that were discussed in Chapter 4: a
deviant's response may be redefined as irrelevant to the group's

function; his discrepant opinion may be minimized (he is really not so different from us as it seemed); or the deviant member may be "differentiated" (as a group of business executives said of the group's only Democrat, "He's basically a good guy, just like the rest of us. Can he help it that he was brought up in the South? Old rebel family, you know").

A number of studies have addressed themselves to the factors that lead a group to use one mechanism rather than another. As we pointed out earlier, changing the group's view in the direction of the deviant is not too likely unless the deviant maintains his position steadfastly, is a very effective persuader, has an established position of leadership, or has otherwise developed some influential bases of power over the other group members. Rejecting the deviant is quite common whenever it is possible, whenever there is great pressure toward uniformity, and especially whenever other means, such as trying to persuade the deviant to change his opinion, prove ineffective. Tolerating the deviant is likely if the deviant has, over a period of time, conformed to the norms of the group and established his right to membership. This has been called building up "idiosyncrasy credit" (Hollander, 1958). Indeed, occasionally the deviant may be given a special role in the group, rather like an official deviant. (The court jester occupied such a role in the medieval court.) Ordinarily, however, being in the minority position is no easy matter.

The Behavior of the Deviant

The deviant group member who is responding to the same pressures toward uniformity also has the same alternatives for reducing these pressures as do the members of the majority, although these devices may not be so effective for him. Ordinarily, his discovery that he is a deviant will be disconcerting and even painful, as was dramatically shown in the photo of Asch's subject (see page 317). Freedman and Doob (1968) reported that when a member of a group learned from a personality test that he differed substantially from the norm, he would first laugh uncomfortably and ask for more information about the test; when he received a second sheet, verifying the initial results, he would become more concerned and then noticeably worried.

The response of the deviant, then, is somewhat parallel to the response of the majority to him. If there is any ambiguity in the deviant's opinion or judgment (particularly if the deviance is not great), the group may minimize the difference, overlook it, view it as a fluke or temporary error, or otherwise distort the difference. This is especially apt to happen if there has been a previous history of agreement. However, if the deviance is unambiguous, consistent, and difficult to disregard, the deviant will probably respond differently.

A study conducted by Festinger and his colleagues (1952) focused on issues rather similar to those explored by Schachter (1951), but it included an examination of the deviants from, as well as the adherents to, group norms. In this study, groups composed of six to nine men or women were given the initial stages of a labor negotiation case to study and then were asked to predict the extent to which the union would adopt a hard or conciliatory position during the later stages. The subjects were to communicate among themselves with written messages; however, these were intercepted and prepared notes were substituted in their place. Thus, it was possible to lead some subjects to believe that they were at the group norm and to let others think that they deviated greatly from the norm. Group cohesiveness was also varied by means of the notes as well as by the experimenter's introductions; some subjects were led to believe that their group had similar interests and backgrounds, while others were told that the experimenter had not been able to group them with others of similar interests.

Those subjects who were informed that their opinions deviated from the norm were less confident of their views than those who believed that theirs was the majority opinion. Moreover, the deviant subjects were more inclined to change their opinions toward the norm, while the others maintained their opinions—especially in the high cohesive groups. Those deviants who did not change their opinions right away tended to communicate with the majority, presumably hoping to persuade them to adopt their (the deviants') views, but later they also tended to stop communicating altogether, particularly with those of the majority who differed the most. These deviants were, in effect, also redefining the boundaries of the group. As in the Schachter study, the deviants tended to reject certain members of the majority, especially in the high cohesive groups. If the deviant liked the other members and believed that they liked him, he was less inclined to reject them and more inclined to alter his opinion toward theirs or, if he felt strongly about his position, to try to convince them that he was right.

The Importance of a Physical Reality Check. Festinger's theory states that there will be less pressure toward uniformity of opinion in a group if there is some physical, outside means for evaluating the correctness of one's opinion. Festinger and his co-workers' experiment attempted to test this by telling some groups that after their discussion they would be informed about how the negotiations actually worked out so that they could see how correct their predictions were; other groups were told that a federal agency had entered the negotiations and substantially altered their course, but these groups were told to make their predictions anyway—as if the negotiations had continued. It was expected that the deviants would cling to their positions more tenaciously if there were an outside check—a correct answer. However, precisely the opposite was found. It would appear that the deviants were not particularly confident of their own opinions, especially since everyone else disagreed with them; if a correct answer was to be revealed, the deviants apparently did not want to be caught making a mistake in front of the others. It was safer to go along with the group. Possibly if the deviants had been able to express their views anonymously and if they could have had the opportunity to check the correct answers privately, they might have held to their position.

Self-confidence, Reactance, and Anticonformity. Other factors also explain why a deviant will choose one means of reducing pressure toward uniformity rather than another. As we mentioned earlier, self-confident people who have high self-esteem are less inclined to conform to a group norm (Crutchfield, 1955). A group that includes "experts" in a relevant field will be more apt to persuade a deviant to change. On the other hand, sometimes a person may be highly sensi-

*Figure 8.9
Anticonformity can
sometimes become an
end in itself.*

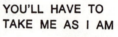
**YOU'LL HAVE TO
TAKE ME AS I AM**

COURTESY WILLIAM STEIG
FROM *THE LONELY ONES.*

tive to, and even feel threatened by, group pressures. If he feels that his freedom and individuality are being threatened, he may demonstrate "reactance" (Brehm, 1966)—a resistance to group influence that can become an end in itself. Carried even further, reactance becomes anticonformity (Willis, 1965). As in the case of adolescent rebellion, there is often a desire to be different just for the sake of being different. Thus, although resistance to conformity can be a healthy sign, showing that a person is thinking and acting on his own —doing what is right despite what others say—it can also be a defensive device, indicating that the person needs to feel in control.

Using Alternative Groups for Self-evaluation. Resisting the pressure toward uniformity in one group may merely mean that the deviant is looking to another group for his basis of self-evaluation. As you may recall (page 311), Sherif's autokinetic study showed that a person who belonged to a group that had established a norm about how far the light had moved tended to be less affected by the judgments of a new and different group. The very same factors that caused the first group to be influential (high cohesiveness, long-term membership, general agreement within that group, and so forth) prevented another group from exercising influence (Gerard, 1954). In that sense, then, a woman from a close, cohesive family with a conservative political viewpoint will not be inclined to change her political opinion if she goes away to a college where most of the students and faculty have liberal views (Newcomb, 1943).

If a deviant can neither convince the majority to change nor permit himself to adopt the majority's viewpoint, he will be inclined to look for another group (unless he already has one) that can serve as a means for self-evaluation and support. This tendency was present, to some extent, in the Festinger et al. (1952) study. The deviants who did not change tended to communicate with other deviants or with those in the majority who differed the least from them. Freedman and Doob (1968) found the same thing among their subjects who believed that they deviated from others on a personality test. Those deviants who scored at the bottom of the personality scale were asked which persons they would like to work with on another experiment dealing with group problem-solving. To a significant degree, these deviants chose other deviants rather than those who were at the norm. But it is interesting to note that the low-scoring deviants seemed to prefer the high-scoring deviants rather than normals bunched in the middle, even though the high-scorers were obviously further removed. It would appear that the deviants felt that associating with other deviants would make them feel more comfortable and that they might receive better treatment, even if their chosen associates differed significantly from them.

Public and Private Conformity of the Deviant. It should be clear that most of the conformity exhibited in studies testing Festinger's theories of pressure toward uniformity are instances of referent power; the subjects were looking at similar others as their basis for self-evaluation. Occasionally expert power was also evident. Interestingly, the need for self-evaluation (see page 46) may sometimes impel a group to use more extreme means, such as coercive power, to bring a deviant into line.

As Asch's subjects stated quite frankly, deviants sometimes anticipate the threat of punishment from a group and try to hide their deviance, if they are not willing or able to change or to defend themselves. The Freedman and Doob (1968) experiments showed that on personality traits (which presumably could not be changed), the deviants tried to hide their differences. If they were given a choice, they said that they would prefer to work alone rather than with others who differed from them. It is, therefore, not surprising that a number of experiments have shown that deviants change their opinions and judgments more quickly if they have to state them publicly (Deutsch and Gerard, 1955; Raven, 1959). Of course, if a deviant feels that he is generally accepted by and has some position or status in his group, he will probably be less frightened by the prospect of punishment or rejection by the group; his "idiosyncracy credit" may protect him from the coercive power of the majority. Thus, Dittes and Kelley (1956) found that if they let a deviant know that he was not too highly valued by the group and therefore might be ejected from it, he tended to shift toward the group in his *public,* but not in his *private,* opinion. This finding parallels a study of physicians showing that those who were only marginally accepted by other physicians in the community were particularly apt to accept a new medical treatment publicly. By accepting innovation early, they demonstrated adherence to medical group norms (Menzel, 1957). In this light, then, we can reexamine the Schanck study of Elm Hollow (see page 202), a community in which any deviance from the public norms of no smoking and no gambling would invariably lead to rejection and punishment by the community. Since the entire community was afraid to deviate, everyone adhered publicly to the norms, even though he might not accept them privately. Consequently, the researchers could not determine whether the public norms differed significantly from the private norms of most of the community.

Reducing dissonance between public and private conformity. The discrepancy between a deviant's public and private opinions or behaviors should increase his dissonance and cause him discomfort. Perhaps that explains why the residents of Elm Hollow quickly changed their public views as soon as these appeared to be acceptable. If the threat of punishment for deviating is sufficiently great, of course, then the threat itself will minimize any dissonance. The deviant has a ready explanation for the discrepancy between his public behavior and his private beliefs. One can think of several historical examples in which the adherents of deviant religions, who faced punishment by death or torture, maintained their beliefs in private for many generations. There were the early Christians in Rome and the Jewish *conversos* or *maranos* in Spain. The threat and resulting difficulty of maintaining private deviance in many cases was the cause of dissonance in its own right ("Why have we subjected ourselves to such difficulties and dangers when a simple act of conversion would release us?"). Many of these people became fanatically devoted to the deviant faith. On the other hand, when the threats are not too great, yet severe enough to produce public conformity, then it is quite probable that later on there will be private acceptance (Raven, 1959).

Private acceptance of one's public behavior. The process of change in the direction of accepting group norms often means that first there is a shift in public statements and behavior and later on private acceptance, as in the case of the politically conservative student who atended a liberal college (Newcomb, 1943); the young, idealistic college graduate who accepted a position with a large industrial organization (Whyte, 1956); or the white Northern liberal undergraduate who transferred to a white Southern university that had strong racist views (Sims and Patrick, 1936). The dissonance reduction model may account for this type of change. However, there is also evidence of a more rational process of change.

The subjects in an experiment conducted by Raven (1959) were assigned to groups of 10 to 14 and were asked to read and discuss a case history. The case was that of the juvenile delinquent, "Johnny Sandron" (modified from Schachter's earlier study [1951]), and the subjects were asked to recommend a course of action. The case history was written in such a manner that the subjects initially tended to recommend leniency. Later they were confronted with the false information that most of the other subjects in their group had advised harsh treatment.

The subjects were told that their own specific recommendation for Johnny Sandron, as shown on a rating scale, would be kept private; it would be seen only by the experimenter. However, they were also asked to write a report summarizing the evidence—as a group of social caseworkers might do—each writing an individual report, discussing it with the others, and then preparing a group report. In one experimental condition, the subjects were led to expect that the individual reports would be passed around the group for everyone to read; in the other condition, the subjects were told that the reports would remain confidential and would not be seen by anyone else.

Raven found that not only the public but the *private* opinion of the deviants (as measured on the rating scale that was seen only by the experimenter) was inclined to change toward the norm (of harshness). This tended to happen especially when the subjects expected their individual reports to be made public. Thus, the *anticipation* of public exposure of their deviant views was enough to alter the subjects' own private opinions.

It seems that a deviant is motivated to change his views in approximately the following manner: First, he may be shocked to find that his opinion differs from that of others. If he likes the group with which he is associated, and if he does not want to be rejected or punished by it, he had better say what the group wants to hear; thus, some self-censoring occurs. Next, he may begin to tune in selectively and remember those opinions that are safe to repeat to others; at the same time, he may also begin to tune out and forget those that he feels contribute to his image as a deviant. Finally, there comes a time when the information that the deviant has selectively perceived and remembered is more consistent with the group norm than with his previous position. At that point, he can change his private opinion and quite honestly say to himself that the change took place as a result of the cogency of all of the evidence that came to his attention.

It can be seen, therefore, that through both dissonance reduction and a process of selective perception and memory, a deviant may experience cognitive change that will justify changing his private opinion as well as his public behavior (Raven, 1959).

THE STRANGE MYSTERY OF THE RISKY SHIFT AND THE RUNAWAY NORM

A critical, dramatic point in the play *Stalag 17* was the discussion by a group of American prisoners of war in a Nazi prison camp about a possible escape attempt. By remaining in the camp, the prisoners might reasonably expect to wait out the war, emerging alive but possibly in poor mental and physical health after some years. By attempting escape, they might find freedom and a healthier life—or they might face death. Which would an individual prisoner choose? But of greater interest to us here, would a group collectively choose a riskier or a more conservative course of action than an individual alone?

Choice Dilemmas and Risky Shifts

Obviously, a number of such "choice dilemmas" exist, where a desirable outcome must be weighed against the risk of a possible undesirable one; here are a few: (1) An electrical engineer must weigh the advantages of giving up his modest but secure job for a much more attractive position with no long-term security; (2) A man with a chronic and moderately debilitating heart ailment could possibly be cured by an operation, but it could also prove fatal; (3) A college senior could go to a top-notch graduate school that has a high flunk-out rate—if successful, though, he could almost certainly enter an illustrious field; or he could go to a mediocre school where he would almost surely be granted an advanced degree; (4) A man of moderate means could invest his money in a stock that might either realize a huge profit or fail completely, or he could choose a stock with a safe but modest return.

These examples are all from the Choice Dilemma Questionnaire (CDQ) (Kogan and Wallach, 1964), that was utilized by James Stoner (1961) in his important initial research on the "risky shift." The CDQ consists of 12 dilemmas together with various probabilities. For example, in the case of the prisoners in the Nazi POW camp, there might be a 1 in 10 chance that the escape would succeed, or 3 in 10, 5 in 10, 7 in 10, or 9 in 10. Each respondent is asked: "Please check the *lowest* probability that you would consider acceptable in order for the prisoner to attempt to escape." A response of "1 in 10" would be a highly risky choice, whereas "9 in 10" would indicate great caution and an unwillingness to take much risk. The numbers chosen for the 12 dilemmas could then be added up to indicate the respondent's general tendency to make risky choices—the lower the total number, the more risky the respondent.

The initial risk choices in Stoner's experiment were made by each respondent alone; nothing was said about any future group discussion. However, after the individual scores had been obtained, the subjects were brought together in groups of six and asked to discuss the 12 choice dilemmas to try to arrive at a unanimous risk choice for each. Thus, a group risk score was also obtained.

One might be tempted to look at the group risk decision in the context of other studies of group norms, such as Sherif's study (1935) of the autokinetic effect. It would seem reasonable to expect that when the behavior of such groups is examined, each group decision would be approximately the average of the individual choices—varying a bit higher or lower depending upon where the more vocal members happened to be. Instead, Stoner found that, almost invariably, the group choice was more risky than the average of the individual choices. It was that dramatic finding, which was totally unexpected, that led to a large series of studies on the "risky shift."

At first, Stoner's findings were challenged because his subjects were largely male business and management students at M.I.T. It was felt that this group, in particular, might have been inculcated with the notion that it is good to take a chance and be risky; after all, nothing ventured, nothing gained. But later studies showed that the group risky shift on the CDQ held true for other subjects as well. The risky shift was found among both men and women undergraduates (Wallach, Kogan, and Bem, 1962) and among grade-school boys and girls (Kogan and Carlson, 1969). It was found among other national groups: British (Bateson, 1966), Canadians (Vidmar, 1970), Israelis (Rim, 1965), Germans (Lamm and Kogan, 1970), and French (Kogan and Doise, 1969). The risky shift was also found among several occupational groups: professional people (Siegel and Zajonc, 1967), workers (Jamieson, 1968), industrial supervisors (Rim, 1965), senior executives (Marquis, 1962), and nurses (Rim, 1965).

Why a Risky Shift?

Later on, a large amount of research was undertaken to try to determine why there was a risky shift and what factors helped to produce it. There are several extensive summaries of these studies (Cartwright, 1971; Dion, Baron, and Miller, 1970; Kogan and Wallach, 1967; Pruitt, 1971a, 1971b). Although a number of explanations of the risky shift have been advanced, we will discuss the four most significant.

The Risky Leader. It has been suggested that those who are more confident, certain, forceful, and direct will also tend to take more chances. Such a person would be the type who would assume leadership in a group; given his talents at persuasion, he would thus tend to try to convince the others to move toward his riskier position. Although this explanation seems intuitively reasonable, it has not been supported in the literature (Wallach, Kogan, and Burt, 1968). Furthermore, there is a risky shift even when there has been no group discussion but simply an indication of each person's prior decision (Myers, Bach, and Schreiber, 1974; Teger and Pruitt, 1967).

Familiarization with the Choices. Perhaps, during the group discussion of choice dilemmas, the individual members become more familiar with the alternatives. With less uncertainty, they may then be more willing to take chances. If so, then the same risky effect could be obtained by having isolated individuals write "briefs" on each item, giving all the pros and cons. Indeed, two experiments found that the risky effect could be obtained through individual familiarization to the same extent as through group discussion (Bateson,

1966; Flanders and Thistlethwaite, 1967). However, other experiments did not replicate this result, and the familiarization theory does not explain the conservative shift that has been found in some experiments.

Diffusion of Responsibility. Another possibility is that the individual may be reluctant to support a risky position; even though he may be intrigued with the possibility of greater gain, he does not want to assume the responsibility for any loss. Group discussion may lead each person to feel less responsible for the decision made, and each member may attribute to the group as a whole the responsibility for any failure or dire consequence (Wallach, Kogan, and Burt, 1968). This explanation has not been definitely ruled out by experimental evidence, but it seems less plausible when we realize that most of the CDQ studies dealt with hypothetical situations; no respondent would actually have been held responsible for the POW's execution or the heart patient's death during the operation. This explanation is also weakened by the fact that the risky shift occurs even when the respondents have not been brought together in a group. Merely hearing a tape-recorded discussion by another group, without knowing its decision, is sufficient to produce it (Kogan and Wallach, 1967), and merely hearing the opinions of others, without participating in a group, also produces it (Teger and Pruitt, 1967). These studies do not rule out the possibility that one may be willing to take a greater risk when the responsibility can be shared, but they do suggest that diffusion of responsibility is not a necessary condition. We might still expect that in some real-life decisions, diffusion of responsibility could increase risky behavior. Remember that the subjects in Milgram's obedience experiment were more willing to deliver a dangerously high electric shock to the "learner" once they were assured that they would not have to bear any responsibility (Milgram, 1974).

Riskiness as a Value. This explanation, which seems to be most clearly supported, is based on the idea that there is a general social or cultural value that favors risk. Indeed, it is this value that leads one to take more risks than one's neighbor and to avoid lagging behind and being overly cautious. In this sense, others serve as a basis for social comparison, as Festinger described it (1954), but the group effects resemble those that apply to abilities rather than opinions. That is, the individual tends to look upward in evaluating himself and tries to surpass the average by being *riskier*. This explanation tallies with much of the research data, which show that simply knowing how the group feels is enough to produce a risky shift (Kogan and Wallach, 1967; Teger and Pruitt, 1967). It has also been found that those who tend to think of themselves as riskier than others are apt to change their opinions in that direction, thereby showing that they are *indeed* riskier; whereas those who see themselves as generally cautious are more apt to shift toward *caution* (Levinger and Schneider, 1969).

Although our culture generally values risk-taking (which may explain why most subjects typically show the risky shift), it would seem reasonable to expect that in another culture where caution is valued, groups should demonstrate a shift toward caution rather than risk. One of the few clear tests of this cross-cultural hypothesis compared Americans with Ugandans. Ugandans have a reputation for being more cautious and less willing to take risks. The results showed that on individual CDQ scores, the Ugandans tended to take more cautious positions than the Americans. It was also found that after a group discussion, the Ugandans tended to become even more cautious, while the Americans demonstrated the risky shift (Carlson and Davis, 1971).

A second version of the risk-as-value explanation emphasizes the information and arguments that emerge during the group discussion. The underlying cultural value may become manifest in the discussion itself, so that the new information presented by the group tends to reflect the cultural norm as well as support the risky alternative (Brown, 1965). This version has received considerable support from studies showing that the subjects' choices are definitely affected by the arguments that are presented to them (Silverthorne, 1971; Ebbesen and Bowers, 1974).

The evidence, then, seems to support the cultural value explanation of the risky shift, although obviously this value does not always win out over caution (see, for example, Kogan and Carlson, 1969; Zajonc, Wolosin, and Wolosin, 1972). Furthermore, if there is a possibility of incurring a real loss by taking a risk, the risky position may not seem as important as reducing the chances of loss. A number of studies based on real, rather than hypothetical, losses seem to produce greater caution. For example, when a group must decide about placing a $2.00 bet at a race track, the shift after the discussion is toward betting on a "sure thing" at low odds rather than a "long shot" with greater possible winnings (McCauley et al., 1973).

It is apparent, then, that groups do not invariably take more risks than individuals; even the CDQ findings bear this out. Most investigators who have used this instrument have reported effects for the sum total of the 12 CDQ items or for a select subset of these. Closer examination of the individual items, however, has revealed that while most of them consistently produce shifts toward riskiness, at least two items generally yield cautious shifts (Vinokur, 1971). In a recent experiment, Malamuth (1975)) found a risky shift on the subject of job selection and a conservative shift on the issue of marriage.

These shifts occurred in both the questionnaire used by Stoner and others and in a situation that had real consequences—where the members of a group believed that they were participating in a peer-counseling session and were actually advising a fellow student.

Shifts similar to those obtained with the CDQ have also been reported on items assessing attitudes that are not related to risk-taking. For example, when French students discussed former President Charles de Gaulle, their initially favorable attitudes became even more positive; when they discussed Americans, their initially critical attitudes became even more negative (Moscovici and Zavalloni, 1969). These findings suggest that groups may "polarize" their attitudes in the direction initially taken by individual group members (Doise, 1969). This group "extremization" has been found on several issues: racial views (Myers and Bishop, 1970), altruistic inclinations (Schroeder, 1973), moral beliefs (Horne and Long, 1972), and legal attitudes (Cvetkovich and Baumgardner, 1973). Risky shifts also occur in situations with real implications, such as peer-group counseling (Malamuth, 1975) and casino gambling (Blascovich, Ginsburg, and Veach, 1975). The risky shift may be one instance of a general group phenomenon; therefore, let us consider additional instances in which such group effects may occur.

Runaway Norms: The Normative Value of Exceeding the Average
An interesting point demonstrated in the research on risky shift is that sometimes there are group pressures that lead one to *exceed* the average on some dimension, rather than merely to converge toward a mean. Roger Brown (1965) postulated that these pressures may be quite common. For example, performance norms often motivate people to try to exceed the average. Years ago, professors were appalled by the students' tendency to try to maintain a "gentleman's C"; those who either exceeded this average grade or fell below it were usually looked down upon by other students. Today the push is generally upward, with students (and often their parents) complaining if they receive only a "C." The effect has been to devalue the grades themselves—with more A's and B's being given—so that the average student's grades appear to be "above average."

Escalation of Aggression in the Stanford Prison. In the Stanford prison simulation (see page 306), the guards initially varied a great deal in their aggressiveness toward the prisoners. If there had been a convergence toward a norm, as in the Sherif autokinetic study, then the more aggressive guards would have gradually reduced their aggressiveness while the more inhibited guards would have become more aggressive. In fact, however, it was observed that there was a continued rise in aggression, with the more hostile guards on each shift assuming leadership and the others looking to them as models for their own behavior. "Not to be tough and arrogant was to be seen as a sign of weakness by the guards, and even those 'good' guards who did not get as drawn into the power syndrome as the others respected the implicit norm of *never* contradicting or even interfering with an action of a more hostile guard on their shift" (Haney, Banks, and Zimbardo, 1973, p. 91).

The Jewish "Blue Book" and the Kwakiutl Potlatch. In small, highly cohesive Jewish communities, generosity and contributions to charity are highly valued. There is subtle (and sometimes not so subtle) pressure on people to increase the percentage of their income that they contribute. In many American cities, the local Jewish "blue book" is one means of exerting such pressure—each year it lists the names of each member of the community, the amount that he or she pledged and gave to charity during the previous year, and the amount that has been pledged for the current year. As a result, the members are inclined to compare their contributions with those of others who are probably in the same income bracket to see how they themselves and others have increased their contributions; apparently there is enough pressure so that contributions nearly always rise. Thus, there is a competitive tendency to try to equal (at least) and possibly exceed the norm; this tendency is somewhat similar to the prisoner's dilemma situation (see Chapter 5).

One of the most striking examples of these runaway norms (as they might be called) is the *potlatch* of the Kwakiutl Indians of the American Northwest. It is highly probable that the *potlatch* ceremony began in the eighteenth century, when the Kwakiutl tribesmen would gather socially. The Kwakiutls valued generosity toward their fellow man, and it became customary for them to give each other gifts—blankets, canoes, jewelry, slaves, and so forth. Each recipient would then feel that he had to reciprocate with a gift of at least equal, and preferably greater, value. Soon a failure to live up to the generosity of a giver was seen as a loss of face—as a sign that the recipient was not as successful or important. Since status was associated with the size of one's gifts, their size grew, and at first fulfilled an important trade function among the tribes when their members met to exchange gifts. Later, however, it became customary to demonstrate one's worth not only by exceeding the next person in the size of one's gifts, but by destroying one's own property; such destruction was viewed as a sign of a person's wealth. At a potlatch in the nineteenth century, it was quite common for a man of status to burn thousands of blankets, destroy a number of canoes, and kill many of his slaves. The escalation of exchange and destruction threatened to completely destroy the economic and social welfare of the Kwakiutl societies before the potlatch faded out, partly as a result of government restrictions (Codere, 1950). Although the runaway norms of the Kwakiutls were extremely dramatic, we have similar norms among the middle class: "Keeping up with the Joneses" is no longer sufficient; one must try to exceed them.

BYSTANDER INTERVENTION AND HELPING BEHAVIOR

```
                              Wino?
                  Sidewalk.        Junkie?
             on                    Hurt?
            face                      Sick?
             on                        Knife
            Man                            in
                                            pocket?
                                         Danger?
                                      Medicine
                                   in
                                   pocket?
                        May
                        die
                     without
                     it?
                     Forget
                     him?

                     Leave
                     him
                     to
                     the
                     cops?

                     Or try
                     to help?
```

FROM STREET POEMS BY ROBERT FROMAN. COPYRIGHT © 1971 BY ROBERT FROMAN. REPRINTED BY PERMISSION OF THE PUBLISHERS, SATURDAY REVIEW PRESS/E. P. DUTTON & CO., INC.

The Tragic Death of Kitty Genovese. The conflict posed so poignantly in this vivid statement (Froman, 1971) is one that most of us have faced, particularly if we live in a large city. When we see a person lying on the sidewalk, questions such as these inevitably come to our mind. There are good reasons to be concerned, of course. An apparently unconscious victim, lying on the sidewalk, could "come to life" and turn on his benefactor. Perhaps it is a cover for a robbery? If the person is seriously ill, we could expose ourselves to a contagious disease. If the person is dirty and grimy, he may be rather repulsive. There are also good legal grounds for caution. If he has a spinal injury, a well-intentioned person who moves him may aggravate his injury, thereby risking a lawsuit at a later time (Kaplan, 1972). Yet there are also positive rewards for helping the person. We are all indoctrinated with the cultural norm that says it is good to help someone who is in need. Most of us know the biblical story of the Good Samaritan, the member of a despised tribe who proved himself more worthy than a priest or a Levite when he helped a poor traveler who was robbed, seriously wounded, and left to die on the road to Jericho (Luke 10:30–37). Surely the cultural norm about helping people would call for risky behavior if we saw an unfortunate man lying on the sidewalk. Therefore, shouldn't we ordinarily try to do something to help a person in distress?

Suppose you found yourself in the following situation: At about 2:30 or 3:00 A.M. you are awakened from your sleep by the sounds of someone screaming and crying in the street below your bedroom window. You get out of bed with some reluctance and anger (who could be making all this noise at such an ungodly hour?) and look out your window. You see a young woman with her hands raised defensively in front of her face, fighting off the apparent attack of a man. The man seems to be wielding something shiny in his right hand— could it be a knife? The woman is screaming, apparently in fear, and crying for help. What should you do? Just then the man runs away, and in a few minutes you are back in bed wondering if what you have seen was all a dream. But alas it was not! Several minutes later the same scene is reenacted. Again there are screams and cries, again the man appears, and again he disappears when the woman calls out for help. Finally, after several more minutes have elapsed, the man returns again; the woman cries for help again, but the attacker (by now it surely must be clear that the man intends to kill her) finally succeeds in his grisly mission—the woman lies inert in the street, bleeding profusely and, as you later discover, is quite dead.

A rather similar incident actually occurred in a quiet residential section of Queens, New York, in 1964; it resulted in the brutal murder of a young woman, Kitty Genovese. When the police finally arrived on the scene and began their investigation, it turned out that this crime had been witnessed by 38 people looking out of the windows of their apartment house—all nice, friendly, charitable people like you and me. Why did no one go outside and attempt to scare off the attacker? Why did no one even try to telephone the police? Why did no one even call out from the safety of his own apartment? When these very questions were asked of the 38 witnesses, they gave reasons like these: "I was afraid of getting involved"; "I thought it was a husband and wife having a lovers' quarrel"; "I was afraid the man would find out who I was and try to kill me too"; "I was afraid I might make things worse for the woman"; "I was afraid of getting involved with the police" (Rosenthal, 1964). Shortly after the death of Kitty Genovese, the New York City newspapers were filled with articles and editorials summarizing the bystanders' responses and interpreting their behavior. Many social scientists were also puzzled by the failure of these people to try to help, and they conducted a large number of studies. There are excellent summaries in Wispé (1972), Staub (1974), Macauley and Berkowitz (1970), and Krebs (1970).

Factors That Influence Helping Behavior

Although it is popularly believed that apathy—an affliction of the urban dweller—explains people's refusal to help those in distress, two social psychologists, John M. Darley and Bibb Latané (1968), were not satisfied with this explanation. They believed that the behavior of the 38 people who witnessed Kitty Genovese's murder was primarily due to the social psychology of the particular situation. Rather than assume that someone should have intervened because there were so many people looking on, they suggested that it was precisely *because* there were lots of people looking on that no one intervened.

In order to test their hunch, Darley and Latané (1968) conducted the following simple but important experiment. Undergraduate men and women were brought to the laboratory one at a time, assigned to individual rooms, and led to believe that they were part of a group of 2, 3, or 6 students who were going to participate in a "discussion about personal problems associated with college life." Each student, in turn, was asked to address the group (the microphone in each room was switched on for two minutes, while those in the other rooms were turned off, permitting only one person to speak at a time). During the second round of talking, each person, in turn, could comment on what the others had said. The subjects were told that the experimenter would *not* be present while they were speaking since "the discussion might be inhibited by his presence." The first person to speak in each group was actually a tape-recorded confederate—the "victim." Just as the second round was beginning, the victim feigned an epileptic seizure:

I-er-um-I think I-I need-er-if-if could-er-er-somebody er-er-er-er-er-er give me a little-er-give me a little help here because-er-I-er-I'm-er-er-h-h-having a-a-a real problem-er-right now and I-er-if somebody could help me out it would-it would-er-er s-s-sure be-sure be good . . . because-er-there-er-er-a cause I-er-I-uh-I've got a-a one of the-er-sei————————er-er-things coming on and-and-and I could really-er-use some help so if somebody would-er-give me a little h-help-uh-er-er-er-er-er c-could somebody-er-er-help-er-uh-uh-uh (choking sounds) . . . I'm gonna die-er-er-I'm . . . gonna die-er-help-er-er-seizure-er-(chokes, then quiet) [Darley and Latané, 1968, p. 379].

Darley and Latané wished to test the following hypothesis: "The more bystanders to an emergency, the less likely, or the more slowly, any one bystander will intervene to provide aid." Therefore, they expected that the subjects in the two-person groups (subject plus victim) would respond more rapidly than those who believed they were in the larger groups. And this is precisely what happened. In the Two-Person Condition, 85 percent of the subjects opened the doors of their rooms (apparently to ask the experimenter for help) before the end of the "epileptic seizure"; in the Three-Person Condition only 62 percent did so; and in the Six-Person Condition only 31 percent. The greater the number of bystanders the subjects believed were present, therefore, the less inclined they were to give assistance.

Diffusion of Responsibility and Diffusion of Guilt. But why should this have been the case? In response, Darley and Latané suggested two possibilities: *diffusion of responsibility* and *diffusion of guilt*. In the Six-Person Condition, for example, the subjects may have said something like the following to themselves: "Why should *I* help? I am no more responsible for what is going on than anyone else" (diffusion of responsibility); or "If something does happen to that poor chap in the next room, I am no more guilty than the next guy. We're all in this together, so no one can put the blame on me" (diffusion of guilt). Notice the resemblance between this type of reasoning and our earlier discussion of deindividuation (see page 301). An individual's justification for allowing harm to come to another person without attempting to help him is somewhat similar to the justification used by a member of a lynch mob when he injures someone.

Number of Bystanders. If there is a greater probability of diffusion of responsibility and guilt when others are present, the reverse is undoubtedly true as well. If you are the *only* person who can offer assistance to a victim, is it not incumbent upon you to do so? After all, you no longer have a group of fellow bystanders upon whom you can deflect your responsibility and potential guilt. In order to test this hypothesis, Latané and Darley (1968) conducted another experiment, in which men students were ushered into the laboratory to discuss problems of urban living. While waiting for the "experiment" to begin, the subjects were asked to fill out a preliminary questionnaire.

When they had completed two pages, the experimenter began to introduce some harmless but frightening white smoke into the subjects' "waiting room" through a vent in the wall. The smoke continued to pour into the room for the entire experimental period of six minutes. Three experimental conditions were run in this study. In one, the subject was the *only* person in the room; in the second, there were three people waiting together, all naïve subjects who had never met one another before; in the third, there were also three people in the room, but two of them were confederates who had been instructed to behave passively—by noticing the smoke but saying nothing about it.

Latané and Darley found that the subjects in the Alone Condition reported the smoke to the experimenter sooner than the subjects in the other two conditions. They also found that, of the two types of three-person groups, the subjects in real groups (with two other naïve subjects) reported the smoke to the experimenter sooner than those who were with two passive confederates. What is the reason for this? Perhaps the calm demeanor of the two confederates suggested that the smoke was not a cause for concern. Or perhaps the subjects were afraid that they would look foolish by asking for help when they were with two people who seemed to be indifferent.

The Presence of Others Who Are Friends. Darley and Latané's findings clearly suggest that when people are alone they are more inclined to help someone who is in need than when they are with others. But, as we have also seen, the characteristics of the group of bystanders are also important. It is reasonable to expect that one would try to be more helpful and think less about appearing foolish if one were among friends rather than among strangers. To test this hunch, Latané and Rodin (1969) arranged for a number of undergraduates to wait either alone, with a friend, or with a stranger before participating in a "market research study." While the subjects were waiting in one of these conditions, they heard the woman experimenter (a "representative of the Consumer Testing Bureau") apparently fall and injure herself in the adjacent room; actually, the subjects were listening to a tape recording. The researchers found that the subjects who were willing to help most quickly and most frequently were generally those in the Alone Condition. They also found that the subjects who were with a friend were more ready to help the woman in distress than those who were with a complete stranger. The experimenters also ran a fourth condition, in which the subject waited with a confederate stranger who, as in the Latané and Darley (1968) study, was instructed to remain completely indifferent. Here, again, Latané and Rodin found that the subjects were least willing to help in this condition; apparently the presence of an indifferent companion serves as a deterrent. It would appear that people will go to some lengths to avoid looking foolish in the eyes of others, even at the expense of a helpless third party, the victim.

A Helping Model. As we have already seen (page 139), people can be motivated to behave aggressively when they are with an aggressive person; this person serves as a role "model" and his behavior is imitated. Conversely, then, perhaps a person could be motivated to act in a helping, altruistic manner if he were exposed to someone who was behaving altruistically. In order to test this idea, John H. Bryan and Maryanne Test (1967) had an undergraduate woman (a confederate) stand next to a car with a flat tire on a busy Los Angeles freeway. In one condition, there was no model present—the woman stood alone next to her car, trying to flag down passing motorists. In another condition (model), a second woman confederate stood next to another car that was located about one quarter of a mile before the first. This car also had a flat tire, but a man was in the act of changing it; although he was a confederate, it appeared as if he had stopped his car in order to help her. Bryan and Test simply kept track of the number of passing motorists who stopped to try to help the woman alone in the two experimental conditions. Of the 4000 vehicles they observed pass by, a total of 93 stopped! Of these, 58 were in the Model Condition, while only 35 were in the Non-Model Condition. In general, then, it appears that very few people were charitable enough to stop at all, although more were willing to give some assistance when they first saw a helping model. Similarly, London (1970) interviewed a number of Christians who had risked their lives in order to help Jews escape from the Nazi terror before and during World War II. He found that these helpers often had moral parents who served as models, or close associates who performed similar deeds. In some cases, a parent was executed for helping Jews escape, and his children then continued his work.

Characteristics of the Person in Need of Help. It is not surprising that some people in need are more apt to receive help than others. We are more inclined to help those whom we like, who appeal to us, and with whom we feel some sort of identification or affiliation. We are more inclined to help someone who seems to be incapable of helping himself—a lost child looks less capable of finding his way than a lost adult; although our views of women are changing, there is still a conception that a woman is less capable of making emergency repairs on her car or protecting herself against a mugger (Gruder and Cook, 1971); an older person may look as if he needs help in crossing the street, while a younger person may not; and so forth. Furthermore, we are more apt to help someone whose condition appears to be due to some socially acceptable cause (sickness, a seizure, or an accident) than someone whose plight seems to be due to his own transgressions or socially inappropriate behavior (drunkenness, drug addiction, or carelessness).

The effects of the gender and affiliation of the person in need were demonstrated in an experiment in a college library and student union carried out by William Howard and William Crano (1974). The "victim," a college student, sat at a table with several other students in the library or union lounge. A confederate (a male who was poorly dressed, unshaven, and unkempt) gave the group the "once over" and then sat some distance away. When the victim left the room, the confederate picked up the victim's books and disappeared. When the victim returned, he or she expressed shock that the books were missing and asked for assistance. Soon the confederate also returned, but without the books. Would the other students sitting nearby help the victim apprehend the surly "thief"? They were clearly more likely to do so if the victim was a woman rather than a man. They were also more apt to help if the prospective victim, before leaving the room, had initiated a brief conversation with a naïve student—perhaps by simply asking for the time. This brief interchange apparently created some feeling of affiliation between the victim and the bystander, increasing his readiness to offer help—even at some risk.

In another experiment in a real-life setting, Piliavin, Rodin, and Piliavin (1969), examined the effects of the social acceptability of the victim's condition and racial similarity on helping behavior in a New York City subway: During the 7½-minute run between two stops, the 43 passengers on the train became unwitting research subjects. Seventy seconds after the train left the station, they saw a man, about 30 years of age, casually dressed, stagger forward and collapse. Unless assisted, he remained motionless staring at the ceiling for the remaining 6 minutes and 20 seconds, until the train reached the next station. Would any passenger help him?

The victim was one of a number of confederates used in this experiment, which was repeated 103 times on different runs between the same two stations. On 38 runs, the victim carried a liquor bottle and reeked of alcohol—he was assisted on only 19 of these runs. On the other 65 trials, he seemed sober and carried a black cane (suggesting illness); he was assisted on 62 of those trials. It seems obvious that receiving assistance was a function of the social acceptability of the victim's condition. On some of the runs, the victim was black and on others he was white. Here similarity and identification were obvious factors—black victims were more apt to be helped by black passengers and white victims by white passengers.

Helping foreigners and compatriots. Frequently a passerby will be in conflict about whether or not to help someone in distress. There may be certain characteristics about the person in need of help that would encourage or discourage the passerby from helping him. For example, suppose that both a foreigner and a compatriot ask for directions. Obviously, the foreigner would seem to be more helpless, and therefore the passerby might be more inclined to help him. On the other hand, since the passerby's identification with the foreigner would be less, he might be less likely to give assistance. One's inclination to help a foreigner may depend upon where the encounter takes place and possibly the attitude of local residents toward the specific foreign country.

Roy Feldman (1968) carried out a field experiment with 401 passersby in Paris, 551 in Athens, and 422 in Boston. Sometimes the person who was asking for directions was a compatriot and sometimes a foreigner (there was a Frenchman in Boston, and an American in Paris and Athens). He found that passersby in Boston were most likely to give assistance (only 20 percent refused to give proper directions), and they did not differentiate between foreigners and compatriots. Forty-five percent of the Parisian sample refused to give correct directions to foreigners (in 10 percent of the cases they even gave wrong directions), while only 24 percent refused to help their compatriots. In Athens, 36 percent refused to help foreigners, and 32 percent would not help other Greeks. Thus, the Parisians were most inclined to discriminate against foreigners. Although language difficulties might account for the discrimination against foreigners, an analysis of the tape recordings showed that the name of the desired street was repeated clearly several times. When the foreigner spoke the native language, there was still significant discrimination. In fairness to the Parisians, it should be pointed out that in a follow-up experiment, in which passersby were asked to mail a letter for the visitor, they were more helpful to Americans than to other Frenchmen.

Summary of Factors in Helping Behavior. The studies discussed here constitute only a fraction of the number that were conducted in the wake of the Kitty Genovese murder. Of course, the situations (and experiments) where help does not occur are usually more dramatic newspaper copy and thus are more likely to appear on the front page. Less newsworthy are those instances in which bystanders do help—where the victim is assisted and recovers. Such incidents are usually not reported, or may be consigned to an inconspicuous place on the lower left-hand column of the financial section. What factors, then, will increase the likelihood of altruism and helping behavior?

1. *The salience of the victim* is important. In the subway experiment, the passengers who were nearer to the victim were more inclined to help than those who were farther away (Piliavin, Rodin, and Piliavin, 1969). (It should also be mentioned that those who

were near the victim but decided not to help often moved to the far end of the car, thereby reducing the salience of the victim and perhaps their own accompanying guilt.) We often manage to overlook the suffering of those who are starving in India or the Sahara, and are far more compassionate toward a neighbor who has lost his job. Thus, the proximity—both physical and psychological—of a victim is an important factor in getting our attention and in determining whether and how we help.

2. *Evaluating a person's need for help.* Having noticed a victim, we next try to decide how serious his condition is. Has this person suffered a heart attack and does he need immediate attention, or has he simply passed out because of drunkenness? Is the smoke coming from a serious fire or merely from a chimney that needs cleaning?

3. *Is helping appropriate?* Although we are all indoctrinated with the moral precept to help those in need, we also know about the counternorm that cautions us to mind our own business ("Am I my brother's keeper?"). Furthermore, most people seem to acquire another view that is quite prevalent in our society—the belief in a "just" world (Lerner, 1970), which holds that people generally get what is coming to them. This is particularly applicable, of course, if we attribute the victim's plight to his own misbehavior. The drunkard, we may believe, doesn't *have* to drink, and thus doesn't deserve help if he faints. The heart patient, on the other hand, did not choose to have an attack, and so perhaps he should be helped.

4. *Costs and rewards for helping.* We next evaluate the costs and rewards of helping someone in distress. The rewards could include social approval as well as gratitude from the victim and others. The costs might include all of the dangers that we mentioned earlier as well as the discomfort of handling someone who might be dirty, bloody, or otherwise repulsive in appearance. We obtain satisfaction in helping someone whom we like or with whom we identify, and far less satisfaction in helping someone whom we dislike or who is different in some respect.

In evaluating a person's need for help, determining whether our assistance is appropriate, and calculating its costs or rewards, the behavior of others may provide some guide for action—a norm against which a potential helper could weigh his decision to help. Thus, the sight of someone else helping a similar victim (for example, the stranded motorist) may suggest that such a person needs help, deserves help, and that the costs would not be too great. By the same token, the sight of others who are standing by passively, not helping someone in distress, may serve to minimize the needs of the victim and suggest that helping is inappropriate or that the costs would outweigh the rewards.

5. *Diffusion of responsibility and guilt.* Finally, there is the dif-

fusion of responsibility and guilt, a factor that contributes to deindividuation, the risky shift, and obedience to authority. This factor may help to explain why people are less inclined to help when others are present. It is interesting to note that with the risky shift, diffusion of responsibility was offered as a reason for people taking riskier actions (although, as pointed out, it was not a *necessary* condition for the risky shift). With helping behavior, diffusion provides an excuse for inaction. The difference, of course, is that the risky shift studies dealt with group decisions and actions, whereas the studies of helping behavior dealt with the behavior of individuals.

Helping and Its Aftermath: Interviews with Kidney Donors. As the result of new developments in transplant surgery, increasing attention is being paid to persons who are willing to donate organs, either before or after their death, for the survival of others. Such donors, as compared with nondonors, appear to be more independent, more secure, and less religious. Although the factors that lead to helping behavior have been examined in many studies, very little attention has been given to the aftereffects of a decision to help. One such study was carried out by Carl Fellner and James Marshall (1970), who conducted intensive interviews with 30 actual or potential donors of kidneys. These included 6 mothers, 1 father, and 23 siblings of patients whose kidneys were so seriously diseased or damaged that their lives could be maintained only by means of expensive and difficult dialytic treatment, and then only for a limited period.

When a transplant is deemed vital, all potential donors—relatives of the patient—are invited to come to the clinic for tests of tissue compatibility and physical health. It is stressed that the testing is only preliminary and that no further commitment is required. Although the voluntary nature of the donation is stressed, there must be tremendous pressures on the potential donor to help. The patient's need is obviously very great and salient. The number of other persons who can help is extremely limited—indeed, often the donor is the *only* one who can help. The feelings of similarity and identification with the "victim" are always great, whether it is a sibling, a child, or a parent. The expectations (stated or implied) of other relatives and friends are usually quite clear. Furthermore, the request to simply undergo a test of tissue compatability, which one can hardly refuse, bears a striking resemblance to the "foot-in-the-door" research (see page 241), where commitment to an initial smaller act prepares one to accept a more extreme act. Despite the care taken by the medical staff to present the final decision to donate a kidney as purely voluntary, and their attempts to provide a dignified, guilt-free opportunity to refuse, it seems that very few do refuse. Nineteen of the 30 said that they had agreed to donate as soon as the idea was mentioned to them by the medical staff over the telephone; 5 others also agreed, although privately hoping that someone else would finally come forth instead.

Following the decision to donate a kidney, the investigators reported that there was a period of substantial uncertainty about the decision, which is consistent with dissonance theory. The preliminary medical tests were viewed as achievement tests that one was quite fortunate to pass—"It is good to know that you are the healthiest of the bunch." Some said that they had carefully avoided discussing their decision with their spouses because they feared that their spouses might tend to dissuade them. Some said that friends and acquaintances had tried to talk them out of it, but that these suggestions were rejected quite firmly. When a doctor would try to present the possible dangers of performing such an operation, in keeping with a policy of informed consent, the potential donor would disregard that information; they believed that the doctors were merely stressing the dangers in an attempt to be honest, but they thought that the doctors were competent to deal with these dangers.

All of the relevant medical personnel stressed the importance of informed consent and the voluntary nature of organ donation. Fellner and Marshall, however, raised serious questions about whether the potential donor's consent could actually be informed and voluntary. They did not deny that the medical staff offered information to the potential donors in good faith, but they suggested that the very nature of the situation, as described above, was such that, psychologically, donors could not really attend to that information— following their decision, a dissonance-reducing process operated to close out important sources of information that would argue against the action. Furthermore, could a donation really be "voluntary" if the process of volunteering elicits a number of subtle social psychological pressures?

What became clear in the post-operative interviews was that the act of donating a kidney in keeping with both dissonance and self-perception theory, led to a striking reevaluation of one's self, with tremendous feelings of elation and self-worth. Donors reported afterward that they developed greater confidence and self-respect, as well as feelings of responsibility and morality. One woman reported that she started going to church more regularly and was more ready to engage in other helping activities that might arise in the future. Several reported that they had developed a more positive and warmer attitude toward their entire family and that, as a result, the family as a whole had become closer. Perhaps not all helping behavior leads to such dramatic changes in self-perception; it may depend upon the significance and danger inherent in the specific helping act.

SUMMARY The group's influence on the individual is an ongoing and ubiquitous phenomenon. Even without interaction, it appears that the mere presence of a group can affect individual performance. Social psychological research indicates that when a person has already mastered some task, the presence of others working on similar tasks has a stimulating, motivating, and generally facilitative effect; when a task has not been mastered, however, the presence of others may prove distracting, may increase the individual's anxiety, and will probably inhibit his performance.

One of the most important ways in which groups influence individual behavior is through the establishment of norms, which constitute a standard against which the person can evaluate the appropriateness of his behavior. Group norms also help to provide order and meaning in what might otherwise be seen as an ambiguous, uncertain, and perhaps threatening situation. In the case of the phenomenon known as social contagion (the spread of a behavior, attitude, or emotional state through a group in a manner resembling the spread of a contagious disease), the group supplies a socially acceptable definition so that the individual will be able to understand the tension he experiences and the symptoms he displays. Similarly, deindividuation (the individual's loss of a sense of identity in a group, which often leads him to act in less moral fashion) occurs when a group's behavior provides norms that increase the social acceptability of individual antisocial acts. Another example of the power of group norms is evident in research using the autokinetic phenomenon (the illusion that a stationary point of light in an otherwise dark room is moving); working with this phenomenon, Muzafer Sherif found that an individual's perception of how far a point of light has moved is affected by the judgments of other group participants.

Groups tend to gravitate toward uniformity of opinion among their members. Such uniformity tends to be greater when: there are fewer differences of opinion within the group, an opinion is more relevant to the group's functioning, and the group is more cohesive; a group's uniformity of opinion is also affected by the personality traits of its members and various cultural factors. If and when there is sufficient similarity of opinion within a group so that a clear group norm exists, any member's deviation from that norm will lead to pressures in the direction of restoring uniformity. Leon Festinger has hypothesized that the other group members may attempt to deal with a deviant by encouraging him to change his views, by rejecting him, or by changing their own views to bring them more in line with those of the deviant. If the deviant can neither convince the majority to change nor permit himself to adopt their viewpoint, he will be inclined to look for another group that can provide support and a basis for self-evaluation.

Groups influence not only the uniformity of opinion but also the decisions made by their members. Thus, it has been repeatedly found that groups tend to make decisions that differ from those made by their members as lone individuals. Although group decisions are sometimes more conservative than those made by individuals, there appears to be tendency for groups to take greater risks. Among the various explanations advanced for the "risky shift," the one that is most clearly supported holds that riskiness is generally valued in our culture, and this value leads group members to take greater risks than one another. The result is a runaway norm in which the socially desirable level of behavior, attitude, or performance exceeds that of the group as a whole.

Another instance of the powerful effect of a group upon the individual can be seen in bystander intervention. Social psychologists have found that a person is less likely to offer assistance to someone in need of help when there are other people present. Rather than explain this phenomenon in terms of apathy, it has been suggested that people want to avoid looking foolish in the eyes of others; therefore, they will not intervene when it may seem inappropriate or dangerous to do so. When other people are present, the bystander can persuade himself that he is no more responsible for refusing to help than the next guy ("diffusion of responsibility") and no more guilty than his neighbor for the hapless victim's fate ("diffusion of guilt").

Having examined the influence of the group upon the individual and his performance, let us now turn to the group itself. Under what circumstances is a group likely to function more effectively than an individual alone? What are some of the factors that affect the quality of group decisions and group solutions? In particular, how is a group's performance affected by the nature and quality of its leadership? What are the determinants of leadership style, and how does this style affect the members of a group? Chapter 9 will address itself to these issues.

Group Decision and Group Performance
Group Norm as a Field of Forces

**The Quality of Group Decisions and Group
    Solutions**
Factors That Affect the Quality of Group Decisions

Leadership
What Is a Leader?
What Factors Produce a Leader?
The Many Functions of Leadership
The Development and Maintenance of Leadership
Leadership Style: The Behavior of Leaders
Leadership and Group Performance

NINE

GROUP PERFORMANCE,
GROUP EFFECTIVENESS,
AND LEADERSHIP

353

"Now for Sweetbreads and Kidneys—All in Favor?" In Chapter 8, many examples were presented in which an individual group member was pressured to conform in his behavior, beliefs, attitudes, or emotions to the norms of his group. It was pointed out that anyone who deviated from those norms could be subjected to direct influence attempts on the part of other group members; these actions could include punishment or even expulsion from the group. From this discussion, one might conclude that groups are essentially conservative, that they develop and maintain norms, and that any new member who joins a group will be pressured to adhere to those norms. Relatively recently, research on the risky shift has suggested that under certain circumstances a group might move its members in a risky, as well as in a conservative, direction. Much earlier, however, a social psychologist, Kurt Lewin, was able to capitalize on the importance of group norms in order to introduce innovation and change among group members.

During World War II the United States, like other countries, found it necessary to institute meat rationing. Actually, this country had a plentiful supply of meat, but the readily available cuts were unpopular and therefore not purchased. These included visceral organs such as sweetbreads, lungs, hearts, and brains. The National Research Council recruited a team of social scientists to try to learn how to interest people in buying these cuts. The anthropologist Margaret Mead provided ample evidence that the discarded cuts of meat were not inherently inedible or distasteful, since people in other cultures consider them delicacies. Sweetbreads and brains, for example, are especially popular among the French and other Western Europeans.

Kurt Lewin analyzed the problem from the perspective of group structure. He assumed that once the unpopular cuts were tastefully prepared for the family table, they would be eaten and eventually might become as accepted in the United States as elsewhere. Therefore, he reasoned that the focus of his research should be on the "gatekeeper," the family member who purchased, prepared, and served food at home. He felt that the problem might be solved if the attitudes and behavior of the homemaker could be changed. But how could that be accomplished when practically all homemakers had a negative attitude toward visceral meats? Although it might be possible to try to meet various women individually in an attempt to convince each one, the woman who actually bought visceral meats would find herself at variance with her friends and neighbors, and so she would inevitably drift back to her previous buying habits. Therefore, Lewin felt that the answer was to try to convince *groups* of women.

The first study was carried out with groups of women Red Cross volunteers. Two methods of change were attempted. Some of the groups were given direct pertinent information by a capable lecturer who stressed that the visceral meats were high in nutritional value, were less expensive, could be prepared in delicious ways, and that using them would represent an important contribution to the war effort. The other groups met with an experienced group worker who managed to convey the same information as the lecturer, but within the context of a group discussion. He ended the group session by asking the women whether they planned to purchase and serve visceral meats; every woman raised her hand. Finally, he said that he would get in touch with them again soon to find out if they had actually followed through with these plans. Several weeks later, all of the women—those who had heard the lecturer and those who had participated in the group discussion—were contacted. Only 3 percent of the women who had heard the lecturer had actually purchased visceral meats, but 32 percent of the women in the discussion group had done so (Lewin, 1943). Later studies that were carried out with a more careful experimental design demonstrated the same essential phenomenon. The group discussion technique was also effective in persuading homemakers to serve more milk, orange juice, and cod liver oil (Radke and Klisurich, 1947) and in motivating college students to select whole wheat instead of white bread (Lewin, 1943). Edith B. Pelz later demonstrated that the group discussion technique would encourage more students to volunteer and participate as subjects in experiments; she also showed that it was the act of making a decision and the feeling of group consensus, rather than the discussion itself, that was the crucial element (Bennett, 1955). Clearly, a group decision can lead to a substantial change in the behavior of those in the group.

GROUP DECISION
AND GROUP
PERFORMANCE

Group Norm as a Field of Forces
Lewin later extended his intial exploratory work by developing a theoretical statement about group behavior that went beyond simple food preferences and included the performance level of industrial workers. As we pointed out in earlier chapters, some of the first experiments in social psychology were carried out in industry, where the goal was to increase worker productivity. Using time-and-motion studies, efficiency experts attempted to determine how men and ma-

chines could be arranged to minimize wasted movement and to maximize productivity.

The Hawthorne effect. The classic study at the Hawthorne Works of the Western Electric Company focused on how improved working conditions—proper temperature, lighting, humidity, length of work day, rest periods, and so forth—might affect productivity. The workers were placed in a separate experimental room, where each of these factors was introduced one by one. Each change seemed to increase productivity. The multi-disciplinary research team was jubilant. However, as a final test, all of the improvements were removed. To the amazement of the researchers, productivity remained at the same high level! Further analyses of the data showed that a number of unexpected changes had taken place among the workers simply because of the establishment of the isolated experimental room: The workers felt freer since the room was in the charge of an "observer" rather than a supervisor. They spoke to one another more often and in a more jovial manner. They became close friends both on the job and during their leisure time. Absenteeism in this work group was low and the morale was generally high. It also seemed that once the higher work norm had been established, it became the accepted level in the group, and there was pressure to maintain it. Those who worked below the norm were pressured to increase their productivity; those who worked far above it were pressured to lower their output (Roethlisberger and Dickson, 1939).

Quasi-Stationary Equilibria. The operation of group norms at the Hawthorne plant was clearly consistent with Lewin's analysis of group norms and group decisions. Lewin suggested that when an individual is seen as behaving in a consistent manner, whether by purchasing only certain cuts of meat or by working at a steady rate in a factory, the apparent stability does not reveal what the underlying processes are. In fact, the person may be subjected to a number of forces that are not at all apparent to the casual observer. The factory worker who consistently produces 60 units per hour may experience certain pressures to increase his output—stemming from a desire for more pay or promotion, pressure from his supervisor, an awareness of his own ability to produce more, and so forth. These, however, are balanced by an equal number and weight of forces to reduce production—fatigue; displeasure at the boss or company; fear that if he produces above a certain level, the boss may change the piece rate; and so forth. Sixty units is the resultant of these forces, and the group exerts pressure to maintain the norm. Occasionally a worker will vary his output, perhaps increasing it; in that case, there will be even greater pressures to return to the earlier output. Indeed, the further he deviates from the 60 units—in either direction—the greater will be the pressures to return to that level. In that sense, then, the apparent stability is really a state of "quasi-stationary equilibrium." These forces are represented by arrows in Figure 9.1; the length of each arrow corresponds to the size of the force.

The concept of underlying forces around an equilibrium point has some interesting implications. For example, two workers may appear to be performing at the same level—both producing around 60 units per hour. However, one of these workers may experience great pressures to increase production—an intense desire to do well, a significant need for additional pay, and a wish to please the supervisor; but these may be balanced by equally strong pressures from the group and from others to keep production down. He thus experiences serious conflict, as compared with the other worker who does not feel any special push either to increase or decrease production. Which worker would be least satisfied, more accident prone, absent more often, and so forth?

It follows, Lewin continued, that if the management of a factory wants to raise production, it might succeed temporarily by increasing the pressure from the supervisor or by offering some type of bonus system for high producers. However, any gains would be countered by stronger forces to reduce production, and so these gains would

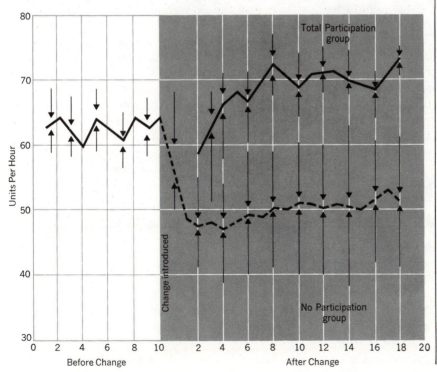

Figure 9.1
Effects of participation on forces to increase or decrease production. *At a pajama factory the workers had been producing about 60 units per hour. Then the management introduced a slight change in the work procedure. Initially there was a drop in the production rate. Coch and French arranged for the change to be made under two experimental conditions. In the Total Participation Condition, the workers had an opportunity to discuss the change with management; in the No Participation Condition, they were simply brought together and told of the change—with no opportunity to discuss it or bring up their own ideas. Their production rate reflected these two conditions.*

produce significant tension among the workers. Thus, when group norms are fixed and strong, productivity could be raised more effectively and with less tension by "unfreezing" the established norm, moving it to a new higher level, and then "refreezing" it at the new level. And how could this be accomplished? Through group discussion and decision-making. Several initial experiments, such as the one conducted by Alex Bavelas at a sewing machine factory, seemed to lend support to the effectiveness of group decisions in changing production levels (Lewin, 1947).

Group Participation in Industrial Change. A more significant test of the effect of group decision-making was conducted in a pajama factory by Lester Coch and John R. P. French, Jr. (Coch and French, 1948). They had been observing the working conditions of the women employees at the Harwood Manufacturing Corporation plant in Marion, Virginia. The effects of group norms soon became quite clear to them when they observed the intense group pressures exerted on the woman who exceeded the usual production level (as described above). Occasionally it was necessary to change a work operation slightly, such as by asking the pajama pressers to stack their finished products by half-dozen lots in a box, instead of placing them on a flat piece of cardboard. Initially it was expected that this change would lead to a drop in the production rate, and this is precisely what happened. However, the time-study experts had calculated that the new method was not essentially more difficult; they believed that once the procedure had been learned, the production rate would return to its earlier level. But this did not happen. In fact, once the production level dropped, it tended to stay low. Applying Lewin's analysis, Coch and French suggested that the downward forces, which corresponded to the greater initial difficulty of the task, had been replaced by the pressures of the group norm, which had now become frozen at the new lower level.

How, then, could the original production level be restored? Coch and French accomplished this with another group by following Lewin's suggestion and arranging for this second group of workers to meet with representatives of management to learn the purpose of the change, examine the new work plan, and discuss the relative ease with which the change could be implemented. There seemed to be general agreement about and acceptance of the change by the workers in this Total Participation Condition, as well as acceptance of the fact that their performance could be maintained at its usual level. As things turned out, this group achieved and maintained an even higher level of production. Concurrently, there was also evidence of reduced tension and conflict, less absenteeism, less expressed hostility, and no resignations. Figure 9.1 presents a schematic diagram of the forces operating on the workers in the Total Participation groups.

By contrast, a group of workers in a No Participation Condition was also asked to make an equivalent change, but the change was presented as follows: The production department modified the job and established a new piece rate; then it called a meeting of the work team to explain the change and the need for it and asked if there were any questions. It was evident that these workers resisted the change almost immediately. They quickly expressed hostility toward management and the supervisor. Grievances were filed against the new piece rate, and 17 percent of these workers quit during the first 40 days. The production level remained low.

Coch and French wondered if the advantages of group discussion and decision could be obtained equally well without having all of the workers present. By bringing together a small group of representatives, chosen by the workers themselves, the discussion could be kept more intimate and direct. The representatives could then convey the sense of the meeting to their fellow workers. It was found that "participation through representation" produced results that were intermediate between the Total Participation and No Participation Conditions. In the case of this pajama factory, at least, maximum change through group decision required the direct participation of all the workers.

Stimulated by the Coch and French study, other investigations were undertaken, providing additional support for the importance of group participation in decisions about social change. However, one significant negative study was conducted in a Norwegian factory by John R. P. French himself, together with Joachim Israel and Dagfinn Ås. Worker participation in a decision on production change (from work on summer footwear to winter footwear) had no significant effect on worker output. However, in this plant, it appears that the workers generally tended to accept the legitimacy of a negotiated agreement through their own union representatives. Group decision-making may have thus appeared to the workers to be a largely irrelevant procedure (French, Israel, and Ås, 1960).

Participation or manipulation? When the studies on group decision and social change were first presented and implemented by social psychologists in various industrial settings, they were hailed as a humanistic approach to human relations in industry. Surely the idea that it was both practically and ethically sound to have workers participate in decisions pertaining to their expected performance should constitute a democratic approach to labor relations. Conservative industrialists, who had felt that workers were paid simply to work, were dubious at first but later impressed with the practical value of worker participation. Soon thereafter, however, labor leaders began to attack the group decision studies on the ground that they were merely another means of manipulating the workers. These critics felt that, instead of paying the workers more to produce more, the workers were being manipulated into making a decision that was really in management's best interest (Gunderson, 1950). Unfortunately, the tools developed and tested by social psychologists, like any other tools, can be subverted and used for selfish purposes. One can only hope that when group participation is not true participation, but manipulation, those who find themselves being used will soon realize it and react accordingly.

A major obstacle to true participation by line workers is the traditional attitudes of management. Management and supervisory personnel are inclined to have their own norms and attitudes, which tend to oppose real participation in decision-making by subordinates. Such management norms often prevail, even in societies where worker participation is an essential aspect of the ideology, such as the Israeli kibbutzim or Socialist factories in Yugoslavia (Tannenbaum et al., 1974). Nancy Morse and Everett Reimer (1956) found that they could alter such supervisory norms in industrial settings, using the same kinds of discussion techniques that Lewin, Coch, and French had utilized earlier in changing workers' attitudes. Units that had had greater worker participation in decision-making enjoyed higher morale, lower turnover rates, less absenteeism, and lower over-all production costs (Katz and Kahn, 1966). Thus, the methods of true participation in decision-making, when accepted and used properly, still provide a promising means for effective and productive social change.

THE QUALITY OF GROUP DECISIONS AND GROUP SOLUTIONS

Intuitively we might expect that several people working together should be more effective in solving problems than one person alone. If there is a correct answer to a problem, and if that answer is not immediately obvious to everyone, then simple probability would suggest that the more people present the greater the likelihood that at least one of them would have the correct solution. Unfortunately, it is not clear that groups are superior to individuals. A group is characterized by interaction among its members, and sometimes the most appropriate solution to a problem may be lost in this sea of interaction. The studies of deindividuation discussed in Chapter 8 certainly suggest that individuals in the context of a group will sometimes select a less moral solution to a problem than if they were alone. Group norms and values may also operate toward a risky or conservative decision, which may not always be the best.

Parkinson's "Law of Triviality." After World War II, when most social psychologists were extolling the wonders of group dynamics, a little-known professor from the University of Northern Malaysia, C. Northcote Parkinson, published a scientific spoof of bureaucracy and committee meetings that contains more than an occasional ring of truth (Parkinson, 1957). For example, his "Law of Triviality" states that when a committee is discussing financial matters, "the time spent on any item of the agenda will be in inverse proportion to the sum involved" (Parkinson, 1957, p. 24). The committee on finance which is considering the construction of a $10 million atomic reactor will quickly survey the subcommittee report and take rapid action. Since the amount is really beyond the ken of the most of the committee members and few know very much about atomic reactors, there is very little to discuss. On the other hand, a sum of $2350 for the construction of a bicycle shed will be discussed at length, since everyone can understand that amount, and everyone can visualize a bicycle shed and thus talk about it extensively. And when it is reported that the refreshments for the meetings have cost $4.75 per month, everyone can calculate that that means $57 per year, and since the cost of coffee and cream is known to everyone, this item could become the subject of a long and acrimonious debate.

Others have also commented wryly on the inefficiency of committee decisions and on the occasional bizarre results. It has even been suggested that a camel is a horse designed by a committee.

Figure 9.2
Parkinson's "law of triviality."

A committee will approve without much discussion a proposal for a $10 million atomic reactor . . .

. . . but it will have an acrimonious debate over the $4.75 per month that it spends on refreshments.

Pressures toward Uniformity May Hamper Problem-solving. There is considerable evidence in support of the criticisms of group effectiveness in decision-making and problem-solving. Irving Janis (1972) described a situation in the mining town of Pitcher, Oklahoma, in 1950, in which the local mining engineer warned that the town had been accidentally undermined and was about to collapse. The next day, the leading citizens met to discuss the implications of his warning. The mining expert was treated very much as "Chicken Little" in the well-known children's story. The citizens' group laughed and joked, breaking into guffaws when one person arrived wearing a parachute. The implicit group decision was to do nothing, and the town settled into complacency. When the collapse eventually occurred shortly thereafter, many people lost their lives. The collective security provided by a group in the face of a threat, which often has positive functions, led in this case to tragic consequences.

In this, as in other instances, group pressures toward uniformity may submerge the minority opinion of the person who happens to have the correct answer. The industrial psychologists Norman Maier and Allen Solem performed a very simple experiment in which subjects were given the following problem: "A man bought a horse for $60 and sold it for $70. Then he bought it back for $80 and sold it again for $90. How much money did he make in the horse business?" The subjects gave a variety of answers, including: that the man lost $10, broke even, or made $10, $20, or $30. Then the subjects were put into discussion groups of five or six and asked to arrive at a unanimous group answer. The number of correct answers rose somewhat, but when the correct answer (which is $20, by the way) was suggested by a minority of the group, the majority incorrect answer still tended to predominate (Maier and Solem, 1952). In a later follow-up study, where unanimity was not insisted upon, the group members were told individually to disregard the group discussion in arriving at their final individual decisions. Nonetheless about half of these groups made a unanimous decision—and half of these groups were unanimously incorrect! Furthermore, the unanimous groups were more satisfied with their decision than were the split groups, regardless of whether the group decision was correct—unanimity seemed to be more rewarding than accuracy (Thomas and Fink, 1961).

Since the 1940s, social psychologists have been analyzing those factors that lead a group to mobilize its resources most effectively in solving problems and arriving at optimal decisions, and those that inhibit effective action. Such analyses must consider several of the basic variables in group problem-solving: (1) *The nature of the task:* Is it difficult or easy? Is the task one that readily permits a division of labor, or does it require coordination? Is there a simple, direct solution, or is it a matter of judgment? (2) *The characteristics of the individuals:* To what extent do they combine skills and competencies? Are the people individualistic or group-oriented, affiliative or achievement-oriented, dominant or submissive? To what extent are the people similar or diverse in these characteristics? (3) *The nature of the group:* How do the individuals combine into one group? What are the processes of interaction? What is the communication, status, sociometric, and role structure of the group? What is the quality of the leadership? What are the group traditions? What is the size of the group?

Factors That Affect the Quality of Group Decisions

Further complicating any conclusions about the factors that enter into effective group problem-solving and decisions are the interactions among these variables: the relationships between the nature of tasks and individuals, tasks and the group, individuals and the group, and the combination of all three—tasks-by-individuals-by-groups. Although detailed accounts of group problem-solving and group decisions can be found in the research literature (for example, Hoffman, 1965; Kelley and Thibaut, 1969; Davis, 1969; Collins and Guetzkow, 1964; Steiner, 1972), a few generalizations will be mentioned here.

Acceptance of Common Goals. Any decision-making or problem-solving task that requires coordination or the exchange of information among members will be completed more effectively if the members accept the goals of the group. This is particularly true if there is a high degree of means-interdependence, where each aspect of the task requires the exchange of activity or information (Deutsch, 1969; Raven and Eachus, 1963). When members of the group do not accept common goals, they tend to withhold information or to be unwilling to participate actively in solving the problem. Therefore, a group composed of individuals whose personalities are such as to make them self-oriented will be less likely to attain an optimal solution than one in which the members are willing to share with one another (Fouriezos, Hutt, and Guetzkow, 1950).

Divisibility of Group Task. Some tasks cannot readily be subdivided. Let us suppose that a group of mental health professionals in a mental hospital must decide whether a patient should be released or given further treatment; or that the president's advisory group is trying to decide what immediate action should be taken in response to a national threat (such as the Soviet Union's installation of nuclear missles in Cuba). In such cases, it would be difficult to subdivide the task of making a decision. On the other hand, an advisory group to

President Eisenhower, in anticipation of the Supreme Court decision abolishing school desegregation, could have effectively divided its task—some members could have concentrated on the impact desegregation would have on federal aid to education, others could have worked on problems of federal enforcement, still others on plans to upgrade schools in segregated black neighborhoods, and so forth. In the latter case, group members could have been assigned to jobs according to their qualifications; each person's expertise could have been utilized to its fullest by assignment to a special subcommittee or individual job. When a task cannot be subdivided, a group decision must be made, although this means that expert opinions may be submerged by group pressures and that some individuals may not be able to participate fully in working on the problem. In order for a group to take full advantage of the divisibility of a task, there must be maximum coordination and assignment of functions. (Steiner, 1972; Kelley and Thibaut, 1969).

Communication and Status Structure. The communication patterns within a group can determine the group's success in solving problems. Communication, in turn, depends upon the status of the individuals in the group. The study by Hurwitz, Zander, and Hymovitch (see page 282) shows that when a status discrepancy exists in a problem-solving group (for example, when one person is designated as an "industrial executive" and another as a "YMCA worker"), the higher-status persons will speak more and have more influence, while the lower-status persons will tend to speak less and defer to those of higher status (Hurwitz, Zander, and Hymovitch, 1953). Consequently, any lower-status person who has something to contribute to the group solution may be inhibited from doing so, and thus the group may be rendered less effective.

Paul Torrance tested this principle in a hierarchy composed of three-man bomber crews. Crews consisting of a pilot (the officer in command), a navigator, and a gunner (an enlisted man, who was lowest in status) were presented with Maier's horse-trading problem. Initially, 50 percent of the navigators, 31 percent of the pilots, and 29 percent of the gunners individually chose the correct answer; thus, most groups had the potential knowledge to solve the problem. The actual number of correct group solutions, however, fell well below what might have been expected from individual performances. Closer analysis showed that it all depended upon *who* had the correct answer to begin with. If it turned out that it was the pilot who was correct, then the group was in luck—94 percent of the pilots were successful in convincing the others when they were correct. The gunners, who were actually as skilled at choosing the right answer as the pilots, could not as readily convince the others—only 63 percent of the accurate gunners were able to persuade the others of their answer. And the navigators, who were the most skilled at choosing the right answer, were not as persuasive as the pilots—only 80 percent of them were successful. Thus, status differences can hamper effective group problem-solving when the high-status person does not have all the answers. We should add that when Torrance used random groups of pilot, navigator, and gunner, each from a different crew, the effect of status was less deleterious (Torrance, 1954).

Status patterns and communication restrictions may not always be counterproductive. There are obvious instances in which an effective leader can help the group to make maximum use of its resources. Also, as noted in our discussion of research on communication networks (see Chapter 7), when a group is working with a simple assembly task—where each person has specific contributions to make and where separate bits of information must be coordinated into one whole—a centralized communication structure may be more rapid and effective (Shaw, 1954). For example, when the director of a small company wants to consider the feasibility of developing a new product, he calls in the production expert, the marketing expert, and the sales expert, gets his information from each and then makes a decision that he passes on to them. If the decisions to be made are more complex—encompassing a greater spread of information—then the centralized structure may have destructive consequences.

Group Size. With a larger group, one might expect that there would be more collective information available and therefore a wiser group decision. Yet group size does have its limitations. As the group gets larger, there is less participation by each person and consequently less efficiency (Thomas and Fink, 1963). Furthermore, in larger groups participation becomes increasingly limited to one or two persons (Bales and Borgatta, 1955; Stephan and Mishler, 1952). Those who tend to dominate or who have a very clear stake in the outcome are able to take over a larger meeting, whereas they might be called to account in a smaller gathering. The proper size of the decision group may vary. Philip Slater studied 24 male groups, ranging in size from two to seven members, that had been asked to solve some human relations problems. The group members seemed to feel that a five-man group would be the best size. Larger groups appeared to be more aggressive, competitive, and inconsiderate, whereas smaller groups seemed to be more tense, constrained, and overly tactful (Slater, 1958).

Composition of Group—Heterogeneity versus Homogeneity. Some research on group problem-solving has dealt with the advantages and disadvantages of groups with similar or different types of people. Should a group be composed of people with diverse skills and expertise, with dissimilar backgrounds, with differing personalities? These considerations recall our discussion of interpersonal attraction in Chapter 4, and the findings are, likewise, by no means simple.

Clearly there are situations in which it is helpful to have a variety of viewpoints in arriving at a solution, particularly when a problem is complex and requires the participants to have substantial background information. How many committees dealing with problems of race and minority relations have failed because they had no members who were black, Mexican American, Asian American, or native American? Yet committees that have had representatives from these diverse groups have often been laden with tensions, hostilities, little satisfaction, and substantial frustration. In some cases, the group has not been able to mobilize enough agreement to arrive at any decision. But is a poor solution better than no solution at all?

Richard Hoffman (1965) reported a series of studies showing that heterogeneous groups generally do tend to be more effective. Not only is there a greater diversity of information available for solving problems, but there is a greater tendency for individual members to question the untested assumptions and opinions of one another. Day in and day out we tend to associate with those who are similar, with those who agree with us and do not question our views. But if we try to solve problems with these same people, we are apt to ignore other—perhaps significant—points of view. Obviously, then, heterogeneity can be advantageous, particularly for difficult tasks in which differing opinions and approaches would be helpful, up to the point where the tensions become so great that the group cannot function at all. For example, Fred Fiedler and his co-workers capitalized on the strong and long-standing religious differences in the Netherlands—between the staunch Calvinists and devout Catholics—in constructing groups. The mixed groups here were so tense and hostile that communication became impossible and the groups functioned ineffectively (Fiedler, Meuwese, and Oonk, 1961).

One way to take full advantage of heterogeneity, while minimizing its harmful effects, is to have some kind of preparation and training before the group task begins. Harry Triandis, Eleanor Hall, and Robert Ewen (1965) compared groups whose members were either all liberal, all conservative, or mixed in their political views. They found that the mixed groups were less effective than the homogeneous ones. However, after having the mixed groups participate in a training program in interpersonal relations, which encouraged members to accept differences in others, the heterogeneous groups became more effective than those that were homogeneous.

Group Cohesiveness. It has generally been assumed that group cohesiveness is a good thing because it leads to more effective, creative, and productive group behavior. Indeed, in Chapter 7 we pointed out that group cohesiveness leads to greater participation and freedom in communication, greater acceptance of the group goals, and less hostility and tension. Other evidence in support of the role of group cohesiveness is available as well.

Field studies of six-man squads in the U. S. army showed that the squads that were most effective in solving tactical problems were also made up of members who were attracted to one another and were especially proud of their squads (Goodacre, 1951; 1953). Similar relationships between cohesiveness and effective group functioning were also found with bomber squads (Hemphill and Sechrest, 1952) and air force maintenance crews (Strupp and Hausman, 1953). Of course, it is not immediately obvious whether cohesiveness increased effectiveness or vice versa. Goodacre, however, obtained measures of interpersonal attraction before the field operation, suggesting that cohesiveness may precede effectiveness. Also, in our discussion of the effects of assigning carpenter crews based on sociometric choice (Chapter 7), cohesiveness clearly increased productivity (Van Zelst, 1952a, 1952b).

There are, however, some instances in which a high degree of cohesiveness can hamper group effectiveness. In a study of the effectiveness of second-grade children in solving spelling problems, for example, some children were grouped with those whom they liked, while others were grouped with those whom they had not chosen. Initially, the cohesive groups were more effective, but this declined later on, especially in the most cohesive groups. It was determined that this loss of effectiveness in the cohesive groups was due to the fact that these children spent more time socializing and less time on the problems (Shaw and Shaw, 1962). Thus, cohesiveness can be detrimental to effectiveness if the group loses sight of its goal. There can be an even stronger negative effect if the group adopts a norm that is opposed to being effective or productive; thus, group cohesiveness can lead to greater adherence to a norm, whether this produces greater or lesser effectiveness (Schachter et al., 1951; in Berkowitz, 1954). Even if a group would like to be effective in solving problems, there will be a greater tendency to submerge minority opinions if the group is cohesive. This is all well and good when the minority is wrong, but is obviously counterproductive if the minority happens to be right (Sakurai, 1975; Thomas and Fink, 1961).

Leadership. The effectiveness of a group often depends upon whether it has a leader and upon the manner in which he organizes and directs the group's activities. Under various conditions a leader can clearly affect each of the preceding variables. He can have some effect on the group goals and on the extent to which they are accepted by the others in the group; he can sometimes assign and divide tasks; he can determine status and communication patterns; he can sometimes divide the group into subgroups of varying size; he can modify the effects of heterogeneity; he can affect the group's cohesiveness; and he can make certain that minority opinions are expressed. Because leaders can exert such a profound influence on group performance and effectiveness, the rest of this chapter will analyze their functions and roles.

LEADERSHIP

Imagine that you have been invited to a dinner party with a number of other people whom you have not met before. You arrive at the appointed hour, talk for a while with the host and hostess (the only people you know), and then are ushered into the living room, where you are introduced to the other guests. You take a seat on the sofa, munch on the hors d'oeuvres, nurse your cocktail, and begin to engage in conversation. Soon dinner is served, and after a delightful meal you and the other guests move back to the living room and ease into more comfortable chairs, while the conversation touches on a variety of topics—ranging from sports and movies to politics and philosophy. As the evening moves along, you begin to notice that several rather obvious but interesting transformations have taken place. For one thing, you observe that this assemblage of almost total strangers has somehow developed into a group. Out of the simple collective act of pushing silverware and food around on plates, out of the shared enjoyment of a good meal and enthusiastic conversation, out of the sheer presence of you and the others in the same room for several hours, a sense of relatedness has somehow emerged among the guests—you have almost become members of a family.

Another thing you notice is that during the course of the evening, there has been a change in the amount of conversation. The often awkward, embarrassed silences over cocktails have now, after a relatively short period of social contact, given way to loud, enthusiastic chatter. Moreover, you observe that there has been a change in the conversational activity of many guests. The woman who seemed so surprisingly comfortable over cocktails, talking away "a mile a minute," has now become strangely silent and withdrawn. In fact, several of the guests seem to be concerned about this fact and occasionally try to draw her into conversation. And then there is Charlie, a young man who seemed so shy and reticent at first, but who now shows a lot of self-confidence as he begins to dominate the conversation. He is not simply a loud buffoon, spouting an unending series of empty phrases; much of what Charlie says makes a lot of sense. Indeed, he is an expert in the art of conversation.

Still, not all of the guests are satisfied with this arrangement. Some have begun to squirm quietly in their seats; others seem to be trying to get a word in edgewise. Joe, for example, has apparently decided that he has had enough of Charlie's domination, and so he takes issue with him. Soon a lively argument begins to rage. The mild seat-squirming among the other guests has by now become a state of acute agitation. Things seem to be breaking apart; this highly civilized middle-class ritual (the dinner party) has deteriorated into an Ionesco farce. Just as the evening is about to disintegrate beyond repair, the hostess interjects, "Actually, you know, you *both* have good points," and she proceeds to explain to Charlie and Joe how they are in closer agreement than they think. Without waiting for either of them to respond, she graciously eases her way into an amusing anecdote or two, the guests laugh uproariously, and the evening is saved. People swap several rounds of jokes and risqué stories. Charlie gingerly resumes his discourse with an occasional cautious glance at Joe; the hostess sits poised and ready. Eventually the evening ends, on a far more pleasant note than seemed possible a short time earlier.

The underlying processes at this hypothetical dinner party are not unlike those that can be observed in a wide variety of other situations. Indeed, whenever people come together in small groups—at fraternities, dormitories, political and social clubs, cocktail parties, T-groups, and so forth—several events occur with rather remarkable regularity. Unless there are proscriptions against communicating, people begin to speak to each other about a variety of things. In the process of interacting, ideas and opinions are exchanged, and influence is exerted. As was pointed out in Chapter 8, the group begins to affect the behavior of its individual members in systematic ways. And similarly, in the course of interaction, individual group members begin to influence the group as a whole. It is this latter process and its consequences that we shall discuss here.

Leadership is often associated with formal groups and organizations—we think of the leaders in a political organization, in a factory or university, in a formally organized social club, or on an athletic team. The point of our example is that leadership also emerges even in the most casual and informal groups. Leaders are often appointed, sometimes by someone who is external to the group—the President is not a member of the State Department, yet he appoints the Secretary of State with the approval of the Senate. Sometimes leaders are formally elected by the group itself—as is the president of a nation or a society. Sometimes there are formal rules of succession to leadership—the eldest son of a tribal chief ascends to the chiefdom upon the death of his father. More often than not, however, especially in small groups, leadership emerges informally. In the process of exchanging ideas and opinions, an inequality of participation begins to develop. As at the dinner party, some person or persons begin to assume a more active role in shaping the behavior of the group. This more active person, then, may be seen as the leader of the group. Let us consider exactly what is meant by leader and leadership.

What Is a Leader?

Although definitions of "leader" and "leadership" vary, they usually include one characteristic—the fact that the leader somehow influences the activities of the other group members. Definitions vary in their focus on one or another aspect of leadership: the leader as a position in the group structure, the leader as a role or set of expected behaviors, the leader as one or more functions in the activities of the group, and the leader as a person. We believe that all of these aspects of leadership are important.

Leader as a position in the group structure. Leadership implies social differentiation—one cannot speak of a leader without a follower. The leader's position thus must be viewed in relation to other non-leadership positions. Particularly in formal organizations, the organization chart will designate one or more leadership positions—the foreman, the supervisor, the platoon sergeant, the principal, and so forth. Yet for certain purposes, there may also be informal leadership, with persons in certain positions establishing behavior for others. The workers at an open-hearth furnace may recognize the formally designated foreman, yet they may look for direction to the old-timer who has been working at that job for many years and "knows the score." Of course, as in our dinner party example, informal leaders may emerge even though there are no formally designated leadership positions. Furthermore, various leadership positions may be occupied by several persons at the same time and at different times.

Leader as a role. As with any position, there is a set of expected behaviors—a role—that characterizes the leader's position. The principal behavior expected of a leader is that of giving direction or providing suggestions—actions that somehow influence others. The leader is expected to communicate more, to speak more authoritatively, and to be more dominant and forceful in his actions. He is expected to be a full member of the group and to behave according to its norms—to set an example for others. But, once having established a model of normative behavior, he also has certain privileges—idiosyncrasy credits—that allow him greater latitude in deviating from the general group norms.

Leader as a set of functions. The leader serves certain functions for the group. These relate particularly to directing and coordinating the activities of others in such a way as to help the group maintain itself and to reach its goals most expeditiously. These functions are more clearly specified in a formal goal-directed group, but, as can be seen in our dinner party example, these functions are still found in less formal groups that have no clear-cut goals (note Charlie's function in moving and directing the conversation, and the hostess's function in resolving conflicts and preserving amicability).

Leader as a person. Finally, although the leader's position may be either formally or informally designated, leadership is not manifested until a person actually occupies that position. As we shall see, certain attributes and personality traits tend to thrust a given individual into leadership. It is also true that being placed in a position of leadership will affect the behavior of the occupant, eliciting certain traits and subduing others. If the personality of an individual in the leadership position is so rigid that he cannot act in accordance with the role behaviors expected of that position, he will ordinarily be replaced by someone else.

Definition of a Leader. Based on the preceding discussion, we may now define a leader as someone who occupies a position in a group, influences others in accordance with the role expectation for that position, and coordinates and directs the group in maintaining itself and reaching its goals.

What Factors Produce a Leader?

A very persistent controversy in psychology concerns the relative influence of heredity and environment. Are an individual's personality, intelligence, and aptitudes determined by his inheritance, or is the individual primarily a product of his environment and his experiences? The corresponding controversy in social psychology concerns the issue of leadership and the extent to which it is the product of trait or situational factors. Some believe that a leader is not born but made, shaped by the situation in which he finds himself. Others assume that a person becomes a leader because he has certain characteristics that make him so.

Personality Traits. The assumption that a person becomes a leader because of certain personality traits has long been held by social theorists. Aristotle prepared the way for the "great man" theory with his observation that "From the hour of their birth some are marked out for subjection and others for command" (Aristotle, *Politics*, I, 5 [trans. Jowett, 1885]). The problem, then, is to discover exactly what these leadership traits are. Once we know and can learn how to measure them, we should have no difficulty ferreting out potential

Figure 9.3
Was Dr. Martin Luther King, Jr.'s leadership of the civil rights movement from the mid-1950s to the late 1960s due more to his personality traits or to the situation in which he found himself? Here, he is entering Jackson, Mississippi, in 1966. From left: Mrs. Bernita Abernathy, Rev. Ralph Abernathy, Mrs. Coretta King, Dr. King, Floyd McKissick, Stokely Carmichael.

leaders. How can these traits be discovered? One way is to examine those who have been successful leaders and compare them with non-leaders to determine how they differ. A large number of studies have been conducted to analyze the characteristics of established leaders (Stogdill, 1948; Mann, 1959; Bass, 1960). Typically, trait theorists have found slight but rather stable differences between leaders and non-leaders, while the anti-trait theorists have gleefully suggested dramatic counter-examples: Leaders tend to be bigger and heavier than followers (Adolf Hitler?); stronger and healthier (Julius Caesar?); handsome and physically more attractive (Abraham Lincoln?); more aggressive and domineering (Mohandas Gandhi?); psychologically well adjusted (Nero?); more intelligent (please provide your own counter-example). In 1972 a political pundit pointed out that Americans prefer taller persons as President and that in every presidential election up until that time the taller of the two candidates had been elected. He predicted, therefore, that George McGovern would handily defeat Richard Nixon.

Leadership traits in the leaderless group. Despite the glaring counter-examples, during World War I the German military accepted the inherent logic of the great man theory of leadership and developed from it a rather clever method of selecting leaders. A group of men was given a controversial topic for discussion. Observers carefully rated the group members according to the number of times they attempted to direct the behavior of others and the effectiveness of those attempts. The one person who exhibited those behaviors most frequently was chosen as a candidate for officer status. This "leaderless group discussion" technique was utilized quite frequently in various other countries, particularly after World War II. In industrial situations, it was found that the "LGD" scores correlated consistently with a supervisor's ratings of a worker's administrative capacity and leadership potential, with leadership ratings by peers, with success ratings by foremen, and with other similar measures. Although the correlations were generally quite positive, they were far from perfect and seldom higher than .50 (Bass, 1960).

The correlations between ratings and performance in leaderless groups have encouraged social psychologists to look for consistencies in the leader who emerges in successive groups. In a typical study, 25 undergraduate men were placed in five five-man discussion groups; later on, each student was asked to rank his fellow members according to his preference for each one to be a leader in another group. The following week, the members were reassembled into five new groups in such a way that all of the members were new to each other. Again no leaders were assigned. The groups discussed a different topic, after which the members' preferences for a leader were again measured. Four additional groupings were arranged; thus, each person participated in six groups, and a total of 30 groups was studied. The results clearly indicated a consistency in leadership—the person who was preferred as a leader in one group tended to be preferred as a leader in subsequent groups, even though the members differed (Bell and French, 1950). A later study with airmen in three-man groups showed similar results; both the answers to a questionnaire and observational data supported the great man theory of leadership. This study of airmen also indicated some of the traits that seem to differentiate leaders from followers: (1) *task ability:* the extent to which the members note that the individual is knowledgeable about the topic being discussed; (2) *assertiveness:* the person's total participation time in interaction, as determined by the observers; and (3) *social acceptability:* the extent to which the other members enjoy working with the individual. The same persons tended to maintain their superiority on each of these measures. The study also showed that when one of the "great men" was included in a group, the group manifested less tension, greater agreement, and higher morale (Borgatta, Couch, and Bales, 1954).

A review of many studies of leadership, including both observational, questionnaire, and experimental studies, points to seven major personality traits that generally seem to be associated with leadership: intelligence, adjustment, extroversion, dominance, masculinity, interpersonal sensitivity, and conservatism. The more of each of these traits (except conservatism) an individual possesses, the greater the likelihood that he will become a leader (Mann, 1959).

One criticism of many of these studies is that they tend to focus on leadership in very similar situations, using similar tasks and similar participants. The studies mentioned above typically employed male subjects, in all-student or all-airmen groups, who were engaged in a problem-solving discussion (although the topics varied somewhat). Consequently, the situational factors that are important in leadership did not have a real opportunity to emerge. One notable exception was a study in which groups of people were given four different tasks—reasoning, mechanical, assembling, and discussion—and it was found that there was consistency in leadership (Carter et al., 1951). In general, however, although leadership does tend to be consistent from one situation to the next, the relationship is far from perfect.

Another difficulty with many of the studies of leadership traits stems from the fact that they often focus on situations such as the leaderless group discussion in which a leader must emerge from an unorganized group. While this method is an interesting way to allow personality traits to manifest themselves, it ignores the fact that sometimes leadership is thrust upon a person and that the leadership position may very well develop his traits. It can be seen, therefore, that although a case can be made for personality traits in leadership, it is also important to consider the situational factors.

Situational Factors in Leadership. Opposed to those who argue for the trait or great man theories of leadership are those who emphasize the importance of the situation in influencing the person who becomes leader. Their viewpoint is also quite well documented.

The leader position shapes the leader. It is clear that sometimes when a person is pressed into becoming a leader as a result of a given situation, the leadership position itself induces him to adopt a leadership role. Group members do behave differently toward the person who is the leader: they communicate their expectations, reinforce his behavior, and in other ways enable him to further reinforce his occupancy of that role. We have already pointed out that members of a group speak more with a person of higher status, show him a certain deference, and change their opinions in the direction of his (see page 282) (Hurwitz, Zander, and Hymovitch, 1953). As a result, the person of higher status feels more confident, recognizes that he is looked up to by the others, usually enjoys this recognition, speaks more, and engages in more directive, influencing behavior (Zander and Cohen, 1955). It has also been demonstrated that a person who can be induced to speak more will be more apt to be viewed and designated as a leader (Bavelas et al., 1965). Thus, once in a position of leadership, a person tends to continue in that position. It is quite understandable that a study of squads of new navy recruits, in which the "acting petty officer" had been randomly assigned at the outset, found that this man tended to be retained in that position. As "acting petty officer," he handled very routine leadership tasks such as lining men up for roll call and leading them to the mess hall; later on, he was chosen by his fellow recruits as the one whom they wanted to lead them into combat (Bell and French, 1950). It may also be true that being a follower in a group for a prolonged period will make it especially difficult to move into the leadership position. During World War II, when the casualty rate for commissioned officers in the infantry was quite high, the U.S. army found it necessary to appoint enlisted men to "field commissions," suddenly promoting them to officer status. Experience soon indicated that these new lieutenants had to be transferred to other units to assume command, for they were having difficulty leading their former buddies.

Position in the communication and interdependence structure. Other group structural factors may also determine leadership. Studies of communication networks have clearly supported the finding that the person who is central in a communication network—the central figure in the "wheel," "Y," or "chain"—is especially apt to become the leader (Bavelas, 1950; Leavitt, 1951). That such centrality leads to leadership in real-life situations has been demonstrated in a study of communication networks among B-29 bomber crews (Kip-

Figure 9.4
Since it has been found that the central person in a communication network is apt to become a leader, and in baseball the catcher is most central, is it any wonder that Yogi Berra became manager of the New York Mets? Here he is shown talking with the Mets' pitchers Tom Seaver (left) and Jon Matlack (right). Since the pitcher changes with each game, it is not surprising that neither of these men succeeded to the manager's position. Berra was replaced in 1975 by Roy MacMillan, shortstop (also a central position).

nis, 1957) and among baseball teams (Grusky, 1963). The latter study focused on both the communication and interdependence network of teams on the field. The outfielders were found to be peripheral, in both their physical location and the amount of interaction they had with others. Infielders, by contrast, were found to be more central because they throw to and receive the ball from more players on the team. The catcher is especially central. The pitcher, though central in a given game, tends to be replaced from game to game. Who, then, would be most apt to become a field manager? Obviously the catcher, with other infielders (except the pitcher) also being strong candidates. The outfielders rarely move into team leadership position.

The effects of group size on leadership development. Leadership is also affected by the size of a group. In a two-person group, problems of coordination are less critical, communication may be free and easy, and although one person may speak more than the other, there is likely to be greater equality of participation. A three-person group is much more complex: there is a greater possibility of tension between two of the members that must be resolved by the third; there is a greater chance of disagreement; and so forth. A ten-person group is even more complex. Thus, as the size of the group increases, there is a greater probability that one or a few members will dominate while the others will become relatively silent (Carter et al., 1951; Bales et al., 1951). As a group becomes larger, there is a greater need for a leader, the demands on the leader become greater, and his influence over others increases (Hemphill, 1950).

Threat and leadership. "On a calm sea, every man is a pilot." This folk saying, taken from a beer coaster in a German hofbrauhaus, implies another important factor in leadership development—its converse, namely, that on a turbulent sea there can be only one pilot. There are numerous examples in history in which a leader whose position had been unstable gained strength because of a crisis. It is believed that Stalin was in an insecure position before Germany attacked the Soviet Union. Nasser offered to resign after Egypt's devastating defeat by Israel in the Six-Day War, but the defeat so threatened Egypt that the nation rallied behind its leader. Franklin D. Roosevelt was encouraged to assume greater power in the face of the severe depression of the 1930s. Earthquakes, floods, and other natural disasters, as well as serious threats to one's belief system, can also serve the same function: For example, the Seekers rallied around Mrs. Keech when their belief in the apocalypse was threatened (see page 19).

Robert L. Hamblin (1958) conducted a clever study of leadership in times of crisis. College students in groups of three were asked to play a modified version of shuffleboard. They were told that the game had a number of special rules, and they were asked to figure out these rules through a process of trial and error by trying out different procedures. Every time a score was made, a green light would flash on a board; whenever a rule was violated, a red light would flash. The groups were told that they were competing with high-school students who had taken part in the experiment earlier, and that both sets of scores would be posted at the end of each of the six playing periods (games). By the end of the third game, all of the groups had been given the fictitious impression that they were comfortably ahead of the high-school competitors.

For half of the groups, the rules remained the same throughout the six games. The other groups, however, were confronted with a "crisis" during the fourth, fifth, and sixth games in the form of sudden, unannounced changes in the rules. The procedures that had formerly produced scores were now illegal, and whenever the players learned one of the new rules, the rules were changed! The members of the crisis groups were thus unable to score at all in the last three games. Throughout the experiment, Hamblin kept track of two things: the relative frequency with which each of the three members of a group suggested a rule or a procedure for testing a rule (the "influence ratio") and the relative frequency with which these suggestions were accepted by the other two group members (the "acceptance ratio").

Hamblin found that during the last three game periods, the influence and acceptance ratios of those who were leaders in the crisis groups were far greater than of those who were leaders in the other groups. The presence of a crisis thus tended to highlight those characteristics associated with leadership. Those persons who had been influential before the crisis became even more so afterward; they made more suggestions, and more of these were accepted. Suggestions that might ordinarily have been challenged were accepted by the crisis groups without hesitation. Of course, there were limits to this crisis-induced leadership; if a leader proved incapable of dealing with the crisis after a reasonable time, he was usually replaced.

Other experimenters have reported similar findings. Earlier we cited the study of Dutch shopkeepers conducted by Mauk Mulder and Ad Stemerding (1963) (see page 124). These shopkeepers were faced with the threat of supermarket chains entering their community, and they were led to believe that this threat would be either very large or small. When the shopkeepers were subsequently asked how important they felt it was to have a strong leader who could champion their views, those who faced a large threat said more often that they wanted a strong leader than did those who faced only a small threat.

Just as an external crisis encourages the emergence of strong leadership, so does an internal upheaval. A group that is experiencing conflict among its members, a shift in ideology, sudden changes in membership, or the withdrawal of its leader is especially inclined to want and to look for a strong, directive leader—someone who can bring events under control. In a field study of this process, William H. Crockett (1955) examined the emergence of leadership in 72 business, governmental, and industrial groups. He found that those groups that faced an internal threat, in the form of conflicting goals among their members, were more apt to have strong leaders take charge than those groups whose members were in substantial agreement.

Trait versus Situational Factors in Leadership. Probably leadership cannot be explained on the basis of either traits alone or situational factors alone; rather, it is the interaction between these factors that must be considered in any analysis of leadership (Hollander and Julian, 1975). Even some of the data supporting traits *or* situational factors as an explanation can be reexamined from an interactionist position: Hitler's leadership traits almost certainly would not have manifested themselves if Germany had not faced serious economic and political problems after World War I. The leaders who emerged in the leaderless discussion groups showed certain leadership traits, but would these traits have become evident if the groups already had leaders? The "acting petty officers" in the navy became leaders because they had been appointed to their positions, but most of them were probably capable young men; after all, would a complete dolt have been able to continue his leadership after appointment?

Obviously some tasks require the special skills or abilities that only certain persons have: the head of a surveying team could not readily exchange positions with the head of a hospital's intensive care unit or the principal of an elementary school. As the situation faced by a group changes, in all likelihood so do the requirements of leadership. In *The Admirable Crichton,* an insightful comedy by James Barrie, a wealthy English family is shipwrecked on an island, together with their faithful and obedient butler, Crichton. The head of the household, a prominent London aristocrat, cannot cope with the basic requirements of leadership for survival on the island. The resourceful Crichton, however, comes forth and gradually assumes all the perquisites of leadership; he wins the family's admiration and the affection of the lord's daughter. On returning to London, the family resumes its former social structure, though not without some uneasiness and pain. Indeed, the only criticism we would make of the play is that the family's return to the status quo ante is a bit *too* simple to be believable (Barrie, 1903).

The interaction between personality traits and situational factors

*Figure 9.5
(Top) In the film,* The
Admirable Crichton
(1957), *the Edwardian
butler Crichton (Ken-
neth More) put every-
one to work when he
and his employers (a
British aristocratic fam-
ily) were shipwrecked
on a deserted, tropical
island. (Bottom) Back in
London again, Crichton
resumed his role as a
butler and refused to
acknowledge his island
experience to Lady
Brocklehurst (Martita
Hunt).*

in leadership cannot easily be disentangled. For a better under-standing of this interaction, we must first look at the functions that the leader serves for the group.

The Many Functions of Leadership

The functions of leadership are many and varied, depending upon the basic problems with which a group must deal; one analysis has listed 14 leadership functions (Krech, Crutchfield, and Ballachey, 1962). These pertain to the manner in which a group establishes and works toward its goals, the problems that arise in maintaining a cohesive and harmonious group, the provision of a common symbol with which group members can identify, and the way in which the group relates to other groups or individuals.

Helping to define and reach group goals. The leader may serve as a policy-maker, helping the group to establish its goals and define its tasks. Having done this, the leader may then formulate a plan that would enable the tasks to be completed and the goals reached. As an executive, the leader may coordinate the activities of the various group members in accordance with the over-all plan. As one with superior knowledge and a better view of the "big picture," the leader may serve as an expert in directing the group toward its goals.

Maintaining the group. During the course of the group's activities, there will inevitably be disagreements among the members, together with tensions and hostilities. The leader may be able to help reduce tensions, arbitrate differences, and generally maintain harmony in the group.

Providing a symbol for identification. Group members sometimes need a common symbol with which they can identify—a flag to rally around, a slogan, a symbol. The leader himself may serve as a symbol for the group. By identifying with the leader, the group can maintain its unity. The leader may also serve as an exemplar—a model that the group members may wish to emulate. Sigmund Freud considered this the primary function of the leader (Freud, 1922; Scheidlinger, 1952). It has also been suggested that the leader may serve as a scapegoat, one on whom personal and group failures may be blamed in order to prevent internally directed tensions.

Representing the group to others. The leader may also represent the group in its relationships with other groups or people; he may help to solve problems and tensions between groups and may help the group work with others toward common goals.

The Problem of Fulfilling Contradictory Functions. These leadership functions are quite varied and sometimes require contradictory skills—which may help account for the explicit differentiation of leadership functions in certain groups. At the national level in Great Britain, the government makes a clear distinction between the symbol and task functions of the nation's top leaders. Over the course of time, the symbol function has come to be assigned to the king or queen, while the prime minister performs more of the task functions. Thus, the monarch can remain an uncontroversial symbol, while the prime minister occasionally provokes disagreement and wrath.

One indication of the leader's importance in coordination and group maintenance can be seen in the study by Maier and Solem (1952) (see page 362). It was found that a group tended to end up with the wrong answer to the horse-trading problem if this wrong answer was initially given by the majority of the group. However, when leaders were assigned to the groups and instructed to facilitate the discussion without contributing anything toward the answer, a larger number of groups answered correctly. The improvement was due to the fact that the leaders managed to get the minority who had the correct answer to speak out. Thus, it can be seen that another important function of the leader is to stand against the tyranny of a majority group norm. Yet the leader must be able to accomplish this with diplomacy and finesse, particularly if he is dealing with an emotionally charged issue; otherwise, by encouraging minority expression, he might find himself rejected.

In his careful observational study of street gangs, William F. Whyte (Whyte, 1943) vividly illustrates the many functions of leaders. Doc and Sam, the leaders of two of the gangs, were at various times expected to make policy decisions, plan gang activities (going bowling, building a camp, waging "war" on rival gangs), and put these plans into operation—often by delegating responsibility to one or more "lieutenants." Although Doc and Sam were not necessarily the biggest or strongest gang members, they were good street fighters who were also expected to be experts at some activity that was important to the group, such as bowling or baseball. Doc and Sam were the gang members who were best known to the police, politicians, and racketeers; outsiders, therefore, had to deal with Doc and Sam in order to influence the gang's behavior. When fights broke out within the gangs, it was Doc and Sam (or one of their lieutenants) who eased things over and managed the reduction of conflict. Finally, it was the gang leaders, with their distinctive hairdos, insignia, and black leather jackets, who symbolized and exemplified the gangs and all that they stood for.

The Development and Maintenance of Leadership

The conflicting demands on a leader, due to the various functions that must be performed, undoubtedly pose problems for him. He is pressed to make changes, yet he must not be too different if he is to serve as an exemplar. He may try to be accepted and liked, yet he may have to order, criticize, and even punish group members. He may need to be dominant, active, and forceful, but then he may be rejected for being too "pushy." The conflicting demands on the leader vary, depending in part upon the way in which he attained leadership.

Emergent versus Appointed Leaders. A leader who is appointed to his position may have some advantages, provided that the members of the group view the appointing agency as legitimate. In that case, the appointed leader can relax, relatively secure in his position, and devote his attention to coordinating the group's activities and working toward its goal. On the other hand, an emergent leader who must win out over other contenders in order to establish his position may behave quite differently. He must be more active and aggressive to both achieve and maintain his position, and he may have to face the resentments and jealousies of other group members (Carter et al., 1951).

Attaining Leadership by Starting Strong. An emergent leader, then, must deal rather forcefully with what has been called the basic dilemma of leadership (Blau, 1964)—how to achieve power while maintaining the approval of others. He may try to cope with this problem sequentially. At the outset, he may behave very competitively, demonstrating his competence over others and emphasizing his expertise. On occasion he may use physical force, while at other times he may demonstrate his superiority at a valued group activity. The street gangs mentioned earlier participated in highly competitive bowling tournaments, which were sometimes used as a means for achieving leadership, together with street fighting (Whyte, 1943). The emergent leader may thus utilize some of the stronger power bases—coercion, reward, and expertise. Once he has established his position and his legitimacy, he can relax a bit. He can then rely more on referent influence and try to win back the support he may have lost in the process of gaining leadership—using his power of office to facilitate his new support (Blau, 1964).

Attaining Leadership by Following. Another way of securing leadership is illustrated in a study of nursery-school children conducted by Ferenc Merei (1949). Groups of three children were placed in separate rooms each day for three to six meetings. During this time, the groups developed various norms and traditions—who should sit where, who should play with what, sequences of games, and rituals. Once these traditions had been established, a potential leader was added to each group—a child, usually a bit older and bigger than the others, whose observed activity on the playground indicated that he tended to direct and influence others. How, then, would these children attempt to become leaders in these groups?

That these dominant children did attempt to gain leadership in the groups was obvious. It was also clear that in the groups with well-developed traditions, the dominant child proved weak. He would suggest a circle game but no one would follow him. He would begin to sing and try to get the others to join him. They would, briefly, but would then return to their usual games, leaving him to sing alone. Some of the dominant children persisted in their direct leadership attempts, but they were repeatedly rebuffed and frustrated. Those who became successful leaders developed a more subtle approach: they became *followers* at first; they carefully observed what the others were doing and joined in their activities. It was as if they knew the words of the legendary French commander whose troops joined the surging mobs in storming the Bastille: "I am their leader. I must follow them!"

Having established his group identity through conformity, the successful leader was then prepared to introduce innovations, but still within the basic traditions of the group. One leader wanted to play "hide and seek," but the group preferred to play its favorite game, "acting with hats." So the leader joined the group in the hat game, but gradually suggested innovations. For example, the child acting with the hat had to look the other way while the others hid, and then he had to find them (Merei, 1949).

By initial conformity, sometimes ultraconformity, the leader may establish his idiosyncrasy credit, which he can then use to introduce change—but only within the limits of group traditions. The issue of precisely when the leader starts strong and then seeks group acceptance, and when he first aims at acceptance before taking over, clearly deserves further exploration. One can speculate that in the nursery-school study, the aspiring leader was inhibited from using physical force because adult teachers were present. He was also faced with a group that had developed firm and clear traditions. In the case of the gang leaders, they may have established their membership at some previous time so that they felt little hesitation in using force to attain their positions of leadership.

Leadership Development in Interaction. A somewhat different approach to the study of leadership development appears in the studies of interaction process analysis conducted by Bales and his co-workers (Bales, 1950, 1970; Bales and Slater, 1955; Bales and Strodtbeck, 1951) (see page 268). A group is given a problem, such as solving a chess game or discussing a human relations case, and then the researcher carefully observes the group and records who speaks to whom and what type of communication is used (whether the person gives or asks for orientation, suggestions, or information; shows tension or tension release, agreement or disagreement, solidarity, or antagonism). Initially, the group typically focuses on problems relating to its assigned task: It determines what the goal is, makes plans for reaching it, and implements the plans. These task and goal activities correspond to the first major function of a leader, as described earlier; indeed, a member of the group typically emerges as the task-leader during this period. The task-leader, however, tends to pay a price for his ascendance since people don't ordinarily enjoy being directed, particularly by someone who is not an established, legitimate leader. The general fatigue of the task also reflects itself in tensions among the group members. Disagreements and hostilities mount. There comes a point at which the group can no longer work effectively on its task until the group's internal problems have been dealt with. At this time, then, the group makes an attempt to reduce tensions, resolve disagreements, and develop group harmony and cohesiveness. Communications begin to center in the socioemotional area. Thus, the second major function of leadership manifests itself, and indeed someone ordinarily does come forth—a socioemotional, or group-maintenance leader—to cope with the tensions. Once the internal problems have been eliminated, the group is ready to move again toward its goal, until further internal tensions arise.

Task-leaders and group-maintenance leaders. Although the differentiation between the task-leader and the group-maintenance leader is particularly clear in problem-solving groups that have specific goals, Bales has also observed a similar differentiation in groups such as therapy groups, where the external task is less obvious. In our dinner party example, the amount of conversation changed during the course of the evening, and some guests began to speak more than others. Charlie emerged as quite a conversationalist, the most active and dominant member of the group. But could one call him a task-leader? Since the guests had no explicit task to perform, it might seem ridiculous to think of Charlie as a task-leader. On the other hand, since the implicit goal of most middle-class dinner parties is to make conversation, and since Charlie certainly moved the group toward this goal, he could well be viewed as the task-leader. Not everybody was pleased with Charlie's dominant behavior, however. Joe began to take issue with him, and then the tension among the guests increased. At this point, the hostess intervened with a soothing remark and an anecdote or two. By serving as the maintenance specialist, she helped to restore harmony and smooth over the conflict, allowing the guests to relieve their tension and Charlie and Joe to speak civilly once more.

The fact that it was the hostess who served as group-maintenance leader makes sense, of course, because she must have felt responsible for keeping her guests happy. It might also be expected that it would be the hostess rather than the host who would assume this role, based on other evidence presented by Bales and his colleagues. Several studies of mixed-sex groups have shown that task-leaders tend to be men while group-maintenance leaders tend to be women; this has been demonstrated in both discussion groups and jury deliberations (Bales and Slater, 1955; Bales and Strodtbeck, 1951). Although the sex roles in our society are now changing dramatically, it has been suggested that role relations in groups are an extension of the roles played in the family. In the traditional family, it is the husband and father who tends to be most concerned with handling the family's external problems—with earning the money required for food and housing, with handling problems related to housing, taxes, moving, and so forth. The wife and mother tends to be most concerned with having a happy, harmonious family—the internal relations of the family.

The task-leader versus maintenance-leader distinction has also been demonstrated in a study of industrial settings conducted by Robert L. Kahn and Daniel Katz (1953). Their data were obtained from a series of standardized interviews with the workers and supervisors in a variety of businesses—an insurance company, a railroad section gang, an electric company, an automobile manufacturer, and so forth. Kahn and Katz found that, in general, the most productive companies had supervisors who performed both task and maintenance functions either by themselves or with others. These men spent more time planning and supervising their employees' work, as well as helping them to satisfy their needs. According to Kahn and Katz:

> The differentiated role of the supervisor apparently affects the productivity of the group in two ways. The attention given to planning has a direct effect upon output in the coordination and organization of the tasks of the group. This is a type of skill of an engineering or institutional sort, in that the technical know-how of the supervisor is brought to bear upon the ordering of the work of the group on a long-range basis. The second way in which the supervisor affects productivity is more indirect. He can increase or decrease the motivation of his employees to produce [p. 616].

Thus, the performance of both task and maintenance functions is not only a characteristic of many groups; it appears to be a prerequisite for effective group performance.

One leader, two, or many? We began by discussing the characteristics of a leader, which might imply that there can only be one such person in a group. However, the research by Bales and his co-workers showed that two leaders typically emerge in a group—a task-leader and a socioemotional leader. They found that these roles are usually performed by two different persons, although on occasion a "great man" may assume both roles. Other social psychologists, however, have suggested that the type of free discussion situations studied by Bales tended to encourage the separation of roles (Verba, 1961). In free discussion groups, leaders must emerge and assume their positions, and thus they may not be accorded legitimate power (this was the case with Charlie, who emerged in the dinner party group). Since ascendance of a task-leader in this way may be resented, the maintenance role must then be filled by another group member. In many real-life groups the leader is appointed or elected, or his rise to a position of authority is seen as proper for other reasons. If the group perceives his assumption of leadership as legitimate, it will have less resentment, and so the task-leader can also serve as the group-maintenance leader. This is frequently the case in industrial leadership (Kahn and Katz, 1953).

A further distinction should be made between groups where accomplishing a task (or reaching a goal) is of primary importance and those where the socioemotional relationship is the most important consideration. At the dinner party, obviously, the only thing that really mattered was friendly interaction. But even in a supposedly task-oriented group, there are times when the members are less concerned about their task than about their interpersonal relations (as, for example, at a poker party, judo class, bowling or bridge club). In one experiment, several groups were given a juvenile delinquency case to discuss. Although the goal was spelled out clearly, the observers noted considerable differences among the groups—some seemed to be primarily interested in reaching a group solution to the problem, whereas others were obviously more interested in socializing. It was found that the task-leader was clearly more disliked in the social-oriented groups; therefore, in those groups, a different socioemotional leader emerged. Since the task-leader was not resented in the task-oriented groups, he could serve as the group-maintenance leader as well (Burke, 1967). Furthermore, by suggesting to a group that it was not doing too well on its task, its task orientation could be increased and the task-leader accepted more warmly; however, if a group was led to believe that it was doing well on its task, then its social needs became more prominent and the task-leader was sometimes rejected (Burke, 1968).

We should also emphasize that, although there may be a tendency for one or two persons to assume more leadership than the others, leadership functions may be performed by many members of the group at various times. As we have seen, it is during periods of stress or other difficult times that leadership seems to become more centralized (Hamblin, 1958).

Leadership Style: The Behavior of Leaders

Regardless of whether the leader performs task functions, maintenance functions, or both, he invariably *influences* behavior. But how does he do this? Also, which methods of influence are most effective for the leader and the group, and which tend to encourage greater acceptance or rejection of the leader? A number of studies have been made of what has been called "leadership style" (the characteristic behavior of leaders), many of which may be fruitfully analyzed in terms of the six bases of power (see page 202).

What difference does it make if the leader relies on coercive power, reward power, legitimate power, expert power, referent power, or informational power? Coercive power tends to promote compliance with the leader's wishes so long as he is present, but noncompliance in his absence; it also encourages people to reject the leader. Expert power may promote greater influence by the leader, but it may also be accompanied by greater social distance and less reference. Referent power may produce a closer relationship between the leader and his followers, but it may also lessen the leader's expertise. Informational power may prove effective if the leader can present the information in a comprehensible and persuasive fashion, but this may require more time and may therefore be impractical when immediate action must be taken. We should expect the bases of power and their effectiveness to vary according to the leader's functional role and the group's situation. The task-leader may be more inclined to use legitimacy, expertise, and possibly reward and coercion; the group-maintenance leader may tend to use referent power.

In one particularly comprehensive study of social power in an industrial setting, Kurt Student (1968) asked the workers in a home-appliance factory to indicate the extent to which their supervisors utilized five bases of power (informational power was not included). He then related the attributed use of the five power bases to other variables. Student found that while legitimate power was cited most often as the reason for compliance with a supervisor's directives, its use was not significantly related to differences in the work performance of the various work groups. Expert power was the only power base whose use significantly reduced the workers' accident rate. Expert and referent power were related to less absenteeism and a higher quality of work. The supervisor who used referent power seemed to encourage the workers to make more suggestions for improving work procedures. The use of reward and coercive power, while sometimes influencing the workers, also produced unintended side effects, such as lower average earnings for a work group and higher maintenance costs. Thus, Student recommended that if a supervisor found it necessary to use legitimate, coercive, and reward power, he should temper these with the effective use of referent and expert power as well.

The number of possible combinations of the various bases of power is quite large—63 to be exact! In reality, however, these often appear together in clusters, so that there are actually far fewer combinations of leadership style.

Two leadership styles in Lord of the Flies. Two distinct leadership styles are exemplified by Ralph and Jack, two characters in William Golding's *Lord of the Flies* (1954). The novel begins on a deserted island, where a plane carrying a number of British boys has recently crashed. As the novel opens, one of the boys, Ralph, meets up with another, Piggy, and the two of them wander around in search of other survivors. (The only adult, the pilot, died in the crash.) Piggy and Ralph find a large sea shell (a conch), and Ralph blows into it, making a loud noise. The noise attracts the attention of the other boys on the island, who begin to gravitate toward its source. Soon many of the boys are huddled around Ralph and Piggy, who move among them exchanging names and comforting the smaller boys (the "littluns"). The group at this point is still in a state of disarray. The littluns are frightened and disheveled, and a leader has not yet really emerged. Suddenly out of the woods another group of boys appears, "marching approximately in step in two parallel lines and dressed in strangely eccentric clothing" (p. 16)—the uniform of choir boys. At the head of this group, dressed like the others but wearing a special cap with a gold badge, is the choir leader, Jack. "Where's the man with the trumpet?" Jack asks. "Isn't there a man here?" "No," Ralph replies, "we're having a meeting. Come and join in." Jack turns to the choir boys and shouts, "Choir! Stand still," and the two groups begin to mingle together (p. 17). Soon Ralph suggests:

"*Seems to me we ought to have a chief to decide things.*"
"*A chief! A chief!*"
"*I ought to be chief,*" *said Jack with simple arrogance,* "*because I'm chapter chorister and head boy. I can sing C sharp.*"
Another buzz.
"*Well then,*" *said Jack,* "*I—*"
He hesitated. The dark boy, Roger, stirred at last and spoke up.
"*Let's have a vote.*"
"*Yes!*"
"*Vote for chief!*"
"*Let's vote—*"

"Him with the shell."
"Ralph! Ralph!"
"Let him be chief with the trumpet-thing."
Ralph raised a hand for silence.
"All right. Who wants Jack for chief?"
With dreary obedience the choir raised their hands.
"Who wants me?"
Every hand outside the choir except Piggy's was raised immediately.
Then Piggy, too, raised his hand grudgingly into the air.
Ralph counted.
"I'm chief then" [p. 19].

Beginning with this initial victory for Ralph and defeat for Jack, the lines are drawn. As the novel progresses, Ralph and Jack continue to struggle for leadership, and eventually Jack prevails.

Without going into the details of their protracted struggle to assume and maintain control, let us examine some of the features of the two boys' leadership styles, for these styles are so different that no real sharing of leadership functions is possible. Jack is a lover of rules: "We'll have rules," he cries. "Lots of rules! Then when anyone breaks 'em—' " (p. 29). He thrives on being the expert—not only can he sing C sharp, he says, but he can hunt and kill; he "knows" things better than anyone else. Jack, moreover, is an expert in the use of promises and threats—coercive and reward power. If you come with me, he says in effect to the undecided boys, we will hunt and kill wild pigs, and I will provide you with plenty of fresh meat and lots of fun. But if you don't join with me, he insinuates, you will be left hungry, cold, and alone—and the strange "beasties" that lurk in the woods will come and get you. Jack, in other words, seems to be most comfortable when he is aloof and distant from his followers and when he is very much in charge.

Ralph's style is quite different. Far more than Jack, he is "one of the boys." He appears to care genuinely about the littluns. He shares many of their concerns and fears and is willing to talk about them in the presence of the others. In addition, though, he has ideas about reality and is willing to check these ideas out and share his findings with the rest of the group. Early in the novel, one of the littluns comes racing out of the woods crying about a "snake-thing" beastie he imagines he has seen. Ralph assures him that there is no beastie, but the littlun continues to be afraid. Then Jack seizes the conch:

"Ralph's right of course. There isn't a snake-thing. But if there was a snake we'd hunt it and kill it. We're going to hunt pigs to get meat for everybody. And we'll look for the snake too—"

"But there isn't a snake!"
"We'll make sure when we go hunting" [p. 32].

Jack learns quite early to play on the littluns' fears. He fosters the belief that there actually are beasties in the woods. Ralph, on the other hand, continually tries to allay the boys' fears by providing them with information about reality. There are no beasties, he points out, after leading a thorough search of the island. In order to increase their chances of being rescued, Ralph suggests that they build a fire on top of the mountain with lots of smoke. He suggests ways in which shelters and lavatories can be built, food and fresh water collected, and the fire kept going. Ralph, in short, is a provider of information. He attempts to exercise leadership by sharing his concerns and fears with the group, as well as by proposing ways in which those concerns and fears can be allayed.

What, then, are the constellations of power bases utilized by these two leaders? Jack seems to make consistent, though not exclusive, use of four bases of power: reward, coercion, expertise, and legitimacy. He tries to influence the others by saying, in effect: "Do what I ask because I am bigger and stronger than you; I can help you or hurt you; I know things that you don't (although I won't tell you what I know); and I have a right to ask these things of you because there are rules that give me the right to be chief. Do what I ask because I direct you to do so." Jack's main objective is to try to elicit compliance—to effect the changes that he considers necessary; he is less interested in being accepted by the others in the group. One might characterize Jack as as "directive" leader (Rogers, 1951; Gordon, 1955).

By contrast, Ralph seems to rely especially on referent and informational power. He says, in effect: "Do what I ask because you value our relationship, because I am fundamentally like you, as you are like me. But more important, do what I ask because what I am saying makes a lot of sense; if you look at the logic and information that I am giving you, I am confident that you will share my point of view as to what should be done." Ralph might be viewed as a "group-centered" leader (Rogers, 1951; Gordon, 1955).

Directive versus Group-centered Leadership Styles. The distinction we have drawn between directive and group-centered styles must be tempered by several considerations. For one thing, this distinction has been taken from a brief analysis of a work of fiction—the leaders are caricatures rather than real people. It is our belief, however, that the analysis rings true. We could just as easily have chosen other fictitious leaders, such as McMurphy and Big Nurse in Ken Kesey's *One Flew over the Cuckoo's Nest* (1962), or Aegistheus and Orestes in Sartre's play *The Flies* (1955), or we could have selected leaders in the real world as our examples. An issue of greater concern is the fact that we have portrayed two ideal types here—extreme cases that do not correspond precisely to the variety of leadership styles one can observe every day. A directive leader may sometimes invoke referent and/or informational power in order to achieve his ends. Similarly, a group-centered leader may sometimes employ reward, coercive, expert, and/or legitimate power. The world is not as neatly organized as our dichotomy suggests. Nevertheless, if you take any leader (a politician, scoutmaster, or university president) and analyze his style in terms of the six bases of power, we believe you will often find one or the other of these two distinct leadership profiles.

Further support for these two leadership styles comes from an Olympian study of leadership conducted at Ohio State University in 1950 (Hemphill, 1950). Using ratings of a leader's behavior in a number of leadership situations, more than 1000 different behavior categories were established. However, when these were subjected to factor analysis using sophisticated correlational techniques (Halpin and Winer, 1952), it turned out that four basic clusters were able to account for the 1000 behavior categories. Two of these clusters were responsible for more than 83 percent of the items, and these corresponded quite closely to the directive versus group-centered distinction. *Group-centered* behaviors (called "consideration") included such things as concern about the warmth of personal relationships, mutual trust, a willingness to listen to subordinates, and encouragement of participation. *Directive* behaviors (called "initiating structure") included making sure that the leader's role in the group was understood, asking the group to follow standard operating procedures, maintaining definite standards of performance, assigning group members to particular tasks, and making the leader's attitude clear to the group. The remaining two clusters were called "production emphasis" and "social awareness." However, it seems clear that if we want to describe how leaders behave, we should see how directive or group-centered they are. We might also mention that, following the original Bales studies, the leaders who scored high on group-centered behaviors tended to be liked better (Hemphill, 1950).

The Leader's Assumptions about the Nature of Man. Assuming that the leader has various means available for influencing the members of his group, what motivates him to select certain bases of power in preference to others? Although there is no clear-cut answer to this question, one particularly insightful analysis has been offered by the industrial social psychologist Douglas McGregor (1960). He argued that "behind every managerial decision or action are assumptions about human nature and human behavior," and that a leader tends to behave in accordance with these assumptions. One assumption (called "Theory X" by McGregor) is that (1) the average person dislikes work and will avoid it if he can; (2) therefore, in order for him to work effectively, he must be controlled, coerced, directed, and threatened with punishment; (3) the average person, in fact, really does not want responsibility, but would rather have security and direction. Leaders who adhere to Theory X tend to be more directive in their behavior. Their approach typifies traditional management principles in industry, such as those set forth in one of the early "bibles" of industrial management (Taylor, 1911).

By contrast, another assumption (called "Theory Y" by McGregor) is that (1) work is as natural as play or rest; (2) external control and the threat of coercion are not the only means of influence; (3) a person's commitment to his work is directly related to the rewards that he expects to receive from the work itself (both material and psychological); (4) the average person is creative and can accept responsibility when this is encouraged; (5) many people have the capacity for imagination and creativity, and not just a few leaders; (6) the full potentialities of the average person are only partially utilized in most work situations. Theory Y is more consistent with the views of most social scientists and modern industrial relations specialists. It is characteristic of the group-oriented approach to leadership.

McGregor's analysis has not yet been fully tested, but it has an intuitive appeal that provides a point of departure for analyzing preferences in leadership style. Examples of Theory X in operation are obvious; most businesses and industries seem to follow these traditional views about the nature of man. Far less common are industrial settings in which the assumptions of Theory Y are put into practice. One notable exception is the Scanlon Plan (Lesieur, 1958), a procedure that appears to encourage a Theory Y leadership style through the introduction of structural changes in the distribution of power and rewards. As Harold J. Leavitt (1965) pointed out, this plan has two distinctive features: besides their standard pay, the workers receive bonuses in proportion to the company's over-all improvement in productivity and efficiency; and the workers' ideas and grievances are regularly taken into account in "work-improvement" committees that cut across the various hierarchical levels—the workers meet not only with other workers from the same section, but with workers from other parts of the plant, foremen, supervisors, and executives. A number of companies have tried to implement the Scanlon Plan and the results have typically been favorable. There have been over-all productivity increases, and the internal relations among the workers—as well as between the workers and the supervisors—have improved dramatically.

Leadership and Group Performance

Democratic, Authoritarian, and Laissez-faire Leadership. One of the earliest and most influential studies of the effects of leadership style was conducted by Kurt Lewin, Ronald Lippitt, and Ralph K. White in 1939. The experimenters organized groups of 10-year-old boys into "clubs" and exposed each club to three different leadership styles: authoritarian, democratic, and laissez-faire. The leaders were adults who had been selected and trained by the experimenters to exercise the three leadership styles. The *authoritarian* leaders were told to make all of the decisions pertaining to group activities by themselves; they were to keep the group uninformed about many matters, to remain aloof from active participation, and to give praise and criticism without explaining their reasons. The *democratic* leaders were instructed to make decisions and policies in collaboration with the group, through the process of group discussion; they were to be friendly, "regular" group members; they were encouraged to help the group establish long-range goals; and they were to "communicate in an objective, fact-minded way the bases for . . . praise and criticism of individual and group activities." Finally, the *laissez-faire* leaders were instructed to assume a friendly but passive posture; they were not to make any suggestions or to evaluate individual or group behavior positively or negatively.

The clubs met once a week for several months; during that time the clubs were exposed to all three leadership styles. During each meeting the behavior of the boys was observed, interviews were conducted with the boys as well as with their parents, and several group "crises" were created—in order to observe the group's reactions to stress. One of these crises consisted of the leader arriving late; another consisted of the leader suddenly being called out of the room for no clear reason.

Lewin, Lippitt, and White found that the leaders varied in their behavior as expected. The authoritarian leaders barked orders at the group ("Get your work aprons on. Today we've got to paint and letter the sign"), and they gave nonobjective praise and criticism ("No, you can't make it like that. That isn't a good job at all"). The democratic leaders tended to give guiding suggestions and information ("Did you ever try going the other way—with the grain?" "That's a knife sharpener so you can have sharp knives to carve wood with"), and they engaged in what the experimenters described as "jovial and confiding" behavior, behavior that communicated that the leaders liked the boys and felt like members of the group themselves. Finally, the laissez-faire leaders did not interact with the group unless they received direct requests for information, which they provided in a friendly way.

With respect to the way in which the groups functioned after having been exposed to these three styles (or social atmospheres), Lewin, Lippitt, and White found that the groups with the democratic leaders were the most effective and efficient. The members seemed to be group-minded and friendly. For example, they exchanged mutual praise, seemed ready to share group property, and used the pronoun "we" (rather than "I") more frequently than did the other groups. The groups with the democratic leaders were also very productive, completing lots of high-quality work although, interestingly, they were not always as productive as the authoritarian groups. The groups with the authoritarian leaders tended to display hostility and aggression toward either the leader or a scapegoat for the leader, and the atmosphere of the groups was strained and tense. The members of these groups were exceedingly dependent upon the leader and continually demanded his attention. When a crisis arose because of the leader's absence, the authoritarian groups simply could not function. When the leader was present, these groups accomplished more than the democratic groups, but when he left the room, these groups just stopped working (by contrast, in a similar situation, the democratic groups continued to work productively). Thus, it appears that the authoritarian group members complied with influence attempts, while the democratic group members internalized them. Of the three leadership styles, the least productive was the laissez-faire. The groups with the laissez-faire leaders engaged in lots of horse play and were friendly with the leaders, but when the boys were interviewed, they said that they preferred the democratic leaders.

Notice that the authoritarian style corresponds to the constellation of social power that we have called "directive" (using reward, coercive, expert, and legitimate power). This style led to compliance with influence, but only so long as the leader was there to maintain surveillance over the group. The democratic style, which relies upon informational and referent power, resembles the group-centered orientation; the results of this style were both compliance and internalization. The group could still function even though the leader was not there. The laissez-faire style finally, does not correspond to either the directive or the group-centered style. It seems to be a special case, utilizing referent power almost exclusively. In real life, the laissez-faire style probably does not occur as often as the other two and is therefore of lesser importance.

Other studies of authoritarianism in leadership. Following the pioneering work of Lewin, Lippitt, and White, a number of other researchers have studied the effects of leadership style, and their findings have generally supported the ones described above. Instead of experimentally manipulating leadership style, some researchers have varied the group communication structure (see page 270) and have found that highly centralized structures (the wheel) result in greater productivity, but also greater dissatisfaction, than less centralized structures (the circle). Other experimenters have attempted to study the effects of leadership style by selecting leaders who either have or do not have authoritarian personalities. William Haythorn (1956), for example, asked four-man groups to watch a film dealing with a human relations problem and then discuss it. The men had previously been tested on a scale designed to measure authoritarianism (the F-scale, developed by Adorno et al., 1950); one in each group who had scored either high in authoritarianism (high-F) or low (low-F) was appointed as leader. The mens' behavior was observed as they discussed the problem in each group. Haythorn found that the high-F leaders demonstrated less egalitarian behavior than the low-F leaders, were less concerned about group approval, and were less sensitive to the needs of the group. The group members with a high-F leader were less likely to express differences of opinion, to influence the group process, or to develop an informal working arrangement than those with a low-F leader.

Fiedler's Contingency Model of Leadership Effectiveness. The results of a wide variety of experiments seem to indicate that a group-centered leader is generally more apt to elicit effective group performance than a directive one. Yet, as we shall see, the picture is much more complex. As soon as one begins to look more closely at a group interacting with its leader, it turns out that the directive leaders are more effective in certain circumstances while the group-centered leaders are more effective in others.

It is always gratifying to a scientist when he can develop a theory and hypotheses, test these hypotheses with a careful research design, and then find that his theory and expectations are supported. Occasionally, however, entire research programs have been established because of results that turned out to be completely contrary to the hypotheses. One example was Asch's line-judgment studies (see page 317). Another is the series of leadership studies initiated by the clinical psychologist Fred Fiedler, who began with a McGregor-like Theory Y model, then switched to a Theory X model, and finally ended up with a Theory XY model of leadership.

From his experience and research in clinical psychology, Fiedler had found that reputedly effective psychotherapists tended to see their patients as similar to themselves, whereas the less effective therapists tended to see their patients as different and thus were less accepting of them (Fiedler, 1951). The same factors, he believed, might also apply to effective leadership. All leaders, good or bad, would appreciate their most effective group members, and the leaders would view them as similar to themselves. But what about the least effective group members? Good leaders, he thought, would feel that their "least preferred co-workers" were really decent people at heart and not actually that different, so that with a little patience and understanding they would improve. Fiedler believed that bad leaders, like poor therapists, would have little patience with ineffective group members and would, therefore, view them as basically different and as generally unattractive people. Thus, the potential value of these members would be lost, and the group would be less effective. This expectation would fit rather well with the findings of the many human-relations-oriented studies suggesting that warm, accepting supervisors tend to have more effective work groups (see, for example, Likert, 1961).

The leader's evaluation of his "least preferred co-worker." Using a simple rating scale, Fiedler categorized leaders as having either a task-oriented (directive) style or a relationship-oriented (group-centered) style. The leader was asked to think of all of the people with whom he had ever worked and to describe the one person with whom he had worked least well. The leader who provided a favorable description of this "least preferred co-worker" (LPC) was viewed as being primarily interested in maintaining good relations with group members and was classified as relationship-oriented. On the other hand, the leader who described the LPC in unfavorable terms was classified as task-oriented.

Fiedler first tested his hypotheses on 14 high-school basketball teams, obtaining measures of how the team captain perceived his best and worst team members and then relating these to the number of games won. To his astonishment, the results were the reverse of his predictions. The warm, accepting captains, who rated even their least preferred players as being essentially good men (although recognizing that their game needed improvement), had teams with the worst records, whereas the less-accepting captains had the winning teams. Was there something peculiar about basketball teams? Fiedler then tested the same hypotheses with surveying teams; he measured the errors made in surveying and related these to the perceptions of the crew leaders. Again the results contradicted the expectations. Then Fiedler tested work teams working in open-hearth furnaces, and again he obtained similar results. Fiedler became increasingly convinced that his original theory was completely wrong. Contrary to what human-relations-oriented researchers had proposed, it appeared that the leader who showed the least consideration, who had no use for the ineffective group member, and who was mainly interested in getting the task done was the most effective.

Fiedler revised his theory and hypotheses, and decided to study the effectiveness of B-29 bomber crews during bombing practice, army tank crews during gunnery practice, and antiaircraft artillery squads. The results of these studies proved to be somewhat more complex. In those cases where the leader had a good relationship with his key-man (for example, the gunner on the tank gunnery crew), the "directive" leader was more effective. But in those cases where the leader did not have a good relationship with the key-man, the "group-centered" leader was more effective. These mixed results, which were repeated in several subsequent studies, led Fiedler back to the drawing board to develop another and somewhat more complex theory.

When are group-centered leaders more or less effective than directive leaders? The revised theory focuses on the behavioral orientation of the directive and the group-centered leader. The directive leader is primarily concerned about completing the group task, especially when the going is rough. His self-esteem is bound up with getting the group's job done and done well. However, when things seem to be going smoothly, he will turn his attention to developing good relations with his co-workers since he feels that this will also help him get the job done in the long run. By contrast, the group-centered leader, although also aware that the group task must be accomplished, gets his major personal satisfaction from being accepted and liked by his co-workers; therefore, he is primarily interested in good interpersonal relations, especially when the group situation is difficult. However, when things are going well with the group, he may be even less interested than usual in the task since (presumably) that is being well handled. At that time the group-centered leader will strive for admiration and prominence—to put himself forward as a great leader. Thus, the behavior of group-centered and directive leaders differs, depending upon the difficulty of leading the group.

Three major factors make the leader's role more or less difficult, thereby affecting the ease with which he can influence the group: The most important is the *leader's relationship with the members.* Do the members like, trust, and respect him or not? The second is the *task structure of the group.* Is the task structured or is it vague? Can a correct decision be verified? Are the goals of the group clearly stated? Can the task be completed using a variety of procedures? Is there more than one correct solution to a problem? The third factor is the *power of the leader.* Does he have legitimate authority over the group? Does he have the power to impose rewards and sanctions? Together these three factors determine whether the group situation will be favorable or unfavorable for the leader. Thus, according to Fiedler, the leader's job in trying to influence the members of his group will be easiest when: he has a positive and friendly working relationship with the members, when the group task is highly structured and unambiguous, and when the leader's position (legiti-

Figure 9.6
Which type of leader
(directive or group-cen-
tered) would probably
be more effective with a
heterogeneous group of
soldiers, such as this
U.N. force (this page)?
With a homogeneous
group, such as these
American troops (op-
posite page)?

macy, expertise, ability to mediate rewards and punishments, and so forth) is strongest.

Whether the directive leader or group-centered leader will be more effective, according to Fiedler's contingency theory, depends upon how difficult the leader's job is. The controlling, managing, directive leader will perform best under either the *most* favorable conditions or the *least* favorable conditions—when his relationship with the group, the structure of the task, and his power position are either very good and easy *or* very poor and difficult. The permissive, considerate, more passive leader will perform best under moderate conditions—when his situation with the group is neither very easy nor very difficult.

The rationale for this theory requires careful attention. (1) Under extremely unfavorable, difficult conditions (such as a highly ambiguous group task), the group-centered leader reacts characteristically by trying to smooth over any interpersonal problems. However, in such circumstances, the group may be more task-oriented—it may be more willing to overlook interpersonal conflicts for the time being in

order to concentrate on the job at hand. By contrast, the directive, task-oriented leader provides more of what the group needs under such unfavorable conditions; he concentrates on the task and relegates interpersonal problems to second place for the moment. (2) When the leader is confronted with moderately favorable or unfavorable conditions (for example, a moderately ambiguous or difficult group task), interpersonal friction may become more of a problem. When the group members are not sufficiently threatened or challenged by a task at hand, they have no incentive to subdue their interpersonal problems or to look up to a strong leader. Thus, under moderate conditions, the group-centered leader can respond more directly to the immediate needs of the group. (3) When conditions are extremely favorable (a relatively simple group task, for example), the directive leader will relax and mend his fences; he will try to make up for any shortcomings in his relationship with the group members. At that time the group can operate even more smoothly and effectively. Since the group-centered leader already has a good relationship with his group and doesn't feel he needs to worry too much about the task (since that is being accomplished anyway), he concentrates on a self-enhancing role—he begins to act like a "leader," tries to demonstrate his expertise, and tries to achieve prominence in the group. By doing this, he may lose some of the goodwill that he had established and he may neglect the task. In this way, the group-centered leader proves to be less effective in the favorable situation than the directive leader (Fiedler, 1971).

Evidence for the contingency model. The rationale for Fiedler's contingency model may seem a bit forced. Although there is evidence of different types of behavior on the part of the two types of leaders, as a function of situation difficulty, that evidence is not conclusive. However, there is an impressive array of support for the contingency model—demonstrating that the directive leader performs most effectively under extremely difficult and extremely easy situations, but that the group-centered leader functions best in moderate situations.

In one study, undergraduate students in a psychology class were divided into groups of four in order to conduct a series of ten animal-learning experiments as part of their course requirement. In each group, a student who had been rated as group-centered or directive on Fiedler's "least preferred co-worker test" was appointed as leader. The leader's job was to assign tasks, supervise the work, conduct a discussion, and write up a final report. Nine of the ten assignments were strictly routine in nature. The tenth one, however, was designed to be stressful: the students were required to complete this exercise without the benefit of their lab manuals and in less time than usual. It was found that the style of the leader did not affect the groups' behavior when they were doing routine assignments. But when the groups were given the stress problem, those that had a directive leader performed better than those that had a group-centered one. Why? It appears that the conditions of stress motivated the group to orient itself toward completing its assignment; these conditions, therefore, favored the directive style of leadership, as predicted by the contingency model (Sample and Wilson, 1965).

In another test of Fiedler's contingency theory, five-person groups were given three problems to solve, each of which had one or more possible solutions. A leader was appointed for each group and was instructed to behave in either a directive or a nondirective way. The experimenters found that the groups were more successful in solving the problems when they had a directive leader and when the problems were highly structured, that is, when they had a single solution. Thus, when a group was given a problem with a single solution (a condition highly favorable for the leader), the directive leader was more effective than the nondirective leader (Shaw and Blum, 1964).

Another study was conducted on a military base, with the members of 55 field artillery sections serving as subjects. Many measures were obtained from the leaders of these groups, including their feelings of acceptance by their section, the amount of training they had received, and their ratings on the "least preferred co-worker" scale. It had been expected that the various tasks of an artillery crew would seem highly structured to a trained leader, but would seem relatively unstructured to an untrained one. Thus, in this study the researchers had an opportunity to see how the leader's relationship with his group and the task structure are related to leadership style and group performance. (Fiedler's third factor, position power, is obviously constant and high in the military.) It was found that when the group situation was either favorable (when there were trained leaders who felt that they were accepted by the group) or unfavorable (when there were untrained leaders who felt inadequate), the directive leaders performed best. On the other hand, when the conditions were moderately favorable (when there were trained leaders who felt inadequate), the group-centered leaders turned out to be more effective (Csoka and Fiedler, 1972).

As Fiedler (1973) has observed, "It makes no sense to speak of a good leader or a poor leader. There are only leaders who perform well in one situation but not well in another" (p. 26). To be effective, a leader must adapt his style to the needs of the group. He must learn which kinds of groups are well suited to his own idiosyncratic style and which ones are not. The directive leader who can be most effective when the group conditions are either extremely favorable or unfavorable to a task-orientation may be at a total loss when the conditions are less clear-cut. Conversely, the group-centered leader who can perform so well when the group conditions are moderate may be totally ineffective under obviously favorable or unfavorable circumstances.

Can We Make Leaders More Effective? In summarizing his research, Fiedler has addressed himself to the crucial question: What can be done to make a leader more effective? Leadership-training programs have had different premises about how to improve leader effectiveness. Earlier in this century (Taylor, 1911), such programs emphasized the directive (Theory X) approach: Leaders were instructed how to plan work schedules, how to recommend raises and influence workers by means of work ratings, and how to maintain their distance and thus their respect. There was little subsequent evidence that these training programs had made any difference in leader effectiveness.

More recent leadership-training programs have emphasized sensitivity and a concern for the workers, following the group-centered

(Theory Y) approach. Workshops have been held throughout the country, bringing together various kinds of leaders—supervisors, administrators, and foremen. Often those who have planned these workshops have followed this approach themselves; they have demonstrated a democratic or even a laissez-faire attitude. The participants have been encouraged to express themselves completely and openly, in the hope that they would thus become more sensitive and accepting of one another, of themselves, and of other people. The participants have had considerable praise for the way in which the workshops have enabled them to change their own personalities as well as their relationships with their superiors and subordinates. However, it is not clear whether there has been any improvement in the productivity of the leaders' work groups or organizations (Dunnette and Campbell, 1968; House, 1967). One training program that was geared to the group-centered approach demonstrated successful results for several weeks after the supervisors returned to their jobs, but the supervisors eventually reverted to their earlier patterns of behavior (Fleishman, Harris, and Burtt, 1955). As psychotherapists have long known, it is extremely difficult to change an individual's basic personality characteristics and social habits, especially when there have been no accompanying changes in the usual environment—his family, his social group, and his work situation—to which he returns (Fiedler, 1973).

Fiedler (1971) has suggested that his contingency model could be used to improve leadership training and to effect change as follows: (1) One could increase the leader's position of power by improving his prestige or authority or reduce it by establishing new communication lines between the group members and the top supervisors. (2) One could alter the task structure; it would become easier if the task were made clear-cut, or it would become difficult if the task carried only general instructions. (3) One could alter the leader-member relations by making the group more heterogeneous or homogeneous, or by shifting around the more "difficult" members. These changes in the leader's position could be engineered according to the leader's personality. The training program for the leader could be designed to increase his knowledge of the job and thus give him more expert power over the work group. Again, it must be remembered that the experience and training that would help to make one supervisor more effective might make another supervisor less effective.

Applying this contingency model in order to improve leader effectiveness is certainly an intriguing possibility. However, many of the technical aspects of implementation have not yet been considered; this approach to leadership improvement remains to be fully tested.

SUMMARY

Intuitively one might expect a group to function more effectively than a person alone; thus, if a problem exists for which there is only one correct answer, simple probability suggests that the greater the number of people present, the greater the likelihood that at least one of them will have that answer. In reality, however, groups are not always superior to individuals. A group is characterized by the nature of the interaction among its members, and sometimes the best solution to a problem may be lost in this sea of interaction. Furthermore, a group may establish norms that subject its members to conflicting forces, and these may lead to a group decision that is less than optimal. The studies of deindividuation and bystander intervention discussed in Chapter 8, for example, suggest that group norms may encourage group members to deal less morally with a problem when they are together than when they are alone.

Just as individuals vary in their effectiveness, so do small groups. Among the more important factors influencing the effectiveness of a group's performance are: the extent to which group members accept common group goals (in general, the greater the acceptance of common goals, the greater the group's effectiveness); the group's ability to divide its task so that individual members can fully utilize their special talents; the group's communication and status structure (in an effectively functioning group, these are fitted to the competencies of its members as well as the type of problem the group wishes to solve); group size (in an effective group, the size is optimal for the amount of information and participation required to make a particular group decision); group heterogeneity (groups whose members have diverse backgrounds are generally better at solving complex problems, whereas more homogeneous groups are generally better at solving simple problems); group cohesiveness, which often—but not always—leads to more effective, creative, and productive group behavior; and finally, a group's leadership.

A leader may be defined as someone who occupies a key position in a group, influences others in accordance with the role expectation for that position, and coordinates and directs the group in maintaining itself and working toward its goals. Some group tasks obviously require the special traits and abilities that only certain persons possess, while other tasks are structured in such a way that situational factors will determine who will emerge as leaders. Thus, leadership probably cannot be explained on the basis of either traits alone or situational factors alone; rather, it must be understood in terms of their interaction.

Leadership functions include (among other things) establishing group goals and tasks, maintaining harmony within the group, serving as a symbol or object of identification for the group, and representing the group in its dealings with other groups or individuals.

These functions sometimes require contradictory skills, which may help to explain the explicit differentiation of leadership functions in some groups.

Regardless of his functions, the leader will invariably influence the behavior of the group in certain ways that characterize his leadership style. Two of these styles—directive and group-centered—appear to be quite common. With reference to our discussion of social influence in Chapter 6, a directive leader makes consistent, though not exclusive, use of four bases of power—reward, coercion, expertise, and legitimacy; a group-centered leader, on the other hand, tends to rely especially on the use of referent and informational power.

Although the results of a number of experiments indicate that a group-centered leader is generally apt to elicit more effective group performance than a directive one, the situation is actually much more complex. Fred E. Fiedler has developed a contingency model of leader effectiveness which asserts that the effectiveness of a directive or group-centered leader seems to vary according to the difficulty of the leader's job. He finds that the directive leader appears to be more effective under both the most favorable and the least favorable circumstances—when the leader's relationship with the group, his power position, and the group's task are either extremely easy *or* extremely difficult for him; the group-centered leader, on the other hand, appears to be more effective under moderate circumstances—when the group situation is neither very easy nor very difficult for him. Thus, to be effective, the leader must adjust his behavioral style to the particular circumstances of the group.

In the three preceding chapters we examined the inner workings of the group. Let us now turn our attention outward and see how a group deals with other groups. How do groups that are in conflict with one another make decisions? How does intergroup conflict develop and perpetuate itself? Finally, what contributions can social psychologists make toward the reduction of intergroup and international tensions? These questions and others will be addressed in the last chapter, Chapter 10.

**Small-Group Research and Its Relevance for
    International Tensions**
Generalizing from Interpersonal to International
    Conflict
Small-Group Decisions Affect International Affairs

How Groups in Conflict Make Decisions
Groupthink
The Nixon Group and the Watergate Affair

The Development of Intergroup Conflict
Studying Intergroup Conflict—Some Pertinent Questions
Field Experimental Studies of Intergroup Conflict
Development and Escalation of Conflict
Competitive and Hostile Conflict: Escalation of
    Conflict between Nations

Reducing Intergroup Conflict
Reducing Tension and Hostility in the Sherif Field
    Experiments
Reducing Conflict between Groups, Organizations,
    and Nations
The GRIT Proposal for De-escalating
    International Conflict

The Threat. If a 20-megaton nuclear bomb were dropped on midtown Manhattan, a person standing outdoors 60 miles away would see a fireball 30 times brighter than the noonday sun, a fireball that would rapidly expand to a diameter of 4½ miles. The heat would burn the clothing of an observer 21 miles away and sear the uncovered skin of someone 31 miles away. An intense wave of pressure, traveling faster than sound, would spread out from the epicenter, crushing to splinters everything within 7.7 miles and severely damaging any objects up to 15 miles. Within hundreds of miles, few could escape the hazards of extreme heat; immediate nuclear radiation; or the effects of the blast, firestorm, and fallout. Millions would die in the holocaust. Those who survived throughout the nation would experience long-lasting and severe economic and social disruption far beyond our present comprehension (Scientists' Committee, 1962). Would the survivors be compensated by the knowledge that the nation that was believed to have been responsible for the attack might have one of its major cities destroyed by a 30-megaton bomb?

As early as 1960, it was definitely known that several adversary nations had a number of 20-megaton bombs in their nuclear stockpiles as well as quite a few larger bombs. Since that date the number has obviously increased, and other nations have also acquired nuclear weapons. Now there are even more sophisticated weapons available in untold numbers: biological weapons that can produce tularemia (a deadly disease transmitted by rodents), botulism, and various psychic and neurologic illnesses; and geophysical weapons that would allow an enemy to trigger earthquakes, create tidal waves, redistribute the Antarctic ice cap, and destroy the protective ozone layer, thereby permitting the sun's ultraviolet rays to destroy directly or indirectly life upon this planet (Perrucci and Pilisuk, 1971).

The threat of a deliberate all-out nuclear war seems less likely today than it had been in the early 1960s, although it is not clear to what extent the reduced threat is real or is due to a psychological defense mechanism. In any event, the stockpiling of weapons and the development of increasingly sophisticated delivery systems continues. In May 1972, Soviet and American representatives met to negotiate a Strategic Arms Limitation Treaty. After considerable haggling, they finally signed an agreement to limit the development of *defensive* weapons, especially antiballistic missiles. They hedged on an agreement to limit offensive weapons. It would appear that, with present technology, it is far more costly and difficult to develop defensive weapons. With large areas of land and people to protect, a huge number of defensive devices would be needed; therefore, it would be much more difficult to keep them secret. Conceivably, the negotiators felt that a deterrent force would be more effective in forestalling war than an equivalent defensive force. Discussions on limiting offensive weapons continued for several years. In November 1974, President Gerald Ford and Prime Minister Leonid Brezhnev met in Vladivostok and agreed on some basic principles for a nuclear arms accord, limiting each nation to no more than 2400 heavy bombers, 1320 missiles with nuclear warheads, and a large array of offensive support weapons. Those who had hoped for greater control of offensive weapons were deeply disappointed and discouraged (Gelb, 1975).

The Dangers in Defensive Strategy. Some strategists have argued that war would be more likely to ensue from developing defensive, as opposed to offensive, strategies. This argument takes the following form: First, given the necessity of protecting an entire nation, a much larger force would be required for defense, including the protection of civilians. Secondly, such an expenditure of energy and resources could produce dissonance and a need to justify the purpose. In the late 1950s, the U.S. Office of Civil Defense, with the President's support, encouraged Americans to take a more active part in civil defense. Specifically, citizens were urged to build bomb shelters as "minimal insurance" against the "unlikely" event of nuclear war. A group of prominent social scientists discussed the implications of the civil defense program and concluded that the program would probably increase people's fear of attack from an enemy nation and consequently increase their attribution of evil intent to that nation. Some social scientists relied upon dissonance theory: A person who invests his time and resources in building an expensive and elaborate bomb shelter may reduce his dissonance by adding cognitive elements—the attribution of evil intent to the enemy, the perceived probability of a disastrous sneak attack, and the knowledge that his shelter would provide protection—which would help him justify his investment in the bomb shelter (Waskow, 1962). These social scientists did not present clear empirical evidence to support their application of dissonance theory to the bomb shelter effects. However, data from a national survey did indicate that the President's appeal for bomb shelters and other civil defense measures was interpreted by people to mean that there was a clear and present danger of nuclear war; otherwise, they couldn't see why the President would issue such a strong appeal (Withey, 1962). The call for bomb shelters suggested that negotiations with the Soviet Union were failing (Waskow, 1962). If at any time Americans are convinced that we are facing an implacable enemy, then the government's ability to negotiate peace may be seriously hampered. In fact, during the 1950s and 1960s a number of previously popular legislators were attacked as being "soft on Communism" and were defeated. While people were being urged to prepare for the possibility of all-out nuclear war, there is good reason to believe that such preparation, whether necessary or not, served to increase international distrust and hostility, thereby making peace negotiations much more difficult.

We will not attempt to document the astronomical costs of war preparations in the United States and elsewhere. Whatever these costs have been since the end of World War II, they are infinitesimal when compared to what the costs of a nuclear war would be. In a world in which there is still widespread hunger and death from natural causes, where the standard of living among a large proportion of the world's population is still at a bare subsistence level or below, the diversion of resources toward destructive ends is all the more dismaying. A number of social scientists have addressed themselves to the problem of world conflict and attempted to study how tensions among groups and nations could be eased.

SMALL-GROUP RESEARCH AND ITS RELEVANCE FOR INTERNATIONAL TENSIONS

Initially one might think that the problems of international war and peace belong only to the provinces of political science and international relations, and indeed most of the research and literature on the subject has been written from these perspectives. A good case can be made, however, for applying research and theory from the social psychology of the small group toward an understanding and resolution of international tensions.

Generalizing from Interpersonal to International Conflict

Some social psychologists have attempted a direct application of the evidence from interpersonal conflict to international conflict. Research on two-person games, such as the Prisoner's Dilemma (see page 166), has been extrapolated to the analysis of U.S.-U.S.S.R. relations, though usually with precautionary statements by the investigators. Each side is presumably attempting to maximize its own gains and minimize its losses, and each distrusts the other. During the interaction process, then, the two parties end up with losses (even the prospect of catastrophic losses in case of a nuclear war), when mutual trust and a willingness to settle for a bit less could lead to substantial mutual gain.

The analogy is indeed inviting, though there has been appropriate criticism of the unrestrained generalization from two individuals and a small prize to two nations locked in a major ideological and economic struggle with nuclear war at stake. Such a generalization from individuals to nations is, of course, not limited to social psychologists. Political cartoonists sometimes try to make their point by taking a complex issue and reducing it to the personal level—the interaction between Uncle Sam and the Russian bear—and we may come away from such cartoons with a distinct feeling of having gained new insight and better understanding. It is evident that major political figures also personify nations, equating international conflicts with interactions among persons (Kelman, 1965). In describing the U.S.-U.S.S.R. confrontation during the Cuban missile crisis, Secretary of State Dean Rusk compared it to two street fighters, in the style of a classic Western cowboy film, who were facing each other in a life-and-death encounter. "Remember, when you report this," he said, "that, eyeball to eyeball they blinked first" (Hilsman, 1964, p. 20). Although it could be argued that Secretary Rusk was merely using this simplified dramatic analogy to communicate with the masses on their own level, some scholars of international affairs believe that certain political leaders really think in this way. If so, then

*Figure 10.1
Political cartoonists often make their point by taking a complex issue in international relations and reducing it to the interpersonal level. Here the artist has captured elements of Goffman's "front stage" and "backstage" behavior in U.S.-U.S.S.R. relations.*

CARTOON BY MIKE LEE/UCLA DAILY BRUIN.

by comparison, the social psychologists' generalization from controlled laboratory experiments would seem much more justifiable, though precautions are obviously required. Once one has gained an insight from experimental research, one must look more carefully at the analogy, review the common elements, and seek further support from other sources.

Small-Group Decisions Affect International Affairs

Although we can gain some insights into international and intergroup conflicts by cautiously examining studies of interpersonal conflict, the generalization leap is somewhat less tenuous if we focus our attention on an analysis of conflict between small groups. The small group offers some insight into the processes of agreement and disagreement within any group, the effects of group leadership, the relationship between interpersonal conflict within a group and conflict among groups, and so forth. Some investigators have considered the small group as analogous to the nation, and they have been criticized in the same way as those who have leaped from individual to nation.

It must be borne in mind, however, that major decisions in international relations are often made by a group of policymakers—a politburo, a cabinet group, a security council, a conference of foreign ministers. In this sense, then, crucial stages of international relations may take place in small groups. Once this point has been recognized, much of our theoretical discussion in previous chapters becomes relevant to the analysis of the policy-making group. A group can be seen as participating in group problem-solving vis-à-vis an opposing group. The ways in which the group members perceive one another and the members of the opposing group are especially relevant. Interpersonal relations assume major importance as the members of a group develop balance and congruity in their perceptions and evaluations of one another and in their evaluation of their antagonist. Any threat from the outgroup increases the feelings of interdependence within the group, both means interdependence and goal interdependence. Social influence and power relationships become more salient as members of the group attempt to resolve their differences in order to present a united front against the opponent, while various bases of power are explored in an attempt to persuade the antagonist to make concessions. The group becomes differentiated in its functions and roles, with various members assuming different positions and attitudes in the process of discussion and organization. The impact of the group on the individual member becomes more evident as the deviant is viewed as a threat to effective group functioning; there will be pressures toward risky positions and toward a more militant stance against the opponent. The leadership role becomes a crucial factor in determining just how the group will deal with its problem; the leader will either attack the opponent or strive toward reconciliation.

This chapter will focus first upon the behavior within a decision-making group, as it interacts with a hostile outgroup. Then it will look more closely at the positive and negative interaction between groups and make suggestions for the improvement of what had initially been hostile intergroup relations.

HOW GROUPS
IN CONFLICT
MAKE DECISIONS

Group Decision and the Bay of Pigs. Suppose you were the President of the United States. As an intelligent, ambitious, and conscientious Chief Executive, you feel the need for a capable group of advisers. Perhaps, in addition to your experience, you have the advantage of having read pertinent books and articles on how to select capable advisers. You, therefore, might feel quite fortunate in being able to assemble the following: (1) as Secretary of State, an experienced administrator with long-term experience in the State Department, a veteran, and proven policymaker; (2) an expert statistician who has been a top executive of a major automobile manufacturing company and has developed effective decision-making procedures within that company; (3) a keen analytic thinker who has had long diplomatic experience; (4) a top-notch Harvard professor and dean who has conducted studies on decision-making in the State Department; (5) a world-renowned Harvard historian who has a keen understanding of international relations; (6) a brilliant economist who is also an expert on intelligence data; (7) two of the nation's top experts on Latin American affairs; and (8) three top military analysts. Suppose, furthermore, that this group has a high sense of purpose, an over-all agreement about goals, and a deep desire to serve their country and President. Obviously this group would be exceptionally well qualified to discuss ideas. The size of the group would not be so large as to stifle participation. There would be some homogeneity in the members' educational and cultural background and in their general agreement on politics, yet there would be heterogeneity in their skills and areas of expertise. There would be a very high level of cohesiveness and conviviality and a tremendous devotion and respect for their leader, the President. And there would be no dearth of experienced leadership. What more could anyone ask?

The group we have described is not some unattainable ideal, for

President John F. Kennedy convened just such an advisory group and assigned it a very important problem: how to deal with a neighboring Latin American country that seemed to be increasingly hostile toward the United States. The decision that was approved by this group for implementation led to one of the most militarily disastrous and morally disgraceful ventures in American history—the Bay of Pigs invasion of Cuba. The advisory group consisted of (1) Dean Rusk, (2) Robert McNamara, (3) Douglas Dillon, (4) McGeorge Bundy, (5) Arthur Schlesinger, Jr., (6) Richard Bissell, (7) Thomas Mann and Adolph Berle, Jr., and (8) three bemedaled and multi-starred members of the Joint Chiefs of Staff.

It is ironic that the U.S.-supported invasion of Cuba by U.S.-trained Cuban exiles had been suggested by President Kennedy's arch-rival, Richard M. Nixon, when he was Vice President. Nixon broached the idea to President Dwight D. Eisenhower in March 1960. Eisenhower directed the Central Intelligence Agency to organize Cuban exile groups in the U.S., and from them select a number of volunteers who would be trained as a guerrilla force to infiltrate their homeland. Two days after his inauguration in January 1961, President Kennedy was briefed on the developing plans by the CIA head, Allen Dulles, and by the Chairman of the Joint Chiefs of Staff, General Lyman Lemnitzer. Thus, many of the plans had already been worked out; Kennedy passed these along to his newly appointed advisory group for consideration. These plans were then discussed quite thoroughly, modified somewhat, and approved for

Figure 10.2
President John F. Kennedy meets with the National Security Council, April 1962.

speedy implementation. The U.S. role in supporting and engineering the invasion was supposed to be covert, but from the outset there were few knowledgeable persons at the United Nations or elsewhere who did not see through the scheme. The air assault on Cuba by U.S. planes with disguised markings was exposed immediately. The expected popular uprising against the Castro regime did not materialize. The small, ill-equipped and poorly trained group of exiles was quickly surrounded and killed or captured by the vastly superior and jubilant Cuban forces. The United States suffered a humiliating defeat in the eyes of the world, and the Castro government became even more firmly entrenched and extremely hostile toward the U.S. The Soviet Union gained even more influence in Cuba and the Western Hemisphere. And the Bay of Pigs fiasco eventually led to the brink of a nuclear war, as the Soviet Union attempted to place nuclear missiles on Cuban soil.

President Kennedy later asked, "How could we have been so stupid?" McNamara marveled at his own extreme lack of judgment. Indeed, each member of the advisory group found it hard to believe that he had gone along with the plan and that such a high-level group could have advocated such a patently stupid decision.

Groupthink

Several years later, Charlotte Janis, at the suggestion of her father, wrote a term paper for her high-school history course on the abortive Bay of Pigs invasion. Her preliminary research so intrigued her father, the social psychologist Irving Janis, that he spent the next two years intensively studying the Bay of Pigs as well as other major decisions of national advisory committees that had led to fiascoes— such as our unpreparedness for the attack on Pearl Harbor, the Korean War, and the escalation of American and French participation in Vietnam. He also studied other national decisions that seemed more laudable, such as resolving the Cuban missile crisis and establishing the Marshall Plan to help Europe after World War II. Janis applied to these studies his knowledge of theory and research in social psychology, especially group problem-solving and decision-making. The result is a particularly interesting example of the blending of social psychology, political science, and history in an attempt to understand important social issues—*Victims of Groupthink: A Psychological Study of Foreign-Policy Decisions and Fiascoes* (Janis, 1972). Given the unique importance of Janis's study, we will discuss it at some length, though, of course, without the rich detail of the full report.

Janis quickly disposed of official explanations for the Bay of Pigs fiasco. Was the adventure an attempt to win popular support in

America by disposing of the "Cuban problem" quickly? This explanation is certainly not adequate. If the group had operated effectively, probably the moral reprehensibility and military stupidity of
the plan would have become evident—scarcely an outcome that
would have won popular support. Was the advisory group merely
composed of some inexperienced men who were caught up in a plan
that had been initiated by the previous administration? No, the background of these men does not support such an explanation. Janis suggested that the members of Kennedy's advisory group were victims
of "groupthink," a term that he coined, in keeping with the new-
speak vocabulary of George Orwell's *1984.* Janis explained that
groupthink is the "deterioration of mental efficiency, reality testing,
and moral judgment that results from in-group pressure" (Janis, 1972,
p. 9). Janis took sharp issue with those social psychologists who assume that high morale and an esprit de corps are the hallmarks of a
healthy and effective group. He pointed out that high-level cohesiveness and positive self-regard among members of policy-making
groups cause them to subtly stifle criticism and dissent, thus leading
to "irrational and dehumanizing actions directed against outgroups."
The process of groupthink is furthered by the group's insulation
from outside opposing views and by the endorsement and encouragement of the group's policy by a popular and persuasive group
leader.

Symptoms of Groupthink. How does groupthink manifest itself?
Janis listed some of the major symptoms and showed how these were
evident in Kennedy's policy-making group. Note how each of these
is due, at least in part, to high morale and an esprit de corps. Each
begins with the assumption: "We are a great team, and therefore . . ."

1. *Illusion of invulnerability and superior morality.* "We are
better and stronger than anyone opposed to us. Nothing and no one
can defeat us." This was the spirit of the New Frontiersmen recruited by the Kennedy Administration. According to Arthur Schlesinger, "Euphoria reigned; we thought for a moment that the world
was plastic and the future unlimited" (Schlesinger, 1965, p. 214).
The feeling of belonging to an influential group that held the future
in its hands was intoxicating. How else could one explain the expectation that 1400 Cuban exiles would be able to defeat a trained army
of 200,000! A feeling of vast moral superiority was intertwined with
the illusion of strength. Castro was described as a stupid, self-seeking leader who was ripe for overthrow by the disgruntled masses. As
a corollary, the illusion of invulnerability fostered a willingness and
desire to take risks—particularly since the Kennedy group felt confident of success.

2. *Illusion of unanimity*. "The course of action we are adopting is one on which we all must agree." Schlesinger said, "Our meetings took place in a curious atmosphere of assumed consensus" (Schlesinger, 1965, p. 250). Note the similarity between this and the pluralistic ignorance in Schanck's study of Elm Hollow (Schanck, 1932) (see page 202). If we are such a great team and have such high respect for one another, how could we possibly disagree? Later, it turned out that there had been occasional expressions of opposing views, though these were not stated very forcefully. The disagreements were ignored or glossed over by the others in the advisory group.

3. *Suppression of personal doubts and pressures toward uniformity*. "If I disagree with my team, then I must be wrong and not they." It follows that anyone who disagreed with the planned course of action would feel that he was the only one out of step and thus would conclude that he must be at fault rather than the others. We examined this phenomenon in the studies by Sherif, Asch, and others (see pages 310–322); this process further encourages the illusion of unanimity. Again, Schlesinger's insightful analysis of his own behavior: "In the months after the Bay of Pigs, I reproached myself for having kept so silent . . . my feelings of guilt were tempered by the knowledge that a course of objection would have accomplished little save to gain me a name as a nuisance" (Schlesinger, 1965, p. 255).

The process operating on the committee member who might have been opposed to the direction of the group's decision is probably quite similar to that which was discussed on page 331 (Raven, 1953, 1959). The "deviant" member may at first be struck by the fact that his views differ from those of the others. Since he likes and admires the other group members, he may be quite reluctant to express his disagreement, and thus he may censor his words to avoid being seen as a "nuisance." As the discussion progresses, he may soon censor his thoughts and look instead for bits of information he can contribute that will be acceptable to the group—things that he can say without fear of ridicule. Eventually, he will fully accept the position taken by the group.

As Schlesinger pointed out elsewhere in his analysis, the pressures on him and the others to accept the Bay of Pigs decision were not merely referent influences; expert and informational influences were also important. The military members of the advisory group, as well as Secretary Rusk, brought with them privileged information— carefully developed reports about the status of the Castro regime in Cuba, the strength of the opposition forces, and so forth. In opposing the plans for a military operation, the non-military members of the group were at a distinct disadvantage, especially Schlesinger, who had just recently joined the group.

Of course, as Schlesinger mentioned, the tendency to follow the group may entail some conflict; after one has decided to accept the group's position, there may be some dissonance: "Why have I sold myself out this way?" Dissonance theory might explain that the deviant who has decided to go along with the group might later become even more convinced that the group's position was right. Indeed, he might even become one of the group's most vehement "mindguards"—those who suppress the dissent of others.

4. *Self-appointed mindguards.* "If any one of us disagrees with the others, he must be whipped into line as soon as possible." It seems that in the advisory group, Secretary of State Dean Rusk played this role particularly well. He was known to reproach any member who even began to challenge the group's opinion. Secretary Rusk was, obviously, a good and loyal group member.

5. *Docility fostered by suave leadership.* "We have a great leader to whom we must look for guidance and direction." President Kennedy was the leader to whom all members of the advisory group looked for general guidance. He had won a series of striking victories in his uphill fight for the nomination and the election. He was the chief New Frontiersman; he used his leadership skills to organize his team, to herd in the wayward followers, to forge them into a cohesive unit, prepared for their glorious crusade. The advisory group seemed to follow docilely.

How Pervasive Is Groupthink? Was the Bay of Pigs fiasco an isolated incident? Was it simply the result of certain unique historical and political events? Janis argues convincingly that it was not. He offers briefer analyses of several other major policy decisions that seem to contain the same essential processes—the decision of President Truman's advisers to authorize General MacArthur's disastrous campaign into North Korea, the failure of the U.S. Pacific Fleet commanders to give due credence to extensive intelligence reports (some gained from cracking the Japanese secret code) that indicated a strong possibility of a Japanese attack on Pearl Harbor, and various decisions to escalate the Vietnam War.

The following are similar events where groupthink processes might also have been operating: (1) The decision by Nazi Germany to invade the Soviet Union in 1941. After Germany had succeeded in defeating France and occupying most of Western Europe, it felt invulnerable and morally superior; it was confident of quick success in defeating the Soviet Union. Groupthink was consciously fostered by Adolf Hitler, who severely punished anyone who disagreed with him too vehemently. (2) The unpreparedness of Israel for the October war in 1973. It is possible that the Israeli cabinet's high morale and esprit de corps, which had been heightened by the country's stunning victory in the 1967 Six-Day War, produced an illusion of invulnerability that caused the Cabinet to view the Arab nations as incompetent, stupid, and morally decadent. (3) The actions of some of President Nixon's closest advisers who were involved in the Watergate affair and who tried to cover it up later on. (4) The 1961 decision of the German firm Grünenthal Chemie to produce and market the tranquilizer thalidomide (groupthink is not limited to government policy decisions). The pharmaceutical house had vouched that this highly profitable drug was safe for pregnant women, though its effects on the unborn had not been tested. As a result, 7000 deformed babies were born in 1962 to mothers who had taken thalidomide (Janis, 1972). (5) The 1956 decision by the Ford Motor Company to market the Edsel, an expensive automobile that was almost completely rejected by the American public.

Is Groupthink Inevitable? Without some positive feelings, high morale, and esprit de corps, it is difficult for any group to function effectively. But is groupthink an inevitable result of group cohesiveness? Clearly, the danger is always present and must be guarded against. Janis presented some well-considered counter-examples indicating how groupthink could be avoided.

Preventing groupthink in the Cuban missile crisis. It is particularly encouraging to note that the leader of the group that had made a disastrous decision was able to restructure the group and its operations in order to try to avoid such pitfalls a second time. A year after the Bay of Pigs fiasco, President Kennedy's reorganized policy-making group was faced with a much more serious crisis. The Soviet Union, in a secret agreement with the Castro regime, had deployed nearly one-third of its atomic warhead potential in Cuba, together with 20,000 fully equipped Soviet troops. Missile installations were being built throughout Cuba. The U.S. military intelligence estimated that the nuclear potential in Cuba could destroy all major American cities and kill 80 million Americans. The Soviet Union initially denied the existence of the missiles in Cuba, but photos from U-2 reconnaissance planes provided indisputable evidence that the missile sites were rapidly being completed, with convoys of Soviet ships bringing in additional forces and matériel. This crisis led President Kennedy to call an emergency meeting of the Executive Committee of the National Security Council, an advisory group that included many of the same high-level men who had participated in the Bay of Pigs decision.

At the first meeting of the Executive Committee, the stage seemed to be set for another decision characterized by groupthink, but the consequences of this decision carried infinitely more risk to the United States than did the Bay of Pigs decision. There was some pressure from military advisers to launch a massive air strike on the missile sites themselves, rendering them inoperative, in order to demonstrate once and for all that the United States would not allow itself to be threatened. There was a sense of extreme urgency; the President counseled the advisory group to put aside its various disagreements in order to take speedy and decisive action. Of course, the secrecy with which the missiles were being installed and the initial unequivocal denial from Soviet Premier Khrushchev and Cuban Premier Castro led many American officials to feel that extreme countermeasures would be justified. The initial response of the Executive Committee was disagreement; some members criticized the first strike proposal as immoral, dangerous, and counter to American policy. This led to further argument and a number of counterproposals, each of which was also subjected to critical evaluation. A student of group behavior might well have missed the significance of what was happening if he had been able to observe the heated argument and division of opinion in the 1962 advisory group, as compared with the more friendly, agreeable 1961 group. Soon a number of alternative proposals were made, ranging from simple acceptance of the existence of missiles in Cuba without taking any countermeasure, through instituting a limited naval blockade to prevent the introduction of additional missiles, or carrying out a limited "surgical" first strike on the missile bases, to a massive all-out attack and invasion to destroy the Castro regime.

Making certain that all alternatives are considered. Each alternative was carefully analyzed, with some members of the advisory group assuming the role of devil's advocate if no one else were critical. Protocol was abandoned, as Assistant Secretaries disagreed with Secretaries, and members of one department opposed others in the same division. The group appeared to be leaderless, and, indeed, former Secretary of State Dean Acheson, who participated in the discussion as a resource person, lamented the apparent absence of group structure and strong leadership. During the course of the discussion, strong opinions were reevaluated—Secretary of the Treasury Douglas Dillon initially favored an air strike, but was persuaded to accept a blockade instead after hearing Robert Kennedy's argument about the immorality of an air strike. It was remarked that some members began as hawks and others as doves, some changed from hawks to doves, but all eventually emerged as "dawks."

The group also appeared to treat the Soviet Union and Cuba with reasonable respect. They assumed that Khrushchev and his associates probably had very similar concerns—that they, too, were aware of the possible extreme actions that the U.S. could take, that they, too, had a range of possible alternatives to weigh, and that their decisions might be determined, in part, by the decisions made by the U.S.; therefore, the group was willing to recommend a conciliatory strategy, in the hopes that it might invoke a nonhostile response.

The group decision, accepted and implemented by President Kennedy, was essentially firm yet cautious and conciliatory. A naval blockade was imposed, with a ban on the further shipment of nuclear weapons. The first ship that was boarded by U.S. naval personnel was a non-Soviet ship that was under Russian charter. It had been determined beforehand that the ship carried no missiles; therefore, in boarding, the U.S. could demonstrate the seriousness of its intentions while avoiding a confrontation. Soon the Soviet ships that were en route carrying missiles to Cuba reversed their direction. Later on, an agreement was worked out: The U.S.S.R. agreed to remove its missiles from Cuba and the U.S. agreed not to invade Cuba. From this point on, the tensions between the Soviet Union and the United States were reduced and the ground was laid for a more amicable relationship.

How did the 1962 advisory group differ from the 1961 group, aside from its membership? To some degree, President Kennedy and his advisers had benefited from the experience of the Bay of Pigs fiasco, and they were determined to have no repetition. Partly because of the recommendations of a 1961 commission of inquiry and partly because of greater experience in government, Kennedy had introduced drastic changes in the decision-making process. He had changed the roles of the group members: each was encouraged to be a critical thinker, to be ready to learn and to criticize suggestions even if these were outside his particular specialty—to be a "skeptical generalist" as well as an informed specialist. The group was protected against insularity by bringing in a number of outside specialists and observers who were encouraged to participate fully. The advisory group had several overlapping subgroups that met periodically and then returned to the larger group with differing insights. President Kennedy was deliberately absent from many of the meetings, for he believed that many of the group members might be reluctant to speak candidly in his presence or express a view that differed from his own.

Preventing Groupthink: Some Recommendations. Based upon his analysis of the Cuban missile crisis and other decisions, Janis has presented a number of valuable suggestions for preventing groupthink.

1. *The leader of a policy-forming group should assign the role of critical evaluator to each member, encouraging the group to give high priority to airing objections and doubts. This practice needs to be reinforced by the leader's acceptance of criticism of his own judgments in order to discourage the members from soft-pedaling their disagreements [p. 209].*

2. *The leaders in an organization's hierarchy, when assigning a policy-planning mission to a group, should be impartial instead of stating preferences and expectations at the outset. The practice requires each leader to limit his briefings to unbiased statements about the scope of the problem and the limitations of available resources, without advocating specific proposals he would like to see adopted. This allows conferees the opportunity to develop an atmosphere of open inquiry and to explore impartially a wide range of policy alternatives [p. 210].*

3. *The organization should routinely follow the administrative practice of setting up several independent policy-planning and evaluation groups to work on the same policy question, each carrying out its deliberations under a different leader [p. 211].*

4. *Throughout the period when the feasibility and effectiveness of policy alternatives are being surveyed, the policy-making group should from time to time divide into two or more subgroups to meet separately, under different chairmen, and then come together to hammer out their differences [p. 213].*

5. *Each member of the policy-making group should discuss periodically the group's deliberations with trusted associates in his own unit of the organization and report back their reactions [p. 213].*

6. *One or more outside experts or qualified colleagues within the organization who are not core members of the policy-making group should be invited to each meeting on a staggered basis and should be encouraged to challenge the views of the core members [p. 214].*

7. *At every meeting devoted to evaluating policy alternatives, at least one member should be assigned to the role of devil's advocate [p. 215].*

8. *Whenever the policy issue involves relations with a rival nation or organization, a sizable bloc of time (perhaps an entire session) should be spent surveying all warning signals from the rivals and constructing alternative scenarios of the rivals' intentions [p. 216].*

9. *After reaching a preliminary consensus about what seems to be the best policy alternative, the policy-making group should hold a "second chance" meeting at which every member is expected to express as vividly as he can all his residual doubts and to rethink the entire issue before making a definitive choice [p. 218].*

These suggestions, viewed from the perspective of the Bay of Pigs and other major policy failures, seem to have good bases not only in historical examples but also in social psychological theory and research. Similar suggestions have been presented in studies of social organizations (for example, Katz and Kahn, 1966, pp. 259–299;

March and Simon, 1958). One can only hope that they might be utilized by those who are entrusted with making important policy decisions on behalf of this country.

The Nixon Group and the Watergate Affair [1]

On June 17, 1972 (prior to the presidential nominating conventions), a group of burglars was apprehended at the Democratic National Committee headquarters in Washington's Watergate office and apartment complex. The intruders were in the process of checking and reinstalling secret listening devices which, it turned out, were providing information for the Republicans' Committee for the Re-Election of the President. The burglars' purpose became known as a result of the notations and telephone numbers found in the notebook of one of the burglars; one entry gave the code name and number of the former CIA agent E. Howard Hunt, who had been prominently associated with both CREEP and the internal security of the White House staff. Later, it was revealed that funds for the wiretapping and other similar activities had originally come from illegal corporate contributions with the encouragement of prominent White House officials; the funds were then channeled through the Committee for the Re-Election of the President and "laundered" by going through a Mexican bank, after which they were reconverted for use by the wiretappers. Thus, the trail of the investigation led to the inner sanctum of the White House itself. These disclosures in turn brought about a further investigation of the activities of the President and the White House staff.

Eventually it was revealed that President Nixon and his close advisers had been involved in a number of perfidious and clandestine operations throughout his first four years in office. The following are some of the disclosures that were made: A secret "enemies" list had been compiled that included many prominent individuals who were viewed by Nixon's advisers as opponents of the administration—it included senators and congressmen, journalists, newspaper publishers, judges, union leaders, professors, and former Cabinet members. The facilities of the Office of the Attorney General, the Federal Bureau of Investigation, the Central Intelligence Agency, and the Internal Revenue Service were used to gather information about these "enemies" and, on occasion, to harass and punish them. Forged letters and documents were used to discredit these "enemies." As part of a "dirty tricks" campaign, political and activist groups were infiltrated by government agents who were gathering information and serving as agents provocateurs to urge these groups to extreme acts. In an attempt to discredit a prominent critic of the Vietnam War, key members of the President's staff sent agents to

[1] This section includes material that was presented in a presidential address to the Society for the Psychological Study of Social Issues and later published in the *Journal of Social Issues* (Raven, 1974). This material is reproduced with the kind permission of SPSSI.

burglarize the confidential files of his psychiatrist. New disclosures of "dirty tricks" have continued to emerge. E. Howard Hunt reports that he and certain White House staff members considered spreading a drug on the steering wheel of the car belonging to the columnist Jack Anderson (a frequent critic of the Nixon Administration). The drug, which enters the body through the skin, would make him babble incoherently during his news broadcast, thereby causing his audience to discredit him. The plan, Hunt continues, was abandoned because it was "too chancy" (*Time*, October 6, 1975).

At the Office of the Attorney General, elaborate plans were presented for using high-paid prostitutes, kidnapings, blackmail, and burglary to compromise and essentially destroy the Democratic Party. Large sums of money were accumulated, sometimes by means resembling extortion, to finance these operations and to bribe those who were later apprehended to remain silent. In order to have a secret record of these activities, the President and a few of his most trusted staff members arranged for secret listening devices to be placed in the Executive Office to record many of the discussions relating to these activities. Apparently, the President believed that he would be able to maintain possession of these recordings. But when congressional and court investigators managed to obtain them by subpoena, the evidence was so conclusive and damaging that the President chose to resign rather than face certain impeachment; most of his closest advisers were tried and convicted. Nixon's resignation occurred less than two years after he had been reelected by the largest majority in American history.

A Small-Group Analysis of the Nixon Group. There have been many attempts to explain how the President and his close associates could plummet from the height of political success to the depth of notoriety. After reading the transcripts of the presidential tapes, the hearings before the House and Senate committees, and various court reports, we believe that much of what happened can be explained by examining the development and operation of the team that President Nixon had assembled to assist him with his responsibilities and to manage his political campaigns. President Nixon and his close associates perceived a conflict between themselves and those who were (actual or potential) critics of the administration. The opposing group (the "enemies") was a diffuse collection of intellectuals, journalists, those in the arts, Democrats, socialists, left-wingers, and others who seemed to be critical of the Nixon Administration. In analyzing the Nixon group, a number of the factors that we have discussed in connection with groupthink are in all likelihood appropriate, as are various other concepts such as group pressures, group structure, sociometry, and the risky shift.

One of the most penetrating analyses of the Nixon group is presented by Theodore H. White in his best-selling book *The Making of the President—1972* and in *Breach of Faith* (White, 1973, 1975). It is instructive to read White's description of Nixon's plans for his teams following his first election in 1968.

The big team. Toward the end of the 1968 campaign, when victory seemed certain, White asked Nixon what type of team he would have with him in the White House. Nixon responded, "I want two teams in the White House—a big team but also a young team." The Big Team would consist of well-known and experienced people who could run the Cabinet, provide prestige for the administration, cement alliances with various powerful groups in the party and in the nation at large—names like Romney, Rockefeller, Scranton, and maybe even Humphrey and Jackson. It was important then that the Big Team be composed of people with prestige who would inspire confidence in the government. The most basic decisions, however, could be entrusted only to those whose loyalty to the President was beyond question. The Young Team would be composed mainly (but not exclusively) of men between 30 and 40, active men who "learned fast," who would be loyal and devoted to the chief, who could be counted on for aggressive action, and presumably who would have no compunctions about hitting the "enemy" hard. Assembling the Big Team proved to be difficult and frustrating for the new President, who had assumed that anyone would be delighted to serve in his administration. Did they distrust him? Did they suspect that they might be used for public relations and window dressing? Were they jealous of him? Did they simply prefer the positions they already held? In any event, Nixon's defeated rival, Hubert Humphrey, rejected his offer to be the U.S. ambassador to the U.N. Senator Henry Jackson, whose appointment would have indicated bipartisanship, declined appointment as Secretary of Defense. David Rockefeller turned down appointment as Secretary of the Treasury and of Defense. William Scranton refused to serve as Secretary of State. Robert Finch was asked to be Attorney General, but he declined. Daniel "Pat" Moynihan might have been willing to serve as Secretary of Labor, but the nation's top labor leaders objected. In short, most of the important people who were asked would not join Nixon's Big Team. Some of those who did, such as Walter Hickel, left before long—disillusioned. Some remained, such as Richardson, Moynihan, Laird, Rogers, and Ruckelshaus. These Big Team members, however, were seen as outsiders by the Nixon group and so were barred from the Oval Office. Haldeman and his Young Team carefully controlled their visits and acted toward them rather condescendingly. Nixon spoke derisively and contemptuously of them, as was shown by the White House tapes (Bernstein and Woodward, 1974).

The young team. If long-time personal loyalty, coupled with a direct, hard-hitting approach to solving problems, was a major consideration in selecting the Young Team, the nucleus for that team was two men—H. R. ("Bob") Haldeman (who became Nixon's chief of staff) and John Mitchell (Attorney General and 1972 campaign director). Since he was also a member of the Cabinet, Mitchell was one of the few members of the Young Team who, for a time, was on the Big Team as well. Mitchell and Nixon had become close friends during Nixon's political exile in New York (1963–1967) following his defeat in the California gubernatorial race. During those years, when Nixon needed support, the Mitchell home provided many a warm social evening; Martha Mitchell served as the charming Southern hostess, Nixon often played the piano, and the other guests sang. Haldeman had been working closely with Nixon since 1956, assisting him in various political campaigns, as well as during his term as Vice President. Both Haldeman and Mitchell had worked in Nixon's 1968 campaign, Mitchell as national campaign manager and Haldeman as personal manager. At that time a bitter rivalry developed between them that continued thereafter. By including both of these men in the nucleus of the Young Team, rival factions developed in this group that continued well beyond Nixon's resignation.

Figure 10.3
This White House Organization Chart was presented at the opening session of the Senate Watergate investigating committee, May 1973.

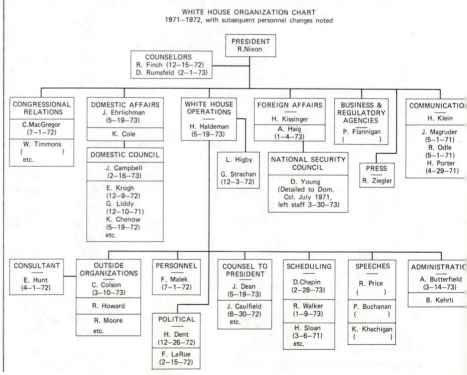

A Sociometric Analysis of the Nixon Group. Those who watched the televised hearings of the Senate Select Committee, chaired by Senator Sam Ervin, had the opportunity to examine several formal organizational charts showing the relationship between the President and his staff. These charts disclosed very little about how decisions were made and provided almost no information about the actual operations of the Nixon team. More revealing is a sociometric analysis of the Nixon group, as shown in Figure 10.4.

The contending factions. Mitchell brought several young men to the team, especially John Dean. Later, when Nixon wanted Mitchell to manage his 1972 campaign, Mitchell agreed provided that he could name his own replacement as Attorney General. Thus, Richard Kleindienst joined the Mitchell-Dean faction.

A much stronger faction developed under Haldeman's aegis. Robert Finch, another longtime California friend of Nixon's, joined the group. Haldeman also added his old friend and classmate from UCLA, John Ehrlichman. Years earlier, Haldeman had managed the campaign of Ehrlichman's wife for vice-president of the student body at UCLA (unsuccessfully, as it turned out). Finch introduced his old friend, Herbert Klein, to the team. Then another young Californian who had participated in a number of Nixon's campaigns, Jeb Stuart Magruder, joined the fold. Not long before, Magruder had left the cosmetics industry and had bounced from job to job. He was now

Figure 10.4
Sociometric diagram of the relationship between President Richard M. Nixon and his staff. Nixon had a positive relationship with nearly everyone listed here (the most significant staff members).

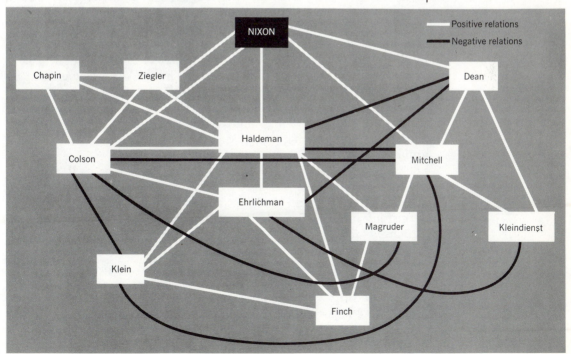

determined that he would make good in this new position, no matter what, since "it might be a springboard toward unlimited success." "You like this job," he told himself, "and you're going to do what they tell you" (Magruder, 1974, p. 56). He thus showed deference and courtesy and, according to Theodore White, "His eager-beaver desire to be helpful made one feel that if he had a tail, he would wag it" (White, 1973, p. 371). Before long he was one of the few people in the Nixon camp who got along very well with both Haldeman and Mitchell. Indeed, it was Magruder's ability to bridge the two contending factions that probably led to his rapid advance in the Nixon group. (Later, it may have contributed to his downfall as well.)

Soon thereafter, another rising star, Charles Colson, joined the team under Haldeman's aegis and very quickly rose through the ranks. His technique, however, was quite different from Magruder's. Instead of trying to win acceptance by both factions, he carefully sized up the situation and allied himself with the group that appeared to be the "winner." While maintaining his loyalty to the Haldeman group, he made a special play for the "big chief." His devotion and dedication to Nixon knew no bounds. He wrote to his own staff: "If I bruise feelings or injure anyone's moral [*sic*], I will be happy to make amends on the morning of November 8 [the day after Election Day]. . . . [To help Nixon's campaign] I would walk over my grandmother if necessary" (White, 1973, p. 368). Magruder noted, somewhat enviously, that Colson "could always see which way the President was leaning, and he would state brilliantly whatever the President wanted to hear. He could devastate those who disagreed with him. His tactic was always the same: He only wished to help the President, so if you disagreed with him [Colson], you must be disloyal to the President" (Magruder, 1974, p. 65). Using this tactic or others, Colson had no uneasiness about challenging anyone except, of course, Haldeman and Nixon, whom he never questioned. The two young rising stars, Magruder and Colson, soon became quite hostile toward one another.

Mitchell was soon at loggerheads with Colson as well. Such opposition from a powerful man like Mitchell might ordinarily devastate a young upstart. Colson, however, was so effective in establishing himself through exaggerated loyalty to the chief (by using driving, hard-hitting methods and by showing contempt for the President's "enemies") that his position was secured. He eventually acquired his own private intelligence system that supplied information on everyone—including Mitchell.

As the situation deteriorated. The sociometric analysis shown in Figure 10.4 helps to explain a number of events that occurred during the testimony of various members of the Nixon group before the Senate Select Committee and the House Judiciary Committee. Initially, there seemed to be competition between the factions, each attempting to show that it was most adept at preserving the presidency and at following the "game plan." As the pressure mounted, however, and the original game plan proved difficult to maintain, there was increasing evidence that each faction tried to protect itself and to shift the responsibility for any wrongdoing to the other. Dean and Mitchell upheld one another steadfastly as a besieged minority, while the others began to place more and more of the blame on them. Mitchell was forced to resign as Attorney General shortly after the Watergate break-in, and there was increasing pressure on him to assume all of the responsibility—to sacrifice himself as a good team member. Dean was asked to help put all of the blame on Mitchell (*White House Transcripts*, 1974). After Mitchell, there was Dean: Haldeman and Ehrlichman met with the President and urged him to accept a strategy whereby Dean would resign and thus admit major guilt by implication. At an earlier time, the President had tried to persuade Dean to sign a prepared letter of resignation (to be kept on hand in case it might be needed). Dean refused to do this unless Haldeman and Ehrlichman also resigned (*White House Transcripts*, 1974).

Jeb Magruder presents a particularly interesting case, since he was one of the few members of Nixon's staff who was able to maintain positive relations with both factions. When the evidence began to mount against Magruder, it became apparent that he would have to testify and admit guilt. (Once Nixon learned this, he wanted very much to receive credit for persuading Magruder to "let it all hang out.") In testifying, Magruder would have to implicate others—but whom? Mitchell was counting on what he thought was a close personal relationship with Magruder; he also knew that, though Magruder was brought in by the Haldeman-Ehrlichman faction, he had very strong negative feelings toward Colson. Magruder, however, was already making plans for the future, having reconciled himself to the idea of leaving Nixon's staff. He had hopes for clemency, or perhaps a pardon, and had flown out to California to test the political waters—to see about the possibility of running for governor. And who could help him achieve these ends? To help Magruder make up his mind, Haldeman had promised him a very attractive position as director of the 1976 Bicentennial Celebration. The choice was then clear—Magruder testified that he had been responsible for illegally concealing information, together with Dean and Mitchell. (Later, he would state that Haldeman and Colson were also guilty, but he did not choose to implicate them.) Even Mitchell, hardened and calloused by many years of political infighting, was shocked by Magruder's betrayal. "How," he asked, "could that All-American boy with that sweet wife and wonderful children turn out to be such a viper?" (White, 1973, p. 397). In the struggle within the Nixon group, the Mitchell-Dean faction was now vanquished; Dean was branded as the "mastermind" of the cover-up and Mitchell as his "patron."

Cohesiveness without esprit de corps. As can be seen, then, a close examination of the Nixon group does *not* show any high-level esprit de corps, any mutual attraction toward one another, or any mutual admiration or identification, which Janis believed was important for groupthink. Instead, there were two major contending and mutually distrusting factions, as well as a number of individuals within each faction who vied for power and disliked each other. The Kennedy policy-making group described by Janis certainly demonstrated some personal antagonisms and competition for power, but these were mild compared with the Nixon group. Furthermore, the members of the Nixon group, who had been selected because they were "young," hard-hitting fighters, often directed their energies to fighting Nixon's "enemies," but sometimes used these tactics in their own mutual struggles.

On the other hand, the Nixon group could still be viewed as highly cohesive in some sense, for every member dearly wanted to be in that group, and hopefully at its center. All of the members were bound to the group through loyalty, acceptance, and identification with their leader, Richard M. Nixon. According to White, they had been specifically selected for their loyalty. Their dependence on Nixon was complete, since none (except Finch) had ever won election to political office, yet each had high political aspirations. Nixon or his immediate followers had brought most of them into the limelight; without him they would have had no status. The members were also bound together by some initial agreement about strategy and tactics; despite their later disclaimers, they had been chosen in part because of their willingness to use whatever tactics would be efficacious in furthering the goals of their leader. So long as Richard Nixon was successful and powerful, and the group members showed the proper loyalty and utilized appropriate tactics, they could be assured of an important role in one of the most powerful offices in the world.

Thus, dependence upon and admiration for their leader was the glue that held the Nixon group together. Janis also pointed out that groupthink is furthered when a group is essentially isolated from contrary outside opinions. The Nixon group certainly demonstrated ample evidence of insulation: They cast out anyone who took strong issue with the group, and they maintained such secrecy about their basic internal operations that individual group members had to hire their own security guards. Herbert Klein (1974) described in some detail how the President gradually became isolated from "outsiders" who had opposing viewpoints. We had noted that the members of the Big Team, Cabinet members (except for Mitchell), and other high officials, were denied access to the President. Republican and Democratic leaders of Congress were also barred. The President held very few press conferences, and so he was seldom questioned by reporters. Anyone who wished to see the President, even a Young Team member, first had to present an exact agenda to Haldeman for his approval, and then he was admonished not to deviate from that agenda (Mollenhoff, 1974). This isolation was due in part to the needs of the office, in part to the President's personality and his wish to have only limited contact with others, and in part to his obsessive concern about security. In trying to keep secret information from getting out, the Nixon group constructed a "Berlin Wall," which also restricted unpleasant information and a variety of viewpoints from getting in, not only to the President but also to the members of the Nixon group.

Groupthink in the Nixon Group. What symptoms of groupthink can be detected in the Nixon group? The illusion of superior morality was clearly evident. The group described the "other side" (liberals and intellectuals) as posing a direct threat to the future of our country and the world; they often used this "danger" to justify the morality of any form of countermeasure. They had the illusion of long-range invulnerability because they felt that ultimately Nixon would win the election and that the group would be secure in its power. Yet they were also afraid of the possibility of an upset, so, again they felt that any means must be used to prevent such a contingency. There was also an illusion of unanimity; although the group acknowledged disagreement on specific details, they believed that everyone agreed that the group's objectives must be accomplished by the quickest and most effective means, without regard for scruples. Any personal doubts about such extreme measures were immediately suppressed, for no one wanted to be a millstone or a nuisance. Haldeman and Colson were obviously self-appointed mindguards, with others performing these functions from time to time. Conformity was facilitated by strong leadership, particularly by the President and sometimes by Haldeman, though such leadership could more appropriately be characterized as forceful rather than suave. So great was the group's dependence upon President Nixon that few disagreements were expressed in his presence and just the invocation of his name by his lieutenants was enough to bring any deviants into line.

The Runaway Norm in the Nixon Group. With respect to runaway norms (see Chapter 8), it appears that the decisions of the Nixon group were often characterized by pressures to at least equal, and preferably exceed, the group average. One norm that had to be equaled or exceeded was taking a tough stand against Nixon's "enemies." One could not appear to be softer than the group average or more concerned about the moral implications of the issue of dealing with the press, liberals, intellectuals, or other such groups. Exceeding the norm was the path to success, while appearing softer than the group average was the road to exile from the Nixon group. Charles Colson's rapid rise, due to his dealing firmly with the "enemies," was not lost on such aspiring young men as Magruder and Dean. Equally instructive were the lessons of the falling "stars," such as Daniel "Pat" Moynihan, an early key member of the team who was exiled with an ambassadorship to India for being too apologetic for liberal causes. Another early "star," Robert Finch, was ridiculed as a "Pasadena Hamlet" for being too soft and was soon banished, along with his associate Herbert Klein; they had advocated taking a mild approach toward the young demonstrators who opposed the Vietnam War. In his determination to reach the top of the Nixon group, Magruder proudly displayed a banner that read, "Winning the election isn't the only thing. It's everything!"

With respect to the risky shift, group pressures on each individual compelled him to adopt a position that was riskier, bolder, stronger, and less inhibited than that taken by the other members of the group. These pressures, however, grew because of the competition between the contending factions, and between certain young men who wanted to rise quickly and certain older men (such as Mitchell) who did not want to fall. Dean later wondered why Mitchell had not taken a stronger stand against the outrageous plan of Gordon Liddy to use high-paid prostitutes, kidnapings, blackmail, and burglaries to help defame the Democrats; Liddy had presented his plan, illustrated with six-color charts, in the Attorney General's office in the presence of Dean, Mitchell, and Magruder. But why had Dean said nothing at this meeting? Or Magruder? Later on, in retrospect, all of them expressed profound shock at the proposal. Mitchell said regretfully, "I not only should have thrown him [Liddy] out of the office; I should have thrown him out of the window." Yet, at the time, the only thing Dean, Mitchell, or Magruder could say was that the plan was not exactly what he had in mind. Why was nothing else said? One reason may be that Liddy had a close relationship with Colson, the superhard fighter. A strong display of disapproval might have been interpreted as a sign of weakness—of not being a good team member. On another, similar occasion, Magruder (who had Liddy and Hunt at his disposal) reported that he had been reluctant to approve their bugging of the Democratic headquarters. That is, until he got a call from Colson who asked if he was going to "fish or cut bait." If Magruder had been at all hesitant about giving the Watergate burglars the go-ahead, this might very well have been interpreted as a sign of weakness (you had better move ahead fast if you "have your head screwed on right").

The Applicability of Small-Group Theory. It would appear that many of the concepts from the social psychology of small groups can be used in trying to understand the Nixon group and the decision processes that led to the Watergate affair and other related scandals. A sociometric analysis of the Nixon team points to the divisions within the Nixon group and the ways in which each member was affected by the social structure of which he was a part. Although Janis believes that high esprit de corps and mutual admiration and respect are essential for groupthink, these did not exist in the Nixon group. The group was held together by mutual identification with a common leader upon whom all members were dependent. The processes of groupthink were fostered by competition between individuals and factions, and by strong runaway norms—pressures to try to at least equal, and preferably exceed, one another in taking strong, unscrupulous, and risky stands in dealing with "enemies." In trying to compare this group with other decision-making bodies, it was in many respects more like the entourage of Adolf Hitler or Joseph Stalin than that of other American presidents. The actions of Nixon's group were, of course, not so extreme, but all three groups were highly dependent upon the leader, and the members of all three groups wanted to outdo one another in taking extreme actions.

If the Nixon group had followed Irving Janis's suggestions for preventing groupthink, possibly the decisions that led to Watergate and the other scandals would have been averted. However, given the basic initial structure and selection of the Nixon team, it is difficult to imagine how these suggestions could have been implemented.

THE DEVELOPMENT
OF INTERGROUP
CONFLICT

Competitive and Hostile Conflict. Having examined some of the processes that occur *within* a group that is in conflict with another group, let us now turn to the interactive process by which such a conflict develops *between* groups. Many of the concepts described in the preceding chapters are applicable here, especially: the development of conflict among individuals (see Chapter 5), interpersonal hostility and aggression (see Chapter 4), the bases of power by which one person attempts to influence another (see Chapter 6), and the role of leadership (see Chapter 9). We defined conflict as a relationship in which people are negatively interdependent with respect to goals, means, or both. In a broader sense, conflict means incompatibility between parties on the issue of the desirability of a state of affairs, actual or potential. Competition was defined more narrowly, as stemming from negative interdependence with respect to goals; in that sense, therefore, competition is a form of conflict. Competitive conflict is particularly obvious: the conflict between two automobile manufacturers with respect to who will control the major share of the market; the conflict between oil-producing nations (whose goal is maximum oil profits) and oil-importing nations (whose goal is minimal oil prices); and the conflict between two top football teams who both desperately want to win a series championship. Conflicts between groups over the means to a mutually accepted goal, while perhaps less obvious, are nonetheless quite prevalent: two groups of mathematics teachers may disagree about whether the "new math" or a more traditional method will lead to more effective learning; two black activist political organizations, both striving for black ascendancy, may disagree about whether a militant (or even violent) approach will be more effective than working through duly constituted legal means—legislation and judicial action; two Latin American nations, both striving for rapid economic development, may disagree about how much economic assistance to seek from the United States for their regional development program.

A particularly difficult form of competitive conflict is that in which the very existence of one party is incompatible with the desired goal of another: For the Palestine Liberation Organization and allied Arab states, the continuation of Israel or the existence of any Jewish state as an entity in the Middle East is incompatible with their goals for that region, while, of course, the elimination of itself is an unacceptable goal for Israel; for any religious group that believes that salvation and the millennium can only be attained if everyone adopts that particular religion, the very existence of other religious groups is opposed to its basic goals (this was the case with Catholicism during the Spanish Inquisition period; somewhat earlier, the same thing had been true in the Islamic world; during the first few centuries A.D., the Romans perceived Christianity as threatening their goals; and today there is a similar conflict between doctrinaire Marxists and die-hard capitalists).

Some conflicts between groups or individuals arise from the fact that one party dislikes or hates the other. There is a parallel here with our discussion of aggression (see Chapter 4), in which we distinguished between instrumental aggression, which strives to achieve a specific end, and aggression that simply stems from dislike. In the latter case, injuring the other party becomes a goal in its own right, and when one party is (or believes he has been) injured by the other, then retaliation is seen as both proper and desirable. Often, of course, the hostile intent behind aggression may be masked or even unconscious, since it is often considered more "acceptable" to attack someone who stands in your path than someone whom you simply dislike. As we shall see, competitive conflict often develops into hostile conflict, and hostile conflict may produce a competitive component, which is consistent with the basic principles of balance theory. As the sociologist Georg Simmel noted many years ago, "It is expedient to hate the adversary with whom one fights [or competes?], just as it is expedient to love a person whom one is tied to" (Simmel, 1908, p. 34). It has been demonstrated experimentally that persons who dislike one another are apt to emphasize or develop incompatible goals (Rapoport, 1965).

Competitive conflict and hostile conflict are so often intertwined that it is difficult to determine which came first. With respect to the conflict between Protestants and Catholics in Northern Ireland, did the incompatibility of political goals precede the hatred of one group for the other, or was it the reverse? Is the conflict between American blue-collar whites and blacks primarily due to racial hostility or to competition for scarce jobs? The same questions can be raised with respect to opposing groups on the school desegregation issue, the Arab-Israeli conflict, the Soviet-American conflict, and the antagonism between the Walloons and Flemish in Belgium. All of these examples include elements of hostility and goal incompatibility, yet any attempt to mitigate these conflicts requires making a distinction between the hostile and the competitive aspects.

Studying Intergroup Conflict—Some Pertinent Questions

In order to unravel the complex relationship between the competitive and hostile aspects of conflict and to understand how it develops, Morton Deutsch (1973) has listed seven questions that ought to be carefully examined—whether the conflict is between husband and wife, the federal government and peace demonstrators, labor and management, or nations.

1. *What are the two parties like? Are they equal or unequal in relative power? What weapons or methods do they have available to them?*
2. *What is the prior history of their relationship? Have the two parties generally been friendly or unfriendly to one aother? Do they have a history of trust or distrust? Here one can ask whether the conflict is primarily due to hostility.*
3. *What issues or disagreements have led to the present conflict? Are they ideological or related to scarce resources? What goals or means are incompatible? Here one can examine the extent to which there is competitive conflict.*
4. *What is the situation or environment in which the conflict occurred? Are there legal or moral restraints that oppose or favor*

the use of certain weapons or strategies? Is there a tradition or ethic that favors cooperation or conflict?

5. *What third parties are involved as audiences or possible participants? Does one of the parties want to save face before a third party, so that a strong nonconciliatory stance might seem appropriate? Or does a third party press for a peaceful resolution? If so, does the third party maintain peace with force or with censure, or does it serve as a conciliator?*

6. *What are the strategies and tactics that have been employed during the course of conflict? Can we characterize the bases of power (reward, coercion, expertise, legitimacy, reference, and information) that each party utilizes in attempting to achieve its ends? Is there free communication, or is interaction restricted?*

7. *How does the conflict affect the participants? How do the techniques, strategies, and weapons used by each party affect both that party and the opposition? Here one should look for the ways in which competitive conflict might lead to hostile conflict. Alternatively, one could examine how a conciliatory strategy might or might not reduce hostility. (Our discussion of groupthink and the Nixon group might be relevant here.)*

Field Experimental Studies of Intergroup Conflict

These questions can be used to examine case histories of intergroup conflict or to guide a conciliator or mediator who is trying to understand a conflict in order to help terminate it. These questions should also be used in setting up laboratory simulations of conflicts or field experiments, and in analyzing the outcome of such studies.

Bull Dogs and Red Devils, Panthers and Pythons, Eagles and Rattlers. Muzafer and Carolyn Sherif and their co-workers (Sherif, 1966; Sherif et al., 1961), conducted a rather dramatic series of field experiments that demonstrated how conflicts develop. They wanted to understand the process, as well as test various means for reducing conflicts. They chose an isolated, controlled field situation for their study so that they could minimize the effects of outside factors and manipulate the social setting. Their subjects were 11- and 12-year-old boys at a summer camp. The researchers conducted three experiments: one in Connecticut in 1949; the second in rural, upstate New York in 1953; and the third in Oklahoma in 1954. The same essential design was followed in each, although variations were introduced in the successive studies based upon the earlier findings. Despite the geographic differences, the processes observed by the researchers were strikingly similar.

Setting the stage for conflict. Through interviews with the boys

and their parents, clinical testing, and observation of the boys while
at play, the researchers selected those who were considered normal
and psychologically healthy, so that the experience would not be
harmful to them, and so that their later behavior would not be interpreted as acting out by maladjusted boys. To minimize the effects
of any prior hostility, at the outset the boys were given three days of
relative freedom in which to become acquainted. Sociometric studies
were conducted to determine friendship patterns. Then the boys
were assigned to either of two groups, and their sleeping accommodations were reassigned so that the two groups were physically separated from each other. This assignment deliberately separated each
boy from those with whom he had been most friendly. Sociometric
measures would thus indicate that each of the two groups was initially low in group cohesiveness.

The activities during the week that followed were planned to try
to develop cohesiveness and solidarity within these two groups; the
boys participated in such enjoyable events as camping out, cooking
meals, improving a swimming hole, clearing athletic fields, boating,
and various games (Sherif and Sherif, 1969). Eventually, each group
achieved its own identity and even selected its own name or
symbol—tough, fighting names—Bull Dogs and Red Devils, Panthers and Pythons, Eagles and Rattlers. Flags and other identifying
symbols were created by each group. The effectiveness of the common pleasurable activities and common goals in fostering group cohesiveness and solidarity was amply illustrated in the Connecticut
study. When the boys were first divided into two groups, they felt
considerable resentment at being separated from their friends—the
boys in the group that was later called Red Devils had 65 percent of
their friends in the opposite group (later called Bull Dogs); the future Bull Dogs had 65 percent of their best friends in the Red Devils
group. Within five days, the initial resentment vanished and new
friendships became firmly established: 95 percent of the Red Devils
now chose fellow Red Devils for friends, and 88 percent of the Bull
Dogs similarly chose friends from their own group.

Experimentally induced conflict. Having established two highly
cohesive groups, the research team focused on trying to foster intergroup conflict through competition and negative interdependence.

Various competitive games, tournaments, and contests were introduced, such as tug-of-war, a treasure hunt (with the winning team
sharing the treasure), baseball, football, competitive tent pitching,
and prizes for the group that had the neatest cabin. The effects of
negative interdependence with the opposite group were heightened
by establishing positive interdependence within groups—if a group
won, *all* of the members would share an attractive prize (each boy
might receive a highly valued pocket knife). The effects of compe-

tition were not immediately apparent. Particularly since the boys still had friends in the opposite group, there was an attempt at "good sportsmanship," which is often emphasized (through lip service) in "friendly" competitive sports. The Bull Dogs, after winning a contest, would demonstrate that they were good winners with a cheer, "Two! Four! Six! Eight! Who do we appree-shee-ate? RED DEVILS!" It did not take very long, however, for such competitive conflict to take its toll. Soon the chant of good sportsmanship was changed: "Two! Four! Six! Eight! Who do we appree-shee-HATE!"

The experimenters also managed to heighten the level of intergroup tension by deliberately introducing events that frustrated one group and appeared to have been caused by the other. At one point during the 1949 study, for example, when there was already quite a bit of hostility between the two groups, the staff gave a party "to let bygones be bygones"; they prepared a table of refreshments (ice cream and cake), half of which were whole and delectable, and the other half crushed, soggy, and unappetizing. Unknown to the boys, the experimenters had arranged for the Red Devils to arrive first, and naturally they took the most appetizing refreshments. The Bull Dogs were furious when they saw what was left for them, and they called the Red Devils "pigs," "Red Bums," and "jerks." In re-

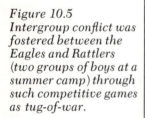

*Figure 10.5
Intergroup conflict was
fostered between the
Eagles and Rattlers
(two groups of boys at a
summer camp) through
such competitive games
as tug-of-war.*

taliation, the next day, the Red Devils deliberately left the breakfast table in a messy state so that the job of cleaning up would be more difficult for the Bull Dogs (who were on K.P. duty). The Bull Dogs then smeared "the table with cocoa, sugar, syrup, and the like . . . leaving it alive with bees and wasps" (p. 242). At lunch that day a fight broke out in the mess hall, with the boys throwing food and utensils around. No one could say exactly who had started this fight, but everyone was quite sure that it must have been someone in the other group.

The state of intergroup tension created by the Sherifs and their team had a number of interesting social psychological consequences, apart from the overt expressions of hostility among the Bull Dogs and Red Devils. In particular, the escalating intergroup conflict seems to have led to a form of *judgmental distortion* that made expressions of hostility virtually inevitable. When asked by the experimenters, for example, to rate their own group and the other group with respect to six adjectives (brave, tough, friendly, sneaky, smart alecks, stinkers), the boys described their own group almost exclusively in favorable terms (brave, tough, and friendly) and the other group as sneaky, smart alecks, and stinkers. The kinds of stereotypes to which intergroup conflict gives rise and the manner in which they reinforce and further intensify a conflict are obviously important issues—to which we shall return.

The Connecticut experiment began to take on more ominous dimensions after the fight in the mess hall; each group became convinced that that fight was only a prelude to an even greater battle. The Bull Dogs felt that they had to defend themselves, and so they raided neighboring orchards for green apples. The Red Devils stockpiled their own arsenal of apples for defense against the Bull Dogs. They were quite certain that the sneaky Bull Dogs, who had defeated them (by using wiles) in most of the competitive sports, must be preparing for a sneak attack. The Red Devils finally decided to undertake a preemptive first strike while the Bull Dogs and the counselors were asleep. Sherif reported that although the Red Devils had not been too well organized during the competitive sports, the physical threat motivated them to organize themselves to deal with their enemies. Differences and disagreements within the group were put aside, and the social structure and leadership were more readily accepted. The Bull Dogs also demonstrated planning and coordination for the purpose of attacking the Red Devils and defending themselves—there were no chance skirmishes consisting of hostile acts between individuals, but rather a coordinated, well-planned attack.

Escalation and runaway norms. Within the two opposing groups of campers could be found the same pressures to conform that we noted earlier in the Kennedy and Nixon advisory groups. As the conflict developed, it became less and less acceptable to maintain contact with the members of the opposing group. Those boys who initially tried to continue their early friendships with those in the other group found that they were being treated as traitors by their new group. The nonconformists were punished by means of the "silent treatment," ridicule, and threats. The Bull Dogs punished their nonconformists by requiring them to improve the swimming hole by removing a specified number of boulders. An initially popular leader who pleaded for understanding and conciliation with the "enemy" was castigated and replaced. At each stage of the escalating conflict, runaway norms within the groups were clearly evident—no boy could afford to appear softer than the other group members in dealing with the "enemy." A boy who had been punished for being a "bully" and pushing others around during the first few days of camp now acquired new status as a hero in his group, in keeping with the group's tougher position toward the "enemy." Thus, as conflict developed, toughness typically became more of a virtue. There was one exception however—among the Eagles in the 1954 experiment. That group developed a norm of "goodness" and deliberately tried to appear "holier than thou," in contrast to the rough, rowdy Rattlers. The "enemy" was cited as a negative referent: When an Eagle was asked, "Do you want to go around swearing, being rough, and selfish like a Rattler?" he replied, "No." Instead of having a boisterous rally before any competition, the Eagles would huddle in solemn prayer—but praying that they would be victorious and that their "enemy" would be vanquished.

In each of the three experiments, there were three stages, each of which lasted about a week. The first stage was devoted to establishing cohesiveness and an in-group feeling among the separate groups of boys; the second stage focused on developing intergroup conflict; and the third dealt with attempts to reduce the conflict. During the second stage in each experiment, the conflict mushroomed to an almost intolerable level. The staff was extremely hard-pressed in trying to prevent an outbreak of serious disorder; before the third stage could be implemented, the staff needed two full days of "preaching and coercion" in order to keep the two groups from attacking each other again.

It should be stressed again that in these experiments the research plan minimized the likelihood that conflict would erupt because of *initial* hostility. As mentioned earlier, hostility is often the source of conflict, as, for example, when there is prejudice between two groups because of differences in language, culture, or religion. In this case, the boys in each group initially had many friends in the counterpart group, and the two groups were not essentially different from one another. Also, as in the Zimbardo et al. (1973) Stanford prison study (see page 306), it appears that the situation (rather than the characteristics of the boys) was largely responsible for their conflict. If observers had been present at one of the camp sites at the height of the hostilities, they might have easily concluded that they were observing vicious, disturbed, neurotic, or basically wicked boys (they might have also reached the same conclusions if they had ventured into the "Stanford County Jail"). Yet the participants in both cases were carefully selected young boys or men from "good" backgrounds who showed no signs of any prior psychological disturbance.

The situation that produced the conflict, as set up by the experimenters, was negative goal interdependence—competition. The boys' competitive conflict eventually led to hostile conflict; they became more interested in injuring the "enemy" than in attaining their own discrepant goals. This same type of conflict seems to arise in so many situations: among business competitors, between husband and wife on the tennis court, among players on the football field, but even more, among those on the hockey rink.

Before we mention some of the devices that Sherif and his coworkers used in order to reduce the hostility among the campers, let us reexamine some of the phenomena observed in the camp studies and their prevalence elsewhere.

Figure 10.6
A competitive conflict can easily become a hostile conflict, as in this rugby match between Richmond and Oxford universities, held at Richmond, Surrey, England.

Development and Escalation of Conflict

In order to understand the implications of the Sherifs' studies for intergroup, interorganizational, and international conflicts, the camp situation can be examined as a process of escalation. The antagonism between the two groups of campers began with competition; as the competitive conflict changed into a hostile conflict, there were mutual threats (which were best exemplified by the accumulation of apple arsenals); there were also changes in intergroup communication and intergroup perception.

Mutual Threats and Conflict. Traditionally, nations have relied upon a superior military force (or the threat of force) in order to deter an enemy attack and thereby assure peace. The justification for large arms expenditures has been held to be their deterrent value—we must be strong so that no enemy would dare attack us. Although this is a logical position, there is evidence that the mere availability of a threat may actually reduce the possibility of mutual cooperation, as the collection of an arsenal of apples by the Red Devils ("in case we need them") led to a similar accumulation by the Bull Dogs—followed by an apple war. When the United States developed its atomic bomb, some people believed that this deterrent would assure us of peace. When the Soviet Union detonated its first nuclear bomb, some people said that now we could *really* be assured of peace because there would be mutual deterrence. A less optimistic picture of the value of threats in achieving accommodation is presented in a series of studies by Morton Deutsch and Robert Krauss (1960, 1962; Krauss and Deutsch, 1966) and later research that was summarized by Deutsch (1973).

The Deutsch and Krauss trucking game. This experimental game consisted of two players, each of whom took the role of a trucking company. Each company, Acme and Bolt, was given the sum of $4.00 in working capital and assigned the task of moving a truckload of merchandise from a starting point to a destination as quickly as possible; the company would be paid according to the time taken to make the trip—$.60 for each completed delivery, minus $.01 per second for operating costs. There were two routes that the company could follow, one a short and direct route, and the other a long and winding route. Although each company's goal was independent, the routes were constructed so that there was a very high degree of means interdependence (see Figure 10.7). The short and direct path for each company included a one-lane road, which was also part of the short and direct path for the other.

The subjects in the first experiments were women clerks at a telephone company. Each subject was given the map shown in Figure 10.7 and a panel containing a switch that could be pushed to

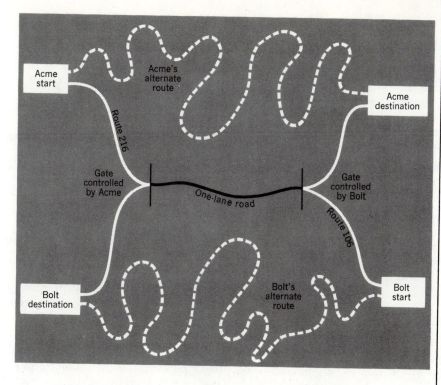

*Figure 10.7
The Acme-Bolt road
map (Deutsch and
Krauss, 1962).*

move the truck forward or backward and a numbered meter that
showed the position of the company's truck on the map. The subject
could not know the position of the other company's truck unless
there was a confrontation on the one-lane road; in this case, a light
would appear on the panels of both players. Each pair of subjects
played the game for 20 turns, or trials. This situation of high means
interdependence and goal independence led to implicit bargaining
and an agreement to take turns on the one-lane road in order to maximize the gains for both players. The profits for both companies improved during successive trials.

In variations of the game, gates were introduced that could be
used as threats. Bolt could push a switch closing a gate at the end of
the one-lane road that was closest to Bolt's starting position; Acme
had a similar gate near her starting position. With this bilateral threat,
which, the players were told, did not have to be used, each of the
companies lost money. The players chose to use the gates, and each
side retaliated against the other by blocking the one-lane road with
her truck. Thus, the short common path—the interdependence in
means—was converted into a counterthreat, though at some expense
to each company, since the longer a truck blocked the path, the
greater the cost for each side. But what if only one company con-

trolled a gate? It might be expected that that company would become quite powerful by manipulating the situation for its own benefit. However, in a Unilateral Threat Condition, where Acme alone could use the gate (although she was informed that she did not have to), her profits, as well as Bolt's, were less than in the No Threat Condition, but were noticeably greater than in the Bilateral Threat Condition. The significant point is that both the Unilateral and Bilateral Threat Conditions could be converted to the No Threat Condition (which provided maximal profits) by simply deciding not to use the gates. In the Bilateral Threat Condition, however, it appears that each player readily inferred the intention of the other from capability alone (if she possesses the threat, she will probably use it); in that condition in particular (although to a lesser extent in the Unilateral Threat Condition as well), the inference led to the actual use of each side's own weapon in defense or retaliation. This phenomenon has also been observed in other experimental situations (Pruitt, 1965; Meeker, Shure, and Moore, 1964).

It should be mentioned that in a critique of this study, some evidence was presented indicating that failure to reach an accommodation in the Unilateral and Bilateral Threat Conditions may have been due to the very small sums of money at stake (Gallo, 1966). However, Deutsch (1973) has reviewed a number of later studies and reports the negative effects of threat potential even when larger amounts of money are at stake.

This simple interpersonal paradigm of threat and conflict seems to reflect a relatively common phenomenon observed in intergroup and international conflict. Frequently, the availability of a threat does not serve to reduce or forestall conflict, but may intensify it. This outcome has been observed in both experimental situations and international events (Katz, 1965; Pruitt, 1965; Schelling, 1960; Meeker, Shure, and Moore, 1964). The evidence from analyses of primitive societies (Eckhardt, 1975) as well as modern nations (Alcock, 1972; Newcombe and Wert, 1972) strongly suggests that preparations for war are more likely to provoke rather than prevent it. The escalation of conflict among the various nations of Europe from the time of the assassination of the Austrian archduke, Francis Ferdinand, in June 1914, to the outbreak of World War I (a war that neither group of nations desired) has been analyzed in terms of the availability and utilization of mutual threats for the purpose of deterrence (North, Brody, and Holsti, 1964). Even when one side appears to have superior force at its disposal, this threat will not necessarily deter the weaker side from increasing its own potential, if it has any hope of forestalling an attack. In 1939, Poland, despite its weakness, mobilized all of its defenses against the threat of a far stronger Nazi Germany (Katz, 1965).

Outside the laboratory, one might hope that the use of available threats could be prevented by means of negotiations. In the first trucking game experiment, the subjects, sitting in separate booths, could not speak to each other. In a later trucking game, Deutsch and Krauss provided an intercom system so that the subjects could speak to each other. Communication was utilized in the No Threat Condition, where it was not really necessary. However, it was not used very often in the Unilateral or Bilateral Threat Conditions and, even when it was, it had little effect on the outcome. The reason for this will be discussed later.

Communication Changes and Autistic Hostility. Theodore Newcomb has examined the development of conflict in relation to the deterioration of communication. First of all, the *amount* of overt communication between the parties decreases. In the Deutsch and Krauss trucking game experiment, the channels for verbal communication were scarcely used once the threat had become evident. Secondly, the affect of the communication changes; available channels are used to send hostile rather than friendly messages. In addition, communications tend to be distorted; what may be intended as a friendly or neutral message will often be interpreted as a hostile one. In a variation of the trucking game, a number of subjects were asked to communicate with each other. The following exchange took place between one pair of subjects: "We're both stopped."/ "Are you going to open your gate?" /"Why should I?"/ "I'll do the same next time."/"Is that a threat?"/ "You playing tricks?" (Deutsch, 1973, p. 242). Note that the words of one subject, "I'll do the same next time," which were probably intended to be conciliatory, were interpreted as being threatening by the other subject. Inadequate communication, particularly in a context that might promote suspicion, leads to a distorted view of the other party. Thus, hostility may develop that is not justified by the reality of the situation; Newcomb calls this "autistic hostility" (Newcomb, 1947). Of course, the point of interest here is that autistic hostility, which is due to inadequate communication, leads to behavior that is hostile, thus providing adequate justification for hostility—but even this behavior tends to be distorted, thereby increasing conflict.

The Kaingáng Indians fight to extinction. The social anthropologist Jules Henry provided a vivid example of the development of autistic hostility and its dire effects in describing his observations of the Kaingáng Indians, who live in the dark, threatening jungles of Brazil (Henry, 1941). The hidden dangers of man, beast, and the elements are so great that the Kaingáng culture, folk tales, and belief systems are imbued with threats of doom and make many references to *lu* (the threatening world). In the jungle the Kaingáng larger family tends to divide into small subunits, and each subunit is then seen as a potential competitor for scarce resources and as a potential mortal threat. When a Kaingáng sees a shadowy form through the thick jungle growth, he is inclined to experience the following thought process:

> *Everything outside threatens. This is my* lu, *my doom. My body is in constant danger of destruction, and I must take action against that threat. Contemplating action I feel guilt. Feeling guilt I project: "The other person fears me because he knows what is in my mind. He fears me and therefore wishes to destroy me." This is my* lu. *I must take action to prevent it. I take action and feel guilt* [p. 121].

And what action does he take? In all likelihood the Kaingáng will throw a spear at the furtive figure. Once he has acted, the other person, who probably went through the same thought process himself, has a reason for his hostility, and his original autistic hostility now becomes justified. If the victim survives, he will try to take his revenge; if he does not, then his family will do so. But even if they do not, the spear-throwing Kaingáng will feel that he must attempt to eradicate the victim's family (a preemptive first strike) since they must certainly be craving revenge. In this way, the Kaingáng Indians have almost become extinct.

Among the Kaingáng Indians, whose scarce resources foster fierce competition, whose natural environment is threatening, and whose physical setting hinders communication and produces suspicion, autistic hostility is especially likely to develop. However, numerous other persons, groups, and nations also experience the spiraling effects of changed and lessened communication (see Chapters 4 and 5). While inadequate communication does not inevitably produce hostility, it definitely appears to enhance conflict. In the Sherif experiments, the disruption of communication between the two competing groups was quite evident. One of the major results of poor communication is the distorted perception of one's opponents, the development of stereotypes, and the increased distinction between "we" and "they."

Stereotypic Thinking and Judgmental Distortion. As mentioned in Chapter 3, the majority of people need to simplify their cognitive world. In order for them to deal with the vast amount of ambiguity they encounter day in and day out, people prefer (or need) to categorize things as polar opposites: black versus white, good versus bad, we versus they, you versus me.

Although stereotyping helps us simplify a complex, disturbing world, unfortunately it also blinds us to the true variability and uniqueness of people and things. Others are either with us or against us, democrat or Fascist, capitalist or Communist; they are not perceived as individuals, groups, or nations—complex, interesting, and continually struggling entities.

Stereotypy thus gives rise to what Charles Osgood (1961) and others have called a "two-valued orientation." One of the most interesting and important consequences of a two-valued orientation is the fact that the same behavior is often perceived and described differently—depending upon *who* performs it. Consider, for example, the following pairs of perceptions suggested by Campbell (1967):

1. *We have pride, self-respect and revere the traditions of our ancestors.*

   They are egotistical and self-centered. They love themselves more than they love us.

2. *We are loyal.*

   They are clannish, exclude others.

3. *We are honest and trustworthy among ourselves, but we're not suckers when foreigners try their tricks.*

   They will cheat us if they can. They have no honesty or moral restraint when dealing with us.

4. *We are brave and progressive. We stand up for our own rights, defend what is ours, and can't be pushed around or bullied.*

   They are aggressive and expansionistic. They want to get ahead at our expense.

5. *We are peaceful, loving people, hating only our vile enemies.*

   They are a hostile people who hate us.

6. *We are moral and clean.*

   They are immoral and unclean [p. 823].

An act that one nation believes it is performing as a defensive maneuver in the cause of peace may be viewed by its opponent as outright aggression. An act that one person believes is a demonstration of love may be experienced by the object of his affection as intrusiveness or possessiveness.

In our discussion of attribution theory (see Chapter 3), it was mentioned that people go out of their way to explain events causally. With respect to stereotyping and its consequences, it appears that people tend to judge the locus of responsibility for behavior quite differently—depending upon who the actor happens to be. Possibly when *we* have performed some particularly desirable or charitable act, we may attribute this act to "good intentions" or to the kind of person we are (our true disposition); however, when *someone else* performs the same act, we may believe that it was done because of necessity or exigency; we may believe that he was nice not because of the kind of guy he is, but because he *had* to be nice or because he wanted something from us. Now consider the kinds of causal attributions we might make when some particularly unattractive, heinous, or dastardly act is performed. If we are the actor, we may attribute our nasty behavior to circumstances (having a bad day at the office, losing a game of poker, burning the cookies we were baking) rather than to a nasty disposition. However, we may perceive another person's dastardly act as attributable to his personality. Thus, "If I'm nice, it's because fundamentally I'm a nice person; if I'm nasty it's because somebody or something made me do it (so it's really not my fault)." But if the other person is nice, it may well mean that he wants something (he has designs); his nasty behavior, of course, is probably a reflection of his truly nasty nature (Jones and Nisbett, 1971).

Why is it that people tend to distort the meaning of their own and others' behavior? As mentioned earlier, stereotyping permits the perceiver to simplify an otherwise complex environment. However, it should be clear that people generally have difficulty taking the role or perspective of others. We tend to view the world from our own perspective, one that has been conditioned by our own personal needs, fears, expectations, and conceptions of reality.

Competitive and Hostile Conflict: Escalation of Conflict between Nations

Dare we draw parallels from the Sherif camp experiments to international relations—from the Red Devils versus the Bull Dogs to the U.S.S.R. versus the U.S.A.? Obviously, the complexity of the relationship and the history of the two small groups of campers can in no way be compared with the two superpowers. Yet, the process of escalation presents some parallels that are readily noted. Despite the fear, distrust, and hostility that had existed between the United States and the Soviet Union from the Bolshevik Revolution to the 1930s, World War II ended with unprecedented good feelings between the two nations; an aura of mutual admiration can be observed in film clips, recorded speeches, historical accounts and documents, and statements made by national leaders soon after the war. Recall the photos of the American soldiers, advancing through Germany from the west, rushing joyously to embrace their Russian counterparts who were moving triumphantly from the east. Recall the happy champagne parties at which Presidents Roosevelt and Truman dined and exchanged toasts with Soviet Premier Joseph Stalin and other

*Figure 10.8
American troops, who
had been advancing
through Germany from
the west, finally met
their Soviet counter-
parts, who had been
moving from the east,
on a wrecked bridge
over the Elbe River in
May 1945. How did this
spirit of camaraderie
give way to the Cold
War following World
War II?*

Soviet leaders; the optimistic pronouncements about mutual prosperity and cooperation in the peaceful development of the world; the
expressions of mutual admiration between Generals MacArthur, Eisenhower, and Marshall on the one side and Generals Bulganin,
Malenkov, and Timoshenko on the other. Although there were persons on each side who still distrusted the motives of the other side,
the over-all spirit was quite friendly and positive, and there were
mutual friendships between the groups—as in the first stage of the
Sherif experiments.

Escalation in the Cold War. Perhaps later historians will be able to
sift through the evidence and reach some conclusions as to whether
one side or the other was primarily responsible for the subsequent
Cold War, which on occasion came dangerously close to a full-scale
war. In any event, the competitive bases for conflict cannot be ignored—the competition for ideological supremacy, for control of critical land and waterways, for control of major world markets and resources, and so forth. We can also observe the steps in escalation:
there was a restriction of movement between the two countries and
in communications; the Soviet Union strengthened its military and
political control over eastern Europe, while the United States bol-
stered its relations with western Europe; both countries committed

Figure 10.9
Two Zax stopped in their tracks.

"Look here, now!" the North-Going Zax said. "I say!
You are blocking my path. You are right in my way.
I'm a North-Going Zax and I always go north.
Get out of my way, now, and let me go forth!"

"Who's in whose way?" snapped the South-Going Zax.
"I always go south, making south-going tracks.
So you're in MY way! And I ask you to move
And let me go south in my south-going groove."

espionage against the other; Czechoslovakia fell into the Soviet orbit; the United States worked rapidly to help create the North Atlantic Treaty Organization and other alliance blocs on the periphery of the Soviet Union; the Soviet Union further strengthened its alliances with eastern Europe; the United States built military bases around the Soviet Union; the Soviet Union constructed missile bases so that the American bases would be within accessible range; America established the Voice of America and Radio Free Europe to "penetrate the Iron Curtain"; the Soviet Union jammed these broadcasts; the Soviets used spies to gather information about the U.S. and its allies; the U.S. used spy planes to fly over Soviet territory; the Soviet Union blockaded West Berlin, while the U.S. airlifted supplies to the city; the Berlin wall was built by the German Democratic Republic with Soviet encouragement; both sides developed their nuclear capabilities and stockpiled weapons; the Soviet Union attempted to build missile bases in Cuba.

What about the Soviet and American mutual misperceptions?

Stereotypic Perception of Other Nations. Charles Osgood has provided the following graphic illustration of the type of double standard with which we, the United States, view both our own actions and those of the Soviet Union. He asks us to imagine that the wise philosopher Socrates has returned in order to teach the average American about the contradictions in his attitudes.

"Suppose," says Socrates, "that Russian Man were to decide that war under present conditions is intolerable and were to publicly junk all of his weapons—would you, American Man, leap to destroy him in a nuclear holocaust?" "Of course not," replies American Man—"we are only concerned with protecting ourselves, not destroying others." "Would you overrun the Soviet Union," asks Socrates, "and make slaves of the Russian people?" "For goodness sake," American Man replies with a grin, "we have no imperialist ambitions—and in any case, a world unified under our way of life would be as good for them as for us. To tell the truth," he adds, "we'd welcome the chance to get rid of our weapons and live in peace." "All right, then," says the wise Socrates, "do you think that Russian Man would leap to destroy you with his nuclear missiles if you were to lay down your weapons and render yourself defenseless?" Here there is a long pause. Finally American Man replies that maybe the Russians wouldn't, but he certainly can't take a chance on it—and in any case, he adds, they would certainly take advantage of our helplessness by over-running the world and making Communists out of everybody. "All I can conclude," says Socrates, shaking his head in puzzlement, "is that Russian Man must be somehow intrinsically different from American Man" [Osgood, 1960, pp. 35–36].

Despite the recent beginning thaw in our relations with the Soviet Union, our attitudes toward that country do not appear to have changed very much from those we held at the height of the Cold War. We continue to adhere to what Osgood has described as a "bogey-man conception of the enemy"—a view in which our adversaries are seen as fundamentally different from us and far less worthy.

The social developmental psychologist Urie Bronfenbrenner visited the Soviet Union during the summer of 1960, spoke with many of its citizens, and returned to this country with vivid impressions of what he has called the "mirror image in Soviet-American relations." According to Bronfenbrenner, the United States has a distorted image of what Russia and the Russians are like, but they, too, view us in equally twisted, unrealistic ways. Bronfenbrenner said that there was a remarkable similarity in the stereotypic views of Americans and Russians. Each side is convinced that the other is the aggressor; that it cannot be trusted; that its people are exploited and deluded by the government; that the vast majority of its people are not really sympathetic to the government; and that its policies verge on madness.

The great danger inherent in such stereotypic views, of course, is (as Bronfenbrenner himself pointed out) that they tend to be self-confirming. We expect the Russians to be wholly untrustworthy; therefore, we tend to treat them (and any peaceful overtures they might make) with suspicion, thereby eliciting from them the very negative, hostile, and untrustworthy behavior that we suspected in the first place. Moreover, we tend to view their attempts to increase our trust and their trustworthiness as further confirmation of our initial conviction—that they must want something of us, or else why would they be nice? Meanwhile, the Russians proceed with an identical set of distortions. It is unfortunate, but probably true, that prophesies of suspicion and untrustworthiness are more readily fulfilled and confirmed by the behavior of others than are prophesies of trust, kindness, and benevolence (Bronfenbrenner, 1961).

Stuart Oskamp demonstrated the process of selective distortion and evaluation (Oskamp, 1965). He presented to a group of American college students two parallel lists of 50 acts, conciliatory and belligerent, that had been undertaken by *both* the United States and the Soviet Union. Each of these acts was correctly attributed to either the U.S. or the U.S.S.R., and the students were asked to rate them on a 6-point scale (0—"strongly unfavorable"; 6—"strongly favorable"). The following act—"The U.S. government has provided military training and assistance to smaller nations"—was rated, on the average, as 4.15 (rather favorable); on the other hand, "The U.S.S.R. has provided military training and assistance to small nations" was rated very unfavorable at 1.85. On 45 out of 50 acts, the evaluation was significantly dependent upon whether it was attributed to the U.S. or the U.S.S.R.

Misperception and Escalation in the Vietnam War.   The perceptual distortion that accompanied escalation of the Cold War was also apparent in America's participation in the Vietnam War. Social psychologist Ralph K. White traced the United States's adventures and misadventures in Southeast Asia to six types of distorted misperception:

1. *A diabolical enemy-image—our view that the Vietcong were inscrutable people who were capable of infinite deception, atrocities, and aggression, and who were resourceful in the worst, most fiendish kind of way.*
2. *A virile self-image—our belief that we and our military policy were determined, unswerving, and unflinching, and that all who did not share this view were gutless, lily-livered chickens.*
3. *Military overconfidence—our belief (not based on a realistic as-*

sessment of the situation) that we would surely "win." Each campaign seemed to bring us just one battle closer to total victory, but that elusive victory could simply not be attained.

4. *Lack of empathy—our inability or unwillingness to take the role of the other, to understand the Weltanschauung of the Vietcong, and thus to be able to wage the conflict more realistically.*

5. *Selective inattention—our tendency to selectively ignore a number of events that might have altered our position and persistence in the war, for example, our role in installing President Ngo Dinh Diem and our implicit support of his undemocratic regime, the large-scale corruption within the government of South Vietnam, the probable outcome of our bombing of North Vietnam (we should have learned from our experience in the Korean War that this would probably stiffen [rather than soften] Communist resistance and morale), and so forth.*

6. *A moral self-image—our view that we were not only strong but right and just—that "God was on our side."*

White's (1966) analysis of our participation in the Vietnam War resembles Janis's later analysis of groupthink. They both emphasized that there was a stereotypic view of the enemy, coupled with a stereotypic view of our own country (our strength, our moral rectitude), selective inattention, and an inability to see the perspective of the other side. Although it is tempting to look at the entire conflict between the U.S. and the U.S.S.R. or the opposing forces in Indochina as merely attributable to mutual errors in perception, such an analysis would grossly oversimplify the situation. Our purpose here has been to examine the escalation of conflict as a dynamic process, with competitive conflict contributing to hostile conflict and vice versa through the interplay of incompatible goals and perceptual errors.

REDUCING INTERGROUP CONFLICT

Thus far we have presented a very pessimistic view of the escalation of conflict. We pointed out that competitive conflict can lead to hostile conflict. As hostility rises, there is increased distortion and distrust of the other; each act of defense is seen as a potential attack; the implication of each attack is exaggerated, thereby leading to counterattack; soon the accelerating spiral produces destruction and mutual loss. Is there any way to stop this and reverse the trend? Some initial clues may be provided by the Sherifs' studies.

Reducing Tension and Hostility in the Sherif Field Experiments

Having created a situation of intergroup tension and perceptual distortion with remarkable ease among the campers, the Sherifs set out to understand how the conflict could be reduced and harmony restored. A number of approaches were tried, almost all of which proved to be ineffective. The researchers tried a rational approach, in which they gave each group of boys favorable information about the other group; however, this information was so dissonant with the boys' well-established negative impressions that it was invariably rejected. Then they placed *all* of the boys from both groups in negative interdependence with one another; the boys were competing individually against others from both their own and the opposing group. Although this approach might have reduced the "we-they" distinction, it didn't; the boys were still hostile toward the competitor in the *other* group, while being friendly toward the competitor in their *own* group. When the group leaders were asked to appeal for understanding of the opposing group, this approach was also rejected since there was evidence that the leaders would find themselves rejected if they did. Even increasing the amount of social contact between the members of both groups failed to reduce intergroup tensions; it produced greater friction instead. During the 1954 study, for example, the Sherifs deliberately introduced pleasant group activities in which both the Eagles and the Rattlers could take part: movies, fireworks displays on the fourth of July, and eating together in the same dining room. According to the Sherifs:

> *Far from reducing conflict, these situations served as occasions for the rival groups to berate and attack each other. In the dining-hall line, they shoved each other, and the group that lost the contest for the head of the line shouted "Ladies first!" at the winner. They threw paper, food, and vile names at each other. An Eagle bumped by a Rattler was admonished by his fellow Eagles to brush "the dirt" off his clothes. The mealtime encounters were dubbed "garbage wars" by the participants [Sherif and Sherif, 1969, p. 256].*

The Use of Superordinate Goals and Common Threats. The *only* clearly effective means for reestablishing friendly relationships between the groups turned out to be the introduction of "superordinate goals" and common threats, that is, goals and threats that superseded those possessed by each group individually and that resulted in positive goal interdependence between the groups. (The manner in which common goals and threats were implemented varied from one experiment to another.) At one of the camps an outside team was brought in to compete in sports with a team made up

*Figure 10.10
The conflict between
the Eagles and Rattlers
was reduced by the in-
troduction of superor-
dinate goals. When the
camp truck "broke
down," both groups
worked together coop-
eratively to tow the
truck to be repaired.
They used the same
rope here that they had
once used competitively
in a tug-of-war (see Fig-
ure 10.5).*

of boys from both groups. The Sherifs later deliberately clogged the
water supply system and led the boys to believe that the clogging
had been done by a common enemy. Thus, they created a hardship
for everybody, necessitating mutual cooperation between the groups
in order to repair the system. On another occasion, when both groups
were on their way to a campout, the camp truck mysteriously "broke
down." Working alone, neither group could tow the truck in for repair, but when the two groups combined their strength and worked
as a single team, they were able to do it. As an interesting symbolic
touch, the very rope that had once been used to wage a nasty tug-of-
war was later used in a cooperative endeavor with all the boys pulling together.

   Initially, the cooperation that brought the boys together was
forced upon them by circumstances—an outside team coming in to
compete in sports; the desperate need for water, which could only be
met by a joint endeavor; and the necessity for working together to
move the truck. Once this type of promotive interdependence had
been established, the way was clear for cooperation on less crucial
matters. When both groups said that they wanted to see a certain film
that was rather expensive to rent, the boys were informed that the
camp could not "afford" it. As a consequence, each group donated
enough money from its own treasury so that the film could be obtained and enjoyed by both groups together.

As positive interdependence increased, the contacts between the groups became more friendly. While waiting in the mess-hall line, the boys were less apt to shove the members of the other group. Mutual entertainment was planned before a common campfire. One group used a $5.00 prize it had won in a competition to treat its opponents to malted milks. On various questionnaire rating scales, the boys showed greater esteem for the members of the opposite group, although they still preferred the members of their own group; it was evident that some boys still tended to avoid sitting with members of the counterpart group on the bus. (At this point we should add that the Sherifs and their colleagues were particularly concerned about possible untoward aftereffects of the camp experience. Later on, they interviewed a large number of the boys and their parents and found no sign of any lasting negative consequences. In most cases, the participants and their parents were very much interested in taking part in another similar camp program the following year [Sherif, 1975].)

Sherif and his colleagues concluded that, contrary to the view held by many students of intergroup relations, simple contact between groups that had been hostile was not sufficient to produce harmony, even if there were equal status contact under pleasurable circumstances. They concluded that it was more important for the two opposing groups to come together in a number of situations that posed a mutual threat or that presented common significant goals requiring the joint effort of both groups. They also concluded that it was much easier to induce and encourage intergroup conflict than it was to reduce or terminate it afterward.

Reducing Conflict between Groups, Organizations, and Nations

The Sherif field experiments concluded that it was important to establish common goals and emphasize common threats in order to mitigate intergroup conflict. Other mechanisms can also help to reduce tensions: (1) improving the channels of communication between the conflicting groups; (2) utilizing representatives or spokespersons to facilitate communication between the groups; (3) introducing third parties; and (4) separating the larger conflict into small and more readily manageable parts. These devices are, of course, utilized in the process of emphasizing common goals and working together in the face of common threats.

Closing the Communication Gap. For those who place their faith in rationality, it is satisfying and convenient to explain social conflict as merely a breakdown in communication and understanding. These people assume that if only the opposing parties could be brought

together to speak openly and freely, many problems could be solved. This faith in rationality has led some social theorists who hope to find a simple way to improve relationships between groups to urge desegregation of schools and housing, and to set up workshops that would bring together various racial, religious, and ethnic groups, or that would bring together those with conflicting interests (the police and representatives of the community, or management and workers). Unfortunately, as the Sherifs' data suggest, such reliance on opportunities for speaking together tend to be disappointing. Ordinarily, such opportunities are not fully utilized, or—even worse—are utilized ineffectively. When a conflict is not too serious, there is some evidence that talking may actually help to mitigate tension. However, when a conflict is more intense, talking is not too effective, and it may even exacerbate a precarious situation. Channels of communication may be used to communicate hostility; furthermore, as Newcomb pointed out in his discussion of autistic hostility, even potentially friendly messages can be misperceived (Newcomb, 1947).

The futility of expecting simple social contact to lead to tension-reducing communication can be seen in a news headline: "TWO SIDES SIT SILENTLY 4½ HOURS AT KOREAN TRUCE MEETING" (*Philadelphia Evening Bulletin,* April 11, 1969). The accompanying article went on to describe an incident in which Major General James B. Knapp (an American negotiator for the United Nations Command) and Major General Ri Choon-sun (a negotiator for the Democratic People's Republic of North Korea) each sat silently waiting for the other to propose a recess at the 289th meeting of the Korean Military Armistice Commission. The truce meeting lasted a total of nearly 12 hours during which time neither general ate nor went to the toilet. Finally, after the 4½-hour silence, General Ri simply got up, walked out, and drove away.

In our earlier discussion of the Deutsch and Krauss trucking game (page 442), we noted that in some conditions, the subjects were given the option of speaking to each other if they wanted to. It was found that the two players utilized the intercom very little, especially when they were in the midst of intense conflict. Thus, in support of Newcomb's autistic hostility hypothesis, intense conflict was accompanied by restricted and distorted communication (Krauss and Deutsch, 1966).

Still hoping to show that serious conflict could be reduced by communication, Deutsch and Krauss used the trucking game with other subjects, and they required each player to communicate with the other ("say anything you want . . . but you must say something"). The results were discouraging; the players used the intercom to mislead, intimidate, insult, and show contempt for one another (Deutsch and Krauss, 1962). In a final attempt, the researchers told another group of adversaries that they must not only speak but must "make a proposal which you think is reasonable and acceptable both to yourself and to the other person . . . which you would be willing to accept." Only in this condition of "tutored communication" was the conflict ameliorated. It thus appears that during an intense conflict, directive intervention from a skilled third party may be necessary before communication can be effective (Krauss and Deutsch, 1966).

Reducing Conflict by Means of Group Representatives. When there is conflict between nations, large groups, or organizations, it is obviously impractical to bring everyone together for direct discussion and negotiation. Even with small groups, a good argument can be made that conflict resolution would be more effective if the discussion took place between a few chosen leaders or representatives rather than involving everyone in both groups. It might reasonably be expected that the leaders would have a broader perspective than the average members. They might also be more effective in interpersonal relations and more sensitive to alternative points of view. With greater responsibility for the welfare of their group, they would probably be less likely to emphasize their own personal needs and prejudices. After reaching an amicable settlement with the opposing group, the leaders, because of their prestige and authority, might be able to persuade their members to accept and reconcile themselves to their opponents. The effectiveness of group leaders in reducing intergroup tensions, then, is probably due in part to their ability to make concessions and demands that are beyond the capabilities of individual members. To the extent that a group empowers its negotiator with decision-making authority (as it must if the representative is to be able to reach an agreement), it grants him the power to speak with the full force and authority of the group behind him and to adopt a more flexible position in dealing with others than would be possible for the group as a whole. Indeed, most peace settlements reached by large conflicting organizations or nations have been negotiated by leaders or group representatives.

The limited idiosyncrasy credit of group representatives. Despite the power and flexibility accorded group negotiators, however, it is important to bear in mind that representatives are ultimately limited by the attitudes of the groups they represent, and they can often be held responsible for the accord reached or for its failure. When there is a serious conflict between groups, a leader who takes a position that is too conciliatory for the group members may find himself displaced and punished. For example, a labor leader may be fired for negotiating a "sweetheart contract" with management, and the agreement will be rejected by the union members. In the

Sherif studies, leaders could not be used to reduce the intergroup conflict because conciliatory leaders would almost certainly have been accused of being traitors by their constituencies.

That accountability to one's group may very well affect a negotiator's behavior can be seen in a series of studies conducted by Robert Blake, Jane Mouton, and their co-investigators (Blake and Mouton, 1961; Blake, Shepard, and Mouton, 1964). One hundred and fifty groups, comprising about 1000 subjects, participated in their studies; the subjects included college students, as well as business and industrial executives who were attending human relations workshops. In a typical study, two groups made up of seven to twelve members, who had been matched on the basis of relevant personal characteristics, were paired, and each group spent 10 to 12 hours together in the human relations training program. When a high degree of group cohesiveness had been developed, each group was asked to solve a human relations problem and prepare a group position statement. Each group then selected a member representative to meet with a representative of the opposing group to discuss their two solutions to the problem and to work out a mutually acceptable joint solution. During the negotiations, which were held in public, the group members could send their representatives notes, instructing them how to proceed or asking them about the opposing group's proposal. These notes seemed to be aimed more at destroying the opposition's position than at comparing similarities and differences. As the investigators had predicted, group loyalty was stronger than reason. When a panel of impartial judges rated the position paper of one group as superior to that of the other, there was overwhelming pressure on the representative from the less favored group to stand firm behind his group's position; in one study, 60 out of 62 representatives refused to back down from their own group's position (Blake and Mouton, 1961). Although the negotiators had all been rated very favorably by their respective groups when they were selected, those who appeared to be too conciliatory during the negotiations were soon viewed as traitors and were evaluated as less mature, less intelligent, and less well-intentioned than formerly.

The pressure on a negotiator to present a tough image. In addition to direct presures from his own group members, a negotiator faces problems that are quite common among those who perform in public, and who are therefore concerned about their image. In our society, as well as in many others, there are strong cultural pressures to appear competent, strong, and effective when dealing with others, especially in public (Brown, 1968; Rubin and Brown, 1975; Goffman, 1959; Kogan, Lamm, and Trommsdorff, 1972). In the Deutsch and Krauss trucking game, the players were much less inclined to be conciliatory and to refrain from making threats if there had been any suggestion that they had been ridiculed for their cooperative behavior by an observing audience (Brown, 1968). Thus, negotiators tend to take a hard line in public. Because of the pressures on a group representative to champion his own group's position, to make a show of competence and strength, and to take an extreme position, his ability to facilitate resolution of intergroup conflict may be drastically curtailed. An effective group conciliator must carefully gauge what his own group will accept, and then either limit his agreements with the opposing group accordingly or first prepare his own group for concessions that will undoubtedly be necessary to reach a peaceful solution. In any event, he must have the personal strength to withstand the criticism and possible loss of esteem that will almost certainly accompany any move toward compromise. Otherwise, it is likely that the negotiator will be pressed to take a much harder line on behalf of his group than he would if he were negotiating only on his own behalf (Benton and Druckman, 1974).

Use of Third Parties in Negotiation. While the Sherif camp experiments were presented as a conflict between two groups, we should not forget that there was also a third group present, namely, the adults who conducted the research and ran the camp. During the experiments, it was the staff's coercive and persuasive power that prevented the conflict from getting completely out of hand; they helped to keep an uneasy though sporadic peace among the campers until they had introduced methods for reducing the conflict. In a similar fashion, a referee in a hockey game is always ready to place a player in the penalty box who has allowed the competitive conflict to become too hostile, and the team that cannot control its hostility may be obliged to forfeit the entire game. At the international level, a major world power from time to time uses its coercive power to maintain peace; for example, there was the *Pax Romana* during the Roman Empire and the *Pax Britannica* during the nineteenth century. Any peace that is maintained by coercion will almost certainly be an uneasy peace, ready to deteriorate into conflict whenever the surveillance or coercion of the third party is reduced. Often, however, the third party may act as the staff did in the Sherif experiments—providing a means of communication between the opposing groups, mediating the conflict, giving an "objective" view of the disagreement, or arranging for a common threat.

Some third-party roles, such as conciliator, mediator, arbitrator, and fact-finder tend to be relatively formal; others, such as intermediary or special envoy (the role Henry Kissinger sometimes played) tend to be more informal. Formal third-party roles are often defined legally or stem from a prior formal agreement between the opposing groups. In the case of a formal arrangement, the two sides are at least obliged to recognize the legitimacy of the third party's role, and they may even be compelled to abide by his recommendations (as in the case of an arbitrator or judge). With respect to an informal third party, there are usually no previously agreed upon specifications for his authority or legitimate range of activity. But his effectiveness will depend upon his ability to demonstrate his authority and legitimacy to the satisfaction of the adversaries.

Experimental studies that demonstrate the value of third parties. Let us now briefly consider some of the experimental work done on the effectiveness of third parties. One particularly pertinent study, conducted by Dean Pruitt and Douglas Johnson, used a paradigm (known as the Bilateral Monopoly game) to study bargaining and negotiation (Siegel and Fouraker, 1960). This game consists of two players—a lone Buyer and a lone Seller—each of whom attempts to maximize his profits by negotiating the particular price and quantity at which imaginary merchandise will be bought or sold. The negotiations are conducted by means of a series of written offers and counteroffers; these are based on a profit table that specifies the amount (in cents) that can be made for each possible transaction between the two players.

Using a version of this game, Pruitt and Johnson assigned their subjects to one of three possible roles—Buyer, Seller, or Recorder. It was the Recorder's job to receive the written messages exchanged between the Buyer and Seller, keep a record of them, and comment on the notes, if he wanted to. Each subject was, in fact, assigned to be the Buyer; the other two persons (unknown to the subject) were research assistants. The Seller's messages followed a prearranged program—during the first half of the session his messages indicated that he was a tough and relentless bargainer who never made an offer that would allow the Buyer to make a profit. These offers were, of course, rarely accepted. Gradually, the Seller's messages became more reasonable, allowing the Buyer to make a profit. Under such conditions, the Buyer still refused the offer and remained adamantly opposed to concessions. Questionnaires that were later given to the Buyer to complete indicated that he was reluctant to be conciliatory largely because he did not want to appear weak, a facesaving device that prevented him from making money. For half the subjects, however, the Recorder, according to the prearranged program, would assume a mediator's role. He would send a brief message to the Buyer saying, "On the basis of my predictions, I suggest that you agree on a price of ———. A copy of this note has also been sent to your opponent." The suggested price was always a perfect compromise, exactly halfway between the Buyer's and the Seller's last offer.

Pruitt and Johnson found that those subjects who were exposed to the intervention subsequently made more frequent and larger concessions than those who were not. What makes these findings particularly interesting is the fact that the intervention was actually rather limited in scope and came from someone who was never explicitly identified as a mediator or third party in the traditional sense. Yet even this rather minimal intervention proved to be quite effective. In explanation, Pruitt and Johnson suggested that third-party intervention is effective largely because it enables two opposing sides to make concessions without viewing themselves as weak for having done so and without running the risk that the other side might view them as foolish (Pruitt and Johnson, 1970). The effectiveness of a third-party mediator in bringing about concessions has also been demonstrated in a number of other similar studies (Podell and Knapp, 1969; Vidmar, 1971; Meeker and Shure, 1969; and Krauss and Deutsch, 1966).

The functions of third-party negotiators. As several investigators have pointed out, third parties serve a number of important functions, including: (1) reducing emotionalism by giving both sides an opportunity to vent their feelings; (2) presenting alternative solutions, by recasting the issues in different or more acceptable terms; (3) providing opportunities for "graceful retreat" or facesaving in the eyes of one's adversary, one's constituency, the public, or oneself; (4) facilitating constructive communication between the opposing sides; and (5) planning the meeting for the two adversaries, including such aspects as the neutrality of the meeting site, the formality of the setting, the time constraints, and the number and kinds of other people (if any) who would be there (Kerr, 1954; Walton, 1969; Rubin and Brown, 1975).

Of these various functions, one—facilitating constructive communication—may deserve special comment. Because of the fact that opposing parties make little use of opportunities to speak with one another, what kind of intervention could a third party provide? Suppose, for example, that a third party was able to persuade the two sides not to commit themselves to a course of action until they had carefully studied the issues? Could this type of intervention, in which the parties are encouraged to speak with one another for the purpose of exploring the issues and alternatives (rather than heaping invective upon one another) prove effective?

The effectiveness of such process intervention was demonstrated in an experiment with college subjects that simulated a contractual dispute between representatives of a school board and representatives of a teachers' union. At issue were questions relating to the number of students in each classroom, the amount of clerical work assigned to the teachers, and extra duties for the teachers. The third party intervened in three ways: *passive* (merely calling a break in the negotiations to allow the representatives time to rest); *content*

(calling a break and then suggesting a specific compromise solution ← content. most effective
to the problem); and *process* (calling a break during which each participant was trained to paraphrase the opponent's position and to
repeat it so that each side clearly understood the other's position).
Both forms of active intervention produced a greater number of
agreements, better joint results, and speedier resolutions than the
passive intervention; the content intervention was the most effective
of all in this study (Bartunek, Benton, and Keys, 1975).

Of course, process intervention can take place in a variety of
ways, and researchers are still examining the effectiveness of each.
One study points to the value of a prenegotiation planning session,
in which the two parties are carefully tutored to examine and understand the positions of the other side and to examine the areas of
agreement and disagreement before any bargaining takes place. It
has been found that this procedure is effective in minimizing later conflict, particularly if both parties have jointly explored their mutual positions. Clearly there is less conflict here than in the more typical situation in which both sides meet privately in a prebargaining session
to perfect their own positions (Bass, 1966; Druckman, 1968a, 1968b).
The negotiator's role in facilitating communication between the two
parties bears a striking resemblance to that of the experimenter in
the trucking game who carefully tutored the communication process
(see page 457) (Krauss and Deutsch, 1966).

As mentioned earlier, third parties can provide a number of valuable services. To do so, however, they must be perceived as authoritative and impartial, and thereby worthy of the opposing parties'
trust and confidence. Only if a third party is seen as competent, endowed with expertise, and reasonably sympathetic (or at least not un-
sympathetic) to each side's position is he likely to be effective. Expressed in terms of social influence and the bases of power (see
Chapter 6), a third party is effective to the extent that he can effectively utilize power bases other than reward or coercion: if he can
impart information (informational power), be knowledgeable (expert
power), be entitled to make certain recommendations (legitimate
power), and be perceived as fair and impartial (referent power). With
these bases of power, a third party can provide a valuable impetus to
the resolution of conflict.

Conflict Fractionation. We suspect that one of the reasons why conflicts between individuals or groups become so protracted and the
participants become so unyielding is that the issues of contention
have become fused into a monolithic whole that is not easily broken
apart. Each side views the issues as so interconnected, and the resulting complex as so overwhelming, that the give-and-take process
of concession and compromise appears impossible. For example, at

the height of the Cold War between the United States and the Soviet Union, or during the conflict between Israel and the Arab states, each side has had a bogey-man stereotypic view of the other, each has seen the disputed issues as monolithic and gargantuan, and each has been unable (or unwilling) to fragment this monolith into smaller issues—some of which could be negotiated.

One of the most obvious and important techniques for mitigating intergroup tensions is the fractionation of conflict—the division of large, all-encompassing issues into smaller, more manageable ones (Fisher, 1964). Using this technique, the contending parties may be able to avoid the negative effects of excessive loyalty and commitment that often accompany attempts to resolve monolithic issues. In other words, the opponents may be able to restructure a competitive, zero sum, "winner take all" conflict into one that includes give and take, some degree of cooperation, and a non zero sum outcome. Just as a third party's effectiveness depends to a large extent upon his ability to defuse a conflict by focusing on such intangible issues as the loss of face, the potential effectiveness of fractionation is also due to the creation of smaller issues on which concessions (without loss of face) can be made. The Cuban missile crisis was an example of conflict resolution by fractionation. At the time of the crisis, the Soviet Union suggested before the United Nations that this would be a good opportunity to discuss the major differences between the U.S. and the U.S.S.R.—the future of Cuba, international spheres of influence, and general relations between the two superpowers. It was unlikely that any headway could have been made on these global points of conflict. However, the more specific issues—the removal of missiles from Cuba and U.S. agreement not to invade Cuba—were manageable at that point and, when resolved, cleared the way for dealing with other issues.

Without a third party, is there anything an active participant in a conflict can do to de-escalate the conflict? For some years after World War II, many Americans were alarmed about the escalation of aggression between the U.S. and the U.S.S.R., and a number of solutions to the problem were proposed. Most Americans felt that we had to show the Soviets that we were more powerful and could match and exceed each of their hostile moves; they felt that by so doing, we could deter them from making a direct attack. Some even proposed a preemptive strike, before the U.S.S.R. was militarily well prepared, in order to end the escalation by totally destroying our adversary. Those who urged strong countermeasures pointed to Nazi Germany under Hitler in the 1930s; he had claimed one territory after another, each of which had been conceded by the weak Western Allies. For many of these Hawks, the justification for maintaining a position of strength and initiating an attack was so clear that they could not understand how anyone could hold any other viewpoint. The Hawks labeled those who advocated negotiation with the Soviet Union "Communist dupes" or something comparable. A certain hysteria, fanned by Senator Joseph McCarthy, swept the nation, and many persons were accused of being traitors—American leaders and various citizens who had been friendly with or cooperated with the Soviet Union either during the 1930s or during the war, especially those who had tried to maintain these long-time friendships.

Meanwhile, others advocated conciliation. Many of these people pointed to the dangers of military escalation, as in the case of the armaments race preceding World War I. They feared the ultimate catastrophe of a worldwide nuclear holocaust. The Doves argued that the Soviets were simply rearming because they feared the power of the West. Therefore, they believed we could ensure peace by disarming unilaterally, at which point the Soviets would do the same. At least it was worth trying, the Doves said, if the only other alternative was worldwide nuclear destruction: "Better red than dead!" To which the Hawks countered that we should never surrender our principles or our cherished way of life even if it meant the total destruction of the United States: "Better dead than red!" In the 1950s the Hawks' position gained strength, as each Soviet aggressive act provided justification for harsh countermeasures, which increased the escalation of hostilities.

As escalation proceeded, the imminent danger of all-out nuclear war became increasingly real. It may have been the Cuban missile crisis that brought both America and the Soviet Union face-to-face with the actual possibility of a nuclear war. In any event, at that time many thoughtful persons began a search for alternatives to all-out war or unilateral surrender. One such alternative was presented by Charles Osgood, an experimental psychologist who faced up to the deteriorating world situation and initially advocated unilateral disarmament but later proposed an intermediate, more flexible approach.

The GRIT Proposal for De-escalating International Conflict

Osgood called his proposal for de-escalation "Graduated Reciprocation in Tension Reduction" or "GRIT" (a quality he felt the party wishing to implement his program would have to possess). This is a plan for reversing the maddening spiral of escalation, for successively undoing each of the increasingly aggressive acts undertaken by two opposing parties. The approach is graduated in that it first requires taking small, not too significant steps (following the principles of conflict fractionation); there is also an expectation of reciprocation by the other party as proof that the conflict is being reduced (Osgood, 1959, 1962).

The entire program is built upon the recognition of common

goals and common threats. The common threat, in this case, was the possibility of mutual annihilation from nuclear war as presented at the beginning of this chapter. This threat was dramatically portrayed in popular literature and films, such as *On the Beach* (Shute, 1957), in which the last survivors of American-Soviet nuclear blasts await their own ultimate death from the radioactive fallout. As for common goals, what could be more attractive than the possibility of a mutual exchange of cultural achievements and mutual cooperation in scientific endeavors; there would be prosperity for both sides, as resources previously committed to armaments were used for the benefit of everyone. It is reasonable to assume that unless both sides were made fully aware of their extreme degree of positive interdependence with respect to goals, means, and threats, neither GRIT nor any other attempt to de-escalate a conflict could succeed.

Once superordinate goals, means interdependence, and common threats were spelled out clearly to both sides, the situation would be ripe for a graduated "peace offensive." This program calls for unilateral acts that would be diversified in nature and substantial enough to establish trust and invite reciprocation, yet not so great as to imply weakness or vulnerability to aggressive acts. The deeds would be broader than "disarmament" or "disengagement"; in fact, they would offer possibilities for positive "engagement" in joint efforts to serve the common good. Osgood proposed that a peace-seeking party follow these principles in selecting its unilateral acts:

1. "Unilateral acts must be seen by the opponent as reducing his external threat." The effectiveness of any unilateral act will depend not only on our choice of an act, but on our ability to present it in such a way that our opponent believes it will reduce his external threat. A unilateral act could range all the way from military disengagement to the sharing of scientific information.

2. "Unilateral acts must be accompanied by explicit invitations to reciprocation." Such invitations would encourage the opponent to think about how he might reduce our tensions, would assure him that his acts would be positively interpreted, and would indicate that the unilateral acts were not undertaken because of fear or weakness. Osgood cautioned, however, that one must be aware of differing perceptions. While we may believe that our action represents a significant concession, the other side may view it as totally insignificant; what our opponent may believe is a major concession on his part may be viewed in a totally different light by us.

3. "Unilateral acts must be executed regardless of prior commitment by the opponent to reciprocate." If we refuse to act unless our opponent has promised to reciprocate, then our freedom of action is restricted: By first acting and then inviting reciprocation, we not only begin the process, thereby inviting trust, but place on our opponent

the responsibility for any failure of these attempts at tension-reduction.

4. "Unilateral acts must be planned in sequences and continued over considerable periods regardless of reciprocation by an opponent." The first move may not be sufficient, particularly since it is likely to be relatively small and cautious. It may even be viewed as a trick by a suspicious adversary. Each successive act, however, will add cumulative pressure toward reciprocation.

5. "Unilateral acts must be announced in advance of execution and widely publicized to ally, neutral, and enemy countries as part of a consistent policy." An advance announcement will give the others time to contemplate the seriousness of our intent and to prepare themselves for the unilateral acts; it may also encourage allies and neutral countries to urge our adversary to consider reciprocal measures. The announcement also makes it clear that the unilateral acts constitute a clear and separate peace-seeking program.

6. "Unilateral acts must be graduated in risk potential" so that they could not be exploited by our opponent. Our initial acts must be of less significance than the later acts in order not to endanger our own security or frighten the more militant members of our own society. Our opponent may well scoff at the insignificance of the first acts, but the subsequent ones should indicate the seriousness of our intentions.

7. "Unilateral acts of a tension-reducing nature must be accompanied by explicit firmness in all areas." Our unilateral acts should not preclude taking a firm stand against anything our adversary might do to exploit our peace-seeking actions; any deterrent measure should be carried out carefully, unemotionally, and firmly, while reiterating our invitation to reciprocate our conciliatory acts.

Testing the Effectiveness of GRIT. After the GRIT proposal was published, several social psychologists who attempted to test it out in the laboratory obtained encouraging results. Typically, the subjects were asked to assume the role of policy-makers of two adversary nations and to interact with each other in such a way that would benefit their own nation. One elaborate study included such realistic devices as allowing the participants to obtain pictures of missiles stockpiled by their opponents (reminiscent of the Cuban missile crisis) and requiring the participants to choose whether to allocate their resources for building factories (to improve their nation's economic status) or for missiles (to improve their defensive position and offensive strength vis-à-vis the adversary). After the subject had made his choice, he received a signal on a light panel indicating the other subject's choice and the outcome, expressed in terms of his economic strength (how many factories he now had operating) and relative military strength (how many missiles he had relative to the number his opponent had). Some subjects played against fellow subjects, while others received their signals according to a prearranged program worked out by the experimenters. During certain phases of the study, the subjects were permitted to announce in advance the actions that they planned to take. Whether the other subject was real or programmed, it appeared that the GRIT strategy was most likely to lead to mutual disarmament and maximum gain for both players. However, in the interactions with a real partner, the GRIT strategy was seldom followed. Since communication tended to be used deceptively, no cooperation or trust was achieved. A player who used an aggressive strategy by increasing his stockpile of missiles was typically met by an aggressive response. A player who used a completely peaceful strategy by unilaterally converting all or most of his missiles into factories was usually taken advantage of. However, a partner who gradually converted four of his five missiles into factories found that he was met quite consistently with even greater disarmament by his opponent, with greatest gain for both. Thus, the GRIT strategy of combining small, consistent, unilateral overtures of good intentions, with honest prior announcement of these moves, led to the most favorable situation for both players (Pilisuk and Skolnick, 1968).

In an even more complex study, five subjects took the role of the leaders of five nations that were competing with one another; two of these nations were especially powerful. As part of their role, the leaders were instructed to act in their own nations' best interests, as they themselves defined this concept. As in the previously cited study, the leaders were free to allocate their nations' resources to consumer goods or armaments. They could also make peace overtures or try to forge military alliances.

The subjects met together for 13 periods of 70 minutes each; during each period they indicated their tension level by means of a self-rating scale. In one of the experimental conditions, the leader of one of the two powerful nations was instructed to adopt a GRIT strategy beginning with the seventh period. This maneuver led to a brief rise in tension among all of the leaders during the seventh period, but then their tension decreased dramatically (Crow, 1963).

Observing GRIT in International Relations. Although these two experiments are encouraging, they are limited by the fact that they are only roughly analogous to actual international conflicts. However, data gathered from various protocols also support the GRIT proposal. A study made of Soviet-American relationships between 1946 and 1963 showed that each conciliatory move made by one side was followed shortly thereafter by a conciliatory move by the other (Gamson and Modigliani, 1971). That study, by its nature, did not analyze the sequential interaction to see if graduated reciprocation was the answer. However, the sociologist Amitai Etzioni (1967, 1969) made a careful analysis of President John F. Kennedy's attempts to apply a gradualist approach in our relations with the Soviet Union between June and November 1963.

The groundwork had been laid in 1962 (before the Cuban missile crisis), when Kennedy gave a major address in which he stressed the concept of world interdependence. He said that we had all gone through a period in which our watchword was "independence" and in which most nations had sought freedom from one another. Now, he continued, we must acknowledge that on our small planet we are all interdependent—with respect to natural resources, with respect to progress in scientific developments, with respect to space exploration, and with respect to the mutual threat of nuclear annihilation. He then elaborated on a portion of his Inaugural Address: "Let both sides seek to invoke the wonders of science instead of its terror. Together let us explore the sky, conquer the desert, eradicate disease, tap the ocean depths, and encourage the arts and commerce" (Kennedy, 1961). It is possible that certain conciliatory actions taken by the Kennedy Administration were misinterpreted by the leaders of the Soviet Union. While indicating that they were ready for cooperation and that they had peaceful intentions, the Soviets secretly began to establish nuclear missile bases in Cuba. The American Hawks then argued that all attempts at rapprochement must be abandoned in favor of the sternest possible action. However, although the Kennedy overtures were not abandoned, the United States took a firm, but cautious, stand in responding to the Soviet missile threat.

In June 1963, eight months after the missile crisis had been resolved, it was announced that the President would make a major foreign policy address. On June 10, before a huge radio and television audience, Kennedy delivered his "Strategy for Peace" speech. He emphasized the "constructive changes" that had taken place since the Cuban crisis and his hopes for the future. "Mankind must put an end to war or war will put an end to mankind. . . . Our problems are man-made . . . and can be solved by man." Building on his earlier "Interdependence" speech, he called on both Americans and Russians to reexamine their views of one another and to visualize what mutual peace could bring in terms of blessings for the whole world. He also announced the first unilateral act—the United States would halt all nuclear tests in the atmosphere—and he urged the Soviet Union to reciprocate. The U.S.S.R. did so almost immediately, announcing its decision in *Izvestia*, where it reprinted the entire text of Kennedy's speech. The U.S.S.R. then withdrew its objection to a U.S. and Western-sponsored proposal to send a United Nations team to help resolve a conflict in Yemen. The U.S. announced that it would no longer oppose reseating the Hungarian delegation at the United Nations. Premier Khrushchev then publicly ordered a halt in the production of strategic bombers. Newspapers in both the U.S.S.R. and the U.S. took a more conciliatory approach in their articles about the other nation, and they emphasized peaceful activities. Trade and cultural missions were exchanged. The Bolshoi Ballet toured the U.S., and major American musicals were presented in the U.S.S.R. The U.S. was given permission to establish a new consulate in Leningrad to balance the new Soviet consulate in Chicago. American surplus wheat was sold to the U.S.S.R. Soviet and American scientists met to discuss possible joint explorations in space. As these less important ventures were undertaken, the two nations reached the point where they could discuss major issues, such as the limited nuclear test ban treaty.

During this period in 1963, some of Osgood's central hypotheses were thus supported: certain unilateral gestures were reciprocated, and these reciprocated gestures reduced tensions; some unilateral acts were followed by bilateral agreements; some of the first initiatives taken were viewed with suspicion by the other side, but as they continued, the suspicion diminished; the spiraling hostility between the two nations at first slowed, then it stopped, and then it reversed itself. Unfortunately, the assassination of President Kennedy and the escalation of the war in Southeast Asia stemmed the momentum of the Kennedy peace initiatives (Etzioni, 1967; 1969). However, since the withdrawal of U.S. troops from hostilities in Southeast Asia, there has been additional conciliation, including such major negotiations as the Strategic Arms Limitation Treaty and important U.S.-Soviet trade agreements.

In July 1975, an event of major symbolic significance contributed to the rapprochement between the United States and the Soviet Union. In a major feat of means-interdependent coordination, the U.S. space capsule Apollo docked with the Soviet capsule Soyuz, which had been launched into space two days earlier. Television pictures were relayed back to earth showing the Soviet cosmonauts and American astronauts smiling, grasping hands, and floating together weightlessly in apparent camaraderie. Thus, the competition in space exploration between the two world powers was finally converted into a cooperative effort. President Gerald Ford made the following comment: "If the Soviet Union and the United States can reach an agreement so that our astronauts can fit together the most intricate scientific equipment, work together, and shake hands 137 miles out in space, we as statesmen have an obligation to do as well on earth."

In August 1975, 35 Eastern and Western nations (including the United States and the Soviet Union) met in Helsinki and signed an

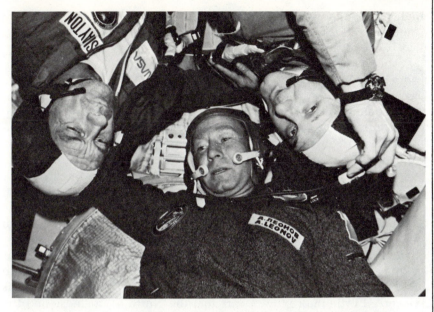

Figure 10.11
After joining their
Soyuz and Apollo cap-
sules, one Russian cos-
monaut and two Ameri-
can astronauts meet
together in outer space.

agreement that was hailed as one of the most promising of recent years. The agreement to accept the de facto post-World War II boundaries was seen as a concession from the West. There was also an agreement on vastly increased cultural exchanges; on a freer flow of information and circulation of foreign newspapers; and on the acknowledgment of human rights, including freedom of emigration and a prohibition against the forceful intervention by one nation in the affairs of another. Following a major confrontation with the Soviet Union over the persecution and limited emigration of Soviet Jews and a history of Soviet intervention in Poland, Czechoslovakia, and Hungary, this agreement seemed to be a major concession from the East, and from the Soviet Union in particular. It was, of course, emphasized that future moves toward true peace would depend upon clear evidence that the agreements were being honored. A further summit meeting was planned for Vienna; President Ford said that, at that time, he might announce a further reduction of U.S. military forces in Europe, and both sides pledged to continue their efforts to control nuclear arms.

Obviously, we should not be so optimistic as to imagine that all conflicts can readily be resolved by means of graduated reciprocation. The GRIT strategy is based on the assumption that both sides can be made aware of the extreme mutual threat that would arise as a result of continuing hostilities and the mutual gain that could be achieved by conciliation. It is difficult to see how GRIT could have reduced the conflict between Nazi Germany and the Western Allies in the late 1930s. Probably Adolf Hitler and his advisers were sufficiently confident of ultimate military victory and of securing all of their objectives that they saw nothing to be gained by concessions, except in the most temporary sense.

In an attempt to end the war in Vietnam in 1968, President Lyndon Johnson seemed to be initiating a GRIT strategy. First there were publicity statements about a forthcoming "major policy announcement." Then Johnson delivered a carefully prepared television address that was quite reminiscent of the Kennedy "Interdependence" and "Strategy for Peace" speeches. He spoke of the horrors of continued war for both the Indochinese people and the U.S., and the possibility of mutual prosperity, with technological and agricultural development in Southeast Asia. He announced a unilateral halt in the bombing of North Vietnam and invited reciprocation. The invitation did not elicit the hoped-for response. Probably the North Vietnamese viewed the halt not as a concession by the U.S., but as the abandonment of a policy that had been widely condemned as inhumane and ineffective. There is reason to believe that the North Vietnamese did not view Johnson's offers of future concessions as sincere. Furthermore, it appears that the North Vietnamese and the Vietcong were confident of securing most of their goals without any concessions, provided that they continued to fight for several years. By 1975, it was clear that their expectation had been justified.

On the other hand, President Nixon's rapprochement with the People's Republic of China did have some of the elements of GRIT. At first the United States innocuously invited the Chinese table tennis team to visit this country in return for a visit to China by the U.S. team; surprisingly, this suggestion was accepted. Later there were other cultural exchanges, a loosening of trade restrictions, modification of the U.S. policy with respect to Taiwan, and so forth.

It is not clear yet exactly when GRIT does or does not work, or how it should be modified to fit specific circumstances. In those cases where it has been successful, improved communication has led to improved perception—the mirror-image distortion cited by Bronfenbrenner has been repaired, thus bringing about better understanding, friendlier interaction, and common perceptions of interdependence.

The quest for commonality and the resolution of differences was aptly stated by President Kennedy (1963):

We must remember that there are no permanent enemies. Let each nation choose its own future so long as that choice does not interfere with the choice of others. If we cannot end our differences, at least we can help to make the world safe for diversity. In the final analysis our most common link is that all breathe the same air. We all cherish our children's future. And we are all mortal.

SUMMARY

We live in a time of rapid technological change and advancement. Yet even as we begin to explore outer space, continue to plummet the depths of our oceans, move closer to an understanding of the causes and control of certain diseases, learn to harness new sources of energy, and so forth, we are plagued by a continuing failure to fully understand ourselves and our relations with one another. Violence still erupts in our crowded urban centers, young children still learn to despise each other because of the color of their skin or the school they attend, our public leaders remain the targets of would-be assassins, and war continues to ravage our world. Our collective insights into social relations have obviously failed to keep pace with our magnificent technological achievements.

Social psychologists (like other social scientists), of course, can provide no panacea for these social ills. The road from controlled laboratory research to generalizations about intergroup and international conflict is a long and treacherous one, and it must be followed with caution and restraint. Nevertheless, it is clear that many of the social psychological principles of interaction between individuals also apply to groups. Decision-making by groups or nations in conflict, the antecedents and consequences of such conflict, as well as some of the factors that are likely to affect the resolution of intergroup conflict are each issues social psychologists have begun to address.

Working from carefully documented historical data, the social psychologist Irving Janis has argued that highly cohesive groups occasionally suffer from a "deterioration of mental efficiency, reality testing, and moral judgment that results from in-group pressure." This phenomenon of faulty group decision-making (dubbed "groupthink" by Janis) is characterized by an illusion of invulnerability and moral superiority, the illusion of unanimity of opinion among group members, the suppression by members of their personal doubts, pressures toward uniformity, the emergence of self-appointed "mindguards" (who "whip" deviant members into line as soon as possible), and docility fostered by suave leadership. Janis suggests that groupthink is a pervasive phenomenon and documents his analysis with accounts of our unsuccessful invasion of Cuba at the Bay of Pigs, our unpreparedness for the Japanese attack at Pearl Harbor, our decision to invade North Korea, and our escalation of the Vietnam War. More recently, Raven has applied the concept of groupthink to the Nixon group's role in the Watergate affair.

Social psychologists have long been interested in trying to understand the factors that lead to the development and escalation of intergroup conflict. As Morton Deutsch has observed, the issues that need to be considered include: the nature and prior history of the parties, the issues underlying the present conflict, the situation in which the conflict occurs, the presence and involvement of third parties, and the strategies and tactics employed by the participants as well as their effects on the opposition. A particularly noteworthy field experimental study of intergroup conflict was conducted by Muzafer and Carolyn Sherif, using as subjects preadolescent boys at a summer camp.

There are many unfortunate consequences of intergroup and international conflict. Besides the obvious physical and/or psychological injury that one side may inflict upon the other, intergroup conflict often leads to distortion in the use of communication channels and to hostility that is unjustified by the reality of the situation ("autistic hostility"). Intergroup conflict may also foster judgmental distortion, as each side comes to view the other in stereotypic ways that sharpen the distinction between "we" and "they." The great danger inherent in such stereotypic views is that they tend to be self-confirming: If we expect our adversary to be untrustworthy, we will treat him with suspicion, thereby eliciting the very behavior we expected in the first place.

Considerable research has been devoted to the study of techniques that may facilitate the resolution of intergroup conflict. One method involves the introduction of "superordinate goals and threats"—goals and threats that are common to the parties in conflict and that outweigh the parties' hostility and divergent goals. Another technique requires the conflicting parties to communicate, although if their conflict is intense, communication could actually exacerbate tensions. Intergroup conflict may also be reduced by means of group representatives who may be able and willing to make concessions and demands that are beyond the capabilities of individual members; the power and flexibility accorded group negotiators, however, will probably be limited by the attitudes of the groups they represent and their accountability to these groups. Yet another technique involves the intervention of third parties; if they are seen as authoritative and impartial, third parties can facilitate constructive communication, reduce emotionalism among the parties in conflict, provide opportunities for graceful retreat or facesaving, and present alternative solutions by recasting the issues in different terms. Finally, intergroup conflict can sometimes be reduced through the technique of "fractionation"—subdividing large or all-encompassing issues into smaller, more manageable ones. Osgood's GRIT proposal for reducing international conflict relies on the use of fractionation to minimize the negative effects of excessive loyalty and commitment that often accompany attempts to resolve monolithic, "winner take all" issues.

RESEARCH METHODS IN SOCIAL PSYCHOLOGY

An Illustrative Example: Third Party Intervention

Try picking up a copy of your local daily newspaper and scanning the headlines on the first page. There is a good chance that you will find at least one article whose primary focus is upon some form of interpersonal, intergroup, or international conflict. Conflict, it is clear, is a ubiquitous and pervasive phenomenon in the lives of all of us, and the development of methods for its effective and expedient resolution continues to be an issue of great importance.

As we briefly indicated in Chapter 10, one technique to help resolve conflict is the introduction and intervention of a third party. Third parties may function effectively at the interpersonal level (a therapist may intervene in the ongoing conflict between a husband and wife), at the intergroup level (a federal mediator may step into a dispute between management and labor or between a teachers' union and a board of education), as well as at the international level (a special envoy or go-between, such as Henry Kissinger, may attempt to pave the way for a reduction in overt hostility between two or more nations in conflict). Although they are not always optimally effective in these various settings, it appears that third parties are often useful in helping to bring about more rapid and effective conflict resolution.

But what is it, exactly, about third parties and their interventions, that makes them effective? Perhaps the key is the *timing* of third party interventions or the *content* of the interventions themselves; perhaps such interventions are effective because of particular *third party attributes* (for example, authoritativeness, expertise, or integrity) or because of the particular *role* third parties are asked to assume (mediator, arbitrator, fact-finder, ombudsman, and so forth); or possibly third party effectiveness stems from the particular *circumstances* in which they intervene (for example, by informal invitation of the disputants rather than by prior formal agreement or legal sanction), or the nature of the *issues* in dispute (tangible or intangible), or certain *attributes of the protagonists* (their willingness to trust a third party, their concern with issues of self-esteem, loss of face, and so forth); finally, it may be that the effectiveness of third parties is due to their *mere presence* during a conflict.

Suppose that, as social psychologists, we wish to understand better the particular reasons why third party intervention seems to work. That is, we wish to devise an *experiment* (literally a "try" or "test") that will help us establish the causes of third party effectiveness. Would it be possible to answer this complex question in a single experiment? Probably not. Each of the factors (or *independent variables*) described above is likely to make a difference, and it would not be feasible in a single experiment to attempt to discover which one or ones is responsible for third party effectiveness. Moreover, even if we could find a way to examine simultaneously the effect of each of the many factors in a single, monolithic study, we couldn't be certain that we understood the underlying cause(s) of our phenomenon. Perhaps we did not fully comprehend the various ways in which the factors interact with one another; or perhaps there are other factors, unrecognized by or unknown to us, that are at least as important as the ones we subjected to study. Experiments do not typically permit us to make cause-and-effect statements with absolute certainty. They do move us in this direction, however, through a process of successive approximation, by which we come to have greater and greater confidence in our understanding of the causes of some phenomenon.

Toward the Test of a Single Hypothesis. While recognizing the complex role of the third party in conflict intervention, we have decided to focus on one relatively simple but important variable—the mere presence of the third party. We may formulate our hypothesis as follows: *The mere physical presence of a third party in a conflict situation between two parties will result in more rapid and greater conflict resolution.* Thus *presence of a third party* is our *independent variable* (the hypothesized cause). *Conflict resolution*, both in speed and degree, is our *dependent variable* (the hypothesized effect). We have purposely attempted to simplify our independent variable, as a starting point in our research, limiting it to the mere *presence* of a third party. Thus, in testing this hypothesis, we will want to control for possible confounding or extraneous variables—communication of the third party with the other two, the relative wisdom attributed to the third party, the possible threat that the third party might exert, and so forth. Maintaining these controls is one of the most difficult aspects of careful social psychological research. The effects of the *mere presence* of a third party, while not immediately obvious, have some plausibility, based on our past experiences and knowledge of social behavior. It seems reasonable to expect, for example, that the mere knowledge of a third party's presence may enable the disputants to make concessions without viewing themselves as weak for having done so. As Pruitt and Johnson (1970) concluded in their study of mediation in negotiation: "Mediation provides the negotiator with a face-saving device whereby he can retreat without feeling that he has capitulated. Presumably, this face-saving results from throwing the blame for one's own concessions onto the mediator" (p. 246). In addition, the actual or anticipated involvement of a third party may help create a climate that increases the prominence and appropriateness of norms of fairness and equity, in which conflict resolution is seen as socially desirable. Thus, as a result of his mere presence, a third party may both *encourage* the disputants to make concessions (by reducing the possibility of loss of face in the eyes of one's adversary) and *pressure* them to do so (by implicitly invoking norms of ethical behavior). These intermediate factors—face-saving, presentation of a climate of "fairness," implicit invocation of norms—are called *intervening variables* (the independent variable affects the intervening variables, which in turn affect the dependent variable). In the course of our research, we may wish to examine or measure the intervening variables as well, in order to see if they do indeed contribute to the relationship between the presence of a third party and conflict resolution.

Social psychologists have available a variety of rather intriguing methods to test hypotheses, each of which has its own unique advantages and limitations. Let us now examine each of these methods in turn, using our simple hypothesis about third party effectiveness as a case in point.

Review of Relevant Historical Documents

Evidence in support of a hypothesis may be obtained by reviewing relevant historical documents, such as biographies, archives, public records, or newspaper accounts. We could, for example, search for accounts of conflict exchanges in which third parties have been absent and compare these with accounts in which third parties have been present but minimally involved. (Obviously what is meant by "minimal involvement" would have to be clearly specified beforehand.) Thus, we might wish to compare the official records of divorce and child custody proceedings that have been settled out of court with those that have been adjudicated in the presence of a judge who intervened either infrequently or not at all. Or we might try to obtain access to the written records of the Federal Mediation and Conciliation Service and compare the outcomes of labor-management disputes that varied in the extent to which a federal mediator was actively involved. Or, if and when the biographies or autobiographies of noteworthy third parties such as Henry Kissinger or Theodore Kheel become available, we might be able to use these accounts to test our hypothesis.

There are several obvious advantages in analyzing historical documents as a means of testing hypotheses. For one thing, the object of study is not disturbed or directly affected by the investigator;

since this form of research is based entirely on written records, the behavior of the participants can in no way be affected by the knowledge that they are being observed. In addition, it is appealing to see one's theories and hypotheses tested in, and borne out by, important historical events. Such tests, however, may turn out to be rather ambiguous since the direction of causal relations is difficult to determine.

Suppose we were consistently to find that conflict is resolved more effectively when a third party is merely present than when he is absent. There thus appears to be a large, positive *correlation* between third party presence and conflict resolution—where "correlation" is defined as the degree of relationship between two variables. (A positive correlation means that the larger one variable, the larger the other tends to be—for example, a person's height and shoe size; a negative correlation means that the larger one variable, the smaller the other—for example, IQ and number of errors on an IQ test.) This positive correlation, unfortunately, like any statement of correlation, would fail to specify the causal relationship between our variables. On the one hand, it is possible (as we hypothesized) that the mere presence of a judge during a divorce proceeding, or a federal mediator in a labor-management dispute, brought about the resolution of conflict. However, it is also possible that the very ability of particular married couples or labor-management negotiation teams to settle their dispute amicably made third party intervention unnecessary, thereby enabling the judge or mediator to take a more passive role.

In general, historical documents can provide the social psychologist with an opportunity to test the plausibility and generality of his theories. They may also reveal some counterexamples that will challenge him to revise and modify his theory at an early stage. Often, however, these sources of data are open to a variety of interpretations and are therefore of somewhat limited usefulness in testing hypotheses. Furthermore, it is possible that the social psychologist's biases may operate (albeit unconsciously) in his selection of particular examples from a large mass of historical data.

The Field Survey

This method of social research, which has become increasingly sophisticated since the 1950s, typically utilizes a large field staff of trained interviewers who question a representative sample of a preselected population. You are undoubtedly familiar with the polls conducted by the Gallup, Harris, and Roper organizations, whose findings are widely publicized in the news media during election campaigns. Based on interviews with a small, carefully chosen national sample, these polls attempt to describe and predict the attitudes of the adult voting population of the United States at a given time. In similar fashion, organizations such as the Survey Research Center of the University of Michigan and the National Opinion Research Center conduct national, regional, and local surveys to ascertain the views of people on any number of social, economic, and political issues.

Most survey studies are descriptive; they simply try to describe the characteristics of a population—its views about certain social issues, its expectations of future economic conditions, its evaluation of government policies, and so forth. Recently, however, as survey methodology has become increasingly sophisticated, field surveys have also been used to test hypotheses.

The use of surveys for hypothesis-testing has several obvious advantages. First, it enables the researcher to reach conclusions by sampling a broad population of participants with diverse backgrounds, rather than a single, highly specialized and idiosyncratic group (college sophomores, for example). Second, it permits the researcher to examine real and meaningful social relationships, as these occur in everyday life, rather than the more artifical (albeit more highly controlled) behavior that occurs in a laboratory. A third advantage of the field survey is that it permits the investigator to inquire directly into the issue of interest, without waiting for a response to occur naturally. Finally, this method enables the researcher to ask about the reasons for a particular response, thereby enabling him to move closer to an understanding of causal relations.

Suppose, for example, that we wish to test our third party intervention hypothesis using a field survey. We might select a broad sample of professional disputants (for example, international negotiators, labor-management spokesmen, or attorneys) who are typically involved in different types of controversies (international, intergroup, or interpersonal) and ask them a series of questions designed to tap their experiences in the absence or mere presence of a third party. Or we might select a representative group of third parties and ask them to report *their* perceptions of the relationship between their absence or minimal involvement and the effectiveness with which a particular conflict had been resolved. Or, if we want a better understanding of the role of third party intervention in the lives of ordinary people, we might wish to draw a sample from the United States adult population and ask them first to recount as many examples as they can from their own experience in which a third party was involved in some conflict; then to describe the nature and extent of the third party's intervention, and finally to report the manner in which each conflict was resolved.

Field surveys, of course, have several limitations. Notice, first of all, that the data collected, like the data available in a review of historical documents, tend to be correlational in nature. Thus, we ask our respondents to report on the role of a third party in conflict (his presence and involvement); we also ask them to describe how a particular conflict was resolved; then we examine the degree of relationship between the two variables. If our hypothesis about third party effectiveness is correct, the correlation between third party presence and conflict resolution should be positive—but, as we saw in the case of historical research, the results may be open to alternative causal explanations. Even though we ask the respondents to state the reasons for their behavior or opinion, we cannot be sure that the mere presence of a third party has *caused* effective conflict resolution. A second potential drawback of this technique stems from the possibility that the respondents may not be particularly insightful observers of their own behavior and attitudes and may, therefore, provide inaccurate or incomplete information about the issue in question; or, for one reason or another, the respondents may deliberately misrepresent their true position. Finally, there is always the danger that the sample will not be truly representative of the population from which it is drawn and will, therefore, lead us to erroneous or unwarranted conclusions about the acceptability of our hypothesis.

The Field Study
Social psychologists have inherited the field study method from cultural anthropologists and have refined it for their own purposes. This technique requires a careful examination of a single social unit—such as a dating couple, a community, a work group, a club or organization, a neighborhood, or some other group or aggregate of individuals—in a real-life setting. Individuals or groups are studied without any attempt to vary or influence their behavior or introduce manipulated variables. Like the field survey and archival research, this method is often purely descriptive, with minimal interpretation. However, field studies have also been used to test hypotheses. As in the case of the other two methods, the investigator takes his object of study where and as he finds it; he does not tamper with, manipulate, or create it. Yablonsky's (1967) account of Synanon (see page 7) and Schanck's (1932) description of life in Elm Hollow (see page 202) are good examples of field studies.

The field study method may entail a series of simple, careful, but informal observations; or it may require the use of an observation schedule with observational categories prepared in advance (as in Bales's [1950] "interaction process analysis"—see page 267); or it may use both questionnaires and interviews. This approach has certain advantages over the traditional field survey since it entails careful observation over an extended period of time. Our hypothesis about the effects of third party presence, for example, could be tested by selecting for observation two conflict situations: one in which a third party is present but minimally involved and a second with no third party at all. We would then carefully observe the subsequent behavior of the disputants in each of the two situations and attempt to trace over time the manner and extent to which they deal with their respective conflicts.

While the field study has the advantages of extended observation, coupled with the study of real-life, meaningful, ongoing phenomena, it does present several potential dangers and disadvantages. For one thing, the fact that only one or a few groups are typically studied raises the issue of the findings' generality: Would the same results have occurred in other groups, in other situations, and at other times? This problem of generalizability is further compounded by the fact that even when several groups are studied (as in our illustration), it is often difficult to obtain the control necessary to make comparisons between groups. We have seen, for example, that a variety of factors, apart from a third party's mere presence, may contribute to his effectiveness. If the two groups we choose for observation differ with respect to such factors (for example, the particular issue in conflict, the number of parties involved, the intensity of conflict), in addition to the role and involvement of the third party, we will have trouble giving our hypothesis a fair test by comparing the two groups. And, unfortunately, it is notoriously difficult to find real-life groups that are exactly comparable in all respects save one.

Another important potential disadvantage of the field study is that in the process of observing behavior, the researcher may somehow affect what is going on. Indeed, if our hypothesis about the effect of a third party's presence is correct, the observer's mere presence at the site of conflict may cast *him* in the role of a third party and may influence the resolution of conflict accordingly. Finally, there is always the danger (present in other research methods as well) that the researcher's knowledge of his hypothesis will somehow unwittingly bias his observations, leading him to overemphasize behavior that is in accord with his hypothesis and to selectively inattend to or underestimate the importance of events that are contrary to his expectations.

The Natural Experiment
Imagine that we received a phone call one day from an official of the Federal Mediation and Conciliation Service, informing us that a particular labor-management dispute has just begun and inviting us to serve as (unobtrusive) observers of the proceedings. Imagine further that a federal mediator would eventually step into the dispute and

assume a minimal role, but only after giving the protagonists a chance to meet for a while in his absence. We thus would have a unique opportunity to study the extent and manner of conflict resolution in the absence of a third party, as well as the effects of his subsequent minimal involvement. Our participation as observers in such a situation would enable us to "conduct" a natural experiment, in which we could take advantage of the fact that the changes we wish to study are occurring as part of the normal course of events in a real-life setting. Instead of observing two groups, in which a third party is present in one and absent in the other (as in a field study), we would now be able to observe the effect of our variable in a single group. Nature, in effect, is conducting an experiment for us, and we can then assess the results in terms of our hypothesis. Obviously, we could give our third party hypothesis an even better test if, in addition to the above situation, we had an opportunity to observe a conflict in which a third party was initially present, but then withdrew or was absent from the proceedings.

As in the case of a field study, the investigator carefully observes a natural group in action. In most field studies and natural experiments, the researcher typically occupies a role that is external to the group—he stands outside and looks in. In others, however, the investigator may be a member of the group he is studying, or he may join the group in order to study it. Sometimes this is done surreptitiously, so that the observer can study the group as it operates naturally, without the group being aware of his observation.

The study of the Seekers (see page 16), described in Festinger, Riecken, and Schachter's (1956) book *When Prophecy Fails*, is a prime example of the use of a natural experiment in social psychological research. In this study, the investigators were able to take advantage of a critical event—the moment when the Seekers' beliefs were disconfirmed. Another advantage was that there was a natural control group, consisting of those students who went home for the Christmas holiday and did not join the main group of Seekers in suburban Lake City.

The natural experiment allows for a more explicit test of causal relationships than is possible in a correlational field study or field survey. This is due to the fact that data can be gathered both before and after an event occurs. As in other field research methods, the selected event may be an important one in the lives of those who are being studied. The ongoing, real-life quality of the situation under study also gives the investigator confidence about generalizing from the results.

The natural experiment, however, also has certain disadvantages. The investigator's control over the group or selected event is not as great as he might like. Could Festinger and his colleagues assume, for example, that the control group of Seekers was similar to the one that waited in suburban Lake City? And can we assume that a particular conflict situation in which a third party is initially absent, and then present, is comparable to another situation where a third party is minimally involved at first and then absent? Yet another limitation of this method has to do with the fact that most, if not all, of the observational, interview, and questionnaire devices must be carefully prepared in advance. Indeed, this method is often referred to as "firehouse" research since the investigators must be ready to go charging to the site of study at a moment's notice.

A third, more serious potential drawback of the natural experiment is that the researcher must wait for events to occur naturally, and these events often occur with unpredictable frequency. For example, if we wanted to study bystander apathy during emergencies (see Chapter 8), it would hardly make sense for us to stand at the corner of 42nd Street and Broadway in New York City and wait for a mugging, rape, or murder to take place. Related to this difficulty is the possibility that since the researcher is at the mercy of the events that occur, these events may not be as "pure" as he would like. Thus, although newsmen tried to secure interviews with the Seekers before the "moment of truth," they sought information with even greater (and therefore different) intensity after the disconfirmation. Finally, when one uses participant-observers, important ethical and methodological issues arise with respect to the effects of deceit in gaining entry to a group. In studying the Seekers, for example, the investigators and their assistants sometimes comprised nearly one-third of the group; since there was secret communication among the three researchers (which meant that one or more of them appeared at crucial moments), this may have provided further support for the Seekers' beliefs in thought transference, the occult, and divine intervention. While the influence of the investigators may not always be so critical (as, for example, in the natural experimental study of third party intervention), it probably cannot be completely eliminated.

The Field Experiment
Several of the problems inherent in the field study and natural experimental methods have led social psychologists to develop yet another, more powerful, technique for studying behavior in real-life settings: the field experiment. Perhaps the most important feature of this method is that, given the approval of those who are in charge, it permits the investigator to deliberately introduce changes in a natural setting. Once again, the researcher acts as the observer of natural behavior, but he also attempts to gain greater control over that behavior, its causes, and consequences by systematically manipulating

certain (independent) variables and examining their effects on various (dependent) measures. Several good examples of field experiments are described in our discussion of helping behavior (see page 339).

Suppose, once again, that we wish to study the influence of third party presence on conflict resolution in labor-management disputes, but, instead of waiting for our colleague at the Federal Mediation and Conciliation Service to contact us, we decide to take the initiative. We give this official a call, persuade him of the value and importance of testing our hypothesis, perhaps offer to provide some service in exchange for his assistance, and succeed in obtaining his permission to conduct a simple experiment.

Toward the beginning of September, around the time that public schools are scheduled to reopen, we call our friend again and are fortunate enough to discover that two different teachers union-board of education disputes are currently in progress. We schedule separate interviews with the spokesmen in these disputes, and they each agree to participate in our study. Each spokesman is individually asked about his perceptions of the underlying issues, the history and intensity of the conflict, his attitudes toward a number of other issues, and so forth, and we find that the two conflicts appear to be following a rather similar course. Thus, initially, the two disputes appear to be rather similar in their history and intensity, and the spokesmen themselves appear to be roughly comparable with respect to a number of attributes. We then arrange for the spokesmen for the teachers union and board of education in one of the disputes to meet together in a room, ask them to try to reach an agreement that is acceptable to both sides, and then let them bargain by themselves for a two-hour period. Meanwhile, a tape recording is made of the interaction, which we can later analyze in terms of such measures as the amount of hostility expressed by the disputants, the number and quality of offers and concessions made, the use of threats and coercion, and the nature of the agreement reached (if any). After the session, we separately interview the spokesmen again and ask the same questions that we posed before. The same procedure is followed with the second group of disputants, except that a third party (perhaps our federal mediator colleague) is in the room with them, but he is instructed to say nothing unless one of the spokesmen asks him a direct question—in which case he is to respond as briefly and impartially as possible, keeping his active participation to a minimum.

How might we now assess the validity of our hypothesis? For one thing, we could compare the nature of the interaction among the two groups; we might find that in the presence of a third party there was less overt hostility, more frequent and "sincere" concession-making, less coercion, and a greater likelihood of agreement being reached. In addition, we could judge the effect of our manipulation (the introduction or absence of a third party) by comparing the disputants' responses to the initial private interview with those given after the two-hour confrontation. Again, if our hypothesis is correct, we might find a greater difference in the responses of the spokesmen who met in the presence of a mediator—with this group perceiving that there had been greater conflict resolution.

One of the useful features of the technique of comparing responses made before and after a manipulation is that it permits the experimenter to reach conclusions about the effect of his manipulation, even when the groups or individuals being studied are *not* exactly comparable. Thus, even if we happened to get two groups that differed in their initial perceptions of the conflict, its history, and intensity, we could still evaluate the effects of third party presence. We would do this by comparing the *difference scores* in the two groups (the pre-manipulation perceptions of conflict size minus post-manipulation perceptions) rather than the absolute magnitude of these perceptions. Each spokesman would, in effect, serve as his own control.

When designed this way, the field experiment obviously represents a rather powerful tool for testing social psychological hypotheses. Since the situation is a real and meaningful one for the participants, they are personally involved. Moreover, by manipulating or determining critical variables and by introducing necessary experimental controls, the researcher is able to indicate with considerable confidence the direction and source of causality. There are, however, several problems with this method that should be borne in mind. First, it is not always possible to get the cooperation needed to implement a study; individuals and groups do not ordinarily enjoy being the object of experimentation. Furthermore, those groups or individuals that do allow such research may well be unique, thereby reducing the generality of our findings. Despite difficulties such as these, the virtues of the field experiment remain considerable.

The Laboratory Experiment

This final research method is perhaps the most important—and certainly the most widely used—technique available to social psychologists. In the laboratory experiment, as in the previous method, the investigator attempts to establish causality by systematically manipulating experimental variables and then examining their effects on particular dependent measures. However, instead of studying some phenomenon in a real-life setting, the researcher transports this phenomenon to an artificial environment (the laboratory), where he can obtain maximum control over the variables of interest.

One of the great advantages of the laboratory experiment is that it permits the investigator enormous flexibility. He no longer has to rely on the occurrence of natural events or on the existence of real groups for the purpose of testing hypotheses. Instead, he can experimentally *create* events and groups in any one of a number of ways and thus devise an enormous variety of experimental settings.

Suppose that we once again wish to examine the effects of third party presence on conflict resolution—but this time in the laboratory. Following a procedure similar to the one used by Meeker and Shure (1969), for example, we might invite pairs of subjects to come to the laboratory to participate in a study of interpersonal bargaining. Upon their arrival, the pairs would be randomly assigned to one of two experimental conditions. In one, the two subjects would be seated together in a room, given a particular bargaining problem (such as the Acme-Bolt trucking game, described on page 442), and asked to work on it for a given number of turns, or for a specified time. In the second experimental condition, pairs of subjects would be asked to perform the same bargaining task, except that it would be in the presence of an older, neutral observer who would monitor the bargainers' behavior and perhaps interview them after the session. If our hypothesis about the effects of a third party's mere presence is correct, we would expect to find that the bargainers behave more cooperatively when the neutral observer is present than when he is not. (As a matter of fact, Meeker and Shure [1969] found that the amount of cooperation in the Third Party Condition—especially at the outset of the session—was more than twice as great as that found in the No Third Party Condition.) As in the field experimental study of third party behavior described earlier, we might increase the amount of data available to test our hypothesis by administering a "conflict" questionnaire to all subjects at both the beginning and the end of the bargaining session, then comparing the responses (as well as the shift in these responses) in the two experimental conditions.

Suppose that, instead of merely presenting the participants with a bargaining problem (such as the Acme-Bolt game) in which we expect conflict to occur, we wish to obtain even more control over the situation by systematically varying the amount of (perceived) conflict in the relationship. It could be, for example, that a third party's presence would be likely to facilitate conflict resolution only, or especially, when a conflict is viewed by the disputants as relatively small; if they view their conflict as large or intractable, perhaps the effect of a third party's presence would be to intensify (rather than diminish) the disputants' concern with potential loss of face and to encourage greater intransigence than if he were absent. If so, then clearly it would be desirable to find some way to manipulate not only third party presence but also conflict size.

One way in which we could test this extension of our hypothesis would be to devise an experiment consisting of two stages. During the first stage, the subjects would come to the laboratory one at a time and would be randomly assigned to one of two experimental conditions. In one, they would be given 15 minutes to work on a bargaining problem by exchanging written offers and counteroffers with a second person (actually a confederate of the experimenter) who would be seated in another room and instructed to consistently adopt a tough, unyielding, hostile stance throughout. In the other experimental condition, the subjects would be given the identical bargaining problem and would exchange messages with the same confederate, but this time the confederate would be instructed to adopt a friendly and conciliatory stance, although not conciliatory enough to permit agreement.

Following this 15-minute period, the second stage of the experiment would begin. The experimenter would publicly observe that no agreement had yet been reached and would suggest that a face-to-face encounter between the disputants might help them to better understand the issues. Half of the subjects in each of the two experimental conditions would then be seated in a room with their "adversary" and given 15 additional minutes to continue negotiating. (During this time, the confederate would be instructed to make a standard series of offers and concessions, responding in kind to those initiated by the subject.) The remaining subjects in the two previous experimental conditions would be seated in a room with the confederate (who would follow the identical pattern of concession-making by responding in kind), but now a third party (the experimenter, perhaps) would also be present and would act as a neutral but silent observer.

There would thus be four experimental conditions created in this simple study: High Conflict-Third Party Absent, Low Conflict-Third Party Absent, High Conflict-Third Party Present, and Low Conflict-Third Party Present. If our hypothesis about third party intervention were correct, we might expect to find more effective conflict resolution over-all (as measured by the subjects' concessions) in the two Third Party Present Conditions. Of these two conditions, however, we might also find that conflict was reduced more effectively when it was manipulated to be low rather than high. Notice that in an experimental design like this, it would obviously be useful to obtain data on the subjects' perceptions of the conflict both before and after the second stage. And since we have manipulated conflict size to be larger in some conditions than in others, we would want to consider the *change* in the subjects' perceptions rather than their absolute magnitude.

To give one final illustration of the laboratory experiment's flexibility, suppose that we wished to compare not simply the effect of a third party's mere presence or absence, but the *extent* of his presence. How might we do this? Instead of creating two experimental Third Party Conditions (present versus absent), we could vary third party presence along a continuum—having him absent in one condition, present for 5 of the 15 minutes in a second, present for 10 minutes in a third, and 15 minutes in a fourth condition. In this way we might be able to make a more precise estimate of the exact effects of third party presence.

Advantages of the Laboratory Experiment. We have already considered one of this technique's great virtues: the fact that it gives the experimenter enormous flexibility in the design of research settings, procedures, and measures with which to test his hypotheses. Perhaps the greatest single advantage of the laboratory experiment, however, is that it allows the investigator to move—with greater confidence than is possible in most other research methods—toward the establishment of cause-and-effect relations. By manipulating those variables he is interested in, while controlling for the effects of all others, the researcher can vary the exclusive set of events that he believes may influence behavior. Suppose he believes that whenever event X occurs (third party presence, for example), event Y (effective conflict resolution) is likely to result. By controlling for the effects of other possible sources of variation (the other letters of the alphabet), he can give his hypothesis a fair test. If, in such a test, the investigator finds that whenever X is introduced Y occurs, that whenever X is absent Y subsequently fails to occur, and that changes in X lead to corresponding changes in Y, he can conclude with considerable confidence that event X has caused event Y.

One of the ways in which the laboratory researcher attempts to control for the effects of potentially important factors that he is not interested in studying for the moment is by exposing the subjects to stimulus situations that are identical in all respects except the particular experimental variable or variables he wishes to introduce. Another extremely important technique by which laboratory researchers control for sources of extraneous variation is through *randomization.* By randomly assigning subjects to experimental conditions, the investigator attempts to create a (statistical) guarantee that people with special or unusual attributes are no more likely to appear in one experimental condition than in another. The problem that often plagues the field study and the natural experiment (namely, that individuals or groups are behaving as they do not because of the correctness of a hypothesis, but because of unassessed differences in other individual or group attributes) is thus handled rather neatly in the laboratory experiment. An important implication of randomization is that it permits the researcher to focus his attention not on particular people as unique individuals with idiosyncratic characteristics (John's effectiveness as a bargainer in relation to Joe, and so forth), but on the particular *process* of interest to him (the effects of a third party's mere presence)—as this process occurs consistently among a number of people.

A final important advantage of the laboratory experiment in comparison with other techniques is that it permits the researcher to quantify more precisely the importance of a particular experimental variable. By varying the treatments to which the subjects are exposed in a systematic manner, the experimenter can explore the dimensions of a potentially complex variable. Thus, by systematically varying the amount of time a third party is present during a dispute, we can more precisely estimate the effect of this variable than would be possible in an either-or (present versus absent) situation.

Disadvantages of the Laboratory Experiment. Although the lab experiment has many virtues and is clearly the most ubiquitous and important technique currently used by social psychologists (as the number of such studies mentioned in this book clearly attests), it is not without certain limitations and liabilities. Some of these disadvantages are unique to laboratory studies, while others apply to virtually any form of research. However, because the laboratory experiment is the tool used most often by social psychologists, and because in many ways it is the best research method we've got, the following litany of dangers and disadvantages may be appropriately considered in terms of this single, important method.

Design difficulty. First of all, good laboratory experiments are often difficult to design. Whereas the investigator of behavior in real-life settings must often settle for what's available and do the best he can with what he's got, the laboratory researcher has far greater choice. He can introduce experimental variables in a variety of ways, devise any one of a number of alternative procedures, and select among a host of possible dependent measures. By creating choices, however, this virtue of flexibility challenges the laboratory researcher to devise the best experiment he can—one that is creative, is involving for the participants, succeeds in controlling for possible extraneous sources of variation, and permits him to give his hypothesis a fair test.

Time constraints. Laboratory experiments are often extraordinarily time-consuming, both for the experimenter and the participants. Aronson and Carlsmith (1968) observe that, besides the countless hours required to design a clever experiment,

A single person must [typically] be seen for an hour or two by an experimenter and one or more assistants or confederates. Frequently

the experimenter goes to elaborate lengths to set the stage, motivate the subject, and, on occasion, to deceive him. After expending all of this time and effort, the investigator may obtain only a single datum, perhaps something as simple as a "yes" or a "no" response [pp. 3–4].

The subject, similarly, may be asked to give of his time rather generously in order to take part in an experiment about which he receives little useful information beforehand.

Artificiality and lack of realism. The criticism is often lodged against laboratory experiments that they are artificial, sterile, and too far removed from the real-life phenomena from which they have been derived. After spending only a few minutes or hours observing subjects immersed in a rather unfamiliar setting, how can one possibly hope to make generalizations that apply to the world at large?

In their chapter on experimentation in social psychology, Aronson and Carlsmith (1968) make a rather useful distinction between "experimental realism" and "mundane realism." Experimental realism refers to the extent to which an experiment is involving or meaningful for the subjects, while mundane realism denotes the degree to which events occurring in the laboratory are likely to happen in the real world. Any single experiment may be high in both forms of realism, low in both, or high in one and low in the other. Of these two forms of realism, Aronson and Carlsmith argue, experimental realism is far more important. If, and only if, a laboratory study is personally involving for the participants can one hope to tap some meaningful underlying process that may be important both in the laboratory and in the real world. Expressed another way, social psychologists are typically less concerned with creating a replica of the real world than with developing an understanding of critical theoretical variables—a purpose for which the laboratory is ideally suited.

Some of the most significant laboratory experiments in social psychology have had remarkably little mundane realism, although they are high in experimental realism. Consider, for example, Stanley Milgram's (1963) study of obedience to authority (see page 219). Have you ever been asked to deliver electric shocks to an innocent victim? Probably not. Yet there is little doubt that the subjects who were requested to do this in Milgram's lab study found their task meaningful and involving—so much so, in fact, that this research has given rise to a host of ethical concerns.

In summary, it would seem that social psychologists' best response to the criticism that their laboratory research is artificial and sterile is to point out that the focus of this research is not upon real events per se, but upon underlying processes. And to the extent that an experiment is involving for the participants, such underlying processes have a fair chance of being better understood.

Reactivity and expectancy effects. Suppose someone were to ask you to stand up for ten minutes and behave naturally, while he carefully observed your behavior. Would you, in fact, behave naturally? Probably not. Unfortunately for researchers, it often happens that the very process of observing an individual may lead him to alter his behavior and react in certain ways. This problem, known as *reactivity*, is extremely important and continues to plague social psychologists. How can we know what a person is really like if, by observing him, we cause him to change his behavior?

The problem of reactivity is likely to arise in field settings whenever we ask respondents to report their feelings, perceptions, and so forth, and even when they are simply aware of the fact that they are being observed. (In fact, the very process of reactivity may help account for the effectiveness of a third party's mere presence during conflict.) Similarly, the likelihood of reactivity may be increased whenever we administer an interview schedule or questionnaire to the same respondent on several occasions. The fact that we are posing similar or identical questions several times may suggest to the respondent that we are particularly interested in certain issues, and this may lead him to vary his response accordingly. It is in the laboratory, however, that problems of reactivity are likely to be especially acute.

As Robert Rosenthal and others have pointed out, when subjects are brought to an experimental laboratory (an unfamiliar, peculiar, and perhaps threatening environment), they rapidly come to the accurate conclusion that their behavior is being observed and that they may be expected to perform in certain, predictable ways (Rosenthal, 1966, 1967, 1969; Rosenthal and Rosnow, 1969, 1974, 1975). As a result, subjects tend to develop expectations or hunches about the nature of the experiment in which they are participating and the hypotheses they believe it is designed to test. If they want to be "good" subjects, they may attempt to behave in accord with what they believe the experimenter's hypothesis to be; or, if they are particularly "ornery," they may do exactly the opposite of what they think is expected! In either case, the experimenter may be unable to measure the participants' *true* perceptions and behavior.

What we have been describing has been referred to as the problem of *subject expectancy effects.* Unfortunately, laboratory research and other forms of experimentation may also give rise to *experimenter expectancy effects.* It often happens, especially when a researcher has helped to design an experiment and develop its hypotheses, that he has certain expectations about how subjects should, or are likely to, behave. These expectations may subtly (even unconsciously) influence the experimenter's own behavior, leading him to vary his behavior in different experimental conditions, and thereby affecting the subjects' behavior and the results of the experiment.

Rosenthal and his colleagues have conducted a rather impressive assortment of experiments over the years on the problems of experimenter bias. They discovered, for example, that when student experimenters were told that some laboratory rats were "maze-bright" while others were "maze-dull," the students found that the "bright" animals learned a standard maze faster than those labeled "dull." The findings are particularly interesting since the animals were randomly assigned to the students and did not differ initially in their maze-learning ability. Somehow, the experimenters' differential expectations must have led to important differences in the handling and care of the animals, which in turn affected the animals' behavior (Rosenthal and Fode, 1963). More recently, in a controversial and important field experiment, Rosenthal and Jacobson (1968) found that elementary-school pupils who had been identified to their teachers at the beginning of the school year as "intellectual bloomers who will show unusual intellectual gain" did better on an achievement test at year's end than those who had not been so identified, despite the fact that the "intellectual bloomers" had been *randomly* chosen in each classroom.

The problems of subject and experimenter expectancies are obviously profound and consequential. What, if anything, can be done to ameliorate their effects? With respect to subject expectancy and reactivity, probably the most effective single solution would be for the experimenter to make use of *unobtrusive measures* whenever possible. By assessing the subjects' behavior without them being aware of this fact, the experimenter can minimize the chances of reactive behavior. Unfortunately, the use of unobtrusive measures could constitute an invasion of privacy (as, for example, if we were to tap someone's phone) and could raise a number of ethical and legal issues.

With respect to experimenter expectancy effects, Rosenthal has a number of useful suggestions. First of all, experiments should be "double-blind" whenever possible, that is, both the subjects and the experimenter should be unaware of (blind to) the experimental hypotheses; at the very least, the experimenter should not be aware of the experimental condition each subject is in. Second, psychologists should increase the number of experimenters who conduct a particular study so that expectancy effects will tend to be randomly distributed—that is, no more likely to occur in one condition with one experimenter than in another. Third, some systematic attempt should be made to study not only the behavior of subjects but that of experimenters as well. Fourth, experimenters should be trained to keep their behavior as constant as possible in the various experimental conditions. Finally, automatic equipment should be used as much as possible, thereby minimizing the amount of "live" contact between experimenter and subject.

Ethical problems. The list of ethical issues in laboratory experimentation as well as in other forms of psychological research is both long and impressive. All too often, laboratory experiments have involved some form of invasion of the participants' privacy, as, for example, when unobtrusive measures of a personal or confidential nature have been obtained without their permission or awareness. In their desire to be scientific and to conduct carefully controlled research, experimenters have occasionally tended to treat the participants as objects rather than as collaborators. All too often, researchers have failed to obtain the informed consent of their subjects, thereby keeping the ignorant about procedures that may be risky, injurious, or disagreeable. After having participated in a laboratory study, the subjects have sometimes not been fully debriefed about the experiment and its underlying purposes. Finally, laboratory experiments have frequently involved the use of deception, leading the participants to believe that a study is about one issue when it is really about another.

The matter of deception in social psychological research deserves special comment. All social psychologists would surely agree that given a choice between two equally effective research designs, the first of which required the use of deception while the second did not, the latter design would be preferable. Why deliberately mislead and dupe people if such deception is unnecessary? The question remains, however, of whether deception is invariably unnecessary. Suppose that instead of conducting his obedience research as he did, Milgram had described the experimental situation to a group of people in considerable detail, asked them to put themselves in the role of the "teacher" (the subject), and then asked them to predict how much electric shock they would deliver to the victim before stopping. Would the results of this study have paralleled those he actually obtained? Probably not. If fact, when Milgram asked a group of students to predict the number of people who would obey authority to the hilt, they predicted that only 1.2 percent would do so, whereas in the laboratory experiment 65 percent of the subjects actually went all the way to the most extreme shock level (Milgram, 1963). Perhaps a more clever or ingenious experimenter could have found a way to study the conditions of obedience to authority without using deception. Would such an experiment be as compelling to us as readers? Would it be as high in experimental realism for the subjects? Would it yield the pattern of results that Milgram obtained? And can such an experiment be devised? These important questions remain largely unanswered with respect not only to Milgram's experiment but to all research that uses deception.

Because of a general concern about the ethics of research on human subjects in psychology and other fields, many major universities and research organizations have established experimental ethics committees to make sure that no research will be harmful to any human participant. The American Psychological Association (1973) recently published a pamphlet entitled *Ethical Principles in the Conduct of Research with Human Participants,* in which the following ten principles are stated and explained:

1. In planning a study the investigator has the personal responsibility to make a careful evaluation of its ethical acceptability. . . .

2. Responsibility for the establishment and maintenance of acceptable ethical practice in research always remains with the individual investigator. . . .

3. Ethical practice requires the investigator to inform the participant of all features of the research that reasonably might be expected to influence willingness to participate and to explain all other aspects of the research about which the participant inquires. . . .

4. . . . When the methodological requirements of a study necessitate concealment or deception, the investigator is required to ensure the participant's understanding of the reasons for this action and to restore the quality of the relationship with the investigator.

5. Ethical research practice requires the investigator to respect the individual's freedom to decline to participate in research or to discontinue participation at any time. . . .

6. Ethically acceptable research begins with the establishment of a clear and fair agreement between the investigator and the research participant that clarifies the responsibilities of each. . . .

7. The ethical investigator protects participants from physical and mental discomfort, harm, and danger. If the risk of such consequences exists, the investigator is required to inform the participant of that fact, secure consent before proceeding, and take all possible measures to minimize distress. . . .

8. After the data are collected, ethical practice requires the investigator to provide the participant with a full clarification of the nature of the study and to remove any misconceptions that may have arisen. . . .

9. Where research procedures may result in undesirable consequences for the participant, the investigator has the responsibility to detect and remove or correct these consequences, including, where relevant, long-term aftereffects.

10. Information obtained about the research participants during the course of an investigation is confidential . . . [pp. 1–2].

The failure to test new and interesting hypotheses. In a brilliant, scathing attack on the current status of experimental social psychology, William J. McGuire (1973) has argued that social psychological research all too often consists of demonstrations of obvious truths. What an experiment too frequently tests, he writes, "is not whether the hypothesis is true but rather whether the experimenter is a sufficiently ingenious stage manager to produce in the laboratory conditions which demonstrate that an obviously true hypothesis is correct" (p. 449). Moreover, he points out, the hypotheses that researchers do honestly set out to test tend to be extremely simple and fail to capture the true complexity of the social world.

So what should social psychologists do instead? First of all, McGuire recommends that we learn to "think big"—to focus on more than one person at a time and to examine relationships that are complex. Also, instead of relying on a single research technique, we should employ a multimethod approach, combining the six techniques described in this Appendix. Second, social psychologists should spend more time creating interesting hypotheses and less time actually testing them. Included among the approaches McGuire suggests for the development of interesting hypotheses are: *case study,* in which a single individual or group is observed carefully and continuously over an extended period of time (Jean Piaget's research in developmental psychology is a good example of this method); *paradoxical incident,* in which people behave in a nonobvious, counterintuitive, or paradoxical way (for example, the behavior of the Seekers when the world did not end as they had expected); *conflicting results,* in which two theories lead to opposing predictions with respect to some phenomenon (for example, the conflicting predictions about the effect of incentives on attitude change made by learning theory and dissonance theory); and finally, *rules of thumb,* in which one finds and learns from those who are practitioners or craftsmen with special social psychological expertise (we could, for example, probably learn a great deal about the strategy and tactics of bargaining by talking with used-car salesmen, politicians, and diplomats).

Social psychology is a young discipline; its theories and research tools are still experiencing the growing pains of early adolescence. Often our theories have proved inadequate, incomplete, or of limited generality, and all too often our favorite investigative techniques have turned out to have serious dangers and drawbacks. The field is young; however, it is vibrant and, as McGuire's commentary is meant to suggest, it is very much alive. So long as social psychologists continue to struggle with the quality of their ideas and the state of their art, and to rework old and faded research techniques into new and more effective tools, the discipline will continue to grow.

Affective structure. See *Sociometric structure.*

Affiliation. The tendency to join or be with others.

Aggression. Behavior by one person that injures another. See *Hostile aggression, Imitative aggression, Instrumental aggression.*

All-channel communication network. A decentralized communication network in which each member of a group may communicate with every other member.

Attitude. The positive or negative evaluation of an object. Associated with this evaluation are (1) a belief about the nature of the object and its relationship to other objects, and (2) behavioral tendencies to act positively or negatively toward the object.

Attribution process. The process of assigning stable, enduring characteristics or dispositions to another person on the basis of his observed behavior. By observing an individual's action and its effects—in relation to the situational demands, and our awareness of his knowledge, abilities, and past behavior—we draw inferences about that person's intentions, and thence about his dispositions or personal characteristics.

Attribution theory. The social psychological theory that attempts to explain the *attribution process.*

Authoritarian leadership. A style of leadership that is somewhat similar to *directive leadership* and to *autocratic leadership,* which was studied by Lewin, Lippitt, and White.

Autistic hostility. Hostility between two parties that arises from fears, fantasies, and negative expectations. By means of a mutual process of escalating aggressive acts and restricting friendly communications, the basis for hostility between the two parties becomes real, although it actually originated with the autistic thinking of each side.

Autocratic leadership. One of the three leadership styles that was studied in the classic experiment by Lewin, Lippitt, and White. The autocratic leader of a group was instructed to make all of the decisions pertaining to the group's activities on his own; to communicate these decisions, plans, and goals piecemeal, without letting the members have an over-all picture or understanding of the group's ultimate goals; to remain aloof from active cooperative participation; and to give praise and criticism arbitrarily. This type of leader resembles the *authoritarian leader* and uses some of the methods of the *task-centered leader.* Compare with *democratic leadership* and *laissez-faire leadership.*

Autokinetic phenomenon. The observation that a stationary pinpoint of light in an otherwise completely dark room appears to move. This phenomenon was utilized by Sherif to study the development of group norms. During the course of successive judgments, groups of subjects tended to agree about how far the light had moved.

496

Balance theory. A theory of interpersonal attraction and attitude change which hypothesizes that people will tend to be consistent in their attitudes and beliefs, and that they will experience discomfort or tension if these are inconsistent. Thus, there are pressures on an individual to change his beliefs and attitudes to bring them into balance. (Example: If I paint a landscape and my best friend doesn't like it, I will experience tension or discomfort. I may then [1] try to convince her that the painting is truly a work of art, [2] change the painting so that she will like it, [3] deny that it was the "real" me who painted it [perhaps I painted it under pressure], [4] conclude that she isn't really such a good friend after all, [5] decide that she is a wonderful friend in many ways, but that she just doesn't know anything about art, and/or [6] decide that she has a right to her own opinion, but that our relationship is based on our common interest in psychology, not art, and thus our differences on this issue are irrelevant.)

Bargaining. The process whereby two or more people attempt to settle a conflict by means of a verbal exchange of offers and counteroffers.

Boomerang effect. A *social influence* situation in which persons who have received a communication that was designed to change their view in a certain direction actually change their attitudes in the opposite direction. It has been suggested that this effect results when the positive influence of the message is overbalanced by the even greater negative influence of the agent himself (suspicion or dislike for the communicator).

Brainwashing. An intensive attitude-change program, notably utilized by the Chinese during the Korean War to try to change the political views of their prisoners of war. This method utilizes isolation and physical strain, as well as political indoctrination, arousal of guilt, peer pressures, and the *foot-in-the-door technique*.

Bystander intervention phenomenon. The observation that a person will be less likely to offer assistance to someone in need of help when there are other people present.

Catharsis. The reduction of frustration-induced tendencies toward aggressive behavior through the expression of hostility or tension in behavior, verbal expression, or fantasy. The catharsis theory holds that the observation of hostility or aggression in others (such as in a football game or a violent film) may serve to dissipate one's tendencies toward more direct aggression.

Centrality. A characteristic of a *position* in a group structure (usually a *communication network*). The fewer the number of communication linkages from a given position to all of the other positions, the greater the centrality. Thus, in a five-person *wheel communication network,* the hub position is most central, since its occupant is only four steps removed (one to each of the other four positions) from reaching the occupants of those positions. Less commonly centrality also applies to other structural dimensions, such as *sociometric* and *structure interdependence.*

Centralized communication network. A *communication network* in which one or a few members of a group (the central members) can readily receive communications from all or most of the others (the peripheral members), but in which the peripheral members cannot communicate well among themselves. This is the opposite of a decentralized communication network in which everyone can fairly easily communicate with everyone else. The degree of centralization in communication affects morale, effectiveness in problem-solving, leadership, and other group variables. The following communication networks range in order from highly centralized to highly decentralized: *wheel, Y, chain, circle,* and *all-channel.*

Chain communication network. A *communication network* in which the channels form a chain ($A \leftrightarrow B \leftrightarrow C \leftrightarrow D \leftrightarrow E$).

Choice Dilemma Questionnaire (CDQ). An instrument that is used to study risky shift. A subject is given a series of problems in which he must choose between one alternative that is safe (with little risk of harm or loss) but that only offers the prospect of a small reward, and another alternative that offers great risk as well as the possibility of a large reward.

Circle communication network. A *communication network* in which the channels of communication form a circle: A communicates with B, B with C, C with D, D with E, and E with A. Thus the circle is a decentralized communication network.

Coalition. A subgroup whose members cooperate with one another in order to work toward a common goal and to exert control over others who are not in the coalition and with whom the subgroup is in *competition.*

Coercive power. *Social power* that derives from the *influencing agent*'s ability to punish the person who is being influenced, and where it is clear that the agent will punish that person if he does not comply. Impersonal coercive power utilizes an impersonal commodity such as a poor grade, a spanking, a fine, or an arrest; personal coercive power utilizes disapproval, hate, or rejection as commodities.

Cognition. See *Cognitive element.*

Cognitive consonance. A state of comfort experienced by an individual because he holds two or more cognitions whose implications are consistent with one another. This is the opposite of *cognitive dissonance*. (Example: The cognition that I am living in Los Angeles is consistent with the cognition that the weather here is very sunny and pleasant [and with the cognition that other parts of the United States are facing blizzards and freezing weather].)

Cognitive dissonance. A state of tension or discomfort experienced by an individual because he holds two or more cognitions whose implications are inconsistent with one another. (Example: The cognition that I am living in Los Angeles is inconsistent with the cognition that smog in Los Angeles can be debilitating.)

Cognitive dissonance, theory of. A theory advanced by Leon Festinger stating that, because cognitive dissonance is unpleasant, an individual experiencing it will tend to change his cognitions or behaviors, or that he will add new cognitive elements in order to reduce his dissonance.

Cognitive element (or **cognition**). A discrete piece of information, thought, belief, observation, or opinion that an individual has about himself or his environment.

Cohesiveness. See *Group cohesiveness*.

Communication network. The pattern of communication channels in a group or social organization. Some of the principal communication networks are the *wheel, Y, chain, circle*, and *all-channel*.

Comparison level (CL). The net level of benefits (rewards minus costs) that an individual considers appropriate in order for him to join or remain in a group—a standard against which the outcomes in a given group are compared. CL may also be viewed as the neutral point on the individual's subjective scale of "satisfaction–dissatisfaction." If the person's experiences in the group are above the CL, then he is satisfied with the group; however, the further his experiences fall below the CL, the greater his dissatisfaction. This term was used by John Thibaut and Harold Kelley in their *analyses of interdependence*.

Comparison level for alternatives (CL$_{alt}$). A standard used by an individual in deciding whether or not to remain in a group; his decision will be based upon the possible benefits that he might receive in various other social relationships (relative to their costs). If his group experiences are below the CL$_{alt}$, he will be inclined to leave the group; if his experiences are above the CL$_{alt}$ but below the CL, he will be dissatisfied with group, but will remain a member. This term was used by John Thibaut and Harold Kelley in their analysis of *interdependence*.

Competition. The behavior toward one another of two or more persons who have *divergent interests* (negative goals interdependence). Since each person perceives that he can only reach his goal at the expense of the other(s), and vice versa, he will behave in such a way as to enhance only his own progress, and he may even attempt to retard the other(s). *Coordination* is extremely unlikely in situations of pure competition.

Competitive conflict. Conflict between two or more parties (individuals, groups, or larger social entities) arising from *competition*, in which each party tries to move toward its goals at the expense of the opposing party (parties). As compared with *hostile conflict*, the major focus is on the incompatibility of extrinsic goals. (Example: Two nations may struggle over a disputed territory that each believes is rightly its own.) Compare *instrumental aggression*.

Complementarity hypothesis. The hypothesis that two or more persons will tend to be attracted to each other to the extent that their needs and traits complement one another. (Example: A dominant person will be more attracted to a submissive person than to another dominant person.) See also *Similarity hypothesis*.

Conflict, interpersonal (or **conflict, intergroup; conflict, social**). The behavior toward one another of two or more parties (individuals, groups, or larger social units) who have negative means interdependence and/or negative goals interdependence. Interpersonal conflict may be subdivided into *competitive conflict* and *hostile conflict;* this subdivision parallels the distinction between *instrumental aggression* and *hostile aggression*.

Conflict, intrapersonal (or **decisional conflict**). The dilemma faced by an individual who must choose between two or more alternative behaviors that are incompatible with one another. (Examples: An individual may be required to choose between two automobiles both of which have positive and negative features; a child may have to decide whether to perform a disagreeable chore or be punished.) According to Festinger's *cognitive dissonance theory*, after making the decision that resolves such a conflict, the individual will invariably experience some dissonance.

Conflict fractionation. See *Fractionation of conflict*.

Conjunctive task. A group task in which success depends upon the performance of the least effective member. (Examples: A team of mountain climbers can move only as fast as the slowest member; a task may be accomplished by dividing the work among the members of a group.)

Contagion, social. See *Social contagion*.

Content analysis. A research technique for the objective, systematic, and quantitative coding of the content of communication. (Example: Coding newspaper editorials according to their stand on the issue of school desegregation.)

Contingency model of leader effectiveness. A theory of leadership proposed by Fiedler relating the effectiveness of *directive leadership* and *group-centered leadership* to a particular group situation. When the group's activities or membership is either extremely favorable or unfavorable to its leader, the *directive leader* tends to be most effective; on the other hand, when the group's activities or membership is moderately favorable, the *group-centered leader* is most effective.

Controlled experiment. A research method in which the experimenter systematically manipulates certain variables (*independent variables*) while he measures others (*dependent variables*), thus allowing him to test causal relationships. (Example: To test the hypothesis that congeniality in groups results in greater productivity, the experimenter may create a congenial relationship in some groups by various methods [the independent variable], leave other groups alone, and then measure and compare the resulting levels of productivity [the dependent variable].)

Convergent interests (or **common interests; positive interdependence**). A relationship in which the movement of one person toward his own goal increases the likelihood that another person or persons will make progress toward their respective goals, and vice versa. Convergent interests may be a function of positive means interdependence and/or positive goals interdependence. Convergent interests usually lead to *cooperation.*

Cooperation. The behavior toward one another of two or more persons who have *convergent interests* (positive interdependence). Each perceives that progress toward his own goal will be enhanced by the progress of the other person or persons as well, and each expects reciprocation. In situations of pure cooperation, there is likely to be *coordination.*

Coordination. The process by which two or more persons implicitly or explicitly attempt to phase their preferences, intentions, and/or expectations with those of others. Queuing (lining up) or taking turns is a common method of coordination. (Example: Working parents and school-age children must coordinate their use of the one family bathroom in the morning as they all prepare for a busy weekday.)

Correlation. The degree to which two *variables* are related or vary together. When an increase in one *variable* is related to a corresponding increase in the other (for example, height and weight), the *variables* are positively correlated. There is a negative correlation between two *variables* when an increase in one is related to a decrease in the other (for example, the amount of money a person withdraws from his savings account and the balance shown in his bankbook). Two *variables* may also be uncorrelated if a variation in one is unrealted to a variation in the other (for example, shoe size and body temperature).

Correlation coefficient. A statistical index (r) that measures the degree of *correlation* between two *variables*. The value of this index is -1.00 if two *variables* are perfectly negatively correlated, 0 if they are uncorrelated, and $+1.00$ if they are perfectly positively correlated.

Deindividuation. The loss of a sense of individual identity in a group, which frequently leads a person to act in a less moral fashion.

Democratic leadership. One of the three leadership styles that was studied in the classic experiment by Lewin, Lippitt, and White. The democratic leader of a group was instructed to participate with the group in making decisions, to be friendly and supportive, to assist the group in focusing upon and developing long-range goals, and to communicate in a fair, objective manner. These behaviors are also associated with *group-centered leadership*.

Dependent variable. A *variable* or measure whose value depends upon a particular *independent variable*. In the expression $Y = f(X)$, Y denotes a dependent variable since its value depends upon the value of X. If $Y = X^2$, and $X = 5$, then $Y = 25$. In experimentation, a researcher attempts to predict the value of the dependent variable on the basis of his hypothesis about the effect of an *independent variable*. See *controlled experiment*.

Diffusion of guilt. The reduced feeling of guilt experienced by someone who is part of a group that has been responsible for an undesirable act. He may feel less guilty because he attributes the act to the group as a whole rather than to himself personally. Diffusion of guilt may be responsible for the *bystander intervention phenomenon* and such extreme group behavior as gang rape, lynching, and atrocities committed by military personnel against helpless civilians.

Diffusion of responsibility. A reduced feeling of responsibility experienced by a person who is a member of a group, so that he may feel free to commit an extreme act or do nothing at all since he shares responsibility with the other members of his group. *Deindividuation* may lead to diffusion of responsibility, and diffusion of responsibility may help to produce the *risky shift* and the *bystander intervention phenomenon*.

Directive leadership. A leadership style characterized by the use of four forms of *social influence: reward power, coercive power, expert power,* and *legitimate power*. The directive leader is mainly interested in eliciting compliance in order to bring about the changes that he feels are necessary; he tends to make decisions himself and is relatively unconcerned about being accepted by the other members of the group. This style is the opposite of *group-centered leadership.*

Dissonance. See *Cognitive dissonance.*

Divergent interests (or **opposed interests; negative interdependence**). A relationship in which the movement of one person toward his own goal decreases the likelihood that another person or persons will make progress toward their respective goals, and vice versa. Divergent interests may be a function of negative means interdependence and/or negative goals interdependence. Divergent interests often lead to *competition* and *conflict.*

Dominance hierarchy. A stable, relatively enduring pattern of *social power* in a group, in which one or more members exert more control than others.

Dominant response. The most likely response that an individual will give when exposed to a specific stimulus or situation. The dominant response was probably learned earlier in life in similar situations.

Ecological manipulation. A form of *manipulation* in which one person influences another by altering some aspect of his environment. (Examples: A hostess may be able to discourage some of her guests from smoking by not providing ashtrays; one person can discourage others from crossing a field by erecting a high electrified fence.)

Encounter group. A group whose major purpose is to encourage personal growth and improved sensitivity and communication among its members. The group provides opportunities for intensive interaction, openness, the expression of emotions, and the honest exchange of opinions and feelings. It is essentially the same as a T-group and sensitivity group.

Equilibrium, quasi-stationary. An apparently stationary pattern of behavior that is actually a balance point between two opposing forces. (Example: A factory worker whose rate of production [number of pieces produced per hour] seems to be stable may actually be responding to pressures to increase his production [such as incentives and personal standards] as well as to equally strong pressures to decrease his production [such as group norms and fatigue].)

Escalation of conflict. The increase in conflict between two persons, groups, or social units, due to the development of competing goals, threats, and autistic hostility.

Esprit de corps (literally, "spirit of a body [of persons]"). The sense of pride in one's group, high cohesiveness, the feeling of common interest and acceptance of group purposes and goals.

Evaluation apprehension. The concern shown by someone whose performance is being evaluated. This concern may cause the person to perform less well or to act in a way that he believes will be approved by an observer.

Evaluative structure. See *Sociometric structure*.

Experiment. See specific type of experiment: *Controlled experiment, Field experiment, Laboratory experiment*.

Experimenter expectancy effects. The undesirable or distorting effects on the outcome and interpretation of an experiment that arise when a researcher's awareness of the hypotheses leads him to subtly vary his behavior in different experimental conditions, thus unconsciously influencing the results in the predicted direction.

Expert power. *Social power* that can be exerted by one person when another person attributes superior knowledge or ability to him.

Field experiment. A *controlled experiment* in a natural setting such as an industrial plant or a school; this contrasts with a *laboratory experiment*.

Field study. The careful examination of a single social unit (such as a community, a work group, a club, a neighborhood, a school). A field study may utilize careful observations or it may also include questionnaires. (Example: Lewis Yablonsky's careful descriptive study of Synanon; a study of leadership practices and productivity in an industrial work group, utilizing observations, interviews with workers, and measurement of productivity.)

Field survey. A social research technique to assess the attitudes, beliefs, behaviors, or other characteristics of a population by means of personal interviews with a representative sample of that population. (Example: Determining people's attitudes toward school desegregation throughout the country by interviewing a representative sample of the adult population.)

Foot-in-the-door technique. A form of manipulation by gradation, in which one person persuades another to engage in a more extreme act after first convincing him to perform a more moderate act. (Example: A political campaign worker may first ask a person to sign a petition allowing his candidate to appear on the ballot, and then he may request a financial contribution.)

Forced compliance. A situation in which a person is compelled to do something that he doesn't want to do. Forced compliance has been utilized in many experiments to study the *cognitive dissonance theory* of attitude change.

Formal social structure. The prescribed structure of a group or social organization. This is the opposite of *informal social structure*. (Example: The table of organization of a business, social group, institution, or government, indicating titles of position, authority relationships, job descriptions, and so forth.)

Fractionation of conflict. A method of resolving intergroup conflict by separating large, all-encompassing issues into smaller, more workable ones (this method was suggested by Roger Fisher). Fractionation is often accomplished by *third-party intervention.*

Frustration. Interference with the attainment of some goal.

Frustration-aggression hypothesis. The hypothesis that frustration inevitably promotes aggression, and that aggression is always the outcome of frustration.

Function of position. The purpose served by a given *position* in a group for maintaining the group and enabling it to move toward its goal.

Gestalt. A unified pattern or configuration. Gestalt theory of perception postulates that "the whole is greater than the sum of its parts" since the configuration of parts takes on meaning in its own right. In gestalt therapy groups, presumably the members try to be aware of the total configuration of the group experience.

Goals interdependence. A relationship among the members of a group in which one person's movement toward his own goal either facilitates or inhibits another person's movement toward his goal. Positive goal interdependence (or *convergent interest*) leads to *cooperation.* Negative goal interdependence (or *divergent interest*) leads to *competition.* Goald interdependence focuses on the goal rather than the means utilized to attain that goal. See *Means interdependence.*

GRIT (Graduated Reciprocation in Tension Reduction). A method (proposed by Charles Osgood) to reverse the *escalation of conflict* between two parties. Both parties must first recognize *superordinate goal* or *superordinate threat*; then the conflict must be fractionated, and one party must make a graduated series of unilateral concessions, announced clearly in advance, and contingent upon reciprocated concessions.

Group. Two or more individuals who have an explicit social psychological relationship with one another; that is, each person both affects and is affected by the other(s).

Group-centered leadership. A leadership style characterized by the use of two forms of *social influence: referent power* and *informational power.* The group-centered leader wants to both elicit compliance and be accepted by the other members of the group; he permits and encourages the group members to participate fully in decision-making and planning. This style is the opposite of *directive leadership.*

Group cohesiveness. The total of all of the pressures acting upon the individual members of a group to remain in that group or leave. A group may be characterized as having high cohesiveness, low cohesiveness, or negative cohesiveness. (Negative cohesiveness might arise if the pressures to leave the group were greater than those to remain, which could come about if there were barriers to leaving the group.)

Group effects. The influence of a group on the individual, motivating him to change or not to change.

Group locomotion. The movement of a group toward its goal. To facilitate this movement, the individual members may need to coordinate their beliefs, attitudes, and behavior, and thus they may experience *interdependence pressures*. Group locomotion may be one source of pressures toward uniformity.

Group norm. A level of performance, pattern of behavior, or belief that is formally or informally established as appropriate by a group. An individual member usually experiences pressure to behave in accordance with group norms, and sometimes a group uses positive and negative sanctions to enforce conformity to its norms.

Groupthink. A word coined by Irving Janis meaning a "deterioration of mental efficiency, reality testing, and moral judgment [among members of a group] which results from in-group pressures." Janis said that groupthink could more readily be found in highly cohesive groups.

Halo effect. The tendency for a person's evaluation of one object to affect his evaluation of another associated object. According to *balance theory*, if we dislike a certain person, we will also tend to dislike what he has created and/or disagree with what he says.

Hawthorne effect. The observation (first noted at the Hawthorne Works of the Western Electric Company) that members of a group will work harder and be more productive if they feel their group has been singled out as important and that they are participating in a new and special activity.

Heterogeneous group. A group composed of members with diverse knowledge, skills, and experience; dissimilar backgrounds; or differing personalities. Heterogeneous groups tend to function more effectively than homogeneous ones, especially when a variety of facts and opinions is required to solve a set of difficult group tasks. On the other hand, the more heterogeneous a group, the more likely that the members will hold contrasting viewpoints, which may lead to group tension and hostility.

Hierarchy. See *Dominance hierarchy*.

Hostile aggression. The type of *aggression* that is primarily intended to harm another person. This contrasts with *instrumental aggression.*

Hostile conflict. Conflict between two or more parties (individuals, groups, or larger social entities) arising from the fact that one party dislikes or hates the other (an attitude that is probably reciprocated). The primary purpose of hostile conflict is to harm the opposing party, over and above (often in addition to) the pursuance of disparate extrinsic goals (as in *competitive conflict*). Hostile conflict thus includes the *hostile aggression* of one party toward the other.

Hypothesis. A predicted relationship derived from a *theory*. The hypothesis, when tested and confirmed, lends support to the *theory.*

Idiosyncrasy credit. The implicit permission granted by a group to one of its members to be somewhat nonconformist; such permission will depend upon the member's *status,* prior long-term pattern of conformity, outstanding contributions to the group, and so forth. (This concept was first presented by Edwin Hollander.)

Illusion of unanimity. The phenomenon in which various members of a group falsely believe that the rest of the group is in unanimous agreement on some issue.

Imitative aggression. *Aggression* that occurs when one person imitates another who is aggressive.

Implicit theories of personality. *Hypotheses* and *theories* that people hold privately about the traits and attributes of others and themselves.

Impression management. The process by which a person selects and controls his own behavior, as well as the situation in which it is displayed, in order to project a desired image of himself to others.

Incentive effect. One form of the *halo effect.* If we are well paid for doing something, the positive value of the payment may carry over to our evaluation of that behavior. In some cases, then, it is hypothesized that if we are well paid to say something, we may eventually believe what we have said. This result differs from what one would expect according to *cognitive dissonance theory.*

Independent variable. A *variable,* controlled or manipulated by the researcher, whose value (according to the *hypothesis* tested) should determine the value of a *dependent variable.* In the expression $Y = f(X)$, X denotes an independent variable since its value determines Y. If $Y = \sqrt{X}$, and $X = 36$, then $Y = 6$. See *Controlled experiment.*

Influence. See *Social influence.*

Influencing agent. The person who attempts to influence another person (the *target person*).

Informal social structure. The structure of a group or social organization that is not formally written down or otherwise prescribed. Thus, patterns of influence in a factory often differ from the formal table of organization; the *position* and *role* of social "smoother" (argument settler) or critical evaluator in a group will generally not be formally prescribed. This is the opposite of *formal social structure.*

Informational power. *Social power* that stems from the persuasive content of a communication. (Example: A doctor persuades a patient to give up smoking by providing evidence that smoking is closely associated with lung cancer and other serious ailments.)

Instrumental aggression. The type of *aggression* used to attain some goal or to defend oneself against a negative act. The primary purpose of instrumental aggression is *not* to harm another person, as it is with *hostile aggression.*

Interaction process analysis. A procedure developed by Robert Freed Bales that can be used to observe and classify the pattern and content of communication in a group, regardless of its history, function, or composition. Using 12 categories, an observer codes the communications of each group member, noting who communicated and the person to whom the message was directed.

Interdependence. (1) The degree to which the results of one group member's activities are either improved (positive interdependence) or made worse (negative interdependence) with respect to the result of another member's activities, and vice versa. Interdependence may be subdivided into *means interdependence* and *goals interdependence.* (2) A dimension of group structure; a pattern of dependence interrelationships among the members of a group. (Example: In an assembly line, each worker is dependent upon the worker who precedes him in line.)

Interdependence pressures. The pressures on an individual who is in a means interdependent relationship with others to coordinate his behavior with theirs. A worker on an assembly line will experience interdependence pressures in the form a "push" from the worker who passes the product on to him and a "pull" from the worker who is waiting for the product next.

Intervention. See *Third party intervention.*

Kibbutz (plural *kibbutzim*). A collective agricultural community in Israel that has a communal, cooperative orientation. In a kibbutz, private property is minimized and competitiveness is viewed as antithetical to a full and happy life. A member of a kibbutz is called a *kibbutznik*.

Laboratory experiment. A *controlled experiment* carried out in a laboratory, which is totally different from one's ordinary living and working situation. Most social psychological laboratory experiments are performed with undergraduate students in campus laboratories. The laboratory experiment allows maximal control over the relevant variables, but the extent to which the findings can be applied to "real-life" situations has been questioned. This contrasts with *field experiment*.

Laissez-faire leadership. One of the three leadership styles that was studied in the classic experiment by Lewin, Lippitt, and White. The laissez-faire leader of a group was instructed to act in a friendly, but passive way with the group; not to make suggestions; and not to evaluate individual members or the group itself either positively or negatively.

Leader. An individual who occupies a key *position* in a group, influences others in accordance with the *role* expectations for that *position,* and coordinates and directs the group in maintaining itself and working toward its goals. Generally, a leader is a group member who consistently exercises greater influence on the goals and activities of the group than do other members.

Leadership functions. The services provided by a leader and the needs that he fulfills for the group to which he belongs. Leadership functions include: helping the group establish its goals and define its tasks, maintaining harmony, serving as a group symbol with whom the members can identify, and representing the group in its dealings with other groups or individuals. Although one or two members generally tend to exercise more leadership than others, the leadership functions may be performed by many different members at various times.

Leadership style. The characteristic manner in which a leader exercises influence. Although many styles are possible, two seem to be quite common: *directive leadership* and *group-centered leadership*.

Least preferred co-worker (LPC). A measure of the leader's attitude toward the group member whom he considers the worst co-worker. This measure was used by Fiedler in developing his *contingency model of leader effectiveness*. A low LPC score, which indicates the leader's personal rejection of the worst co-worker, characterizes a *directive leader;* a high LPC score, which indicates that a leader is favorably disposed toward a poor co-worker, characterizes a *group-centered leader.*

Legitimate power. *Social power* that arises when one person accepts an *influencing agent*'s right to influence him and thereby feels an obligation to comply. Legitimate power can be due to acceptance of a formal structure (a worker accepts the legitimate power of his supervisor); formal obligation (the right of a person who has done a favor to expect one in return); and the legitimate power of those in need who cannot ordinarily expect help from those in power.

Manipulation. An indirect form of *social influence,* in which an *influencing agent* succeeds in changing another person's belief, attitude, emotion, or behavior by first changing some other aspect of the person or his environment. (Example: A parent can influence a child to eat some cereal that the child does not especially like by serving it in the child's favorite bowl, which has a picture of Goldilocks and the three bears on the bottom.) See also *Ecological manipulation.*

Matrix representation. A method of representing patterns of interpersonal and intergroup relationship, used especially by *social exchange* theorists. The various behavior options available to one party are listed along the horizontal dimension, and the options available to the other are listed along the vertical dimension. The intersecting squares show the costs and rewards for each of the parties, according to the combination of behavior options. Matrix representation has also been utilized for other analyses of social structure, including *sociometric, interdependence,* and communication. In these analyses, the members of the group are listed along the horizontal and vertical dimensions, and the form of the relationship (for example, positive, negative, or neutral) is shown in the intersecting squares.

Means interdependence. A relationship between members of a group in which the means used by one person to reach his own goal are positively or negatively affected by the means used by another person to reach his goal. Compare *goals interdependence.* The goals of the two members may be common or different. (Example of negative means interdependence: Two women who are in a workshop, one building a radio and the other an air conditioner, must share one Phillips-head screwdriver. Example of positive means interdependence: Two men who are working in a carpentry shop, one building a door and the other a boat, must both use the power saw to complete the project, but each needs the assistance of the other in order to operate it.)

Mixed-motive relationship. A relationship in which the participants have both cooperative and competitive tendencies; both *convergent interests* and *divergent interests* exist simultaneously.

Natural experiment. A research method similar to the *controlled experiment,* except that the researcher does not manipulate the *independent variable* himself; he takes advantage of a natural occurrence that manipulates the variable for him. (Example: In testing the hypothesis that fearful events increase people's tendencies to affiliate, the researcher might compare those who live in a community that had experienced an earthquake with those who live in a comparable one that had not, and examine the closeness of family life before and after the event.)

Negative goals interdependence. See *Goals interdependence* and *Interdependence.*

Negative influence. *Social influence* in which a person changes his attitudes or behavior in a direction that differs from the one desired by the *influencing agent.* This is the opposite of *positive influence.*

Negative means interdependence. See *Interdependence* and *Means interdependence.*

Norm. See *Group Norm.*

Pecking order. A *dominance hierarchy.* This term is derived from the observation that chickens seem to follow a stable pattern that gives certain chickens the ability to peck others and not be pecked in return. Typically, the dominant chicken in the pecking order, *a,* will be able to peck all of the others (and not be pecked in return); *b* will peck all except *a; c* will peck all except *a* and *b,* and so forth. Similar pecking orders, including both aggressive behavior and influence, have been observed in nursery-school playgrounds, boys' gangs, and industrial hierarchies.

Peer. A person of equal or similar rank, status, age, class, race, and so forth. A peer or peer group may serve as a basis for *social comparison* and have *referent power* over a given individual.

Pluralistic ignorance. A phenomenon in which various members of a group or social unit share the same false impression of what the group norm is, and, while disagreeing with it, tend to behave publicly in accordance with it. (Example: In the classic Hans Christian Anderson tale, *The Emperor's Clothes,* all of the adult citizens thought that everyone else believed that the emperor was wearing beautiful new clothes; therefore, no one spoke up to say that the emperor was naked, for fear of being treated as a deviant.)

Position. A location within the differentiated structure of a group. The person who occupies that position is expected to fulfill a particular *role* and is accorded the degree of *status* considered appropriate for that position. A position also tends to have a specified function for the group. (Examples: leader, follower, supervisor, father, mother, child, policeman, arbitrator, joker.)

Positive goals interdependence. See *Goals interdependence* and *Interdependence*.

Positive influence. *Social influence* in which a person changes his attitudes or behavior in the direction desired by the *influencing agent* or in such a way that the person becomes more similar to the agent. This is the opposite of *negative influence*.

Positive means interdependence. See *Interdependence* and *Means interdependence*.

Potlatch. A ceremony that was once common among Northwest American Indians, particularly the Kwakiutl, in which the participants vied with one another to give increasingly expensive gifts that were then destroyed to demonstrate that the recipient had no need for the gifts. This is an example of a *runaway norm*.

Power. See *Social power*.

Power of the powerless. A form of *legitimate power* based on the concept that those who are helpless and in need have a right to expect assistance from those who are in a position to help them.

Primacy effect. The principle that information that is presented to someone first will have a greater impact than information presented to him later on. The primacy effect applies particularly to attitude change and to the formation of impressions about people. This is the opposite of *recency effect*.

Prisoner's Dilemma game. This is a paradigm for the study of *mixed-motive relationships* and is taken from a hypothetical situation in which each of two suspects in a crime is confronted with the dilemma of whether to implicate his partner (and thus receive more favorable treatment) or remain silent (thus assuring his partner of more favorable treatment, but subjecting himself to punishment). It is of interest because the best individual choice leads to the worst joint result. Thus, a player's strategy is determined in part by the degree of trust he has for his partner.

Private dependent influence. *Socially dependent influence* in which the maintenance of an individual's changed position does not require the *influencing agent* to be aware that any change has occurred. *Expert power, legitimate power,* and *referent power* lead to private dependent influence. This is the opposite of *public dependent influence*. (Example: A student who solves a problem according to his teacher's instructions because he believes that the teacher probably knows the best way will continue to relate his change to the teacher, but he will not care whether the teacher knows about it.)

Programmed social interaction. A technique commonly utilized in simulation experiments whereby a subject interacts with either an assistant (whom he assumes to be another subject) or a computer. The programmed behavior, by assistant or computer, follows a predetermined script, which may remain the same or vary according to the subject's responses. Thus, in a simulated bargaining study, the assistant or computer can match the offer made by the subject, make a counteroffer that is higher or lower than the one made by the subject, or follow a more complex bargaining strategy—as predetermined by the experimenter. The programmed behavior may constitute the *independent variable* and the subject's behavior the *dependent variable*.

Public dependent influence. *Socially dependent influence* in which the maintenance of an individual's changed position depends upon his belief that the change will be noticed or brought to the attention of the *influencing agent*. *Reward power* and *coercive power* lead to public dependent influence. (Example: A student follows his teacher's instructions in working on a problem, but only because he is afraid that the teacher will notice what he is doing, and because his course grade is dependent upon following the instructions.)

Push and pull. A form of *interdependence pressure* on a worker in an assembly line.

Quasi-stationary equilibrium. See *Equilibrium, quasi-stationary.*

Randomization. A statistical technique in laboratory experimentation that is used to control for sources of extraneous variation by randomly assigning subjects to experimental conditions. Through randomization, the researcher attempts to guarantee that subjects with special or unusual attributes are no more likely to appear in one experimental condition than another.

Reactance. A form of *negative influence* that comes about when someone is afraid that his freedom and individuality may be threatened by the attempt to influence him.

Reactivity. The degree to which the very process of measuring a *variable* may bias the resulting score. Asking a job candidate to describe his qualifications to an interviewer may constitute a reactive measure, whereas inspecting his dossier does not.

Recency effect. The principle that information that is presented to someone at a later time will have a greater impact than information presented earlier. This is the opposite of *primacy effect*.

Referent power. *Social power* that arises when the person who is being influenced identifies with the *influencing agent*, perceives some communality, or wants to form a unit with him. (Example: Adolescents often look to their peers in deciding what type of clothes to wear; a young man may adopt the hairstyle of his favorite sports hero.)

Reinforcement hypothesis. A *hypothesis* derived from learning theory stating that individuals tend to repeat any behavior that has been rewarded and avoid any behavior that has been punished.

Reward power. *Social power* that comes from the *influencing agent*'s ability to mediate rewards or benefits for the person who is being influenced (the *target person*), and where it is clear that the agent will reward the person only if he complies with the request. Impersonal reward power refers to a reward of some impersonal commodity such as money, a good grade in a course, a recommendation for promotion; personal reward power uses approval, love, and acceptance as commodities.

Risky shift. The tendency for people in groups, under certain circumstances, to make more risky and less conservative decisions than they would as lone individuals. When it occurs, the risky shift may be an instance of a *runaway norm*.

Role. A pattern of behavior that characterizes and is expected of a person who occupies a certain *position* in a group or social organization. (Example: The behaviors expected of a person who is identified as a father, mother, man, woman, teacher, student, and so forth.)

Role conflict. The situation that arises when a person simultaneously occupies two *roles* that have conflicting demands. (Example: A woman who is married and has young children may experience a role conflict if she also has a job as a traveling salesperson—the demands of these two *roles* are not complementary.)

Runaway norm. A social norm in which the desired level of behavior, attitude, or performance *exceeds* that of the group as a whole. The *risky shift* phenomenon may be a special instance of a runaway norm.

Self-appointed mindguards. Members of a group who take it upon themselves to urge conformity on any members who deviate. According to Irving Janis, self-appointed mindguards are especially likely to contribute to the *groupthink* process.

Self-disclosure. The process of revealing oneself to others fully and honestly.

Self-esteem. A person's assessment of his own value, competence, or adequacy.

Self-perception theory. An extension of *attribution theory,* advanced by Daryl Bem, stating that individuals make inferences about their own beliefs and attitudes by observing their own behavior and the context in which it occurs. Bem suggests that self-attribution analysis may explain dissonance reduction in a *forced compliance* situation.

Sensitivity group. See *Encounter group.*

Similarity hypothesis. The *hypothesis* that two or more persons will tend to be attracted to each other to the extent that they have similar traits, needs, and other characteristics. See also *Complementarity hypothesis.*

Simulation. The creation in an experimental laboratory of a social situation that is analogous in its basic elements (though not necessarily in specifics) to a situation in the real world. Social scientists have attempted to simulate prisons, international conflict, urban communities, factories, and other social organizations. Simulation is often achieved by means of *programmed social interaction* using computers or assistants.

Sleeper effect. A positive influence exerted by a communication that is designed to change an attitude or opinion, but whose effect cannot be seen immediately. (Example: A man is given a very persuasive sales message from an encyclopedia salesman, who argues for the advantages of having a good encyclopedia at home. The man refuses to place an order. He is not going to be taken in by a slick sales pitch from someone who simply wants to earn money from him. Sometime later, however, the man sees an encyclopedia on sale in a store and decides to purchase it. It is possible that the sleeper effect was due to the negative dependent influence of the salesman [the man's rejection of the communicator], which was dissipated over time, while the positive influence of the content of the communication [which was socially independent] was more stable.)

Social comparison. The general process by which an individual evaluates his own opinions, attitudes, beliefs, emotions, or behaviors by referring to those of others. Festinger developed a social comparison theory for the purpose of studying *group effects* on opinions and abilities; the theory was later extended to emotions.

Social contagion. The spread of a behavior, attitude, or emotional state among the members of a group or social organization in a manner resembling the spread of a contagious disease.

Social exchange theory. A *theory* that analyzes interpersonal and group interaction in terms of interdependence. The process of interaction is examined according to the individual's inputs (or costs) and the rewards and/or punishments he anticipates and receives in the social relationship.

Social facilitation. An increase in the activity or productivity of one person that can be attributed to the actions of one or more other persons who are performing a parallel activity. See also *Social inhibition.*

Social influence. A change in one person—in his beliefs, attitudes, behavior, emotions, and so forth—that is due to the behavior or simply the presence of another person.

Social inhibition. A decrease in the activity or productivity of one person that can be attributed to the actions of one or more other persons who are performing a parallel activity. See also *Social facilitation.*

Socially dependent influence. *Social influence* in which the person who has changed continues to relate his new behavior, belief, or attitude to the *influencing agent*. This is the opposite of *socially independent influence*. (Example: A doctor who wishes his patient to give up smoking can simply rely on his expertise—"You'll have to take my word for it, since I have studied these things and know what is best for you." The patient who accepts the influence continues to relate it to the doctor—"I stopped smoking, but only because my doctor told me to do so." Socially dependent influence can be subdivided into *public dependent* and *private dependent influence.*

Socially independent influence. *Social influence* in which the person who has changed stops relating his new behavior, belief, or attitude to the *influencing agent*. This is the opposite of *socially dependent influence*. (Example: If a mathematics teacher explains the logic behind solving a problem in a particular manner and the student understands the explanation, then the influenced change will no longer be socially dependent upon the teacher. It will, however, depend upon other cognitions—the student's previous knowledge about mathematics and its logic, his understanding of the symbols used and the concepts involved, and so forth.)

Social power. Potential *social influence*. The ability of one person or group to influence another. French and Raven have listed six major bases of social power: *coercion, reward, legitimacy, expertise, reference,* and *information.*

Social psychology. A discipline that attempts to understand, explain, and predict how the thoughts, feelings, and actions of individuals are influenced by the perceived, imagined, or implied thoughts, feelings, and actions of others.

Social reality. A belief about truth that is based on an awareness of what others believe to be true. A need for social reality will produce pressures toward uniformity in a group, especially when it is not possible to check physical reality. (Example: If I am not sure why the price of oil has gone up, I may look to my associates to see what explanation they accept.)

Social structure, group. The pattern of relationships that various members of a group establish with one another. Among the most prominent dimensions of social structure are: evaluation (or *sociometric*), *interdependence, influence, status, role,* and communication (or *communication network*). Social structure may be subdivided into formal and informal structure.

Socioemotional group. A group whose members view the purpose of the group as satisfying certain social and emotional needs (for example, friendship, prestige, self-understanding), rather than as accomplishing some task (as in a *task-oriented group*). An *encounter group* is an example of a socioemotional group.

Socioemotional specialist. A particular group *role*, whose occupant assumes responsibility for maintaining harmony and good feelings in the group, thereby reducing interpersonal conflict. (This observation was made by Bales.) This is the opposite of a *task specialist.*

Sociometric analysis. An analysis of a group's *sociometric structure* in terms of the pattern of interpersonal attraction and rejection among its members. This is typically carried out by means of a sociometric questionnaire, in which each member is asked to indicate whom he likes and whom he dislikes in the group. This analysis may be done informally by observing the members' likes and dislikes or by examining other indications of sociometric choice.

Sociometric structure (or **evaluative structure; effective structure**). The pattern of interpersonal attraction and rejection among the members of a group.

Status. The amount of respect, prestige, and privilege that is accorded to the person who occupies a particular *position.* One of the privileges may be *idiosyncrasy credit.*

Stereotype. A preconceived idea about the characteristics of some grouping of people; it is often oversimplified, rigid, and uncomplimentary. Once a person is identified with that group, his own individuality tends to be overlooked, and the characteristics of the group are attributed to him with little qualification. (Example: According to common stereotypes, Jews are sometimes viewed as ambitious and clannish; blacks as athletic and musical; professors as absentminded and impractical.)

Subjects. The people or animals that participate in experiments.

Superordinate goals. The common goals shared by the parties to a conflict that are larger and more significant than their hostility and divergent goals. (This concept was proposed by Muzafer Sherif as an important factor in reducing intergroup conflict.)

Superordinate threats. The common threats shared by the parties to a conflict that are larger and more significant than their hostility and divergent goals.

Survey research. See *Field survey.*

Target person. The person whom an *influencing agent* tries to influence.

Task-centered leader. A group leader who is primarily interested in seeing that his group accomplishes its given task.

Task divisibility. The extent to which a group task can be subdivided in order to permit a division of labor.

Task-oriented group. A group whose members are directed primarily toward the accomplishment of a given task. This is the opposite of a *socioemotional group.*

Task specialist. A particular group *role,* as observed by Bales, whose occupant assumes responsibility for generating ideas and for moving the group toward accomplishment of its task. This is the opposite of a *socioemotional specialist.*

T-group. See *Encounter group.*

Thanatos. The death instinct—a tendency toward self-destruction—which Freud believed exists in everyone from birth. Turned outward, it can manifest itself as hostility, aggression, and war; turned inward, it leads to suicide.

Theory. A systematic statement setting forth the apparent relationships and underlying principles of certain observed phenomena. A *hypothesis* is derived from a theory.

Theory X. An assumption held by some supervisors and employers that their subordinates do not want responsibility, dislike their jobs, and avoid working if they can. Thus, employers must arrange for their workers to be carefully monitored, controlled, and coerced. This term was used by Douglas McGregor. Compare with *Theory Y.*

Theory Y. An assumption held by some supervisors and employers that people seek out responsibility, enjoy their work, and will be committed to it if they have the proper opportunity. Thus, employers do not need to coerce their workers by means of surveillance, external control, or threat. This term was used by Douglas McGregor. Compare with *Theory X.*

Third party intervention. The intervention by a third party to try to help resolve a conflict between two other parties. The third party may utilize any means, including the various bases of *social power.* The third party can also serve as a conciliator, mediator, arbitrator, fact-finder, or message carrier (where communication between the parties has become difficult). Another method used by third parties is *fractionation of conflict.*

Trait theory of leadership. The view that a person emerges as a leader because of certain of his personality traits. The concept that "great men are born, not made" is the opposite of the more common social psychological position that a leader emerges because of a particular group situation and its effect upon individual members ("great men are made, not born"). Recent research indicates that leadership is actually best understood as a product of the interaction between personality and situational factors.

Unit-forming relationship. According to *balance theory,* two objects have a unit-forming (or U) relationship if they appear to be one unit. (Examples: Since I wrote this book, I have a U-relationship with the book. Sometimes U-relationships depend upon the context: A New York delegate to a national convention would probably have a non-U relationship with a California delegate; at an international convention, however, they would probably have a positive U-relationship [as Americans].)

Unobtrusive measure. A measure obtained without the awareness of the individual being assessed, thereby minimizing the possibility of measurement *reactivity.* (Example: One social researcher suggested that the popularity of a television special could be gauged by comparing the city water consumption immediately after the show with the consumption at the same time one week earlier.)

Value. A basic standard or criterion that serves as a guide to action and to the development and maintenance of attitudes toward events, people, and objects. Values are general criteria, and do not apply to specific objects. (Examples: freedom, equality, wisdom.)

Variable. Any attribute that varies or has different levels. Sex is typically considered a *variable* with two levels—male and female. Voting preference in the United States has two major levels—Democratic and Republican—although other levels (corresponding to less popular political parties) may also be identified. A *variable* may have many levels, depending upon how it is defined. Age, for example, may be defined in years, months, weeks, days, and so forth. See also *independent variable* and *dependent variable*

Wheel communication network. A *centralized communication network* in which one person is at the center of all communication channels, and the other members of the group can communicate only with him; his position is comparable to the hub of a wheel.

Y communication network. A *communication network* arranged in such a way that it forms a "Y." In a five-person Y network, three persons can communicate directly with one central person, and the fifth person can communicate only with one of the three peripheral persons (as at the bottom of the Y). The Y is a *centralized communication network,* but less so than the *wheel communication network.*

REFERENCES

Abelson, Robert P., and Miller, James C. 1967. Negative persuasion via personal insult. *Journal of Experimental Social Psychology, 3,* 321–333.

Adorno, Theodor W.; Frenkel-Brunswick, Else; Levinson, Daniel J.; and Sanford, R. Nevitt. 1950. *The authoritarian personality.* New York: Harper & Row.

Alcock, N. Z. 1972. *The war-disease.* Oakville, Ontario: Canadian Peace Research Institute Press.

Alinski, Saul. 1971. *Rules for radicals.* New York: Random House.

Allport, Floyd H. 1924. *Social psychology.* Boston: Houghton Mifflin.

Allport, Gordon. 1968. The historical background of modern social psychology. In Gardner Lindzey and Elliot Aronson, eds., *The handbook of social psychology,* 2nd ed., Vol. 1. Reading, Mass.: Addison-Wesley. Pp. 1–80.

Allport, Gordon, and Postman, Leo. 1947. *The psychology of rumor.* New York: Holt, Rinehart and Winston.

Altman, Irwin, and Taylor, Dalmas A. 1973. *Social penetration: the development of interpersonal relationships.* New York: Holt, Rinehart and Winston.

American Psychological Association. 1973. *Ethical principles in the conduct of research with human participants.* Washington, D.C.: American Psychological Association.

Anderson, Norman H. 1968. Likableness ratings of 555 personality-trait words. *Journal of Personality and Social Psychology, 9,* 272–279.

Aristotle. 1885. *Politics.* Translated by B. Jowett. Oxford: Clarendon Press.

Aronfreed, Justin. 1964. The origin of self-criticism. *Psychological Review, 71,* 193–218.

Aronson, Elliot. 1969. The theory of cognitive dissonance: a current perspective. In Leonard Berkowitz, ed., *Advances in experimental social psychology,* Vol. 4. New York: Academic Press. Pp. 1–34.

——. 1972. *The social animal.* San Francisco: Freeman.

Aronson, Elliot (with Blaney, Nancy; Sikes, Jev; Stephan, Cookie; and Snapp, Matthew). 1975. The jigsaw route to learning and liking. *Psychology Today,* February, 43–50.

Aronson, Elliot, and Carlsmith, J. Merrill. 1968. Experimentation in social psychology. In Gardner Lindzey and Elliot Aronson, eds., *Handbook of social psychology,* 2nd ed., Vol. 2. Reading, Mass.: Addison-Wesley. Pp. 1–79.

Aronson, Elliot, and Linder, Darwyn. 1965. Gain and loss of esteem as determinants of interpersonal attractiveness. *Journal of Experimental Social Psychology, 1,* 156–171.

521

Aronson, Elliot, and Mills, Judson. 1959. The effect of severity of initiation on liking for a group. *Journal of Abnormal and Social Psychology, 59,* 177–181.

Aronson, Elliot; Willerman, Ben; and Floyd, Joanne. 1966. The effect of a pratfall on increasing interpersonal attractiveness. *Psychonomic Science, 4,* 227–228.

Asch, Solomon E. 1946. Forming impressions of personality. *Journal of Abnormal and Social Psychology, 41,* 258–290.

———. 1952. *Social psychology.* Englewood Cliffs, N.J.: Prentice-Hall.

———. 1955. Opinions and social pressure. *Scientific American,* November.

———. 1956. Studies of independence and conformity: I. A minority of one against a unanimous majority. *Psychological Monographs, 70* (9, Whole No. 416).

Bach, George R., and Wyden, Peter. 1968. *The intimate enemy: how to fight fair in love and marriage.* New York: Avon Books.

Back, Kurt W. 1948. Interpersonal relations in a discussion group. *Journal of Social Issues, 4,* 61–65.

———. 1951. Influence through social communication. *Journal of Abnormal and Social Psychology, 46,* 9–23.

Backman, Carl W., and Secord, Paul F. 1959. The effect of perceived liking on interpersonal attraction. *Human Relations, 12,* 379–384.

———. 1968. *A social psychological view of education.* New York: Harcourt Brace Jovanovich.

Baker, Robert K., and Baker, Sandra J. 1969. *Violence and the media: a staff report to the National Commission on the Causes and Prevention of Violence.* Washington, D.C.: U.S. Govt. Printing Office.

Bales, Robert Freed. 1950. *Interaction process analysis: a method for the study of small groups.* Reading, Mass.: Addison-Wesley.

———. 1958. Task roles and social roles in problem-solving groups. In Eleanor E. Maccoby; Theodore M. Newcomb; and Eugene L. Hartley, eds., *Readings in social psychology,* 3rd ed. New York: Holt, Rinehart and Winston. Pp. 437–447.

Bales, Robert Freed, and Borgatta, Edgar F. 1955. A study of group size: size of group as a factor in the interaction profile. In A. Paul Hare; Edgar F. Borgatta; and Robert Freed Bales, eds., *Small groups: studies in social interaction.* New York: Knopf. Pp. 396–413.

Bales, Robert Freed, and Slater, Philip E. 1955. Role differentiation in small decision-making groups. In Talcott Parsons and Robert

Freed Bales, *Family, socialization, and interaction process.* New York: Free Press. Pp. 259–306.

Bales, Robert Freed, and Strodtbeck, Fred L. 1951. Phases in group problem solving. *Journal of Abnormal and Social Psychology, 46,* 485–495.

Bandura, Albert. 1965. Influence of models' reinforcement contingencies on the acquisition of imitative responses. *Journal of Personality and Social Psychology, 1,* 589–595.

Bandura, Albert; Ross, Dorothea; and Ross, Sheila A. 1961. Transmission of aggression through imitation of aggressive models. *Journal of Abnormal and Social Psychology, 63,* 575–582.

———. 1963. Vicarious reinforcement and imitative learning. *Journal of Abnormal and Social Psychology, 67,* 601–607.

Banuazizi, Ali, and Movahedi, Siamak. 1975. Interpersonal dynamics in a simulated prison: a methodological analysis. *American Psychologist, 30,* 152–161.

Barrie, James M. 1968. *The admirable Crichton* (1903). In Henry F. Salerno, ed., *English drama in transition: 1880–1920.* Indianapolis, Ind.: Bobbs-Merrill (Pegasus).

Bartunek, Jean M.; Benton, Alan A.; and Keys, Christopher B. 1975. Third party intervention and the bargaining behavior of group representatives. *Journal of Conflict Resolution, 19,* 532–557.

Bass, Bernard M. 1960. *Leadership, psychology and organizational behavior.* New York: Harper & Row.

———. 1966. Effects on the subsequent performance of negotiators of studying issues or planning strategies alone or in groups. *Psychological Monographs, 80* (Whole No. 614).

Bateson, Nicholas. 1966. Familiarization, group discussion, and risk-taking. *Journal of Experimental Social Psychology, 2,* 119–129.

Bavelas, Alex. 1950. Communication patterns in task oriented groups. *Journal of the Acoustical Society of America, 22,* 725–730.

Bavelas, Alex; Hastorf, Albert H.; Gross, Alan E.; and Kite, W. Richard. 1965. Experiments on the alteration of group structure. *Journal of Experimental Social Psychology, 1,* 55–70.

Bayer, E. 1929. Beiträge zur Zweikomponententheorie des Hungers. *Zeitschrift für Psychologie, 112,* 1–54.

Bell, Graham B., and French, Robert L. 1950. Consistency of individual leadership position in small groups of varying membership. *Journal of Abnormal and Social Psychology, 45,* 764–767.

Bem, Daryl J. 1965. An experimental analysis of self-persuasion. *Journal of Experimental Social Psychology, 1,* 199–218.

———. 1967. Self-perception: an alternative interpretation of cognitive dissonance phenomena. *Psychological Review, 74,* 183–200.

———. 1972. Self-perception theory. In Leonard Berkowitz, ed., *Ad-*

vances in experimental social psychology, Vol. 6. New York: Academic Press, Pp. 2–62.

Bem, Sandra L. 1974. The measurement of psychological androgyny. *Journal of Consulting and Clinical Psychology, 42,* 155–162.

———. 1975. Sex role adaptation: one consequence of psychological androgyny. *Journal of Personality and Social Psychology, 31,* 634–643.

Bem, Sandra L., and Bem, Daryl J. 1970. Case study of a nonconscious ideology: training the woman to know her place. In Daryl J. Bem, *Beliefs, attitudes, and human affairs.* Monterey, Calif.: Brooks-Cole. Pp. 89–99.

Bennett, Edith B. 1955. Discussion, decision, commitment and consensus in group decision. *Human Relations, 8,* 251–273.

Benton, Alan A., and Druckman, Daniel. 1974. Constituent's bargaining orientation and intergroup negotiations. *Journal of Applied Social Psychology, 4,* 141–150.

Bergum, Bruce O., and Lehr, Donald J. 1963. Effects of authoritarianism on vigilance performance. *Journal of Applied Psychology, 47,* 75–77.

Berkowitz, Leonard. 1954. Group standards, cohesiveness, and productivity. *Human Relations, 7,* 509–519.

———. 1956. Personality and group position. *Sociometry, 19,* 210–222.

———. 1960. Manifest hostility level and hostile behavior. *Journal of Social Psychology, 52,* 165–171.

———. 1965. Some aspects of observed aggression. *Journal of Personality and Social Psychology, 2,* 359–369.

———. 1971. Reporting an experiment: a case study in leveling, sharpening, and assimilation. *Journal of Experimental Social Psychology, 7,* 237–243.

———. 1973. The case for bottling up rage. *Psychology Today,* July, 24–31.

Berkowitz, Leonard, and Daniels, Louise R. 1963. Responsibility and dependency. *Journal of Abnormal and Social Psychology, 66,* 429–436.

Berkowitz, Leonard, and Geen, Russell G. 1966. Film violence and the cue properties of available targets. *Journal of Personality and Social Psychology, 3,* 525–530.

———. 1967. Stimulus qualities of the target of aggression: a further study. *Journal of Personality and Social Psychology, 5,* 364–368.

Berkowitz, Leonard, and Green, James A. 1962. The stimulus qualities of the scapegoat. *Journal of Abnormal and Social Psychology, 64,* 293–301.

Berkowitz, Leonard, and LePage, Anthony. 1967. Weapons as aggression-eliciting stimuli. *Journal of Personality and Social Psychology, 7,* 202–207.

Bernstein, Carl, and Woodward, Bob. 1974. A passion for the covert: the response to the threat of discovery. In *Washington Post* Staff, *The fall of a president.* New York: Dell. Pp. 30–37.

Berscheid, Ellen, and Walster, Elaine H. 1969. *Interpersonal attraction.* Reading, Mass.: Addison-Wesley.

Bettelheim, Bruno. 1943. Individual and mass behavior in extreme situations. *Journal of Abnormal and Social Psychology, 38,* 417–452.

Bexton, William H.; Heron, William; and Scott, T. H. 1954. Effects of decreased variation in the sensory environment. *Canadian Journal of Psychology, 8,* 70–76.

Biddle, Bruce J., and Thomas, Edwin J., eds. 1966. *Role theory: concepts and research.* New York: Wiley.

Bjerstedt, Ake. 1961. Preparation, process, and product in small group interaction. *Human Relations, 14,* 183–189.

Blake, Robert R., and Mouton, Jane S. 1961. Loyalty of representatives to ingroup positions during intergroup competition. *Sociometry, 24,* 177–183.

Blake, Robert R.; Shepard, Herbert A.; and Mouton, Jane S. 1964. *Managing intergroup conflict in industry.* Houston, Texas: Gulf Publishing Co.

Blascovich, Jim; Ginsburg, Gerald P.; and Veach, Tracy L. 1975. A pluralistic explanation of choice shifts on the risk dimension. *Journal of Personality and Social Psychology, 31,* 422–429.

Blascovich, Jim; Veach, Tracy L.; and Ginsburg, Gerald P. 1973. Blackjack and the risky shift. *Sociometry, 36,* 42–55.

Blau, Peter. 1964. *Exchange and power in social life.* New York: Wiley.

Blood, Robert O., Jr., and Wolfe, Donald M. 1960. *Husbands and wives: the dynamics of married living.* New York: Free Press.

Bombard, Alain. 1953. *The Bombard story.* Translated by Brian Connell. London: Andre Deutsch.

Borgatta, Edgar F.; Couch, Arthur S.; and Bales, Robert Freed. 1954. Some findings relevant to the great man theory of leadership. *American Sociological Review, 19,* 755–759.

Bowerman, Charles E., and Bahr, Stephen J. 1973. Conjugal power and adolescent identification with parents. *Sociometry, 36,* 366–377.

Bramel, Dana; Taub, Barry; and Blum, Barbara. 1968. An observer's reaction to the suffering of his enemy. *Journal of Personality and Social Psychology, 8,* 384–392.

Brehm, Jack W. 1966. *A theory of psychological reactance.* New York: Academic Press.

Brehm, Jack W., and Cohen, Arthur Robert. 1962. *Explorations in cognitive dissonance.* New York: Wiley.

Brigham, John C., and Weissbach, Theodore A., eds. 1972. *Racial at-*

titudes in America: analysis and findings of social psychology. New York: Harper & Row.

Brissenden, Paul F. 1957. *The I.W.W.: a study of American syndicalism.* 2nd ed. New York: Russell & Russell.

Brock, Timothy C. 1965. Communicator-recipient similarity and decision change. *Journal of Personality and Social Psychology, 1,* 650–654.

Bronfenbrenner, Urie. 1961. The mirror image in Soviet-American relations: a social psychologist's report. *Journal of Social Issues, 17*(3), 45–56.

———. 1962. Soviet studies of personality development and socialization. In Raymond Bauer, ed., *Some views of Soviet psychology.* Washington, D.C.: American Psychological Association.

Brown, Bert R. 1968. The need to maintain face in interpersonal bargaining. *Journal of Experimental Social Psychology, 4,* 107–122.

Brown, Roger. 1965. *Social psychology.* New York: Free Press.

———. Further comment on the risky shift. *American Psychologist, 29,* 468–470.

Bryan, James H., and Test, Mary Ann. 1967. Models and helping: naturalistic studies in aiding behavior. *Journal of Personality and Social Psychology, 6,* 400–407.

Burke, Peter J. 1967. The development of task and social-emotional role differentiation. *Sociometry, 30,* 379–392.

———. 1968. Role differentiation and the legitimation of task activity. *Sociometry, 31,* 404–411.

———. 1972. Leadership role differentiation. In Charles G. McClintock, ed., *Experimental social psychology.* New York: Holt, Rinehart and Winston. Pp. 514–546.

Burney, Charles. 1952. *Solitary confinement.* New York: Coward, McCann & Geoghegan.

Burnstein, Eugene, and McRae, Adie V. 1962. Some effects of shared threat and prejudice in racially mixed groups. *Journal of Abnormal and Social Psychology, 64,* 257–263.

Buss, Arnold H. 1966. Instrumentality of aggression, feedback, and frustration as determinants of physical aggression. *Journal of Personality and Social Psychology, 3,* 153–162.

Byrd, Richard E. 1938. *Alone.* New York: Putnam.

Byrne, Donn. 1971. *The attraction paradigm.* New York: Academic Press.

Byrne, Donn; Ervin, Charles R.; and Lamberth, John. 1970. Continuity between the experimental study of attraction and real-life computer dating. *Journal of Personality and Social Psychology, 16,* 157–165.

Byrne, Donn, and Nelson, Don. 1964. Attraction as a function of attitude similarity-dissimilarity: the effect of topic importance. *Psychonomic Science, 1*, 93–94.

Byrne, Donn; Nelson, Don; and Reeves, Keith. 1966. Effects of consensual validation and invalidation on attraction as a function of verifiability. *Journal of Experimental Social Psychology, 2*, 98–107.

Campbell, Donald T. 1967. Stereotypes and the perception of group differences. *American Psychologist, 22*, 817–829.

Carlsmith, James Merrill; Collins, Barry E.; and Helmreich, Robert L. 1966. Studies in forced compliance: I. The effect of pressure for compliance on attitude change produced by face-to-face role playing and anonymous essay writing. *Journal of Personality and Social Psychology, 4*, 1–13.

Carlsmith, James Merrill, and Gross, Alan E. 1969. Some effects of guilt on compliance. *Journal of Personality and Social Psychology, 11*, 232–239.

Carlson, Earl R. 1956. Attitude change through modification of attitude structure. *Journal of Abnormal and Social Psychology, 52*, 256–261.

Carlson, Julia A., and Davis, Clive M. 1971. Cultural values and the risky shift: a cross-cultural test in Uganda and the United States. *Journal of Personality and Social Psychology, 20*, 392–399.

Carnegie, Dale. 1936. *How to win friends and influence people.* New York: Simon & Schuster.

Carter, Launor F.; Haythorn, William; Shriver, Beatrice; and Lanzetta, John. 1951. The behavior of leaders and other group members. *Journal of Abnormal and Social Psychology, 46*, 589–595.

Cartwright, Dorwin. 1965. Influence, leadership, control. In James G. March, ed., *Handbook of organizations.* Chicago: Rand McNally. Pp. 1–47.

———. 1971. Risk taking by individuals and groups: an assessment of research employing choice dilemmas. *Journal of Personality and Social Psychology, 20*, 361–378.

Cartwright, Dorwin, and Harary, Frank. 1956. Structural balance: a generalization from Heider's theory. *Psychological Review, 63*, 277–293.

Centers, Richard; Raven, Bertram H.; and Rodrigues, Aroldo. 1971. Conjugal power structure: a re-examination. *American Sociological Review, 36*, 264–278.

Chaffee, Steven H., and McLeod, Jack M. 1971. Adolescents, parents and television violence. Paper presented at annual meeting of the American Psychological Association, Washington, D.C., September.

Chapman, Antony J. 1973. *Social facilitation of laughter in children. Journal of Experimental Social Psychology, 9,* 528–541.

Charters, W. W., Jr., and Newcomb, Theodore M. 1952. Some attitudinal effects of experimentally increased salience of a membership group. In Guy E. Swanson; Theodore M. Newcomb; and Eugene L. Hartley, eds., *Readings in social psychology.* New York: Holt, Rinehart and Winston. Pp. 415–420.

Chen, S. C. 1938. Social modification of the activity of ants in nest building. *Physiological Zoology, 10,* 420–436.

Clark, Walter van Tilburg. 1940. *The Ox-Bow incident.* New York: New American Library.

Cleaver, Eldrige. 1968. *Soul on ice.* New York: Dell.

Clore, Gerald L.; Wiggins, Nancy H.; and Itkin, Stuart. 1975. Gain and loss in attraction: attributions from nonverbal behavior. *Journal of Personality and Social Psychology, 31,* 706–712.

Coch, Lester, and French, John R. P., Jr. 1948. Overcoming resistance to change. *Human Relations, 1,* 512–532.

Codere, Helen. 1950. *Fighting with property: a study of Kwakiutl pot-latching and warfare, 1792–1930.* American Ethnological Society Monograph No. 18. Locust Valley, N.Y.: J.J. Augustin.

Collier, Rex M. 1944. The effect of propaganda upon attitudes following a critical examination of the propaganda itself. *Journal of Social Psychology, 20,* 3–17.

Collins, Barry E., and Guetzkow, Harold. 1964. *A social psychology of group processes for decision-making.* New York: Wiley.

Collins, Barry E., and Raven, Bertram H. 1969. Group structure: attraction, coalitions, communication, and power. In Gardner Lindzey and Elliot Aronson, eds., *The handbook of social psychology,* 2nd ed., Vol. 4. Reading, Mass.: Addison-Wesley. Pp. 102–204.

Cooley, Charles Horton. 1902. *Human nature and the social order.* New York: Scribner.

Costanzo, Philip R. 1970. Conformity development as a function of self-blame. *Journal of Personality and Social Psychology, 14,* 366–374.

Crockett, Walter H. 1955. Emergent leadership in small, decision-making groups. *Journal of Abnormal and Social Psychology, 51,* 378–383.

Crow, Wayman J. 1963. A study of strategic doctrines using the Inter-Nation Simulation. *Journal of Conflict Resolution, 7,* 580–589.

Crutchfield, Richard S. 1955. Conformity and character. *American Psychologist, 10,* 191–199.

Csoka, Louis S., and Fiedler, Fred E. 1972. The effect of military leadership training: a test of the contingency model. *Organizational Behavior and Human Performance, 8,* 395–407.

Cvetkovich, George, and Baumgardner, Steve R. 1973. Attitude polarization: the relative influence of discussion group structure and reference group norms. *Journal of Personality and Social Psychology, 26,* 159–165.

Darley, John M., and Aronson, Elliot. 1966. Self-evaluation vs. direct anxiety reduction as determinants of the fear-affiliation relationship. *Journal of Experimental Social Psychology,* Supplement 1, 66–79.

Darley, John M., and Berscheid, Ellen. 1967. Increased liking as a result of the anticipation of personal contact. *Human Relations, 20,* 29–40.

Darley, John M., and Latané, Bibb. 1968. Bystander intervention in emergencies: diffusion of responsibility. *Journal of Personality and Social Psychology, 8,* 377–383.

Dashiell, John F. 1930. An experimental analysis of some group effects. *Journal of Abnormal and Social Psychology, 25,* 190–199.

Davis, James H. 1969. *Group performance.* Reading, Mass: Addison-Wesley.

Davitz, Joel R. 1952. The effects of previous training on postfrustration behavior. *Journal of Abnormal and Social Psychology, 47,* 309–315.

deCharms, Richard. 1968. *Personal causation: the internal affective determinants of behavior.* New York: Academic Press.

Deutsch, Morton. 1949a. A theory of cooperation and competition. *Human Relations, 2,* 129–152.

————. 1949b. An experimental study of the effects of cooperation and competition upon group process. *Human Relations, 2,* 199–231.

————.1958. Trust and suspicion. *Journal of Conflict Resolution, 2,* 265–279.

————. 1960. The effect of motivational orientation upon trust and suspicion. *Human Relations, 13,* 123–139.

————. 1973. *The resolution of conflict: constructive and destructive processes.* New Haven: Yale Univ. Press.

Deutsch, Morton, and Collins, Mary E. 1951. *Interracial housing: a psychological evaluation of a social experiment.* Minneapolis: Univ. of Minnesota Press.

Deutsch, Morton, and Gerard, Harold B. 1955. A study of normative and informational social influences upon individual judgment. *Journal of Abnormal and Social Psychology, 51,* 629–636.

Deutsch, Morton, and Krauss, Robert M. 1960. The effect of threat upon interpersonal bargaining. *Journal of Abnormal and Social Psychology, 61,* 181–189.

———. 1962. Studies of interpersonal bargaining. *Journal of Conflict Resolution, 6,* 52–76.

Deutsch, Morton, and Solomon, Leonard. 1959. Reactions to evaluations by others as influenced by self-evaluations. *Sociometry, 22,* 93–112.

Dickoff, H. 1961. Reactions to evaluations by another person as a function of self-evaluation and the interaction context. Unpublished doctoral dissertation, Duke University.

Dion, Karen K. 1972. Physical attractiveness and evaluation of children's transgressions. *Journal of Personality and Social Psychology, 24,* 207–213.

Dion, Karen; Berscheid, Ellen; and Walster, Elaine. 1972. What is beautiful is good. *Journal of Personality and Social Psychology, 24,* 285–290.

Dion, Kenneth L.; Baron, Robert S.; and Miller, Norman. 1970. Why do groups make riskier decisions than individuals? In Leonard Berkowitz, ed., *Advances in experimental social psychology,* Vol. 5. New York: Academic Press. Pp. 306–378.

Dittes, James E., and Kelley, Harold H. 1956. Effects of different conditions of acceptance upon conformity to group norms. *Journal of Abnormal and Social Psychology, 53,* 100–107.

Doise, Willem. 1969. Intergroup relations and polarization of individual and collective judgments. *Journal of Personality and Social Psychology, 12,* 136–143.

Dolci, Danilo. 1959. *Report from Palermo.* Translated by P. D. Cummins. New York: Orion Press. (Reprinted, 1970, by Viking Press.)

Dollard, John; Miller, Neal E.; Doob, Leonard W.; Mowrer, O. Hobart; and Sears, Robert R. 1939. *Frustration and aggression.* New Haven: Yale Univ. Press.

Dreiser, Theodore. 1929. *A gallery of women.* New York: Liveright.

Druckman, Daniel. 1968a. Prenegotiation experience and dyadic conflict resolution in a bargaining situation. *Journal of Experimental Social Psychology, 4,* 367–383.

———. 1968b. Ethnocentrism in the inter-nation simulation. *Journal of Conflict Resolution, 12,* 45–68.

Dunnette, Marvin D., and Campbell, John P. 1968. Laboratory education: impact on people and organization. *Industrial Relations, 8,* 1–44.

Ebbesen, Ebbe B., and Bowers, Richard J. 1974. The effects of proportion of risky to conservative arguments in a group discussion on risky shift. *Journal of Personality and Social Psychology, 29,* 316–327.

Eckhardt, William. 1975. Primitive militarism. *Journal of Peace Research, 12,* 55–62.

Eisenhower, Milton, et al. 1969. *Commission statement on violence in television entertainment programs.* National Commission on the Causes and Prevention of Violence. Washington, D.C.: U.S. Govt. Printing Office.

Elms, Alan C., and Janis, Irving L. 1965. Counter-norm attitudes induced by consonant versus dissonant conditions of role-playing. *Journal of Experimental Research in Personality, 1,* 50–60.

Emerson, Robert M. 1954. Deviation and rejection: an experimental replication. *American Sociological Review, 19,* 688–694.

Eron, Leonard D. 1963. Relationship of TV viewing habits and aggressive behavior in children. *Journal of Abnormal and Social Psychology, 67,* 193–196.

Esquire. 1972. September, 125–129.

Etzioni, Amitai. 1967. Nonconventional uses of sociology as illustrated by peace research. In Paul F. Lazarsfeld; William H. Sewell; and H. L. Wilensky, eds., *The uses of sociology.* New York: Basic Books. Pp. 806–838.

———. 1969. Social psychological aspects of international relations. In Gardner Lindzey and Elliot Aronson, eds., *Handbook of social psychology,* 2nd ed., Vol. 5. Reading, Mass.: Addison-Wesley. Pp. 538–601.

Eysenck, Sybil B. G. 1965. *Manual for the Junior Eysenck Personality Inventory.* San Diego, Calif: Educational and Industrial Testing Service.

Fantz, Robert L. 1963. Pattern vision in newborn infants. *Science, 140,* 269–297.

Faucheux, Claude, and Moscovici, Serge. 1967. Le style de comportement d'une minorité et son influence sur les réponses d'une majorité. *Bulletin du Centre d'Études et Recherches Psychologiques, 16,* 337–360.

Feldman, Roy E. 1968. Response to compatriot and foreigner who seek assistance. *Journal of Personality and Social Psychology, 10,* 202–214.

Fellner, Carl H., and Marshall, John R. 1970. Kidney donors. In Jacqueline Macaulay and Leonard Berkowitz, eds., *Altruism and helping behavior.* New York: Academic Press. Pp. 269–281.

Feshbach, Seymour. 1955. The drive-reducing function of fantasy behavior. *Journal of Abnormal and Social Psychology, 50,* 3–11.

———. 1956. The catharsis hypothesis and some consequences of interaction with aggressive and neutral play objects. *Journal of Personality, 24,* 449–462.

Feshbach, Seymour, and Singer, Robert. 1957. The effects of personal and shared threats upon social prejudice. *Journal of Abnormal and Social Psychology, 54,* 411–416.

———. 1970. *Television and violence.* San Francisco: Jossey-Bass.

Festinger, Leon. 1954. A theory of social comparison processes. *Human Relations, 2,* 117–140.

———. 1957. *A theory of cognitive dissonance.* Stanford, Calif.: Stanford Univ. Press.

Festinger, Leon, and Carlsmith, James Merrill. 1959. Cognitive consequences of forced compliance. *Journal of Abnormal and Social Psychology, 58,* 203–211.

Festinger, Leon; Gerard, Harold B.; Hymovitch, Bernard; Kelley, Harold H.; and Raven, Bertram H. 1952. The influence process in the presence of extreme deviates. *Human Relations, 5,* 327–346.

Festinger, Leon; Pepitone, Albert; and Newcomb, Theodore. 1952. Some consequences of de-individuation in a group. *Journal of Abnormal and Social Psychology, 47,* 382–389.

Festinger Leon; Riecken, Henry W.; and Schachter, Stanley. 1956. *When prophecy fails.* Minneapolis: Univ. of Minnesota Press.

Festinger, Leon; Schachter, Stanley; and Back, Kurt. 1950. *Social pressures in informal groups: a study of human factors in housing.* New York: Harper & Row.

Fiedler, Fred E. 1951. A method of objective quantification of certain counter-transference attitudes. *Journal of Clinical Psychology, 7,* 101–107.

———. 1958. *Leader attitudes and group effectiveness.* Urbana, Ill.: Univ. of Illinois Press.

———. 1964. A contingency model of leadership effectiveness. In Leonard Berkowitz, ed., *Advances in experimental social psychology,* Vol. 1. New York: Academic Press. Pp. 150–191.

———. 1971. Leadership. Morristown, N.J.: Silver Burdett Co. (General Learning Press).

———. 1973. The trouble with leadership training is that it doesn't train leaders. *Psychology Today,* February, 23–29, 92.

Fiedler, Fred; Meuwese, W.; and Oonk, S. 1961. Performance of laboratory tasks requiring group creativity. *Acta psychologica, 18,* 100–119.

Fischer, Louis. 1954. *Gandhi: his life and message for the world.* New York: New American Library (Mentor Books).

Fishbein, Martin. 1963. An investigation of the relationships between beliefs about an object and the attitude toward that object. *Human Relations, 16,* 233–240.

Fisher, Roger. 1964. Fractionating conflict. In Roger Fisher, ed., *International conflict and behavioral science: the Craigville papers.* New York: Basic Books.

Flanders, James P., and Thistlethwaite, Donald L. 1967. Effects of familiarization and group discussion upon risk taking. *Journal of Personality and Social Psychology*, 5, 91–97.

Fleishman, E. A.; Harris, E. F.; and Burtt, H. E. 1955. Leadership and supervision in industry: an evaluation of a supervisory training program. *Ohio studies in personnel*, No. 33. Columbus: Bureau of Educational Research Monographs, Ohio State University.

Fouriezos, Nicholas T.; Hutt, Max L.; and Guetzkow, Harold. 1950. Measurement of self-oriented needs in discussion groups. *Journal of Abnormal and Social Psychology*, 45, 682–690.

Frank, Arlene F., and Rubin, Jeffrey Z. 1974. The role of information in a convergent interest coordination game. Unpublished manuscript, Tufts University.

———. 1975. The effects of the spiral of reciprocal perspectives on coordination game behavior. Unpublished manuscript, Tufts University.

Frank, Jerome D. 1944. Experimental studies of personal pressure and resistance: I. Experimental production of resistance. *Journal of Genetic Psychology*, 30, 23–41.

Fraser, M. 1972. Article on work. *New York Post*, October 4, p. 40.

Freedman, Jonathan L., and Doob, Anthony N. 1968. *Deviancy*. New York: Academic Press.

Freedman, Jonathan L., and Fraser, Scott C. 1966. Compliance without pressure: the foot-in-the-door technique. *Journal of Personality and Social Psychology*, 4, 195–202.

Freedman, Jonathan L.; Wallington, Sue Ann; and Bless, Evelyn. 1967. Compliance without pressure: the effect of guilt. *Journal of Personality and Social Psychology*, 7, 117–124.

French, John R. P., Jr. 1944. Organized and unorganized groups under fear and frustration. *University of Iowa Studies of Child Welfare*, 20, 231–308.

French, John R. P., Jr.; Israel, Joachim; and Ås, Dagfinn. 1960. An experiment on participation in a Norwegian factory: interpersonal dimensions of decision-making. *Human Relations, 13*, 3–20.

French, John R. P., Jr., and Raven, Bertram H. 1959. The bases of social power. In Dorwin Cartwright, ed., *Studies in social power*. Ann Arbor: Institute for Social Research, Univ. of Michigan. Pp. 150–167.

Freud, Sigmund. 1922. *Group psychology and the analysis of the ego*. Longon: Hogarth Press.

Frieze, Irene; Johnson, Paula; Parsons, Jacquelynne E.; Ruble, Diane N.; and Zellman, Gail L., eds. 1976. *Women and sex roles: a social psychological perspective*. New York: Norton.

Froman, Robert. 1971. *Street poems*. New York: Saturday Review Press (Dutton).

Fromm, Erich. 1939. Selfishness and self-love. *Psychiatry, 2,* 507–523.

———. 1941. *Escape from freedom.* New York: Holt, Rinehart and Winston.

Fülöp-Miller, René. 1928. *Rasputin: the holy devil.* New York: Viking Press.

Gallo, Philip S., Jr. 1966. Effects of increased incentives upon the use of threat in bargaining. *Journal of Personality and Social Psychology, 4,* 14–20.

Gamson, William A., and Modigliani, Andre. 1971. *Untangling the cold war: a strategy for testing rival theories.* Boston: Little, Brown.

Gandhi, Mohandas K. 1949. *The story of my experiments with truth.* London: Phoenix Press.

Geen, Russell G., and Berkowitz, Leonard. 1966. Name-mediated aggressive cue properties. *Journal of Personality, 34,* 456–465.

Gelb, Leslie H. 1975. Ford briefs team for A-arms pact. *New York Times,* January 30, page 6.

Gerard, Harold B. 1954. The anchorage of opinions in face-to-face groups. *Human Relations, 7,* 313–326.

Gerard, Harold B., and Matthewson, Grover C. 1966. The effects of severity of initiation on liking for a group: a replication. *Journal of Experimental Social Psychology, 2,* 278–287.

Gergen, Kenneth J. 1965. The effects of interaction goals and personalistic feedback on the presentation of self. *Journal of Personality and Social Psychology, 1,* 413–424.

———. 1972. Multiple identity: the healthy, happy human being wears many masks. *Psychology Today,* May, 31–35, 64–66.

Gergen, Kenneth J., and Wishnov, Barbara. 1965. Others' self-evaluations and interaction anticipation as determinants of self-presentation. *Journal of Personality and Social Psychology, 2,* 348–358.

Gewitz, Jacob L., and Baer, Donald M. 1958. The effect of brief social deprivation on behaviors for a social reinforcer. *Journal of Abnormal and Social Psychology, 56,* 49–56.

Goffman, Erving. 1959. *The presentation of self in everyday life.* New York: Doubleday (Anchor Books).

Golding, William. 1954. *Lord of the flies.* New York: Putnam (Capricorn Books).

Goodacre, Daniel M. 1951. The use of a sociometric test as a predictor of combat unit effectiveness. *Sociometry, 14,* 148–152.

down on smoking. *Journal of Personality and Social Psychology,* *17,* 25–35.

Janis, Irving L., and Hovland, Carl I. 1959. An overview of persuasibility research. In Carl I. Hovland and Irving L. Janis, eds., *Personality and persuasibility.* New Haven, Conn.: Yale Univ. Press. Pp. 1–28.

Janov, Arthur. 1970. *The primal scream.* New York: Putnam.

Johnson, Paula. 1974. Social power and sex-role stereotyping. Unpublished doctoral dissertation, University of California, Los Angeles.

————. 1976. Women and interpersonal power. In Irene Frieze; Paula Johnson; Jacquelynne E. Parsons; Diane N. Ruble; and Gail L. Zellman, eds., *Women and sex roles: a social psychological perspective.* New York: Norton.

Jones, Edward E. 1964. *Ingratiation.* New York: Appleton-Century-Crofts.

Jones, Edward E., and Davis, Keith E. 1965. From acts to dispositions: the attribution process in person perception. In Leonard Berkowitz, ed., *Advances in experimental social psychology,* Vol. 2. New York: Academic Press.

Jones, Edward E.; Davis, Keith E.; and Gergen, Kenneth J. 1961. Role playing variations and their information value for person perception. *Journal of Abnormal and Social Psychology, 63,* 302–310.

Jones, Edward E., and Gerard, Harold B. 1967. *Foundations of social psychology.* New York: Wiley.

Jones, Edward E., and Nisbett, Richard E. 1971. The actor and the observer: divergent perceptions of the causes of behavior. Morristown, N.J.: Silver Burdett Co. (General Learning Press).

Jones, Robert A. 1975. Short-handle hoe: a history of agony for dubious advantages. *Los Angeles Times,* April 14, Part II, p. 1.

Josephus, Flavius. 1959. *Jewish war.* Translated by Geoffrey A. Williamson. Baltimore: Penguin Books.

Jourard, Sidney M. 1964. *The transparent self: self-disclosure and well-being.* New York: Van Nostrand.

Julian, James W.; Regula, Robert; and Hollander, Edwin P. 1968. Effects of prior agreement from others on task confidence and conformity. *Journal of Personality and Social Psychology, 9,* 171–178.

Julian, James W.; Ryckman, Richard M.; and Hollander, Edwin P. 1969. Effect of prior group support on conformity: an extension. *Journal of Social Psychology, 77,* 189–196.

Kahn, Robert L., and Katz, Daniel. 1953. Leadership practices in relation to productivity and morale. In Dorwin Cartwright and

Alvin Zander, eds., *Group dynamics: research and theory.* New York: Harper & Row. Pp. 612–628.

Kaplan, John. 1972. A legal look at prosocial behavior: what can happen for failing to help or trying to help someone. *Journal of Social Issues, 28*(3), 219–226.

Katz, Daniel. 1965. Nationalism and strategies of international conflict resolution. In Herbert C. Kelman, ed., *International behavior: a social psychological analysis.* New York: Holt, Rinehart and Winston. Pp. 354–390.

Katz, Daniel, and Kahn, Robert L. 1966. *The social psychology of organizations.* New York: Wiley.

Katz, Elihu, and Danet, Brenda. 1966. Petitions and persuasive appeals: a study of official-client relations. *American Sociological Review, 31,* 811–822.

Katz, Elihu; Gurevitch, Michael; Danet, Brenda; and Peled, Tziyona. 1969. Petitions and prayers: a method for the content analysis of persuasive appeals. *Social Forces, 47,* 447–463.

Katz, Irwin. 1967. The socialization of academic motivation in minority group children. In David Levine, ed., *Nebraska Symposium on Motivation.* Lincoln: Univ. of Nebraska Press. Pp. 133–192.

Katz, Irwin, and Cohen, Melvin. 1962. The effects of training Negroes upon cooperative problem solving in biracial teams. *Journal of Abnormal and Social Psychology, 64,* 319–325.

Katz, Stuart, and Burnstein, Eugene. 1973. Is an out-of-role act credible to biased observers and does it affect the credibility of neutral acts? Unpublished manuscript, University of Michigan.

Kelley, Harold H. 1950. The warm-cold variable in first impressions of persons. *Journal of Personality, 18,* 431–439.

———. 1951. Communication in experimentally created hierarchies. *Human Relations, 4,* 39–56.

———. 1966. A classroom study of the dilemmas in interpersonal negotiations. In K. Archibald, ed., *Strategic interaction and conflict.* Berkeley, Calif.: Institute of International Studies, University of California. Pp. 49–73.

———. 1967. Attribution theory in social psychology. In David Levine, ed., *Nebraska Symposium on Motivation,* Vol. 15. Lincoln: Univ. of Nebraska Press. Pp. 192–240.

Kelley, Harold H., and Schenitzki, Dietmar P. 1972. Bargaining. In Charles G. McClintock, ed., *Experimental social psychology.* New York: Holt, Rinehart and Winston. Pp. 298–337.

Kelley, Harold H., and Thibaut, John W. 1969. Group problem solving. In Gardner Lindzey and Elliot Aronson, eds., *Handbook of social psychology,* 2nd ed., Vol. 4. Reading, Mass.: Addison-Wesley. Pp. 1–101.

Kelman, Herbert C. 1958. Compliance, identification, and internalization: three processes of attitude change. *Journal of Conflict Resolution, 2,* 51–60.

———. 1965. Social-psychological approaches to the study of international relations: the question of relevance. In Herbert C. Kelman, ed., *International behavior: a social-psychological analysis.* New York: Holt, Rinehart and Winston. Pp. 565–607.

Kelman, Herbert C., and Hovland, Carl I. 1953. "Reinstatement" of the communicator in delayed measurement of opinion change. *Journal of Abnormal and Social Psychology, 48,* 327–335.

Kelman, Herbert C., and Lawrence, Lee H. 1972. Assignment of responsibility in the case of Lt. Calley: preliminary report on a national survey. *Journal of Social Issues, 28*(1), 177–212.

Kennedy, John F. 1961. Inaugural address, January.

———. 1963. American University commencement address, June 11.

Kerckhoff, Alan C., and Back, Kurt W. 1968. *The June bug: a study of hysterical contagion.* New York: Appleton-Century-Crofts.

Kerckhoff, Alan C., and Davis, Keith E. 1962. Value consensus and need complementarity in mate selection. *American Sociological Review, 27,* 295–303.

Kerr, Clark, 1954. Industrial conflict and its resolution. *American Journal of Sociology, 60,* 230–245.

Kesey, Ken. 1962. *One flew over the cuckoo's nest.* New York: Viking Press.

Kipnis, David. 1958. The effects of leadership style and leadership power upon the inducement of attitude change. *Journal of Abnormal and Social Psychology, 57,* 173–180.

Klein, Herbert G. 1974. The fall began when deceit replaced truth. *Los Angeles Times,* August 16, Part II, p. 7.

Koffka, Kurt. 1935. *Principles of gestalt psychology.* New York: Harcourt Brace Jovanovich.

Kogan, Nathan, and Carlson, Julia A. 1969. Group risk taking under competitive and noncompetitive conditions in adults and children. *Journal of Educational Psychology, 60,* 158–167.

Kogan, Nathan, and Doise, W. 1969. Effects of anticipated delegate status on level of risk-taking in small decision-making groups. *Acta Psychologica, 29,* 228–243.

Kogan, Nathan; Lamm, Helmut; and Trommsdorff, Gisela. 1972. Negotiation constraints in the risk-taking domain: effects of being observed by partners of higher or lower status. *Journal of Personality and Social Psychology, 23,* 143–156.

Kogan, Nathan, and Wallach, Michael A. 1964. *Risk-taking: a study in cognition and personality.* New York: Holt, Rinehart and Winston.

———. 1967. Risk-taking as a function of the situation, the person, and the group. In George Mandler; Paul Mussen; Nathan Kogan; and Michael A. Wallach, eds., *New directions in psychology,* Vol. 3. New York: Holt, Rinehart and Winston. Pp. 224–266.

Köhler, Wolfgang. 1929. *Gestalt psychology.* New York: Liveright.

Komarovsky, Mirra. 1946. Cultural contradictions and sex roles. *American Journal of Sociology, 52,* 184–189.

Krauss, Robert K., and Deutsch, Morton. 1966. Communication in interpersonal bargaining. *Journal of Personality and Social Psychology, 4,* 572–577.

Krebs, Dennis L. 1970. Altruism: an examination of the concept and a review of the literature. *Psychological Bulletin, 73,* 258–302.

Krech, David; Crutchfield, Richard S.; and Ballachey, Egerton L. 1962. *Individual in society: a textbook of social psychology.* New York: McGraw-Hill.

Kruglanski, Arie W. 1970. Attributing trustworthiness in supervisor-worker relations. *Journal of Experimental Social Psychology, 6,* 214–232.

Laird, David A. 1923. Changes in motor control and individual variations under the influence of "razzing." *Journal of Experimental Psychology, 6,* 236–246.

Lamm, Helmut, and Kogan, Nathan. 1970. Risk-taking in the context of intergroup relations. *Journal of Experimental Social Psychology, 6,* 361–363.

Lanzetta, John T. 1955. Group behavior under stress. *Human Relations, 8,* 29–53.

Larsson, K. 1956. *Conditioning and sexual behavior in the male albino rat.* Stockholm: Almquist & Wiksells.

Latané, Bibb, and Darley, John M. 1968. Group inhibition of bystander intervention in emergencies. *Journal of Personality and Social Psychology, 10,* 215–221.

Latané, Bibb, and Rodin, Judith. 1968. A lady in distress: inhibiting effects of friends and strangers on bystander intervention. *Journal of Experimental Social Psychology, 5,* 189–202.

Laumann, Edward O. 1969. Friends of urban men: an assessment of accuracy in reporting their socioeconomic attributes, mutual choice, and attitude agreement. *Sociometry, 32,* 54–70.

Leavitt, Harold J. 1951. Some effects of certain communication patterns on group performance. *Journal of Abnormal and Social Psychology, 46,* 38–50.

———. 1960. Task ordering and organizational development in the common target game. *Behavioral Science, 5,* 233–239.

———. 1965. Applied organizational change in industry: structural, technological and humanistic approaches. In James G. March, ed., *Handbook of organizations.* Chicago: Rand McNally. Pp. 1144–1170.

LeBon, Gustav. 1896. *Psychologie des foules.* London: Unwin.

Leff, Walda F.; Raven, Bertram H.; and Gunn, Robert L. 1964. A preliminary investigation of social influence in the mental health professions. *American Psychologist, 19,* 505.

Lerner, Melvin J. 1970. The desire for justice and reactions to victims. In Jacqueline Macaulay and Leonard Berkowitz, eds., *Altruism and helping behavior.* New York: Academic Press.

Lesieur, Frederick G., ed. 1958. *The Scanlon plan: a frontier in labor-management cooperation.* Cambridge, Mass.: M.I.T. Press.

Levinger, George. 1964. Note on need complementarity in marriage. *Psychological Bulletin, 61,* 153–157.

Levinger, George, and Breedlove, James. 1966. Interpersonal attraction and agreement: a study of marriage partners. *Journal of Personality and Social Psychology, 3,* 367–372.

Levinger, George, and Schneider, David J. 1969. Test of the "risk is a value" hypothesis. *Journal of Personality and Social Psychology, 11,* 165–170.

Levinger, George; Senn, David J.; and Jorgensen, Bruce W. 1970. Progress toward permanence in courtship: a test of the Kerckhoff-Davis hypotheses. *Sociometry, 33,* 427–443.

Lewin, Kurt. 1935. Psycho-sociological problems of a minority group. *Character and Personality, 3,* 175–187.

———. 1936. Some social psychological differences between the United States and Germany. *Character and Personality, 4,* 265–298.

———. 1941. Self-hatred among Jews. *Contemporary Jewish Record, 4,* 219–232.

———. 1943. Forces behind food habits and methods of change. *Bulletin of the National Research Council, 108,* 35–65.

———. 1947. Frontiers in group dynamics: I. Concept, method and reality in social science: social equilibria and social change. *Human Relations, 1,* 5–41.

———. 1948. Some social-psychological differences between the United States and Germany. In G. Lewin, ed., *Resolving social conflicts: selected papers on group dynamics, 1935–1946.* New York: Harper & Row.

———. 1951. *Field theory in social science.* New York: Harper & Row.

———. 1952. Group decision and social change. In Guy E. Swanson; Theodore M. Newcomb; and Eugene L. Hartley, eds., *Readings in social psychology,* 2nd ed. New York: Holt, Rinehart and Winston. Pp. 459–473.

Lewin, Kurt; Lippitt, Ronald; and White, Ralph K. 1939. Patterns of aggressive behavior in experimentally created "social climates." *Journal of Social Psychology, 10,* 271–299.

Lewis, Michael. 1972. Culture and gender roles: there's no unisex in the nursery. *Psychology Today,* May, 54–57.

Lewis, Oscar, 1961. *Life in a Mexican village: Tepoztlan revisited.* Urbana, Ill.: Univ. of Illinois Press.

Likert, Rensis. 1961. An emerging theory of organization, leadership, and management. In Luigi Petrullo and Bernard Bass, eds., *Leadership and interpersonal behavior.* New York: Holt, Rinehart and Winston. Pp. 290–309.

Lilly, J. C. 1956. Mental effects of reduction of ordinary levels of physical stimuli on intact, healthy persons. *Psychiatric Research Reports, 5,* 1–9.

Linton, Robert. 1936. *The study of man.* New York: Appleton-Century-Crofts.

Lombroso-Ferrero, Gina. 1911. *Criminal man according to the classification of Cesare Lombroso.* New York: Putnam.

London, Perry. 1970. The rescuers: motivational hypotheses about Christians who saved Jews from the Nazis. In Jacqueline Macaulay and Leonard Berkowitz, eds., *Altruism and helping behavior.* New York: Academic Press. Pp. 241–250.

Loomis, J. L. 1959. Communication, the development of trust, and cooperative behavior. *Human Relations, 12,* 305–315.

Lorge, Irving. 1936. Prestige, suggestion, and attitudes. *Journal of Social Psychology, 7,* 386–402.

Luce, R. Duncan, and Raiffa, Howard. 1957. *Games and decisions: introduction and critical survey.* New York: Wiley.

Luchins, Abraham S. 1957. Experimental attempts to minimize the impact of first impressions. In C. Hovland, ed., *The order of presentation in persuasion.* New Haven: Yale Univ. Press.

Macaulay, Jacqueline, and Berkowitz, Leonard, eds. 1970. *Altruism and helping behavior.* New York: Academic Press.

McCauley, Clark; Stitt, Christopher L.; Woods, Kathryn; and Lipton, Diana. 1973. Group shift to caution at the race track. *Journal of Experimental Social Psychology, 9,* 80–86.

McDonough, John J. 1975. One day in the life of Ivan Denisovich: a study of the structural requisites of organization. *Human Relations, 28,* 295–328.

McGrath, Joseph E. 1964. *Social psychology: a brief introduction.* New York: Holt, Rinehart and Winston.

McGregor, Douglas. 1960. *The human side of enterprise.* New York: McGraw-Hill.

McGuire, William J. 1973. The yin and yang of progress in social psychology: seven koan. *Journal of Personality and Social Psychology, 26,* 446–456.

Madsen, Millard C. 1967. Cooperative and competitive motivation of children in three Mexican sub-cultures. *Psychological Reports, 20,* 1307–1320.

Magruder, Jeb Stuart. 1974. *An American life: one man's road to Watergate.* New York: Atheneum.

Maier, Norman R. F., and Solem, Allen R. 1952. The contribution of a discussion leader to the quality of group thinking: the effective use of minority opinions. *Human Relations, 5,* 277–288.

Malamuth, Neil M. 1975. A systematic analysis of the relationship between group shifts and characteristics of the choice dilemmas questionnaire. Unpublished doctoral dissertation, University of California, Los Angeles.

Mallick, Shahbaz Kahn, and McCandless, Boyd R. 1966. A study of catharsis of aggression. *Journal of Personality and Social Psychology, 4,* 591–596.

Mann, Richard D. 1959. A review of the relationships between personality and performance in small groups. *Psychological Bulletin, 56,* 241–270.

March, James G., and Simon, Herbert A. 1958. *Organizations.* New York: Wiley.

Marquis, Donald G. 1962. Individual responsibility and group decisions involving risks. *Industrial Management Review, 3,* 8–23.

Marquis, Donald G.; Guetzkow, Harold; and Heyns, Roger W. 1951. A social psychological study of the decision-making conference. In Harold Guetzkow, ed., *Groups, leadership, and men: research in human relations.* New Brunswick, N.J.: Rutgers Univ. Press, Pp. 55–67.

Maslow, Abraham H. 1942. Self-esteem (dominance feeling) and sexuality in women. *Journal of Social Psychology, 16,* 259–294.

———. 1970. *Motivation and personality.* 2nd ed. New York: Harper & Row.

Mead, George Herbert. 1934. *Mind, self, and society.* Chicago: Univ. of Chicago Press.

Mead, Margaret. 1935. *Sex and temperament in three primitive societies.* New York: Morrow.

———, ed. 1937. *Cooperation and competition among primitive peoples.* New York: McGraw-Hill.

Meeker, Robert J., and Shure, Gerald H. 1969. The influence of "outsiders" on the effectiveness of pacifist tactics in a bargaining game. *Journal of Conflict Resolution, 13,* 478–493.

Meeker, Robert J.; Shure, Gerald H.; and Moore, W. H., Jr. 1964. Real-time computer studies of bargaining behavior: the effects of threat upon bargaining. *American Federation of Information Processing Societies Conference Proceedings, 24,* 115–123.

Menzel, Herbert. 1957. Public and private conformity under different conditions of acceptance in the group. *Journal of Abnormal and Social Psychology, 55,* 398–402.

Merei, Ferenc. 1949. Group leadership and institutionalization. *Human Relations, 2,* 23–39.

Merton, Robert K., and Rossi, Alice S. 1957. Contributions to the theory of reference group behavior. In Robert K. Merton, ed., *Social theory and social structure,* rev. ed. New York: Free Press. Pp. 225–280.

Mettee, David R., and Wilkins, Paul C. 1972. When similarity "hurts": effects of perceived ability and a humorous blunder on interpersonal attractiveness. *Journal of Personality and Social Psychology, 22,* 246–258.

Michotte, Albert. 1963 (originally published in French in 1946). *The perception of causality.* New York: Basic Books.

Milgram, Stanley. 1961. Nationality and conformity. *Scientific American, 205,* 45–51.

———. 1963. Behavioral study of obedience. *Journal of Abnormal and Social Psychology, 67,* 371–378.

———. 1965a. Liberating effects of group pressure. *Journal of Personality and Social Psychology, 1,* 127–134.

———. 1965b. Some conditions of obedience and disobedience to authority. *Human Relations, 18,* 57–75.

———. 1974. *Obedience to authority: an experimental view.* New York: Harper & Row.

Miller, Neal E., and Bugelski, B. R. 1948. Mirror studies of aggression: the influence of frustration imposed on the in-group on attitudes expressed toward out-groups. *Journal of Psychology, 25,* 437–442.

Mills, Judson. 1958. Change in moral attitudes following temptation. *Journal of Personality, 26,* 517–531.

Mills, Theodore M. 1953. Power relations in three-person groups. *American Sociological Review, 18,* 351–357.

Mintz, Alexander. 1946. A re-examination of correlations between lynchings and economic indices. *Journal of Abnormal and Social Psychology, 41,* 154–160.

———. 1951. Non-adaptive group behavior. *Journal of Abnormal and Social Psychology, 46,* 150–159.

Moede, W. 1920. *Experimentelle massenpsychologie.* Leipzig: S. Hirzel.

Mollenhoff, Clark R. 1974. The problem was Haldeman's iron control. *Los Angeles Times,* August 16, Part II, p. 7.

Monahan, Florence. 1941. *Women in crime.* New York: Ives Washburn. (Reprinted by Finch Press, Ann Arbor, Mich.)

Moreno, Jacob L. 1934. *Who shall survive? A new approach to the problem of human interrelations.* Washington, D. C.: Nervous & Mental Diseases Publishing Co.

Morse, Nancy C., and Reimer, Everett. 1956. The experimental change of a major organizational variable. *Journal of Abnormal and Social Psychology, 52,* 120–129.

Morse, Stanley J., and Gergen, Kenneth J. 1970. Social comparison, self-consistency, and the concept of self. *Journal of Personality and Social Psychology, 16,* 148–156.

Moscovici, Serge; Lage, E.; and Naffrechoux, M. 1969. Influence of a consistent minority on the responses of a majority in a color perception task. *Sociometry, 32,* 365–380.

Moscovici, Serge, and Zavalloni, Marisa. 1969. The group as a polarizer of attitudes. *Journal of Personality and Social Psychology, 12,* 125–135.

Moss, Peter D., and McEvedy, Colin P. 1966. An epidemic of overbreathing among schoolgirls. *British Medical Journal, 2,* 1295–1300.

Mulder, Mauk, and Stemerding, Ad. 1963. Threat, attraction to group, and need for strong leadership. *Human Relations, 16,* 317–334.

Myers, David G.; Bach, Paul J.; and Schreiber, F. Barry. 1974. Normative and informational effects of group interaction. *Sociometry, 37,* 275–286.

Myers, David G., and Bishop, G. D. 1970. Discussion effects on racial attitudes. *Science, 169,* 778–779.

Nemeth, Charlan, and Wachtler, Joel. 1974. Creating the perceptions of consistency and confidence: a necessary condition for minority influence. *Sociometry, 37,* 529–540.

Newcomb, Theodore M. 1943. *Personality and social change: attitude formation in a student community.* New York: Dryden.

——. 1947. Autistic hostility and social reality. *Human Relations, 1,* 69–86.

——. 1953. An approach to the study of communicative acts. *Psychological Review, 60,* 393–404.

——. 1961. *The acquaintance process.* New York: Holt, Rinehart and Winston.

——. 1963. Stabilities underlying changes in interpersonal attraction. *Journal of Abnormal and Social Psychology, 66,* 376–386.

——. 1965. Interpersonal constancies: psychological and sociological approaches. In Otto Klineberg and Richard Christie, eds., *Perspectives in social psychology.* New York: Holt, Rinehart and Winston. Pp. 38–49.

Newcombe, A. G., and Wert, J. 1972. *An internation tensiometer for the prediction of war.* Oakville, Ontario: Canadian Peace Research Institute Press.

North, R. C.; Brody, Robert A.; and Holsti, Ole R. 1964. Some empirical data on the conflict spiral. *Peace Research Society (International) Papers, 1,* 1–14.

Orne, Martin T., and Evans, Frederick J. 1965. Social control in the psychological experiment: antisocial behavior and hypnosis. *Journal of Personality and Social Psychology, 1,* 189–200.

————. 1966. Inadvertent termination of hypnosis with hypnotized and simulating subjects. *International Journal of Clinical and Experimental Hypnosis, 14,* 61–78.

Orwell, George. 1951. *Down and out in Paris and London.* London: Secker & Warburg.

Osgood, Charles E. 1959. Suggestions for winning the real war with communism. *Journal of Conflict Resolution, 3,* 295–325.

————. 1960. *Graduated reciprocation in tension-reduction: a key to initiative in foreign policy.* Urbana, Ill.: Institute of Communications Research, University of Illinois.

————. 1961. An analysis of the cold war mentality. *Journal of Social Issues, 17*(3), 12–19.

————. 1962. *An alternative to war or surrender.* Urbana, Ill.: Univ. of Illinois Press.

Osgood, Charles E., and Tannenbaum, Percy H. 1955. The principle of congruity in the prediction of attitude change. *Psychological Review, 62,* 42–55.

Oskamp, Stuart. 1965. Attitudes toward U.S. and Russian actions—a double standard. *Psychological Reports, 16,* 43–46.

Parkinson, C. Northcote. 1957. *Parkinson's law.* Boston: Houghton Mifflin.

Patterson, Gerald R.; Littman, Richard A.; and Bricker, William. 1967. Assertive behavior in children: a step toward a theory of aggression. *Monographs of the Society for Research in Child Development, 32,* 1–43.

Patterson, T. T., and Willett, E. J. 1951. An anthropological experiment in a British colliery. *Human Organization, 10,* 19–23.

Pelton, Leroy H. 1974. *The psychology of non-violence.* Elmsford, N.Y.: Pergamon Press.

Perlman, Daniel, and Oskamp, Stuart. 1971. The effects of picture content and exposure frequency in evaluation of Negroes and whites. *Journal of Experimental Social Psychology, 7,* 503–514.

Perls, Fritz. 1969. *Ego, hunger, and aggression.* New York: Random House.

Perrucci, Robert, and Pilisuk, Marc, eds. 1971. *The triple revolution emerging: social problems in depth.* Boston: Little, Brown.

Pessin, J. 1933. The comparative effects of social and mechanical stimulation on memorizing. *American Journal of Psychology, 45,* 263–270.

Philp, Alice J. 1940. Strangers and friends as competitors and co-operators. *Journal of Genetic Psychology, 57,* 249–258.

Piaget, Jean. 1948. *The moral judgment of the child.* New York: Free Press.

Piliavin, Irving M.; Rodin, Judith; and Piliavin, Jane Allyn. 1969. Good samaritanism: an underground phenomenon? *Journal of Personality and Social Psychology, 13,* 289–299.

Pilisuk, Marc, and Skolnick, Paul. 1968. Inducing trust: a test of the Osgood proposal. *Journal of Personality and Social Psychology, 8,* 121–133.

Pilisuk, Marc; Winter, J. Alan; Chapman, Reuben; and Hass, Neil. 1967. Honesty, deceit, and timing in the display of intentions. *Behavioral Science, 12,* 205–215.

Podell, Jerome E., and Knapp, William M. 1969. The effect of mediation on the perceived firmness of the opponent. *Journal of Conflict Resolution, 13,* 511–520.

Pruitt, Dean G. 1965. Definition of the situation as a determinant of international action. In Herbert C. Kelman, ed., *International behavior: a social psychological analysis.* New York: Holt, Rinehart and Winston. Pp. 391–432.

———. 1971a. Choice shifts in group discussion: an introductory review. *Journal of Personality and Social Psychology, 20,* 339–360.

———. 1971b. Conclusions: toward an understanding of choice shifts in group discussion. *Journal of Personality and Social Psychology, 20,* 495–510.

Pruitt, Dean G., and Johnson, Douglas F. 1970. Mediation as an aid to facesaving in negotiation. *Journal of Personality and Social Psychology, 14,* 239–246.

Quarantelli, Enrico L., and Dynes, Russell R. 1970. Organizational and group behaviors in disasters. *American Behavioral Scientist, 13,* 325–426.

Radke, Miriam, and Klisurich, D. 1947. Experiments in changing food habits. *Journal of American Dietetic Association, 24,* 403–409.

Radloff, Roland. 1961. Opinion evaluation and affiliation. *Journal of Abnormal and Social Psychology, 62,* 578–585.

Rapoport, Anatol. 1962. The use and misuse of game theory. *Scientific American, 207,* 108–118.

———. 1965. Game theory and intergroup hostility. In M. Berkowitz and P. G. Bock, eds., *American national security: a reader in theory and policy.* New York: Free Press. Pp. 368–375.

Raven, Bertram H. 1953. The effects of group pressures on opinions, perception, and communication. Unpublished doctoral dissertation, University of Michigan.

———. 1959. Social influence on opinions and the communication of related content. *Journal of Abnormal and Social Psychology, 58,* 119–128.

———. 1965. Social influence and power. In Ivan D. Steiner and Martin Fishbein, eds., *Current studies in social psychology.* New York: Holt, Rinehart and Winston. Pp. 371–382.

———. 1974a. The comparative analysis of power and power preference. In James Tedeschi, ed., *Perspectives on social power.* Chicago: Aldine.

———. 1974b. The Nixon group. *Journal of Social Issues, 29*(4), 297–320.

Raven, Bertram H., and Eachus, H. Todd. 1963. Cooperation and competition in means-interdependent triads. *Journal of Abnormal and Social Psychology, 67,* 307–316.

Raven, Bertram H., and French, John R. P., Jr. 1958. Legitimate power, coercive power, and observability in social influence. *Sociometry, 21,* 83–97.

Raven, Bertram H., and Gallo, Philip S. 1965. The effects of nominating conventions, elections, and reference group identification upon the perception of political figures. *Human Relations, 18,* 217–229.

Raven, Bertram H., and Leff, Walda F. 1965. The effect of partner's behavior and culture upon strategy in a two-person game. *Scripta Hierosolymitana, 14,* 148–165.

Raven, Bertram H.; Mansson, Helge H.; and Anthony, Edwin. 1962. The effects of attributed ability upon expert and referent influence. Technical Report No. 10, Contract Nonr 233 (54). University of California, Los Angeles.

Raven, Bertram H., and Rietsema, Jan. 1957. The effects of varied clarity of group goal and group path upon the individual and his relation to his group. *Human Relations, 10,* 29–47.

Read, Peter B. 1974. Source of authority and legitimation of leadership in small groups. *Sociometry, 37,* 189–204.

Riesman, David. 1950. *The lonely crowd.* New Haven: Yale Univ. Press.

Rim, Yeshayahu. 1965. Leadership attitudes and decisions involving risk. *Personnel Psychology, 18,* 423–430.

Ring, Kenneth, and Kelley, Harold H. 1963. A comparison of augmentation and reduction as modes of influence. *Journal of Abnormal and Social Psychology, 66,* 95–102.

Roby, Thornton B., and Rubin, Jeffrey Z. 1973. An exploratory study of competitive temporal judgment. *Behavioral Science, 18,* 42–51.

Roethlisberger, Fritz J., and Dickson, William J. 1939. *Management and the worker.* Cambridge, Mass.: Harvard Univ. Press.

Rogers, Carl R. 1951. *Client-centered therapy.* Boston: Houghton Mifflin.

Rokeach, Milton. 1971. Long-range experimental modification of values, attitudes, and behavior. *American Psychologist, 22,* 453–459.

———. 1975. Long-term value change initiated by computer feedback. *Journal of Personality and Social Psychology, 32,* 467–476.

Rosenberg, Milton J. 1956. Cognitive structure and attitudinal affect. *Journal of Abnormal and Social Psychology, 53,* 367–372.

———. 1960. Cognitive reorganization in response to the hypnotic reversal of attitudinal affect. *Journal of Personality, 28,* 39–63.

———. 1965. When dissonance fails: on eliminating evaluation apprehension from attitude measurement. *Journal of Personality and Social Psychology, 1,* 28–42.

Rosenberg, Seymour, and Jones, Russell. 1972. A method for investigating and representing a person's implicit theory of personality: Theodore Dreiser's view of people. *Journal of Personality and Social Psychology, 22,* 372–386.

Rosenhan, David L. 1973. On being sane in insane places. *Science, 179,* 250–258.

Rosenthal, Abraham M. 1964. *Thirty-eight witnesses.* New York: McGraw-Hill.

Rosenthal, Robert. 1966. *Experimenter effects in behavioral research.* New York: Appleton-Century-Crofts.

———. 1967. Covert communication in the psychological experiment. *Psychological Bulletin, 67,* 356–367.

———. 1969. Interpersonal expectations: effects of the experimenter's hypotheses. In R. Rosenthal and R. L. Rosnow, eds., *Artifact in behavioral research.* New York: Academic Press. Pp. 181–277.

Rosenthal, Robert, and Fode, K. 1963. The effect of experimental bias on the performance of the albino rat. *Behavioral Science, 8,* 183–189.

Rosenthal, Robert, and Jacobson, Lenore. 1968. *Pygmalion in the classroom.* New York: Holt, Rinehard and Winston.

Rosenthal, Robert, and Rosnow, Ralph L. 1974. *The volunteer subject.* New York: Wiley.

————. 1975. *Primer of methods for the behavioral sciences.* New York: Wiley.

Rosenthal, Robert, and Rosnow, Ralph L., eds. 1969. *Artifact in behavioral research.* New York: Academic Press.

Rubin, Jeffrey Z., and Brown, Bert R. 1975. *The social psychology of bargaining and negotiation.* New York: Academic Press.

Rubin, Jeffrey Z.; Greller, Martin; and Roby, Thornton B. 1974. Factors affecting the magnitude and proportionality of solutions to problems of coordination. *Perceptual and Motor Skills, 39,* 599–618. (Monograph supplement 2-V39.)

Rubin, Jeffrey Z., and Lewicki, Roy J. 1973. A three-factor experimental analysis of interpersonal influence. *Journal of Applied Social Psychology, 3,* 240–257.

Rubin, Jeffrey Z.; Lewicki, Roy J.; and Dunn, Lynne. 1973. Perception of promisers and threateners. *Proceedings of the 81st Annual Convention of the American Psychological Association, 8,* 141–142.

Rubin, Jeffrey Z.; Provenzano, Frank J.; and Luria, Zella. 1974. The eye of the beholder: parents' views on sex of newborns. *American Journal of Orthopsychiatry, 44,* 512–519.

Rubin, Jeffrey Z.; Steinberg, Bruce D.; and Gerrein, John R. 1974. How to obtain the right of way: an experimental analysis of behavior at intersections. *Perceptual and Motor Skills, 39,* 1263–1274.

Rubin, Zick. 1973. *Liking and loving: an invitation to social psychology.* New York: Holt, Rinehart and Winston.

————. 1975. Disclosing oneself to a stranger: reciprocity and its limits. *Journal of Experimental Social Psychology, 11,* 233–260.

Rule, Brendan G., and Percival, Elizabeth. 1971. The effects of frustration and attack of physical aggression. *Journal of Experimental Research in Personality, 5,* 111–188.

Saegert, Susan; Swap, Walter; and Zajonc, Robert B. 1973. Exposure, context, and interpersonal attraction. *Journal of Personality and Social Psychology, 25,* 234–242.

Sakurai, Melvin M. 1975. Small group cohesiveness and detrimental conformity. *Sociometry, 38,* 340–357.

Sample, John A., and Wilson, Thurlow R. 1965. Leader behavior, group productivity, and rating of least preferred co-worker. *Journal of Personality and Social Psychology, 1,* 266–270.

Sartre, Jean-Paul. 1955a. The flies. In Jean-Paul Sartre, *No exit and three other plays.* New York: Random House (Vintage Books). Pp. 49–128.

———. 1955b. *No exit and three other plays*. New York: Random House (Vintage Books).

Schachter, Stanley. 1951. Deviation, rejection, and communication. *Journal of Abnormal and Social Psychology, 46,* 190–207.

———. 1959. The psychology of affiliation. Stanford, Calif.: Stanford Univ. Press.

Schachter, Stanley; Ellertson, Norris; McBride, Dorothy; and Gregory, Doris. 1951. An experimental study of cohesiveness and productivity. *Human Relations, 4,* 229–238.

Schachter, Stanley, and Singer, Jerome E. 1962. Cognitive, social, and physiological determinants of emotional state. *Psychological Review, 69,* 379–399.

Schaffer, H. R. 1971. *The growth of sociability*. Baltimore: Penguin Books.

Schanck, Robert L. 1932. A study of a community and its groups and institutions conceived of as behaviors of individuals. *Psychological Monographs, 43.*

Scheidlinger, Saul. 1952. *Psychoanalysis and group behavior: a study in Freudian group psychology*. New York: Norton.

Schein, Edgar H. 1961. *Coercive persuasion*. New York: Norton.

Schein, Edgar H.; Schneier, Inge; and Barker, Curtis H. 1961. *Coercive persuasion: a socio-psychological analysis of the "brain-washing" of American civilian prisoners by the Chinese Communists*. New York: Norton.

Schelling, Thomas C. 1960. *The strategy of conflict*. Cambridge, Mass.: Harvard Univ. Press.

Schenitzki, Dietmar P. 1962. Bargaining, group decision making, and the attainment of maximum joint outcome. Unpublished doctoral dissertation, University of Minnesota.

Schiller, Belle. 1932. A quantitative analysis of marriage selection in a small group. *Journal of Social Psychology, 3,* 297–319.

Schiller, J. C. F. 1882. *Essays, esthetical and philosophical, including the dissertation on the "Connexions between the animal and the spiritual in man."* London: Bell.

Schjelderup-Ebbe, T. 1935. Social behavior of birds. In C. Murchison, ed., *A handbook of social psychology*. Worcester, Mass.: Clark Univ. Press. Pp. 947–972.

Schlesinger, Arthur M., Jr. 1965. *A thousand days*. Boston: Houghton Mifflin.

Schneirla, T. C. 1971. *Army ants: a study in social organization*. San Francisco: Freeman.

Schroeder, Harold E. 1973. The risky shift as a general choice shift. *Journal of Personality and Social Psychology, 27,* 297–300.

Scientists' Committee for Radiation Information. 1962. The effects of a 20-megaton bomb. *New University Thought,* 24–32.

Scodel, A.; Minas, J. S.; Ratoosh, Philburn; and Lipetz, Milton E. 1959. Some descriptive aspects of two-person and non-zero-sum games. *Journal of Conflict Resolution, 3,* 114–119.

Scott, T. H.; Bexton, William H.; Heron, William; and Doane, B. K. 1959. Cognitive effects of perceptual isolation. *Canadian Journal of Psychology, 13,* 200–209.

Sears, Robert R.; Maccoby, Eleanor E.; and Levin, Harry. 1957. *Patterns of child rearing.* New York: Harper & Row.

Sears, Robert R.; Whiting, John W. M.; Nowlis, Vincent; and Sears, Pauline S. 1953. Some child-rearing antecedents of aggression and dependency in young children. *Genetic Psychology Monographs, 47,* 135–236.

Seashore, Stanley E. 1954. *Group cohesiveness in the industrial group.* Ann Arbor: Institute for Social Research, Univ. of Michigan.

Shakespeare, William. 1936. The tragedy of Julius Caesar. In William A. Wright, ed., *The complete works of William Shakespeare* (Cambridge ed.). New York: Doubleday. Pp. 629–662.

Shapira, Ariella. 1970. Competition, cooperation, and conformity among city and kibbutz children in Israel. Unpublished doctoral dissertation, University of California, Los Angeles.

Shapira, Ariella, and Madsen, Millard C. 1969. Cooperative and competitive behavior of kibbutz and urban children in Israel. *Child Development, 40,* 609–617.

Shapiro, David, and Leiderman, P. Herbert. 1964. Acts and activation: a psychophysiological study of social interaction. In P. Herbert Leiderman and David Shapiro, eds., *Psychological approaches to social behavior.* Stanford, Calif.: Stanford Univ. Press. Pp. 110–126.

Shaw, Marvin E. 1954. Some effects of problem complexity upon problem solution efficiency in different communication nets. *Journal of Experimental Psychology, 48,* 211–217.

Shaw, Marvin E., and Blum, J. Michael. 1964. Effects of leadership style upon group performance as a function of task structure. Technical Report No. 3, Contract Nonr 580 (11). University of Florida.

Shaw, Marvin E., and Shaw, L. M. 1962. Some effects of sociometric grouping upon learning in a second grade classroom. *Journal of Social Psychology, 57,* 453–458.

Sherif, Muzafer. 1935. A study of some social factors in perception. *Archives of Psychology, 27,* No. 187.

———. 1966. *In common predicament: social psychology of intergroup conflict and cooperation.* Boston: Houghton Mifflin.

———. 1975. Personal communication, September.

Sherif, Muzafer; Harvey, O. J.; White, B. J.; Hood, William R.; and

Sherif, Carolyn W. 1961. *Intergroup conflict and cooperation: the Robbers Cave experiment.* Norman, Okla.: University Book Exchange.

Sherif, Muzafer, and Sherif, Carolyn W. 1953. *Groups in harmony and tension.* New York: Harper & Row.

——. 1969. *Social psychology.* New York: Harper & Row.

Shor, Ronald E. 1957. Effect of preinformation upon human characteristics attributed to animated geometric figures. *Journal of Abnormal and Social Psychology, 54,* 124–126.

Shouval, Ron; Venaki, Sophie Kav; Bronfenbrenner, Urie; Devereux, Edward C.; and Kiely, Elizabeth. 1975. Anomalous reactions to social pressure of Israeli and Soviet children raised in family versus collective settings. *Journal of Personality and Social Psychology, 32,* 477–489.

Shute, Nevil. 1957. *On the beach.* New York: Bantam Books.

Sidowski, Joseph B.; Wyckoff, L. B.; and Tabory, L. 1956. The influence of reinforcement and punishment in a minimal social situation. *Journal of Abnormal and Social Psychology, 52,* 115–119.

Siegel, Alberta E. 1958. The influence of violence in the mass media upon children's role expectations. *Child Development, 29,* 35–56.

Siegel, Alberta E., and Siegel, Sidney. 1957. Reference groups, membership groups, and attitude change. *Journal of Abnormal and Social Psychology, 55,* 360–364.

Siegel, Sidney, and Fouraker, L. E. 1960. *Bargaining and group decision making: experiments in bilateral monopoly.* New York: McGraw-Hill.

Siegel, Sidney, and Zajonc, Robert B. 1967. Group risk-taking in professional decisions. *Sociometry, 30,* 339–350.

Silverthorne, Colin P. 1971. Information input and the group shift phenomenon in risk taking. *Journal of Personality and Social Psychology, 20,* 456–461.

Simmel, Georg. 1902. The number of members as determining the sociological form of the group. *American Journal of Sociology, 8,* 158–196.

——. 1955. *The web of group affiliations* (1908). Translated by K. H. Wolff. New York: Free Press.

Sims, V. M., and Patrick, J. R. 1936. Attitude toward the Negro of northern and southern students. *Journal of Social Psychology, 7,* 192–204.

Singer, Jerome E.; Brush, Claudia A.; and Lublin, Shirley C. 1965. Some aspects of deindividuation: identification and conformity. *Journal of Experimental Social Psychology, 1,* 356–378.

Slater, Philip E. 1958. Contrasting correlates of group size. *Sociometry, 21,* 129–139.

Smith, Anthony J. 1957. Similarity of values and its relation to acceptance and the projection of similarity. *Journal of Psychology, 43,* 251–260.

Smith, Anthony J.; Madden, E. H.; and Sobel, R. 1957. Productivity and recall in cooperative and competitive discussion groups. *Journal of Psychology, 43,* 193–204.

Smith, Ewart E. 1961. The power of dissonance techniques. *Public Opinion Quarterly, 25,* 626–639.

Solomon, Leonard. 1960. The influence of some types of power relationships and game strategies upon the development of interpersonal trust. *Journal of Abnormal and Social Psychology, 61,* 223–230.

Solzhenitsyn, Alexander. 1963. *One day in the life of Ivan Denisovich.* New York: Dutton.

Sommer, Robert. 1969. *Personal space: the behavioral basis of design.* Englewood Cliffs, N.J.: Prentice-Hall.

Spitz, René A. 1945. Hospitalism: an inquiry into the genesis of psychiatric conditions in early childhood. In A. Freud; H. Hartman; and E. Kris, eds., *The psychoanalytic study of the child,* Vol. 1. New York: International Universities Press. Pp. 53–74.

Staub, Ervin. 1974. Helping a distressed person: social, personality, and stimulus determinants. In Leonard Berkowitz, ed., *Advances in experimental social psychology,* Vol. 7. New York: Academic Press. Pp. 294–341.

Steig, William. 1970. *The lonely ones.* New York: Windmill Books.

Stein, David D. 1966. The influence of belief systems on interpersonal preference: a validation study of Rokeach's theory of prejudice. *Psychological Monographs, 80,* 1–29.

Steiner, Ivan D. 1972. *Group process and productivity.* New York: Academic Press.

Steiner, Ivan D., and Peters, Stanley C. 1958. Conformity and the A-B-X model. *Journal of Personality, 26,* 229–242.

Steinzor, Bernard. 1950. The spatial factor in face to face discussion groups. *Journal of Abnormal and Social Psychology, 45,* 552–555.

Stephan, Frederick F., and Mishler, Elliot G. 1952. The distribution of participation in small groups: an exponential approximation. *American Sociological Review, 17,* 598–608.

Stock, Dorothy. 1949. An investigation into the intercorrelations between the self-concept and feelings directed toward other persons and groups. *Journal of Consulting Psychology, 13,* 176–180.

Stogdill, Ralph M. 1948. Personal factors associated with leadership: a survey of the literature. *Journal of Psychology, 25,* 35–71.

Stoner, James A. F. 1961. A comparison of individual and group decisions involving risk. Unpublished master's thesis, Sloan

School of Management, Massachusetts Institute of Technology.

Stouffer, S. A.,; Lumsdaine, A. A., Lumsdaine, M. H.; Williams, R. M., Jr.; Smith, M. B.; Janis, I. L.; Star, S. A.; and Cottrell, L. S., Jr. 1949. *Studies in social psychology in World War II: the American soldier, combat and its aftermath.* Princeton, N.J.: Princeton Univ. Press.

Strickland, Lloyd H. 1958. Surveillance and trust. *Journal of Personality, 26,* 200–215.

Strodtbeck, Fred L.; James, Rita J.; and Hawkins, Charles. 1957. Social status in jury deliberations. *American Sociological Review, 22,* 713–719.

Strupp, Hans H., and Hausman, Howard J. 1953. Some correlates of group productivity. *American Psychologist, 8,* 443–444.

Student, Kurt R. 1968. Supervisory influence and work-group performance. *Journal of Applied Psychology, 52,* 188–194.

Sudnow, David. 1967. Dead on arrival. *Trans-action, 5,* 36–44.

Surgeon General's Advisory Committee on Television and Social Behavior. 1972. *Television and growing up: the impact of televised violence.* Washington, D.C.: U.S. Govt. Printing Office.

Swap, Walter C. 1973. Effects of repeated exposure of meaningful stimuli on attitude formation and change. *Proceedings of the 81st Annual Convention of the American Psychological Association, 8,* 107–108 (Summary).

———. 1975. Interpersonal attraction and repeated exposure to rewarders and punishers. Unpublished manuscript. Tufts University, Medford, Mass.

Tagiuri, Renato; Bruner, Jerome S.; and Blake, Robert R. 1958. On the relation between feelings and perception of feelings among members of small groups. In Eleanor E. Maccoby; Theodore M. Newcomb; and Eugene L. Hartley, eds., *Readings in social psychology.* New York: Holt, Rinehart and Winston. Pp. 110–116.

Tannenbaum, Arnold S.; Kavčič, Bogdan; Rosner, Menachem; Vianello, Mino; and Weiser, Georg. 1974. *Hierarchy in organizations.* San Francisco: Jossey-Bass.

Taylor, Frederic W. 1911. *Principles of scientific management.* New York: Harcourt Brace Jovanovich.

Teger, Allan I., and Pruitt, Dean G. 1967. Components of group risk taking. *Journal of Experimental Social Psychology, 3,* 189–205.

Tharp, Roland G. 1963. Psychological patterning in marriage. *Psychological Bulletin, 60,* 97–117.

———. 1964. Reply to Levinger's note. *Psychological Bulletin, 61,* 158–160.

Thibaut, John W., and Kelley, Harold H. 1959. *The social psychology of groups.* New York: Wiley.

Thibaut, John W., and Riecken, Henry W. 1955. Some determinants and consequences of the perception of social causality. *Journal of Personality, 24,* 113–133.

Thomas, Edwin J. 1957. Effects of facilitative role interdependence on group functioning. *Human Relations, 10,* 347–366.

Thomas, Edwin J., and Fink, Clinton F. 1961. Models of group problem-solving. *Journal of Abnormal and Social Psychology, 63,* 53–63.

———. 1963. Effects of group size. *Psychological Bulletin, 64,* 371–384.

Tolman, Charles W. 1964. Social facilitation of feeding behavior in the domestic chick. *Animal Behavior, 12,* 245–251.

Torrance, E. Paul. 1954. Some consequences of power differences on decision making in permanent and temporary three-man groups. *Research Studies* (Washington State College), *22,* 130–140.

Triandis, Harry C. 1960. Cognitive similarity and communication in a dyad. *Human Relations, 13,* 175–183.

Triandis, Harry C., and Fishbein, Martin. 1963. Cognitive interaction in person perception. *Journal of Abnormal and Social Psychology, 67,* 446–454.

Triandis, Harry C.; Hall, Eleanor R.; and Ewen, Robert B. 1965. Member heterogeneity and dyadic creativity. *Human Relations, 18,* 33–55.

Triplett, N. 1898. The dynamogenic factors in pace-making and competition. *American Journal of Psychology, 9,* 507–533.

Trollope, Frances. 1832. *Domestic manners of the Americans,* 2 vols. London: Whitaker, Treacher.

Tuchman, Barbara. 1963. *The guns of August.* New York: Dell.

Van Zelst, R. H. 1952. Sociometrically selected work teams increase production. *Personnel Psychology, 5,* 175–185.

———. 1952b. Validation of a sociometric regrouping procedure. *Journal of Abnormal and Social Psychology, 47,* 299–301.

Verba, Sidney. 1961. *Small groups and political behavior.* Princeton, N.J.: Princeton Univ. Press.

Vidmar, Neil. 1970. Group composition and risky-shift. *Journal of Experimental Social Psychology, 6,* 163–166.

———. 1971. Effects of representational roles and mediators on negotiation effectiveness. *Journal of Personality and Social Psychology, 17,* 48–58.

Vinokur, Amiram. 1971. Review and theoretical analysis of the effects of group processes upon individual and group decisions involving risk. *Psychological Bulletin, 76,* 231–250.

Vogel, H. H.; Scott, John Paul; and Marston, M. 1950. Social facilitation and allelomimetic behavior in dogs. *Behavior, 2,* 121–143.

von Neumann, John; and Morgenstern, Oscar. 1944. *Theory of games and economic behavior.* Princeton, N.J.: Princeton Univ. Press.

Wakil, S. Parvez. 1973. Campus mate selection preferences: a cross-national comparison. *Social Forces, 51,* 471–476.

Wallach, Michael A.; Kogan, Nathan; and Bem, Daryl J. 1962. Group influence on individual risk-taking. *Journal of Abnormal and Social Psychology, 65,* 75–86.

————. 1964. Diffusion of responsibility and level of risk-taking in groups. *Journal of Abnormal and Social Psychology, 68,* 263–274.

Wallach, Michael A.; Kogan, Nathan; and Burt, Roger B. 1968. Are risk takers more persuasive than conservatives in group discussion? *Journal of Experimental Social Psychology, 4,* 76–88.

Walster, Elaine. 1965. Effects of self-esteem on romantic liking. *Journal of Experimental Social Psychology, 1,* 184–197.

————. 1966. Assignment of responsibility for an accident. *Journal of Personality and Social Psychology, 3,* 73–79.

Walster, Elaine; Aronson, Vera; Abrahams, Darcy; and Rottmann, Leon. 1966. Importance of physical attractiveness in dating behavior. *Journal of Personality and Social Psychology, 4,* 508–516.

Walster, Elaine, and Festinger, Leon. 1962. The effectiveness of "overheard" persuasive communications. *Journal of Abnormal and Social Psychology, 65,* 395–402.

Walters, Richard H., and Brown, Murray. 1963. Studies of reinforcement and aggression: III. Transfer of responses to an interpersonal situation. *Child Development, 34,* 563–571.

Walton, Richard E. 1969. *Interpersonal peacemaking: confrontations and third-party consultation.* Reading, Mass.: Addison-Wesley.

Washburn, S. L., and DeVore, Irven. 1961. The social life of baboons. *Scientific American* (Offprint No. 614).

Waskow, Arthur I. 1962. The shelter-centered society. *Scientific American, 206*(34), 46–51.

Watson, Robert I. 1973. Investigation into deindividuation using a cross-cultural survey technique. *Journal of Personality and Social Psychology, 25,* 342–345.

Weingarten, Murray. 1959. *Life in a kibbutz.* Jerusalem: Jerusalem Post Press.

Welty, J. C. 1934. Experiments in group behavior of fishes. *Physiological Zoology, 7,* 85–128.

Wertheimer, Max. 1923. Untersuchungen zur Lehre von der Gestalt: II. *Psychologische Forschung, 4,* 301–350.

————. 1945. *Productive thinking.* New York: Harper & Row.

Wheeler, Ladd, and Caggiula, Anthony R. 1966. The contagion of aggression. *Journal of Experimental Social Psychology, 2,* 1–10.

Wheeler, Ladd; Shaver, Kelly G.; Jones, Russell A.; Goethals, George R.; Cooper, Joel; Robinson, James E.; Gruder, Charles L.; and Butzine, Kent W. 1969. Factors determining choice of a comparison other. *Journal of Experimental Social Psychology, 5,* 219–232.

White, Ralph K. 1966. Misperception and the Vietnam war. *Journal of Social Issues, 22* (Whole No. 3).

White, Robert W. 1958. When prophecy fails. *American Psychologist, 13,* 656–657.

White, Theodore H. 1973. *The making of the president—1972.* New York: Bantam Books.

———. 1975. *Breach of faith: the fall of Richard Nixon.* New York: Atheneum.

White House transcripts. 1974. New York: Bantam Books.

Whyte, William Foote. 1943. *Street corner society: the social structure of an Italian slum.* Chicago: Univ. of Chicago Press.

———. 1948. *Human relations in the restaurant industry.* New York: McGraw-Hill.

———. 1961. *Men at work.* Homewood, Ill.: Irwin.

Whyte, William H., Jr. 1956. *The organization man.* New York: Simon & Schuster.

Willis, Richard H. 1965. Conformity, independence, and anticonformity. *Human Relations, 18,* 373–388.

Wilson, P. R. 1968. The perceptual distortion of height as a function of ascribed academic status. *Journal of Social Psychology, 74,* 97–102.

Winch, Robert F. 1955. The theory of complementary needs in mate-selection: a test of one kind of complementariness. *American Sociological Review, 20,* 52–56.

Winch, Robert F.; Ktsanes, T.; and Ktsanes, Virginia. 1954. The theory of complementary needs in mate selection: an analytic and descriptive study. *American Sociological Review, 19,* 241–249.

Wispe, Lauren G., ed. 1972. Positive forms of social behavior. *Journal of Social Issues, 28* (Whole No. 3).

Withey, Stephen B. 1962. *The U.S. and the U.S.S.R.: a report on the public's perspectives on United States-Russian relations in late 1961.* Ann Arbor, Mich.: Survey Research Center, Univ. of Michigan.

Wolfe, Donald M. 1959. Power and authority in the family. In Dorwin Cartwright, ed., *Studies in social power.* Ann Arbor: Institute for Social Research, Univ. of Michigan. Pp. 99–117.

Wolosin, Robert J. 1975. Cognitive similarity and group laughter. *Journal of Personality and Social Psychology, 32,* 503–509.

Woodworth, Robert S. 1925. A review of *Social Psychology* by F. H. Allport. *Journal of Abnormal Psychology, 20*, 92–106.

Worchel, Philip, and Schuster, Stephen D. 1966. Attraction as a function of the drive state. *Journal of Experimental Research in Personality, 1*, 277–281.

Xenophon. 1969. *The Persian expedition.* Translated by Rex Warner. Harmondsworth, Middlesex, England: Penguin Books. Pp. 52–56.

Yablonsky, Lewis. 1967. *Synanon: the tunnel back.* Baltimore: Penguin Books.

Zajonc, Robert B. 1965. Social facilitation. *Science, 149*, 269–274.

———. 1968a. Attitudinal effects of mere exposure. *Journal of Personality and Social Psychology* (Monograph Supplement, Part 2), 1–27.

———. 1968b. Social facilitation in cockroaches. In Edward C. Simmel; Ronald A. Hoppe; and G. Alexander Milton, eds., *Social facilitation and imitative behavior.* Boston: Allyn & Bacon. Pp. 73–88.

———. 1970. Brainwash: familiarity breeds comfort. *Psychology Today*, February, 32–35, 60–64.

Zajonc, Robert B.; Wolosin, Robert J.; and Wolosin, Myrna A. 1972. Group risk-taking under various group decision schemes. *Journal of Experimental Social Psychology, 8*, 16–30.

Zander, Alvin F., and Cohen, Arthur R. 1955. Attributed social power and group acceptance: a classroom experimental demonstration. *Journal of Abnormal and Social Psychology, 51*, 490–492.

Zander, Alvin; Cohen, Arthur R.; and Stotland, Ezra. 1957. *Role relations in the mental health professions.* Ann Arbor: Institute for Social Research, Univ. of Michigan.

———. 1959. Power and the relations among professions. In Dorwin Cartwright, ed., *Studies in social power.* Ann Arbor: Institute for Social Research, Univ. of Michigan. Pp. 15–34.

Zander, Alvin, and Wolfe, Donald. 1964. Administrative rewards and coordination among committee members. *Administrative Science Quarterly, 9*, 50–69.

Zborowski, Mark, and Herzog, Elizabeth. 1952. *Life is with people.* New York: International Universities Press.

Zillman, Dolf. 1971. Excitation transfer in communication-mediated aggressive behavior. *Journal of Experimental Social Psychology, 7*, 419–434.

Zimbardo, Philip G. 1969. The human choice: individuation, reason and order versus deindividuation, impulse, and chaos. In William J. Arnold and David Levine, eds., *Nebraska Symposium on Motivation*. Lincoln: Univ. of Nebraska Press. Pp. 237–308.

———. 1970. The psychology of police confessions. In J. V. McConnell, ed., *Readings in social psychology today*. Del Mar, Calif.: CRM Books, Pp. 102–107.

Zimbardo, Philip G., and Formica, R. 1963. Emotional comparison and self-esteem as determinants of affiliation. *Journal of Personality, 31*, 141–162.

Zimbardo, Philip G.; Haney, Craig; Banks, W. Curtis; and Jaffe, David. The psychology of imprisonment: privation, power and pathology. Unpublished manuscript, Stanford University.

Zimbardo, Philip G.; Weisenberg, Matisyohu; Firestone, Ira; and Levy, B. 1965. Communicator effectiveness in producing public conformity and private attitude change. *Journal of Personality, 33*, 233–255.

Zucker, Robert A.; Manosevitz, Martin; and Lanyon, Richard I. 1968. Birth order, anxiety, and affiliation during a crisis. *Journal of Personality and Social Psychology, 8*, 354–359.

Brown, R., 188, 336, 337, (526)
Bruner, J. S., 125, (557)
Brush, C. A., 304, (555)
Bryan, J. H., 344, (526)
Bugelski, B. R., 136, (546)
Burke, P. J., 386, (526)
Burney, C., 36, (526)
Burnstein, E., 84, 125, (526, 540)
Burt, R. B., 334, (559)
Burtt, H. E., 402, (533)
Buss, A. H., 142, (526)
Butzine, K. W., 48, (560)
Byrd, R. E., 35, (516)
Byrne, D., 118, (526, 527)

C

Caggiula, A. R., 142, (560)
Campbell, D. T., 314, 447, (527, 538)
Campbell, J. P., 402, (530)
Carlsmith, J. M., 231, 234, 240, 489, 490, (521, 527, 532)
Carlson, E. R., 110, 207, (527)
Carlson, J. A., 334, (527, 541)
Carnegie, D., 102, (527)
Carter, L. F., 374, 376, 382, (527)
Cartwright, D., 103, 105, 239, 334, (527)
Centers, R., 284, (527)
Chaffee, S. H., 147, (527)
Chapman, A. J., 291, (528)
Chapman, R., (549)
Charters, W. W., 215, (528)
Chen, S. C., 290, (528)
Clark, W. v. T., 303, (528)
Cleaver, E., 89, (528)
Clore, G. L., 126, (528)
Coch, L., 296, 358, (528)
Codere, H., 339, (528)
Cohen, A. R., 115, 280, 374, (525, 561)
Cohen, M., 275, (540)
Collier, R. M., (528)
Collins, B. E., 255, 363, (527, 528)
Collins, M. E., 132, (529)
Cook, T. D., 345, (535)
Cooley, C. H., 93, (528)
Cooper, J., 48, (560)

Costanzo, P. R., 319, (528)
Cottrell, L. S., 125, (557)
Couch, A. S., 373, (525)
Crano, W. D., 345, (537)
Crockett, W. H., 378, (528)
Crow, W. J., 468, (528)
Crutchfield, R. S., 75, 317, 319, 328, 380, (528, 542)
Csoka, L. S., 401, (528)
Cvetkovich, G., 337, (529)

D

Dalrymple, S., (536)
Danet, B., 201, 218, 219, (540)
Daniels, L. R., 217, (524)
Darley, J. M., 53, 132, 341, 342, 343, 344, (529, 542)
Dashiell, J. F., (529)
Davis, C. M., 336, (527)
Davis, J. H., 363, (529)
Davis, K. E., 75, 76, 84, 121, 236, (539, 541)
Davitz, J. R., 148, (529)
deCharms, R., 77, (529)
Deutsch, M., 125, 128, 132, 172, 181, 182, 183, 184, 317, 330, 363, 442, 443, 444, 445, 457, 458, 462, 463, (529, 530, 542)
Devereux, E. C., 322, (555)
De Vore, I., 278, (559)
Dickoff, H., 126, (530)
Dickson, W. J., 356, (551)
Dion, K., 112, 114, (530)
Dion, K. L., 334, (530)
Dittes, J. E., 330, (530)
Doane, B. K., 38, (554)
Doise, W., 334, 337, (530, 541)
Dolci, D., 6, (530)
Dollard, J., 134, 136, (530)
Doob, A. N., 118, 138, 326, 329, 330, (533)
Doob, L. W., 134, 136, (530)
Dreiser, T., 69, (530)
Druckman, D., 460, 463, (524, 530)
Dunn, L. A., 210, (552)
Dunnette, M. D., 402, (530)
Dynes, R. R., 124, (549)

ILLUSTRATION CREDITS

CHAPTER ONE

Figure 1.1: (top) United Press International; (bottom) Wide World Photos. **Figure 1.2:** (top) Synanon News Service; (bottom) Hap Stewart/Jeroboam. **Figure 1.3:** Culver Pictures.

CHAPTER TWO

Figure 2.1: Wide World Photos. **Figure 2.2:** David Powers/Jeroboam. **Figure 2.3:** Wide World Photos. **Figure 2.4:** Reprinted by special permission of The Philadelphia Evening & Sunday Bulletin.

CHAPTER THREE

Figure 3.1: David Linton. **Figure 3.2:** Dan Budnick/Woodfin Camp. **Figure 3.3:** Fashion Eyewear Group of America.

CHAPTER FOUR

Figure 4.4: Burt Glinn/Magnum. **Figure 4.7:** By permission of Stanley Kramer. **Figure 4.8:** Reproduced from Bandura, Ross & Ross, 1963, p. 8. Copyright by American Psychological Association and reproduced by permission. **Figure 4.9:** Courtesy Dr. George Bach. Photo by William C. Groves.

CHAPTER FIVE

Figure 5.6: Ian Berry/Magnum. **Figure 5.8:** David Stickler/Monkmeyer. **Figure 5.9:** Philip Jones Griffiths/Magnum.

CHAPTER SIX

Figure 6.5: Copyright 1965 by Stanley Milgram. From the film OBEDIENCE, distributed by the New York University Film Library.

CHAPTER SEVEN

Figure 7.5: Henri Cartier-Bresson/Magnum. **Figure 7.6:** Culver Pictures. **Figure 7.10:** Erika Stone/Peter Arnold. **Figure 7.12:** Jon Raven.

CHAPTER EIGHT

Figure 8.1: Rick Winsor/Woodfin Camp. **Figure 8.2:** The Bettmann Archive. **Figure 8.3:** (top) Courtesy Professor Philip G. Zimbardo,

Stanford University; (bottom) Roy Pinney/Monkmeyer. **Figure 8.4:** (top) Courtesy Professor Philip G. Zimbardo, Stanford University; (bottom) Leonard Freed/Magnum. **Figure 8.7:** William Vandivert.

CHAPTER NINE

Figure 9.3: Bob Fitch/Black Star. **Figure 9.4:** United Press International. **Figure 9.5:** Copyright © 1957 Columbia Pictures Corporation. **Figure 9.6:** (left) United Nations; (right) Burk Uzzle/Magnum.

CHAPTER TEN

Figure 10.2: Arthur Rickerby/Time Life Picture Agency, © Time, Inc. **Figure 10.5:** Courtesy Muzafer Sherif, The Pennsylvania State University. **Figure 10.6:** Gerry Cranham/Rapho-Photo Researchers. **Figure 10.8:** United Press International. **Figure 10.9:** From *The Sneetches and Other Stories*, by Dr. Seuss. Copyright 1953, 1954, © 1961 by Dr. Seuss. Reprinted by permission of Random House, Inc. **Figure 10.10:** Courtesy Muzafer Sherif, The Pennsylvania State University. **Figure 10.11:** Wide World Photos.

AUTHOR INDEX

The page numbers in parentheses pertain to the References.

A

Abelson, R. P., 205, (521)
Abrahams, D., 113, (559)
Adorno, T. W., 395, (521)
Alcock, N. Z., 444, (521)
Alinski, S., 15, (521)
Allport, F. H., 291, 292, (521)
Allport, G., 10, (521)
Altman, I., 89, (521)
Anderson, N. H., 111, (521)
Anthony, E., 226, (550)
Arensberg, C. M., 254, (537)
Aristotle, 371, (521)
Aronfreed, J., 295, (521)
Aronson, E., 25, 53, 119, 120, 126, 127, 132, 264, 489, 490, (521, 522, 529)
Aronson, V., 113, (559)
Ås, D., 359, (533)
Asch, S. E., 62, 64, 66, 317, 319, 325, (522)

B

Bach, G. R., 148, 149, (522)
Bach, P. J., 334, (547)
Back, K. W., 126, 132, 255, 300, (522, 532)
Backman, C. W., 103, 125, 297, (522)
Baer, D. M., 38, (534)
Bahr, S. J., (525)
Baker, R. K., 133, (522)
Baker, S. J., 133, (522)
Bales, R. F., 365, 373, 376, 383, 385, 480, (522, 523, 525)
Ballachey, E. L., 75, 380, (542)
Bandura, A., 140, 146, 147, (523)
Banks, W. C., 306, 338, 440, (535, 562)
Banuazizi, A., 309, (523)
Barker, C. H., (553)
Baron, R. S., 334, (530)
Barrie, J. M., 378, (523)
Bartunek, J. M., 463, (523)
Bass, B. M., 372, 373, 463, (523)
Bateson, N., 334, (523)
Baumgardner, S. R., 337, (529)

Bavelas, A., 270, 374, 375, (523)
Bayer, E., 291, (523)
Becker, H., 297, (538)
Bell, G. B., 373, 375, (523)
Bem, D. J., 94, 123, 236, 237, 334, (523, 559)
Bem, S. L., 123, (524)
Bennett, E. B., 355, (524)
Benton, A. A., 460, 463, (524)
Bergum, B. O., 294, (524)
Berkowitz, L., 26, 137, 138, 140, 147, 149, 217, 255, 277, 341, 367, (524, 534, 535, 545)
Bernstein, C., 425, (525)
Berscheid, E., 43, 112, 128, 132, (525, 529, 530, 538)
Bettelheim, B., 309, (525)
Bexton, W. H., 37, 38, (525, 554)
Biddle, B. J., 274, (525)
Bishop, G. D., 337, (547)
Bjerstedt, A., 254, (525)
Blake, R. R., 125, 459, (525, 557)
Blaney, N., 264, (521)
Blascovich, J., 337, (525)
Blau, P., 165, 382, (525)
Bless, E., 240, (533)
Blood, R. O., 115, 283, (525)
Blum, B., 150, (525)
Blum, J. M., 400, (554)
Bombard, A., 35, 36, (525)
Borgatta, E. F., 365, 373, (522, 525)
Bowerman, C. E., (525)
Bowers, R. J., 336, (530)
Braden, M., (535)
Bramel, D., 150, (525)
Breedlove, J., 119, (543)
Brehm, J. W., 205, 329, (525)
Bricker, W., 150, (548)
Brigham, J. C., 230, (525)
Brissenden, P. F., 225, (526)
Brock, T. C., 213, (526)
Brody, R. A., 444, (548)
Bronfenbrenner, U., 262, 322, (526, 555)
Brotzman, E., (536)
Brown, B. R., 169, 190, 193, 459, 460, 462, (526, 552)
Brown, M., 150, (559)
Brown, P., 147, (535)

E

Eachus, H. T., 125, 184, 185, 187, 258, 259, 260, 261, 363, (550)
Ebbesen, E. B., 336, (530)
Eckhardt, W., 444, (531)
Eisenhower, M., 145, (531)
Ellertson, N., 255, 367, (553)
Elms, A. C., 230, (531)
Emerson, R. M., 119, (531)
Eron, L. D., 145, (531)
Ervin, C. R., 118, (526)
Etzioni, A., 469, 470, (531)
Evans, F. J., 143, (548)
Ewen, R. B., 366, (558)
Eysenck, S. B. G., 300, (531)

F

Fantz, R. L., 59, (531)
Faucheux, C., 313, (531)
Feldman, R. E., 346, (531)
Fellner, C. H., 348, (531)
Feshbach, S., 125, 146, 148, 149, (531, 532)
Festinger, L., 17, 22, 23, 46, 125, 132, 231, 233, 234, 297, 303, 304, 319, 327, 329, 335, 482, (532, 559)
Fiedler, F., 366, 395, 400, 401, 402, (528, 532)
Field, P. B., 319, (538)
Fink, C. F., 362, 365, 367, (558)
Firestone, I., 236, (562)
Fischer, L., 3, (532)
Fishbein, M., 110, 119, (532, 558)
Fisher, R., 464, (532)
Flanders, J. P., 335, (533)
Fleishman, E. A., 402, (533)
Floyd, J., 120, (522)
Fode, K., 492, (551)
Formica, R., 53, (562)
Fouraker, L. E., 461, (555)
Fouriezos, N. T., 363, (533)
Frank, A. F., 158, (533)
Frank, J. D., 219, 241, (533)
Fraser, M., 70, (533)
Fraser, S. C., 241, (533)

Freedman, J. L., 118, 138, 241, 326, 329, 330, (533)
French, J. R. P., 202, 224, 230, 296, 358, 359, (533, 550)
French, R. L., 373, 375, (523)
Frenkel-Brunswick, E., 395, (521)
Freud, S., 380, (533)
Frieze, I., (533)
Froman, R., 340, (534)
Fromm, E., 41, 127, (534)
Fülop-Miller, R., 11, (534)

G

Gallo, P. S., 215, 444, (534, 550)
Gamson, W. A., 468, (534)
Gandhi, M. K., 2, (534)
Geen, R. G., 138, (524, 534)
Geer, B., 297, (538)
Gelb, L. H., 409, (534)
Gerard, H. B., 132, 317, 327, 329, 330, (529, 532, 534, 539)
Gergen, K. J., 84, 96, 97, 119, (534, 539, 547)
Gerrein, J. R., 163, (552)
Gewirtz, J. L., 38, (534)
Ginsburg, G. P., 337, (525)
Glass, D. C., 294, (536)
Goethals, G. R., 48, (560)
Goffman, E., 81, 87, 92, 459, (534)
Golding, W., 388, (534)
Goodacre, D. M., 367, (534, 535)
Goranson, R. E., 217, (535)
Greenburg, D., 240, (535)
Gordon, T., 390, (535)
Graves, N., (536)
Green, J. A., 138, (524)
Gregory, D., 255, 367, (553)
Greller, M., 161, (552)
Gross, A. E., 240, 374, (523, 527)
Gruder, C. L., 48, 345, (535, 560)
Grusky, O., 376, (535)
Guetzkow, H., 254, 276, 363, (535, 545)
Gunderson, R. G., 360, (535)
Gunn, R. L., 280, (543)
Gurevitch, M., 201, 219, (540)

H

Haber, I., 210, (537)
Hall, E. R., 366, (558)
Halloran, R., 137, (535)
Halpin, A. W., 391, (535)
Hamblin, R. L., 376, 387, (535)
Haner, C., 147, (535)
Haney, C., 306, 338, 440, (535, 562)
Harari, H., 66, (535)
Harary, F., 103, 105, (527)
Hardyck, J. A., (535)
Harlow, H. F., 291, (535)
Harris, E. F., 402, (533)
Harvey, O. J., 436, (554)
Hass, N., (549)
Hastorf, A. H., 374, (523)
Hausman, H. J., 367, (557)
Hawkins, C., 282, (557)
Haythorn, W., 374, 376, 382, 395, (527, 536)
Heider, F., 11, 26, 74, 75, 103, 104, 105, 106, 202, (536)
Helmreich, R. L., (527)
Hemphill, J. K., 367, 376, 391, (536)
Henchy, T. P., 294, (536)
Henry, J., 445, (536)
Herbst, P. G., 283, (536)
Heron, W., 37, 38, (525, 554)
Herzog, E., 217, (561)
Heyns, R. W., 254, (545)
Hill, D., 102, (536)
Hilsman, R., 411, (536)
Hobbes, T., 134, (536)
Hoffman, D. B., 227, (538)
Hoffman, L. R., 363, 366, (536)
Hofling, C. K., (536)
Hokanson, J. E., 149, (536)
Hollander, E. P., 319, 326, 378, (537, 539)
Holsti, O. R., 444, (548)
Homans, G. C., 165, (537)
Hood, W. R., 436, (554)
Horai, J., 210, (537)
Horne, W. C., 337, (537)
Horner, M. S., 276, (537)
Horsfall, A. B., 254, (537)
House, R. J., 402, (537)
Hovland, C., 135, 204, 214, 227, 228, 319, 320, (537, 539, 541)

Howard, W., 345, (537)
Hoyt, M. F., 124, (537)
Hughes, E., 297, (538)
Hurwitz, J. I., 282, 364, 374, (538)
Husband, R. W., 254, (538)
Hutt, M. L., 363, (533)
Hyman, H. H., 214, (538)
Hymovitch, B., 282, 327, 329, 364, 374, (532, 538)

I

Iklé, F. C., (538)
Inbau, F., 237, (538)
Israel, J., 359, (533)
Itkin, S., 126, (528)

J

Jacobs, L., 128, (538)
Jacobs, R. C., 314, (538)
Jacobson, L., 492, (551)
Jaffee, D., 306, 440, (562)
James, R. J., 282, (557)
Jamieson, B. D., 334, (538)
Janis, I. L., 14, 125, 227, 230, 319, 320, 362, 415, 416, 419, (537, 538, 539)
Janov, A., 149, (539)
Johnson, D. F., 462, 476, (549)
Johnson, P., 276, (533, 539)
Jones, E. E., 75, 76, 84, 128, 236, 448, (539)
Jones, Robert A., 230, (539)
Jones, Russell A., 48, 69, (551, 560)
Jorgensen, B. W., 121, (543)
Josephus, F., (539)
Jourard, S. M., 89, 90, 91, 94, (539)
Julian, J. W., 319, 378, (539)

K

Kahn, R. L., 360, 385, 386, 422, (539, 540)
Kaplan, J., (540)
Katz, D., 360, 385, 386, 422, 444, (540)
Katz, E., 201, 218, 219, (540)
Katz, I., 275, 295, (540)
Katz, S., 84, (540)

Kavčič, B., 360, (557)
Kelley, H. H., 64, 75, 94, 129, 165, 188, 191, 194, 210, 281, 319, 327, 329, 363, 364, (530, 532, 537, 551, 557)
Kelman, H. C., 80, 88, 204, 223, 227, 228, 411, (541)
Kennedy, J. F., 469, 472, (541)
Kerckhoff, A. C., 121, 300, (541)
Kerr, C., 462, (541)
Kesey, K., 391, (541)
Keys, C. B., 463, (523)
Kiely, E., 322, (555)
Kipnis, D., 210, 376, (541)
Kite, W. R., 374, (523)
Klein, H. G., 430, (541)
Klisurich, D., 355, (549)
Knapp, W. M., 462, (549)
Koffka, K., 26, (541)
Kogan, N., 333, 334, 335, 336, 459, (541, 542, 559)
Köhler, W., 26, (542)
Krauss, R., 125, 172, 442, 443, 457, 458, 462, 463, (529, 542)
Krebs, D. L., 341, (542)
Krech, D., 75, 380, (542)
Kruglanski, A. W., 212, (542)
Ktsanes, T., 121, (560)
Ktsanes, V., 121, (560)

L

Lage, E., 313, (547)
Laird, D. A., 295, (542)
Lamberth, J., 118, (526)
Lamm, H., 334, 459, (541, 542)
Lanyon, R. I., 124, (562)
Lanzetta, J. T., 124, 374, 376, 382, (542)
Larsson, K., 291, (542)
Latané, B., 341, 342, 343, 344, (529, 542)
Laumann, E. O., 115, (542)
Lawrence, L. H., 80, 88, (541)
Leavitt, H. J., 270, 272, 375, 392, (542)
LeBon, G., 302, 303, (543)
Leff, W. F., 174, 280, (543, 550)
Lehr, D. J., 294, (524)
Leiderman, P. H., 293, (554)

LePage, A., 137, (524)
Lerner, M. J., 347, (543)
Lesieur, F. G., 392, (543)
Levin, H., 134, (554)
Levinger, G., 119, 121, 122, 336, (543)
Levinson, D. J., 395, (521)
Levy, B., 236, (562)
Lewicki, R. J., 210, (552)
Lewin, K., 26, 91, 124, 239, 296, 355, 358, 393, (543, 544)
Lewis, M., 72, (544)
Lewis, O., 178, (544)
Likert, R., 396, (544)
Lilly, J. C., 37, (544)
Linder, D., 126, (521)
Linton, R., (544)
Lippitt, R., 393, (544)
Lipetz, M. E., 172, (554)
Lipton, D., 336, (544)
Littman, R. A., 150, (548)
Lombroso-Ferrero, G., 112, (544)
London, P., 344, (544)
Long, G., 337, (537)
Loomis, J. L., 172, (544)
Lorge, I., (544)
Lublin, S. C., 304 (555)
Luce, R. D., 167, (544)
Luchins, A. S., 67, (544)
Lumsdaine, A. A., 125, 204, 227, (537, 557)
Lumsdaine, M. H., 125, (557)
Luria, Z., 72, (552)

M

Macauley, J., 341, (544)
McBride, D., 255, 367, (553)
McCandless, B. R., 148, (545)
McCauley, C., 336, (544)
Maccoby, E. E., 134, (554)
McDavid, J. W., 66, (535)
McDonough, J. J., 309, (544)
McEvedy, C. P., 300, (547)
McGrath, J. E., 255, (544)
McGregor, D., 391, (544)
McGuire, W. J., 495, (545)
McLeod, J. M., 147, (527)
McRae, A. V., 125, (526)
Madden, E. H., 258, (556)

Madsen, M. C., 175, 176, 178, (545, 554)
Magruder, J. S., 428, (545)
Maier, N. R. F., 362, 381, (536, 545)
Malamuth, N. M., 336, 337, (545)
Mallick, S. K., 148, (545)
Mann, R. D., 372, 374, (545)
Manosevitz, M., 124, (562)
Mansson, H. H., 226, (550)
March, J. G., 423, (545)
Marquis, D. G., 254, 334, (545)
Marshall, J., 348, (531)
Marston, M., 291, (558)
Maslow, A. H., 123, 127, (545)
Matthewson, G. C., 132, (534)
Mead, G. H., 93, (545)
Mead, M., 123, 173, (545)
Meeker, R. J., 444, 462, 486, (545)
Menzel, H., 330, (546)
Merei, F., 382, 383, (546)
Merton, R. K., 214, (546)
Mettee, D. R., 120, (546)
Meuwese, W., 366, (532)
Michotte, A., 73, (546)
Milgram, S., 126, 142, 219, 221, 320, 335, 490, 493, (546)
Miller, J. C., 205, (521)
Miller, N., 334, (530)
Miller, N. E., 134, 136, (530, 546)
Mills, J., 25, 132, 234, (522, 546)
Mills, T. M., 265, (546)
Minas, J. S., 172, (554)
Mintz, A., 135, 188, (546)
Mishler, E. G., 365, (556)
Modigliani, A., 468, (534)
Moede, W., (546)
Mollenhoff, C. R., 431, (546)
Monahan, F., 112, (546)
Moore, W. H., 444, (545)
Moreno, J. L., (546)
Morgenstern, O., 164, (559)
Morse, N. C., 360, (547)
Morse, S. J., 97, 119, (547)
Moscovici, S., 313, 337, (531, 547)
Moss, P. D., 300, (547)
Mouton, J. S., 459, (525)
Movahedi, S., 309, (523)
Mowrer, O. H., 134, 136, (530)
Mulder, M., 124, 377, (547)
Myers, D. G., 334, 337, (547)

N

Naffrechoux, M., 313, (547)
Nelson, D., 118, (526, 527)
Nemeth, C., 313, (547)
Newcomb, T. M., 103, 115, 117, 125, 215, 303, 304, 329, 331, 445, 457, (528, 532, 547)
Newcombe, A. G., 444, (548)
Nisbett, R. E., 448, (539)
North, R. C., 444, (548)
Nowlis, V., 148, (554)

O

Oonk, S., 366, (532)
Orne, M. T., 143, (548)
Orwell, G., 82, (548)
Osgood, C. E., 103, 447, 451, 465, (548)
Oskamp, S., 452, (548)

P

Parkinson, C. N., 361, (548)
Parsons, J. E., (533)
Patrick, J. R., 331, (555)
Patterson, G. R., 150, (548)
Patterson, T. T., 254, (548)
Peled, T., 201, 219, (540)
Pelton, L. H., 147, (548)
Pepitone, A., 303, 304, (532)
Percival, E., 136, (552)
Perlman, D., (548)
Perls, F., 149, (549)
Perrucci, R., 408, (549)
Pessin, J., 294, (549)
Peters, S. C., 107, 119, (556)
Philp, A. J., 254, (549)
Piaget, J., 77, (549)
Pierce, C. M., (536)
Piliavin, I. M., 345, 347, (549)
Piliavin, J. A., 345, 347, (549)
Pilisuk, M., 408, (549)
Podell, J. E., 462, (549)
Postman, L., (521)
Provenzano, F. J., 72, (552)
Pruitt, D. G., 334, 335, 336, 444, 462, 476, (549, 557)

Q

Quarantelli, E. L., 124, (549)

R

Radke, M., 355, (549)
Radloff, R., 49, (550)
Raiffa, H., 167, (544)
Rapoport, A., 435, (550)
Ratoosh, P., 172, (554)
Raven, B. H., 124, 125, 174, 184, 185, 187, 202, 215, 224, 226, 230, 255, 258, 259, 260, 261, 280, 284, 327, 329, 330, 331, 332, 363, 417, 423, (527, 528, 532, 533, 537, 543, 550)
Read, P. B., (550)
Reeves, K., 118, (527)
Regula, R., 319, (539)
Reid, J. E., 237, (538)
Reimer, E., 360, (547)
Riecken, H. W., 22, 85, 482, (532, 557)
Riesman, D., 320, (550)
Rietsema, J., (550)
Rim, Y., 334, (551)
Ring, K., 210, (551)
Robinson, J. E., 48, (560)
Roby, T. B., 161, (551, 552)
Rodin, J., 343, 345, 347, (542, 549)
Rodrigues, A., 284, (527)
Roethlisberger, F. J., 356, (551)
Rogers, C. R., 127, 390, (551)
Rokeach, M., 207, 208, (551)
Rosenberg, M. J., 109, 110, 295, (551)
Rosenberg, S., 69, (551)
Rosenhan, D. L., 70, (551)
Rosenthal, A. M., 341, (551)
Rosenthal, R., 219, 491, 492, (551, 552)
Rosner, M., 360, (557)
Rosnow, R. L., 491, (552)
Ross, D., 140, 147, (523)
Ross, S. A., 140, 147, (523)
Rossi, A. S., 214, (546)
Rottmann, L., 113, (559)
Rubin, J. Z., 72, 159, 161, 163, 169, 190, 193, 210, 459, 462, (551, 552)
Rubin, Z., 90, (552)
Ruble, D. N., (533)
Rule, B. G., 136, (552)
Ryckman, R. M., 319, (539)

S

Saegert, S., 131, (552)
Sakurai, M., 367, (552)
Sample, J. A., 400, (552)
Sanford, R. N., 395, (521)
Sartre, J.-P., 255, 391, (552)
Schachter, S., 22, 38, 44, 96, 117, 119, 125, 126, 132, 133, 141, 255, 322, 327, 331, 367, 482, (532, 553)
Schaffer, H. R., 42, 59, 60, 61, (553)
Schanck, R. L., 202, 417, 480, (553)
Scheidlinger, S., 380, (553)
Schein, E. H., 38, (553)
Schelling, T. C., 12, 13, 157, 158, 163, 165, 444, (553)
Schenitzki, D. P., 193, 194, (540, 553)
Schiller, B., 115, (553)
Schiller, J. C. F., 112, (553)
Schjelderup-Ebbe, T., 279, 284, (553)
Schlesinger, A. M., 416, 417, (553)
Schneider, D. J., 336, (543)
Schneier, I., (553)
Schneirla, T. C., (553)
Schreiber, F. B., 334, (547)
Schroeder, H. E., 337, (553)
Schuster, S. D., 119, (561)
Scodel, A., 172, (554)
Scott, J. P., 291, (558)
Scott, T. H., 37, 38, (525, 554)
Sears, P. S., 148, (554)
Sears, R. R., 134, 135, 136, 148, (530, 537, 554)
Seashore, S. E., 254, 296, (554)
Sechrest, L., 367, (24)
Secord, P. F., 103, 125, 297, (522)
Senn, D. J., 121, (543)
Shakespeare, W., (554)
Shapira, A., 175, 177, (554)
Shapiro, D., 293, (554)

Shaver, K. G., 48, (560)
Shaw, L. M., 367, (554)
Shaw, M. E., 271, 365, 367, 400, (554)
Sheffield, F. D., 204, 227, (537)
Shepard, H. A., 459, (525)
Sherif, C. W., 436, 437, 454, (555)
Sherif, M., 312, 318, 333, 436, 437, 454, 456, (554, 555)
Shor, R. E., 75, (555)
Shouval, R., 322, (555)
Shriver, B., 374, 376, 382, (527)
Shure, G. H., 444, 462, 486, (545)
Shute, N., 466, (555)
Sidowski, J. B., 156, (555)
Siegel, A. E., 145, (555)
Siegel, S., 334, 461, (555)
Sikes, J., 264, (521)
Silverthorne, C. P., 336, (555)
Simmel, G., 264, 435, (555)
Simmel, M., 74, (536)
Simon, H. A., 423, (545)
Sims, V. M., 331, (555)
Singer, J. E., 141, 304, (553, 555)
Singer, R. D., 125, 146, 148, (532)
Skolnick, P., 468, (549)
Slater, P. E., 365, 383, 385, (522, 555)
Smith, A. J., 119, 258, (556)
Smith, E. E., 236, (556)
Smith, M. B., 125, (557)
Smith, R. B., 210, (537)
Snapp, M., 264, (521)
Sobel, R., 258, (556)
Solem, A. R., 362, 381, (545)
Solomon, L., 128, 172, (530, 556)
Solzhenitsyn, A., 309, (556)
Sommer, R., (556)
Spitz, R., 37, 42, (556)
Star, S. A., 125, (557)
Staub, E., 341, (556)
Steig, W., (556)
Stein, D. D., 119, (556)
Steinberg, B. D., 163, (552)
Steiner, I. D., 107, 119, 260, 295, 363, 364, (556)
Steinzor, B., (556)
Stemerding, A., 124, 377, (547)
Stephan, C., 264, (521)

Stephan, F. F., 365, (556)
Stitt, C. L., 336, (544)
Stock, D., 127, (556)
Stogdill, R. M., 372, (556)
Stoner, J. A. F., 333, (556)
Stotland, E., 115, 280, (561)
Stouffer, S. A., 125, (557)
Strickland, L. H., 212, (557)
Strodtbeck, F. L., 282, 376, 383, 385, (523, 557)
Strupp, H. H., 367, (557)
Student, K. R., 387, (557)
Sudnow, D., 114, (557)
Swap, W. C., 131, (552, 557)

T

Tabory, L., 156, (555)
Tagiuri, R., 125, (557)
Tannenbaum, A. S., 360, (557)
Tannenbaum, P. H., 103, (548)
Taub, B., 150, (525)
Taylor, D. A., 89, (521)
Taylor, F. W., 392, 401, (557)
Tedeschi, J. T., 210, (537)
Teger, A. I., 334, 335, 336, (557)
Test, M. A., 344, (526)
Tharp, R. G., 122, (557)
Thibaut, J. W., 85, 129, 165, 188, 210, 363, 364, (540, 557)
Thistlethwaite, D. L., 335, (533)
Thomas, E. J., 182, 258, 274, 362, 365, 367, (525, 558)
Tolman, C. W., 291, 292, (558)
Torrance, E. P., 365, (558)
Triandis, H. C., 119, 366, (558)
Triplett, N., 184, 291, (558)
Trollope, F., 87, (558)
Trommsdorff, G., 459, (541)
Tuchman, B., (558)

V

Van Zelst, R. H., 254, 367, (558)
Veach, T. L., 337, (525)
Venaki, S. K., 322, (555)
Verba, S., 386, (558)
Vianello, M., 360, (557)
Vidmar, N., 334, 462, (558)

Vinokur, A., 336, (558)
Vogel, H. H., 291, (558)
von Neumann, J., 164, (559)

W

Wachtler, J., 313, (547)
Wakil, S. P., 114, (559)
Wallach, M. A., 333, 334, 335, 336, (541, 559)
Wallington, S. A., 240, (533)
Walster, E. H., 43, 79, 112, 113, 128, (525, 530, 538, 559)
Walters, R. H., 150, (559)
Walton, R. E., 462, (559)
Washburn, S. L., 278, (559)
Waskow, A. I., 409, (559)
Watson, R. I., 306, (559)
Weingarten, M., 174, (559)
Weisenberg, M., 236, (562)
Weiser, G., 360, (557)
Weiss, W., 204, 214, 227, (537)
Weissbach, T. A., 230, (525)
Welty, J. C., 291, (559)
Wert, J., 444, (548)
Wertheimer, M., 26, 164, (559)
Wheeler, L., 48, 142, (560)
White, B. J., 436, (554)
White, R. K., 393, 453, (544, 560)
White, R. W., 23, (560)
White, T. H., 215, 425, 428, 430, (560)
Whiting, J. W. M., 148, (554)
Whyte, W. F., 273, 381, 382, (560)
Whyte, W. H., 331, (560)
Wiggins, N. H., 126, (528)
Wilkins, P. C., 120, (546)
Willerman, B., 119, (522)
Willett, E. J., 254, (548)
Williams, R. M., 125, (557)

Willis, R. H., 329, (560)
Wilson, P. R., 62, (560)
Wilson, T. R., 400, (552)
Winch, R. F., 120, 121, (560)
Winer, B. J., 391, (535)
Winter, J. A., (549)
Wishnov, B., 97, (534)
Wispe, L. G., 341, (560)
Withey, S. B., 409, (560)
Wolfe, D. M., 115, 258, 283, (525, 560, 561)
Wolosin, M. A., 336, (561)
Wolosin, R. J., 291, 336, (560, 561)
Woods, K., 336, (544)
Woodward, B., 425, (525)
Woodworth, R. S., 178, (561)
Worchel, P., 119, (561)
Wyckoff, L. B., 156, (555)
Wyden, P., 148, 149, (522)

X

Xenophon, 11, 134, (561)

Y

Yablonsky, L., 7, 9, 480, (561)

Z

Zajonc, R. B., 129, 131, 291, 293, 334, 336, (552, 555, 561)
Zander, A. F., 115, 258, 280, 282, 364, 374, (538, 561)
Zavalloni, M., 337, (547)
Zborowski, M., 217, (561)
Zellman, A. L., (533)
Zillman, D., 140, (561)
Zimbardo, P. G., 53, 144, 236, 237, 302, 304, 306, 338, 440, (562)
Zucker, R. A., 124, (562)

SUBJECT INDEX

A

Aalsmeer flower auction, 160–161
Acheson, Dean, 420
Acme-Bolt trucking game, 442–445, 457–458
Adamski, George, 18
Admirable Crichton, The, 378–380
Affection. *See* Attraction, interpersonal
Affiliation, definition of, 496
  and anxiety, 43–45
  and fear-reduction, 43–45
  need for, 41
  need for information and, 45–46
  need for love and approval and, 42–43
  and physical needs, 41–42
  and social comparison, 49–51
  See also Attraction, interpersonal; Cohesiveness
Age, and attribution of causality, 77–79
  and power, 284
Aggression, 133–150
  definition of, 134, 496
  and autistic hostility, 445–446
  and catharisis, 146, 148–150
  on command, 142–144, 219–222
  and deindividuation, 303–306
  and diffusion of responsibility, 142–144, 219–222
  displacement of, 135
  and emotional arousal, 140–141
  escalation of, 338
  Freudian theory of, 146, 148–150
  and frustration-aggression hypothesis, 134–135
  and group effects, 144
  and guns, 137
  hostile, 134
  under hypnosis, 143
  and imitation, 139–140, 142
  inhibition of, 147–148
  instrumental, 142, 433
  and obedience, 142–144, 219–222
  and self-attribution, 141
  social facilitation of, 139–140
  as a social role, 144
  in Stanford prison experiment, 306–310, 338
  television and, 144–147
Alcoholics Anonymous, 9
Alienation, 39
Aloneness, characteristics of, 34–41
  in presence of others, 38–41
Altruism, 339–350
  See also Helping behavior
Androgynous society, 122–123
Anger. *See* Aggression; Hostility
Anticonformity, 328–329
Anxiety, and affiliation, 52
  negative effects of on performance, 295
  and social comparison, 52–54
Apollo-Soyuz mission, 470
Appearance, and interpersonal attraction, 111–114
Armstrong, Dr. Thomas, 16–22
Artificiality in research, 485, 490
Aspiration level, and social comparison, 47–49
Assertiveness, of leader, 373
  training in, 275
Attitude change, and boomerang effect, 204–205, 227, 230
  and brainwashing, 38
  dissonance and, 231
  inconsistency and, 207, 231
  long-term effects of, 207, 224, 228–230
  pluralistic ignorance and, 203
  and police interrogation, 237–238
  positive and negative, 204–205
  and primacy and recency effects, 66–68
  public and private, 203
  reactance and, 205–206, 329–330
  and sleeper effect, 204–205, 227, 230
  and source credibility, 204–205
Attitudes, 109–110, 116, 117
  definition of, 109–110, 496
  and behavior, 230
  dissonance of with beliefs, 231
  and interpersonal attraction, 117–119

positive and negative, 204–205
public and private, 203
Attraction, interpersonal, 111–132
 and appearance, 111–114
 and being liked, 127–128
 and coercion, 210
 and common goals and threats,
  124–125
 in communications, 267
 and competence, 119, 396–397
 and complementary needs, 120–
  122
 of deviant, 329
 and familiarity, 129–132
 and gain-loss hypothesis, 125–
  127
 and group effectiveness, 367
 and group structure, 253
 and identification, 115–117
 of leader, 373
 and power, 284
 and primacy and recency effects,
  67–68, 125–127
 and reward, 210
 and similarity, 120–122
 See also Affiliation; Cohesiveness; Sociometric structure
Attractiveness, physical, and interpersonal attraction, 111–114
Attribution, 73–89
 definition of, 75, 496
 and aggression, 148
 of causality, 73–75, 77–81
  and intergroup conflict, 447–
   448
 and demands and pressures from
  others, 85–86
 of dispositions, 95–96
 of evil intent of enemy, 409–410
 of responsibility,
  for frustration, 136
  and intergroup conflict, 447–
   448
  for transgression, 114
 and role demands, 82–85
 of self and forced compliance,
  236–238
 and situational demands, 82–85
 and social power, 212

and social status, 86
 theory of, 75–89
  definition of, 75, 496
  and self-perception, 94–96
Auctions, 160–161
Audience, effects of on performance, 293–295
Authoritarian leadership, 393–395
 definition of, 496
Authoritarian personality, 395
Autistic hostility, 445, 457
 definition of, 445, 496
Autocratic leadership, 393–394
 definition of, 393, 496
Autokinetic phenomenon, 310–313
 definition of, 310, 496

B

Backstage behavior, 81–82, 86–88
 in U.S.-U.S.S.R. relations, 411–
  412
Balanced relationships, achievement of, 105–108
 and attitudes, 109–110, 205
 in *No Exit*, 225–257
 and social influence, 205
Balance theory, 26, 108–111, 125,
  132
 definition of, 497
 and attitude change, 205
Bargaining, definition of, 190–191,
  497
 communication in, 192–193, 456–
  458
 and conflict, 189–190
 and interdependence, 191
 offers and counteroffers in, 192–
  193
 requirements for, 191–193
 role-taking in, 193–194
 successful, 193–194
 third parties in, 461–463
Baseball team, leadership of and
  communication, 375–376
Battle of Britain, 204, 227
Bay of Pigs fiasco, 413, 415–416
Beauty and interpersonal attraction, 111–114

576

Behavior, and attitudes, 230
social influence on, 226–227
Beliefs, disconfirmation of, 21–23
dissonance of with attitudes, 231
similarities of and interpersonal attraction, 117–119
social influence on, 226–227
See also Attitudes; Values
Berle, Adolph, Jr., 414
Berra, Yogi, 375
Bilateral monopoly game, 461–462
Bissell, Richard, 414
Blaming, 76–79, 114
Bomb shelters, 409
Boomerang effect, 204–205, 227, 230
definition of, 204, 497
Brainwashing, 38
definition of, 497
Brutus, 108
Bulganin, General Nikolai, 449
Bundy, McGeorge, 414
Bystander intervention, 339–348
definition of, 497
and Kitty Genovese case, 340–341
See also Helping behavior

C

Caesar, Julius, 108, 134, 372
Calley, Lt. William, 79–81, 88, 222
Cantril, Hadley, 19
Cartoons, political, 411–412
Caste, 246–250
Castro, Fidel, 417, 419
Catharsis, 146, 148–150
definition of, 497
Causality, attribution of, 73–75, 77–81
Central Intelligence Agency, 414, 423
Centrality, definition of, 270–271, 497
in communication structure, 270–273
Champion, The, 138, 145
Chavez, Cesar, 229

Choice Dilemma Questionnaire (CDQ), 333–334
definition of, 333, 498
Choon-sun, Major General Ri, 457
Churchill, Winston, 261
Circus, social structure of, 246–250
Cleaver, Eldridge, 89
Coalition, 260–262
definition of, 260–261, 498
and group size, 264–265
and interdependence, 260–266
Coercive power, 208–212
definition of, 209, 498
See also Social power, bases of
Cognitive change, through informational influence, 206–208
Cognitive dissonance. *See* Dissonance, cognitive
Cohesiveness, definition of, 253
and behavior of deviant, 327
and deindividuation, 303–306
and effective decision-making, 366
and group effectiveness, 366–367
and group structure, 253
and Hawthorne effect, 356
and helping behavior, 343
in intergroup conflict, 459
and leadership, 394
and morale, 254
in Nixon group, 430–431
in *No Exit,* 256
and pressures toward uniformity of opinion, 323–324
in the Sherifs' studies of intergroup conflict, 438
Coldness, in behavior, 126–127
as central personality trait, 64–65
Cold War, 449–452
Colson, Charles, 428, 432
Commitment, and attitude change, 4–5, 16–25, 409–410
Committees, decisions of, 361
Communes, 39
See also Kibbutz
Communication, 251–252, 364
and conflict, 445–446, 456–458
with deviant member, 324

as dimension of group structure, 251–252

and interaction process analysis, 267–270

and interpersonal attraction, 323–324

and leadership, 374–375

in Prisoner's Dilemma game, 168–169, 172

restriction of Nixon group, 431

in social hierarchies, 281–283, 364–365

among psychiatrists, psychologists, and psychiatric social workers, 280

See also Attitude change; Social influence

Communication networks, 270–272, 276–277

definition of, 270, 499

and contagion, 299–301

and group decisions, 365

and leadership of baseball team, 375–376

Comparison level for alternatives (CL_alt), definition of, 499

in bargaining, 191–192

Competence, and interpersonal attraction, 119, 396–397

and leadership, 373, 378, 381, 385

Competition, definition of, 433–434, 499

and group effects, 290–292

and inducement of intergroup conflict, 437–439

in kibbutz, 175–177

in Prisoner's Dilemma game, 169–173

and productivity, 183–184

urban-rural differences in, 177–178

See also Bargaining; Cooperation; Cooperation and competition; Divergent interests

Competitive conflict, 433–435, 500

Complementarity, in interpersonal attraction, 120–122

Concentration camps, 309–310

Confessions, false, belief in, 236–238

Conflict, definition of, 189, 433, 500

competitive, 433–435

generalizing from interpersonal to international, 410–413

hostile, 433–435

and interdependence, 189

interpersonal, 285

research on, 484, 486–488

Conflict, intergroup, 433–442

and autistic hostility, 445–446

and bases of power, 436

and communication, 445–446

and competition, 441

escalation of, 442–446

between labor and management, 458–459

in Nixon group, 426–431

reduction of, 453–456

through fractionation, 463–465

through group representatives, 458–460

through third-party intervention, 460–463, 475–476, 479

and the Sherifs' field experiments, 436–441, 454–456

and stereotyping, 447–448

and third parties, 436, 475, 479, 481, 482, 484, 486–487

Conflict, international, 442

escalation of, 448–453

and the Cold War, 449–452

in the Vietnam War, 452–453

reduction of,

through fractionation, 463–465

GRIT proposal for, 465–472

through superordinate goals, 466

and stereotyping, 450–453

Conjunctive tasks, 260, 500

Consistency of attitudes and behavior, 26

See also Balanced relationships; Dissonance, cognitive; Inconsistency

Contact (social) hypothesis, 132, 454, 456

Contagion, social, definition of, 515
and group effects, 299–301

Content analysis, 477–478
definition of, 500

Contingency model of leadership, 395–402,
definition of, 500

Controlled experiment, 485–493
definition of, 501

Convergent interests, 157–169
definition of, 501

Conversos, 331

Cooperation, definition of, 181–182, 501
and culture, 172–178
and interdependence, 181–182, 186–187
in kibbutz, 175–177
and morale, 259
and productivity, 183–184
and reduction of intergroup conflict, 454–456
urban-rural differences in, 177–178

Cooperation and competition, 181
in the classroom, 297
and effectiveness, 258–259
and interdependence, 186–187
and productivity, 184–186
in Soviet boarding schools, 262–263
See also Bargaining; Convergent interests; Coordination; Divergent interests

Coordination, 12–13, 156–178
definition of, 501
in Apollo-Soyuz mission, 470
and convergent interests, 157–169
and decision-making, 363–364
and divergent interests, 161–163

Correlation, 478
definition of, 501
and causality, 304, 478, 480

Cost-benefits, in bargaining, 191–192
in interpersonal attraction, 129

and social exchange, 128, 164–166

Crowd behavior, 302–303

Crusoe, Robinson, 40–41

Cuban missile crisis, 419, 464, 467, 469

Culture, and cooperation, 172–178
and deindividuation, 306
and pressures toward uniformity of opinion, 320–322
and risk-taking, 336
and role definition, 275–276
and self-disclosure, 91
and sex roles, 122–123
in small group, 314–315
and social power, 218–219

Cyrus (King of Persia), 11, 14, 134

D

Dating and interpersonal attraction, 113–114

Dean, John, 429, 432

Death instinct, 134

Death of a Salesman, 226–267

Decisions, group, and the Bay of Pigs fiasco, 413–423
and changing food habits, 354–355
cohesiveness of, 366–367
and common goals, 363
and communication network, 364–365
and divisibility of task, 363–364
factors affecting quality of, 363–368
in family, 283–284
and group pressures, 362–363
homogeneity of, 365–366
in international relations, 412–413
and leadership, 367
as manipulation, 359–366
and performance, 355–360
and size of group, 365
and status structure, 364–365
training for, 366

Decisions, individual, and dissonance, 231–232

Dederich, Charles E., 6–9, 14, 201
Deindividuation, 144
  definition of, 303, 502
  and cohesiveness, 303–306
  and group effects, 301–310
  laboratory studies of, 303–310
  in lynch mobs, 303
  of prisoners and guards, 306–310
  and reduction of social restraints, 302–310
Democratic leadership, 393–394
  definition of, 393, 502
Dependence, power of, 217–219
Dependent variable, 476, 477, 484
  definition of, 502
Desegregation, 132, 230, 263–364, 456
Deutsch-Krauss trucking game, 442–445, 457–458
Deviance, in cohesive groups, 327
  and mutual attraction, 329
  and personality, 326, 328–329
  in policy-making groups, 417, 422, 428, 432
  and pressures toward uniformity of opinion, 322–326, 417
  and public and private conformity, 203, 330, 417
  and responses to majority pressure, 326–332
  and tyranny of the majority, 324–326
Dharsana Salt Works, 4, 23
Diffusion, of guilt, 342–348
  definition of, 502
  of responsibility. See Responsibility, diffusion of
Dillon, Douglas, 414, 420
Discussion, group. See Group discussion
Disliking, and coercion, 210
  See also Attraction, interpersonal; Liking
Dispositions, attribution of, 76–79
Dissonance, cognitive, 111, 203, 237
  definition of, 231, 499
  between attitudes, beliefs, and behavior, 203, 231

  and bomb shelters, 409–410
  and commitment, 4–5, 16–25, 409–410, 418
  and forced compliance, 231–236
  and helping behavior, 349–350
  and influence by gradations, 241
  and initiations, 23–25
  post-decisional, 231–232
  in public and private conformity, 330–332
  versus self-perception analyses, 237–238
  theory of, 23–25, 132, 231
Divergent interests, 161–169, 179
  definition of, 161, 503
Dominance, in autokinetic judgment, 313
  in family 283
  and leadership, 382–383
Dominance hierarchy, definition of, 278–280, 503
  See also Pecking order
Douglas, Kirk, 138
Drug addiction, 6–9, 14
Dyads. See Group size

E

Ecological manipulation, definition of, 239, 503
Effectiveness, group, in communication networks, 277
  and goal interdependence, 258–259
  and leadership, 385, 393–402
Ehrlichman, John, 426, 429
Eichman, Adolf, 222
Eisenhower, General Dwight D., 414, 449
Elections, and familiarity of candidate, 129–130
  and positive and negative reference groups, 215–217
Emotions, and aggression, 140–141, 145
  arousal of, 145
  and mob behavior, 302–303
  self-attribution of, 51–54
  social comparison and, 51–54

1

Encounter groups, 39
  definition of, 503
Escalation of conflict, definition of, 503
  between groups, 439–442
  See also Conflict, intergroup; Conflict, international
Ethics in research, 222, 490, 493–494
Evaluation, as dimension of group structure, 251–252
Evaluation apprehension, 295, 504
Exchange theory, 128
Expectancy effects, 491–493
Experiment, field, 27, 483–485
  definition of, 27, 504
  on intergroup conflict, 436–441
Experiment, laboratory, 27, 485–493
  definition of, 27, 509
Experiment, natural, 17, 27, 481–483
  definition of, 27, 511
Experimenter, and expectancy effects, 491–493
  definition of, 504
  legitimate power of, 142–143, 219–222
Expert influence, definition of, 50–51, 504
  See also Social power, bases of
Exposure, frequency of and interpersonal attraction, 129–132
Expressiveness of individual, 81
Extraneous variable, 488, 489

F

Familiarity, and interpersonal attraction, 129–132
Familiar objects, preference for, 61
Family, group structure of, 354
  power in, 283
  roles in, 283–284
Fear and social comparison, 52–54
Feelings and social comparison, 51–54
Females, labeling of, 71–72

roles of, 122–123, 275–276
  stereotyping of, 69
Fiedler, Fred, and contingency model of leadership, 395–402
Field experiment, 27, 483–485, 504
Field study, 27, 480–481, 504
Field survey, 27, 478–480, 504
Finch, Robert, 425, 426, 432
Flower auction, 160–161
Foot-in-the-door technique, 241, 348–349, 504
Forced compliance, and dissonance, 231–236, 504
Ford, Gerald R., 471
Formal social structure, 272, 426–427, 504
Fractionation of conflict, 463–465
  definition of, 463, 505
Friendship choices, 115
Front stage behavior, 81–85, 213, 411–412
Frustration, nonaggressive responses to, 147–148
Frustration-aggression hypothesis, 134–135
  definition of, 134, 505
  in intergroup conflict, 438–439

G

Gain-loss factor, in interpersonal attraction, 125–127
Gandhi, Mohandas K., 2–6, 14, 132, 201, 372
Genovese, Kitty, 340–341
Gestalt theory of perception, 26, 62, 72
Goals, common, 124–125
  and group decisions, 363
  dilemma of, 191
  of group and leadership, 380
  superordinate, 454–456
Goals interdependence, 178–181, 258–259, 261–262
  definition of, 505
Graduated Reciprocation of Tension Reduction, (GRIT), 465–472, 505

Group-centered leadership, 390–391, 505
Group cohesiveness. *See* Cohesiveness
Group decisions. *See* Decisions, group
Group discussion, 267–270, 274–275, 355
   leaderless, 372–374
Group effectiveness, and communication networks, 271–274
   and goals interdependence, 258–259
Group effects, definition of, 506
   and aggression, 144
   on animal performance, 290–291
   and anxiety, 295
   and arousal, 293–295
   on behavior, 226–227
   on beliefs, 226–227
   on bicycle racers, 291
   and contagion, 299–301
   on deindividuation, 301–310
   on emotions, 299–310
   influence of on uniformity of opinion, 319–325
   on judgment, 310–332
     and forms of yielding, 318–319
   on meat-eating habits, 239
   on productivity in industry, 291
   on risky shift, 332–337
   on sharks, 302
   and social comparison, 319–325
Group judgment, convergence of, 311–312
   effect of stubborn minority on, 313–315
   and the lone deviant, 315–319
Group membership, and mutual identification, 115–117
Group norms. *See* Norms, group
Group pressures, 327–328
   and power of experimenter, 222
   See also Pressures toward uniformity of opinion
Group size, and coalitions, 264–267
   and communication structure, 273–274
   and dyads, 264–265

   effect of on group decisions, 365
   and leadership, 376
   and triads, 265–267, 376
Group structure. *See* Structure, group
Groupthink, 415–423
   definition of, 416, 506
   examples of, 418–419
   in Nixon group, 431
   symptoms of, 416
Guilt, arousal of and social influence, 239–241
   diffusion of
     definition of, 502
     and helping behavior, 342–348
   suppression of and groupthink, 417

H

Haldeman, H. R., 425, 426, 428, 429, 431, 432
Halo effect, definition of, 230, 506
Hawthorne effect, 356,
   definition of, 506
Helping behavior, 339–350
   aftermath of, 348–349
   factors that influence, 341–348
   and power, 217–219
Helsinki Agreement, 470–471
Henry, O., 14
Hickel, Walter, 425
Historical documents, use of in research, 27, 477–478
Hitler Adolf, 372, 378, 418, 433, 464, 471
Homogeneity, group, and effective decision-making, 365–366
Hostile conflict, 433–435, 507
Hostility, aggressive, 134, 506
   autistic, 445, 457
   and deindividuation, 303–304
   See also Aggression; Conflict, intergroup; Conflict, international
Humphrey, Hubert, 425
Hunt, E. Howard, 423–424
Hypnosis, and aggression, 143
Hypothesis, 476–477, 495, 507

I

Identification, and balance theory, 115–117
  with leader, 380
  with victim and helping behavior, 344–346
Idiosyncrasy credit, 383, 458
  definition of, 507
  and deviance, 330
Imbalanced relationships, 104–110, 205
  See also Balanced relationships
Imitation, and aggression, 139–140, 143, 144, 147, 148
  and helping behavior, 344
Impression formation, 59–72
  and the Asch-Lorge controversy, 63–64
  effect of eyeglasses on, 62–63
  effect of names on, 65–66
  effect of status and prestige on, 62–64
  of integrated whole, 62
  from single attribute, 62
  and stereotyping, 68–72
  of warmth and coldness traits, 64–65
Impressions, of infants, 59–61
  initial, 66–68, 125–127
  management of, 91–93
Inconsistency, between attitudes and values, 207
  between beliefs and behavior, 226
Independence, need for, 205–206
Independent variable, 476, 477, 484
  definition of, 507
Industry, assembly line in, 260–298
  communications in, 272
  division of labor in, 297–299
  group effectiveness in, 291, 385, 392
  group norms and productivity in, 355–360
  leadership in, 385, 392
Infant, effects of labeling, 71–72
  first impressions of, 59–61
  first love relationship of, 61

Influence. *See* Social influence
Informational power, 206–208, 227–228, 508
  See also Social power, bases of
Initiation, severity of and attraction to group, 24–25
Inner-directedness, 84–85
Instrumental aggression, 134, 142
  definition of, 508
Intentions, attributed, 75–77, 409–410
Interaction process analysis, 267–270, 383–385, 480
  definition of, 508
  and roles, 274–275
Interdependence, 154
  definition of, 508
  and bargaining, 189–191
  and conflict, 434
  and cooperation and competition, 181–182, 186–187, 433–434
  as dimension of group structure, 251–252
  in escape attempts, 187–190
  of goals, 178–181, 258–259, 261–262
    in bargaining, 192
    in Deutsch-Krauss trucking game, 443–445
    and morale, 254
  and jigsaw-puzzle method, 263–264
  of means, 178–181, 182–183, 259–260, 261–262
    in Apollo-Soyuz mission, 470
    in competition, 184–186
    in decision-making, 363
    in Deutsch-Krauss trucking game, 443–445
  negative, 179–181, 437
  positive, 179–181, 455–456
  pressures of, 297–299
    definition of, 508
  and productivity, 186–187
  structure of, 257–266
Intergroup conflict. *See* Conflict, intergroup
Intermediaries, use of to resolve conflicts, 460–463
International relations, and appli-

cation of small-group research, 410–413

Interpersonal attraction. *See* Attraction, interpersonal

Interracial relations, 70, 125, 275–276, 295, 345
  reducing conflict in, 25, 132, 263–264, 454, 456

Intervening variable, 477

Intervention, third-party, 436, 460–463
  definition of, 518

Intimacy, and self-disclosure, 90

Invulnerability, illusion of, 416–417

Isolation, 34–38
  experimental studies of, 37
  and psychopathology, 36

J

Jackson, Henry, 425

Janis, Charlotte, 415

Jewish "Blue Book," 338

Jigsaw-puzzle method for reducing interracial tensions, 263–264

Johnson, Lyndon, 472

Judgment. *See* Group judgment

Jury deliberations, group effects on, 322
  social influence on, 282

K

Kaingáng Indians, 445–446

Keech, Mrs. Marian, 16–23, 376

Kennedy, John F., 14, 414, 419, 469–470, 472

Kennedy, Robert, 420

Khrushchev, Nikita, 470

Kibbutz, definition of, 173, 508
  cooperation and competition in, 173–177
  group decisions in, 360
  and pressures toward uniformity of opinion in, 322

Kissinger, Henry, 460

Klein, Herbert, 426, 430, 432

Knapp, Major General James B., 457

Korean War, 415

Kwakiutl potlatch, 338–339

L

Labeling, 70–73

Labor, division of, efficiency of, 260
  in industry, 297–299
  in restaurant, 273–274

Laboratory experiment, 27, 485–493
  definition of, 509

Laissez-faire leadership, 393–394,
  definition of, 509

Leadership, 368–402
  definition of, 370–371, 509
  appointment of, 382
  and assertiveness, 373
  attainment of, 382–383
  authoritarian, 393–395, 496
  autocratic, 393–395, 496
  and communication networks, 272, 276–277
  and conflict, 440
  contingency model of, 395–402
  and crisis situations, 376–378
  democratic, 393–394, 502
  development of, 372–374, 376–378, 381–387
  effects of group size on, 376
  emergence of, 368–370
  factors that produce, 371–380
  functions of, 370–371, 380–381, 509
  great man theory of, 371–380
  group-centered versus directive, 390–400
  and group effectiveness, 367–368, 385, 387
  and group maintenance, 380, 384–387
  and groupthink, 418, 421–422
  idiosyncrasy credit of, 383, 507
  in international relations, 413
  laissez-faire, 393–394, 509
  maintenance of, 381–385
  in Nixon group, 430–431
  and personal attractiveness, 373
  and personality, 371–374, 378–380

Leadership (*continued*)
position of in group structure, 272, 370–371
role of, 370
role of in reducing conflict, 454
role of in risky shift, 334
and self-esteem, 374–375
shaping of by position, 374–376
single or multiple, 385–387
situational determinants of, 374–380
and social power, 394, 397–400
socioemotional, 384–387
styles of, 387–395, 509
and tasks, 384–387
and Theory X and Theory Y, 392, 395, 401
training for, 401–402
trait versus situational factors in, 378–380
Least preferred co-worker (LPC), 396–401, 509
Legitimate power, definition of, 510
of experimenter, 142–144
See also Social power, bases of
Lemnitzer, General Lyman, 414
Liddy, Gordon, 432
Liking of others, reasons for, 111–133
and reward power, 210
and social influence, 236
Lincoln, Abraham, 372
Looking glass self, 93–94
Lord of the Flies, 40–41, 387–390
Love, infants, 61
in marriage, 127
omens of, 102
L (liking) relationship, 103, 110
Lynch mobs, and deindividuation, 303, 306

M

MacArthur, General Douglas, 449
McCarthy, Senator Joseph, 465
McGovern, George, 372
McGregor, Douglas, and Theory X and Theory Y, 391–392, 395
Machiavelli, Niccolò, 15

McMillan, Roy, 375
McNamara, Robert, 414
Magruder, Jeb Stuart, 426, 428, 429, 432
Majority, tyranny of, 324–326
Malenkov, General Georgi M., 449
Males, labeling of, 71–72
roles of, 122–123
Manipulation, ecological, 239
definition of, 503
of group decision, 359–360
Mann, Thomas, 414
Maranos, 331
Marriage, 121
love in, 127
Marshall, General George D., 449
Marshall Plan, 415
Mass media, and violence, 133–134, 144–147
Matlack, Jon, 375
Matrix representation, 165–167
definition of, 510
Means interdependence, 178–181, 182–183, 259–260, 261–262
definition of, 510
Military service, group effectiveness in, 367
leadership in, 374–375, 396–401
social influence in, 204
status differences in, 364–365
Misperception, 106, 452–453
Mitchell, John, 426, 428, 429, 432
Mixed-motive relationships, 163–169, 191
definition of, 510
Mob behavior, 302–303
Morale, group, 254–255
and cohesiveness, 254
and communication networks, 272
and cooperation, 259
and effectiveness, 254–255, 416
and groupthink, 416–417
and Hawthorne effect, 356
Morality, and dissonance, 233
and groupthink, 416–417
Moynihan, Daniel, 425, 432
Mutual identification, 115–117, 125
Mutual threat, 124–125, 189, 465–472
My Lai massacre, 79–81, 88

N

Natural experiment, 17, 27, 481–483
  definition of, 511
Nazi Germany, 309–310, 464, 471
Negative correlation, 478
Negative influence, 204–205, 215–217
  definition of, 511
Negotiation, 456–465
Nero, 372
Nightingale, Florence, 14
Nixon, Richard, M., 372, 414, 423–433, 472
Nixon group, the, 423–433
  formal structure of, 426
  groupthink in, 431
  leadership in, 430
  risky shift in, 432
  runaway norm in, 431–432
  sociometric analysis of, 427
No Exit, 93, 255–257, 265–267
  pecking order in, 284–285
Norms, group, definition of, 506
  and academic performance, 297
  and autokinetic effect, 310–313
  development of, 311–315
  as field of forces, 355–358
  and Hawthorne effect, 356
  and leadership, 382–383
  in microculture, 314–315
  and productivity, 296–297
  as quasi-stationary equilibria, 356–358
  and social comparison, 297
Norms, runaway. *See* Runaway norms

O

Obedience, to command of experimenter, 142–144, 219–222
  of guards and prisoners, 306–310
  and role demands, 309
On the Beach, 466
Organization chart, in industry, 272
Osgood, Charles, and GRIT proposal, 465–472
Other-directedness, 84–85

Other person, taking role of, 12–13
Overconformity, 225

P

Panel survey, 478, 479
Panic behavior, 187–190
Parkinson's law, 361
Pax Britannica, 460
Pax Romana, 460
Pearl Harbor, 415
Pecking noise and social facilitation, 292
Pecking order, 279
  definition of, 511
  circular, 284–285
  in family, 283–284
Peer influence, 50–51, 227, 318
Personality, and behavior of deviant, 326, 328–329
  and effective group decisions, 363
  and group effects, 313
  implicit theories of, 68–69
  and leadership, 371–374, 378–380, 395–402
  and pressures toward uniformity of opinion, 319
  and roles in group, 277
  and self-disclosure, 91
  and trust toward others, 172
Persuasion, 106
  See also Attitude change; Informational power; Social influence
Physical reality check, and social comparison, 327–328
Pluralistic ignorance, 203, 330, 417
  definition of, 511
Police interrogations, 237–238
Political science, 28, 129–130, 215–217
Position in group, 276
  definition of, 512
  in communication network, 271–273, 276–277, 375–376
  and leadership, 374–376, 382
  and social status, 282
  See also Leadership; Role, social; Status, social

Positive correlation, 478
Potlatch, Kwakiutl, 338–339
  definition of, 512
Power. *See* Social power
Powerlessness, legitimate power of, 217–219
Pratfall, and interpersonal attraction, 119–120
Prejudice, racial, 230, 263–264, 275–276
  See also Conflict, intergroup; Interracial relations; Stereotyping
Presentation, of information, order of, 67–68, 125–127
  of self, 81–85, 89–93, 213
Pressures toward uniformity of opinion and aggression, 222
  on deviants, 322–326, 417
  effect of on group decisions, 362–363
  and groupthink, 415–423
  and leadership, 381
  and physical reality check, 327–328
  as quasi-stationary equilibria, 323, 356–358
  and social comparison, 47–55, 319–325
  See also Norms, group; Social comparison; Social influence
Prestige, and communication, 281–283
  and power, 278
Primacy effects, 66–68
Prisoner's Dilemma game, 166–173
  definition of, 167, 512
  cultural factors in, 172–178
  and international conflict, 410
  partner's strategy in, 172
Problem-solving group, 268–269
  in international relations, 412–413
  and pressures toward uniformity of opinion, 362–363
Productivity, group, in industry, 355–360
  and morale, 254–255
Psychiatric social workers, in status hierarchy, 280

Psychiatrists, in status hierarchy, 280
Psychologists, in status hierarchy, 280
Psychology, as discipline, 27–28
Psychotherapy, group, 39
Public and private attitudes, 203
Public and private conformity, 330–332
Punishment and coercion, 208–212
Push and pull in assembly line, 260, 298
  definition of, 513

Q

Quasi-stationary equilibria, 322, 356–358,
  definition of, 503
Queuing, 188

R

Randomization, 488–489
  definition of, 513
Rasputin, Grigori Efimovich, 10, 14
Reactance, 205–206, 329–330
  definition of, 513
Reactivity of measurement, 491
  definition of, 513
Reality, physical, 327–328
  social, 516
Recency effects, 67–68
  definition of, 513
Reciprocation, in self-disclosure, 90
Referent power. *See* Social power, bases of
Reference groups, 214–217
Relevance of issue, and pressures toward uniformity of opinion, 106, 322–324
Research, deception in, 493–494
  ethics in, 222, 490, 493–494
  use of field experiment in, 483–485
  use of field study in, 480–481
  use of field survey in, 478–480
  use of historical documents in, 477–478

use of laboratory experiment, in 485–493
use of natural experiment in, 481–483
Responsibility, diffusion of, definition of, 502
and aggression, 142–144, 219–222
in attribution of causality, 148
in bystander intervention, 342–348
and obedience, 144
in risky shift, 334–335
Reward, for performing act, 231
Reward power. *See* Social power, bases of
Richardson, Elliot, 425
Risky shift, 332–336
definition of, 514
and Choice Dilemmas Questionnaire, 333–334
explanations for, 334–337
and group counseling, 337
and helping behavior, 348
Rivalry, 290–292
Rockefeller, David, 425
Role, social, 251–252
definition of, 274, 514
and aggression, 144
and attribution, 82–85, 96
and bargaining, 193–194
and communication networks, 276–277
conflict in, 276
definition of, 514
of critical evaluator, 421
and cultural factors, 275–276
development of through interaction, 274–275
of devil's advocate, 421–422
as dimension of group structure, 251–252
in family, 283–284
in impression management, 91–93
and leadership, 370, 378–380, 383–387
and legitimate power, 217
of prisoners and guards, 306–310
of psychiatrists, psychologists,

and psychiatric social workers, 280
of socioemotional and task specialists, 274–275, 384–387
See also Sex roles
Romney, George, 425
Roosevelt, Franklin D., 448
Runaway norms, 337–339
definition of, 514
and escalation of conflict, 439–442
in Kwakiutl potlatch, 338–339
in Nixon group, 431–433
Rusk, Dean, 414, 417

S

Salt March, 2–6, 14, 132
Scanlon Plan, 392
Schizophrenics, effects of labeling on, 70–71
Scranton, William, 425
Seaver, Tom, 375
Seekers, the, 16–23, 376
Self, impressions of, 93–98
presentation of, 81–85, 89–93, 213
Self-attribution, and emotions, 141
Self-concept, 97
Self-disclosure, 89–93
definition of, 514
Self-esteem of leader, 374–375
Self-evaluation, 46–54, 93–98, 133
and opinions of others, 96–98
Self-perception, 95
and attribution, 94–96
and emotions, 141
and helping behavior, 349–350
theory of, 237–238
definition of, 515
Sensitivity groups, 39
Sex differences, and helping behavior, 345
in self-disclosure, 91
See also Sex roles
Sexism, 69, 71–72
Sex roles, 72, 91, 122–123, 275–277, 283, 385
Sex stereotyping, 69

Sherif, Muzafer and Carolyn, experiments of in intergroup conflict, 436–441, 454–456
Similarity of people, and competence, 119
and helping behavior, 345–346
and insecurity, 123–124
and interpersonal attraction, 120–122, 515
and referent influence, 225–227
Simulation, definition of, 515
of prison, 306–310
Situational demands, and attribution, 82–85
and self-attribution, 96
Social comparison, 46–55
definition of, 46–47, 515
and abilities, 47–49
and emotions, 51–55
and group norms, 297
and interpersonal attraction, 47–55, 125
and opinions, 49–51
and pressures toward uniformity of opinion, 47–55, 319–325
theory of, 46–54, 125
definition of, 515
Social dependence, and group influence, 318
and social influence, 202, 228
Social exchange theory, 128, 164–166
definition of, 515
Social facilitation, definition of, 291–292, 516
and aggression, 139–140
in the Camponotus ant, 290
and chicken pecking, 291–292
Social influence, 201, 251–252
definition of, 201, 516
on behavior, 226–227
and coercion, 318
dependent, 208–222
definition of, 516
as dimension of group structure, 251–252
enhancement of, 238–241
expert, 313, 318

by gradations (foot-in-the-door-technique), 241
and guilt arousal, 239–241
independent, 206–208
definition of, 516
informational, 206–207, 318
and inconsistencies, 207–208
and interpersonal attraction, 236, 255
and leadership, 394
legitimate, 318
and manipulation, 239
negative, 204–205
boomerang effect of, 204–205
expert, 214, 227
and imbalance, 205
referent, 215–217
and new perceptions, 228–230
positive, 204–205
and power structure, 277–284
public and private, 203, 223–224
referent, 318
and reward, 318
secondary effects of, 228–238
and surveillance, 202–203, 208–212
unintended effects of, 206
See also Social power
Social inhibition, 293–294
definition of, 516
Social power, 201
definition of, 202, 516
and aggression, 129–222
cultural differences in use of, 218–219
as dimension of group structure, 251–252
effect of on attitude change, 223–224, 227–228
of experimenter, 219–222
exploitative use of, 15, 359–360
and helping behavior, 217–219
in intergroup conflict, 436
of leader, 397–400
as potential influence, 202
and sex roles, 276–277
and social structure, 277–284
pecking order in, 279–280

among psychiatrists, psychologists, and psychiatric social workers, 280
and surveillance, 223–225
Social power, bases of, 206–228
coercion, 218, 219, 223–225, 228–230, 233
and intergroup conflict, 436
and leadership, 382, 387, 389, 394–400
comparison of, 222–228
effect of on one another, 230
expertise, 212–214, 222–228, 230, 239
in intergroup conflict, 436
and leadership, 373, 382, 387, 394, 397–400
information, 227–228
in intergroup conflict, 436
and leadership, 387, 394, 397–400
legitimacy, 217–222, 224–225, 228–230, 239
in intergroup conflict, 436
and leadership, 387, 394, 397–400
reference, 214–217, 223–224
in intergroup conflict, 436
and leadership, 387, 394, 397–400
research on, 222
reward, 208–212, 228, 233
in intergroup conflict, 436
and leadership, 382, 387, 389, 394, 397–400
Social psychologist, definition of, 9–10
Social psychology, definition of, 9–10, 516
discipline of, 27–28
reasons for studying, 15–16
Social reality, definition of, 516
Social role. See Role, social
Social structure. See Structure, group
Sociology, 27–28
Socioemotional specialist, definition of, 275, 517

Sociometric structure, 252–254
definition of, 517
and contagion, 301
and morale, 254
in Nixon group, 426–431
in No Exit, 255–257
in the Sherifs' studies of intergroup conflict, 437
Soviet Union, cooperation and competition in, 262–263
pressures toward uniformity of opinion in, 322
prison camps in, 309–310
Spatial location, and social status, 248–250
Sports, competition in, 441
leadership in, 396–297
Stalin, Joseph, 433, 448
Stage-setting, and legitimate power, 222
in social influence, 238, 240
Stanford prison experiment, 306–310, 338, 440–441
Status, social, 246–250
definition of, 517
and attribution, 86
and communication, 264–265
and influence, 282–283
and leadership, 374–377
and spatial location, 248–250
Stereotyping, 68–72
definition of, 517
ethnic, 70
in intergroup conflict, 439, 446–448, 450–453
sex, 69
Strategic Arms Limitation Treaty, 408, 470
Strategies, defensive and offensive, 409–410
Streetcar Named Desire, A, 265–267
Stress. See Anxiety; Threats
Structure, group, definition of, 517
and communication, 267–274
networks of, 270–272
networks of and roles, 276–277, 375–376
and power, 281–283

Structure (*continued*)
  dimensions of, 250–252
  and evaluation, 252–257
    in *No Exit*, 255–257
  of family 354
  formal, 272, 426–427, 504
  and influence, 277–284
  and interdependence, 251–252, 257–266
    and coalitions, 260–266
    of goals, 258–259
    and jigsaw-puzzle method, 263–264
    of means, 259–260
    in Soviet boarding schools, 262–263
  interrelationship among dimensions of, 251–252
  and leadership, 370, 374–377
  of Nixon group, 424–431
  and power, 268, 277–284
    in family, 283–284
    inconsistencies in, 274
    See also Social power
  of a restaurant, 273–274
  and roles, 274–277
    in communication networks, 276–277, 375–376
    in family, 283–284
  sociometric, 252–257, 426–431
Study, field, 27, 480–481, 504
Subjects, 486–494
  definition of, 517
  role of, 142–144, 219–222
Success, and morale, 254–255
Suicide, 134
Surveillance, and social influence, 202–203, 212
  and social power, 208–212, 224–225
Survey field, 27, 478–480
  definition of, 504
  panel, 478, 479
Synanon, 6–9, 14

T

Task, divisibility of and group decisions, 363–364
  importance of and communication, 281
  performance of and morale, 254–255
  specialization of, 260
Task specialist, 275
  definition of, 518
Television, and aggression, 133–134, 144–147
Tensions, interracial, jigsaw-puzzle method for reducing, 263–264
Tepoztlan (Mexico), 178
T-groups, 39
Thanatos, 134, 518
Third-party intervention in conflicts, 430, 460–463, 475–476, 479
  definition of, 518
  research on, 475–476, 479, 481, 482, 484, 486–487
Theory, definition of, 518
  construction and development of, 25–26, 476–477, 495
  formal methods for testing, 26–27, 477–491, 495
Theory X in leadership, 391–392, 518
Theory Y in leadership, 391–392, 518
Threats, common, 124–125, 454–456
  in conflict, 444–445
  and leadership, 376–378
Timoshenko, General Simeon K., 449
Training, for effective decision-making, 366
  for effective leadership, 401–402
Traits, personal, 111–114
Triads, 108, 265–267, 376
Truman, Harry S., 448
Trust, and conflict, 445–446
  interpersonal, 90
  in Prisoner's Dilemma game, 169, 172
  and self-disclosure, 90
  and surveillance, 212
Twelve Angry Men, 322

U

Uniformity. See Pressures toward uniformity of opinion
United Farm Workers, 229
Urbanization, and competition, 177–178
U (unit-forming) relationship, 103–104, 110
  definition of, 103, 519
Unobtrusive measure, 492
  definition of, 519
U.S.-China relations, 472
U.S.-U.S.S.R. relations, 411–412, 448–452, 463–464
  and GRIT proposal, 468–472

V

Values, 109–110, 117
  definition of, 519
  and informational influence, 207–208
  and riskiness, 335–337
Variable, definition of, 519

dependent, 476, 477, 484, 502
independent, 476, 477, 484, 507
intervening, 477
extraneous, 488, 489
Vietnam War, 452–453, 472
Violence. *See* Aggression; Conflict, intergroup; Conflict, international; Hostility
Voting, 129–130, 215–217

W

Warmth, in behavior, 126–127
  as central personality trait, 64–65
Watergate affair, 423–424, 432
Who's Afraid of Virginia Woolf?, 269–270, 279–280
Women, stereotyping of, 69
World War I, 465
World War II, 415, 448–449, 464–465

Z

Z'vi, Shabbetai, 17